Hands-On Microsoft® Windows® Server 2008

Michael Palmer

COURSE TECHNOLOGY
CENGAGE Learning™

Australia • Brazil • Japan • Korea • Mexico • Singapore • Spain • United Kingdom • United States

COURSE TECHNOLOGY
CENGAGE Learning

**Hands-On Microsoft® Windows®
Server 2008**
Michael Palmer

Vice President, Publisher: Dave Garza

Executive Editor: Steve Helba

Managing Editor: Marah Bellegarde

Acquisitions Editor: Nick Lombardi

Senior Product Manager: Michelle Ruelos
  Cannistraci

Developmental Editor: Deb Kaufmann

Editorial Assistant: Claire Jeffers

Marketing Director: Deborah Yarnell

Marketing Manager: Erin Coffin

Marketing Coordinator: Shanna Gibbs

Production Director: Carolyn Miller

Production Manager: Andrew Crouth

Content Project Manager: Jessica McNavich

Art Director: Kun-Tee Chang

Technology Project Manager: Joseph Pliss

Production Technology Analyst: Jamison
  MacLachlan

Manufacturing Manager: Denise Powers

Quality Assurance Testing: John Bosco,
  GreenPenQA

Copyeditor: Gary Michael Spahl

Proofreader: Karen Annett

Compositor: International Typesetting and
  Composition

For product information and technology assistance, contact us at
Cengage Learning Customer & Sales Support, 1-800-354-9706
For permission to use material from this text or product,
submit all requests online at **cengage.com/permissions**
Further permissions questions can be emailed to
permissionrequest@cengage.com

Microsoft® and Windows® are registered trademarks of the
Microsoft Corporation.
ExamView is a registered trademark of eInstruction Corp.

Library of Congress Control Number: 2008935568

ISBN-13: 978-1-423-90234-8

ISBN-10: 1-423-90234-3

Course Technology
25 Thomson Place
Boston, MA 02210
USA

Cengage Learning is a leading provider of customized learning solutions
with office locations around the globe, including Singapore, the United
Kingdom, Australia, Mexico, Brazil, and Japan. Locate your local office at:
international.cengage.com/region

Cengage Learning products are represented in Canada by Nelson
Education, Ltd.

For your lifelong learning solutions, visit **course.cengage.com**
Visit our corporate website at **cengage.com.**

Microsoft and Windows are either registered trademarks or trademarks of
Microsoft Corporation in the United States and/or other countries. Course
Technology, a part of Cengage Learning, is an independent entity from the
Microsoft Corporation, and not affiliated with Microsoft in any manner.

Course Technology and the Course Technology logo are registered trademarks used under license.

Course Technology, a part of Cengage Learning, reserves the right to
revise this publication and make changes from time to time in its content
without notice.

Printed in the United States of America
4 5 6 7 8 9 14 13 12 11 10

Brief Table of Contents

Table of Contents

Introduction

Hands-On Microsoft® Windows® Server 2008 gives you practical experience with Microsoft's latest server operating system as you learn about its capabilities and features. Windows Server 2008 offers more server roles, more flexibility, more security, and more manageability than any previous Microsoft server operating system. With this book, you gain a broad understanding of Windows Server 2008. You learn how to choose the right server edition for your needs and then you learn how to install, configure, customize, manage, and troubleshoot your server. If you are new to server administration, this book gives you the knowledge you need to manage servers on small to large networks. If you are an experienced server administrator, the book provides a fast way to get up to speed on Windows Server 2008.

This book is written for easy understanding and contains over 130 hands-on activities to help your learning come to life. *Hands-On Microsoft Windows Server 2008* includes an evaluation DVD so that you can install Windows Server 2008 and complete the hands-on activities using the Enterprise Edition of Windows Server 2008. The hands-on activities give you the experience you need to truly learn Windows Server 2008 and retain what you have learned.

In addition to the hands-on activities, the book is filled with many learning aids to help you maximize what you learn. The objectives at the start of each chapter give you an overview of what you will be able to accomplish and can be used for a fast review of the chapter contents. At the end of each chapter, there are chapter summaries for more in-depth point-by-point review. There also are review questions and realistic case studies to enable you to stretch your learning. The case studies put you in the shoes of a Windows Server 2008 consultant who works in all kinds of situations fulfilling the needs of clients. Other learning tools include a list of key terms that you have encountered in the chapter and application examples provided throughout to help you understand different ways to use Windows Server 2008.

The goal of this book is to give you the knowledge and confidence to be a capable server administrator. The book also can serve as a foundation for readers who want to go on to achieve Microsoft certifications, such as the Microsoft Certified IT Professional (MCITP) certification.

Intended Audience

Hands-On Microsoft Windows Server 2008 is intended for anyone who wants to learn and practice using Windows Server 2008. It also can be used as a starting block in preparing for the

Microsoft Certified IT Professional (MCITP) Server or Enterprise Administrator certification track. Computer concepts and skills that you need are explained as you go along. Each chapter is written in clear, easily understood language. No prior computer operating system experience is required, but it is helpful to have some prior experience with a Windows operating system such as Windows XP or Windows Vista.

This Book Includes

- A Windows Server 2008 Enterprise Edition evaluation DVD (bundled with the book), which can be installed directly on a computer or installed in a virtual machine, such as in Microsoft Hyper-V, Microsoft Virtual Server, and VMware Server

- Step-by-step hands-on activities for learning nearly every phase of Windows Server 2008, with all activities tested by a technical editor, reviewers, and validation experts

- Extensive review and end-of-chapter materials to strengthen your learning

- Broad training in planning, installation, configuration, security, networking, monitoring, and troubleshooting

- Coverage of features new to Windows Server 2008, including Windows Server Core, Windows PowerShell, Hyper-V, Server Manager, new security features, new network services, new role services, new monitoring tools, and much more

- New appendices to cover using Windows Server 2008 with virtualization systems, including VMware, Microsoft Hyper-V, Microsoft Virtual Server, and Microsoft Virtual PC

- Abundant screen captures and graphics to visually reinforce the text and hands-on activities

Chapter Descriptions

The chapters are balanced to provide a similar amount of coverage. There are twelve chapters and two appendices. The beginning chapters introduce the Windows Server 2008 operating system, and show how to plan for, install, and configure Windows Server 2008. Because it can be vital to a server installation, you also learn about Active Directory in the early portion of the book. The middle chapters address how to configure key services, such as file and folder services, printing, data storage, network services, and remote access. The chapters at the end of the book focus on configuring security, server and network monitoring, and ensuring server reliability. The appendices provide supplementary information about using virtualization through Hyper-V, Microsoft Virtual PC, Microsoft Virtual Server, and VMware Server and Workstation.

Chapter 1, "Introduction to Windows Server 2008," explains and compares each of the Windows Server 2008 editions: Standard Edition, Enterprise Edition, Datacenter Edition, Web Server 2008, and Itanium-Based Edition. The chapter discusses client systems that can be used with Windows Server 2008, identifies new features, and shows how to plan a network model to use.

Chapter 2, "Installing Windows Server 2008," discusses how to prepare for an installation, describes different installation methods (including using virtualization), and steps through an actual installation. The chapter additionally discusses how to implement Windows Server Core, how to implement Windows Deployment Services, how to install service packs, how to troubleshoot installation problems, and how to uninstall the operating system.

Chapter 3, "Configuring the Windows Server 2008 Environment," starts by introducing the new Server Manager management tool. You also learn how to install and uninstall server roles, configure hardware, and configure the operating system. Other topics include understanding the Registry, using the Security Configuration Wizard, and using Windows PowerShell.

Chapter 4, "Introduction to Active Directory and Account Management," presents an extensive introduction to Active Directory, including how to install and configure it. You additionally learn how to create and manage user accounts and security groups.

Chapter 5, "Configuring, Managing, and Troubleshooting Resource Access," teaches you how to manage folders and files, particularly in relation to setting up security. You learn how to create shared objects, such as folders, and how to publish them in Active Directory. You additionally learn how to implement the Distributed File System and how to establish disk quotas. For UNIX and Linux users, you learn how to set up UNIX compatibility features in Windows Server 2008.

Chapter 6, "Configuring Windows Server 2008 Printing," provides information about the inner workings of Windows Server 2008 printing, including how to install local, network, and Internet printers. You learn how to manage print jobs and how to troubleshoot printing problems. You also learn to use the newly designed Print Management tool.

Chapter 7, "Configuring and Managing Data Storage," shows you how to configure basic and dynamic disks, plus how to manage disks and troubleshoot problems. You learn how to use fault tolerance such as RAID, and how to perform disk backups and restores.

Chapter 8, "Managing Windows Server 2008 Network Services," focuses on how to configure the essential services needed for a smooth functioning Windows Server 2008 network, including DNS, WINS, DHCP, and Internet Information Services (Web Server).

Chapter 9, "Configuring Remote Access Services," enables you to learn how to set up and troubleshoot Windows Server 2008 as a virtual private network (VPN) and remote access server for network, Internet, and dial-up remote access. You also learn about new features in Terminal Services and how to configure and manage a terminal server for running applications directly on the server.

Chapter 10, "Securing Windows Server 2008," shows you a wealth of new and time-tested security features. You learn how to configure security policies, set up Active Directory rights, manage security on clients, create security templates, encrypt files and folders, use the new BitLocker Drive Encryption, implement Network Address Translation, configure Windows Firewall, and set up the new Network Access Protection capabilities.

Chapter 11, "Server and Network Monitoring," teaches you how to monitor a server and a network for troubleshooting and to prevent problems. You learn how to use monitoring tools such as the Computer Management tool, Task Manager, Resource Monitor, Performance Monitor, Data Collector Sets, Reliability Monitor, and the SNMP service. Many of these tools are new to Windows Server 2008 or have been enhanced to offer more functionality.

Chapter 12, "Managing System Reliability and Availability," enables you to develop problem-solving strategies for handling server difficulties. You learn how to resolve boot problems, use the Advanced Boot Options, use repair tools on the installation DVD, protect critical systems, use and configure Event Viewer, troubleshoot network problems, administer a server using Remote Desktop, and manage multiple servers through the Remote Server Administration Tools.

Appendix A, "Windows Server 2008 Virtualization," provides a foundation for understanding virtualization and virtual machines. After you learn about virtualization, you learn the ins and outs of the new Hyper-V, which is virtualization software that can be included with Windows Server 2008 at a very minimal cost.

Appendix B, "A Step-by-Step Guide to Using Server Virtualization Software," shows you how to use several popular virtual systems besides Microsoft Hyper-V, including Microsoft Virtual PC, Microsoft Virtual Server, and VMware. You learn how to download these systems, how to install and configure them, and how to use them to set up a virtual machine, such as Windows Server 2008.

Features

To help you better understand how Microsoft Windows Server 2008 and network management concepts and techniques are applied in real-world organizations, this book includes the following learning features:

Chapter Objectives—Each chapter begins with a detailed list of the concepts to be mastered. This list provides you with a quick reference to the chapter's contents and is a useful study aid.

Hands-On Activities—Over 130 hands-on activities are incorporated throughout the text, giving you practice in setting up, managing, and troubleshooting a server. The activities give you a strong foundation for carrying out server administration tasks in the real world. Many of the activities present questions for you to investigate and blank space is provided after each question so you can record your answers in the book. This is intended to help retention and to provide a study aid that you can go back to.

Screen Captures, Illustrations, and Tables—Numerous reproductions of screens and illustrations of concepts aid you in the visualization of theories, concepts, and how to use tools and desktop features. In addition, many tables provide details and comparisons of both practical and theoretical information and can be used for a quick review of topics.

Chapter Summary—Each chapter's text is followed by a summary of the concepts introduced in the chapter. These summaries provide a helpful way to recap and revisit the ideas covered in each chapter.

Key Terms—All of the terms within the chapter that were introduced with boldfaced text are gathered together in the Key Terms list at the end of the chapter. This provides you with a method of checking your understanding of all of the terms introduced.

Review Questions—The end-of-chapter assessment begins with a set of review questions that reinforce the ideas introduced in each chapter. Answering these questions will ensure that you have mastered the important concepts.

Case Projects—Each chapter closes with a multipart case project. In this realistic case example, as a consultant at Aspen Consulting, you implement the skills and knowledge gained in the chapter through real-world setup and administration scenarios.

On the DVD—On the DVD you will find a free 120-day evaluation copy of Microsoft Windows Server 2008 Enterprise Edition.

Text and Graphic Conventions

Additional information and exercises have been added to this book to help you better understand what's being discussed in the chapter. Icons throughout the text alert you to these additional materials. The icons used in this book are described below:

Tips offer extra information on resources, how to attack problems, and time-saving shortcuts.

Notes present additional helpful material related to the subject being discussed.

The Caution icon identifies important information about potential mistakes or hazards.

Each Hands-On Activity in this book is preceded by the Activity icon.

Hands-On Activities specially tailored for virtual servers are preceded by the Virtual Activity icon.

Case project icons mark the end-of-chapter case projects, which are scenario-based assignments that ask you to independently apply what you have learned in the chapter.

Instructor's Resources

The following supplemental materials are available when this book is used in a classroom setting. All of the supplements available with this book are provided to the instructor on a single Instructor Resources CD (ISBN: 1423902777).

Electronic Instructor's Manual—The Instructor's Manual that accompanies this textbook includes additional instructional material to assist in class preparation, including suggestions for classroom activities, discussion topics, and additional activities.

Solutions—The instructor's resources include solutions to all end-of-chapter material, including the Review Questions, Hands-On Activities, and Case Projects.

ExamView—This textbook is accompanied by ExamView, a powerful testing software package that allows instructors to create and administer printed, computer (LAN-based), and Internet exams. ExamView includes hundreds of questions that correspond to the topics covered in this text, enabling students to generate detailed study guides that include page references for further review. The computer-based and Internet testing components allow students to take exams at their computers and to also save the instructor time by grading each exam automatically.

PowerPoint presentations—This book comes with Microsoft PowerPoint slides for each chapter. These are included as a teaching aid for classroom presentation, to make available to students on the network for chapter review, or to be printed for classroom distribution. Instructors, please feel at liberty to add your own slides for additional topics you introduce to the class.

Figure files—All of the figures and tables in the book are reproduced on the Instructor Resources CD, in bitmap format. Similar to the PowerPoint presentations, these are included as a teaching aid for classroom presentation, to make available to students for review, or to be printed for classroom distribution.

System Requirements

Hardware

- Listed in the Windows Server Catalog of Tested Products or has the Certified for Windows Server 2008 sticker
- 1 GHz CPU or faster for an x86 computer or 1.4 GHz CPU or faster for an x64 computer
- 512 MB RAM or more (for x86 and x64 computers)
- 15 GB or more disk space (for x86 and x64 computers)
- DVD drive
- Super VGA or higher resolution monitor
- Mouse or pointing device
- Keyboard
- Network interface card connected to the classroom, lab, or school network for on-ground students—or Internet access (plus a network interface card installed) for online students
- Printer (to practice setting up a network printer)

Software Windows Server 2008 Standard or Enterprise Edition

Virtualization Windows Server 2008 can be loaded into a virtual server environment, such Microsoft Hyper-V, VMware, or Microsoft Virtual Server or PC.

Acknowledgments

I've had the good fortune to work with an outstanding team of people on this book. I am very grateful to Course Technology / Cengage Learning and Acquisitions Editor Nick Lombardi for their support and vision for the book project. Michelle Ruelos Cannistraci, the Product Manager, has brought together the many people who have contributed to the project and she has provided important guidance and support from start to finish. Many thanks also go to Deb Kaufmann, the Development Editor who has not only helped turn words into understanding, but is a vital source of guidance, good will, and excellent ideas. Deb helps authors know there really is light at the end of every day of hard work. Thanks also go to Rajni Pisharody and Jessica McNavich who have coordinated the production tasks for the book. I'm also grateful to Gary Michael Spahl who has provided very clean copyediting.

Every word, mouse click, and keystroke has been evaluated, tested, and retested by John Bosco and his outstanding Green Pen Quality Assurance staff, who are true technical professionals. I am also grateful to the peer reviewers who have throughout provided all kinds of essential advice, ideas, insights, and help. They have been important to helping ensure that the book is technically accurate and that it is tailored to the needs of students and teachers as well as general readers. These reviewers are Brian Bridson, Zarreen Farooqi, Joseph Hart, and Hermine Turner.

Finally, I'm grateful to my wife Sally for her support and patience.

Dedication

I dedicate this book to Shawn, Kristy, and Ian, who are all working to make a difference.

chapter 1

Introduction to Windows Server 2008

After reading this chapter and completing the exercises, you will be able to:

- Identify the key features of each Windows Server 2008 edition
- Understand client systems that can be used with Windows Server 2008
- Identify important general features of Windows Server 2008
- Plan a Windows Server 2008 networking model
- Understand and implement networking protocols used by Windows Server 2008

Microsoft Windows Server systems are at the core of information access, productivity, and entertainment all over the world. Chances are that you access a Windows server when you purchase music on the Internet, open a spreadsheet at work, watch a movie on a plane, or send an e-mail. Windows Server 2008 is Microsoft's newest server platform that offers more roles for servers, better security, easier server management, and more reliable computing than its predecessors.

This book is intended to give you a solid grounding in how to install and use Windows Server 2008 for all types of computing situations. In this chapter, you begin your journey by learning about the different Windows Server 2008 platforms, from the Standard Edition to the Itanium-based version. You also learn how Windows Server 2008 works in tandem with client desktop systems such as Windows Vista.

Windows Server 2008 incorporates many new features, which you learn about in this chapter and go on to master in later chapters. After exploring the features, you review the networking models used by Windows Server 2008, from peer-to-peer to server-based networking. Finally, you learn how to implement protocol communications for effective Windows Server 2008 networking.

Windows Server 2008 Platforms

Servers have a wide variety of uses designed to match the needs of a variety of users from small businesses to international corporations. They are also finding their way into homes and home offices. Because one size does not fit all needs, it is important to offer different types of server operating systems. Windows Server 2008 comes in eight versions. All versions are built on the same foundation, but offer unique capabilities to suit a home office or a business with branches all over the world.

The Windows Server 2008 platforms are as follows:

- Windows Server 2008 Standard Edition
- Windows Server 2008 Enterprise Edition
- Windows Web Server 2008
- Windows Server 2008 Datacenter Edition
- Windows Server 2008 for Itanium-Based Systems
- Windows Server 2008 Standard Edition without Hyper-V
- Windows Server 2008 Enterprise Edition without Hyper-V
- Windows Server 2008 Datacenter Edition without Hyper-V

These platforms are discussed in the next sections.

Windows Server 2008 Standard Edition

Windows Server 2008 Standard Edition is the most basic server version on which the other versions are based. It is designed to meet the everyday needs of small to large businesses. Standard Edition provides file and print services, secure Internet connectivity, and centralized management of network resources. This platform is built on technology from previous Windows Server systems, such as Windows Server 2003, but includes many new features. Also, the program coding of old features is enhanced for security and efficiency.

A small company or a department in a larger company might use Windows Server 2008 Standard Edition to manage its accounting and payroll software, for example. A medium-sized or large company might use it to manage e-mail or network resources. Small to large companies might use Standard Edition to manage users' access to application software, such as Microsoft Office.

Windows Server 2008 can be used on x86 and x64 computers, which is true of all editions of Windows Server 2008. An x86 computer has a 32-bit processor and is based on the architecture of the original 80386 processor family. Intel, Advanced Micro Devices (AMD), and VIA manufacture

x86-compatible processors. An x64 computer uses a 64-bit processor in personal computers and servers for faster, industrial-strength processing and is also manufactured by Intel, AMD, and VIA. In Standard Edition, an x86 server can use up to 4 GB of RAM whereas an x64 server can have up to 32 GB.

> **NOTE** 32-bit and 64-bit refer to the number of bits the processor can receive and transmit at one time (in parallel). Because a 64-bit computer can transport twice as many bits at one time, it is faster than a 32-bit processor (depending on the ability of the operating system to take advantage of 64-bit processing). Also, a 64-bit processor can handle more RAM than a 32-bit processor (again depending on the capabilities of the operating system). Microsoft is projecting at this time that future releases of desktop and server operating systems after Windows Server 2008 and Windows Vista will be written only for x64 processors.

Standard Edition provides basic server elements that enable file and printer sharing, essential network services, application sharing, and other server services. In addition to x86 and x64 processors, Standard Edition supports multiprocessor computers and multiprocessor clients. A multiprocessor computer is known as a **symmetric multiprocessor (SMP) computer**, which is a computer that uses more than one processor.

For companies that develop their own software, all editions of Windows Server 2008 are compatible with the common language runtime used in Microsoft .NET Framework and Microsoft Visual Studio .NET, and Windows Server 2008 enables computer programmers to develop and use program code in several programming languages.

Included with Standard Edition is **Hyper-V**. Hyper-V enables Windows Server 2008 to offer a **virtualization** environment, which is a way to run more than one operating system on a single computer at the same time. Historically, organizations have used multiple servers for different operating systems, such as one server for Windows Server 2003, one for Windows Server 2008, and one for Linux. The disadvantage of this approach is the cost of multiple computers. In organizations that require tens or hundreds of servers, the hardware costs rise fast. Also, additional costs are associated with housing the computers in temperature-controlled computer rooms, including the cost of security and cooling the machines. Virtualization offers a way to cut costs by using fewer computers.

The advantages of Hyper-V compared with Microsoft's earlier Virtual Server 2005 R2 include the following capabilities:

- Can run 32-bit and 64-bit operating systems at the same time
- Can run on SMP computers
- Can access larger memory segments

When you purchase Windows Server 2008 Standard Edition, you can select whether to have Hyper-V included (but currently Hyper-V only runs on x64 computers).

Windows Server 2008 Enterprise Edition

Windows Server 2008 Enterprise Edition is designed to meet the everyday needs of networks with applications and Web services requiring high-end servers and a high level of productivity. It is intended for midsized and large organizations that want the option to continue scaling their server operations upward. Enterprise Edition also has more management and consolidation features for company-wide software applications.

Medium-sized to large organizations might use this platform to host large-scale accounting, manufacturing, or inventory systems. A college might use this platform for a student information or registration system. A bank might take advantage of this platform because of its reliability and availability.

Enterprise Edition supports both x86 and x64 computers. On an x86 computer, it supports up to 64 GB of RAM and on a x64 computer, it supports up to 2 terabytes (TB; a terabyte is about 1024 GB or one trillion bytes). Enterprise Edition also can handle SMP computers.

Windows Server 2008 Enterprise Edition enables clustering. **Clustering** is the ability to increase the access to server resources and provide fail-safe services by linking two or more discrete computer systems so they appear to function as though they are one (see Figure 1-1). An immediate advantage of server clustering is the increase in computer speed to complete server tasks faster. Also, server clustering provides more computing power for handling resource-hungry applications. With clustering, as an organization adds more users and requires more demanding applications, one or more computers can be added to the cluster to handle the growth. This is a faster, less-expensive approach than having to purchase a larger computer and transfer users and applications to a new system because the old one is overwhelmed. Enterprise Edition supports clusters of up to 16 computers.

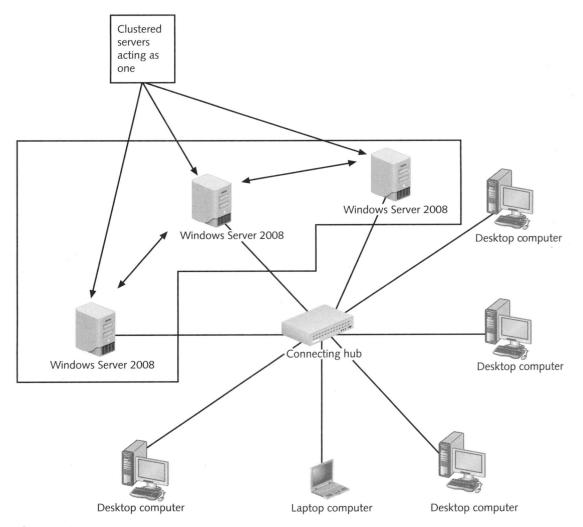

Figure 1-1   Three servers acting as one in a cluster

Another advantage of Enterprise Edition is that it supports hot-add memory. **Hot-add memory** is the ability to add RAM without shutting down the computer or operating system. In addition to this capability, Enterprise Edition has **fault tolerant memory sync,** which enables memory to resynchronize after transient memory problems so there is no interruption to current computing activities. This is an important feature because it is estimated that memory errors occur up to 100 times more frequently than memory failures.

Some enterprise networks have servers with different operating systems and directory services. Enterprise Edition provides Microsoft Metadirectory Services to facilitate multiple directory services to track and manage access to such resources as user accounts, shared folders, and shared printers. This means less work for users because they can use one account to log on to all servers, instead of having different accounts for different operating systems. Simplifying access for users in this way also simplifies the work of server administrators.

Yet another option in Enterprise Edition is the ability to have unlimited numbers of users remotely access a server. In Standard Edition, remote access is limited to 250 connections or fewer, depending on the type of access.

Windows Web Server 2008

Windows Web Server 2008 is designed for hosting and deploying Web services and applications. For scalability, this platform supports multiple processors. Windows Web Server 2008 is particularly optimized to run Microsoft Internet Information Services.

Small to large companies, or departments within an organization that develop and deploy a single Web site, are examples of the intended users of this platform. They can employ it to develop a Web site that takes advantage of the .NET Framework tools and XML Web services.

Windows Web Server 2008 can be used on x86 and x64 computers. It supports up to 4 GB of RAM on an x86 computer and up to 32 GB on an x64 computer.

A limitation of Windows Web Server 2008 is that it cannot be used to manage directory resources via hosting Active Directory, a function that is available to all other Windows Server 2008 platforms (you'll learn more about Active Directory later in this chapter). Windows Web Server 2008 also does not support some of the extra capabilities of Enterprise Edition. For example, it does not support clustering, hot-add memory, fault-tolerant memory sync, or Metadirectory Services. Further, Windows Web Server 2008 does not come with Hyper-V.

Windows Server 2008 Datacenter Edition

Windows Server 2008 Datacenter Edition is designed for environments with mission-critical applications, very large databases, and information access requiring high availability. This platform offers support for clustering with up to 16 computers. Also, for SMP computers it supports from 2 to 64 processors. Datacenter Edition enables hot-add memory for increased server availability and adds two other capabilities: hot-add processor and hot-replace processor. **Hot-add processor** means that a processor can be added to an empty processor slot while the system is running. With **hot-replace processor**, you can replace a processor in an SMP system without taking the system down.

At this writing, Microsoft licensing includes a per-processor charge for the Datacenter Edition and the Itanium-Based Systems Edition.

The RAM capabilities for the Datacenter Edition are identical to Enterprise Edition at 64 GB for x86 processor computers and 2 TB for x64 processor computers. Windows Server 2008 Datacenter Edition is designed for large database applications in any organization. A university alumni association might use it to house a database that tracks information on thousands of alumni all over the world. A large company might use it for an integrated accounting system that stores information in a complex database. A national investment firm might use it to track and manage the investment holdings of its customers.

Windows Server 2008 for Itanium-Based Systems

Microsoft also offers a Windows Server 2008 edition intended for use on Intel Itanium computers. An Itanium processor is a 64-bit processor that uses a design different than typical x86 and x64 processors, which allows it to process more instructions per processor cycle. Both 32-bit and 64-bit applications can be run on an Itanium computer.

The design of an Itanium processor enables it to be scaled up to 512 processors and handle one petabyte (PB) of RAM (1024 TB). However, the maximum RAM supported by Windows Server 2008 for Itanium-Based Systems is 2 TB. The Itanium-Based Edition supports hot-add memory, hot-add processor, hot-replace processor, and SMP computers. This edition also supports server clustering for up to eight servers in one cluster.

An Itanium system is intended for resource-intensive applications. For example, it might be used for an accounting system at a large corporation. Another example is as a server for research scientists who do resource-intensive computing. Another possible application is for an organization that has a large Web site accessed by a huge population, such as a Web site used by students at a university to access student information systems and e-mail. Because the Itanium processor is so scalable, it is also a good candidate for a company that is starting out but anticipates rapid growth, such as one offering new Internet-wide Web search engine capability.

Windows Server 2008 Versions Without Hyper-V

It is not necessary to pay extra for Hyper-V if your organization has no need for it. The following non-Hyper-V versions of Windows 2008 are available:

- Windows Server 2008 Standard Edition without Hyper-V
- Windows Server 2008 Enterprise Edition without Hyper-V
- Windows Server 2008 Datacenter Edition without Hyper-V

When you purchase a version without Hyper-V, the cost savings is very small. If your organization is growing or its computer strategy might change in the next few years, purchasing a Windows Server 2008 version with Hyper-V can save money and installation headaches in the future.

Table 1-1 summarizes the minimum recommended hardware requirements for each of the Windows Server 2008 editions.

Table 1-1 Minimum hardware requirements for the Windows Server 2008 editions

Hardware	Standard Edition	Enterprise Edition	Web Server	Datacenter Edition	Itanium-Based Edition
CPU	1 GHz (x86) 1.4 GHz (x64) (2 GHz or faster is recommended)	1 GHz (x86) 1.4 GHz (x64) (2 GHz or faster is recommended)	1 GHz (x86) 1.4 GHz (x64) (2 GHz or faster is recommended)	1 GHz (x86) 1.4 GHz (x64) (2 GHz or faster is recommended)	Intel Itanium 2
Disk space	10 GB (40 GB or more recommended)	10 GB (40 GB or more recommended)	10 GB (40 GB or more recommended)	10 GB (40 GB or more recommended)	10 GB (40 GB or more recommended)
RAM	512 MB (2 GB or more recommended)*	512 MB (2 GB or more recommended)*	512 MB (2 GB or more recommended)*	512 MB (2 GB or more recommended)*	512 MB (2 GB or more recommended)*
Drive	DVD	DVD	DVD	DVD	DVD
Display	Super VGA or better	Super VGA or better	Super VGA or better	Super VGA or better	Super VGA or better
Interactive devices	Keyboard and pointing device	Keyboard and pointing device	Keyboard and pointing device	Keyboard and pointing device	Keyboard and pointing device

*On x86 systems, the RAM maximums are 4 GB for Standard and Web Server 2008 and 64 GB for Enterprise and Datacenter Editions. On x64 systems, the RAM maximums are 32 GB for Standard and Web Server 2008 and 2 TB for Enterprise and Datacenter Editions. For Itanium-based systems, the RAM maximum is 2 TB.

You can do the hands-on activities in this book from a Windows Server 2008 server with or without virtualization. If you are not working from a virtual server, just follow the steps as written. If you are using a virtual server, such as Hyper-V, you first need to access the server from within the virtual environment. The following steps show how to start and access a Hyper-V virtual server that is already installed. You learn how to install a virtual server in Microsoft Hyper-V in Chapter 2, "Installing Windows Server 2008."

To access a virtual server in Microsoft Hyper-V, follow these general steps:

1. Click **Start**, point to **Administrative Tools**, and click **Hyper-V Manager**.

2. In the middle pane of the Hyper-V Manager window, click the server, such as Windows 2008.

3. If the server is not already started, click the **Action** menu and click **Start** (otherwise skip to Step 5).

4. Wait for the server to start up.

5. If necessary, double-click the name of the server in the middle pane to open its working window, which is the Virtual Machine Connection window.

6. When you see the screen that says Press CTRL+ALT+DELETE to log on (don't press CTRL+ALT+DELETE yet), click the **Action** menu under the title bar and click CTRL+ALT+DELETE.

7. Log on using your account and password, and click the right-pointing arrow.

8. Click the **Maximize** square in the upper-left corner of the window to go into the full screen mode (you'll see a yellow bar at the top).

9. Whenever you are finished (and logged off your account) and want to leave the full screen mode, click the **Restore Down** (two boxes) button in the yellow bar.

10. Close the Virtual Machine Connection window.

11. If you want to shut down the server, click the server in the middle pane, click the **Action** menu, and click **Shut Down**. Or, to leave the server running, skip to Step 12.

12. Close Hyper-V Manager.

Some steps in the activities in this book include bulleted questions with space for you to record your responses/answers.

Activity 1-1: Determining the Windows Server 2008 Edition

Time Required: Approximately 5 minutes
Objective: Determine the Windows Server 2008 edition installed on a computer.

Description: A computer room might have only a few or hundreds of servers. Sometimes it is important for a server administrator to verify which edition of Windows Server 2008 is running on a particular server. In this activity, you learn how to make a quick determination. You will need a server account provided by your instructor or server administrator.

1. Log on to Windows Server 2008 using your account.

2. Click **Start**, right-click **Computer**, and click **Properties**.

3. The window that is displayed provides basic information about the computer system.

4. Under the Windows edition section, you'll see the edition of Windows Server 2008, such as Windows Server Enterprise, as shown in Figure 1-2.

   • Which version of Windows Server 2008 is installed on your computer? Record your answer in the space below.

5. Notice the other information available in this window.

   • How much RAM is in the computer? Is the computer running an x86 or x64 version of Windows Server 2008? Record your answer below.

6. Close the System window.

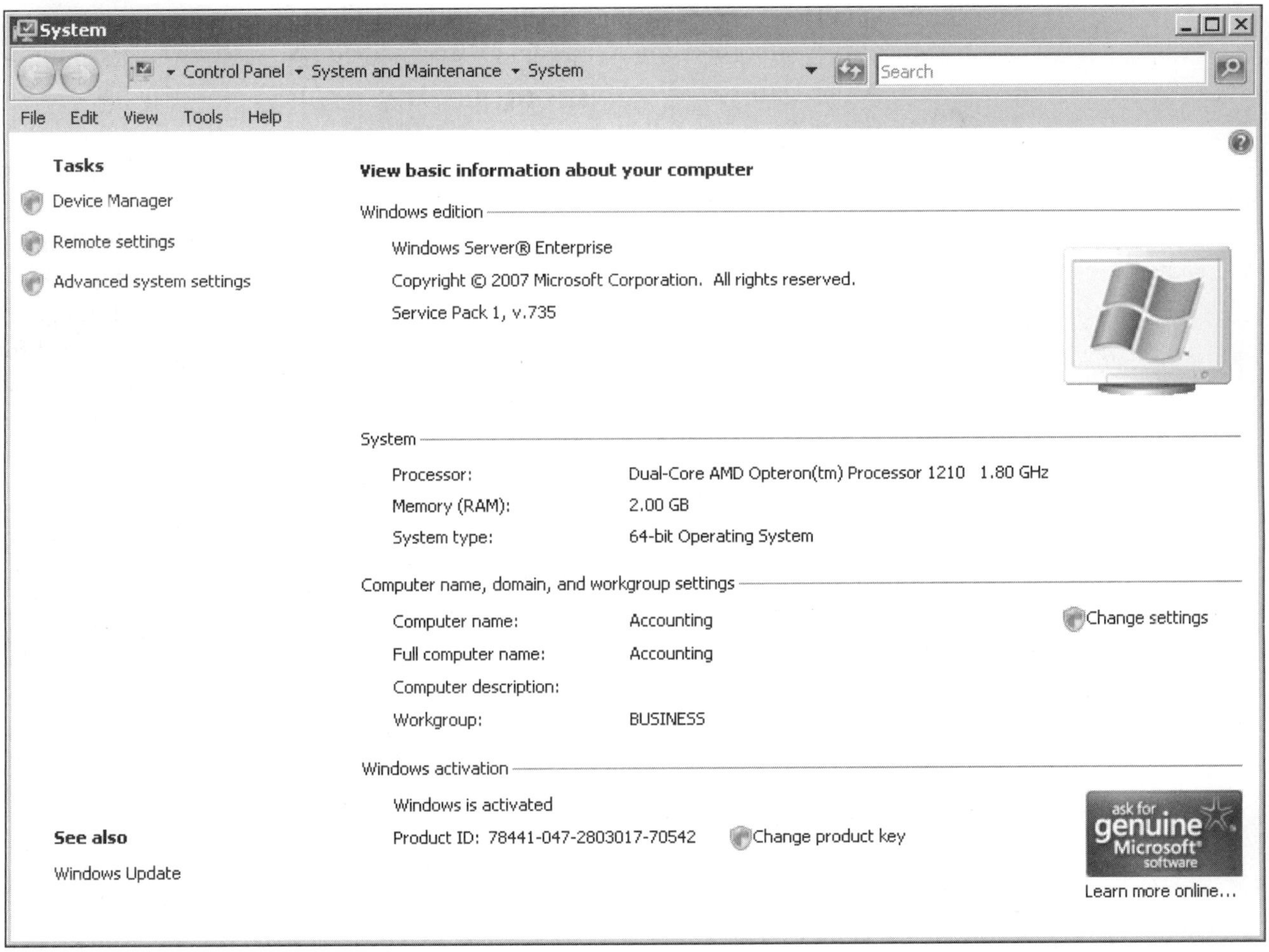

Figure 1-2 Viewing information about the Windows Server 2008 system

Using Windows Server 2008 with Client Systems

The client workstation operating system most compatible with Windows Server 2008 is Windows Vista. A **client** is a computer that accesses resources on another computer via a network or direct cable connection; a **workstation** is a computer that has its own central processing unit (CPU) and can be used as a stand-alone or network computer (often used for a combination of word-processing, spreadsheet, scientific, and other individual applications).

The overall goal of Microsoft is to use the Windows Server 2008 platforms and Windows Vista on the same network to achieve a lower TCO. The **total cost of ownership (TCO)** is the full cost of owning a network, including hardware, software, training, maintenance, and user support costs. Windows Vista is designed to be a reliable and secure workstation operating system to be used in a business environment in a peer-to-peer network or as a member of a domain. A **domain** is a grouping of network objects, such as computers, servers, and user accounts, that provides for easier management. Computers and users in a domain can be managed to determine what resources they can access, such as printers and shared folders. A domain is given a name, such as Microsoft.com for Microsoft. In addition, computers within a domain are given a unique name, which often parallels the name of a user, such as Brown, or is a favorite name or word, such as antelope or popcorn. You learn more about domains in Chapter 4, "Introduction to Active Directory and Account Management."

Recognizing that professionals are highly mobile, Windows Vista is designed to work equally well on a desktop computer or on a laptop computer.

In terms of networking advancements, some of the advantages of using Windows Server 2008 and Windows Vista together include the following:

- New capabilities to recover from many types of network communications problems
- Newly written code for more efficient network communications
- More network diagnostic capabilities
- New code for better use of the network communications protocols, IPv4 and IPv6, with special emphasis on IPv6
- Use of Windows PowerShell commands and scripts in both Windows Server 2008 and Vista (you learn more about Windows PowerShell later in this chapter)

Windows Server 2008 is intended to play a key management role on a network by hosting **Active Directory**—a database of computers, users, groups of users, shared printers, shared folders, and other network resources—and by offering a multitude of network services. Windows Vista offers the best compatibility with the newest version of Active Directory in Windows Server 2008. By combining Windows Vista client workstations and Windows Server 2008 under the management of Active Directory, it is possible to centralize security, applications, application updates, and automated client configuration via a server, thus reducing the TCO.

Another Microsoft long-term objective is to encourage users to convert all workstation operating systems on a network to Windows Vista, because the TCO for Windows Vista is less than for other workstation operating systems such as Windows XP and Windows 2000. The TCO is less because Windows Vista is able to use automated installation, configuration, desktop, and management policy features controlled through Windows Server 2008. Also, although Windows XP and Windows 2000 support Active Directory, they don't support some newer elements. Many desktop configuration settings (including software deployment) can be automated from Windows Server 2008 to Windows Vista, so that the user can set up a client workstation with less technical knowledge or assistance.

Windows XP supports more Active Directory management features than its predecessor Windows 2000. Although Windows XP and Windows 2000 don't support some of the new Active Directory and other Windows Server 2008 features, they still support many of them and can compose a very functional network as clients to Windows Server 2008.

In addition to Windows clients, Windows Server 2008 supports UNIX and Linux clients using the **Subsystem for UNIX-based Applications (SUA)**. For a UNIX or Linux client, SUA creates a multiuser environment complete with commands, case-sensitive abilities (important to UNIX/Linux), programming tools, shells (runtime environments), and scripts. With SUA installed, even UNIX/Linux programs can be ported over to Windows Server 2008.

Scripts are files that contain commands to be run by a computer operating system. Scripts save time because commands don't have to be typed individually by the user each time a particular set of activities needs to be accomplished, such as adding new data to a file.

Windows Server 2008 Features

Windows Server 2008 offers many features that make it a solid server and network operating system. The following list is a sampling of features in Windows Server 2008 that deserve special focus:

- Server Manager
- Security
- Clustering
- Enhanced Web services
- Windows Server Core
- Windows PowerShell
- Virtualization
- Reliability
- Multitasking and multithreading

Each of these features is introduced in the sections that follow. You will learn more about these features as you continue through this book.

Server Manager

Windows Server 2008 comes with a new tool called Server Manager. **Server Manager** enables the server administrator to manage critical configuration features from inside one tool. In earlier versions of Windows Server, you might have to look in several places to do different tasks. Server Manager puts the management tasks together in one place. For example, if you configure several parameters during the initial installation and later decide to modify some of those settings, it's likely you can modify them all in Server Manager. Server Manager is used to:

- View computer configuration information.
- Change properties of a system.
- View network connections.
- Configure Remote Desktop.
- Configure security, including the firewall and how to obtain updates.
- Configure a multitude of server roles, from a basic file server to advanced network services.
- Add and remove features.
- Run diagnostics.
- Manage storage and backups.

In many cases, when the administrator selects a management function, Server Manager starts a wizard for step-by-step guidance through the task. Wizards are helpful for learning tasks and for reducing configuration errors. Server Manager is particularly useful for beginning and intermediate administrators, but also centralizes common tasks for advanced administrators.

Security

Windows Server 2008 is built to be more secure than previous Windows Server systems. One important feature that enables this to happen is **Network Access Protection (NAP)**. NAP is an umbrella of security protection features that monitor and manage a server and its clients. As attackers and malicious software become more sophisticated, so must managing a server to block their attacks. NAP has the following capabilities:

- Identifies clients and other computers on a network that do not comply with the security policies set through Windows Server 2008

- Limits access by noncompliant computers, such as by not allowing access to resources, not permitting logon, or by quarantining a noncompliant computer to specific resources or portions of a network

- Automatically updates or configures a noncompliant computer to match the security policies required for access, such as by changing policy settings on the client or updating the client operating system to have the latest security patches

- Continuously checks throughout the entire network and server connection session to ensure that computers remain in compliance, even after they have been given access to the network, server, and resources

Another security approach built in to Windows Server 2008 is implementing security by default. When you install Windows Server 2008, add a feature, or install a Windows component, an essential level of security is automatically implemented. This helps to ensure that no back doors are left open for an attacker.

Windows Server 2008 also comes with the Security Configuration Wizard (SCW), which simplifies security configuration to ensure the server is properly configured for the role it serves. SCW poses questions about security needs and configures security on the basis of the responses to the questions. This not only makes it easy to use, but more likely that it will be used.

Windows Server 2008 additionally includes many basic security features, such as:

- File and folder permissions

- Security policies

- Encryption of data

- Event auditing

- Various authentication methods

- Server management and monitoring tools

Clustering and Clustering Tools

Clustering is an important feature of Windows Server 2008 because it not only makes a server system more powerful, but it also provides failover capabilities, so that if one server in a cluster fails, its work is automatically taken over by other servers in the cluster. Clustering also enables a large amount of disk storage to be made available to users, with failover for disk storage as well.

The power of clustering is only as good as the tools used to configure it. Windows Server 2008 offers tools to:

- Test a cluster to ensure it is set up to accomplish the tasks for which it is intended.

- Migrate configuration settings from one cluster to another.

- Quickly configure a cluster and troubleshoot problems.

- Set up storage used in a cluster.

- Create better cluster storage performance and reliability.

- Secure a cluster and enable it to use new network capabilities.

Enhanced Web Services

Windows Server 2008 comes with Microsoft **Internet Information Services (IIS)** to transform the server into a versatile Web server. Consistent with Microsoft's emphasis on security, IIS has been redesigned to consist of over 40 modules. The new design is intended to enable IIS to have a lower attack surface (vulnerable openings exposed to network attackers and malicious software). In addition to reducing the attack surface, eight modules handle specific security issues.

Another security feature is easier application of IIS patches. Microsoft often issues patches for its software as new attack techniques against its operating systems and applications are discovered. Easier patching means that system administrators are more likely to apply security patches in a timely way.

IIS is also redesigned to make it easier for network programmers to write network applications and configure applications for the Web. Also, complementing the applications development enhancements, IIS has better management tools that are incorporated into the IIS Manager. Administrators also can manage IIS remotely for greater convenience and access.

Windows Server Core

Windows Server Core is best understood not by what it has, but by what it does not have. Windows Server Core is a minimum server configuration, designed to function in a fashion similar to traditional UNIX and Linux servers. One of the advantages of UNIX and Linux systems is that they can be installed with a simple command-line interface and only the minimum services needed to get the job done. This offers three distinct advantages. First, there is no huge overhead from having a graphical interface, which means the CPU can be devoted to accomplishing the essential work of the computer. A second advantage is that less disk space and memory are needed for everyday tasks. The third advantage is that the computer has a much smaller attack surface. Some UNIX and Linux server administrators appreciate the flexibility, simplicity, and power of working at a command line. Now Windows server administrators can install the same type of system.

When you install Windows Server Core, you don't have the following:

- A graphical interface, just a command line
- Graphical tools to configure the server, such as Server Manager
- Extra services that you do not need
- A mouse pointer on the screen
- Windows Mail, Microsoft Word, search windows (in fact no windows), and other software

What you do have are the essential or core services needed to run a server. You can still create server accounts through commands at a command line. You can configure security measures and get operating system and software updates. You can install and configure hardware. You can configure a combination of roles for the server, such as file serving, print serving, or handling distributed shared files across multiple computers. You can open the Notepad screen editor to create and edit files.

Windows Server Core is an installation mode available in the Standard, Enterprise, and Datacenter Editions of Windows Server 2008.

Windows PowerShell

Server administrators who want command-line capability, but also want to install the full-fledged Windows Server 2008 operating system with the graphical user interface (GUI), can use **Windows PowerShell**. Windows PowerShell is a command-line interface that offers a **shell**, a customized environment for executing commands and scripts. Recall that a script is a file of commands to be executed by the operating system.

 Using scripts can save a computer user or administrator a lot of time because an involved sequence of commands is stored in a file to use time and time again—so you don't have to memorize the sequence. It's not unusual to hear a computer user (including this author) comment that he spent considerable time trying to figure out how to accomplish a task and a month later does not remember what the specific steps were. Recording the commands in a script solves this problem.

By using the commands available in Windows PowerShell, you can do the following types of tasks:

- Work with files and folders.
- Manage disk storage.
- Manage network tasks.

- Set up local and network printing options.
- Install, list, and remove software applications.
- View information about the local computer, including user accounts.
- Manage services and processes.
- Lock a computer or log off.
- Manage IIS Web services.

Windows PowerShell offers over 130 command-line tools, also called **cmdlets**. A scripting language is also implemented in Windows PowerShell. Windows Server 2008 comes with Windows PowerShell, which you can install through Server Manager. Also, you can download Windows PowerShell for Windows XP SP2, Windows Server 2003 R2, and Windows Vista. For people who manage an enterprise of different Windows computers, Windows PowerShell can be important for automating all kinds of tasks. Figure 1-3 shows Windows PowerShell using the get-childitem cmdlet to list the files in the current directory, which is the directory of the Administrator account.

```
Select Windows PowerShell
Windows PowerShell
Copyright (C) 2006 Microsoft Corporation. All rights reserved.

PS C:\Users\Administrator> get-childitem


    Directory: Microsoft.PowerShell.Core\FileSystem::C:\Users\Administrator


Mode                LastWriteTime     Length Name
----                -------------     ------ ----
d-r--         2/13/2008   12:46 PM            Contacts
d-r--         2/13/2008   12:46 PM            Desktop
d-r--         2/13/2008   12:46 PM            Documents
d-r--         2/13/2008   12:46 PM            Downloads
d-r--         2/13/2008   12:46 PM            Favorites
d-r--         2/13/2008   12:46 PM            Links
d-r--         2/13/2008   12:46 PM            Music
d-r--         2/13/2008   12:46 PM            Pictures
d-r--         2/13/2008   12:46 PM            Saved Games
d-r--         2/13/2008   12:46 PM            Searches
d-r--         2/13/2008   12:46 PM            Videos


PS C:\Users\Administrator> _
```

Figure 1-3 Using Windows PowerShell for a directory listing

Windows PowerShell for Windows XP, Windows Server 2003, and Windows Vista can be downloaded from Microsoft's Web site, *www.microsoft.com*.

Virtualization

The Hyper-V addition to Windows Server 2008 provides the ability to run two or more operating systems on a single computer. Virtualization has become important to organizations because it offers a way to save expenses and to provide more uptime for computing. Consider a scenario in which an organization has 30 servers and they want to reduce this number to 10 so they can put the servers in a smaller central computer room and use the space of the old room for other purposes. They can do this by using Hyper-V to install three operating systems on each server. Besides gaining space, virtualization simplifies server management by reducing the number of computers to manage. This offers cost savings because 10 computers use less energy than 30.

Another situation that is common to organizations is the need to have a test platform for the development of new applications. Consider a small company that provides a nationwide database service to agricultural colleges. This company has four servers, one for applications and three containing databases. Two programmers develop specialized software for the database service. This type of software development must be done in a test environment before it is brought live for production. The company can use Hyper-V on the single applications server to create one system for production and one for testing.

Or, consider a retail business that takes product orders through Web services, over the telephone, and through surface mail. It has four different servers running different versions of Windows Server. The company needs to back up information several times a day. One way to perform the backups is to use Hyper-V on one or two servers that are in a different location. This not only accomplishes the regular backups, but also provides disaster recovery, so that operations could be continued from the backup location.

The Hyper-V capabilities include the following:

- Compatible with clustering
- Able to handle up to a four-processor SMP computer
- Can be used with Windows and Linux operating systems, which are commonly implemented for servers
- Compatible with different types of disk storage methods
- Enables fast migration from one computer to another
- Can house 64-bit and 32-bit operating systems

Reliability

Several features make Windows Server 2008 reliable and powerful. The operating system kernel runs in **privileged mode,** which protects it from problems created by a malfunctioning program or process. The **kernel** consists of the core programs and the computer code of the operating system. Privileged mode gives the operating system kernel an extra level of security from intruders and prevents system crashes due to poorly written applications.

In addition to privileged mode, Microsoft has introduced typical and protected processes in both Windows Server 2008 and Windows Vista. A **process** is a computer program or portion of a program that is currently running. One large program might start several smaller programs or processes. A typical process is like one on previous Windows systems in which the process can be influenced by a user or other processes. A protected process is one for which outside influences are restricted. The concept of a protected process is important because some activities shouldn't be interrupted prematurely, such as updating a database.

Another feature that contributes to reliability is the implementation of better management tools, including Server Manager and a host of wizards that provide step-by-step guidance. These tools help ensure that the server administrator does not introduce errors or problems when configuring and managing a server. Server administrators can also use the Windows Reliability and Performance Monitor to identify trouble spots so they can be addressed.

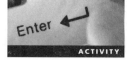

Activity 1-2: Viewing Running Processes

Time Required: Approximately 5 minutes

Objective: View the processes running in Windows Server 2008.

Description: Windows Server 2008 runs many processes at any one time. Some of the processes are used by a program you are using, such as Windows Explorer. Other processes are running in the background, such as a process for your desktop background. In this activity, you view the running processes using a tool called Task Manager. (You can also do this activity in Windows XP and Windows Vista.)

1. With your computer logged on, right-click the **taskbar** at the bottom of your screen (in an open area) and click **Task Manager**.

2. Click the **Processes** tab (see Figure 1-4).

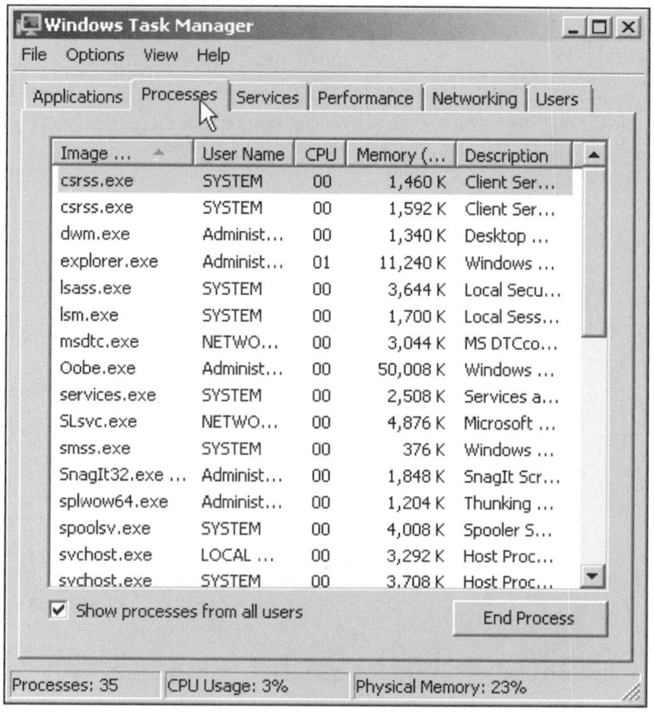

Image ...	User Name	CPU	Memory (...	Description
csrss.exe	SYSTEM	00	1,460 K	Client Ser...
csrss.exe	SYSTEM	00	1,592 K	Client Ser...
dwm.exe	Administ...	00	1,340 K	Desktop ...
explorer.exe	Administ...	01	11,240 K	Windows ...
lsass.exe	SYSTEM	00	3,644 K	Local Secu...
lsm.exe	SYSTEM	00	1,700 K	Local Sess...
msdtc.exe	NETWO...	00	3,044 K	MS DTCco...
Oobe.exe	Administ...	00	50,008 K	Windows ...
services.exe	SYSTEM	00	2,508 K	Services a...
SLsvc.exe	NETWO...	00	4,876 K	Microsoft ...
smss.exe	SYSTEM	00	376 K	Windows ...
SnagIt32.exe ...	Administ...	00	1,848 K	SnagIt Scr...
splwow64.exe	Administ...	00	1,204 K	Thunking ...
spoolsv.exe	SYSTEM	00	4,008 K	Spooler S...
svchost.exe	LOCAL ...	00	3,292 K	Host Proc...
svchost.exe	SYSTEM	00	3,708 K	Host Proc...

☑ Show processes from all users   End Process

Processes: 35 | CPU Usage: 3% | Physical Memory: 23%

Figure 1-4 Using Task Manager to view running processes

3. How many processes are currently running? The processes are shown under the Image... (Image Name) column on the left and you can use the scroll bar on the right to count them.

   • Record below the number of running processes and note the names of two of the processes:

4. Close Task Manager.

Multitasking and Multithreading

Windows Server 2008 and other recent Windows systems take full advantage of the multitasking and multithreading capabilities of modern computers. **Multitasking** is the ability to run two or more programs at the same time. For example, Microsoft Word can print a document at the same time that a Microsoft Excel spreadsheet can calculate the sum of a column of numbers. **Multithreading** is the capability of programs written to run several program code blocks, or "threads," at the same time. For instance, a Microsoft Access database query runs a thread to pull data out of the database, while another thread generates a subtotal of data already obtained.

The multitasking in Windows Server 2008 is called **preemptive multitasking**. This means each program runs in an area of memory separate from areas used by other programs. Early versions of Windows used cooperative multitasking, in which programs shared the same memory area. The advantage of preemptive multitasking is that it reduces the risk of one program interfering with the smooth running of another program, which increases reliability.

Planning a Windows Server 2008 Networking Model

In its simplest form, a network is two or more computers linked together. This provides users with the ability to share devices and applications, exchange files, and communicate via e-mail or videoconferencing. The following sections introduce you to the two basic networking models used with Windows Server 2008 and its workstation clients (such as Windows Vista): the peer-to-peer model and the server-based model.

As a network operating system, Windows Server 2008 is used to coordinate the ways computers access resources available to them on the network. A **network** is a communications system enabling computer users to share computer equipment, application software, and data, voice, and video transmissions. Physically, a network contains computers joined by communications cabling or sometimes by wireless devices. Networks can link users who are in the same office or building, in a different state, or anywhere in the world (see Figure 1-5).

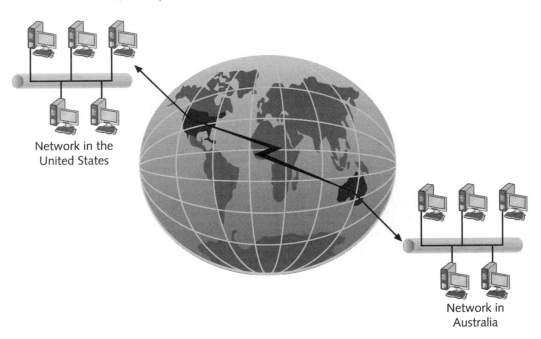

Network in the
United States

Network in
Australia

Figure 1-5   Networking across continents

A workstation or client network operating system is one that enables individual computers to access a network, and in some cases to share resources on a limited basis. As you learned earlier, a workstation is a computer that has its own central processing unit (CPU) and can be used as a stand-alone or network computer for word processing, spreadsheet creation, or other software applications. A client is a computer that accesses resources on another computer through a network or by a direct connection.

Windows Server 2008 can be implemented using either peer-to-peer networking, server-based networking, or a combination of both. **Peer-to-peer networking** focuses on spreading network resource administration among server and nonserver members of a network, whereas **server-based networking** centralizes the network administration on one or more servers. Often small organizations use the peer-to-peer networking model, whereas medium-sized and large networks use the server-based model.

Peer-to-Peer Networking

A peer-to-peer network is one of the simplest ways to configure a network, and is often used for home offices and small businesses. On a peer-to-peer network, workstations are used to share resources such as files and printers and to connect to resources on other computers. Windows Server 2008 and Windows Vista are examples of operating systems that can be used for peer-to-peer network communication. Files, folders, printers, applications, and devices on one computer can be shared and made available for others to access. No special computer, such as a mainframe computer or server, is needed to enable workstations to communicate and share resources, although in some cases a server can be used as a powerful workstation (see Figure 1-6).

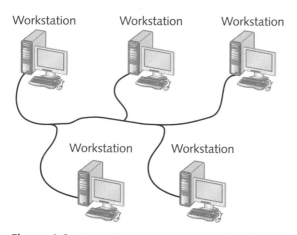

Figure 1-6 A simple peer-to-peer network without a server

Peer-to-peer networking can be effective for very small networks, but it does present some disadvantages. With this model, management of network resources is decentralized. As the network increases in size and the number of shared network resources increases, administration becomes more difficult.

Security of the resources is another important issue. Each of the users is responsible for the security of their own resources and must know how to set the proper permissions and security. Also, a client operating system is not designed to handle a growing load of clients in the same way as a server operating system.

Peer-to-peer networks are generally designed for about 10 workstations or less. As the number of workstations surpass this number, this model becomes less effective for the following reasons:

- Peer-to-peer networking offers only moderate network security because user account information must be managed on each workstation.

- This model provides no centralized storage of information for account management. As the number of network users grows, so does the need to have a central place to store and manage information. It is much easier to manage files by locating them on a central file server.

- Network management becomes more difficult because there is no point of centralized administrative control from which to manage users and critical files, including backing up important files.

- Peer-to-peer networks can often experience slow response times because this model is not optimized for multiple users accessing one computer. If many workgroup members decide to access one shared drive or some other shared resource at the same time, all members are likely to experience slow response. On Microsoft networks, a **workgroup** is a number of users who share drive and printer resources, and it represents an alternative (generally for small networks) to organizing resources in a domain.

Activity 1-3: Determining if a Computer Is in a Domain or a Workgroup

Time Required: Approximately 5 minutes
Objective: Discover if a particular computer is in a domain or a workgroup.

Description: Some networks combine the use of domains and workgroups. Often workgroups are less secure and less tightly managed than a domain, leaving workgroup resources more susceptible to intruders and more likely to have problems with reliable access to shared resources, such as files. In this activity, you learn how to determine if a computer is a member of a domain or workgroup. For this activity, you can use either Windows Server 2008 or Windows Vista.

1. With your computer logged on, click **Start**, and then right-click **Computer**.

2. Click **Properties**.

3. Look for the section, Computer name, domain, and workgroup settings (refer back to Figure 1-2).

   - Is your computer identified as being in a workgroup or a domain? What names are in the Computer name and the Full computer name lines? Record your answer here:

4. Close the System window.

Server-Based Networking

Windows Server 2008 is a more scalable network operating system than Windows Vista or XP, and unlike Windows Vista and XP, it has features that make it a true server operating system. A **server** is a single computer that provides extensive multiuser access to network resources. For example, a single server can act as a file and print server, a Web server, a network administration server, a database server, an e-mail server, or a combination of any of these. Depending on the hardware capabilities, the server can handle hundreds of users at once, providing fast response when delivering the shared resource, and less network congestion when multiple workstations access that resource. Figure 1-7 illustrates a Windows Server 2008 server-based network.

The server-based model offers a wide array of options for networking. For instance, implementing this model can provide the following advantages:

- Users only need to log on once to gain access to network resources.

- Security is stronger because access to shared resources and to the network itself can be intentionally managed from one place—the server—rather than randomly managed on many independent peer-to-peer computers.

- All members can share computer files.

- Printers and other resources can be shared; they can also be located in a central place for convenience.

- All members can have electronic mail (e-mail) and send messages to other office members through an e-mail server such as Microsoft Exchange Server.

- Software applications, such as an accounting package or word-processing software, can be stored and shared in a central location.

- Important databases can be managed and secured from one computer.

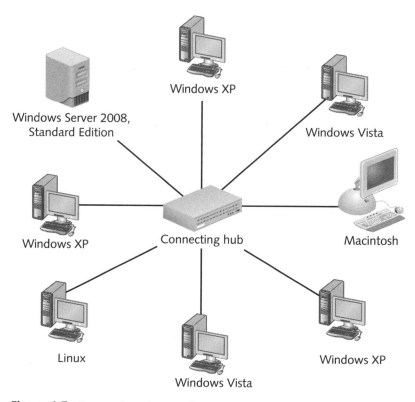

Figure 1-7 A server-based network

- All computers can be backed up more easily. With a network and server, the backups can be performed from one location and regularly scheduled to run from the server.

- Computer resource sharing can be arranged to reflect the work patterns of groups within an organization. For example, managing partners in a legal firm can be one group for the purpose of sharing management and financial information on the server.

- The server administrator can save time when installing software upgrades. For example, to implement the latest version of Word, the administrator upgrades the software installation files on the server. Then Word users on the network can upgrade their versions from the server.

Protocols for the Windows Server 2008 Networking Model

Servers and clients on a Windows Server 2008 network communicate through a set of communications guidelines that are similar to using a language, but the language used by computers is in a binary format of zeros and ones that is sent through network communications cables. The communication languages of computers are called protocols. A **protocol** consists of guidelines for the following:

- How data is formatted into discrete units called packets and frames
- How packets and frames are transmitted across one or more networks
- How packets and frames are interpreted at the receiving end

Packets and **frames** are units of data transmitted from a sending computer to a receiving computer. These units might be compared with words in a language. In a language, people communicate by using words to compose sentences and paragraphs to convey a thought. The words by themselves do not convey the full thought until they are placed in the context of a sentence or paragraph. Like words, packets and frames usually do not convey full meaning until the complete stream of information is received; and just as words must be properly placed in sentences and paragraphs, packets and frames must be received in the proper order to be understood.

 Sometimes the terms <u>packet</u> and <u>frame</u> are used as if they have the same meaning. However, a packet operates at a higher level of communication than a frame. A packet's higher level of communication enables it to contain routing information so that it can be forwarded from one network to another.

Windows Server 2008 and its clients primarily use the **Transmission Control Protocol/Internet Protocol (TCP/IP)**, which is actually a suite of protocols and utilities that support communication across LANs and the Internet. A **local area network (LAN)** is a network of computers in relatively close proximity, such as on the same floor or in the same building. TCP/IP has become the worldwide protocol of choice. One reason for this is that TCP/IP is the protocol used for Internet communication. As companies continue to utilize the Internet as an essential component of their businesses, it makes sense to use TCP/IP as the internal protocol, rather than dedicating additional network resources to use another one. TCP/IP is also popular because it is designed as an open standard, that is, no one owns TCP/IP. It can also be used to connect computers running almost any operating system. In addition, many people around the world are working on improving the standards on which TCP/IP is based.

Transmission Control Protocol

The **Transmission Control Protocol (TCP)** portion of TCP/IP provides for reliable end-to-end delivery of data by controlling data flow. Computers or network stations agree upon a "window" for data transmission that includes the number of bytes to be sent. The transmission window is constantly adjusted to account for existing network traffic. TCP/IP monitors for requests to start a communications session, establishes sessions with other TCP stations, handles transmitting and receiving data, and closes transmission sessions when they are finished. TCP is also considered a **connection-oriented communication** because it ensures that packets are delivered, that they are delivered in the right sequence, and that their contents are accurate.

 Some applications use the **User Datagram Protocol (UDP)** with IP instead of using TCP. These are typically applications in which the reliability of the communication is not a major concern, such as for information used to boot diskless workstations over a network. UDP is a **connectionless communication** because it does not provide checking to make sure that a connection is reliable and that data is sent accurately. The advantage of UDP is that it is formatted as a smaller frame with less header information than TCP and so can be processed faster through network communications.

Internet Protocol

The **Internet Protocol (IP)** portion of the TCP/IP protocol provides network addressing to ensure data packets quickly reach the correct destination. **Internet Protocol Version 4 (IPv4)** and **Internet Protocol Version 6 (IPv6)** are the two versions of IP in use. In this section, you learn about IPv4; IPv6 is described in the section "Internet Protocol Version 6."

IPv4 is used by default on most networks because it has been in existence for years and is well understood. It uses a system of addressing that consists of four numbers separated by a period, such as 129.77.15.182. IP also provides for routing data over different networks, so that data sent from one network only goes to the appropriate destination network instead of to all networks that are linked together. Routing is accomplished through a device called a **router** (or a network device with router capabilities), which connects networks, is able to read IP addresses (see the next section), and can route or forward packets of data to designated networks, as shown in Figure 1-8. IP also handles fragmenting packets because the packet sizes might vary from one network to another. IP is a connectionless communication because it relies on TCP to provide connection-oriented communications.

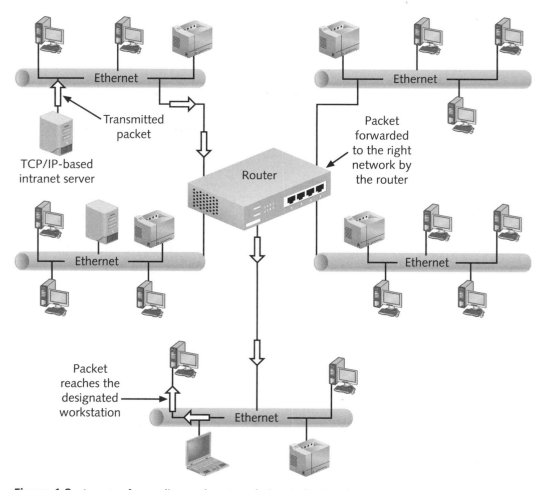

Figure 1-8 A router forwarding packets to a designated network

The combined TCP/IP protocol is particularly well suited for medium-sized and large networks, but it becomes important on any enterprise network or on a local area network that connects to a wide area network.

IP Addressing The **IP address** format is called the **dotted decimal notation**. It is 32 bits long and contains four fields of decimal values representing eight-bit binary octets. An IP address in binary octet format looks like this: 10000001.00000101.00001010.01100100, which converts to 129.5.10.100 in decimal format. Part of the address is the network identifier (NET_ID), and another part is the host identifier (HOST_ID), depending on the size of the LAN, how the LAN is divided into smaller networks, and if the packet is unicast or multicast. A **unicast** is a transmission in which one packet is sent from a server to each client that requests a file or application, such as a video presentation. Thus, if five clients request the video presentation, the server sends five packets per each transmission to the five clients. In the same example, a **multicast** means that the server is able to treat all five clients as a group and send one packet per transmission that reaches all five clients (see Figure 1-9). Multicasts can be used to significantly reduce network traffic when transmitting multimedia applications. A third type of communication is called a **broadcast**, which sends a communication to all points on a specific network (routers are often configured so that they do not forward broadcasts to other networks).

In a unicast on a typical medium-sized LAN (with up to 65,534 actual connections), the first two octets are normally the network ID and the last two are the host ID. In a multicast transmission on the same network, the four octets are used to specify a group of nodes to receive the multicast. Such a group usually consists of nodes that are multicast subscription members.

Another special-purpose form of addressing is the subnet mask. A **subnet mask** is used for two purposes: to show the class of addressing used and to divide a network into subnetworks or

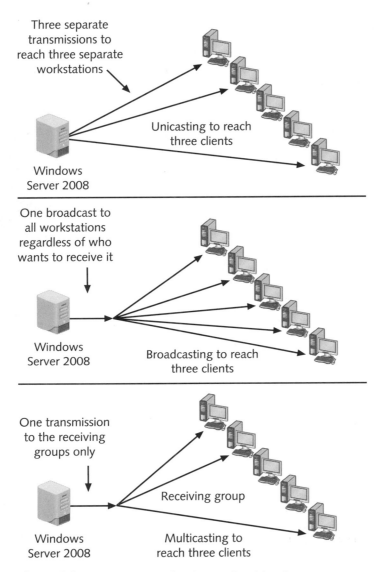

Figure 1-9 Unicasting, broadcasting, and multicasting

subnets to control network traffic. In the first instance, the subnet mask enables an application to determine which part of the address is for the network ID and which is for the host ID. For example, a subnet mask for a Class A network is all binary 1s in the first octet and all binary 0s in remaining octets: 11111111.00000000.00000000.00000000 (255.0.0.0 in decimal).

To divide the network into subnetworks, the subnet mask consists of a subnet ID within the network and a host ID, which is determined by the network administrator. For example, the entire third octet in a Class B address could be designated to indicate the subnet ID, which would be an octet of 11111111.11111111.11111111.00000000 (255.255.255.0). Another option would be to designate only the first five bits in the third octet as the subnet ID and the last three bits (and last octet as well) for the host ID, which would be 11111111.11111111.11111000. 00000000 (255.255.248.0). This approach might be used to reduce the number of unused IP addresses, so that they are not wasted.

Many server administrators use TCP/IP because the ability to create subnets provides important versatility in controlling network congestion and in setting up security so that only authorized users can reach specific parts of a network or specific intranets.

IP Address Considerations

When planning your TCP/IP implementation, you will need to consider a few specific rules. First, the network number 127.0.0.0 cannot be assigned to any network. It is used for diagnostic purposes. For example, the address 127.0.0.1 is known as the loopback address, and is used for diagnostic testing of the local TCP/IP installation. You might use the TCP/IP-based utility, *pathping*, as shown in Figure 1-10, to test connectivity using the loopback address.

```
Administrator: Command Prompt                                          _ □ X
Microsoft Windows [Version 6.0.6001]
Copyright (c) 2006 Microsoft Corporation.  All rights reserved.

C:\Users\Administrator>pathping 127.0.0.1

Tracing route to accounting.jpcomp.com [127.0.0.1]
over a maximum of 30 hops:
  0  accounting.jpcomp.com [127.0.0.1]
  1  accounting.jpcomp.com [127.0.0.1]

Computing statistics for 25 seconds...
              Source to Here   This Node/Link
Hop  RTT     Lost/Sent = Pct  Lost/Sent = Pct  Address
  0                                            accounting.jpcomp.com [127.0.0.1]

                               0/ 100 =  0%  |
  1    0ms    0/ 100 =  0%    0/ 100 =  0%  accounting.jpcomp.com [127.0.0.1]

Trace complete.

C:\Users\Administrator>_
```

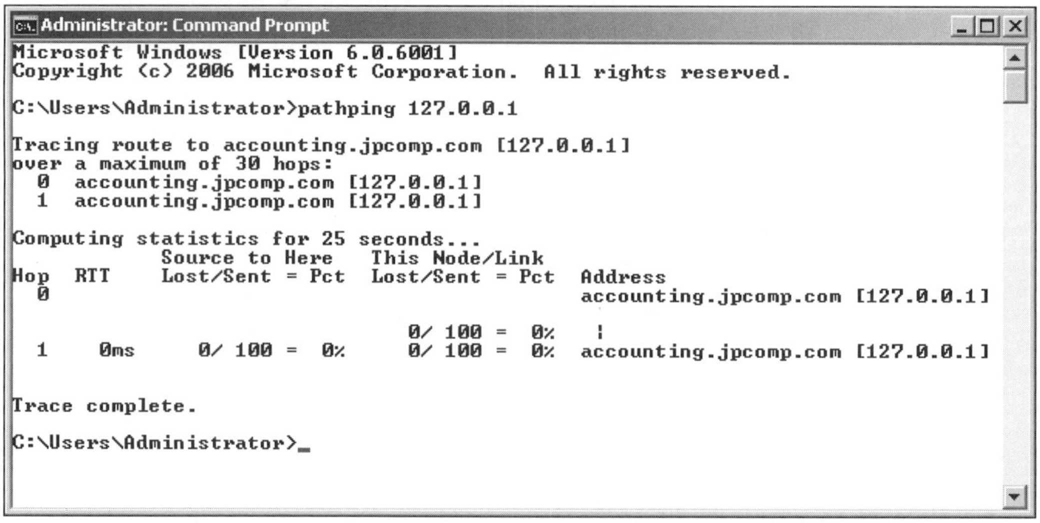

Figure 1-10 Testing a local TCP/IP installation using the loopback address

The standard implementation of TCP/IP also reserves a series of addresses known as private addresses. Table 1-2 shows the IP network numbers that have been reserved for such purposes.

Table 1-2 Reserved IP network numbers

Network number	Subnet mask	IP address range
10.0.0.0	255.0.0.0	10.0.0.1–10.255.255.255
172.16.0.0–172.31.0.0	255.255.0.0	172.16.0.1–172.31.255.255
192.168.0.0	255.255.255.0	192.168.0.1–192.168.255.255

No one can use these IP addresses on the Internet. They are designed for use on a private network behind a **Network Address Translation (NAT)** device, such as a firewall or proxy server, or some routers. If you do have a NAT device, you can use any of these addresses on your own private network. A NAT device is used to disguise local or internal IP addresses from outside networks, such as the Internet. You learn more about NAT in Chapter 10, "Securing Windows Server 2008."

You cannot assign a network number to a computer or any other host on the network. For example, your network number might be 198.92.4.0 (subnet mask 255.255.255.0). You cannot assign this number to a computer on the network.

You also cannot assign the highest number on a network to a host. In the preceding example, you cannot assign 198.92.4.255 to a host on the network. This address is interpreted as a broadcast message for the subnet, and all of the computers on the subnet would receive the packet. On the network referred to here, any numbers from 198.92.4.1 to 198.92.4.254 are valid numbers for hosts.

Activity 1-4: Testing for IP Address and Connectivity

Time Required: Approximately 10 minutes
Objective: Practice using the Windows Server 2008 Command Prompt window with the *pathping* and *tracert* commands.

Description: Two tools that enable you to test IP-addressing issues and connectivity on a network are *pathping* and *tracert. pathping* is used to test connectivity to another network by using IP address information. *pathping* can also calculate the number of IP packets returned from each router through which *pathping* passes. *tracert* simply determines the number of routers, called hops, through which it passes. Because both utilities report IP addressing for the hops, you can use them not only to determine connectivity, but also to identify malfunctioning routers by IP address. This activity enables you to practice both commands from the Windows Server 2008 Command Prompt window. Before you start, obtain from your instructor an off-site network address or name that you can use, or use a name from a favorite Web site in the form of myfavoritesitename.com.

1. Click **Start**, click **All Programs,** click **Accessories,** and click **Command Prompt.**

2. At the prompt, type **pathping** plus the name or address of the computer you are contacting, such as *pathping myfavoritesitename.com.*

   - What results do you see?

3. Next, type **tracert** plus the name or address of the computer you are contacting, such as *tracert myfavoritesitename.com.*

   - What are the results?

4. Close the Command Prompt window.

Internet Protocol Version 6 IPv4 is a product of the early 1980s. By the mid-1990s, network professionals recognized that IPv4 had some limitations. Chief among the limitations was the 32-bit address, particularly when there were thousands of networks and millions of network users. IPv4 was literally running out of addresses. It was also limited because it had no provision for network security or for implementing sophisticated routing options, such as creating subnets based on specific levels of network service and performance. Also, IPv4 did not have many options, other than broadcast and multicast addressing, for handling different kinds of multimedia applications, such as streaming video or videoconferencing.

In response to the exploding use of networks and IP, the IP Next Generation (IPng) initiative was started by the Internet Engineering Task Force (IETF). By 1996, IPng resulted in a newly defined standard called IP Version 6 (IPv6). The purpose of IPv6 is to provide a logical growth path from IPv4 so that applications and network devices can handle new demands as they arise. Currently, IPv4 is used on most networks throughout the world, and the transition to IPv6 is moving slowly. In one survey of Fortune 1000 companies and of many midsized companies, few of the companies surveyed had plans to convert to IPv6. In fact, only about 5 percent of companies are using it now. Some of the delay is related to the widespread use of NAT and internal network addressing enabled by NAT.

This section provides an introduction to IPv6 so you are aware of its existence, but the emphasis in this chapter is on IPv4 because it is so firmly entrenched in current network use.

Among the new features of IPv6 are:

- A 128-bit address capability
- A single address associated with multiple network interfaces

- New IP extension headers that can be implemented for special needs, including more routing and security options

IPv6 addressing enables one IP identifier to be associated with several different interfaces, so it can better handle multimedia traffic. Instead of broadcasting or multicast grouping, under IPv6 networks transmitting multimedia traffic designate all the recipient interfaces as the same address.

IPv6 is designed so that addresses can be configured using a wide range of options. This enables better communications for routing and subnetting. Plus, it offers options to create distinctions within a single address for network size, network location, organization, organization type, workgroups within an organization, and so on. IPv6 addressing is autoconfiguring, which reduces the workload of the network administrator in managing and configuring addresses.

Considering today's concern about network attackers, the IPv6 packet can be encrypted for security. An encrypted packet makes snooping on networks more difficult, which can help to thwart attackers.

The downside to using IPv6 encryption is that it can increase the communication delays on a network, which is another reason why some organizations are slow to adopt it.

Static and Dynamic Addressing Each server and workstation needs a unique IP address, either specified at the computer or obtained from a server that assigns temporary IP addresses. Before setting up TCP/IP, you need to make some decisions about how to set up IP addressing on the network. The options are to use what Microsoft calls static addressing or dynamic addressing. **Static addressing** involves assigning a dotted decimal address that becomes each workstation's permanent, unique IP address. This method is used on networks, large and small, where the network administrator wants direct control over the assigned addresses. Direct control might be necessary where network management software is used to track all network nodes and the software depends on each node having a permanent, known IP address. Permanent addresses give consistency to monitoring network statistics and to keeping historical network performance information. The disadvantage is that IP address administration can be a laborious task on a large network. Most network administrators have an IP database to keep track of currently assigned addresses and unused addresses to assign as new people are connected to the network.

Dynamic addressing automatically assigns an IP address to a computer each time it is logged on. An IP address is leased to a particular computer for a defined period of time. This addressing method uses the **Dynamic Host Configuration Protocol (DHCP)**, which is supported by Windows Server 2008 for dynamic addressing. The protocol is used to enable a Windows Server 2008 server with DHCP services to detect the presence of a new workstation and assign an IP address to that workstation. On your network, this would require you to load DHCP services onto a Windows Server 2008 server and configure it to be a DHCP server. It would still act as a regular server for other activities, but with the added ability to automatically assign IP addresses to workstations. A Windows Server 2008 DHCP server leases IP addresses for a specified period of time, which might be one week, one month, one year, or a permanent lease. When the lease is up, the IP address is returned to a pool of available IP addresses maintained by the server.

When you use DHCP, plan to apply it to client workstations and not to servers. Make each server's IP address permanent. It is important for server IP addresses to always remain the same so there is no doubt about how to access a server. For example, consider how hard a Web server would be to find on the Internet if its IP address changed periodically.

Default Gateway In Windows Server 2008, if you statically configure the IP address, plan to supply the subnet mask information as well as the default gateway. The **default gateway** is the IP address of the router that has a connection to other networks. The default gateway address is used when the host computer you are trying to contact exists on another network. This could be compared with a room that has only one door. If you are in the room, you can talk to anyone else who is also in the room, but if you ever want to go to another room, you must use the door. The default gateway is like the door. If a computer is connecting only to local computers, it will never need the default gateway; but as soon as it needs to go outside the network, it needs to know the exit point.

For example, Table 1-3 shows the TCP/IP configuration for ComputerA and ComputerC and their default gateways.

Table 1-3 Sample TCP/IP configurations

Computer	IP address	Subnet mask	Default gateway
ComputerA	133.229.143.72	255.255.0.0	133.229.1.1
ComputerC	133.225.143.92	255.255.0.0	133.225.1.1

When ComputerA tries to communicate with ComputerC, it determines that ComputerC is on a different network. ComputerA has to send the packet to a remote network, so it uses its default gateway as the exit to that network. Because the default gateway is set as the router (133.229.1.1), ComputerA sends the packet to the router, and the router forwards the packet to ComputerC. When ComputerC replies to the message, it sends the packet to its side of the router (133.225.1.1), and the router forwards the packet to ComputerA.

Most of the time the default gateway (and the router IP address) is set as the first valid host number on a subnet, such as 133.229.1.1. There is no technical reason to do this; it simply makes it easier to remember the configuration.

Name Resolution   Even when using the decimal notation for the IP address instead of the 32-bit number, most users still have difficulty remembering the IP addresses for their computers. Generally, computers are referred to by their names, which are **NetBIOS names** for older Windows-based systems and/or host names for computers on networks that use DNS servers. **Domain Name System (DNS)** is a TCP/IP application protocol that enables a DNS server to resolve (translate) domain and computer names to IP addresses, or IP addresses to domain and computer names.

Examples of names include CORPDC1, RAMRZ, ACCOUNTANT, or any name that an organization or user chooses to uniquely identify a computer on the network. The problem with using names is that they cannot be used by TCP/IP, which can only use the IP address when contacting another computer. Therefore, if computer names are going to be used to connect to other computers, there must be some method of determining the IP address that matches a computer name. Windows Server 2008 enables use of both NetBIOS and host names to resolve IP addresses to computer names.

NetBIOS Names   Prior to Windows 2000 Server, the primary means of locating computers on a Windows-based network was by the computer's NetBIOS name. The Browse list and mapped drives were also based on NetBIOS names.

Windows Server 2008 still supports NetBIOS names for backward compatibility with previous versions of Windows. Every Windows Server 2008 computer can still be accessed using the NetBIOS name.

A number of methods are available to resolve NetBIOS names to IP addresses, but the preferred method is using a **Windows Internet Naming Service (WINS)** server. WINS is a Windows Server (all versions) service that enables the server to convert NetBIOS workstation names to IP addresses. A WINS server stores a database of computer names and their corresponding IP addresses. The biggest advantage of WINS is its dynamic nature. When a WINS client computer is connected to the network and turned on, it automatically registers its name and IP address with the WINS server. Then, any other WINS client can query the WINS server for the IP address using the computer name.

NetBIOS names can also be resolved through the use of broadcasts and files called LmHosts files (Lm stands for LAN Manager, which was an early server operating system offered through Microsoft and 3COM). However, these methods present two main problems. First, broadcasts can create a significant amount of network traffic, as all computers on a network have to look at the broadcast packets. Second, in most cases, broadcast messages do not cross routers. LmHosts are text files stored on each computer that list computer names and IP addresses. One problem with LmHosts files is that they are located on all computers and must be manually updated whenever computer names or IP addresses change (although it is also possible to centralize LmHosts to one file that all other LmHosts files use as a reference). In most cases, WINS is the best solution only if NetBIOS names are used.

WINS and NetBIOS are legacy network services that have been kept in recent server operating systems mostly for compatibility with older client systems, such as Windows NT, Windows 95, and Windows 98. Many organizations are retiring the use of WINS and NetBIOS. Also, WINS and NetBIOS are not compatible with IPv6.

Host Names Using host names is the preferred method of resolving computer names to IP addresses in Windows Server 2008. In fact, you can turn off NetBIOS on a Windows Server 2008 computer so that host name resolution is the only method of name resolution that is available.

The best method in Windows Server 2008 for resolving host names to IP addresses is to use **Dynamic Domain Name System (DDNS)**. DDNS is a modern DNS application that enables client computers to automatically register their IP addresses in DNS without intervention by a user or network administrator.

If a DNS server is not available, broadcasts and HOSTS files can also be used to resolve IP addresses to host names. These methods, however, require far more effort to administer.

You learn much more about using DHCP, DNS, WINS, and DDNS in Chapter 8, "Managing Windows Server 2008 Network Services."

Physical Addresses and the Address Resolution Protocol

In addition to the IP address, each network station also has a unique physical or device address. The **Address Resolution Protocol (ARP)** is used to acquire the physical addresses associated with a computer's **network interface card (NIC)**. Every NIC has a physical address, or **media access control (MAC) address**. A NIC is a card in a networked device that attaches that device to the network, through a wired or wireless connection. The MAC address is programmed on the NIC when it is manufactured, and no two NICs have the same MAC address. For computers to communicate with each other, they must know the MAC addresses of each other's network interface cards. Proper communications using TCP/IP rely on both IP addresses and MAC addresses.

For example, suppose that ComputerA is trying to connect with another computer on the same network (ComputerB) with an IP address of 192.168.1.200. In making the connection, the following occurs:

1. By examining the IP address and subnet mask, ComputerA determines that the two computers are on the same network. ComputerA then checks its ARP cache (storage area) to see if it already has the MAC address for the IP address of ComputerB.

2. If ComputerA does not have the address, then ARP sends out a packet to look for the address. The packet is a request for the MAC address for host 192.168.1.200 (see Figure 1-11).

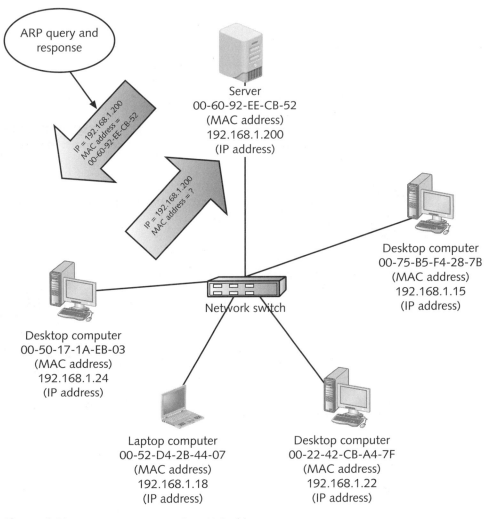

Figure 1-11 Using ARP to query the MAC address

3. All of the computers on the network examine the packet, but only the computer with the right IP address (ComputerB) responds. When ComputerB sees this request, it puts the MAC address for ComputerA into its own ARP cache and then sends back its MAC address to ComputerA.

4. ComputerA puts the MAC address into its ARP cache, and communication continues. The MAC address remains in the cache for 2 to 10 minutes, depending on how often the address is used. If the two computers are not on the same network and the information needs to cross a router, a similar process occurs, except that the ARP request asks for the MAC address of the router.

Every computer running Windows Server 2008 has an ARP cache that can include the recently resolved MAC addresses as well as statically assigned values in the ARP cache. To view the information in the ARP cache, open a Command Prompt window and then type *arp -a*.

The *arp -a* command shows you the MAC addresses along with the corresponding IP addresses that the local computer currently has in its ARP cache. The dynamic entries are stored in the ARP cache for two minutes, unless the entry is used during those two minutes. If the entry is used within two minutes, then the entry will be stored for 10 minutes. The static entries stay in the ARP cache until the computer is rebooted or until the entry is removed using the *arp -d* command.

Activity 1-5: Using Sample Utilities for IP Address and Connectivity Testing

Time Required: Approximately 10 minutes
Objective: Practice using the Windows Server 2008 Command Prompt window and ARP command.

Description: The ARP command is a great addition to your toolkit of utilities for diagnosing a network problem. In this activity, you practice using the ARP tool with the *-a* option to view the contents of the ARP cache and the */?* option to view a listing of all ARP options. You need to be logged on to a computer running Windows Server 2008 (or Windows Vista/XP) using an account provided by your instructor or an account with administrator privileges.

1. Click **Start,** click **All Programs,** click **Accessories,** and click **Command Prompt.** (Alternatively, in Windows Server 2008 and Windows XP, you can click Start, click Run, enter cmd in the Open text box, and click OK. In Windows Vista, you can click Start, click All Programs, click Accessories, click Run, enter cmd in the Open text box, and click OK.)

2. At the prompt, type **arp -a.** Your screen should look similar to the one in Figure 1-12.

```
Administrator: Command Prompt                                          _ □ ×
Microsoft Windows [Version 6.0.6001]
Copyright (c) 2006 Microsoft Corporation.   All rights reserved.

C:\Users\Administrator>arp -a

Interface: 192.168.0.8 --- 0xa
  Internet Address       Physical Address       Type
  192.168.0.1            00-0f-b3-8b-05-70       dynamic
  192.168.0.9            00-19-d2-4a-07-0b       dynamic
  192.168.0.255          ff-ff-ff-ff-ff-ff       static
  224.0.0.22             01-00-5e-00-00-16       static
  224.0.0.252            01-00-5e-00-00-fc       static
  255.255.255.255        ff-ff-ff-ff-ff-ff       static

C:\Users\Administrator>
```

Figure 1-12   Using the ARP command

3. Type **arp /?** at the prompt.

   • What switches are displayed other than /? and -a?

4. Close the Command Prompt window.

Implementing TCP/IP in Windows Server 2008

Implementing TCP/IP in Windows Server 2008 involves two tasks: verifying it is enabled and configuring it. Verifying that TCP/IP is enabled is the easiest part of the implementation. Configuring TCP/IP can be more complex, depending on whether your network uses static or dynamic addressing. You learn about enabling and configuring in the next sections.

Enabling TCP/IP

One of the most essential elements in network setup is understanding how to enable TCP/IP. TCP/IP is the only protocol that is installed by default when you install Windows Server 2008 (and, in fact, the option to remove it is disabled). However, TCP/IP itself can be disabled, which blocks network communication with Windows Server 2008.

Activity 1-6: Verifying TCP/IP Is Enabled

Time Required: Approximately 10 minutes
Objective: Ensure that TCP/IP is enabled in Windows Server 2008.

Description: If your network connection is not working, you can check to ensure that TCP/IP is enabled. It is important to know where to enable or disable TCP/IP to help troubleshoot network problems. Also, there might be times when you want to disable TCP/IP so users do not access a server while you are working on it. The following steps show you where to enable or disable TCP/IP. You will need to log on using an account that has Administrator privileges.

1. Click **Start** and click **Control Panel.**

2. If you are at the Control Panel Home view, click **View network status and tasks** (under Network and Internet). If you are in the Classic View, double-click the icon for **Network and Sharing Center.**

3. Click the link for **Manage network connections**.

4. Right-click the appropriate connection, such as **Local Area Connection** (for a wired connection) or **Wireless Network Connection** (for a computer with wireless network connectivity).

5. Click **Properties.**

6. Check to see if TCP/IP is enabled. If it is currently enabled, you'll see one or both of Internet Protocol Version 6 (TCP/IPv6) and Internet Protocol Version 4 (TCP/IPv4) with check marks in their boxes, as shown in Figure 1-13.

> If you want to prevent users from accessing the server, you can remove the check marks from both Internet Protocol Version 6 (TCP/IPv6) and Internet Protocol Version 4 (TCP/IPv4) and click OK. Next, click Yes in the information box. When you disable both TCP/IPv4 and TCP/IPv6, Windows Server 2008 also disables Client for Microsoft Networks and File and Printer Sharing for Microsoft Networks. When you're ready to enable networking, you'll need to enable these services as well as TCP/IPv4 and TCP/IPv6.

   - What can you do to initiate configuring your NIC from the currently open window?

7. Leave the Connection Properties dialog box open for the next activity (unless you can't complete the next activity at this time).

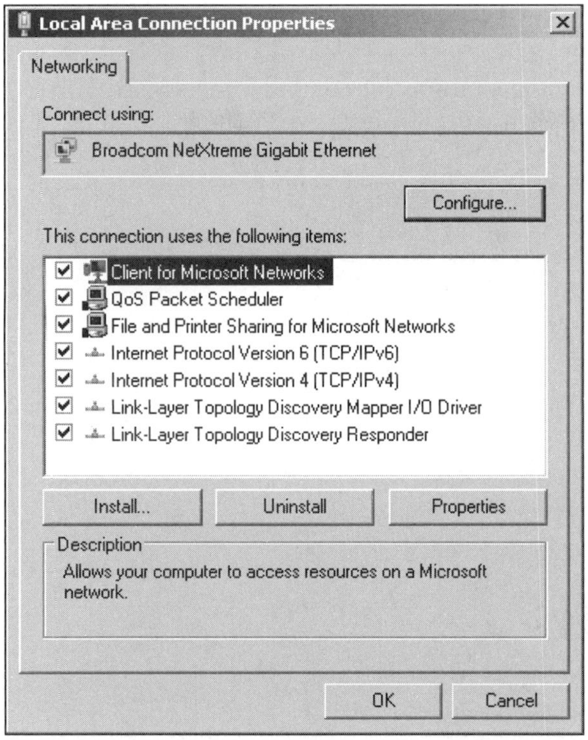

Local Area Connection Properties

Networking

Connect using:

Broadcom NetXtreme Gigabit Ethernet

Configure...

This connection uses the following items:

- ☑ Client for Microsoft Networks
- ☑ QoS Packet Scheduler
- ☑ File and Printer Sharing for Microsoft Networks
- ☑ Internet Protocol Version 6 (TCP/IPv6)
- ☑ Internet Protocol Version 4 (TCP/IPv4)
- ☑ Link-Layer Topology Discovery Mapper I/O Driver
- ☑ Link-Layer Topology Discovery Responder

Install...   Uninstall   Properties

Description
Allows your computer to access resources on a Microsoft network.

OK   Cancel

Figure 1-13   Viewing the network connection properties

Configuring TCP/IP

As you learned earlier in this chapter, two basic approaches can be used to configure the TCP/IP settings, in Windows Server 2008: static addressing and dynamic addressing. In the following sections, you learn how to use each approach.

Using static addressing for all computers on a network can be time consuming. However, some organizations prefer this approach to maintain the ability to track network problems by IP address. Other organizations use static addressing for servers and certain other network devices, such as routers, but use dynamic addressing for their users' computers. When you use static addressing, ensure that all of the parameters are correctly entered to avoid duplicate or conflicting entries that might result in one or more computers that cannot access the network. This is particularly true when configuring a server that must be reliably available to a large number of users.

Activity 1-7: Configuring TCP/IP for Static Addressing

Time Required: Approximately 10 minutes
Objective: Learn how to manually configure TCP/IP for situations in which static addressing is used.

Description: Some organizations prefer to use a static IP address for some or all of the computers on the network. For example, servers are often given a static IP address that does not change, because if it did, there might be confusion about how to reliably access a particular server. In this activity, you learn how to configure the TCP/IP address information manually. Before you start, obtain an IP address, subnet mask, and default gateway from your instructor. Furthermore, obtain an IP address for the preferred DNS server, and if needed, an address for the alternate DNS server. For this activity, assume you are configuring IPv4. Also, you will need to log on using an account that has Administrator privileges.

1. Make sure that the Connection Properties dialog box is still open from the previous activity. If it is not, review Steps 1–5 in Activity 1-6.

2. Double-click **Internet Protocol Version 4 (TCP/IPv4)**.

3. Click **Use the following IP address**, and then type the IP address, Subnet mask, and Default gateway provided by your instructor for this computer (see Figure 1-14). (If necessary, enter periods after each number set to advance from box to box.)

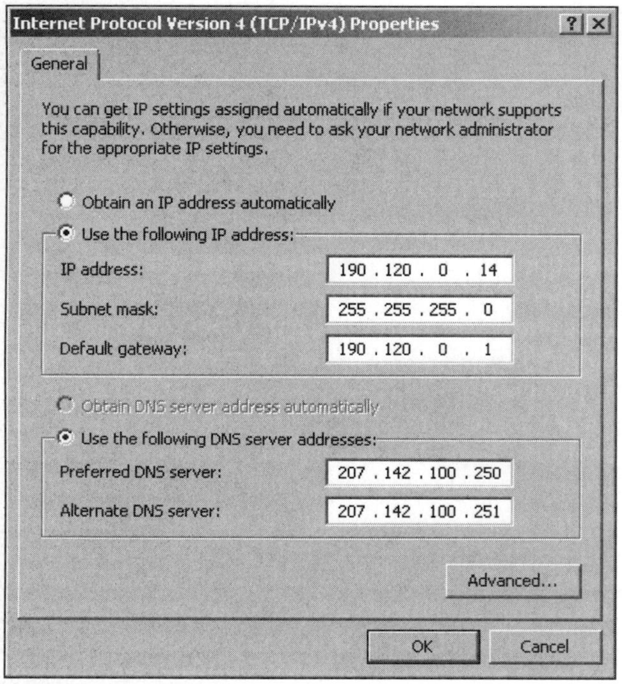

Figure 1-14   Static IP address configuration

4. If necessary, click **Use the following DNS server addresses**.

5. Type the IP address for the **Preferred DNS server** and, if needed, type the IP address for the **Alternate DNS server**.

6. Click the **Advanced** button.

   • What tabs are available for advanced information?

7. Click each tab to see the specific information that you can enter. Click **Cancel**.

8. Click **OK**.

   • What would you click to start configuring IPv6?

9. Click **OK** in the Connection Properties dialog box.

Automated Address Configuration Windows Server 2008 supports two automated addressing approaches. One is **Automatic Private IP Addressing (APIPA)**, which is used to automatically configure the TCP/IP settings for a computer without using a Dynamic Host Configuration Protocol (DHCP) server. The other approach is to use dynamic addressing through the use of a DHCP server.

Automated Addressing Through Automatic Private IP Addressing Notice in Figure 1-14 that you have the option to obtain an IP address automatically. When a computer that is configured to automatically obtain an IP address is switched on, it tries to find a DHCP server to obtain an IP address. As you learned earlier in this chapter, a DHCP server is a server that uses software and DHCP to automatically assign or lease an IP address from a pool of possible addresses. If there is no DHCP server available, the computer automatically assigns itself an IP address from the reserved range of 169.254.0.1 to 169.254.255.254 and a subnet mask of 255.255.0.0. The computer is not able to assign itself a default gateway or the IP address for a Windows Internet Naming Service (WINS) or Domain Name System (DNS) server. As you learned earlier, WINS is a Windows Server 2008 service that enables the server to convert Net-BIOS workstation names to IP addresses for Internet communication. DNS is a TCP/IP application protocol that enables a DNS server to resolve domain and computer names to IP addresses, or IP addresses to domain and computer names. The main problem with automatic configuration is that the computer can only communicate with other computers on the same network that are also automatically configured.

Automatic configuration is appropriate for small organizations that have only one network segment and where the computers do not need to use DNS or access another network. In an environment where a DHCP server is set up, but might be temporarily unavailable, automatic configuration can result in some computers having different IP addresses than the others on the network, which results in the computers not being able to communicate. In a situation like this, automatic configuration should be disabled.

Automatic configuration can be disabled through the Windows Server 2008 Registry. The **Registry** is a database used to store information about the configuration, program setup, devices, drivers, and other data important to the setup of Windows operating systems, such as Windows Server 2008. To disable automatic configuration, you use a Registry editor, such as regedit. The following are general steps you can follow to disable automatic configuration, but note that these are presented for your information and not as a hands-on activity. You will need access to the network using an account with administrator privileges to modify the Registry.

Always use great caution in the Registry editor to avoid inadvertently changing a value that might corrupt the operating system.

1. Click Start and then click Run.

2. Enter regedit in the Open text box, and click OK.

3. In the Registry, browse to the key HKEY_LOCAL_MACHINE\System\CurrentControlSet\ Services\Tcpip\Parameters\Interfaces*adaptername* (the adaptername is the reference to the network interface card in your computer).

4. Click Edit, point to New, and click DWORD (32-bit) Value.

5. Create the value IPAutoconfigurationEnabled as a Reg_Dword value. Assign the data as 0.

6. Repeat Step x but click QWORD (64-bit) value and assign the data as 0.

7. Close regedit.

Dynamic Addressing Through a DHCP Server

Dynamic addressing through a DHCP server is a very common way to configure TCP/IP on many networks, particularly medium-sized and large networks. To enable this type of configuration, you must first install and configure a DHCP server on the network. This server can be configured to dynamically assign an IP address to all the client computers that are set up to automatically obtain an IP address. In addition to assigning the IP address, the DHCP server can also assign the subnet mask, default gateway, DNS server, and other IP settings.

Using a DHCP server can save you a great deal of administrative effort. You only need to configure one server and most of your TCP/IP tasks are done. You learn how to configure a DHCP server in Chapter 8, "Managing Windows Server 2008 Network Services."

To configure a Windows-based computer for dynamic configuration, you select Obtain an IP address automatically in the Internet Protocol (TCP/IP) Properties dialog box shown in Figure 1-14. After this option is configured, the computer contacts a DHCP server on its network to obtain an IP address.

Chapter Summary

- The Windows Server 2008 platforms include Standard Edition, Enterprise Edition, Datacenter Edition, Windows Web Server 2008, and Windows Server 2008 for Itanium-Based Systems. The Standard, Enterprise, and Datacenter Editions can be purchased with or without Hyper-V for creating a virtual server.

- Windows Server 2008 includes many vital features for security, clustering, virtualization, reliability, and multitasking and multithreading. Other important features include the new Server Manager management tool, Windows Server Core, Windows PowerShell, and enhanced Web services.

- The two types of networking models used by Windows Server 2008 are peer-to-peer networks and server-based networks.

- Peer-to-peer networking is intended for small networks. For most networks, a server-based networking model offers increased performance, scalability, security, and centralized management.

- TCP/IP is the default protocol installed with Windows Server 2008.

- TCP/IP is an industry-standard suite of protocols and application utilities that enable communication across local and wide area networks.

- The two versions of IP are IPv4 and IPv6. IPv4 is used in most places because IPv6 has been slow to take hold. IPv6 offers the ability to have more network addresses and better security.

- Every network device, such as a computer or router, must have a unique IP address to ensure network connectivity and the delivery of data. An IP address consists of two parts: the network identifier and the host identifier. Each IP address also has an associated subnet mask to distinguish between the network part and the host part and to enable creating subnets for traffic management.

- IP addresses can be manually configured using static addressing or automatically configured, using APIPA or dynamic addressing through a DHCP server.

Key Terms

Active Directory   A central database of computers, users, shared printers, shared folders, other network resources, and resource groupings that is used to manage a network and enable users to quickly find a particular resource.

Address Resolution Protocol (ARP)   A protocol in the TCP/IP suite that enables a sending station to determine the MAC or physical address of another station on a network.

Automatic Private IP Addressing (APIPA)   Windows Server 2008 supports Automatic Private IP Addressing (APIPA) to automatically configure the TCP/IP settings for a computer. The computer assigns itself an IP address in the range of 169.254.0.1–169.254.255.254, if a DHCP server is not available.

broadcast   A message sent to all computers on a network (but usually blocked to other networks by a router).

client   A computer that accesses resources on another computer via a network or direct cable connection.

clustering   The ability to increase the access to server resources and provide fail-safe services by linking two or more discrete computer systems so they appear to function as though they are one.

cmdlet   A command-line tool available in Windows PowerShell. *See* Windows PowerShell.

connectionless communication   Also called a connectionless service, a communication service that provides no checks (or minimal checks) to make sure that data accurately reaches the destination node.

connection-oriented communication   Also called a connection-oriented service, this service provides several ways to ensure that data is successfully received at the destination, such as requiring an acknowledgement of receipt and using a checksum to make sure the packet or frame contents are accurate.

default gateway   The IP address of the router that has a connection to other networks. The default gateway address is used when the host computer you are trying to contact exists on another network.

domain   A grouping of resource objects—for example, servers, computers, and user accounts—to enable easier centralized management of these objects. On Windows Server 2008 networks, a domain is contained within Active Directory as a higher-level representation of how a business, school, or government agency is organized.

Domain Name System (DNS)   Also called Domain Name Service, a TCP/IP application protocol that enables a DNS server to resolve (translate) domain and computer names to IP addresses, or IP addresses to domain and computer names.

dotted decimal notation   An addressing technique that uses four octets, such as 10000110.11011110.01100101.00000101, converted to decimal (e.g., 134.222.101.5) to differentiate individual servers, workstations, and other network devices.

dynamic addressing   An IP address that is automatically assigned to a client from a general pool of available addresses and that might be assigned each time the client is started, or it might be assigned for a period of days, weeks, months, or longer.

Dynamic Domain Name System (DDNS)   A form of DNS that enables client computers to update DNS registration information so that this does not have to be done manually. DDNS is often used with DHCP servers to automatically register IP addresses on a DNS server.

Dynamic Host Configuration Protocol (DHCP)   A network protocol that provides a way for a server to automatically assign an IP address to a workstation on its network.

fault tolerant memory sync   Enables memory to resynchronize after transient memory problems so there is no interruption to current computing activities.

frame   A unit of data that is transmitted on a network that contains control and address information, but not routing information.

hot-add memory   Memory that can be added without shutting down the computer or operating system.

hot-add processor   The ability to add a processor to an empty processor slot on a multiprocessor system while the system is running.

hot-replace processor   The ability to replace a processor in an SMP system without taking the system down.

Hyper-V   Virtualization software developed by Microsoft that can be included with most versions of Windows Server 2008. *See* virtualization.

Internet Information Services (IIS)   A Microsoft Windows Server component that provides Internet, Web, FTP, mail, and other services to make the server into a full-featured Web server.

Internet Protocol (IP)   The Internet layer protocol responsible for addressing packets so that they are delivered on the local network or across routers to other networks or subnets.

Internet Protocol Version 4 (IPv4)   The most commonly used version of IP, which has been in use for many years. IPv4 has a limitation in that it was not designed to anticipate the vast numbers of networks and network users currently in existence.

Internet Protocol Version 6 (IPv6)   The newest version of IP that is designed for enhanced security and that can handle the addressing needs of growing networks.

IP address   A logical address assigned to each host on an IP network. It is used to identify a specific host on a specific network.

kernel   An essential set of programs and computer code that allows a computer operating system to control processor, disk, memory, and other functions central to its basic operation.

local area network (LAN)   A network of computers in relatively close proximity, such as on the same floor or in the same building.

media access control (MAC) address   Also called a physical or device address, the hexadecimal number permanently assigned to a network interface, and used by the MAC sublayer (a communications sublayer for controlling how computers share communications on the same network).

multicast   A single message is sent from one location and received at several different locations that are subscribed to receive that message.

multitasking   The capability of a computer to run two or more programs at the same time.

multithreading   Running several program processes or parts (threads) at the same time.

network   A communications system that enables computer users to share computer equipment, software, and data, voice, and video transmissions.

Network Access Protection (NAP)   A collection of security protection features that monitor and manage a server and its clients so that access to network and server resources is carefully controlled to match security policies.

Network Address Translation (NAT)   Sometimes used by firewalls, proxy servers, and routers, NAT translates IP addresses on an internal or local network so that the actual IP addresses cannot be determined on the Internet, because the address seen on the Internet is a decoy address used from a pool of decoy addresses.

NetBIOS name   A name or identifier used in older Windows systems to uniquely identify a computer.

network interface card (NIC)   An adaptor board or device to connect a workstation, server, or other network device to a network medium. The connection can be wired or wireless.

packet   A unit of data transmitted on a network that contains control and address information as well as routing information.

peer-to-peer networking   A network on which any computer can communicate with other networked computers on an equal or peer basis without going through an intermediary, such as a server or host.

preemptive multitasking   Running two or more programs simultaneously so that each program runs in an area of memory separate from areas used by other programs.

privileged mode   A protected memory space allocated for the Windows Server 2008 kernel that cannot be directly accessed by software applications.

process   A computer program or portion of a program that is currently running. One large program might start several smaller programs or processes.

protocol   A strictly defined set of rules for communication across a network that specifies how networked data is formatted for transmission, how it is transmitted, and how it is interpreted at the receiving end.

Registry   A database used to store information about the configuration, program setup, devices, drivers, and other data important to the setup of Windows operating systems, such as Windows Server 2008.

router   A device that connects networks, is able to read IP addresses, and can route or forward packets of data to designated networks.

script   A file of shell commands that are run as a unit within the shell. The shell interprets the commands to the operating system one line at a time. Usually to run the contents of a script, the name of that script must be entered at the command line. Scripts save time because commands don't have to be typed individually by the user. Another advantage is that the users do not have to memorize the exact sequence of a set of commands each time they want to accomplish a certain task.

server   A single computer that provides extensive multiuser access to network resources.

server-based networking   A model in which access to the network and resources, and the management of resources, is accomplished through one or more servers.

Server Manager   A comprehensive server management tool offered through Windows Server 2008.

shell   A command-line environment, also called a command interpreter, that enables communication with an operating system. Commands that are run within a shell are typically specific to that shell (although different shells sometimes use the same or similar commands, particularly in UNIX and Linux).

static addressing   An IP address that is assigned to a client and remains in use until it is manually changed.

subnet mask   Used to distinguish between the network part and the host part of the IP address and to enable networks to be divided into subnets.

Subsystem for UNIX-based Applications (SUA)   A set of services that can be installed in Windows Sever 2008 to create a UNIX-like environment for UNIX and Linux clients.

symmetric multiprocessor (SMP) computer   A computer that uses more than one processor.

total cost of ownership (TCO)   The cost of installing and maintaining computers and equipment on a network, which includes hardware, software, maintenance, and support costs.

Transmission Control Protocol (TCP)   This transport protocol, which is part of the TCP/IP suite, establishes communication sessions between networked software application processes and provides for reliable end-to-end delivery of data by controlling data flow.

Transmission Control Protocol/Internet Protocol (TCP/IP)   The default protocol suite installed with Windows Server 2008 that enables network communication.

unicast   A message that goes from one single computer to another single computer.

User Datagram Protocol (UDP)   A connectionless protocol that can be used with IP, instead of TCP.

virtualization   Software that enables one computer to run two or more operating systems that are live at the same time and in which one application running in one operating system does not interfere with an application running in a different operating system.

Windows Internet Naming Service (WINS)   A Windows Server service that enables the server to convert NetBIOS computer names to IP addresses for network and Internet communications. (NetBIOS is an applications programming interface to provide programs with a consistent command set for using network services.)

Windows PowerShell   A Windows command-line interface that offers scripting capabilities as well.

workgroup   As used in Microsoft networks, a number of users who share drive and printer resources in an independent peer-to-peer relationship.

workstation   A computer that has its own central processing unit (CPU) and can be used as a stand-alone or network computer for word processing, spreadsheet creation, or other software applications.

Review Questions

1. The small company where you work needs to implement a second server for its accounting system, but does not have the funds to purchase another computer until next year. Which of the following is a solution?

    a.   Implement Active Directory.

    b.   Use virtualization.

    c.   Change to IPv6 with NAT.

    d.   Replace the x86 processor in the computer with an x64 processor.

2. You are consulting for an organization that has UNIX, Linux, and Windows Server 2008 servers. What feature in Windows Server 2008 enables coordination between systems that have different directory services?

    a. memory sync

    b. Microsoft DNS

    c. Microsoft Metadirectory Services

    d. Windows Directory Replication

3. You are the administrative assistant for the Psychology Department in your college, and they have assigned you to set up a small server to provide basic file services to faculty, staff, and students in that department. For example, faculty will use the server to post and receive class assignments. Which edition of Windows Server 2008 is most appropriate for this situation?

    a. Standard Edition

    b. Enterprise Edition

    c. Datacenter Edition

    d. Datacenter Edition without Hyper-V

4. Your company has a Web server, and sometimes when the network administrator uses tools to test the Web server by IP address there is no response from the server. Which of the following might be the problem?

    a. The Web server is set up with dynamic addressing and so its IP address changes periodically.

    b. The Web server has a NIC that is configured to go offline periodically when the server has over 50 users at one time.

    c. The Web server's NIC is set up to use octal addressing instead of binary addressing.

    d. The Web server is using IPv4 with periodic packet encryption.

5. _____ enables a Windows Server 2008 system to run more than one program at the same time.

    a. task managing

    b. power shelling

    c. micromanaging

    d. multitasking

6. Which of the following can you accomplish with Windows PowerShell? (Choose all that apply.)

    a. Set up printing.

    b. Install software.

    c. View information about local user accounts.

    d. View a listing of files in a folder.

7. Your company has many telecommuters who work at home three days a week and in their offices two days a week. In both places, they work with a laptop computer provided by the company. Although the management team supports telecommuting, they are concerned about telecommuters who make changes to the security settings on their computers that do not match the security policies on the company's network. Which of the following offers a solution for enforcing good security on this company's network?

   a. Secure Domain Name System (SDNS)

   b. Network Access Protection (NAP)

   c. IPvng2

   d. Windows client for networks

8. _____ is used to enable Windows Server 2008 to support UNIX and Linux clients.

9. A server administrator can use the _____ tool to view network connections, configure a firewall, and configure storage on a Windows Server 2008 computer.

10. Your company needs to set up a new server that acts as a general file and print server and that has a small attack surface to reduce the risk of attackers obtaining company secrets. Which of the following installation options offers a reduced attack surface?

   a. Windows Server Simplicity

   b. Network Access Protection in Windowless Mode

   c. Windows Server Core

   d. GUI Mode

11. The management in your company has a disagreement over which client operating system offers the best compatibility with Windows Server 2008 Active Directory. Which of the following operating systems do you mention in your report to management to clear up the dispute?

   a. Windows 2000

   b. Windows XP

   c. Windows Me

   d. Windows Vista

12. Hyper-V enables Windows Server 2008 to operate as a _____ server.

13. One of the managers in your organization has seen older servers crash because of one malfunctioning program. What feature in Windows Server 2008 can help prevent this from happening?

   a. tunneling

   b. privileged mode for the kernel

   c. protected shell

   d. permissions for the shell

14. Which of the following is/are network design models used with Windows Server 2008? (Choose all that apply.)

   a. static promotion

   b. server-based

   c. monolithic-based

   d. peer-to-peer

15. Your small office network has no DHCP server to lease IP addresses. What happens when the network connections of all clients and the servers are configured to obtain an IP address automatically? (Choose all that apply.)

    a. Each computer assigns itself an IP address.

    b. The server uses the static address 127.10.10.1 automatically.

    c. The subnet mask 255.255.0.0 is used for all computers.

    d. Each computer uses a TCP address pointer of 20.

16. The physical address of a NIC is its _____ address.

17. You are training a new computer support person who does not know how to configure a static TCP/IP network connection. Which of the following elements do you show the support person how to configure? (Choose all that apply.)

    a. IP address

    b. TCP address pointer

    c. default gateway

    d. subnet mask

18. _____ is the ability to add RAM without powering down Windows Server 2008.

19. Your IT manager wants you to set up three computers to appear to users as one powerful Windows Server 2008 server. What capability in Windows Server 2008 accomplishes this?

    a. merging

    b. NAPing

    c. gateway converging

    d. clustering

20. Which of the following would you find in the central database called Active Directory? (Choose all that apply.)

    a. users

    b. shared printers

    c. groups of users

    d. computers

Case Projects

One of the best ways to make the most of what you have learned is to apply that knowledge in practical experience. The case projects at the end of each chapter are designed to reinforce your learning by working through realistic situations that involve using Windows Server 2008. In the case projects, you are asked to step into the shoes of an employee in a consulting firm. In this role, you work with Windows Server 2008 in many different kinds of organizations from small to large. Your cases and tasks are varied, just as they would be for any versatile consultant.

Your role involves working for Aspen Consulting, which has clients throughout the United States and Canada. Their staff specializes in server and network implementation, application development, and providing on-site and remote support. Aspen Consulting works with small businesses, departments in organizations, corporations, schools, universities, and government agencies.

Case Project 1-1: Choosing a New Operating System

Cutting Edge is a company with 122 employees who make cutting boards and a full line of knives and knife sets for home and commercial kitchens. The company is divided into several departments, including Development, Marketing, Business, Manufacturing, Information Systems (IS), and Inventory and Shipping. There is also a management team consisting of the company president, vice president, chief financial officer, and the managers of each department. The company is housed in one building that is fully networked. All employees have access to a desktop or laptop computer. These computers are a mixture of Windows 2000, Windows XP, and seven Windows Vista machines. At this point, there is a Windows 2000 Server in each department, and the company is planning to gradually upgrade each server to Windows Server 2008. The IS Department is the smallest department, consisting of four very overworked employees. Considering the IS workload, the IS manager hires you to help assess the server needs of the company and make recommendations for the future.

1. The Marketing Department uses large name and address databases for catalog and other promotions. Some of the databases are ones they own and others are purchased from other catalog sales companies and from Internet companies. The databases are currently on a standard Windows 2000 Server computer, which is overloaded. When they perform sorts and queries of addresses, the computer operates extremely slowly. Which Windows Server 2008 system do you recommend for them? Provide a justification for your recommendation.

2. The Marketing Department wants to establish an Internet business to supplement Cutting Edge's catalog and outlet businesses. Which Windows Server 2008 system would work for the Internet portion of the business? Be sure to justify your recommendation.

3. The Business Department has a Windows 2000 Server system and is concerned about security and reliability. To which Windows Server 2008 edition do you recommend they upgrade? Note some features that would be important for the Business Department.

Case Project 1-2: Management Tools

The IS staff wants to know about important management tools built into Windows Server 2008. Prepare a summary of two management tools that will be of use to them.

Case Project 1-3: Windows Server 2008 Features

The Cutting Edge management team wants to know more about Windows Server 2008 before proceeding with upgrades. In response to their questions, the IS manager asks you to deliver a presentation of Windows Server 2008 features. In your presentation, you should cover elements such as:

- Security
- Reliability
- Expansion options
- Other features valuable to Cutting Edge

If you have the access to Microsoft Office PowerPoint, consider putting your presentation in a slide show for the managers.

Case Project 1-4: IP Addressing Issues

Cutting Edge has been using static IP addressing for all computer systems on their network. One of the difficulties is that because the IS Department is understaffed, they give written NIC configuration instructions to employees, so that employees do their own network configurations. Often employees make mistakes that cause conflicts on the network, and the IS staff has to check out many connections anyway. Further, if the company decides on a wholesale upgrade to Windows Vista, this means all employees will be reconfiguring their computers at the same time. In this context, do you recommend staying with the practice of static addressing? How might an alternative method save time for the IS staff? Create a short report of your recommendations for the IS manager.

Installing Windows Server 2008

After reading this chapter and completing the exercises, you will be able to:

- Plan and make the appropriate preparations for installing Windows Server 2008
- Understand the different installation methods used and install Windows Server 2008
- Set up Windows Server 2008 from the Initial Configuration Tasks window
- Activate Windows Server 2008
- Install and configure Windows Deployment Services
- Install service packs
- Troubleshoot installation problems
- Uninstall Windows Server 2008

Installing a server operating system might sound daunting because servers now offer so many options and features. At one time it was true that installing a server could be like going through a labyrinth with complex steps and confusing paths. Fortunately, the installation of Windows Server 2008 is highly automated to help avoid pitfalls. The Windows Server 2008 installation program takes much of the guesswork out of an installation by detecting hardware and simplifying how to respond by providing windows that step you through the process. Still, installation problems can occur. With advanced preparations as described in this chapter, you can sidestep most installation problems.

In this chapter, you begin with the planning steps needed to help ensure a successful Windows Server 2008 installation. Next, you learn the installation methods that can be used and then install Windows Server 2008. Following the installation, you use the Initial Configuration Tasks window to complete essential configuration tasks, such as naming the server. You also activate the server with Microsoft. You learn how to use Windows Deployment Services to install multiple servers, and to install servers in unattended mode. You also learn to implement service packs to update the operating system. In case there are any problems with the installation, you learn troubleshooting tips to solve them. Finally, you learn how to uninstall Windows Server 2008 so that a computer can be used with a different operating system in the future.

Preparing for Installation

Just as a trip goes better with advanced planning, so does an operating system installation. You are likely to work with the operating system for some time, so it makes sense to get off on a solid footing. When you follow the preinstallation tasks outlined in this section, you can ensure a more successful result and avoid problems later.

The following preinstallation tasks should be completed before installing any edition of Windows Server 2008:

- Identify the hardware requirements and check hardware compatibility.
- Determine disk partitioning options.
- Understand the file system.
- Determine upgrade options.
- Plan user licensing.
- Determine domain or workgroup membership.
- Choose a computer name.
- Determine whether to install Server Core or the full version.
- Identify the server roles to implement.
- Determine the immediate preparations.

Identifying Hardware Requirements and Determining Compatibility

The first step in planning the installation of any operating system is to determine the hardware requirements. Most operating systems come with a list of minimum hardware requirements, which must be met for the operating system to run, and often a list of recommended requirements. It is always better to exceed the minimum recommendations; by how much will be determined by what role the Windows Server 2008 server will play on the network. For example, if your server will play the role of a file server, hosting things such as home folders and company-shared files and printers, additional hard drive space is needed beyond what is required to simply run the operating system. Exceeding the minimum requirements also makes your server more scalable and able to meet increased requirements as the organization grows.

With this in mind, you need to plan hardware based on the server role and projected growth, so as to exceed what is needed to:

- Accommodate the clients that will access the server.
- Provide for extra software and services.
- Match data storage needs.

In Table 1-1 in Chapter 1, "Introduction to Windows Server 2008," you reviewed the minimum requirements for a computer to run an edition of Windows Server 2008. When you develop the specifications for the server hardware you are planning to use, it is better to overestimate than to underestimate. In nearly all cases, this means purchasing much more computer than specified in the minimum requirements. In terms of speed, plan to pay particular attention to the speed of the CPU and the amount of RAM. For example, a small business using one server with Standard Edition should consider purchasing a 2 GHz or faster x64 processor. The cost of an x64 processor is not much more than that of an x86 processor. An x64 processor gives the small business room to grow in the future, too.

A corporation or university that has large databases might consider running the Datacenter Edition on an SMP x64 computer with fast processors. The number of processors depends on the size of the databases and the frequency of performing large queries and reports. The corporation or university might start with two processors, but with the option built into the computer to easily add more in the future.

Another factor in terms of speed is the amount of RAM. More RAM usually equals a faster computer. The small business mentioned earlier might start with 2 to 4 GB of RAM. The corporation or university might consider 16 GB of RAM or more, again depending on the number of processors and the anticipated load from queries and reports, which can be considerable.

The amount of disk space is another important consideration. It doesn't take long to use up disk space, even in a small business. For a starter server, a small business might begin with 250–500 GB or more depending on the intended use. A large corporation or university might start with a **redundant array of inexpensive disks (RAID)**. This is an array of multiple hard drives designed to extend the life of disk drives and to prevent data loss from a hard disk failure. Each drive in the array might hold 300 GB or more of disk space. You learn more about RAID in Chapter 7, "Configuring and Managing Data Storage."

Hardware Compatibility Testing Before any final decisions are made in selecting hardware, you should check the hardware for the Certified for Windows Server 2008 sticker or consult the **Windows Server Catalog of Tested Products**. The most up-to-date listing of compatible hardware (and software) is the Catalog of Tested Products on Microsoft's Web site, which is at *www.windowsservercatalog.com* at this writing. Microsoft reviews all types of hardware to determine whether it will work with Windows Server editions and other Microsoft operating systems.

To avoid installation difficulties, it is recommended that you select hardware listed on the Catalog of Tested Products or labeled with the Certified for Windows Server 2008 logo. Further, avoid hardware from small companies that build individual computers from generic parts. Most established computer manufacturers have products compatible with Windows Server 2008, although their prices might be higher than those of the smaller companies. Cutting expenses when buying server hardware could prove to be costly later on if it results in unreliable equipment and difficult software installations.

If you are upgrading a computer that has been used for a different operating system, such as one currently running Windows Server 2003, that computer might already be in the Catalog of Tested Products, but it might still be necessary to upgrade the **basic input/output system (BIOS)**. The BIOS is a program on a read-only or flash memory chip that establishes basic communication with components such as the monitor and disk drives. Before you upgrade, contact the computer manufacturer or visit the manufacturer's Web site to determine if a BIOS upgrade is needed prior to installing Windows Server 2008. If an upgrade is needed, the manufacturer will provide an upgrade file and instructions about how to perform the upgrade.

Some steps in the activities in this book include bulleted questions with space for you to record your responses/answers.

Activity 2-1: Determining the BIOS Version of a Computer

Time Required: Approximately 10 minutes
Objective: Learn how to determine the BIOS version on a computer.

Description: Before you check with a computer manufacturer about which BIOS version on an older computer is compatible with Windows Server 2008, you will need to determine the BIOS version currently used on the computer. Also, before installing a new operating system on a new or older computer, it is always wise to have the most current BIOS installed on that computer. Some computers display the BIOS version at boot up. On nearly all computers, you can determine the BIOS version by entering the BIOS setup for the computer. This activity provides general instructions for determining the BIOS version.

1. Find out from your instructor or lab assistant how to access the computer's BIOS setup. On most computers, you access the BIOS setup screen by typing a specific key right after turning on the computer's power. For example, some computers use the F1, F2, or Del keys. Also, some computers display a brief message at boot up (before the operating system is loaded) that tells you what key sequence to use.

2. In most cases, the BIOS version number is displayed on the first setup screen. If it is not, follow the on-screen instructions to view or access the various BIOS setup menu(s) for the BIOS version information. You will most likely use the arrow keys on your keyboard to advance through the menus. *Make absolutely certain that you do not change any of the parameters in the BIOS setup.*

   • What is the BIOS version?

3. Exit the BIOS setup without making any changes. On some computers, you can exit by pressing Esc and typing No to the query about saving your changes.

Determining Disk Partitioning Options

Knowing how you plan to partition your hard disks and on which partition you plan to install the operating system can make the Windows Server 2008 installation much smoother. Creating a partition is a process in which a hard disk section or a complete hard disk is prepared for use by an operating system. A disk can be formatted after it is partitioned. When you format a disk, this process divides the disk into small sections called tracks and sectors for the storage of files by a particular file system. During the installation, the Windows Server 2008 installation program will detect how your hard disk is currently partitioned (see Figure 2-1). The installation program will allow you to install the operating system on an existing partition or create a new one on which to install. Depending on how your hard disk is currently partitioned, you will be presented with options to put the operating system on an existing disk partition or on unallocated disk space. A link is also provided to enable you to load a driver for your disk drive, if you want to use a more recent driver or if some drives are not properly recognized by the installation program.

After the installation is complete, you can use Server Manager to create additional partitions, such as on any remaining unallocated disk space or on disks you add later. The Server Manager tool was introduced in Chapter 1 and is further explained in Chapter 3, "Configuring the Windows Server 2008 Environment." Figure 2-2 shows Server Manager starting the Disk Management tool.

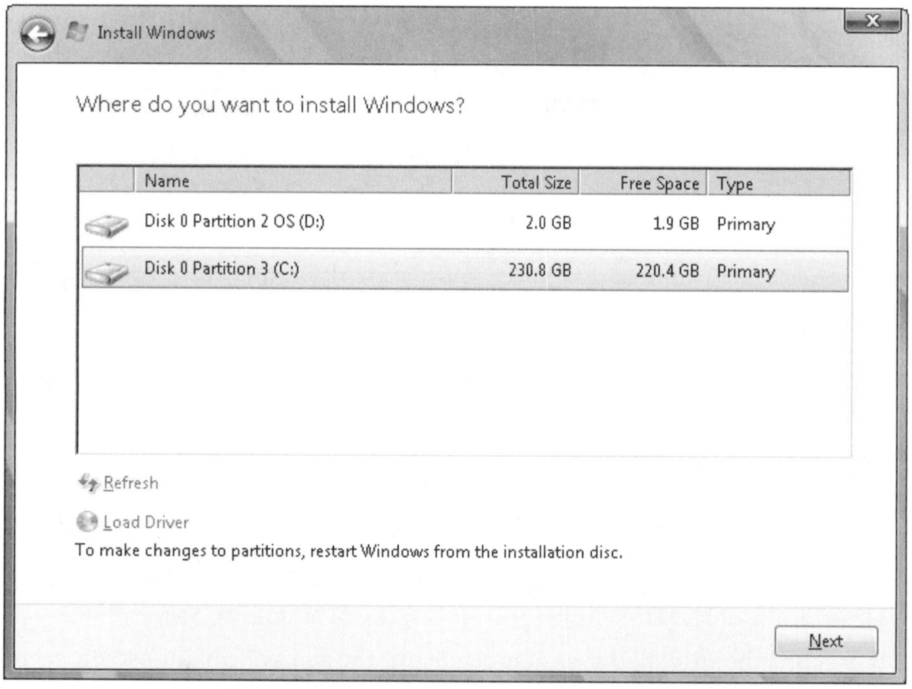

Figure 2-1 Installation program detecting existing partitions

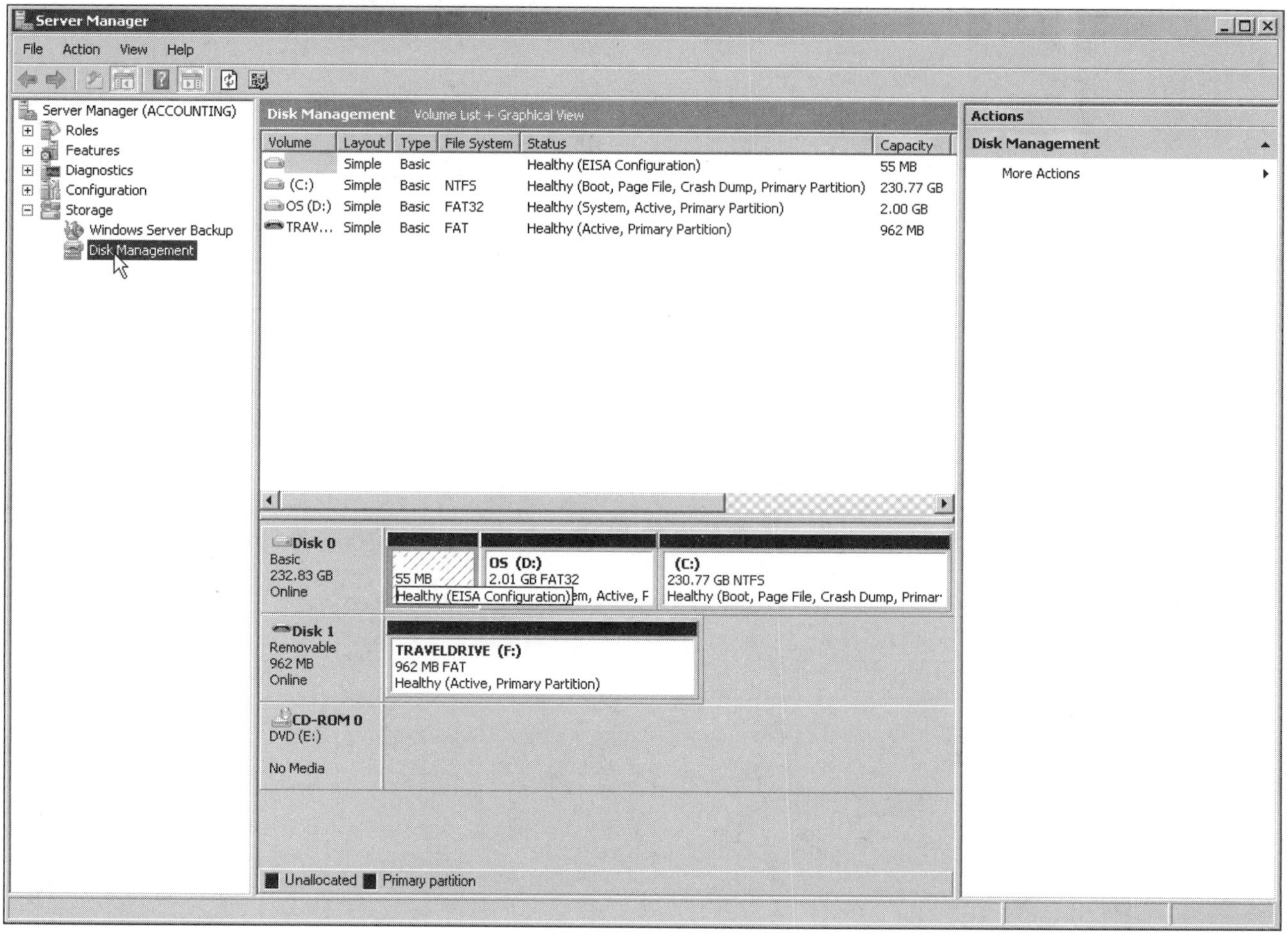

Figure 2-2 Using Server Manager to manage disks after an installation

Activity 2-2: Determining How an Existing Windows Server 2003 Server Is Partitioned

Time Required: Approximately 15 minutes
Objective: Determining the space on disks in a Windows Server 2003 server and how the disks are partitioned.

Description: If you are upgrading a Windows Server 2003 server to Windows Server 2008, it is wise to check the available disk space and the partitioning before you start. This enables you to make plans about partitioning, including how to change existing partitions, before you begin the upgrade. You will need access to a computer running Windows Server 2003 with an account that has Administrator privileges. If a Windows Server 2003 server is not available, you can use similar steps in Windows Server 2008 for practice.

For Windows Server 2003

1. Click **Start** and then right-click **My Computer**.

2. Click **Manage**.

3. Click the **Disk Management** option listed under Storage in the left pane. Figure 2-3 shows an illustration of the Disk Management display in Windows Server 2003.

   • Record the drive letter assignments and the file systems in use on each partition. Also, record the size of each partition.

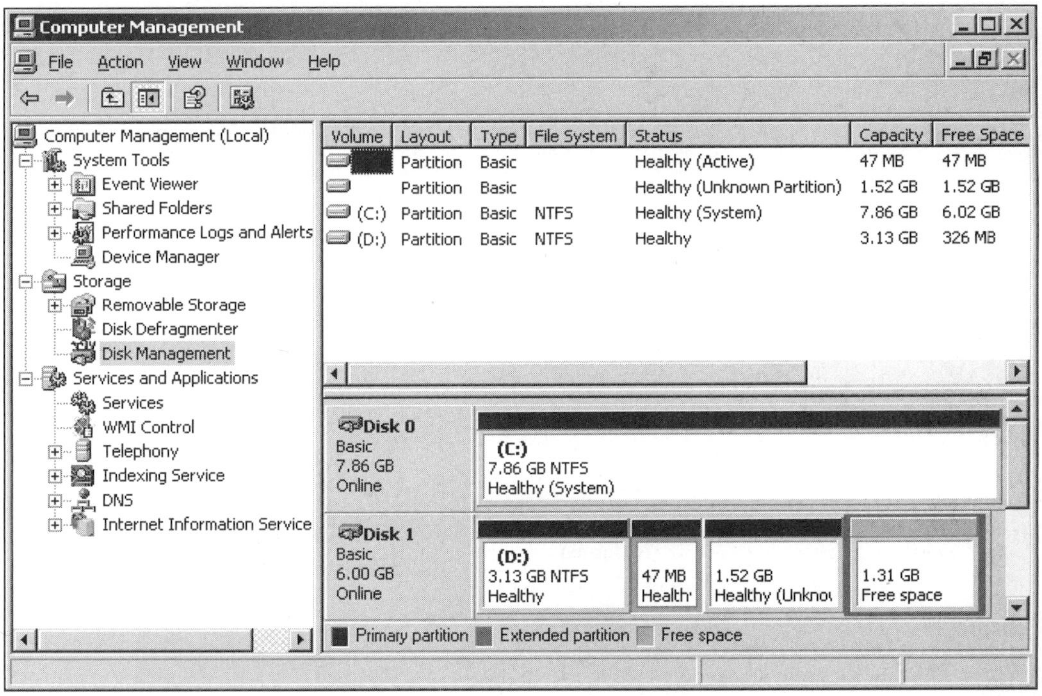

Figure 2-3   Sample disk partitioning in a Windows Server 2003 server

For Windows Server 2008

1. Click **Start** and then right-click **Computer**.

2. Click **Manage** to open Server Manager.

3. Double-click **Storage** in the left pane.

4. Click **Disk Management** listed under Storage in the left pane.

• Record the drive letter assignments and the file systems in use on each partition, as well as the size of each partition.

Understanding NTFS

The **New Technology File System (NTFS)** is the native Windows Server file system. Understanding NTFS before you start an installation is important so that you know its capabilities on your new server. Also, you might need to convert from an older FAT32 file system to NTFS prior to upgrading to Windows Server 2008.

NTFS has been supported in Windows Server systems from when Windows NT Server was introduced in the early 1990s to Windows 2000 Server and Windows Server 2003. Windows Server 2008 also uses NTFS, which includes the following traditional NTFS features:

• Local security through file and folder permissions

• Compression

• Disk quotas

• Encryption

• Indexing

• POSIX.1 support

• Journaling

• Large volume capacity

• Hard links

• Self-healing

NTFS offers an important security advantage by providing folder- and file-level security. Permissions can be set on folders and individual files to protect resources from users accessing them from across the network or locally.

File compression is a process that significantly reduces the size of a file by techniques such as removing unused space within a file or using compression algorithms. Some files can be compressed by more than 40 percent, saving valuable disk space for other storage needs. This is particularly useful for files that are accessed infrequently. NTFS provides the ability to compress files as needed. File compression can be used on specified files after the server is installed. A disadvantage is that compressed files take longer to access because they must be decompressed when retrieved.

NTFS also supports disk quotas. Disk quotas allow an administrator to monitor disk space being consumed by users on the network and to control the amount of disk space being consumed on a per-user or per-group basis.

Data encryption is also included with NTFS. Folders and files can be encrypted so that only the designated user can view the contents, adding yet another level of security. For example, should someone remove a hard drive and place it in another system in an attempt to gain access to the data, they would be unable to view the contents of any folders and files that are encrypted.

Identity theft has experienced a huge increase beginning in 2007, in part because of unencrypted files on servers and other computers that were stolen.

Indexing is used in conjunction with Active Directory to make file searching and retrieval faster. Indexing uses the Indexing Service, which creates a catalog of information about documents accessed through the Search option from Windows Explorer. Also, indexing and the

Indexing Service can be replaced with the Windows Search Service for even faster searches in Windows Server 2008.

NTFS provides support for the **portable operating system interface (POSIX)**. POSIX is a set of standards designed to enable portability of applications from one computer system to another and has been used particularly for UNIX and Linux systems. NTFS follows the POSIX.1 standard, which includes case-sensitive filenames and the use of multiple filenames (called hard links). For example, the files Myfile.doc and MYFile.doc are considered different files (except when using Windows Explorer or the Command Prompt window).

Journaling by a file system means that it tracks changes to files and keeps a record of these changes in a separate log file. Journaling can be important, for example, when the computer crashes due to a power failure in the middle of updating or changing files. The logged journal information makes it possible to restore a file to its original condition prior to the power failure. Journaling enhances both the security and reliability of a system.

The storage needs for computers, and particularly for servers, are growing constantly. NTFS supports large disk volumes of up to 16 TB, which exceeds the 2 TB maximum volume capacity of Windows Server 2008 Enterprise, Datacenter (on x64 computers), and Itanium-Based Editions. A volume is a portion of a storage area, such as a hard disk, that has been set up for one file system. A volume often exists on a single partition, but this is not always the case, so partition and volume are not interchangeable terms (in some cases, a partition might not be recognized as a volume).

Windows NTFS supports the use of hard links. A **hard link** enables you to create one file and then establish links to that file in other folders, as though the file is in all of the folders. For example, an organization might have a document about its rules and regulations for employees. There might be a master copy in a Human Resources Department folder. Links to the master copy are placed in folders for each department in the organization, so that employees from all departments can read the rules and regulations. The advantage of this approach is that when changes are made to the rules and regulations, they only need to be made to the master copy.

Self-healing disks is a new feature to NTFS introduced in Windows Server 2008. Self-healing means that when software in Windows Server 2008 runs into a damaged disk area, NTFS can heal the area without having to take down the server. NTFS self-heals by generating a "worker thread" that repairs data from the damaged area. The data is not available to the software until the worker thread completes its work. The next time the software wants to access that data, it is available for use. Prior to Windows Server 2008, a damaged disk area meant that you had to take down the server and then bring it back up offline to users to run the *chkdsk* utility that rebuilt the data in the damaged area.

If you are moving from Windows Server 2003 to Windows Server 2008, check to ensure that any File Allocation Table (FAT) volumes are first converted to NTFS. FAT, which comes in different versions, is an older file system supported by previous Windows Server systems including Windows Server 2003 and Windows 2000 Server. FAT is not as secure as NTFS and is not a good choice for larger volume systems.

At this writing, you cannot install Windows Server 2008 on a FAT volume (you'll see a message that the volume is not an NTFS volume). Windows Server 2003 has a command-line interface that enables you to convert FAT to NTFS, as shown in Figure 2-4. In this figure, the command *convert f: /fs:ntfs* means "convert volume f: to NTFS (ntfs)."

In some cases, such as on some 64-bit servers, the server installation uses a small FAT formatted system partition for hardware-specific files. You should leave this partition as is and not try to convert it.

To open the Command Prompt window in Windows Server 2003:

1. Click Start.
2. Point to All Programs.
3. Point to Accessories.
4. Click Command Prompt.

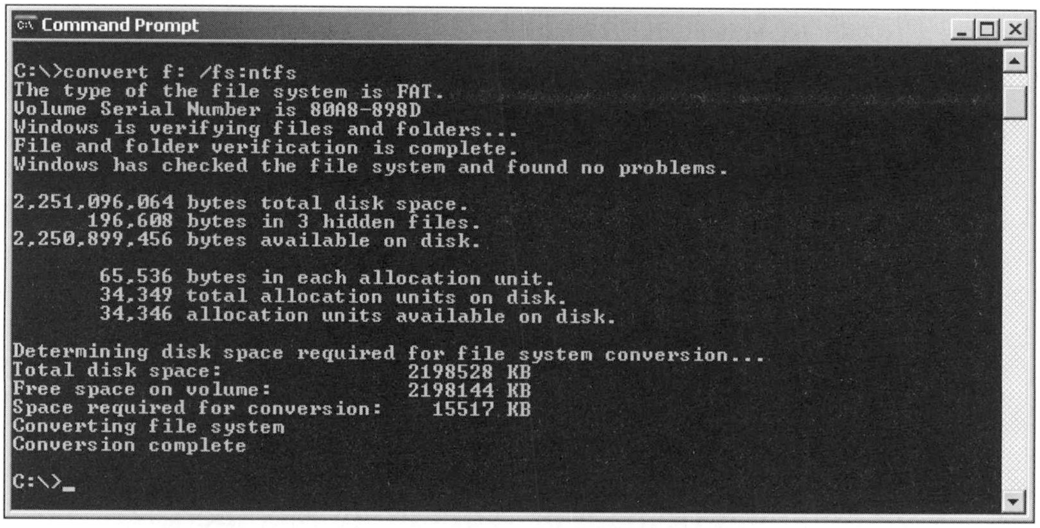

Preparing for Installation

Figure 2-4 Converting a FAT volume to NTFS in Windows Server 2003

After the Command Prompt window is open, you can type in commands. Also, you can view online documentation about the *convert* command by entering *convert /?* at the command line.

Upgrading to Windows Server 2008

Windows Server 2003 can be upgraded to Windows Server 2008 if you are upgrading from compatible edition to compatible edition. For example, you can upgrade Windows Server 2003, Standard Edition to Windows Server 2008 Standard Edition or Windows Server 2008 Enterprise Edition.

Even when you are upgrading using compatible editions, you might have other concerns, such as the service pack level implemented in Windows Server 2003. A **service pack** (**SP**) is a major update for a Windows operating system and includes many updated and enhanced components and functions.

Another issue for upgrading is whether Windows Server 2003 has already been upgraded to Release 2 (R2). R2 is an interim version of Windows Server 2003 developed as a way to offer a newer server version while waiting for Windows Server 2008. Windows Server 2003 R2 contains some of the early features implemented in Windows Server 2008 and is designed for more compatibility with Windows Vista clients than Windows Server 2003 without R2.

Importantly, when you upgrade to Windows Server 2008, you use a full version of the new operating system and not a special upgrade version sold at a reduced price. Table 2-1 provides the specifics about upgrading Windows Server 2003 systems to Windows Server 2008.

Table 2-1 Windows Server upgrade paths

Windows Server 2003 Edition	Windows Server 2008 Edition upgrade path
Windows Server 2003, Enterprise Edition with SP1 or SP2 installed	Windows Server 2008 Standard Edition or Windows Server 2008 Enterprise Edition
Windows Server 2003 R2, Standard Edition	Windows Server 2008 Standard Edition or Windows Server 2008 Enterprise Edition
Windows Server 2003, Enterprise Edition with SP1 or SP2 installed	Windows Server 2008 Enterprise Edition
Windows Server 2003 R2, Enterprise Edition	Windows Server 2008 Enterprise Edition
Windows Server 2003, Datacenter Edition with SP1 or SP2 installed	Windows Server 2008 Datacenter Edition
Windows Server 2003 R2, Datacenter Edition	Windows Server 2008 Datacenter Edition

Planning User Licensing

When you purchase Windows Server 2008, you also need to plan how many workstations will be accessing the server on the basis of the server edition. For the Standard and Enterprise editions, you currently can purchase your initial edition with five or 25 **client access licenses (CALs)**. One CAL is a license for one workstation to access the server. Additional CALs can be added as needed. As a general rule, it is better to purchase a few more CALS than are needed immediately because the number of users connecting to servers tends to grow.

For the Datacenter and Itanium-Based editions, you pay one flat cost per processor. For example, if the server computer has four processors, you pay four times the single processor rate. All clients who can connect are allowed to connect without first having a CAL for each client.

When there is a virtual server set up for Windows Server 2008 Standard Edition, users may have one virtual access per CAL. Windows Server 2008 Enterprise Edition provides up to four virtual accesses per CAL. Finally, for Windows Server 2008 Datacenter Edition, a workstation can have unlimited virtual accesses per processor license.

Determining Domain or Workgroup Membership

During the installation process, you will need to determine the type of network access for which your computer will be configured. As you will recall from Chapter 1, a computer running Windows Server 2008 can be configured in a workgroup model or as a member of a domain.

You can specify a domain or workgroup on the Initial Configuration Tasks window that is displayed when the computer reboots after the actual installation process is completed. This means the server can be booted and connected to the network without first having configured the workgroup or domain choice. By default, the initial installation configures a workgroup with the name Workgroup.

If you choose to add the computer to a domain, the following requirements should be met:

- You will need to provide the DNS name of the domain you want to join, for example, northwest.company.com.

- You must have a computer account in the domain you want to join.

- One domain controller (computer with Active Directory) and a DNS server must be online before you can join the domain.

If the server you are configuring is the first one in a proposed domain, configure the server in a workgroup. After the server is installed and started, you can install Active Directory and configure the first domain as you are installing Active Directory. Active Directory requires at least one active domain.

Choosing a Computer Name

When you install Windows Server 2008, the installation process assigns a randomly generated name for the server computer, such as WIN-CLPHLZFCPUG. The randomly assigned name is clumsy to type and doesn't tell users much about the server. It's easier on the users if you change the name to one that matches your organization's naming scheme or that says something about the purpose of the server.

Some organizations have a predetermined naming scheme for computers on their network. The scheme might be determined by a committee or by a group of administrators and is often one that represents the function of the server or that follows a particular theme. For example, a bank might have servers named Accounts, Loans, and Databases. A college might use server names that reflect the names of specific divisions or departments, such as Business, Student-Services, Sciences, SocialSciences, English, and so on. A small college in the mountains might use a theme-based naming scheme that reflects the names of animals, including Bear, Marmot, Deer, Elk, and so on.

Microsoft's recommendations for creating a computer name include the following:

- The maximum length is 63 characters, but if Windows NT computers are on the network, the Windows NT computers will only recognize the first 15 characters.
- Use shorter names up to 15 characters for easier typing.
- The computer should have a name that is different from any other computer name on the local network or in the domain.
- If no DNS server exists on the network, use only standard Internet characters, which include upper- and lowercase letters, numbers, and the hyphen (-) character, but do not use only numbers.
- If a DNS server is present on the network, use standard Internet characters plus additional characters such as $, %, &, *, and others.

Determining Whether to Install Server Core or the Full Version

Before you install Windows Server 2008, you'll need to consider the purpose for the server so you can determine whether to install Server Core or the full version (for Standard, Enterprise, and Datacenter editions). As you learned in Chapter 1, Server Core is designed to have a small footprint on a network, making it less vulnerable to Internet attackers. It is also for those who want to manage the server using command-line commands and scripts, without a GUI interface of windows, menus, icons, and other features. Additionally, Server Core does not support .NET Framework or Windows PowerShell. Some experienced server administrators prefer using the command line and writing server management scripts as in Server Core, because this environment offers direct control of the server. Also, scripts can automate many mundane management tasks, such as creating a group of user accounts.

The full version of Windows Server 2008 offers many GUI management tools, including Server Manager. It also offers wizards to guide you through server configuration and management. New and experienced administrators like this type of environment for its ease of use and intuitive interface. Also, the full version comes with features such as Microsoft Internet Explorer for Internet access, graphical tools for monitoring the server and network, Windows Mail, the Search window, Microsoft Paint, and many more applications. Other applications, such as Microsoft Office, can be installed in the full version.

Here are some scenarios that could be considered for a Server Core installation:

- Your organization is medium or large in size and wants to dedicate one server to operate as a DHCP or combined DHCP and DNS server (see Chapter 1 for an introduction to DHCP and DNS, and Chapter 8, "Managing Windows Server 2008 Network Services").
- Your organization offers many shared folders to users for their work and the organization wants to centralize all of the shared folders on one computer, such as for distributed file sharing.
- The server contains only centralized databases accessed by users, but does not require software that uses .NET Framework.
- The server holds critical files for the organization and needs to have the smallest attack surface with fewer services and fewer constant updates.
- The server is dedicated to one narrow task, such as frequently backing up important files so they can quickly be brought online for fail-safe protection or after a disaster.

Sample scenarios for installing the full version are:

- Your organization is a small or medium-size business and does not plan to dedicate a server for a specific function, such as for DHCP.
- You prefer to work in a GUI environment for managing the server instead of at the command line.

- Your organization needs to have GUI-based software on the server, such as Microsoft Office.
- The server administrator is relatively new to Windows Server 2008 and wants to use wizards for guidance in configuring the server.
- The server must have .NET Framework for the applications on it.

Identifying Server Roles

The server role is the reason for having a server. Modern servers function in one or a combination of roles. One of the most basic roles is to serve files to users over a network. Another role is to offer printers and fax servers to network users. Servers are also used to offer a range of network services, with Web services as the most visible and a DHCP server operating behind the scenes for smooth network operations.

Windows Server 2008 can function in many roles. In fact, this new version of the operating system offers more roles than in previous Windows Server systems. The next sections offer a brief review of the roles available at this writing.

 Expect Microsoft to continue adding roles through updates or service packs.

Active Directory Certificate Services Role Active Directory (see Chapter 1 and Chapter 4, "Introduction to Active Directory and Account Management") offers the ability to establish digital certificates for enhanced security. A **digital certificate** is a set of unique identification information that is typically put at the end of a file, or that is associated with a computer communication. Its purpose is to show that the source of the file or communication is legitimate. A digital certificate is encrypted by the sender and decrypted by the receiver. The digital certificate ensures that the file or communication comes from an authentic source. The entity that issues the certificate is the certification authority, which in this case is Active Directory. Active Directory can issue certificates for computer users and computers that are managed within Active Directory. Active Directory can also be used to manage Web security.

Four services are incorporated into this role, as shown in Table 2-2.

Table 2-2 Active Directory Certificate Services

Service	Purpose
Certification Authority Web Enrollment	Enables requesting digital certificates for Web communications, sets up smart card digital certificates, and can obtain lists of revoked certifications
Certification Authority	Used to set up the use of digital certificates for user accounts and computers
Microsoft Simple Certificate Enrollment Protocol	Enables routers and network devices to access digital certificates
Online Certificate Status Protocol (OCSP)	Enables detention of a revoked certificate without the need to access a revocation list

Active Directory Domain Services Role The Active Directory Domain Services (AD DS) role is central to implementing Active Directory and creating one or more domains. As you'll recall from Chapter 1, a domain is like a storehouse of computers, servers, user accounts, and other elements. A domain is a vital management tool for network resources and for determining who can access those resources. When you enable the Active Directory Domain Services role on a server, you can set up one or more domains. Also, the server becomes a domain controller, which houses a database of information about computers, users, and network resources (see Chapter 4).

If your network includes UNIX or Linux computers and you want to enable those computers to access a Windows Server 2008 server on your network, you'll need to install Active Directory Domain Services first.

When you install Active Directory Domain Services, you have access to two central services: Active Directory Domain Controller and Identity Management for UNIX.

Active Directory Domain Controller is the service that turns the Windows Server 2008 server into a domain controller. When users log on to a Windows Server 2008 network, their computers first check in with a domain controller for permission to log on. The domain controller also determines which resources a logged-on computer can access.

Identity Management for UNIX enables Windows and UNIX/Linux network clients to access shared directories on UNIX and Linux computers. **Shared directories** are directories on one or more computers that users on other computers can access through the network.

Identity Management for UNIX also enables passwords to be synchronized for Windows Server and UNIX/Linux access. When a user changes her password for a Windows user account, the password to access UNIX/Linux computer resources is changed at the same time.

Active Directory Federation Services
Active Directory Federation Services is used to manage security tokens and security services on a Windows Server 2008 Web-based network. For example, consider a Web server that is used by students at a college to obtain information about their grades, transcripts, tuition payments, and more. This server uses Active Directory Federation Services to issue security tokens that manage which applications and specific information a student can access. Students only access the programs and information that pertains to them, keeping other access restricted. The security tokens are used to manage access for browser clients and for Web applications.

Active Directory Lightweight Directory Services
Active Directory Lightweight Directory Services (AD LDS) is intended for servers that primarily manage applications for users. Some applications need to store configuration and or critical data in a central database. This might be true, for example, of a customer service system application that is accessed by many different people in an organization. Another example is a student registration system in a college.

If Active Directory Domain Services are installed on the server that runs the application, it might be necessary to modify portions of Active Directory Domain Services to customize Active Directory for the database information needed by that application. Modifying Active Directory Domain Services can be complex and result in unexpected consequences if you make a mistake.

Active Directory Lightweight Directory Services offers an alternative to modifying Active Directory Domain Services for an application. AD LDS is a greatly reduced version of Active Directory Domain Services because it contains only those portions necessary for central configuration and data management required by applications, including directory replication and security services. It does not contain services for managing domains and domain resources, such as user accounts and computers. AD LDS is easier to modify for applications, and if you make a mistake in a modification, the result is not likely to affect how users access resources in a domain.

When you install AD LDS, you can use a wizard to create an "instance," which is an application directory. The new instance is separate from Active Directory Domain Services. This means that AD LDS can be installed on a server that either does or does not have Active Directory Domain Services installed.

Active Directory Rights Management Services Role
The Active Directory Rights Management Services (AD RMS) role is for information protection. It uses security capabilities such as encryption, user authentication, and security certificates to help safeguard information. AD RMS works with word processors, spreadsheet, and other programs to build in an extra layer of protection so there are multiple ways to control how information is used and distributed.

The extra layer of protection is in addition to the protection of files through security permissions and of a computer through a firewall.

Consider a situation in which a famous bakery of holiday cakes and breads has decided it wants to carefully protect the recipes so they do not go beyond the eyes of those bakers who must use them. Each recipe document can be protected through AD RMS so that it can only be seen by specific people who are on the local network. Also, the recipe document can be secured through AD RMS so that it cannot be copied, forwarded through e-mail, printed, pasted, or generally reproduced in any way.

In another scenario, the president of a college sends out the college financial audit results to the dean of faculty and department heads. She wants this information kept confidential until she meets with the college trustees, and so she uses an e-mail format enabled by AD RMS that prohibits forwarding, printing, copying, and editing her e-mail after it is sent.

Application Server Role The Application Server role places the Windows Server 2008 server in the role of a computer that makes applications available to users on a network or over the Web. This applies to distributed applications, such as client/server applications in which the client does some of the work and the server does some. The Application Server role is intended for use with Windows Component Object Model + (COM+) applications. **Component Object Model (COM)** consists of standards for building software from individual objects or components; COM provides the basis for Object Linking and Embedding (OLE) and ActiveX for creating applications, for example. **COM+** is an enhancement to COM that enables features such as publishing application services and the ability to subscribe to these services for users and systems on a network. COM+ also enables load balancing across multiple servers of client requests for applications.

The Application Server role supports applications written through .NET Framework and Web server applications. This server role also supports distributed transactions, which means that data can be stored on multiple databases on multiple network computers.

DHCP Server Role Dynamic Host Configuration Protocol (DHCP, see Chapter 1) Server is a server role in which the server leases IP addresses to network clients. This service means that users do not have to configure their computer's IP address and other IP addressing information to access the network. The DHCP capability does the configuration automatically to avoid user configuration error and other addressing problems. This is important because no two computers can use the same IP address; they would be unable to communicate on a network. DHCP avoids this problem and ensures that all computers have an appropriate IP address for their network.

DNS Server Role As you learned in Chapter 1, the reason you don't have to memorize IP addresses to communicate on a network is because the server does the work for you. Domain Name System (DNS) maintains tables from which this service translates domain and computer names into IP addresses and vice versa.

For easier administration, plan to implement both the Active Directory Domain Services and DNS roles so they can work together.

Fax Server Role Through the Fax Server role, you can manage all fax resources on a network. This service not only enables sending and receiving faxes, but managing them as well. It enables configuring fax settings, producing reports about fax activities, and managing fax jobs.

File Services Role The File Services role has traditionally been the "bread and butter" for servers. At the core, this service enables users to access and share files through one or more servers. For example, one of the services contained within the File Services role is for **Distributed File System (DFS)**. DFS enables folders shared from multiple computers to appear as though they exist in one centralized hierarchy of folders instead of on many different computers. For example, consider a network used by atmospheric science researchers. One server contains shared folders for weather research, and another server contains shared folders of geographical data. A third server has shared folders with maps, and a fourth server has shared folders with project information. Remembering which server houses which shared information can be a chore. With DFS, all of the shared folders still reside on different servers, but to the user it looks like all are on one server in one place.

This role also includes Services for Network File System (NFS) so that UNIX and Linux client computers can go to shared folders on Windows systems. For backward compatibility, the Windows Server 2008 File Services role enables file replication and indexing for Windows Server 2003 services on a network that has both Windows Server 2003 and Windows Server 2008 systems.

Hyper-V Role The Hyper-V role enables Windows Server 2008 to function as a virtual server (also see Chapter 1 and Appendix A, "Windows Server 2008 Virtualization"). The virtual server role supports both 32-bit and 64-bit operating systems. However, the Hyper-V server itself must be an x64 computer. Some of the advantages of using the Hyper-V role include:

- Lowers server costs by consolidating operating systems on less hardware
- Provides the ability to have separate program development and test environments on the same hardware as production environments
- Increases disaster recovery options
- Enables network load balancing
- Supports Linux integration

Network Policy and Access Services Role A network is kept secure and healthy by having policies governing who can access it. The Network Policy and Access Services role offers services to:

- Set up and manage network policy by creating and using a Network Policy Server (NPS).
- Set up Routing and Remote Access Services (RRAS) and Virtual Private Network Services (VPNs) to enable users to remotely and securely access network resources through a Web or dial-up connection, for example (you learn about RRAS and VPNs in Chapter 9, "Configuring Remote Access Services").
- Offer support for different types of routing services.
- Validate health certificates used by Network Access Protection (NAP, see Chapter 1).

 Microsoft uses the concept of a healthy network to mean one in which all of the computers on the network use security measures to avoid security problems. This includes creating security policies, maintaining security updates, using antivirus software, configuring a firewall, backing up data, and other measures.

Print Services Role Managing network printing activities is a classic role for a server. The Print Services role includes a service to make a Windows Server 2008 server a formal Print Server that manages print jobs and network printers from one place. Another service manages Internet printing, including sharing Web-based printers. A third role is the Line Printer Daemon (LPD) service for managing printing activities for UNIX and Linux computers.

Terminal Services Role The Terminal Services role is used to enable client computers to run services and software applications on the server instead of on the client. Terminal Services can save an organization money because the client computers do not require much in terms of processing, memory, and storage. The client operates like an old-fashioned **terminal** (a keyboard and monitor with no CPU) connected to a mainframe or, in this case, connected to a server. Besides saving money on computers, user support costs can be lower because there are fewer traditional PC operating systems support needs. You learn more about terminal services in Chapter 9.

UDDI Services Role Universal Description, Discovery, and Integration (UDDI) Services are used in conjunction with Web applications. UDDI enables the discovery of existing Web services and program resources that can be used over and over in different Web applications. UDDI enables the creation of a database that catalogs program resources and how Web applications are configured or linked (bound) to other applications. With UDDI, Web developers can find Web services and programs to implement in current projects, without creating new services or programs. UDDI works with Web developer tools including Visual Studio .NET and Office Web Services Toolkit.

For example, a research organization might have a series of Web programs that perform standard statistical procedures on the data for one project. Through UDDI, the statistical procedures can be cataloged so they can be reused in another project. UDDI not only catalogs the procedures but also provides the binding configuration information so they can be run for the other project.

Web Server (IIS) Role The Web Server role enables Windows Server 2008 to provide an ever-expanding range of Web services. The services are offered through Internet Information Services (IIS); these services turn Windows Server 2008 into a full-featured Web server. When you enable the Web Server role, you enable the following general services: Web Server (IIS), IIS Manager, and Web diagnostics tools. You can also add modules for specific Web functions, such as FTP Publishing.

IIS Web Server services offer Web sites and full Web communications through protocols such as **Hypertext Transfer Protocol (HTTP)**. HTTP is a protocol in the TCP/IP suite of protocols that is used to transport document and other data transmissions over networks and the Internet for access by Web browsers.

The FTP publishing services enable uploading and downloading files from an FTP server over the Internet. **File Transfer Protocol (FTP)** is a TCP/IP application protocol that transfers files in bulk data streams and is commonly used on the Internet.

The Web management tools are for management of IIS Web Server, FTP publishing, and other Web-related tasks, such as Web scripts and remote management of a Web server. There are also diagnostics tools to monitor Web activity.

Windows Deployment Services Role When an organization purchases many new server computers at once or plans to do a widespread Windows server operating system upgrade, Windows Server 2008 can be installed on the computers through automated means via **Windows Deployment Services (WDS)**.

WDS enables an organization to purchase multiple computers without operating systems and then install Windows Server 2008 on all of the computers. This approach can save money and time because it enables the server administrator to be more productive. The following are some advantages of WDS:

- Lowers server operating system installation costs by automating the deployment of servers

- Enables servers to be deployed and configured in a consistent way

- Provides the ability to administer hundreds of servers on a mass scale with the help of scripts

- Takes advantage of network speed options for faster deployment

Activity 2-3: Viewing Server Roles

Time Required: Approximately 15 minutes
Objective: Determine server roles already implemented and view all available server roles.

Description: When you work with a server, it can be important to know which server roles are implemented. In this activity, you use Server Manager to first check what server roles are implemented and then to view the server roles that can be installed. You will need to use an account that has Administrator privileges. (Also, if you don't have access to a computer running Windows

Server 2008 at this point, you can complete this activity after you install Windows Server 2008 in Activity 2-4.)

1. Click **Start** and then right-click **Computer**.

2. Click **Manage**.

3. In Server Manager, find the section Roles Summary. Click the link **Go to Roles**.

   • What roles are installed?

4. Click the link **Add Roles** in the right portion of the window.

5. If you see a Before You Begin dialog box, click **Next**.

6. You should see the Select Server Roles dialog box that lists the roles that can be installed. Figure 2-5 shows the list of roles.

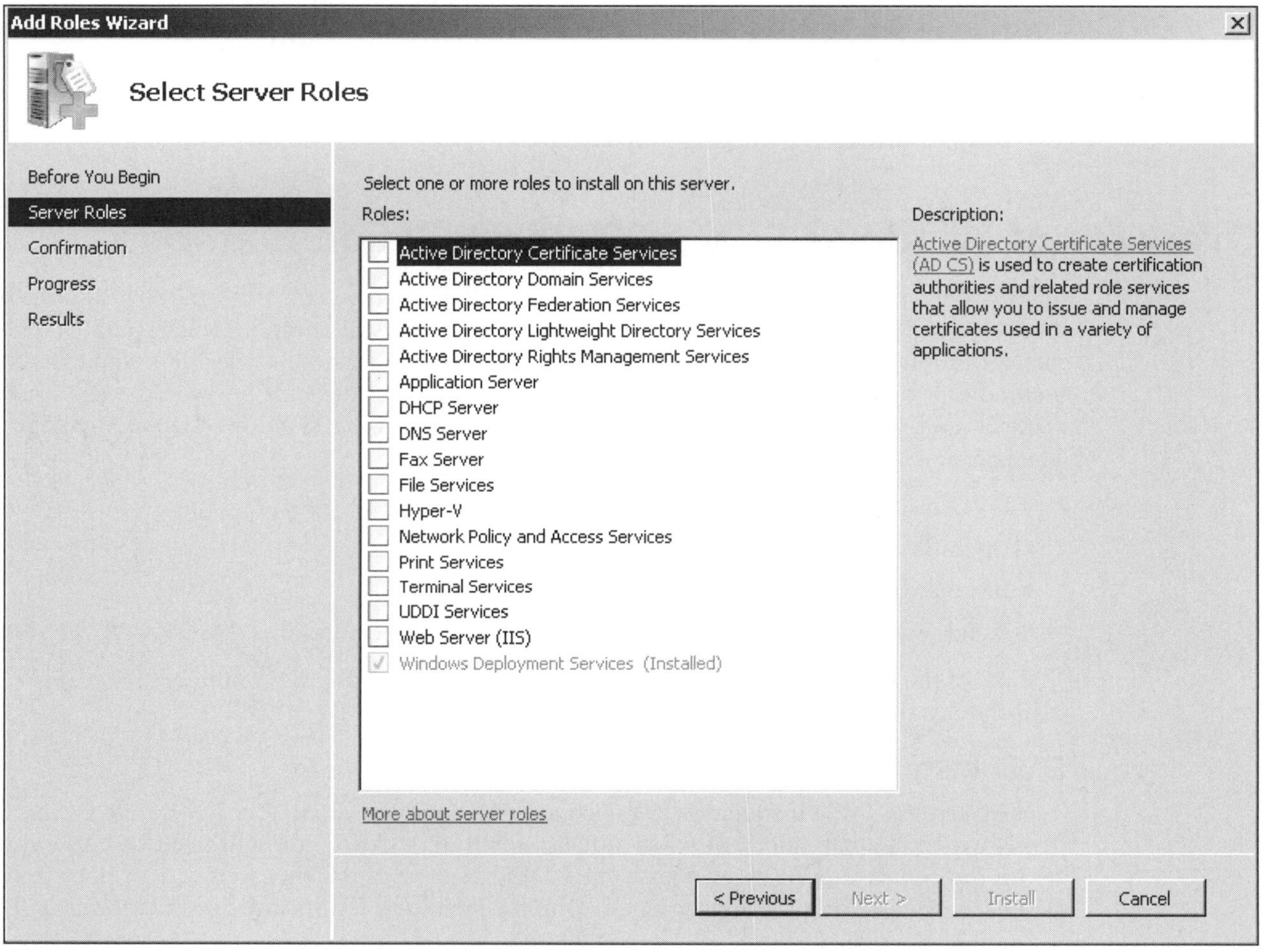

Add Roles Wizard   ✕

Select Server Roles

Before You Begin

Server Roles

Confirmation

Progress

Results

Select one or more roles to install on this server.

Roles:

- ☐ Active Directory Certificate Services
- ☐ Active Directory Domain Services
- ☐ Active Directory Federation Services
- ☐ Active Directory Lightweight Directory Services
- ☐ Active Directory Rights Management Services
- ☐ Application Server
- ☐ DHCP Server
- ☐ DNS Server
- ☐ Fax Server
- ☐ File Services
- ☐ Hyper-V
- ☐ Network Policy and Access Services
- ☐ Print Services
- ☐ Terminal Services
- ☐ UDDI Services
- ☐ Web Server (IIS)
- ☑ Windows Deployment Services (Installed)

Description:

Active Directory Certificate Services (AD CS) is used to create certification authorities and related role services that allow you to issue and manage certificates used in a variety of applications.

More about server roles

                                            [< Previous] [Next >] [Install] [Cancel]

Figure 2-5 Viewing server roles that can be installed

7. Click **Cancel**.

8. Click **Yes**.

9. Close Server Manager.

Making Immediate Preparations

Just before you install Windows Server 2008, it is good practice to make some immediate preparations as follows:

- If you are upgrading an existing Windows Server 2003 system, back up the files before starting. Also consider testing the backup before you start to ensure you have working backup media for a restore. Besides backing up regular data and program files, back up the system configuration information by creating an Automated System Recovery backup set.

- Ensure that the NIC, hard drives, RAID drives, and all other important hardware are preinstalled so that Windows Server 2008 can detect these devices.

- Disconnect or remove removable storage devices, particularly flash drives, so they do not create possible problems during the installation.

- Disconnect any connection for communications with an uninterruptible power supply (UPS).

- Have on hand CD/DVDs or other media with drivers for new peripherals, in case these are needed for configuring the peripherals during or after the installation.

- Use the test software disc that comes with the server to verify that the CPU, memory, and disk drives are working properly.

Overview of Windows Server 2008 Installation Methods

Once you have completed all the necessary preinstallation tasks, you are ready to install the operating system. The following sections outline the different installation methods available and step through a full installation of Windows Server 2008; you just need to decide on an installation method that best meets your needs. The method you choose depends on your specific situation. For example, if you are installing many servers, consider using Windows Deployment Services. The primary installation methods are as follows:

- DVD installation
- Upgrade from Windows Server 2003
- Installation for a virtual server using Hyper-V
- Windows Deployment Services

Each of the installation methods consists of techniques to boot the computer and enable you to load the installation files.

DVD Installation

To perform the DVD installation, your computer should be capable of booting from the DVD drive, which is a capability of most modern computers. Also, you will need to know how to set up the computer's BIOS to boot from a DVD or how to tell the computer to boot from the DVD drive by pressing the appropriate key on the keyboard. To start the installation from DVD:

1. Make sure the computer's BIOS is set to boot first from the CD/DVD drive (see Activity 2-1 to learn how to access the BIOS setup on a computer).

2. Insert the Windows Server 2008 installation DVD.

3. Power off the computer.

4. Turn on the computer, and if necessary press the key combination to boot from the CD/DVD drive.

5. Follow the instructions for installing Windows Server 2008 (see the section, "Performing a DVD–based Installation").

Upgrading from Windows Server 2003

If your computer is running a previous version of Windows, you can perform an upgrade instead of doing a start-from-scratch installation. The benefit of performing an upgrade is that most of your settings, files, and applications are upgraded as well and do not need to be reinstalled. It's important to note that Windows Server 2008 does not come in an upgrade version, but instead you select to perform an upgrade after the installation starts. Also, check the information in Table 2-1 to ensure that you purchase the correct Windows Server 2008 edition for the edition of Windows Server 2003 that you plan to upgrade.

The general steps to begin an upgrade are as follows:

1. Boot the computer to use its current operating system.

2. Insert the Windows Server 2008 installation DVD.

3. If you see the Autoplay window, click the option to Run setup.exe.

4. When you see the Install Windows window, click Install now (see Figure 2-6). Follow the instructions for installing Windows Server 2008 (see the section "Performing a DVD-Based Installation"). Ensure that you select Upgrade when you come to the window with choices for Upgrade or Custom (advanced).

Figure 2-6 Starting the installation

After you insert the DVD, if you see the message, "The computer cannot run this version of the operating system," this means you do not have the right Windows Server 2008 edition for the Windows Server 2003 version on your computer or that you are trying to upgrade from a Windows Server version earlier than Windows Server 2003.

Installation for a Virtual Server Using Hyper-V

Virtual servers are in common use, and Windows Server 2008 can be installed as a virtual server, such as in Microsoft Hyper-V. As you learned in Chapter 1, Hyper-V can be included with the Standard, Enterprise, and Datacenter Editions of Windows Server 2008 for a minor extra cost—but only on an x64 computer. The actual installation steps of Windows Server 2008 as a virtual server are nearly the same as those for a DVD installation, but first you need to go through the steps to set up a virtual server. The following are the general steps for installing and using Hyper-V:

1. Windows Server 2008 must already be installed as a main server, such as by using the DVD installation method in Activity 2-4.

2. After Windows Server 2008 is installed, use the Initial Configuration Tasks tool or Server Manager to install the Hyper-V server role. (See the section later in this chapter, "Using the Initial Configuration Tasks Window for Setup" or in Chapter 3 see the section, "Installing and Removing Server Roles.")

3. Start the Hyper-V Manager by clicking **Start**, clicking **Administrative Tools**, and clicking **Hyper-V Manager.**

4. Click the server in the tree in the left pane.

5. Click the **Action** menu, point to **New**, and click **Virtual Machine** to start the New Virtual Machine Wizard.

6. If you see the Before You Begin dialog box, click **Next**.

7. In the Specify Name and Location window, enter the name for the virtual server, such as *Server 2008*. Click **Next**.

8. In the Assign Memory window, enter the amount of memory to be used for the virtual server in MB, such as *1024 or higher* (remember that the virtual server will be sharing memory with the main server host). Click **Next**.

9. In the Configure Networking window, select the way the server will be connected, such as by selecting the NIC it will use in the *Connection* box. Click **Next.**

10. Select the virtual hard disk option from the following:
    - Create a virtual hard disk (and provide the name, location, and size of the virtual hard disk)
    - Use an existing virtual hard disk
    - Attach a virtual hard disk later

11. Click **Next**.

12. Insert the Windows Server 2008 installation DVD.

13. Select **Install an operating system from a boot CD/DVD-ROM** and provide the location of the Windows Server 2008 installation DVD, such as *Physical CD/DVD drive: E:*. Click **Next**.

14. Click **Finish**.

15. If you don't see the connection window, double-click the name of the server in the middle pane. Click the **Action** menu and click **Start.**

16. Follow the steps for installing Windows Server 2008, starting at Step 3 in Activity 2-4.

17. After the Windows Server 2008 virtual server is installed, you can configure it using the Initial Configuration Tasks window as in Activity 2-5.

You can shut down a virtual server while in Hyper-V Manager by clicking that virtual server in the center pane, clicking the Action menu, and clicking Shut Down. To start a virtual server in Hyper-V Manager, click the server, click the Action menu, and click Start.

Windows Deployment Services

You've already learned that Windows Deployment Services or WDS is a role that can be enabled in Windows Server 2008. This role is designed to enable the installation of Windows operating systems, Windows Vista and Windows Server 2008, on multiple computers. When you use WDS, it's not necessary to stay at the computer during the operating system installation because it can be done unattended. WDS is not really new because it is based on redesigned programming code formerly used in Remote Installation Services from Windows Server 2003.

An installation DVD is not necessary for each computer because the installation files are sent over a network from the Windows Server 2008 Windows Deployment Services server. However, you do need to have licenses for all of the operating systems you install through WDS. You learn how to use WDS in the section of this chapter called, "Using Windows Deployment Services."

Performing a DVD-Based Installation

After you've gathered all your information, determined which options you will use to install Windows Server 2008, and made your immediate preparations, you can proceed with the installation. This section outlines the steps for a typical installation from DVD. The installation is performed by the Setup program on the DVD, which takes you through the installation process step-by-step.

Activity 2-4: Installing Windows Server 2008 from DVD

Time Required: Approximately 30–60 minutes (depending on the speed of your computer)
Objective: Install Windows Server 2008 from DVD.

Description: In this activity, you install Windows Server 2008. The installation steps provided here are for Windows Server 2008 Standard or Enterprise Edition. These steps are for an installation that is done from scratch and in which you install the full version of Windows Server 2008 and not a Server Core installation. However, the steps for upgrading from Windows Server 2003 to Windows Server 2008 are very similar to the steps described here. You will need a Windows Server 2008 installation DVD. Also, make sure that you have the Product Key available, which is typically printed on a label on the jewel case or sleeve that houses the DVD.

1. Follow Steps 1–5 in the section, "DVD Installation" in which you ensure the BIOS is set to boot from the CD/DVD drive. Insert the Windows Server 2008 installation DVD, and boot the computer from the DVD.

2. The DVD might take a few moments to load.

3. When the Install Windows window appears, specify the language to install, such as **English**, in the *Language to install* drop-down box. In the Time and currency format box, make your selection, such as **English (United States)**. In the Keyboard or input method box, make your selection, such as **US**.

4. Click **Next**.

5. The next window enables you to commence the installation. Before you get started, notice there are links for *What to know before installing Windows* and *Repair your computer*. The *Repair your computer* link is for after Windows Server 2008 is installed and a problem arises, such as when the computer won't boot after a power failure. You can use this link to repair problems with boot files.

6. Click the **Install now** button (refer to Figure 2-6).

7. Enter the Product Key.

8. Click **Next**.

9. In the next Install Windows window, you can select one of the following under the Operating System column (this example is for an Enterprise Edition installation, as shown in Figure 2-7):

   • Windows Server 2008 Enterprise (Full Installation)

   • Windows Server 2008 Enterprise (Server Core Installation)

   Depending on your version, select **Windows Server 2008 Standard (Full Installation)** or **Windows Server 2008 Enterprise (Full Installation)** and click **Next**.

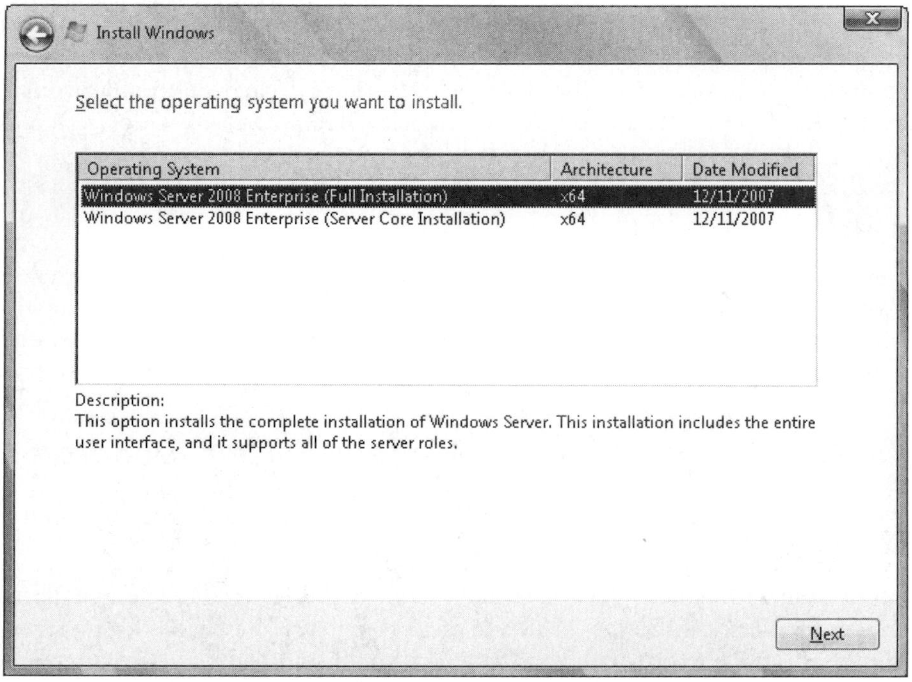

Install Windows

Select the operating system you want to install.

Operating System	Architecture	Date Modified
Windows Server 2008 Enterprise (Full Installation)	x64	12/11/2007
Windows Server 2008 Enterprise (Server Core Installation)	x64	12/11/2007

Description:
This option installs the complete installation of Windows Server. This installation includes the entire user interface, and it supports all of the server roles.

Next

Figure 2-7   Selecting the operating system

10. Read the license terms, click the box for **I accept the license terms**, and click **Next**.

11. In the next window, you'll select (click) the type of installation you want to perform from the following options (see Figure 2-8):

   • Upgrade
   Keep your files, settings, and programs and upgrade Windows.
   Be sure to back up your files before upgrading.

   • Custom (advanced)
   Install a clean copy of Windows, select where you want to install it, or make changes to disks and partitions.
   This option does not keep your files, settings, and programs.

 If you are installing a virtual server in Hyper-V, the Upgrade option is likely to be disabled.

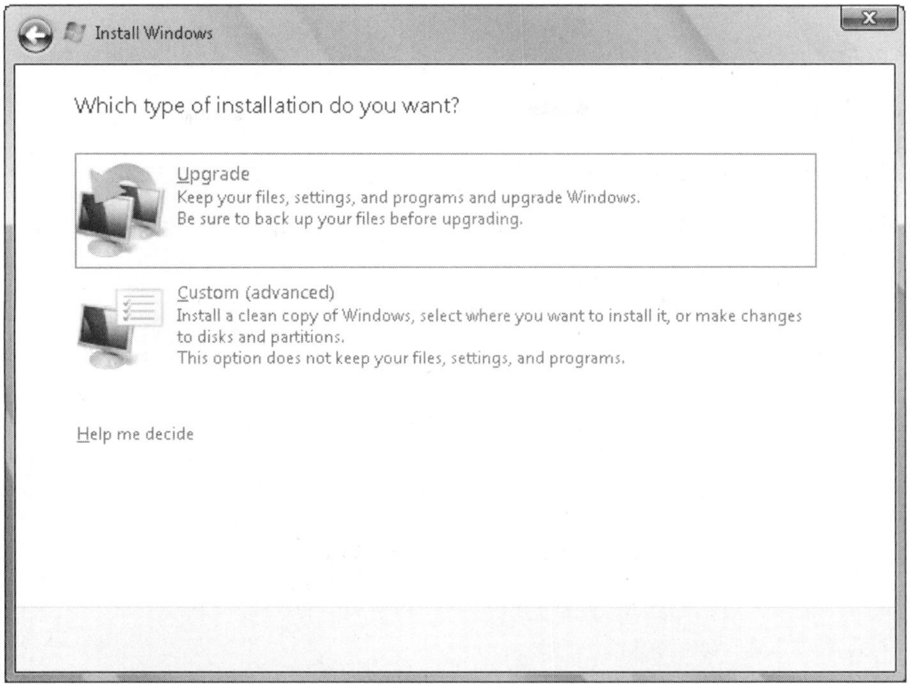

Figure 2-8 Selecting the installation type

12. Click **Custom (advanced)**

13. You might see the Compatibility Report window to report possible compatibility conflicts and direct you to check the Windows Server Catalog at *go.microsoft.com/fwlink/?LinkID=85172* (takes you to the general Windows Server 2008 page).

14. The Windows Installation program displays disk partitions, including existing partitions and unallocated disk space. Select the disk partition or unallocated space you want to use. For example, click Disk 0 Unallocated Space on a new computer. (Note that the window displays an informational message at the bottom, if you highlight a partition that is too small or one that contains a non-NTFS partition. Further, there might be a *Load Driver* link at the bottom of the window so you can install a more recent hard disk driver or a driver for a disk that is not properly recognized by Windows Server 2008. You can click the *Load Driver* link or press F6 at this point to load a new driver.) Also, you might see a *Drive options (advanced)* link, which enables you to set up customized drive options. Figure 2-9 shows a disk with two partitions (both already allocated to NTFS), from which to select. Click **Next** after you've made your selection.

15. The installation program begins installing Windows Server 2008 (you'll see progress information about Copying files, Expanding files, Installing features, Installing updates, Completing installation).

16. The installation program restarts the computer. Let it boot from the hard drive.

17. You see the message: Please wait while Windows sets up your computer.

18. Next you see the Install Windows window as in Step 15, but in the Completing installation phase.

19. The system reboots again. Let it boot from the hard drive. (This might take a little extra time when performing an installation in Hyper-V or in another virtual server.)

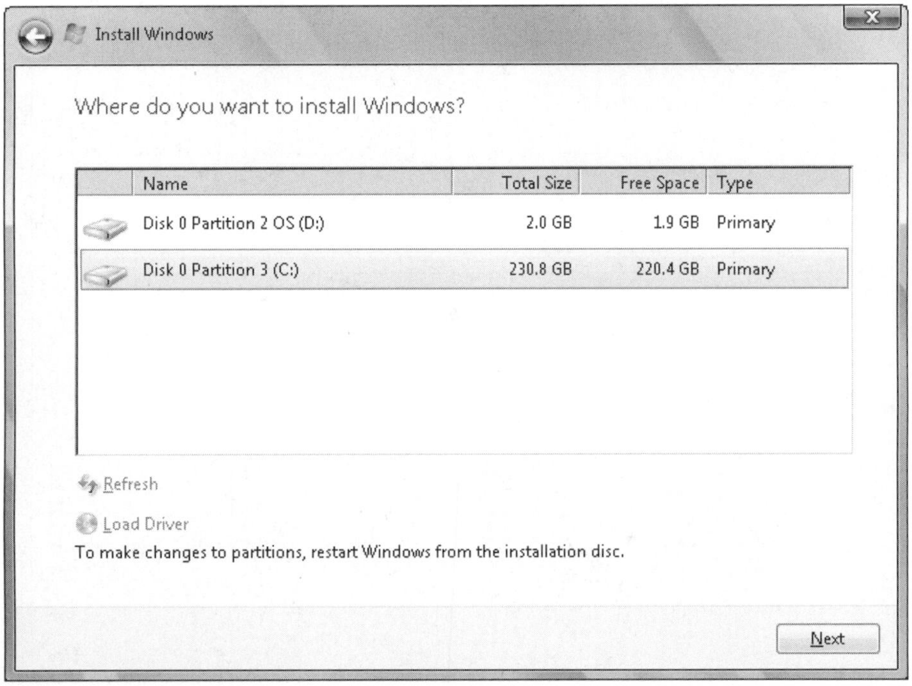

```
←  🗗 Install Windows                                          [ X ]

    Where do you want to install Windows?

    ┌──────────────────────────┬────────────┬─────────────┬──────────┐
    │ Name                     │ Total Size │ Free Space  │ Type     │
    ├──────────────────────────┼────────────┼─────────────┼──────────┤
    │ 💾 Disk 0 Partition 2 OS (D:)  │   2.0 GB   │   1.9 GB    │ Primary  │
    │ 💾 Disk 0 Partition 3 (C:)     │  230.8 GB  │  220.4 GB   │ Primary  │
    │                          │            │             │          │
    └──────────────────────────┴────────────┴─────────────┴──────────┘

    ✦ Refresh

    🌐 Load Driver
    To make changes to partitions, restart Windows from the installation disc.


                                                          [ Next ]
```

Figure 2-9   Selecting the partition

20. You see the message (a red circle with a white x in it): *The user's password must be changed before logging on the first time.* Click **OK**.

21. Enter a new password for the Administrator account and then enter the same password again to confirm the password. Click the blue circle with the white right-pointing arrow inside.

22. If you enter a password that is not a strong password, you see the message: (with a white x in a red circle) *Unable to update the password. The value provided for the new password does not meet the length, complexity, or history requirements of the domain. Click OK and enter a different password.*

For a strong password, consider creating one that is at least eight characters long and that includes numbers, uppercase and lowercase letters, and characters such as $, !, and #.

23. When you see the message *Your password has been changed*, click **OK**.

24. At this point, the Windows desktop is opened and the Initial Configuration Tasks window is displayed.

25. Leave the computer logged on for the next activity (including if you are installing Windows Server 2008 in Hyper-V).

From this point on, if you log off, you can log back on to the Administrator account using the password you entered in Step 21. The Administrator account has complete privileges to manage Windows Server 2008.

Using the Initial Configuration Tasks Window for Setup

You can use the Initial Configuration Tasks window (see Figure 2-10) to begin configuring the server. In this window, you can do the following:

- *Provide Computer Information*—Set the time zone, configure networking, and provide computer name and domain or workgroup information.
- *Update This Server*—Configure how updates are made.
- *Customize This Server*—Set up server roles, implement features, enable Remote Desktop, and configure the firewall.

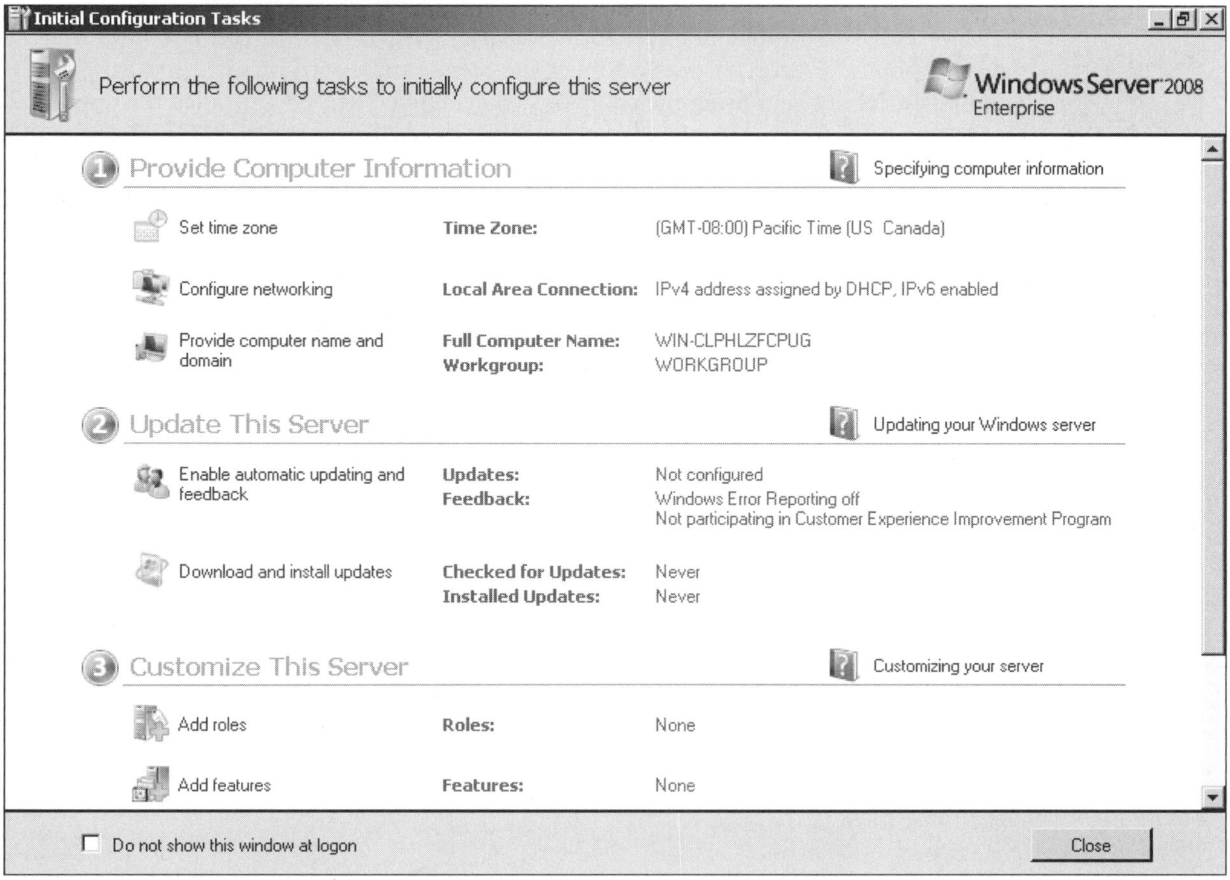

Figure 2-10 The Initial Configuration Tasks window

You don't need to complete all of the tasks at this time, but you should complete some preliminary tasks right away. For example, begin by reviewing and configuring the basic information about the server. Notice in Figure 2-10 that the computer has been assigned a random name of WIN-CLPHLZFCPUG in a workgroup called WORKGROUP. Also, the computer has been automatically set up to have an IP address automatically leased by DHCP. Typically, a server should have a static address that you assign or a permanent address assigned when you configure DHCP to give the server a permanent address.

After configuring the computer information, plan to configure how to update the computer. Regularly obtaining the latest updates is important to ensure that the latest system and security patches are applied. Finally, at this stage ensure that the Windows Firewall is initially configured. Also, if you already know some roles that the server is to perform or features you want to add, you can add those roles and features from the Initial Configuration Tasks window. (You'll learn more about configuring server roles and features in Chapter 3.)

Activity 2-5: Performing Initial Configuration Tasks

Time Required: Approximately 15–20 minutes
Objective: Use the Initial Configuration Tasks window to start configuring Windows Server 2008.

Description: Now that you've installed Windows Server 2008, it's important to configure the server so that it is set for the correct time zone, has an appropriate name, is a member of a workgroup or domain, is regularly updated, and is secured through Windows Firewall. In this activity, you complete all of these tasks. The server should already be logged on to the Administrator account with the Initial Configuration Tasks window open. Also, you'll need a computer name and a domain or workgroup name.

1. Ensure that the Initial Configuration Tasks window is open. If it is not, click **Start**, click the right-pointing arrow at the bottom of the menu, and click **Log Off**. Log back on to the Administrator account using the password you entered when you installed the operating system. (In Hyper-V, if you need to log back on, click the **Action menu**, click **CTRL+ALT+DELETE**, enter your password, and click the **right-pointing arrow**. If you don't see an Action menu and you see a yellow bar at the top of the screen, click the double boxes to the right of the x to switch out of the full screen mode, then click the Action menu, etc.)

2. Examine the setting for Time Zone. If it is set for the wrong time zone, click **Set time zone**. In the Date and Time dialog box, notice that you can change the time and date and change the time zone. Click **Change time zone**. Select the correct entry in the Time zone drop-down box. Click **OK** in the Time Zone Settings dialog box. Click **OK** in the Date and Time dialog box.

3. Click **Configure networking**. Right-click the network connection, such as **Local Area Connection**, and click **Properties**. Double-click the IP version in use on your network, such as **Internet Protocol Version 4 (TCP/IPv4)**, as in Figure 2-11. The Connection Properties dialog

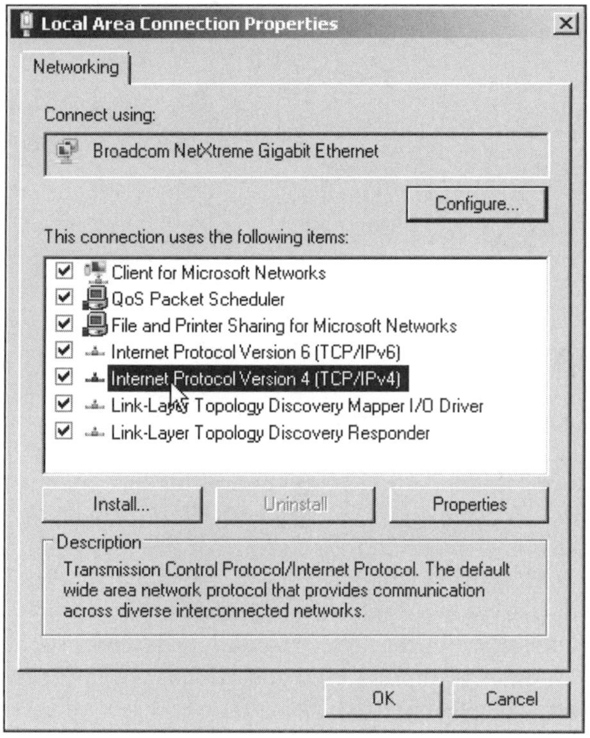

Figure 2-11 Configuring networking

box can be configured in the same way as you did in Activity 1-7 in Chapter 1. If you want to configure a static IP address now, enter the IP address, subnet mask, and default gateway for this computer. Also, enter the IP address for the Preferred DNS server and the IP address for the Alternate DNS server (if there is one). Click **OK**. Click **OK** again in the Connection Properties dialog box. Close the Network Connections window.

4. Back in the Initial Configuration Tasks window, click **Provide computer name and domain**.

5. Ensure the Computer Name tab is displayed and click the **Change** button.

6. Enter the name of the computer in the **Computer name** text box.

7. Click the option button for **Domain** or **Workgroup** (depending on how your network is set up, but if you select domain then there should already be a domain set up on the network for the server to join). Enter the domain or workgroup name and click **OK**. (If you enter a domain name, Windows Server 2008 checks the network to verify there is such a domain; if it does not find the domain, you'll see a warning box that the domain could not be contacted. Click **OK**. Check to ensure you correctly spelled the domain name, correct the name and try again. Or if you spelled it correctly, you might not have access to the domain, in which case you'll need to enter a workgroup name for now.) If you see the Computer Name/Domain Changes box with the white background, click **OK**. Next, click **OK** in the information box that you must restart the computer to apply the changes. Click **Close** to close the System Properties dialog box. You'll see a message box that you must restart the computer to apply the changes. Click **Restart Now**. Wait for the computer to reboot and log back into the Administrator account. The Initial Configuration Tasks window will display automatically.

8. In the Initial Configuration Tasks window, click **Enable automatic updating and feedback**.

9. In the Enable Windows Automatic Updating and Feedback window, click **Enable Windows automatic updating and feedback (recommended)**, as in Figure 2-12.

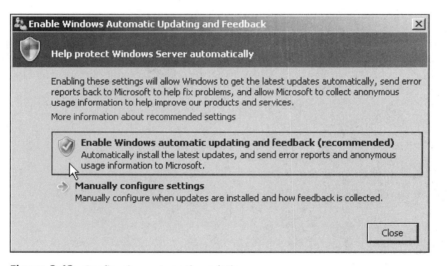

Figure 2-12 Configuring automatic updating

10. From the Initial Configuration Tasks window, notice the Configure Windows Firewall parameter at the bottom of the window. The firewall should be turned on.

11. Click **Configure Windows Firewall**.

12. Click **Turn Windows Firewall on or off** to turn it on. Ensure that the **General** tab is displayed. Notice that if Windows Firewall were not turned on, you can enable it by clicking the **On** option button (see Figure 2-13).

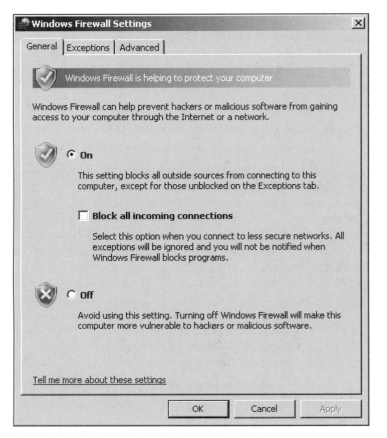

Figure 2-13 Windows Firewall Settings dialog box

13. Click the **Exceptions** tab. Notice the entries under Program or port. These are programs or ports that are blocked by the firewall unless you check one to make it an exception so that it is not blocked. You can also add a program or port to block by using the Add program or Add port buttons.

   • Record the names of any programs or ports that are already checked as exceptions.

14. Click **Cancel** to close the Windows Firewall Settings dialog box.

15. Close the Windows Firewall window.

16. Leave the Initial Configuration Tasks window open.

Server Activation

After Windows Server 2008 is installed, it is necessary to activate the copy of the operating system. Microsoft uses activation as one more step beyond providing the product key to ensure the installed copy of the operating system is legitimate. Activation also enables Microsoft to be sure a single copy is not running on more than one computer.

You need to activate your copy of Windows Server 2008 before the short activation period expires, or else many functions of the operating system are disabled. Windows Server 2008 can be activated through the Internet or by telephone, but the easiest method is through the Internet.

The general steps for activating Windows Server 2008 through the Internet are as follows:

1. Click Start, right-click Computer, and click Properties to open the System window. (Another way to access the System window is from Control Panel. To open it from Control Panel, click Start and click Control Panel. If you are in the Control Panel Home view, click System and Maintenance, and then click System. If you are in the Classic View, double-click System.)

2. Click the link to Activate Windows now.

3. Click Activate Windows online now (you'll need an Internet connection).

4. Click the Close button and restart your computer (close any open windows or work).

Using Windows Deployment Services

Windows Deployment Services is an alternative to physically taking a DVD to each computer that needs to have Windows Server 2008 installed. This is a good alternative when there are many servers (or workstations if you are installing Windows Vista) that need to be installed at once or over a specific time interval.

Windows Deployment Services is based on Windows Server 2003 Remote Installation Services (RIS). The upgraded code in Windows Deployment Services offers the following benefits:

- Installs Windows Server 2008 and Windows Vista
- Retains the ability to install Windows Server 2003 and Windows XP
- Enhances performance
- Provides updated boot format
- Uses image-based installation techniques
- Can utilize multicasting for network efficiency
- Offers a redesigned presentation for choosing which operating system to install

Windows Deployment Services operate in a **Preboot Execution Environment (PXE)**. This means that the target computer on which to install the operating system already has software to be PXE-enabled. A PXE-enabled client can connect to the network and communicate with a server (or boot from the server) without first having to boot from an operating system on the client's hard disk. Some computers come with PXE capabilities. Microsoft uses Windows Pre-installation Environment (WinPE) to enable PXE on the client. Windows PE is a very stripped-down version of a Windows operating system.

Installing and Configuring Windows Deployment Services

The first step is to install the Windows Deployment Services role on a computer that already has Windows Server 2008 installed. Before installing Windows Deployment Services, several requirements must be met:

- A DNS server already configured on the network
- A DHCP server already configured on the network
- Active Directory Domain Services already installed on a network server and the Windows Deployment Services server is part of the domain managed by Active Directory (the Deployment Services server can also house Active Directory)
- NTFS as the file system on the Windows Deployment Services server

You can install the Windows Deployment Services role from either the Initial Configuration Tasks window or from Server Manager. In the following activity, you use the Initial Configuration Tasks window.

At this writing, Windows Deployment Services works only on networks using IPv4. IPv6 functionality is not enabled.

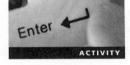

Activity 2-6: Installing and Configuring the Windows Deployment Services Role

Time Required: Approximately 15 minutes
Objective: Use the Initial Configuration Tasks Window to install the Windows Deployment Services role.

Description: The first step in using Windows Deployment Services is to install this role on an existing Windows Server 2008 server. This activity shows you how to install the role. Before starting, ensure that your network has DNS and DHCP servers, Active Directory installed on a server, and that the computer to be used for Windows Deployment Services is formatted for the NTFS file system. Also, you will need to use the Administrator account and you'll need to know the location of the Windows image file to use.

1. Ensure that the Initial Configuration Tasks window is open, or log off and then log back on to the Administrator account.

2. Under Customize This Server, click **Add roles.**

3. If you see the Before You Begin window, click **Next.**

4. In the Select Server Roles window, click the box for **Windows Deployment Services** (refer back to Figure 2-5).

5. Click **Next.**

6. Read the introductory information about Windows Deployment Services and click **Next.**

7. Ensure that both **Deployment Server** and **Transport Server** are selected and click **Next,** as in Figure 2-14.

8. Click **Install.** The installation will take a few moments.

9. In the Installation Results window, make sure that you see the message: Installation succeeded.

10. Click **Close.**

11. In the Initial Configuration Tasks window, you'll see Windows, Deployment Services listed as a role of this server (look under Customize This Server).

12. Click **Start,** point to **All Programs,** and click **Administrative Tools.**

13. Click **Windows Deployment Services.**

14. In the left pane, click the **plus** sign next to Servers to display the Windows Deployment Server.

15. Right-click the server and click **Configure Server.**

16. Click **Next** in the Windows Deployment Services Configuration Wizard.

17. In the Remote Installation Folder Location dialog box, leave the default selection, \Remote-Install (see Figure 2-15). This is a shared folder that will contain the operating system images to be installed on future servers. Click **Next.**

18. If you see a warning about using the System Volume, click **Yes.**

19. Select **Respond only to known client computers** for the PXE setting to govern which computers can be used.

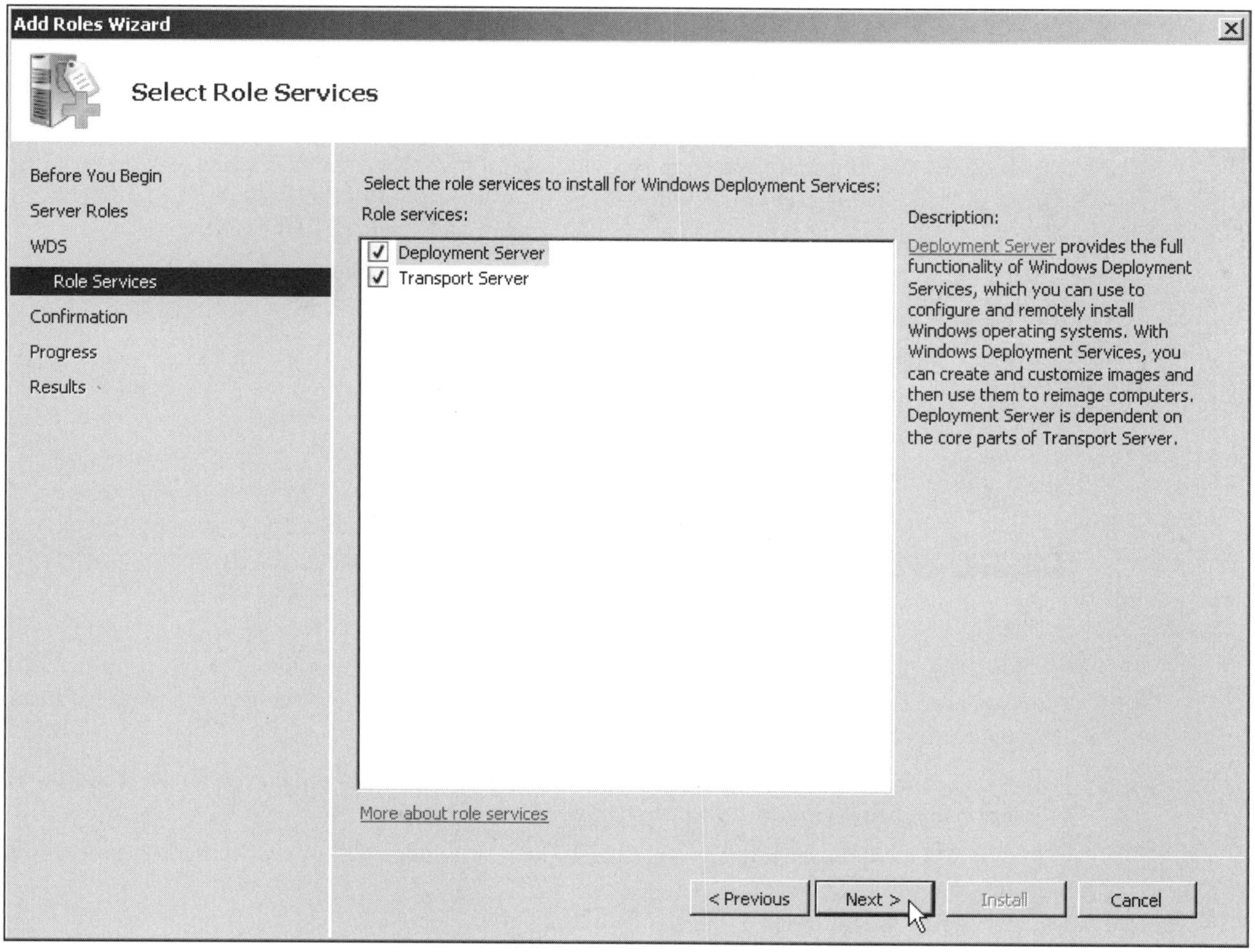

Figure 2-14 Selecting role services

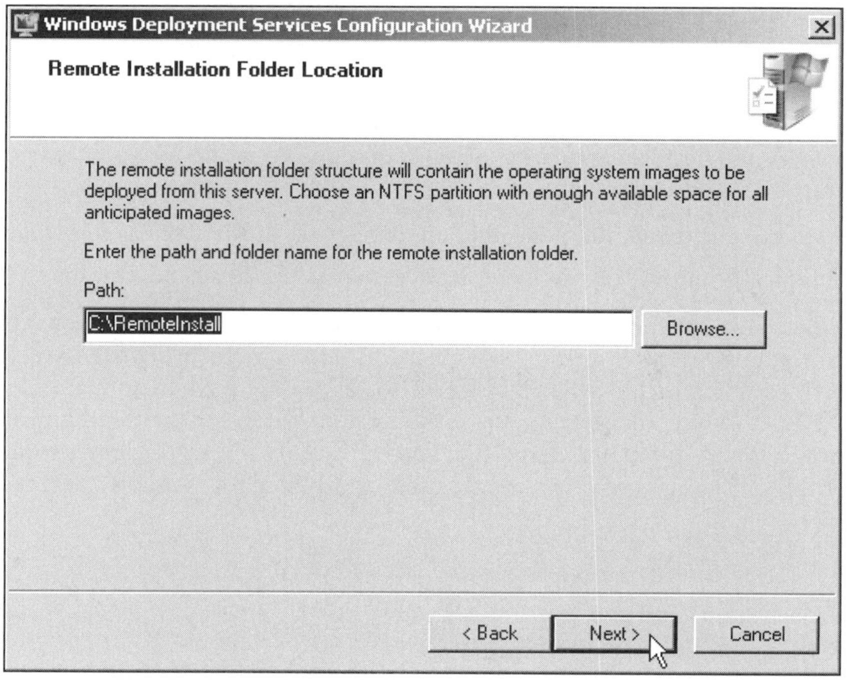

Figure 2-15 Specifying the shared folder location

20. Click **Finish**.

21. Ensure that the **Add images to the Windows Deployment Server now** box is checked. Click **Finish**.

22. Insert the Windows Server 2008 installation DVD. (The operating system image used to deploy to other computers is from the installation DVD that you use, which can be an edition of Windows Server 2008 or Windows Vista, for example.) In the *Path* text box, enter the drive letter of the DVD and the sources folder, such as *E:\sources*. Click **Next**.

23. Leave ImageGroup1 as the new image group and click **Next**.

24. Review the settings and click **Next**.

25. Click **Finish**.

26. Close the Windows Deployment Services window.

 In Steps 12 and 13, you start the configuration wizard from the Administrative Tools menu. As an alternative, you can also use the *wdsutil* command from the Command Prompt window. The Command Prompt window is opened by clicking Start, clicking All Programs, clicking Accessories, and clicking Command Prompt. To learn about options you can use with *wdsutil*, enter *wdsutil /?*.

After you have installed and configured Windows Deployment Services, you can install Windows Server 2008 on a computer through the network. These are the general steps for installing the operating system:

1. Access the BIOS setup program on the client computer. Set the computer so it can do a PXE boot from the network. Save the changes and reboot.

2. When the computer boots, press the F12 key (or whichever key is specified on your computer to start the PXE boot).

3. At the boot menu, select to install the image for Windows Server 2008.

4. Specify the locale for the setup program.

5. Provide a username and the associated password.

6. Follow the setup instructions to complete the installation.

Elements for an Unattended Installation

If you don't want to have to interactively respond when you use Windows Deployment Services, you can choose to perform an unattended installation. To set up for an unattended installation, it is necessary to do the following:

- Create the client-side unattend file, unattend.xml, in the \WDSClientUnattend folder.
- Configure Windows Deployment Services to use the unattend.xml file.

The unattend.xml file is in XML format. There is not enough space in this book to teach XML, but you can visit Microsoft's Web site at *www.microsoft.com* to see sample XML files along with explanations of what they do. Also, if you are a Microsoft TechNet member, go to the TechNet Web site at *technet.microsoft.com* and search for unattend.xml file samples.

When you create an unattend.xml file, you can specify several variables for customized installation. Table 2-3 summarizes commonly used variables for a Windows Server 2008 unattended installation.

Table 2-3 Variables for the unattend.xml file

Variable	Description
%ORGNAME%	Name of the organization using Windows Deployment Services
%MACHINEDOMAIN%	Domain name for the computer when creating a computer account
%USERDOMAIN%	Domain name when creating a user account
%MACHINENAME%	Name for the computer
%USERNAME%	User account name for creating a user account
%USERPASSWORD%	Password for the user account that is created during installation (for the sake of security, the password should be changed during the initial login)

After the unattend.xml file is created, it should be stored in the \RemoteInstall\WDSClient-Unattend folder. The next step is to configure Windows Deployment Services for the unattend.xml file. These are the general steps for configuring Windows Deployment Services for this purpose:

1. Click Start, point to All Programs, and click Administrative Tools.

2. Click Windows Deployment Services.

3. In the left pane, click the plus sign next to Servers to display the Windows Deployment Server.

4. Right-click the server and click Properties.

5. Click the Client tab.

6. Click Enable unattended installation, as shown in Figure 2-16.

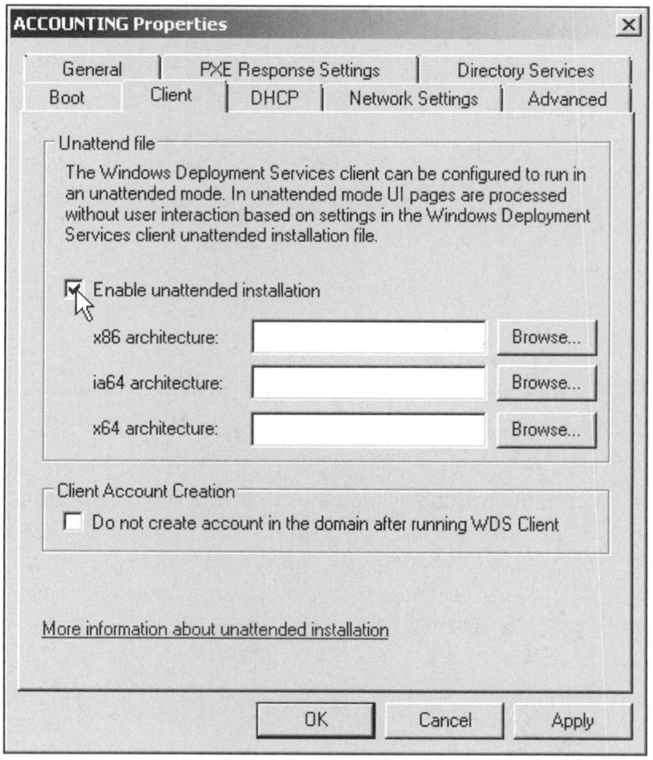

Figure 2-16 Configuring Windows Deployment Services for unattended installation

7. Click OK.

8. Close the Windows Deployment Services window.

Installing Windows Server Core

The steps for installing Windows Server Core are nearly identical to the steps for a full installation, until you reach the end of the process when you need to log on to the newly installed system. Here are the general steps for installing Windows Server Core:

1. Refer to Activity 2-4, "Installing Windows Server 2008 from DVD" and follow Steps 1–8.

2. In the step to select the operating system to install (Step 9 in Activity 2–4), select to install the Server Core Installation, such as Windows Server 2008 Standard (Server Core Installation) or Windows Server 2008 Enterprise (Server Core Installation).

3. Follow Steps 10–19 in Activity 2-4.

4. Press CTRL+ALT+DELETE to log on.

5. Enter Administrator as the account to log on to. Leave the password blank. Click the right-pointing arrow.

6. Enter a new password, confirm it, and click the right-pointing arrow.

7. Click OK.

8. Your new system boots into a command-line window, as shown in Figure 2-17.

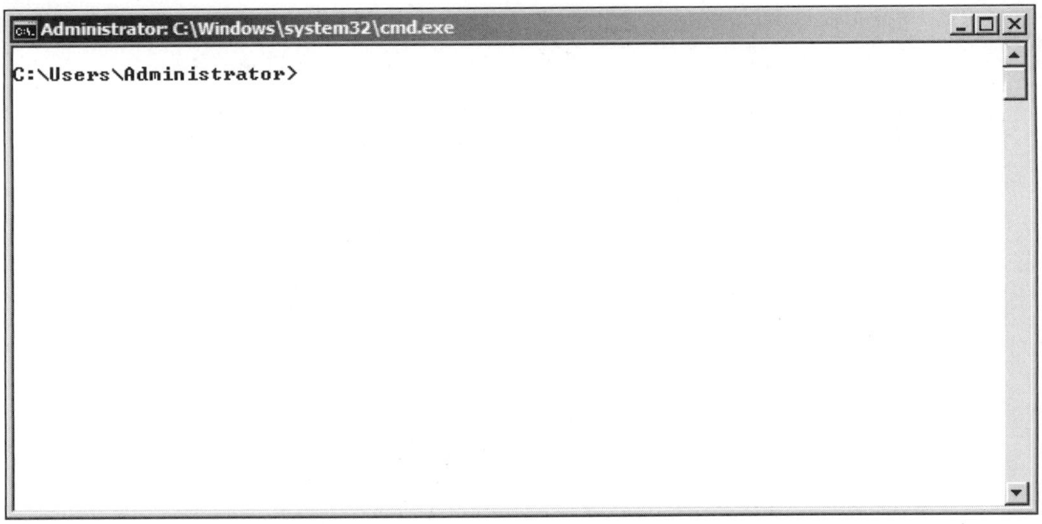

Figure 2-17 Windows Server Core command-line window

After Windows Server Core is installed, you can implement all or portions of the following server roles (at this writing):

- Active Directory Domain Services
- Active Directory Lightweight Directory Services
- DHCP Server
- DNS Server
- File Services
- Print Services
- Web Server

For many of these roles, not all role services can be installed as in the full installation of Windows Server 2008. This is in keeping with the design concept of having a smaller attack surface to discourage attackers and malicious software. For example, the File Server role primarily includes basic DFS (Distributed File System) Namespaces services, DFS Replication services, and services for NFS (Network File System). Examples of the File Server role services not included are File Server Resource Manager, Windows Search Service, and Windows Server 2003 File Services.

Use the *start* command to install a particular role. For instance, to start the DNS server role, enter:

```
start /w ocsetup DNS-Server-Core-Role
```

To install the Active Directory Lightweight Directory Services role, enter:

```
start /w ocsetup DirectoryServices-ADAM-ServerCore
```

If you want to uninstall a role, use the /uninstall option as in the following command to uninstall the Active Directory Lightweight Directory Services role:

```
start /w ocsetup DirectoryServices-ADAM-ServerCore /uninstall
```

Many other commands are available in Windows Server Core. At the command line, enter *help* to view a listing of commands. To learn more about a specific command, enter *help* plus the name of the command, such as *help start* to see the online documentation for the *start* command.

Besides the commands listed via *help,* there are a host of other commands for managing and using the server that are not listed. For example, to open a dialog box to set the time and date, enter *control timedate.cpl.* The *netsh* command enables you to view and configure network interfaces. To change the administrator account password, enter *net user administrator*.* To activate the server, enter *slmgr.vbs -ato.* Use the *netdom join* command to join an existing domain on the network. Finally, use the *logoff* and *shutdown* commands to log off an account or to shut down the computer.

Installing and Managing Service Packs

By the time you install an operating system, chances are there have already been reported problems and bugs with it. Service packs are designed to correct things such as security issues as well as problems affecting stability, performance, or the operation of features included with the operating system. Once you've installed the operating system, it is generally good practice to download and apply the latest service pack to fix any known issues and patch any security holes.

Installing a service pack is considered a major upgrade and should be given serious consideration because some of the operating system files will be replaced. There is always a chance that the upgrade will fail or new problems will be caused by installing the service pack. This is more of an issue for those servers that are already running on the network and being used by clients.

Use the following guidelines when installing the latest service packs for Windows Server 2008 (or any other Microsoft operating systems):

- Download the latest service pack from Microsoft's download site. The service pack is also usually available for order on CD or DVD.

- Review the documentation that comes with the service pack. This will detail the installation procedures and alert you to any problems associated with installing the service pack.

- If the server is already in the production environment, be sure to perform a full backup before you do the service pack installation.

- If the server is already available to clients, schedule when the service pack will be installed because the server will need to be rebooted during the installation. This will alert clients to any downtime.

- Once the service pack is installed, document any problems that occurred and how you fixed them for future reference.

You can install the latest service pack by using Windows Update. Alternatively, the latest service packs for different Microsoft operating systems can be found at *www.microsoft.com/downloads*.

To use Windows Update for obtaining a service pack (and all of the most recent updates), follow these general steps:

1. Ensure that you are connected to the Internet.

2. Click Start and click All Programs.

3. Click Windows Update.

4. Click Check for updates.

5. If a new service pack is available and your computer does not have it installed, follow the steps to install it.

Troubleshooting Installation Problems

With proper planning, many installation problems can be avoided, but even the most experienced installers can still experience difficulty. Following the preinstallation tasks outlined previously in this chapter can help to ensure a successful installation. Also keep the following points in mind to avoid problems:

- Ensure that the hardware has the Certified for Windows Server 2008 sticker or is in the Windows Server Catalog of Tested Products.

- Test all hardware before installing the operating system.

- Run the computer manufacturer's diagnostics before installing the operating system.

- Run a comprehensive test of the hard disk to ensure it is functioning properly.

Sometimes prevention is not enough and installation problems occur. Most problems are related to hardware drivers or to the actual hardware. For example, the computer might contain a hard drive, CD/DVD drive, or display adapter that is newly marketed and not contained in the installation selection list. If Windows Server 2008 Setup does not contain the driver or it is not included on a disk with the hardware, it is necessary to contact the computer vendor for a new driver. Sometimes an adapter card, such as a network interface card or hard disk adapter, is loosened when the computer is moved and the card simply needs to be reseated.

If SCSI adapters are used, the SCSI cable might be loose or it might not be properly terminated. A network interface card or sound card driver might be needed because new models are often introduced to the market. Table 2-4 provides a list of common problems and steps to solve the problems.

Table 2-4 Troubleshooting a Windows Server 2008 installation

Problem description	Solution steps
Installation fails when connecting to the domain controller	Make sure you have previously created an account in the domain or have a user account with administrative privileges and provided the right domain name. Also, make sure the computer is connected to the network and that the domain controller (the server with Active Directory) and the DNS server are working.
Setup did not find any mass storage devices on the computer	The most common cause is that Setup does not have a driver for a SCSI device or is detecting storage devices in the wrong order, such as the CD/DVD drive first. Press F6 or click the *Load Driver* link in the Where do you want to install Windows window, and provide a driver for the mass storage device that will hold the operating system files. Check to make sure all adapters and controllers are working properly. Check power to all devices. Reseat adapters and controllers. For SCSI devices: (1) Ensure the SCSI cabling is properly installed, (2) check that SCSI devices are terminated, (3) ensure SCSI devices are correctly addressed, and (4) verify the BIOS correctly recognizes all SCSI adapters. Also, be sure the SCSI boot drive is addressed as 0. Check the manufacturer's recommendations for configuring SCSI adapters and hard disk drives. Try replacing the adapter before replacing the drive(s). For EIDE/SATA/ATA drives: (1) Check the controller, (2) ensure file I/O and disk access are set to standard, and (3) ensure the system drive is the first device recognized by the controller. For IDE and ESDI drives: (1) Check the cabling and controller, (2) check the drive setup in the BIOS for master/slave relationships, and (3) ensure the drive is properly recognized in the BIOS.
Media errors are reported	If you receive media errors when installing from DVD, try installing from another CD/DVD drive. If the problem still persists, use another Windows Server 2008 installation DVD.
The system will not connect to the network	Use the Initial Configuration Tasks window to ensure that networking is correctly configured. Check the network interface card to be certain it is working. Reseat or replace the card, if necessary. Use the diagnostic software provided with the card to test for problems. If this does not work, try a card from a different manufacturer, in case there is a hardware incompatibility.
The operating system will not install or will not start after installation	Verify that the hardware you are using is supported by Windows Server 2008.
A STOP message appears during the installation	Start the installation again. If the STOP message appears a second time, record the message and consult a Microsoft technician.
The computer locks up	Check the IRQ and I/O settings for conflicts among hardware components and cards (check the NIC and any specialized cards in particular).

Uninstalling Windows Server 2008

At some point, it might be necessary to uninstall Windows Server 2008. For example, if your server is being replaced with a newer model, you might want to install a different operating system on the old server. Uninstalling Windows Server 2008 is a relatively straightforward process and requires you to format the partition on which it has been installed.

Before uninstalling Windows Server 2008, be sure to back up any important data.

If you are installing another operating system, you are usually given an opportunity to format the hard drive for that operating system. Format the drive and install the other operating system. You can also use the FDISK and FORMAT utilities on a startup disk from an older Windows operating system to delete and format the partition. Another option is to use the DISKPART utility. Once the partition has been formatted, you can install a new operating system.

Chapter Summary

- Before you install Windows Server 2008, complete the preinstallation tasks to help ensure the best result. These tasks include checking hardware requirements and compatibility, determining disk partitioning, understanding the implementation of NTFS, looking at upgrade options, planning the number of user licenses needed, deciding on domain or workgroup membership, determining which version to install, and identifying the server roles.

- Windows Server 2008 has many server-based roles, from housing Active Directory functions to offering DNS or DHCP services to providing file and print services. In many cases, one server can have a combination of roles.

- Windows Server 2008 can be installed using any of several methods, which include DVD installation, upgrading from Windows Server 2003, using Hyper-V for a virtual server, and Windows Deployment Services. Fortunately, the installation follows a logical step-by-step process that automates many activities, such as detection of hardware. Although you might need to troubleshoot a specific installation problem, the likelihood of having to deal with a problem is reduced in proportion to how well you have planned in advance.

- After Windows Server 2008 is installed, you can perform basic configuration activities from the Initial Configuration Tasks window. These tasks include providing computer information, configuring networking, naming the server, joining the server to a workgroup or domain, determining how to regularly update the server, installing server roles and features, and configuring a firewall.

- So that you can retain full use of Windows Server 2008, plan to activate the operating system immediately.

- If your organization is planning to install multiple servers or many Windows Vista computers, you can use Windows Deployment Services to save time and effort. Through using Windows Deployment Services, you can even perform installations unattended.

- Service packs should be installed to fix any known problems with the operating system.

- If you run into installation problems, try the troubleshooting suggestions in Table 2-4.

- To uninstall Windows Server 2008, use the installation of another operating system to overwrite the Windows Server 2008 installation or use tools such as FDISK, FORMAT, and DISKPART.

Key Terms

basic input/output system (BIOS)   A program on a read-only or flash memory chip that establishes basic communication with components such as the monitor and disk drives. The advantage of a flash chip is that you can update the BIOS.

client access license (CAL)   A license to enable a workstation to access a Windows server.

COM+   An enhancement to COM that enables publishing and subscriber services for applications, load balancing, and other services.

Component Object Model (COM)   A set of standards for building software from individual objects or components; COM provides the basis for Object Linking and Embedding (OLE) and ActiveX, for example.

digital certificate   A set of unique identification information that is typically put at the end of a file, or that is associated with a computer communication. Its purpose is to show that the source of the file or communication is legitimate.

Distributed File System (DFS)   A system that enables folders shared from multiple computers to appear as though they exist in one centralized hierarchy of folders instead of on many different computers.

File Transfer Protocol (FTP) A TCP/IP application protocol that transfers files in bulk data streams and that is commonly used on the Internet.

hard link Enables you to create one file and then establish links to that file in other folders, as though the file is in all of the folders.

Hypertext Transfer Protocol (HTTP) A protocol in the TCP/IP suite of protocols that is used to transport Hypertext Markup Language (HTML) documents and other data transmissions over networks and the Internet for access by Web-compliant browsers.

journaling The process of keeping chronological records of data or transactions so that if a system crashes without warning, the data or transactions can be reconstructed or backed out to avoid data loss or information that is not properly synchronized.

New Technology File System (NTFS) File system that is native to Windows Server systems and that supports features such as security, compression, disk quotas, encryption, self-healing from disk damage, and others.

portable operating system interface (POSIX) Standards set by the Institute of Electrical and Electronics Engineers (IEEE) for portability of applications.

Preboot Execution Environment (PXE) An environment in which a client computer has software or hardware to enable its network interface card to connect to the network and communicate with a server (or boot from the server) without having to first boot from an operating system on the client's hard disk.

redundant array of inexpensive (or independent) disks (RAID) A set of standards designed to extend the life of hard disk drives and to prevent data loss from a hard disk failure.

service pack (SP) A major update for an operating system that includes fixes for known problems and provides product enhancements.

shared directory A directory on a networked computer that other computers on the network can access.

terminal A device that consists of a monitor and keyboard to communicate with host computers that run the programs. The terminal does not have a processor to use for running programs locally.

Windows Deployment Services (WDS) Services in Windows Server 2008 that enable Windows Server 2008 and Windows Vista (and certain other Windows operating systems) to be installed on multiple computers using automated techniques.

Windows Server Catalog of Tested Products A list of computer hardware and software tested by Microsoft and determined to be compatible with a specific Windows Server operating system, such as Windows Server 2008.

Review Questions

1. Your colleague is trying to upgrade from Windows Server 2003, Datacenter Edition to Windows Server 2008 Standard Edition, but the Setup program won't allow the upgrade. Which of the following is the problem?

   a. Active Directory is set up on the network, but needs to be configured to identify this computer as running Windows Server 2008 Standard Edition.

   b. The Datacenter Edition had only a three-year license, and it has expired.

   c. Windows Server 2003, Datacenter Edition cannot be upgraded to Windows Server 2008 Standard Edition.

   d. The DNS server on the network must first be reconfigured to recognize Windows Server 2008.

2. Your IT director heard about a fast but inexpensive new computer and purchased it to be the new Windows Server 2008 server on the network. When you attempt to install Windows Server 2008, the operating system won't install because there seems to be a problem with the BIOS in the new computer. How might this dilemma have been avoided?

   a. The new computer should have been purchased with no BIOS, which is a requirement of Windows Server 2008.

   b. The new computer is too fast for Windows Server 2008 and should have been purchased with a CPU restrictor option.

   c. The IT director should have first had a system programmer make changes to the BIOS.

   d. The IT director should have checked to see if the computer hardware and BIOS were certified for Windows Server 2008.

3. You have installed Windows Server 2008, but when the computer reboots you only see a command-line screen. However, you intended to implement a full version of the operating system with the normal Windows GUI. What has happened?

   a. For Windows Server 2008, you need a 1399 cable for the display monitor.

   b. You have installed Web Edition, which only has a command-line interface.

   c. The Windows Setup program did not properly identify the type of display monitor.

   d. During the installation, you selected to install Server Core instead of the full installation.

4. Which of the following are roles that can be implemented in Windows Server 2008? (Choose all that apply.)

   a. Active Directory Printer Spooling Services

   b. Application Server

   c. Fax Server

   d. Terminal Services

5. You have installed Windows Deployment Services, but the installation does not properly work. Which of the following might be the problem? (Choose all that apply.)

   a. No DHCP server is present on the network.

   b. Active Directory is not installed on a network server.

   c. Windows Deployment Services only works with IPv6, but your network is configured for IPv4.

   d. No File Services server is present on the network.

6. Before you install Windows Server 2008, the company's management team has expressed a concern about the Marketing Department using too much disk space on the server, because they don't regularly delete old files. What feature(s) of NTFS in Windows Server 2008 can be used to help address this concern? (Choose all that apply.)

   a. indexing

   b. compression

   c. journaling

   d. disk quotas

7. The maximum length for a Windows Server 2008 computer name is _____.

8. The _____ server role is used to manage security tokens and security services for a Web-based network.

9. Your company plans to purchase and implement 21 new servers in the next few months and then add 10 more over the next year. You want to make a case for using Windows Deployment Services. Which of the following do you mention as you make the case? (Choose all that apply.)

   a. lowers installation costs

   b. enables consistent deployment and configuration

   c. requires the purchase of only one server license, even after the servers are installed

   d. enables the servers to be administered together through the help of scripts

10. You have installed Windows Server 2008, but during the installation no screen was provided on which to enter the name of the server computer. What tools enable you to name the server? (Choose all that apply.)

    a. Initial Configuration Tasks window

    b. Role Manager tool

    c. *naming* command in the Command Prompt window

    d. Network Install window

11. When you configure a server to be a member of a domain, at the time of configuration the server checks the network to verify _____.

12. Which of the following must you do shortly after installing Windows Server 2008 to keep the server functions enabled?

    a. Activate Windows Server 2008.

    b. Install the Server Control role.

    c. Click Start and click License Verification.

    d. Reenter the Product Key code when you register with Active Directory.

13. The _____ file is needed for an unattended installation via Windows Deployment Services.

14. The latest service pack has some patches that you need for Windows Server 2008 security. Your assistant says the only way to get a service pack is to order a CD from Microsoft. Is there a faster way to obtain the service pack? (Choose all that apply.)

    a. Purchase it on tape at an office supply retailer.

    b. Use Windows Update.

    c. Check Microsoft's Web site for a download of the service pack.

    d. Connect the computer to the Internet, insert the Windows Server 2008 installation DVD, and on the first screen, click Obtain service pack.

15. You are installing Windows Server 2008, but the Setup program does not find any hard disk drives on the computer. What step or steps are best to take initially? (Choose all that apply.)

    a. Abort the installation and immediately turn the computer back into the vendor even though the hard drives are already installed.

    b. Stop the installation and then restart it pressing F11 on the first installation window.

    c. Press F6 when the installation displays storage device information and provide a driver for the hard disks.

    d. Reseat the disk adapters/controllers.

16. The target client computer which is to install an operating system via Windows Deployment Services should be _____ enabled.

17. Your assistant is about to install the latest service pack for Windows Server 2008 on a production server. What is your advice before he starts? (Choose all that apply.)

    a. Put the server in fast mode to make the process go faster.

    b. Back up the server before starting.

    c. Use Server Manager to turn on Service Pack Enable.

    d. First take down the server and reboot it into Update Environment.

18. When you install Windows Server 2008, you enter a password and confirm it for the _____ account.

19. You are going to perform a Windows Server 2008 installation early in the morning before a meeting and decide to make yourself a checklist of things to do immediately before you start. Which of the following are on your checklist? (Choose all that apply.)

    a. Disconnect any flash drives.

    b. Have on hand drivers for new peripherals in the computer.

    c. Use the test software disc that came with the computer to verify key hardware elements, such as the CPU.

    d. Ensure that all necessary hardware, such as the NIC, is preinstalled.

20. The server you are installing is to be used for the Distributed File System. Which role should be installed on the server?

    a. File Services

    b. UDDI

    c. Active Directory Lightweight Directory Services

    d. DHCP

Case Projects

CASE PROJECTS

This week you work with Gym Masters, a company that makes equipment for fitness centers and gyms. Gym Masters makes treadmills, stair steppers, cross trainers, exercise bikes, free weights, and stationary exercise devices. They supply fitness and recreation centers throughout the United States and Canada. Gym Masters has two locations, one in Chicago and one in Toronto. Both locations have computer centers currently filled with Windows 2000 Server and Windows Server 2003 servers. The Chicago location consists of an office building and a manufacturing building, both fully networked. The Toronto location has a single large building that houses offices and a manufacturing center. The Toronto building is also fully networked. All networks use IPv4 for communications.

The Chicago location has a combination of Windows XP and Windows Vista workstations. In Toronto, they have fully upgraded to Windows Vista. However, the Toronto location is to receive 24 new computers that will need to have Windows Vista installed.

In both locations, the servers are centralized in a controlled computer center environment. The Gym Masters management wants to upgrade the 22 servers in the Chicago location and the 18 servers in Toronto to Windows Server 2008. A combination of Standard, Enterprise, and Datacenter Edition computers must be upgraded. Also, the company is planning to add 12 new servers in Chicago and 14 new ones in Toronto. As is common in many organizations, the information technology (IT) staff are overworked and understaffed. Gym Masters has hired you through Aspen Consulting to coordinate and assist with the transition to Windows Server 2008.

Case Project 2-1: Advance Preparations

The IT managers from Chicago and Toronto have decided the first step is to form a transition committee to plan and track the progress of the server upgrades. The committee consists of both IT managers (from each location), two department heads from each location, the chief financial officer, the director of operations, a senior applications programmer, and a senior systems programmer.

During the kickoff meeting, you briefly mention a few advance preparation steps the committee needs to know about. In response, the committee asks you to create a full report or slide presentation of the steps that need to be considered in advance for Windows Server 2008 installations. In your report or slide show, present all of the steps appropriate to Gym Masters' situation.

Case Project 2-2: Server Roles

The committee has recently been discussing the functions of each server. They are not familiar with server roles, but they do know how specific servers are used. Some of the server functions they mention include:

- Providing a Web site
- Offering applications that users can run on the server through accessing the server over the network
- Offering shared files on large scale
- Managing Active Directory functions for the domain
- Offering VPNs
- Coordinating printing
- Providing Web-based applications to internal users

Create a short report for the committee that translates each of these functions into server roles offered through Windows Server 2008. Also, suggest some other roles that are likely necessary on the company's networks (*Hint*: Consider managing IP address assignments and translating computer names and IP addresses). Include a short explanation of each server role you mention.

Case Project 2-3: Initial Configuration

A Gym Masters system programmer has just installed the first Windows Server 2008 system and now needs to do an initial configuration of the server. Discuss which tool she can use for the initial configuration and briefly discuss the configuration tasks that should be performed at this point.

Case Project 2-4: Installing Multiple Servers

The Toronto IT Department wants to install Windows Server 2008 Standard Edition on all 14 new servers in its location. The servers have arrived, are unpacked, and have been tested. Also, the preliminary preparations have been completed. Now they want to install Standard Edition on a mass scale to complete this part of the project right away. What Windows Server 2008 capability enables them to do the mass installation quickly and efficiently? What general steps are involved in setting up this capability? Can the capability also be used to install Windows Vista on the 24 new client workstations arriving soon? Explain the answers to these questions in a memo to the IT manager in Toronto that you also copy to the transition committee.

chapter 3

Configuring the Windows Server 2008 Environment

After reading this chapter and completing the exercises, you will be able to:

- Use Server Manager and ServerManagerCmd.exe to manage a server
- Install and remove server roles
- Configure server hardware
- Configure the operating system
- Understand and configure the Registry
- Use the Security Configuration Wizard to harden a server
- Install and use Windows PowerShell

A successful Windows Server 2008 installation is certainly the first step in preparing a server for prime time. The next step is to customize the server for your organization's needs. A server can be customized in hundreds of ways, including configuring server roles, hardware, software, and security. Fortunately, Windows Server 2008 has tools that make these tasks go smoothly. Some of the tools are time tested, such as Control Panel, whereas others are newer, such as Server Manager. All of the tools presented here help take the guesswork out of server management.

This chapter introduces the powerful Server Manager tool and shows you how to use it to install and remove server roles, along with other tasks. Next, you learn to use Control Panel and Device Manager to configure hardware and verify key files in Windows Server 2008. You also learn to tune the operating system for peak performance and to set up key functions such as startup and recovery. Because Windows Server 2008 relies on the Registry for vital system information, you learn the Registry's structure and how to configure it. Security is another critical server configuration task, and in this chapter you learn how to use the Security Configuration Wizard as both a GUI and command-line tool. Finally, you learn to install and use Windows PowerShell to manage one or more servers.

Using Server Manager

Server Manager is a new tool introduced with Windows Server 2008. This tool consolidates administrative functions to make a server easier to manage. Other tools are still available, such as the individual tools listed on the Administrative Tools menu and the Microsoft Management Console (MMC), which you learn about in Chapter 4, "Introduction to Active Directory and Account Management." Server Manager, though, is both convenient and powerful for managing a server. It's also a good place to start after you've done the initial configuration tasks described in Chapter 2, "Installing Windows Server 2008."

 If you have managed Windows Server 2003 or Windows 2000 Server, you might be familiar with the Computer Management tool. The Computer Management tool is still available from the Administrative Tools menu, but Server Manager offers a fresh approach that combines many more tools and capabilities in one place.

Whether you are a novice or an experienced server administrator, you'll find something to like about Server Manager. Server Manager does more than the Initial Configuration Tasks window you used in Chapter 2. One important feature you'll notice right away is that the Roles Summary feature prominently displays log information to alert you to warnings or problems.

Server Manager typically has two main panels (see Figure 3-1). The left panel is in a tree format that has the following management areas:

- *Roles*—Shows the server roles currently installed and enables management of the roles, including adding or removing roles. This management capability can be very deep. For example, if Active Directory is installed, there is access to a huge range of tools for managing Active Directory, including creating new user accounts and user groups.

- *Features*—Shows the features that are installed on the server, which often are features associated with the roles of the server. Some features include those for managing server policies, message queuing, TCP/IP services, Internet mail and printing services (for a Web-based server), wireless services, printer port monitoring, and many more.

- *Diagnostics*—Provides access to server diagnostic tools, including Event Viewer for monitoring server logs, Reliability and Performance Monitor for monitoring server and network performance, and Device Manager for configuring devices.

- *Configuration*—Enables configuration of server services, task scheduling, the Windows Firewall and other security features, and Windows Management Instrumentation, which enables management programs to share information.

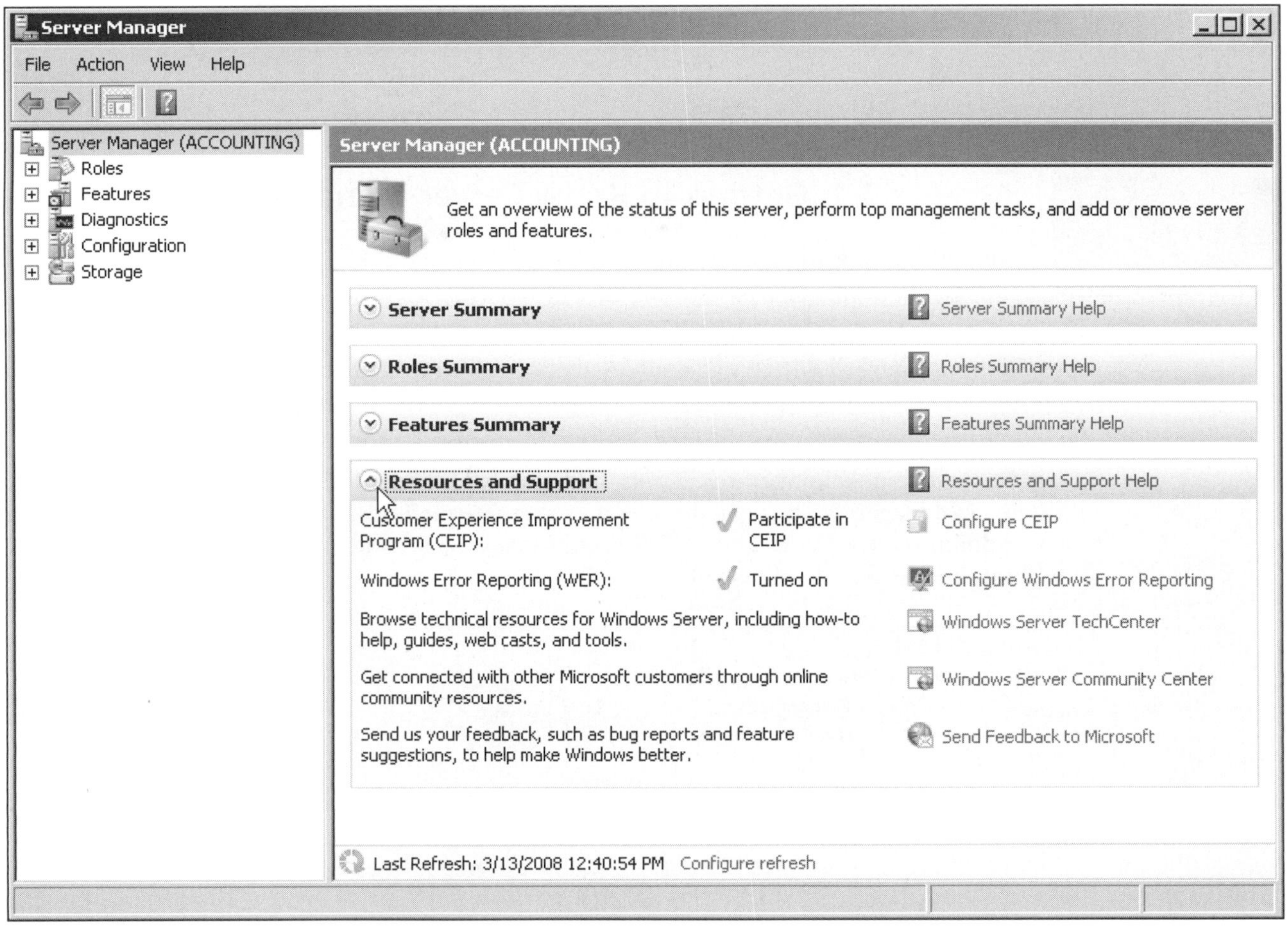

![Server Manager window screenshot]

Server Manager
File   Action   View   Help

Server Manager (ACCOUNTING)
  Roles
  Features
  Diagnostics
  Configuration
  Storage

Server Manager (ACCOUNTING)

Get an overview of the status of this server, perform top management tasks, and add or remove server roles and features.

⌄ **Server Summary**   ? Server Summary Help

⌄ **Roles Summary**   ? Roles Summary Help

⌄ **Features Summary**   ? Features Summary Help

⌃ **Resources and Support**   ? Resources and Support Help

Customer Experience Improvement   ✓ Participate in   Configure CEIP
Program (CEIP):   CEIP

Windows Error Reporting (WER):   ✓ Turned on   Configure Windows Error Reporting

Browse technical resources for Windows Server, including how-to   Windows Server TechCenter
help, guides, web casts, and tools.

Get connected with other Microsoft customers through online   Windows Server Community Center
community resources.

Send us your feedback, such as bug reports and feature   Send Feedback to Microsoft
suggestions, to help make Windows better.

Last Refresh: 3/13/2008 12:40:54 PM   Configure refresh

Figure 3-1 Server Manager window

- *Storage*—Manages disk storage and can back up the server using any of several backup options.

The right panel is divided into these sections:

- *Server Summary*—Shows basic information about the computer and security information, including firewall, Windows Updates, and Internet Explorer security information

- *Roles Summary*—Displays the installed server roles with information about the roles, server log information, and the ability to add or remove roles

- *Features Summary*—Lists the installed features with options to access wizards for adding or removing features

- *Resources and Support*—Shows help and informational resources that are available and includes links to quickly go to a specific type of resource

When you drill down into a specific Server Manager function, a third panel titled Actions often opens displaying specific actions that are appropriate to the management task. For instance, if you are working in Active Directory, you can create a new user account, set up a shared folder, or change to a different domain, just to mention a few possibilities.

For all of the activities in this chapter, you'll need an account with Administrator privileges. Also, all of these activities can be completed on a virtual server or computer, such as in Hyper-V.

Some steps in the activities in this book include bulleted questions with space for you to record your responses/answers.

Activity 3-1: Getting to Know Server Manager

Time Required: Approximately 15 minutes
Objective: Learn how to start and use Server Manager.

Description: Server Manager is a one-stop tool for managing a server. In this activity, you learn to open Server Manager and then you survey its possibilities. This activity is just an introduction; you'll use Server Manager more in this chapter and in chapters that follow.

1. Open Server Manager from the Administrative Tools menu by clicking **Start**, clicking **All Programs**, clicking **Administrative Tools**, and clicking **Server Manager**, as shown in Figure 3-2. (Server Manager can be opened using two alternate methods. One way is to click **Start**, point to **Administrative Tools**, and click **Server Manager**. A second way is to click **Start**, right-click **Computer**, and click **Manage**.)

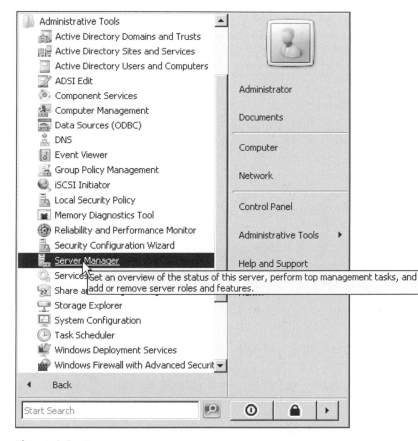

Figure 3-2 Starting Server Manager

2. Notice that the Computer Information area in the right pane shows information such as the computer's name, the domain name, the network connection, whether remote desktop is enabled, and the Product ID.

   • What are the three links to the right of this information?

3. Click **Change System Properties**. Review the information on the Computer Name tab, which enables you to provide a description for the computer and to change its name. Click each of the **Hardware, Advanced,** and **Remote** tabs and read what they do.

4. Click **Cancel**.

5. Examine the Security Information area in the right pane.

    • Is the firewall turned on? How can you go to the firewall to turn it on or configure it? Also, when was this computer last checked for updates?

6. Click the link for **Configure Updates**. (The first time you click the Configure Updates link, the Choose how to install updates dialog box may appear. If you see this dialog box, click **Have Windows install updates automatically** for this activity. Click the link for **Configure Updates** again in Server Manager.)

7. Notice that you could click *Check for updates* to immediately update Windows Server 2008. Also, the link *Change settings* enables you to configure the way in which to automatically update the operating system. Close the Windows Update window.

8. Check out the Roles Summary area in the right pane. The Windows Deployment Services role should still be installed from your work in Chapter 2. Notice any icons in front of this role, such as a circle with the letter *i* inside. This means there is at least one informational entry for this service stored in the server's logs. The logs keep track of ongoing events on the server. Click **Windows Deployment Services**.

9. Under Events in the right pane, you'll find a listing of any recorded events related to Windows Deployment Services. For example, at least one informational event will be listed. If you double-click this event, you'll likely see the time when Windows Deployment Services successfully started. (If you double-click the event, you'll see the Event Properties window. Click Close to close it.)

10. Below the Events area, you'll see the System Services that are associated with running Windows Deployment Services. From here, you can click to Stop, Start, or Restart the WDSServer service. This is a good place to troubleshoot a possible problem with Windows Deployment Services, such as if its WDSServer service is stopped. You'll learn more about working with services throughout this book.

11. Scroll down in the right pane to view the remaining contents.

12. Click the **left arrow** under the File menu to go back to the main Server Manager window display.

13. In the right pane, scroll to the Features Summary area. This area displays the installed features. Notice that you can add new features or remove features by using the *Add Features* or *Remove Features* links. Click **Add Features**.

14. Scroll through the Features box to review the features that you can add. Click **Cancel** and click **Yes**.

15. Scroll to the Resources and Support area in the right pane.

    • What link can you use to find technical resources for Windows Server 2008?

16. Notice that the tree in the left pane has options for the Roles and Features functions you have explored already.

17. Click the plus sign in front of Diagnostics, unless it is already opened.

    • What three tools are listed under Diagnostics?

18. Click the plus sign in front of Configuration, unless it is already opened. Notice the tools listed here, which are Task Scheduler, Windows Firewall with Advanced Security, Services, and WMI Control.

19. Click the plus sign in front of Storage, unless it is already opened. Under Storage, you can access tools to back up the server and to manage the disk.

20. Double-click **Disk Management** under Storage. This action divides the display into three panes: the tree, the Disk Management pane in the middle, and the Actions pane to the right. The Disk Management pane shows the disks that are mounted on the system, including hard drives, CDs/DVDs, flash drives, and other removable drives.

21. Click the **left arrow** under the File menu to go back to the main Server Manager display.

22. Leave Server Manager open for the next activity (unless you have to stop now and restart your work later).

Installing and Removing Server Roles

In Chapter 2, you learned about the many server roles that can be implemented in Windows Server 2008. One of the first steps in managing server roles is to learn how to install and how to remove server roles using Server Manager. Also, for some services associated with a role, you can select to install different portions or components of the services without installing all of the components.

Two common roles for a Windows Server 2008 server are those of a file server and a print server, which are offered through the File Services and Print Services roles. This is especially true in a small to medium-sized organization. The File Services role focuses on sharing files from the server or using the server to coordinate and simplify file sharing through Distributed File System (DFS).

In the Print Services role, the Windows Server 2008 server can be used to manage network printing services and it can offer one or more network printers connected to the network through the server itself. You learn more about DFS in Chapter 5, "Configuring, Managing, and Troubleshooting Resource Access," and about network printing in Chapter 6, "Configuring Windows Server 2008 Printing." For now, we are simply focusing on the steps for installing and removing roles.

There are times when the role or roles of a server change. Consider, for example, an organization that has one server housing File Services, Print Services, DHCP, and DNS. As the organization grows, it decides to dedicate that server to only the File and Print Services roles and to add a new server for the DNS and DHCP roles.

Activity 3-2: Installing and Removing Two Server Roles

Time Required: Approximately 20 minutes
Objective: Install and then remove the File Services and Print Services roles in Windows Server 2008.

Description: Windows Server 2008 offers a wide range of roles on a server-based network. In this activity, you use Server Manager to install two roles: File Services and Print Services. Next, you remove these server roles. The activity is designed to give you a taste of how to install and remove roles via Server Manager. (In Chapters 5 and 6, you'll learn more about the specific steps for configuring the services offered through these roles.)

1. Ensure that Server Manager is open. If you need to open it, click **Start**, right-click **Computer**, and click **Manage**.

2. In the Roles Summary area of the right pane, click **Add Roles**.

3. If you see the Before You Begin window, click **Next**.

4. Click **File Services** (if this service is not yet installed).

5. Click **Print Services** (if this service is not yet installed).

6. Click **Next**.

7. Read the Introduction to Print Services and Things to Note sections of the Print Services page for future reference.

   • What are the topics for additional information?

8. Click **Next**.

9. Leave Print Server checked by default in the Select Role Services window and click **Next**.

10. Read the Introduction to File Services and Things to Note sections in the File Services window. Click **Next**.

11. Leave File Server checked and click **Next**.

12. Review the services to be installed and click **Install**.

13. Note the installation results and click **Close**.

14. View the Roles Summary area of Server Manager to verify that the roles have been installed.

15. Click **Remove Roles**.

16. Click **Next** if you see the Before You Begin window.

17. Remove the checks from the boxes in front of **File Services** and **Print Services**, and click **Next**.

18. Leave the default selection to Delete printers installed on the server and click **Next**.

19. Click **Remove**.

20. Click **Close**.

21. View the Roles Summary area in the right pane to ensure that the roles are removed.

22. Close Server Manager.

Using ServerManagerCmd.exe

In addition to the Server Manager GUI tool, you can also use the ServerManagerCmd.exe command-line tool for managing server roles. ServerManagerCmd.exe also can be used to manage features that are to be added or removed. Microsoft offers this command-line capability so that a server administrator can set up multiple servers identically. Instead of individually running Server Manager on each server, an XML answer file can be created containing the parameters of roles and features to set up. ServerManagerCmd.exe can then be used to run the parameters in the xml answer file on all of the servers to save configuration time and ensure that the servers are configured the same way.

The management activities you can accomplish with ServerManagerCmd.exe include the following:

• Install a role or feature.

• Remove a role or feature.

• Query to determine what roles and features are installed.

- Use the *whatif* option to determine which features and services will be installed by a specific role, before actually installing that role.
- Restart the computer after installing or removing a role or feature.
- Specify particular features or services to install with a role.
- Use an XML-based answer file to have ServerManagerCmd.exe install or remove server roles.

ServerManagerCmd.exe is executed from the command line through the Command Prompt window. For the sake of security, the Command Prompt window should be accessed from the Administrator account and it should be run as the Administrator. When you use the Server-ManagerCmd.exe command, roles and features are identified by IDs, such as Print-Server for the Print Server role or Print-Internet for the Internet Printing feature within the Print Server role. Table 3-1 lists examples of common options used with the ServerManagerCmd.exe command. Also, Table 3-2 lists all of the current IDs for server roles (but not for services within roles, because there are too many to list here).

Table 3-1   ServerManagerCmd.exe options

Option	Description
-install <ID>	Installs a server role or feature that is specified by the ID of the role
-remove <ID>	Removes a server role that is specified via the role ID
-query <file.xml>	Displays a list of the roles and features that can be installed and indicates those that are installed already, plus the results can optionally be saved in an XML file
-inputPath <answer.xml>	Uses the contents of an XML file to determine which roles and features to install or remove
-restart	Restarts the computer after a role has been installed or removed (used with the *-install* or *-remove* option; also, use only if it is necessary to restart the computer following action on a specific role or feature)
-allSubFeatures	Installs all of the services and features associated with a specific role (used with the *-install* option)
-setting	Configures a particular installation setting (used with the *-install* option)
-help or *-?*	Displays help documentation for ServerManagerCmd.exe

Table 3-2   Major IDs for server roles

ID	Server role
Application-Server	Application Server
DHCP	DHCP Server
NPAS	Network Policy and Access Services
Print-Server	Print Services
Terminal-Services	Terminal Services
Web-Server	Web Server (IIS)

Many server roles, such as the File Services role, do not have an ID for that role. Instead, there are IDs for major services or features within the role, such as FS-Fileserver to install a file server and FS-DFS to install DFS.

To find out more about ServerMangerCmd.exe along with the available options and IDs, click Start, click Help and Support, and search for Server-ManagerCmd.exe.

Activity 3-3: Running ServerManagerCmd.exe

Time Required: Approximately 10 minutes

Objective: Use the ServerManagerCmd.exe command to install and query server roles.

Description: ServerManagerCmd.exe is designed to help automate the installation of multiple servers and for the server administrator who prefers to work from the command line. In this activity, you use ServerManagerCmd.exe to install the Print Services role, query the installed roles and features, and then remove the Print Services role.

1. Click **Start**, click **All Programs**, click **Accessories**, and right-click **Command Prompt**.

2. Click **Run as administrator**.

3. On the command line, type **servermanagercmd -install print-server -allsubfeatures** and press **Enter**. Your resulting Command Prompt window should look similar to Figure 3-3.

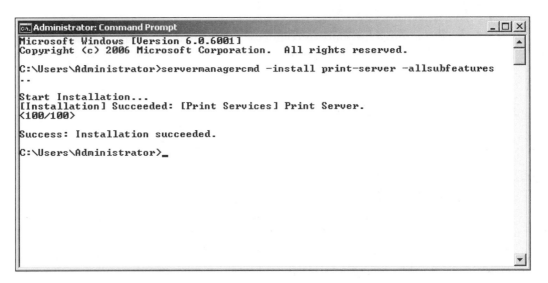

Figure 3-3 Using ServerManagerCmd.exe to install the Print Services role

4. On the command line, type **servermanagercmd -query** and press **Enter**. Use the scroll bar to scroll back over the results. You'll see the roles and features that can be installed. Also, notice that the installed roles are checked and highlighted in color.

You could also write the results of the command in Step 4 to the query.xml file by entering *servermanagercmd -query query.xml*.

5. On the command line, type **servermanagercmd -remove print-server** and press **Enter**.

6. Close the Command Prompt window.

Configuring Server Hardware Devices

Sometimes you will need to replace existing hardware in a server due to failure of a component, or sometimes you'll need to upgrade the hardware. Additionally, you simply may be adding another component such as a second network adapter. Windows Server 2008 offers both Plug and Play services and the Add Hardware Wizard to enable the installation of hardware. Hardware devices can include the following:

- Disk drives
- Disk controllers
- Network adapters
- CD/DVD drives
- Keyboard
- Pointing devices
- Monitor

For those times when you add or replace hardware, you'll need to be familiar with how to install and configure new hardware on your server.

Plug and Play

One important capability in computer hardware and operating system software is the ability to automatically detect and configure newly installed hardware devices, such as a disk or tape drive. This is called **Plug and Play (PnP)**. For this capability to work, PnP must be:

- Built into the device
- Enabled in the target computer's BIOS
- Built into the computer operating system kernel

Microsoft developed PnP, which has now been supplemented by **Universal PnP (UPnP)**, an open standard that is used in all types of systems and that enables connectivity through networks and network protocols. UPnP supports server-based networking, wireless networking, peer-to-peer networking, and other networking services.

Modern hardware, including both computers and peripherals, almost universally supports PnP. PnP eliminates hours of time that server administrators and computer users once spent installing and configuring hardware. When you purchase a computer or a new device, make sure that it is PnP compatible and that the PnP compatibility conforms to the PnP capabilities used by the operating system.

Installing a Plug and Play device is a relatively simple process of attaching the device and then waiting for Windows Server 2008 to detect it and install the appropriate drivers. In some cases, once the device is installed you might need to configure its properties and settings. Keep in mind that you should review the manufacturer's installation instructions before attempting to connect the device to your computer.

Depending on your computer system, it might be necessary to power down before installing some types of devices. Also, even if it is not necessary to power down to install a device (such as one connected to a universal serial bus port), you still might have to restart your computer for Windows to detect the new device. Further, some computer manufacturers prefer that you use the CD/DVD they have supplied to ensure the most recent driver or operating system software is installed, such as special options for configuring or troubleshooting the device.

Using Control Panel and the Add Hardware Wizard

If Windows Server 2008 does not automatically detect newly installed hardware, or if the device you are installing is non-Plug and Play, you can use the Add Hardware Wizard to manually launch PnP or to manually install the device without PnP.

The Add Hardware Wizard is used for the following tasks:

- Invoke the operating system to use PnP to detect new hardware.
- Install new non-PnP hardware and hardware drivers.
- Troubleshoot problems you might be having with existing hardware.

The Add Hardware Wizard is started from Control Panel. Similar to a control center, Control Panel allows you to customize Windows Server 2008 for devices, network connectivity, dial-up capabilities, and many other functions.

Windows Server 2008 provides two Control Panel view options: Control Panel Home and Classic View. Control Panel Home view groups functions under topical areas as follows:

- System and Maintenance
- Security
- Network and Internet
- Hardware and Sound
- Programs
- User Accounts
- Appearance and Personalization
- Clock, Language, and Region
- Ease of Access
- Additional Options

Each topical area contains tools for configuring the server. For example, when you open System and Maintenance, it displays tool selections for configuring the system, Windows Updates, power options, indexing, devices, and administration of the system. It also contains options for sending problem reports to Microsoft and for finding problem solutions.

Classic View displays configuration tools as individual applets or icons, such as Add Hardware to add new hardware, Device Manager for configuring devices, Keyboard to configure the keyboard, and so on.

When you have hardware that does not start PnP services automatically or that you want to configure manually, the easiest way to start the wizard is through the following steps:

1. Click Start and click Control Panel.
2. Click Classic View.
3. Double-click the Add Hardware applet, as shown in Figure 3-4.
4. Follow the instructions for adding the hardware. During the installation process, the wizard enables you to have it search for new hardware or to manually install the hardware from a list of common hardware types.

If you are installing hardware that is new to the market or that has new software drivers, it is often best to configure it manually so that you can use the software CD/DVD that comes with the hardware or the software driver files that you've obtained from the manufacturer's Internet site.

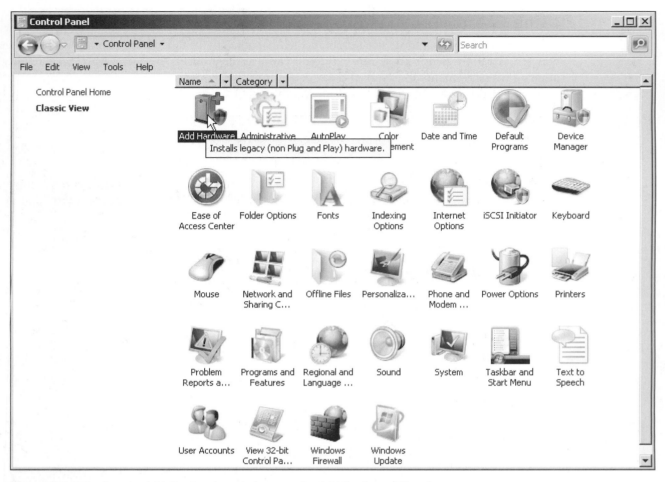

Figure 3-4   Selecting the Add Hardware applet to start the Add Hardware Wizard

Device Manager PnP and the Add Hardware Wizard are very effective for automatically setting up hardware parameters, such as **resources**. A server's resources include the **interrupt request (IRQ) line** (which is a channel for communication with the CPU) and other elements such as the **I/O address** and reserved memory range. For example, a computer contains a limited number of IRQ lines, 01–15. The video display, each disk drive, each serial and parallel port, and the sound card each use a dedicated IRQ to communicate with the processor. Each component also needs reserved memory addresses for I/O operations. Resource conflicts can sometimes occur when a network adapter, a new SCSI device adapter, or some other hardware is automatically configured.

One approach to address the limited number of IRQ lines is the development of Advanced Programmable Interrupt Controllers (APICs), which offer more extensive interrupt management capabilities, including more IRQ line options. Intel provides this technology for symmetric multiprocessor (SMP) computers, for example.

You can use Device Manager to check for a resource conflict and to examine other properties associated with a device. Device Manager provides a graphical view of all hardware currently installed on your computer. It can also be used to:

- Verify if hardware installed on your computer is working properly.
- Update device drivers.
- Disable a device.

- Uninstall a device.
- Configure the settings for a device.

For example, consider a situation in which there is an IRQ line conflict between the network interface card (NIC) and a modem that you have just installed. The conflict is apparent because the NIC will no longer communicate with the network and the modem will not connect through the telephone line you attached to it. The place to go to determine the problem and resolve it is Device Manager.

You can start Device Manager either from Control Panel (in various places) or Server Manager.

Activity 3-4: Resolving a Resource Conflict

Time Required: Approximately 10 minutes
Objective: Use Device Manager to resolve a resource conflict.

Description: Sometimes a resource conflict is subtle, such as a NIC locking up intermittently because it uses a portion of an I/O address range that is also used by another device. In this activity, you learn how to check for a resource conflict.

1. To start Device Manager from Control Panel, click **Start** and click **Control Panel**. From Control Panel Home view, click **Open Device Manager** under System and Maintenance; or from Classic View, double-click the **Device Manager** applet. To start Device Manager from Server Manager, click **Start**, point to **Administrative Tools**, and click **Server Manager**. Double-click **Diagnostics** in the left pane and click **Device Manager**.

2. Double-click **Network adapters**, as shown in Figure 3-5.

Figure 3-5 Device Manager

3. Right-click the adapter installed in your computer and then click **Properties**.

4. Notice that the Device status box reports whether the device is working properly. Keep this in mind as a troubleshooting tool for future use.

5. Observe the tabs that appear in the properties dialog box.
   - Check out each tab to see what it is for, and record your observations about the purpose of each tab.

6. Select the **Resources** tab and notice the resource settings that are used for the NIC.
   - Are any resource conflicts reported? How would you solve a resource conflict?

7. Click **Cancel** on the NIC properties dialog box.
8. Before you exit Device Manager, find out what resources are used by another device, such as a communications port or the display adapter.
9. Close the Device Manager window and any other windows that are open.

Driver Signing When you install a device such as a pointing device or a NIC, Windows Server 2008 checks to make sure that the driver for that device has been verified as secure. When a driver is verified, a unique digital signature is incorporated into it in a process called **driver signing**.

When Windows Server 2008 determines that a device driver is not signed, it gives you a warning, such as "Windows can't verify the publisher of this driver software." Another type of warning might indicate that the driver is altered. If you see such a warning, contact the manufacturer of the device to see if they can provide a signed driver.

Device drivers that are unsigned cannot be loaded in x64 versions of Windows Server 2008. In x86 versions, the Administrator account has authority to bypass driver signing warnings and install the drivers anyway. However, good security practice is to not load unsigned drivers for devices.

It is possible to deactivate checking for signed drivers in x86 computers via the Registry (you learn about the Registry in the section "Understanding the Windows Server 2008 Registry"). Some system administrators do this to enable legacy hardware to work with Windows Server 2008. This is one way in which many unsigned drivers may reside on a system, although it is not advised from the perspective of good security.

Using the System File Checker If you copy an inappropriate file for a device—such as one that is unsigned or outdated or from a different operating system—over a system or driver file, for example a .dll, .exe, or .sys file, Windows Server 2008 offers the System File Checker to scan system files for integrity. You can run this utility to scan all system files to verify integrity, to scan and replace files as needed, or to scan only certain files. When you opt to scan and replace, the System File Checker locates the original system file, which is stored in the Windows\ System32 folder, and then copies it over the inappropriate or damaged file. The System File Checker can be manually run from the Command Prompt window.

Using the System File Checker is one way to restore system files that have been corrupted because of a hardware power problem or a power failure.

Activity 3-5: Manually Running the System File Checker

Time Required: Approximately 5 minutes to learn about the command options and 10–30 minutes to run the test

Objective: Use the System File Checker to verify system files.

Description: The System File Checker is an excellent tool for verifying your system, particularly if you feel it is not responding quite right or that a driver or system file has become corrupted. These problems might occur when there is a power failure on a system that is not on a battery backup or when the power filter for the system is not working properly to ensure quality power. This activity shows you how to start the System File Checker. Note that the best practice is to run the System File Checker only when there are no users on the system.

1. Click **Start**, point to **All Programs**, click **Accessories**, right-click **Command Prompt**, and click **Run as administrator**.

2. Type **sfc /?** in the Command Prompt window, and press **Enter** to view the switch options you can use to check and replace files.

   - What are the switch options? Which option or options would you use to perform a check of the files in the offline mode?

3. If you don't have permission from your instructor to run the System File Checker or if there are users on your system, close the Command Prompt window at this point.

Remember that it is safest to have users off the system when you check files, and you might need to reboot before a replaced file goes into effect. In some cases, the checker might request that you insert the Windows Server 2008 DVD to obtain a file.

4. At the prompt, type **sfc /scannow** and press **Enter**.

5. The checker displays the results in the Command Prompt window, as shown in Figure 3-6. (If the System File Checker finds a file that needs to be replaced, it prompts you.)

```
Administrator: Command Prompt                                        _ | □ | x |
/OFFWINDIR        For offline repair specify the location of the offline windows d ▲
irectory

e.g.

        sfc /SCANNOW
        sfc /VERIFYFILE=c:\windows\system32\kernel32.dll
        sfc /SCANFILE=d:\windows\system32\kernel32.dll /OFFBOOTDIR=d:\ /OFFWINDI
R=d:\windows
        sfc /VERIFYONLY

C:\Users\Administrator>sfc /scannow

Beginning system scan.  This process will take some time.

Beginning verification phase of system scan.
Verification 100% complete.

Windows Resource Protection did not find any integrity violations.

C:\Users\Administrator>
```

Figure 3-6 Running System File Checker

Using Sigverif to Verify System and Critical Files Windows Server 2008 includes another tool, called **Sigverif**, which verifies system and critical files to determine if they have a signature. This tool only scans files and does not overwrite inappropriate files, enabling you to use the tool while users are logged on. After the scan is complete, the results are written to a log file, called sigverif.txt. If the tool finds a file without a signature that you believe needs to be replaced, you can replace the file when users are off the system.

Activity 3-6: Verifying Critical Files for a Signature

Time Required: Approximately 15 minutes
Objective: Use Sigverif to find unsigned files.

Description: After you upgrade a server or if you bypass a driver signature warning, you can check Windows Server 2008 for driver files that are unsigned, which is a good security precaution. Further, you might experience a situation in which unsigned drivers interfere with the normal function of the server—a file that is missed even by the System File Checker. For example, you might install a new disk drive, install the drivers from the manufacturer's CD/DVD, and then find that some other peripheral is not working right because it shares a common .dll file. This activity shows you how to use the Sigverif tool to locate the unsigned files that might be the source of the problem and that should be replaced.

1. Click **Start** and click **Run**.
2. Type **sigverif** in the Open text box and click **OK**.
3. Click the **Advanced** button. Notice the log file that will contain the results of the scan, which is sigverif.txt by default.
4. Click **OK.**
5. Click **Start**. Figure 3-7 shows the summary results of a scan.

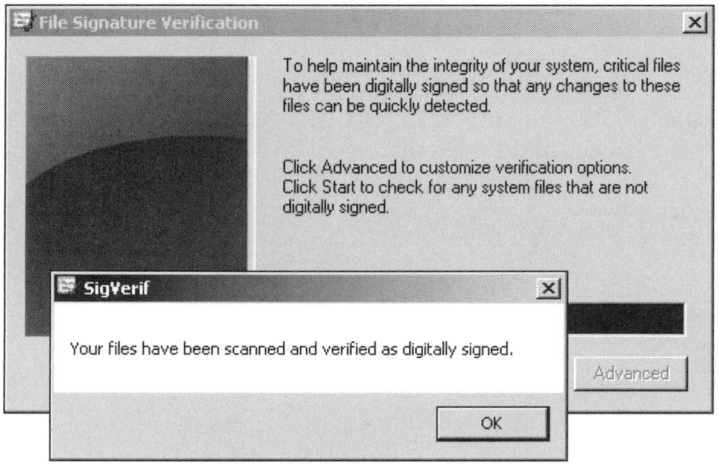

Figure 3-7   Scanning with Sigverif

6. Click **OK** when the scan is completed and then click **Close**.
7. Click **Start**, click **Computer**, and then browse to the drive on which the Windows folder is located. Go to \Users\Public\Public Documents and double-click the SIGVERIF file.
8. Examine the Status column to see which files are signed or not signed (see Figure 3-8).
9. Close Notepad. Click **No** if asked to save your changes. Close the Public Documents window.

```
SIGVERIF - Notepad                                          _ □ ×
File  Edit  Format  View  Help
OS Platform:  Windows (x64), Version:  6.0, Build: 6001, CSDVersion:  S ▲
Scan Results:  Total Files: 78, Signed: 78, Unsigned: 0, Not Scanned: 0

File                      Modified        Version         Status
------------------        ------------    -----------     ------------
[c:\windows\system32]
batt.dll                  12/11/2007      2:6.0           Signed       ▯
clfs.sys                  12/11/2007      2:6.0           Signed
hal.dll                   12/11/2007      2:6.0           Signed
hccoin.dll                11/2/2006       2:6.0           Signed
hcrstco.dll               12/11/2007      2:6.0           Signed
iscsilog.dll              12/10/2007      2:6.0           Signed
storprop.dll              12/11/2007      2:6.0           Signed
streamci.dll              11/2/2006       2:6.0           Signed
[c:\windows\system32\drivers]
acpi.sys                  12/11/2007      2:6.0           Signed
afd.sys                   12/10/2007      2:6.0           Signed
amdk8.sys                 12/10/2007      2:6.0           Signed
asyncmac.sys              12/10/2007      2:6.0           Signed
atapi.sys                 12/11/2007      2:6.0           Signed
ataport.sys               12/11/2007      2:6.0           Signed
b57nd60a.sys              5/10/2007       2:6.0           Signed
cdrom.sys                 12/10/2007      2:6.0           Signed
crcdisk.sys               12/11/2007      2:6.0           Signed
disk.sys                  12/11/2007      2:6.0           Signed
hidclass.sys              12/10/2007      2:6.0           Signed       ▼
◄                                                                   ► //
```

Figure 3-8   Viewing the Sigverif log file for detailed scan results

Configuring the Operating System

After the operating system has been installed, it can be configured to optimize performance and meet very specific requirements. Using tools included with Windows Server 2008, you can configure elements of the operating system, such as performance options, environment variables, startup and recovery options, power options, and protocols. The following sections discuss important ways in which you can configure the operating system, focusing on configuration tools accessed from Control Panel.

Configuring Performance Options

Windows Server 2008 enables you to configure and optimize your server for performance. You can configure three basic areas of performance:

- Processor scheduling and memory usage
- Virtual memory
- Memory for network performance

Configuring Processor Scheduling and Data Execution Prevention   Processor scheduling allows you to configure how processor resources are allocated to programs. The default is set to Background services, which means that all programs running will receive equal amounts of processor time. The Programs setting refers to programs you are likely to be running at the server console, such as a backup program. Normally you will leave the default setting for Background services. Sometimes, though, you might need to give Programs most of the processor's resources, for instance when you determine that a disk drive is failing and you want to back up its contents as fast as possible using the Backup tool.

Another performance (and security) option that is good to know about is **Data Execution Prevention (DEP)**. When programs are running on the server, DEP monitors how they use memory to ensure they are not causing memory problems. This is intended to foil malware, such as computer viruses, Trojan horses, and worms. Malware sometimes works by trying to invade the memory space allocated to system functions. If DEP notices a program trying to use system memory space, it stops the program and notifies the system administrator.

Some types of applications might not work with DEP. For example, applications that use dynamic code generation ("in the moment" code), in which portions of the code are not flagged as executable, might not work with DEP. Another example is program code that runs exception handlers and other code requiring executable locations in memory.

Activity 3-7: Configuring Processor Scheduling and DEP

Time Required: Approximately 10 minutes
Objective: Learn where to set up processor scheduling and system memory protection.

Description: Sometimes it is important to temporarily reconfigure a server to function more like a workstation, so that applications in the foreground have the most resources. This is true, for example, if you need to perform an immediate backup to save vital data during a system emergency. Also, it is important to use DEP to protect how system memory is used. In this activity, you learn where to set the system resources for processor scheduling and you learn to configure DEP.

1. Click **Start** and click **Control Panel**.
2. Ensure that **Classic View** is displayed and double-click **System**.
3. Click **Advanced system settings**.
4. Click the **Advanced** tab, if necessary.
5. In the Performance section, click the **Settings** button.
6. Click the **Advanced** tab. Notice the options that can be set under Processor scheduling, which are Programs and Background services.
7. Click the **Data Execution Prevention** tab. Ensure that **Turn on DEP for all programs and services except those I select** is enabled, as shown in Figure 3-9.

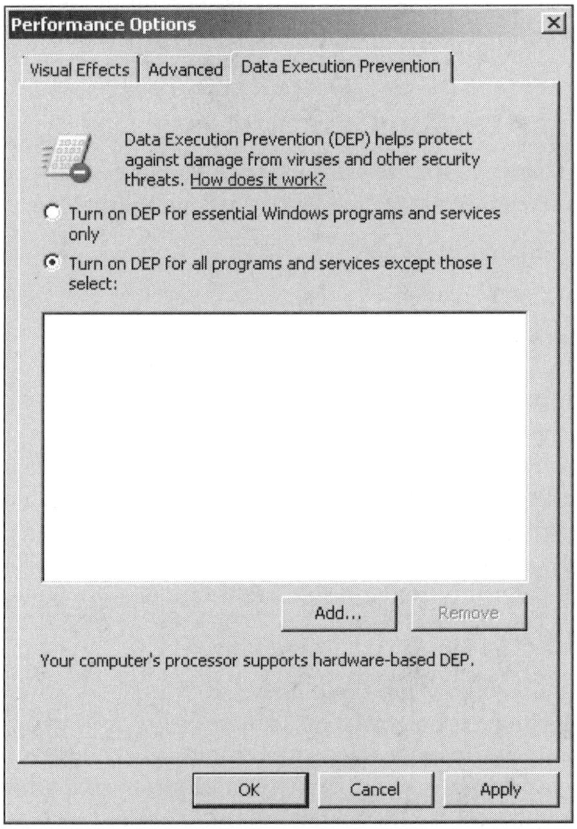

![Performance Options dialog box showing the Data Execution Prevention tab. Data Execution Prevention (DEP) helps protect against damage from viruses and other security threats. How does it work? Radio button: Turn on DEP for essential Windows programs and services only. Selected radio button: Turn on DEP for all programs and services except those I select. An empty list box with Add... and Remove buttons. Your computer's processor supports hardware-based DEP. OK, Cancel, Apply buttons.]

Figure 3-9   Configuring Data Execution Prevention

8. Click **OK**.

9. Close the System Properties dialog box and the Control Panel window.

Configuring Virtual Memory   **Virtual memory** is disk storage used to expand the capacity of the physical RAM installed in the computer. When the currently running programs and processes exceed the RAM, they treat disk space allocated for virtual memory just as if it were real memory. The disadvantage of this is that memory activities performed through virtual memory are not as fast as those performed in RAM (although disk access and data transfer speeds can be quite fast). Virtual memory works through a technique called **paging**, whereby blocks of information, called pages, are moved from RAM into virtual memory on disk. On a typical x86 computer, data is paged in blocks of 4 KB. For example, if the system is not presently using a 7 KB block of code, it divides the code block between two pages, each 4 KB in size (part of one page will not be completely full). Next, both pages are moved to virtual memory on disk until needed. When the processor calls for that code block, the pages are moved back into RAM.

Before virtual memory can be used, it must first be allocated for this purpose by tuning the operating system. The area of disk that is allocated for this purpose is called the **paging file**. A default amount of virtual memory is always established when Windows Server 2008 is installed, but the amount should be checked by the server administrator to ensure that it is not too large or too small.

The location of the paging file is also important. Some tips for placement of the paging file are:

- Server performance is better if the paging file is not placed on the boot partition (the one with the \Windows folder) of basic disks or the boot volume of dynamic disks (you'll learn more about the types of disks later in this book).

- If there are multiple disks, performance can be improved by placing a paging file on each disk (but avoid placing the paging file on the boot partition or volume that contains the system files in the \Windows folder).

- In a mirrored set or volume, place the paging file on the main disk, and not on the mirrored (backup) disk.

- Do not place the paging file on a stripe set, striped volume, stripe set with parity, or RAID-5 volume—because these are all disks specially set up to increase performance and fault tolerance (see Chapter 7, "Configuring and Managing Data Storage").

When you tune the size of the paging file, two parameters must be set: initial size and maximum size. A general rule for configuring the initial size is to multiply the amount of installed RAM times 1.5. For a server with 2 GB of RAM, the initial paging file size should be at least 3 GB. Set the maximum size so it affords plenty of room for growth—such as twice the size of your initial paging file setting. For example, if your initial setting is 3 GB, then consider setting the maximum size to 6 GB. Windows Server 2008 always starts using the initial size and only expands the size of the paging file as additional space is needed.

Activity 3-8: Configuring the Paging File

Time Required: Approximately 5 minutes

Objective: Learn where to configure the initial and maximum size of the paging file.

Description: One way to inexpensively improve the performance of a server is to adjust the size of the paging file. If a server seems to run a little slower than desired because the memory (RAM) is often used to the maximum, consider increasing the maximum paging file size. This activity shows you where to configure the paging file.

1. Click **Start** and click **Control Panel**.

2. If you're in the Control Panel Home view, click **System and Maintenance**, and click **System**. If you're in the Classic View, double-click **System**.

   - Look under the System section and record the amount of RAM in the computer.

3. Click **Advanced system settings**.

4. Click the **Advanced** tab, if it is not already selected.

5. In the Performance section, click the **Settings** button.

6. Click the **Advanced** tab and then click the **Change** button (see Figure 3-10).

   - What are the current settings on your computer? Are the settings appropriate for the amount of memory in the computer?

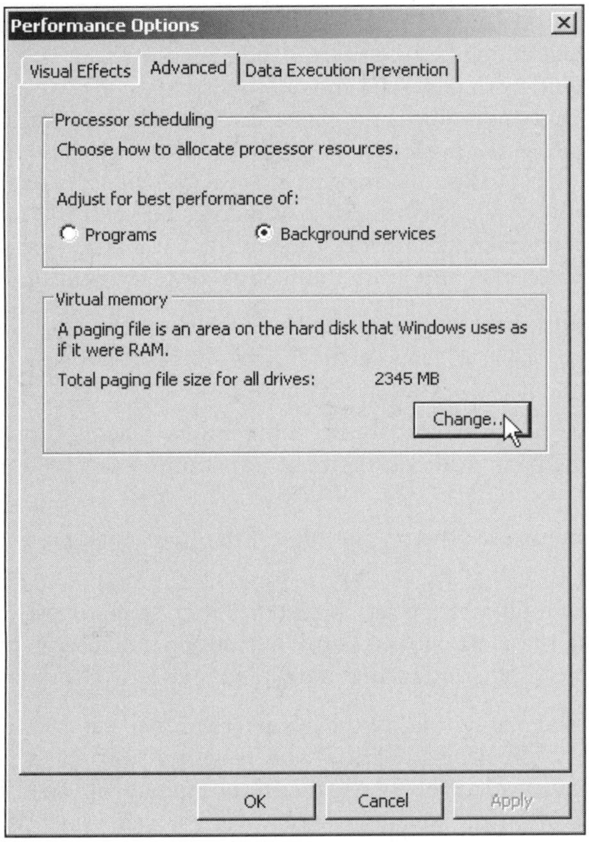

Figure 3-10 Configuring virtual memory

7. Notice that if your computer is running slow because of demands on RAM, you can turn off the automatic virtual memory configuration, which is the default setting, and set the parameters higher. You would do this by removing the check from **Automatically manage paging file size for all drives**, clicking **Custom size**, configuring the **Initial size** and **Maximum size** boxes, and clicking **Set**.

8. Click **Cancel** to leave the Virtual Memory dialog box, and then click **Cancel** to exit the Performance Options dialog box. Close the **System Properties** dialog box and any open windows.

If you change the virtual memory settings, the new settings do not go into effect until the server is rebooted.

Configuring Direct Memory Access for Hard Disks
If your server has Integrated Device Electronics (IDE)/Advanced Technology Attachment (ATA) or Serial Advanced Technology Attachment (SATA) hard disk drives, the drives can be set up in two transfer modes: Program Input/Output (PIO) and Direct Memory Access (DMA). PIO uses CPU memory registers and RAM during the process of transferring data for disk reads and writes. DMA bypasses the use of CPU memory and writes to and reads directly from RAM, which makes it much faster than PIO.

When you install Windows Server 2008, it configures IDE/ATA/SATA drives to use the DMA transfer mode by default (if the disk controllers are compatible with DMA). However, sometimes when you install a drive or have to supply a new driver for that drive, the PIO mode may be set up instead. For the sake of faster performance, it is a good idea to check the transfer mode for IDE drives. Device Manager enables you to check and configure the hard drives.

Small Computer System Interface (SCSI) drives by default generally don't use PIO mode.

Activity 3-9: Configuring the DMA Transfer Mode

Time Required: Approximately 5 minutes
Objective: Determine the transfer mode used by a hard drive and set it to DMA, if necessary.

Description: In this activity, you determine the transfer mode used by an IDE/ATA drive in a server. If the mode is not configured for DMA, then you change the mode for faster disk access performance. You need a computer that has IDE/ATA drives, and should log on using an account that has Administrator privileges.

1. Click **Start**, point to **Administrative Tools,** and click **Server Manager.**

2. Double-click **Diagnostics** in the tree in the left pane, and click **Device Manager** under Diagnostics.

3. Double-click **IDE ATA/ATAPI controllers.**

4. Right-click **ATA Channel 0** and click **Properties.**

5. Click the **Advanced Settings** tab. Ensure that the **Enable DMA** box is checked, as shown in Figure 3-11. If it isn't checked, click the box to select it. Click **OK.**

6. If there are two options for ATA Channel 0 or there are options for ATA Channel 1, repeat Steps 4 and 5 for these options.

7. Close Server Manager.

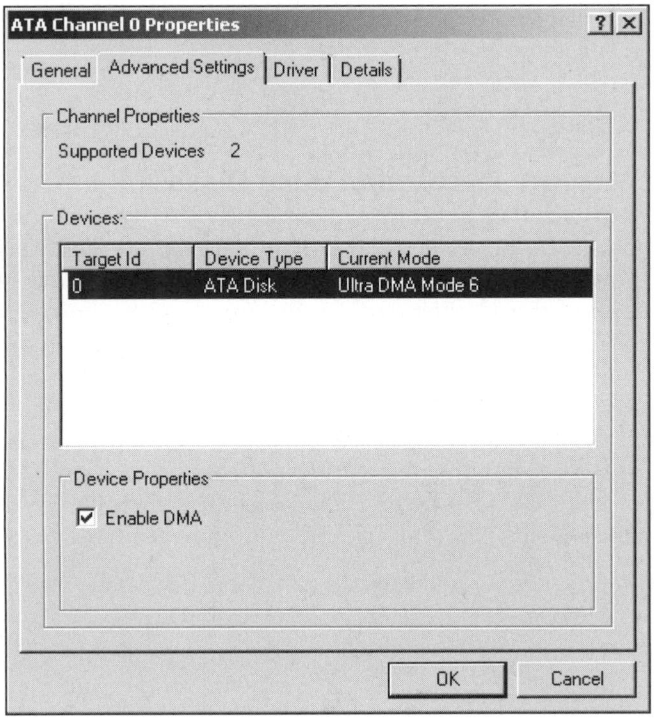

Figure 3-11   Configuring the DMA transfer mode

Configuring Environment Variables

Environment variables are used to tell the operating system where to find certain programs and how to allocate memory to programs, and to control different programs. Environment variables can be broken down into two categories: system environment variables and user environment variables. **System environment variables** are defined by the operating system and apply to any user logged onto the computer. Administrators can add new system environment variables or change the values of existing ones. **User environment variables** can be defined on a per-user basis, such as specifying the path where application files are stored.

Keep the following points in mind when you are working with environment variables:

- System environment variables are always set first.

- User environment variables are set next, overriding any conflicting system environment variables.

Activity 3-10: Configuring System and Environment Variables

Time Required: Approximately 5 minutes
Objective: Learn where to configure system and user environment variables.

Description: A newly installed Windows Server 2008 operating system has several system and user environment variables that are set up by default. In this activity, you learn where to configure the system and user environment variables and at the same time determine which ones are currently configured on your system.

1. Click **Start** and click **Control Panel**. If you are in the Control Panel Home view, click **System and Maintenance** and click **System**. If you are in the Classic View, double-click **System**.

2. Click **Advanced system settings**.

3. Open the **Advanced** tab, if it is not already open.

4. Click **Environment Variables** to display a dialog box showing the environment variables.

   - Which user and system environment variables are defined already on your system? How would you add a new variable?

5. Click **Cancel** to close the Environment Variables dialog box.

6. Click **Cancel** to close the System Properties dialog box.

7. Leave the System window open for the next project (unless you cannot complete the project at this time).

Configuring Startup and Recovery

Windows Server 2008 enables you to configure parameters that dictate the startup sequence and how the system recovers from errors. You can configure the following system startup options:

- Which operating system to boot by default, if more than one operating system is installed
- How long to display a list of operating systems from which to boot
- How long to display a list of recovery options, if the computer needs to go into recovery mode after a system failure

In the event of a system failure, you can configure these options:

- Writing information to the system log (hard configured so you cannot change this)
- Whether to start automatically after a system failure
- How and where to write debugging information

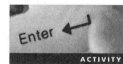

Activity 3-11: Configuring Startup and Recovery

Time Required: Approximately 5 minutes
Objective: Configure startup and recovery options.

Description: Soon after you install Windows Server 2008, it is important to customize the system startup and recovery options to match how your organization operates. This activity shows you how to configure these parameters on a non-dual-boot system so that the system does not automatically start up after a system failure. The advantage of not automatically restarting is that the system administrator has time to examine the system before it is rebooted. This is important, for example, when a disk drive is failing, so that the drive can be replaced before users resume work.

1. Open Control Panel into the System window if it is not already open.

2. Click **Advanced system settings**.

3. Open the **Advanced** tab, if necessary.

4. Find the Startup and Recovery section on the tab and click the **Settings** button in that section.

5. Set the **Time to display list of operating systems** parameter to **15** seconds (see Figure 3-12), so that you still have time to access recovery options when the system boots, but to reflect that you do not need time to select another operating system at boot up because this is not a dual-boot system.

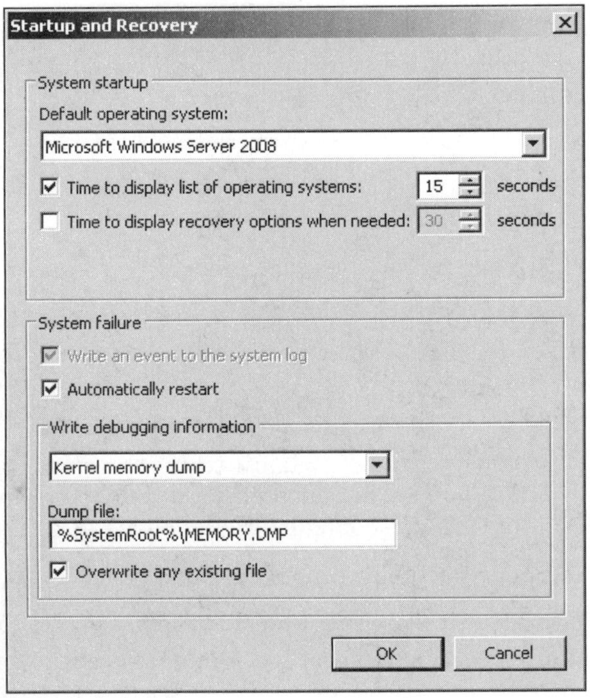

Startup and Recovery

System startup

Default operating system:

| Microsoft Windows Server 2008 |

☑ Time to display list of operating systems: [15]   seconds

☐ Time to display recovery options when needed: [30]   seconds

System failure

☑ Write an event to the system log

☑ Automatically restart

Write debugging information

| Kernel memory dump |

Dump file:
| %SystemRoot%\MEMORY.DMP |

☑ Overwrite any existing file

[OK]   [Cancel]

Figure 3-12   Configuring a system startup option

6. If **Automatically restart** is checked, remove the check mark (which means the system will not reboot after a failure until you do this manually).

7. Click **OK** in the Startup and Recovery dialog box.

8. Click **OK** in the System Properties dialog box.

9. From the System window, click the **back** (left pointing) **arrow** as many times as necessary under the title bar to go back to Control Panel.

10. Leave Control Panel open for the next activity.

Configuring Power Options

After you have installed Windows Server 2008, check the power management options to make sure that they are set appropriately for the computer and the way you are using the computer on the network. The Power Options that you can set are as follows:

- Select a power plan.
- Require a password on wakeup.
- Choose what the power button does.
- Create a power plan.
- Choose when to turn off the display.

 If Windows Server 2008 is installed in a virtual machine, you might not see *Require a password on wakeup* or some other options.

Three power plans are already created: balanced, power saver, and high performance. Each plan consists of a combination of power options including how soon to turn off the display, whether to require a password on wakeup, how soon to turn off the hard disk, sleep/hibernate settings, USB settings, PCI card settings, and processor settings. The balanced setting offers equal emphasis to energy savings and performance. Power saver favors energy savings over performance, and high performance favors performance over energy savings. For example, with the balanced and high performance plans, the hard disk drives are never turned off. However, with the power saver plan, the hard disk drives are turned off after 20 minutes of inactivity. In another example, the processor activity state is set higher (more activity) for the high performance plan than it is for balanced or power saver.

The option to require a password determines whether a password is needed to access the system after it wakes up from sleep/hibernate. Choosing what the power button does enables you to specify one of three options for when the power button is pressed:

- Shut down
- Do nothing
- Hibernate

The option to create a power plan enables you to customize a power plan, if one of the three existing power plans does not meet your needs. Before customizing a power plan, keep in mind that you can change the default settings for the three power plans already created, and so creating a new power plan might not be necessary.

The option to choose when to turn off the display enables you to turn off the display after a specific period of inactivity, in minutes or hours, or to set the display to never turn off. This option can also be configured when you modify an existing power plan or create a new one.

Activity 3-12: Configuring Power Options

Time Required: Approximately 5 minutes
Objective: Configure the balanced power plan.

Description: Many server administrators have specific power options they want to set up. In this activity, you configure the balanced power plan to customize power options.

1. Open Control Panel, if it is not already open. If you are in the Control Panel Home view, click **System and Maintenance**. If you are in the Classic View, go to Step 2.

2. Click or double-click **Power Options**.

3. Notice the options on the left side of the window that enable you to *Require a password on wakeup, Choose what the power button does, Create a power plan,* and *Choose when to turn off the display*.

4. Click **Choose what the power button does** and ensure that **When I press the power button** is set to **Shut down**. If you had to make a change to the setting, click the **Save changes** button. If you didn't make any changes, click **Cancel**.

5. Click the **Balanced** option button, if it is not already selected.

6. Click **Change plan settings** under the Balanced selection.

7. Click **Change advanced power settings** to see the Power Options dialog box, as shown in Figure 3-13.

8. Click the **plus sign** in front of **Hard disk** and the plus sign for **Turn off hard disk after**.

9. Click **Setting** and configure the **Setting (Minutes)** box to **40**.

10. Click the **plus sign** in front of **USB settings** and the **plus sign** in front of **USB selective suspend setting**.

11. Click **Setting** and configure it to **Enabled**.

12. Click the **plus sign** in front of **Display** and click the **plus sign** for **Turn off display after**.

13. Click **Setting** and configure the **Setting (Minutes)** box to **10**.

14. Click the **Apply** button and then click **OK**.

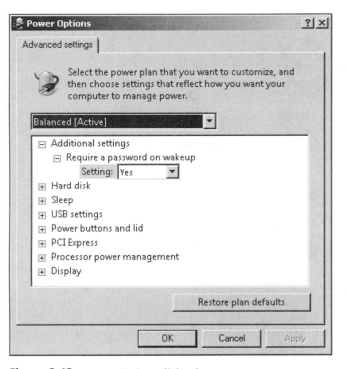

Figure 3-13 Power Options dialog box

15. In the Edit Plan Settings window, click the **back arrow** (left pointing arrow) under the title bar to go back to the Power Options window.

16. Click the **back arrow** as many times as necessary in the Power Options window to go back to Control Panel, and leave Control Panel open for the next activity.

Installing a Protocol

Knowing how to install a protocol is a skill that is similar to knowing how to change a flat tire; you don't need it often but it is important to know how when you need it. Chapter 1, "Introduction to Windows Server 2008," discussed manual TCP/IP configuration. However, you might need to add other protocols to customize the server for your network. Control Panel enables you to install or uninstall protocols from the Network and Sharing Center. Two examples of protocols you might need to install are Microsoft Virtual Network Switch Protocol and Reliable Multicast Protocol.

If TCP/IP is inadvertently uninstalled, it is important to know how to reinstall it, as well as how to install new protocols.

Microsoft Virtual Network Switch Protocol is used when the Hyper-V role is installed in Windows Server 2008. When Windows Server 2008 is operating as a virtual server, Microsoft Virtual Network Switch Protocol is used at the server's NIC (or NICs) to bind or associate the virtual network services to the NIC. Microsoft Virtual Network Switch Protocol enables the use of a software virtual switch between the main operating system and the operating systems on virtual partitions. It also reduces the overhead in network communications when Hyper-V is installed.

If Hyper-V is in use and users find they cannot stay connected to a virtual server, the reason is often because Microsoft Virtual Network Switch Protocol is not installed.

Reliable Multicast Protocol is used for multimedia transmissions, such as a combined voice and video transmission to provide user training to multiple people. In Chapter 1, you learned that in a multicast, the server sends one IP communication to multiple clients (see Figure 1-8 in Chapter 1). For example, if five users are watching a training video at their PCs, the server can use multicasting to make one transmission that goes to all five at once, instead of sending five separate network transmissions. Multicasting can improve network efficiency on networks that provide multimedia transmissions. Reliable Multicast Protocol runs on top of IP and simplifies multicast communications because multicasting can be done even without routers to direct network traffic.

Activity 3-13: Installing a Protocol

Time Required: Approximately 10 minutes
Objective: Learn to install a protocol.

Description: Installing a protocol is not difficult, but it is important to know how to do this task, not only for when you need to install a new protocol, but should you need to reinstall TCP/IP.

1. Open Control Panel, if it's not already open. If you are in the Control Panel Home view, click **View network status and tasks** under Network and Internet. If you are in Classic View, double-click **Network and Sharing Center.**

2. Click **Manage network connections.**

3. Right-click the network connection, such as **Local Area Connection,** and click **Properties.**

4. Click the **Install** button.

5. Double-click **Protocol** (see Figure 3-14).

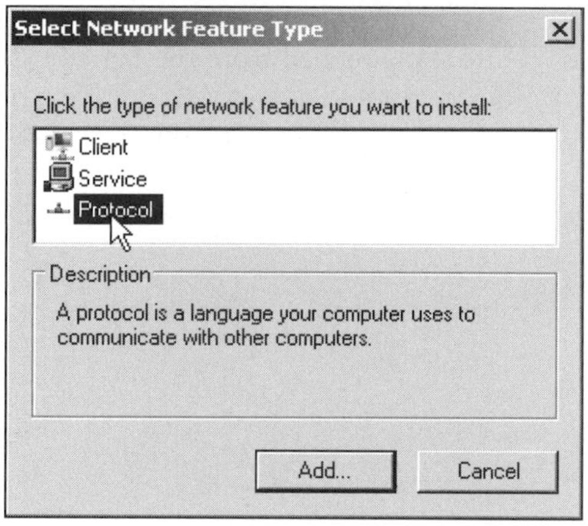

Select Network Feature Type

Click the type of network feature you want to install:

- Client
- Service
- Protocol

Description

A protocol is a language your computer uses to communicate with other computers.

[Add...]   [Cancel]

Figure 3-14 Selecting to install a protocol

6. Double-click **Reliable Multicast Protocol** (note that you can install any protocol at this time, including Internet Protocol Version 4 or 6 if one of these is uninstalled).

7. In the Connection Properties dialog box, notice that Reliable Multicast Protocol is now listed in the *This connection uses the following items* box.

8. Close the Connection Properties dialog box and the Network Connections window.

9. In the Network and Sharing Center window, click the **back arrow** under the title bar to go back to Control Panel.

 You can use similar steps to install a service or client access for networking, such as Client for Microsoft Networks, which enables connecting to networks, and File and Printer Sharing for Microsoft Networks, which enables access to shared files, folders, and printers over the network. In Step 5, you would double-click Client or Service instead of Protocol.

Understanding the Windows Server 2008 Registry

The Windows Server 2008 Registry is a very complex database containing all information the operating system needs about the entire server. For example, the initialization files used by earlier versions of Windows operating systems, including the critical System.ini and Win.ini files, are contained in the Registry. Just as Active Directory can be the coordinating center for network services, the Registry is the coordinating center for a specific server. Without the Registry, Windows Server 2008 cannot function. Some examples of data contained in the Registry are as follows:

- Information about all hardware components, including the CPU, disk drives, network interface cards, CD/DVD drives, and more
- Information about Windows Server 2008 services that are installed, which services they depend on, and the order in which they are started
- Data about user profiles and Windows Server 2008 group policies
- Data on the last current and last known setup used to boot the computer
- Configuration information about all software in use
- Software licensing information
- Server Manager and Control Panel parameter configurations

In Windows Server 2008, the Registry Editor is launched from the Start button Run option as either regedt32 or regedit. The Registry Editor window is very straightforward, with common menu utilities such as File, Edit, View, Favorites, and Help (see Figure 3-15).

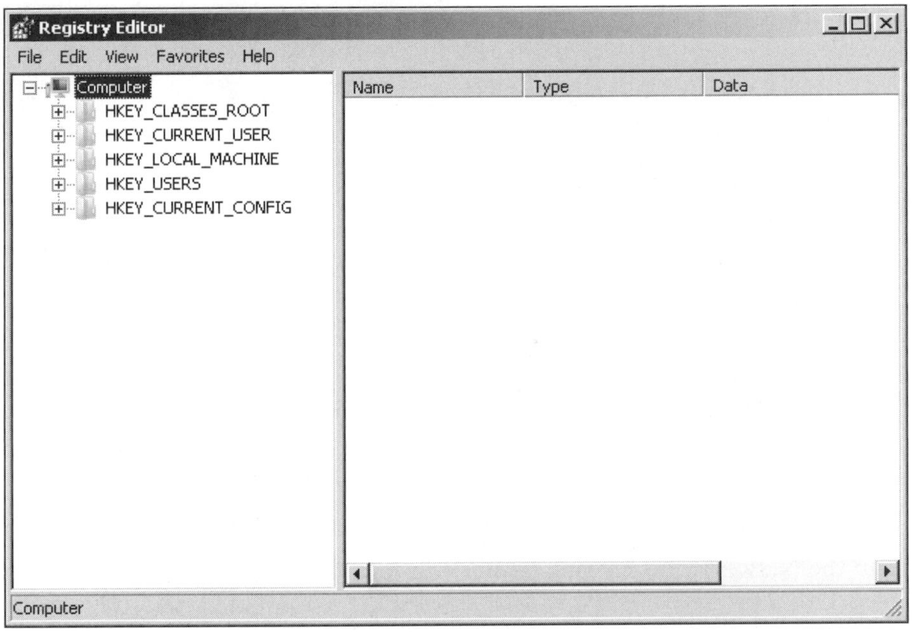

Figure 3-15 Registry Editor

 The Registry Editor has two command names because Windows 2000 Server had two different Registry Editors with different capabilities. At this writing, Windows Server 2003 and 2008 continue with the same editor names, but both open the same program.

Making incorrect changes to the Registry can have profound consequences for and possibly disable your operating system. Use the following precautions when working with the Registry:

- Establish a specific group of administrators who have privileges to open and modify the Registry. Take away Registry modification privileges from all others by controlling who can use the Registry Editor and .reg files.

- Only make changes to the Registry as a last resort, such as those changes recommended in a technical document from Microsoft. It is safer to use tools such as the Control Panel options or the Server Manager tool for changes to information in the Registry.

- Regularly back up the Registry as part of backing up the Windows Server 2008 Windows folder. Further, consider backing up the Registry prior to reconfiguring it through the Registry Editor.

- Never copy the Registry from one Windows-based system over the Registry of a different system, regardless of whether they use the same operating system or version, because each Registry and its contents is unique to the computer and operating system on which it resides. (This does not apply in situations where you create a replica Active Directory domain controller by using a removable hard drive, tape, or DVD backup of a domain controller to restore to a computer from scratch.)

 The Registry folders and files are stored in two main places. System information for the Registry is stored in \Windows\System32\config, and information for user accounts is stored in \Users in files within folders for specific user accounts, such as \Users\Administrator for the Administrator account (in hidden files with the name ntuser.dat).

Registry Contents

The Registry is hierarchical in structure (see Figure 3-16) and is made up of keys, subkeys, and entries:

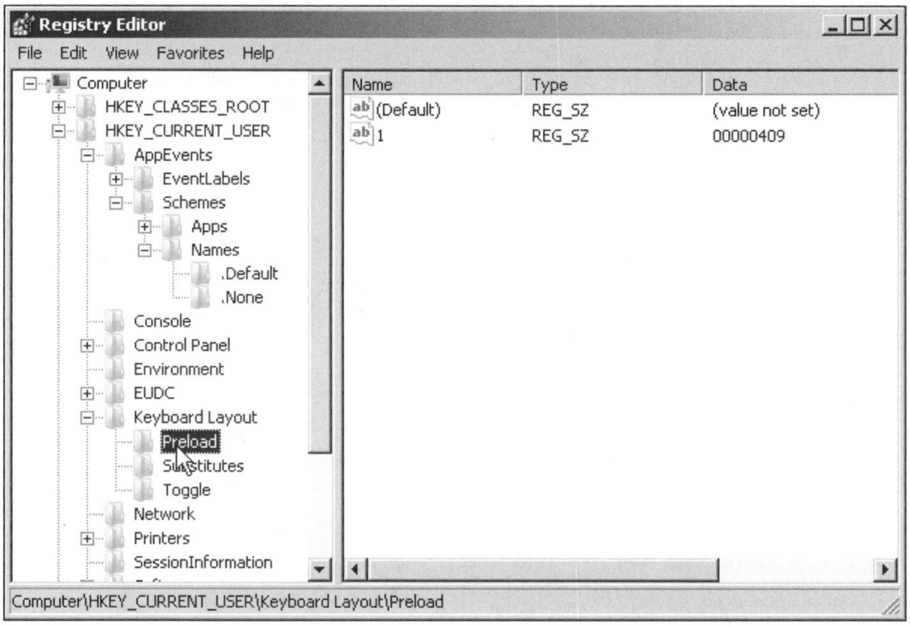

Figure 3-16 Registry's hierarchical structure

- *Key*—A folder that appears in the left pane of the Registry Editor and can contain sub-keys and entries, for example, HKEY_CURRENT_USER.

- *Subkey*—A part of the Registry that is below a key. A Subkey can contain entries or other subkeys.

- *Entry or value*—An item that appears in the details pane and is the lowest level in the Registry. An entry consists of an entry name, its data type, and its value.

A **Registry key** is a category or division of information within the Registry. A single key may contain one or more lower-level keys called **Registry subkeys,** just as a folder may contain several subfolders. A **Registry entry** is a data parameter associated with a software or hardware characteristic under a key (or subkey). A Registry entry consists of three parts—a name, the data type, and the configuration parameter—for example, ErrorControl:REG_DWORD:0 (ErrorControl is the name, REG_DWORD is the data type, and 0 is the parameter setting). In this Registry entry, the option to track errors is turned off if the parameter is 0, and error tracking is turned on if the value is 1. Registry entries can have three data formats: DWORD is hexadecimal, string is text data, and binary is two hexadecimal values.

The Windows Server 2008 Registry is made up of five root keys:

- HKEY_LOCAL_MACHINE
- HKEY_CURRENT_USER
- HKEY_USERS
- HKEY_CLASSES_ROOT
- HKEY_CURRENT_CONFIG

A **root key,** also called a **subtree,** is a primary or highest level category of data contained in the Registry. It might be compared with a main folder, such as the \Windows folder, which is at the root level of folders. All root keys start with HKEY to show they are the highest level key.

HKEY_LOCAL_MACHINE

Information on every hardware component in the server is provided under the HKEY_LOCAL_MACHINE root key. This includes information about what drivers are loaded and their version levels, what IRQ (interrupt request) lines are used, setup configurations, the BIOS version, and more. Figure 3-17 shows the Registry contents, using the Registry Editor to view the HKEY_LOCAL_MACHINE root key information about video settings.

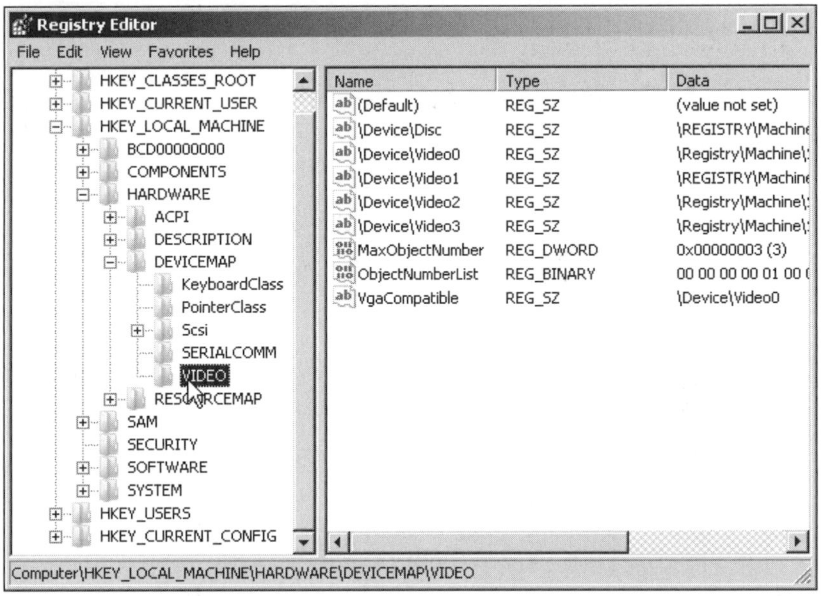

Figure 3-17   The HKEY_LOCAL_MACHINE root key

Under each root key are subkeys, which are BCD00000000, COMPONENTS, HARDWARE, SAM, SECURITY, SOFTWARE, and SYSTEM for the root key shown in Figure 3-17. Each subkey may have subkeys under it, such as ACPI, DESCRIPTION, DEVICEMAP, and RESOURCEMAP under the HARDWARE subkey in Figure 3-17.

A few subkeys are stored as a set, called **hives**, because they hold related information. This is true for the SOFTWARE subkey, which holds information about installed software. You can make hardware configuration changes directly from the Registry, although this is not recommended (see the following Caution).

 Although it is possible to make hardware configuration changes directly from the Registry, this is a dangerous undertaking because a wrong deletion might mean you cannot reboot your server into Windows Server 2008. It is better to use other options first, such as Control Panel. Make changes in the Registry only under the guidance of a Microsoft technical note or a Microsoft support person.

HKEY_CURRENT_USER

The HKEY_CURRENT_USER key contains information about the desktop setup for the account presently logged on to the server console, as opposed to the HKEY_USERS key, which contains profile settings for all users who have logged onto the server. It contains data on color combinations, font sizes and type, the keyboard layout, the taskbar, clock configuration, and nearly any setup action you have made on the desktop. For example, if you want to change the environment parameter governing where temporary files are stored for applications, you could do it from here. The new path is set by clicking the Environment subkey under the HKEY_CURRENT_USER root key and changing the path shown as the value in the right pane. The sounds associated with a given event can be set by clicking the path \HKEY_CURRENT_USER\AppEvents\Event Labels and then changing the sound value for a particular event, such as the event to close a window, which is a single value in the Close subkey (\HKEY_CURRENT_USER\AppEvents\EventLabels\Close).

Another example is to change the delay in the response of the keyboard. For example, click the following path: \HKEY_CURRENT_USER\Control Panel\keyboard. If the KeyboardDelay data value is 0, this means there is minimum delay. You could slow down the response a little by setting the delay to 1. This has the same effect as going into Control Panel in Classic View, double-clicking Keyboard, and setting the Repeat delay slider bar one notch to the left of the Short setting. (This is just an example. Again it is strongly recommended that you rely on tools like Control Panel instead of making configuration changes in the Registry.)

HKEY_USERS

The HKEY_USERS root key contains profile information for each user who has logged onto the computer. Each profile is listed under this root key. Within each user profile is information identical to that viewed within the HKEY_CURRENT_USER root key. The profile used when you are logged on is one of the profiles stored under HKEY_USERS. You can make the same changes just examined by finding the subkey for your profile and making the changes here instead of under the HKEY_CURRENT_USER root key.

HKEY_CLASSES_ROOT

The HKEY_CLASSES_ROOT key holds data to associate file extensions with programs. This is a more extensive list than the one viewed under HKEY_CURRENT_USER. Associations exist for executable files, text files, graphics files, Clipboard files, audio files, and many more. These associations are used as defaults for all users who log on to Windows Server 2008, whereas the associations in HKEY_CURRENT_USER and HKEY_USERS are those that have been customized for a given user profile.

HKEY_CURRENT_CONFIG

The last root key, HKEY_CURRENT_CONFIG, has information about the current hardware profile. It holds information about the monitor type, keyboard, mouse, and other hardware characteristics for the current profile. On most servers, there is only one default hardware profile set up. Two or more profiles could be used, but this is more common for a portable computer running Windows Vista that is used with and without a docking station. One profile would have the keyboard and monitor used when on the road, and another would have a larger keyboard and monitor used when the computer is docked.

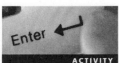

Activity 3-14: Using the Registry Editor

Time Required: Approximately 10 minutes
Objective: Practice using the Registry Editor to view the Registry contents.

Description: It is a good idea to have some experience with the Registry Editor before you make changes to the Registry, such as changes recommended through a Microsoft TechNet document. In this activity, you use the Registry Editor to view where Control Panel settings are stored.

1. Click **Start**, click **Run**, and type **regedit** in the Open text box. Click **OK**.
2. In the tree in the left pane, double-click **HKEY_CURRENT_USER** and double-click **Control Panel**.
   - What Control Panel subkeys do you see?

3. Double-click **Accessibility**.
   - What subkeys are displayed?

4. Click **MouseKeys** to view the values set for that subkey.
5. Click two or three other subkeys to view their values.
6. Click a value and then click the **Edit** menu to view how to modify a value, delete a value, or add a new one.

   Absolutely do not make any changes.

7. Close the Registry Editor.

Using the Security Configuration Wizard

The **Security Configuration Wizard (SCW)** steps you through analyzing and configuring security settings on a server. This tool is automatically installed when you install Windows Server 2008 and provides an interactive interface for analyzing and configuring security on a server.

3

Plan to run the SCW and test its results before you bring a server live into production. This gives you time to ensure that security is set properly and that the SCW security settings do not interfere with any programs or types of access needed on the server.

SCW examines the roles a server plays and then tries to adjust security to match these roles; for this reason, it is also called a role-based security tool. When you install a server role using Server Manager, the elements associated with that role are configured for strong security by default. You can then use SCW to verify that you have the desired level of security and to make modifications, if necessary. Through SCW you can:

- Disable unnecessary services and software.
- Close network communication ports and other communication resources that aren't in use.
- Examine shared files and folders to help manage network access through access protocols.
- Configure firewall rules.

These elements can help you establish a security policy for reducing the attack surface on your computer as a way to thwart attackers and malicious software or malware.

SCW has three components:

- GUI interactive wizard
- Database
- Command-line tool called *scwcmd*

The interactive wizard provides a step-by-step interface that presents information about current security and gives you configuration options. The Security Configuration Database (SCD) is a group of XML files that establish a security policy. Using the wizard you can perform these tasks:

- Create a new security policy.
- Edit an existing security policy.
- Apply an existing security policy.
- Roll back the last applied security policy.

The default action is to create a new security policy. When you select this option, SCW creates the SCD (see Figure 3-18). After the database is created, the wizard identifies server roles, such as DNS, domain controller, file server, and others. You can disable or add roles. Next, you select client features to use, such as DNS client. You can additionally disable or add services. SCW shows ports that are open and in use, so you can block ports that shouldn't be available to the outside world. Next, SCW establishes what types of clients access the server, such as legacy Windows 2000 clients and newer Windows XP/Vista clients, so that it can configure the right network security. Finally, it steps you through creating a basic system audit policy.

The SCW command-line tool, *scwcmd*, can be used to analyze and configure security on the local server or on remote servers, which means the server administrator can configure security on multiple servers from one location. The advantage of *scwcmd* is that it makes server administration easier and enables multiple servers to have consistent security settings. Another important advantage of *scwcmd* is that it has the transform option to convert the SCD XML settings into a Group Policy Object, which is an element of Active Directory that contains policies for using a server. The transform option is powerful because it enables you to customize security policy for different Active Directory management groupings, such as domains and organizational units (OUs). You learn all about domains, OUs, and other management groupings in Chapter 4, "Introduction to Active Directory and Account Management."

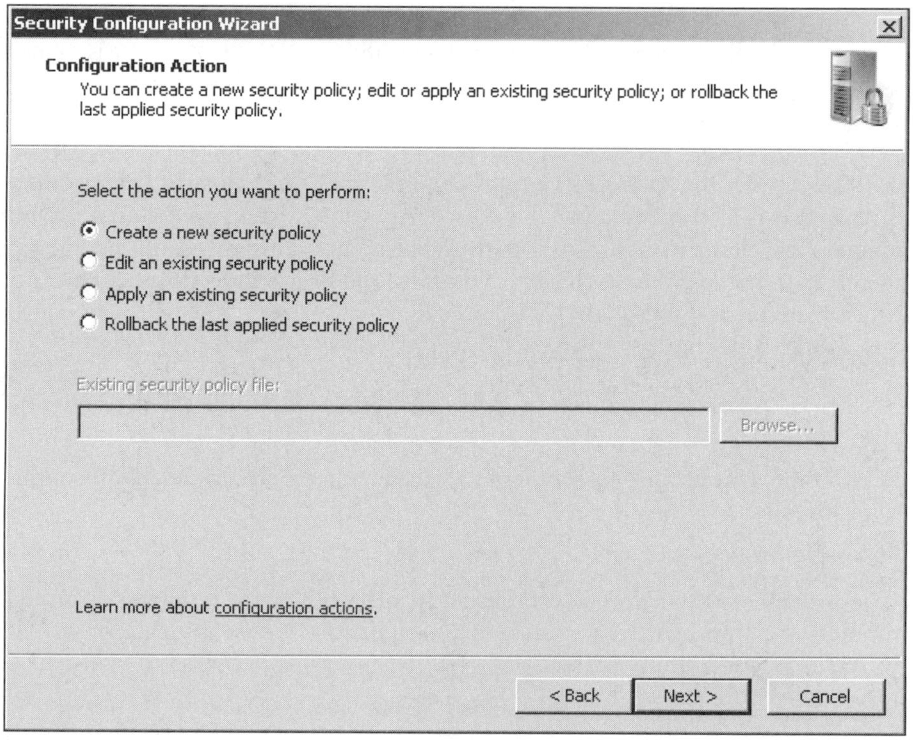

Figure 3-18   Creating a new security policy

When the SCW command-line tool is used to analyze security, you can view the results in an HTML presentation. Further, if you want to roll back SCW security policies to a previously configured set of security settings, you can do so using the SCW command-line tool. You might need to roll back settings, for example, if you find that some services or software cannot function because of the security you have applied.

Table 3-3 lists the options you can use with *scwcmd*.

Table 3-3   *scwcmd* command-line options

Option	Description
analyze	Analyzes current security settings in the SCD
configure	Configures security settings and writes them to the SCD
register	Registers new SCD extensions
rollback	Rolls back security settings to the previously configured settings
transform	Converts the XML security settings in the SCD into a Group Policy Object (GPO) usable in Active Directory
view	Enables you to view the current security settings in the SCD

CAUTION

If you use transform to convert security settings to a Group Policy Object (GPO), then you cannot use the rollback option to undo the GPO settings. Also, some services, including firewall and IPsec services, might not respond correctly when you perform a rollback. Finally, do not apply SCD settings for a 32-bit computer to a 64-bit computer and vice versa.

Activity 3-15: Using SCW to Configure a Security Policy

Time Required: Approximately 20–30 minutes
Objective: Create a new security policy.

Description: One of the first steps in configuring a server should be to configure a security policy. In this activity, you configure a new security policy using SCW in the GUI interactive format.

1. Click **Start**, point to **Administrative Tools**, and click **Security Configuration Wizard**.

2. After the wizard starts, click **Next**.

3. Ensure that **Create a new security policy** is selected and click **Next**.

4. Leave the default server selected in the Select Server window and click **Next**.

5. Click the button to **View Configuration Database**. Click **Yes** if you see a message box warning that the ActiveX control on this page might be unsafe. (Note that it might take a few minutes to generate the SCD.)

6. Click **Server Roles** in the SCW Viewer window. Scroll to and open **DNS Server**.

   • What are the required firewall rules for DNS Server?

7. Click **Server Roles** again to close the listing of roles.

8. Click **Client Features, Administration and Other Options, Services, Windows Firewall** individually to view the items listing under each one.

9. Close the SCW Viewer.

10. In the Processing Security Configuration Database window, click **Next**.

11. Click **Next**.

12. Notice the installed server roles that are checked. There are more roles listed than were described in Chapter 2 because some of the "roles" listed are additional functions, such as Password Synchronization with other servers on a network. Click **Next**.

13. Scroll to view the installed features and then click **Next**.

14. Review the installed options and click **Next**.

15. Notice the additional services listed and click **Next**.

16. In the next window, you can select to have SCW disable services not specified via SCW (as in the previous window in Step 15). When you are first starting to use SCW, it's safest to click **Do not change the startup mode of the service** to avoid unexpected problems with services that have been disabled. Ensure this option is selected and click **Next**.

17. In the Confirm Service Changes window, you can review the services that currently start automatically or through manual intervention via the administrator. These are listed under the Current Startup Mode column. Notice that the startup modes of these services are changed, as shown under the Policy Startup Mode column (see Figure 3-19). For instance, in Figure 3-19 notice that the Application Experience service is currently set to start in the Automatic mode. If you confirm the change, this service will be in the Disabled startup mode when the new security policy is created. These changes help reduce the attack surface of the server. Click **Next**.

18. Read the information in the Network Security window and then click **Next**.

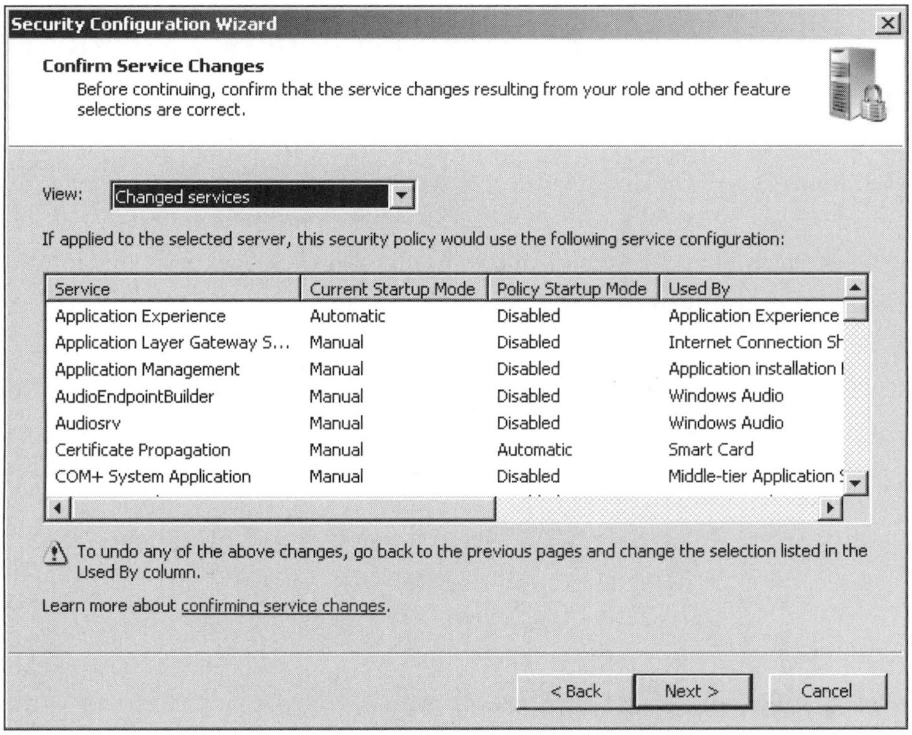

Figure 3-19   Confirming changes to services

19. Scroll through the network security rules, which are Windows Firewall rules applied to protect the functions of server roles and options.

    • How can you disable a rule or add an additional rule?

20. Click **Next**.

21. Read the information for Registry Settings and click **Next**.

22. The Require SMB Security Signatures window applies to the Server Message Block (SMB) protocol, which enables sharing files and folders over a network. Notice the selections made, which are tailored to your server, and click **Next**.

23. Next, you might see the Require LDAP Signing window. This window enables you to require servers with Windows 2000 Service Pack 3 or later for LDAP signing. Lightweight Directory Access Protocol (LDAP) is a protocol used for directory services, such as Active Directory. Leave the default configuration and click **Next**.

24. The Outbound Authentication Methods window is used to configure authentication methods, which are tailored to the specific computer. The following are examples of selections when Active Directory is installed:

    • Domain Accounts

    • Local Accounts on the remote computers

    • File-sharing passwords on Windows 95, Windows 98, or Windows Millennium Edition

    Leave the default selections and click **Next**.

25. If you are working on a computer with Active Directory installed, you'll see the window, Outbound Authentication using Domain Accounts. This screen is used to specify attributes for computers with domain user accounts. Leave the default selections and click **Next**.

26. If you are working on a stand-alone server without Active Directory, you might see the window, Outbound Authentication using Local Accounts. Leave the defaults and click **Next**.

27. If you see an Inbound Authentication Methods window, which includes security for inbound connections from the Internet, leave the default selections and click **Next**.

28. Review the Registry settings you've configured and click **Next**.

29. Read the information about Audit Policy and click **Next**.

30. In the System Audit Policy window, click **Audit successful and unsuccessful activities**. This selection gives you the most versatility for security auditing, and you can change the selection later, if needed. You learn about auditing in Chapter 10, "Securing Windows Server 2008." Click **Next**.

31. Review the Audit Policy Summary window. Notice under the Current Setting column that Not audited is listed (when you are configuring a new installation). This is because you'll later need to configure specific activities to audit, as shown in later chapters of this book. Also, notice that under the Policy Setting column Success, failure is enabled per Step 29 for most items. Click **Next**.

32. In the Save Security Policy window, click **Next**.

33. In the Security policy file name window, enter **Security** plus your initials, such as SecurityJP for the name of the security policy (you don't need to type .xml at the end of the name). Click **Next**.

34. Click **Apply now** and click **Next**.

- Record the folder location (such as C:\Windows\security\msscw\Policies\SecurityJP.xml) of the security policy in the Completing the Security Configuration Wizard window and click **Finish**.

Activity 3-16: Using *scwcmd*

Time Required: Approximately 30 minutes
Objective: View security policy settings using the *scwcmd* command-line command.

Description: The *scwcmd* command also enables you to configure and modify security settings, as well as convert them to Active Directory Group Policy Objects and to apply them to multiple servers. In this activity, you use *scwcmd* to view the security settings in the SCD that you created in the last activity.

1. Click **Start**, point to **All Programs**, and click **Accessories**.
2. Right-click **Command Prompt** and click **Run as administrator**.
3. At the command line, type **scwcmd /?** and press **Enter**.
4. Notice the command options.
5. Type **scwcmd view /x:C:\Windows\security\msscw\Policies***myfile.xml*, where myfile.xml is the name of the database file you created in Activity 3-15, Step 33, such as SecurityJP.xml (you must specify .xml at the end of the filename).
6. If you see a message box warning about an unsafe ActiveX control, click **Yes**.
7. Figure 3-20 shows the SCW Viewer window. In the window, click **Services, Windows Firewall, Registry Settings, Audit,** and **Templates** individually to view the settings in your security policy.
8. Close the SCW Viewer window.
9. Close the Command Prompt window and any other open windows.

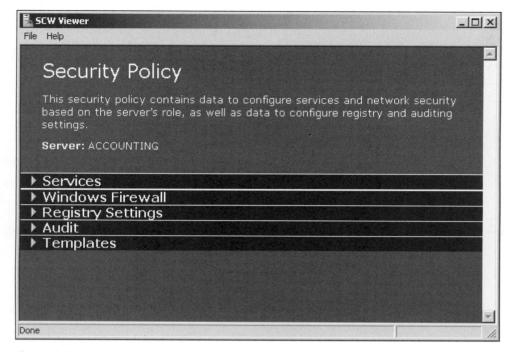

Figure 3-20 SCW Viewer

Windows PowerShell

Windows PowerShell is a command-line interface or shell. As you learned in Chapter 1, a shell is a customized environment for executing commands and scripts. Two important features of Windows PowerShell are scripts and cmdlets. A script is a file of commands that is run when you run the script; cmdlets are specialized commands for completing common tasks in PowerShell. Windows PowerShell is particularly intended for situations in which there are multiple servers and it is more efficient to manage them using a consistent set of scripts. It is also ideal for managing servers with the Application Server role installed in situations where the applications need to be configured in the same way and regular updates are required.

You can create your own cmdlets for PowerShell. Visit *msdn2.microsoft .com/en-us/library/cc136006(VS.85).aspx* to learn more about creating cmdlets.

Some of the tasks you can complete using Windows PowerShell include the following:

- Manage files and folders.
- Manage network tasks.
- Manage fixed and removable storage.
- Configure printing services.
- Manage software applications and updates.
- Manage Terminal Services.
- Manage server services and features.
- Manage Web server services.
- Work with the Registry.

Windows PowerShell is not installed by default when you install Windows Server 2008. You must install it in Server Manager as a feature. Here are the general steps for installing it:

1. Click Start, point to Administrative Tools, and click Server Manager.
2. Scroll to the Features Summary section and click to open it, if necessary.
3. Click Add Features.
4. Under Features, scroll to find Windows PowerShell and then check its box.
5. Click Next and then click Install.
6. Click Close.
7. Close Server Manager.

Over 130 cmdlet tools are available through Windows PowerShell. Windows PowerShell also recognizes some traditional Command Prompt window commands. The following activity gives you an opportunity to try out PowerShell.

Activity 3-17: Using Windows PowerShell

Time Required: Approximately 15 minutes
Objective: Use traditional Command Prompt commands and cmdlets in Windows PowerShell.

Description: Learning how to use Windows PowerShell can be an important way to expand your server administration toolbox. In this activity, you take several traditional commands and cmdlets for a test drive. Windows PowerShell must be installed before you start.

1. Click **Start**, click **All Programs**, and click **Windows PowerShell 1.0**.
2. Click **Windows PowerShell** under Windows PowerShell 1.0.
3. To view the files in the current folder, such as \Users\Administrator, one page at a time type the traditional command, **dir | more** and press **Enter**. Press the **Spacebar**, if necessary, to advance to additional screens.
4. To change to the \Users directory, enter **cd \users** and press **Enter**. Your Windows Powershell window will look similar to Figure 3-21.
5. View a listing of cmdlets. Type **get-command | more** and press **Enter**. You see the commands one screen at a time. Press the **Spacebar** to advance to the next screen, and repeat this step until you've viewed all of the screens. (Note that you can also press **q** to exit back to the command line, if you decide not to view all of the screens of commands.)
6. Press the **up arrow** and notice that the last command you entered is placed on the command line so that you can repeat the command. Press the **up arrow** again and you'll see the second-to-last command you entered. Press **Enter** to run that command.
7. Type **get-process** and press **Enter** to view the processes running on the server.
8. Next, type **get-process | where { $_.WS -gt 500MB } | stop-process** and press **Enter**. If you have any processes using over 500 MB of memory, this command will stop those processes.
9. Type **get-service** and press **Enter** to view services that are running or are stopped. (Or you can enter **get-service | more** to display the services one screen at a time.)
10. You can view more about the main or core Windows PowerShell cmdlets. Type **get-help about_core_command** and press **Enter**.
11. Also, you can view the online help about a specific cmdlet by typing *get-help* plus the cmdlet. For example, type **get-help join-path** and press **Enter**.
12. Close the Windows PowerShell window.

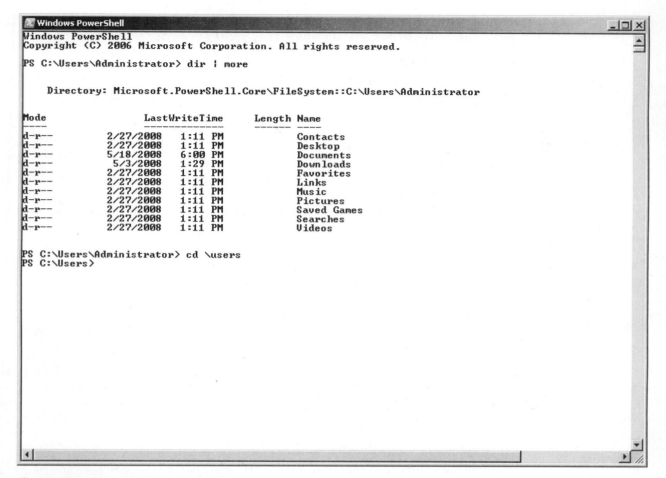

Figure 3-21   Using Windows PowerShell

There is not enough room in the chapter to give you a full grounding in Windows PowerShell. This section is only meant to give you an idea of its capabilities. To fully appreciate Windows PowerShell, you will need to be familiar with writing scripts as well as the PowerShell cmdlets. For tutorials and more resources about Windows PowerShell, try the following Web sites:

- *www.powershellpro.com/powershell-tutorial-introduction* (for a set of tutorials)

- *msdn2.microsoft.com/en-us/library/ms714674.aspx* (for the Windows PowerShell Programmer's Guide)

- *msdn2.microsoft.com/en-us/library/aa973757(VS.85).aspx* (for the Windows PowerShell Getting Started Guide)

- *msdn2.microsoft.com/en-us/library/ms714469(VS.85).aspx* (for the Windows Power-Shell SDK)

Chapter Summary

- Server Manager is a new tool offered in Windows Server 2008. This tool enables you to install and remove roles, install and remove features, access diagnostic and reliability tools, configure services and the Windows Firewall, manage disk storage, and start Device Manager to manage hardware.

- ServerManagerCmd.exe is a command-line version of Server Manager and has the ability to manage multiple servers.

- The Add Hardware Wizard enables the installation of hardware devices not properly detected by PnP.
- Device Manager is a tool you can access from Server Manager or Control Panel to manage hardware.
- The System File Checker and Sigverif are tools for verifying system files.
- After Windows Server 2008 is installed, you can tune performance by configuring processor scheduling and memory use, virtual memory, and memory for network performance.
- To help protect your system from power problems, configure startup and recovery options as well as power options.
- Knowing how to install a protocol is a skill that is similar to knowing how to change a flat tire; you don't need it often but it is important to know how when you need it. Use Control Panel to install or uninstall protocols.
- The Registry is a database that is at the foundation of Windows Server 2008. It's important to know the structure of Registry keys, subkeys, and values so you can carefully make Registry changes as might be called for in technical bulletins.
- The Security Configuration Wizard helps you protect Windows Server 2008 from problems caused by attackers and malicious software. This tool comes in an interactive GUI and a command-line version called *scwcmd*. Use this wizard and then test its results before you bring a server live for production use.
- Windows PowerShell is a command-line tool that enables a system administrator to manage a server using commands, cmdlets, and scripts.

Key Terms

Data Execution Prevention (DEP) A security feature that monitors how programs use memory and stops programs that attempt to use memory allocated for system programs and processes. This is intended to foil viruses, Trojan horses, and worms that attempt to invade system memory.

driver signing A digital signature incorporated into driver and system files as a way to verify the files and to ensure that they are not inappropriately overwritten.

hive A set of related Registry keys and subkeys stored as a file.

interrupt request (IRQ) line A hardware line that a computer component, such as a disk drive or serial port, uses to communicate to the processor that it is ready to send or receive information. Intel-based computers have 16 IRQ lines, with 15 available for computer components to use.

I/O address The address in memory through which data is transferred between a computer component and the processor.

Microsoft Virtual Network Switch Protocol Used with the Hyper-V role at the server's network interface card(s) (NICs) to bind or associate the virtual network services to the NIC and enable the use of a virtual switch between the parent partition containing the main operating system, Windows Server 2008, and child partitions containing other operating systems.

paging Moving blocks of information, called pages, from RAM to virtual memory (the paging file) on disk.

paging file Disk space, in the form of a file, for use when memory requirements exceed the available RAM.

Plug and Play (PnP) Ability of added computer hardware, such as an adapter or modem, to identify itself to the computer operating system for installation. PnP also refers to the Intel and Microsoft specifications for automatic device detection and installation. Many operating systems, such as Windows-based, Macintosh, and UNIX/Linux support PnP.

Registry entry A data parameter in the Registry stored as a value in hexadecimal, binary, or text format.

Registry key   A category of information contained in the Windows Registry, such as hardware or software.

Registry subkey   A key within a Registry key, similar to a subfolder under a folder.

Reliable Multicast Protocol   Used on Windows-based networks to facilitate multicast transmissions for multimedia communications.

resource   On a network, this refers to an object, such as a shared printer or shared directory, which can be accessed by users. On workstations as well as servers, a resource is an IRQ line, I/O address, or memory that is allocated to a computer component, such as a disk drive or communications port.

root key   Also called a subtree, the highest category of data contained in the Registry. There are five root keys.

Security Configuration Wizard (SCW)   A configuration tool that creates or modifies security policies for Windows Server 2008 servers.

Sigverif   A tool used to verify system and other critical files to determine if they have a signature.

subtree   Same as root key.

system environment variables   Variables defined by the operating system and that apply to any user logged onto the computer.

Universal PnP (UPnP)   A supplementation to PnP that enables automated configuration for devices connected through a network.

user environment variables   Environment variables that are defined on a per-user basis.

virtual memory   Disk storage allocated to link with physical RAM to temporarily hold data when there is not enough free RAM.

Review Questions

1. You have installed Windows Server 2008 and had to provide a new driver file for the disk drives in your computer. Now it seems like the disk drives are not responding as quickly as advertised. What can you do?

   a. Check the disk controllers for a switch you can set for faster disk rotation.

   b. Ensure that the DMA transfer mode is configured for the drives.

   c. Allocate more RAM for disk transfers.

   d. Use the Control Panel Disk applet to double the disk transfer speed.

2. Each time that you access files on a disk, the monitor blinks or goes blank for several seconds. What might be the source of the problem and possible solution?

   a. The disk and monitor are connected to the same controller, and you should use Control Panel to configure a hardware link bridge.

   b. This is called a "RAM pause" and you need to use Control Panel to allocate more RAM specifically for the data bus inside the computer.

   c. There is not enough RAM allocated for RAM disk reads, and you need to use Server Manager to reallocate the RAM.

   d. There is an IRQ conflict, and you need to use Device Manager to resolve the problem.

3. You have just used the *servermanagercmd* command to install two server roles. Which of the following commands can you use now to verify that the roles are installed?

   a. *servermanagercmd -query*

   b. *roles -d*

   c. *servermanagercmd /r:display*

   d. *role /v*

3

4. You want to confirm how space is allocated on the disk drives installed in your server. Which of the following tools enables you to do this?

    a. Disk Services

    b. Storage Monitor

    c. Server Manager

    d. WMI Control

5. Which of the following can be installed using the Add Hardware Wizard? (Choose all that apply.)

    a. CD/DVD drive

    b. keyboard

    c. monitor

    d. disk drive

6. You've obtained a new driver from the Internet for your server's NIC. What tool enables you to install the driver?

    a. Device Manager

    b. SCSI Updater

    c. Driver icon in Control Panel

    d. Task Manager

7. You have noticed lately that your server is running very slowly, especially when switching between programs. You see that the C: partition is running low on space, limiting the size of your paging file. You have a second partition, D:, that has 100 GB of free space. How can you move the paging file from partition C: onto partition D:?

    a. Use Device Manager to drag the paging file from partition C: to partition D:.

    b. Move the Paging directory to partition D: via Device Manager.

    c. Configure it from the System window opened through Control Panel.

    d. Use the Paging file option in Control Panel and access the Size link in the Paging window.

8. A _____ variable is defined by the operating system and is applied to every user when logged on.

9. Your organization has consolidated servers through virtualization and now needs to remove the Windows Deployment Services server role from one of its servers. Which of the following tools enable you to remove a server role? (Choose all that apply.)

    a. Control Panel System window

    b. Control Panel Server Roles window

    c. *exclude* command-line command

    d. ServerManagercmd.exe

10. _____ enables Windows Server 2008 to verify that a device driver is secure.

11. When programs are running in Windows Server 2008, _____ monitors their use of memory to be sure they do not cause memory problems.

12. Your server keyboard sometimes hesitates or seems like it is disconnecting from the computer. Which of the following tools enables you to run a quick check on whether the keyboard is working properly?

    a. Control Panel Check Components window

    b. *sysconfig* command

    c. Device Manager

    d. PnP

13. _____ Protocol is used for combined voice and video transmissions.

14. The purpose of the *scwcmd rollback* command is to _____.

15. Your server has a virus with elements of the virus embedded in the Registry. The virus checker has located these elements, but cannot delete them. What tool can you use to delete these virus elements in the Registry?

    a. *scwcmd*

    b. *regedit*

    c. *sigverif*

    d. *scw*

16. You are working in PowerShell and receive a call that users cannot use the print services through the server. What command can you run to quickly determine services that are running or are stopped?

    a. *core_services*

    b. *get-service*

    c. *scwcmd*

    d. *dir services*

17. Which of the following can be accomplished through using the Security Configuration Wizard? (Choose all that apply.)

    a. disable unused services

    b. configure firewall rules

    c. install a software application using security settings

    d. analyze security settings

18. Which of the following are Registry elements? (Choose all that apply.)

    a. OUs

    b. keys

    c. values

    d. markers

19. Your server has 4 GB of RAM. What should the initial amount of virtual memory be set to when you manually configure it?

    a. 1024 MB

    b. 2048 MB

    c. 4096 MB

    d. 6144 MB

20. Your company is working to save costs by conserving the power consumption of its servers. Which of the following default power plans should you select for Windows Server 2008 servers?

   a. high performance

   b. miser

   c. power saver

   d. controlled consumption

Case Projects

Light Crafters is a small company that makes light fixtures for fluorescent bulbs and the newer LED lights. The company is installing two new Windows Server 2008 servers, one using Standard Edition and the other using Enterprise Edition. Both operating systems are freshly installed and now it's time to configure them. Light Crafters has hired you to consult with their IT staff about the installation and configuration of the servers. They recently had turnover in the IT staff, leaving only two personnel who formerly supported users with desktop computers.

Case Project 3-1: Server Manager Training

The two IT staff members responsible for the servers have heard about Server Manager and are requesting training in its use. Prepare a brief report or slide presentation for them, to cover the following:

- An overview of Server Manager's capabilities
- How to start Server Manager
- How to install roles and features

Case Project 3-2: Troubleshooting a NIC

As you are working, a network interface card (NIC) in one of the servers seems to be working erratically. Explain how you can:

- Test the NIC
- Determine if there is an IRQ conflict
- Determine the name of the driver used by the NIC

Case Project 3-3: Troubleshooting a Configuration Problem

As you are working on the Enterprise Edition server, you install a card to connect a set of RAID drives. After the card and drives are set up, you run the installation disc that accompanies the RAID drives and card. When you reboot the server, you get a message about problems with two .dll files. What has most likely happened and how can you fix it?

Case Project 3-4: Understanding the Registry

The Light Crafters IT staff has never worked with the Registry. Create a brief report or slide presentation for them to explain its contents. Also, they need to know how to access the tool used to edit the Registry.

Case Project 3-5: Creating a Security Policy

You want to make certain that Light Crafters creates a security policy on each server before it is brought into production. What tool can you use for this task, and what security elements does it configure? What step should you take after using the tool before a server is made available to users? Create a brief report of this information for the IT staff.

Introduction to Active Directory and Account Management

After reading this chapter and completing the exercises, you will be able to:

- Understand Active Directory basic concepts
- Install and configure Active Directory
- Implement Active Directory containers
- Create and manage user accounts
- Configure and use security groups
- Describe and implement new Active Directory features

Just as the central nervous system coordinates the activities of different parts of the human body, Active Directory coordinates servers, client computers, printers, shared files, and other resources in a Windows Server 2008 network. In addition to coordinating activities, Active Directory secures network resources. Active Directory accomplishes these tasks by providing a hierarchy of management elements that enable you to organize resources, control who accesses them, and advertise their existence—making the lives of users easier. Knowledge of Active Directory is invaluable to you as an administrator because it enables you to capably orchestrate your network.

In this chapter you learn the basics of Active Directory, including Active Directory elements such as the schema and global catalog. You also learn how to install Active Directory. Once Active Directory is installed, you learn how to set up and use containers, including forests, trees, domains, organizational units, and sites. You also become familiar with delegating control over containers to fit the management structure of your organization. Next, you learn to set up security groups to manage access to resources. Finally, you review and use Active Directory features new to Windows Server 2008, including Read-Only Domain Controllers.

Active Directory Basics

Active Directory is a **directory service** that houses information about all network resources such as servers, printers, user accounts, groups of user accounts, security policies, and other information. As a directory service, Active Directory (also referred to as Active Directory Domain Services or AD DS in this chapter) is responsible for providing a central listing of resources and ways to quickly find and access specific resources and for providing a way to manage network resources.

Windows Server 2008 uses Active Directory to manage accounts, groups, and many more network management services. Writable copies of information in Active Directory are contained in one or more **domain controllers (DCs)**, which are servers that have the AD DS server role installed. Servers on a network managed by Active Directory that do not have Active Directory installed are called **member servers** (and are not domain controllers).

 Microsoft recommends that at least two DCs should be present in any organization using Active Directory. This ensures that if one DC goes down, the other is still available to service user account requests to log on and access resources.

In Active Directory, a domain is a fundamental component or container that holds information about all network resources that are grouped within it—servers, printers, and other physical resources, users, and user groups. A domain usually is a higher-level representation of how a business, government, or school is organized, for example reflecting a geographical location or major division of that organization. Every resource is called an **object** and is associated with a domain (see Figure 4-1). When you set up a new user account or a network printer, for instance, it becomes an object within a domain.

In Windows Server 2008, each DC is equal to every other DC in that it contains the full range of information that composes Active Directory. If information on one DC changes, such as the creation of an account, it is replicated to all other DCs in a process called **multimaster replication**. The advantage of this approach is that if one DC fails, Active Directory is fully intact on all other DCs, and there is no visible network interruption.

In Windows Server 2008, you can set replication of Active Directory information to occur at a preset interval instead of as soon as an update occurs. Also, you can determine how much of Active Directory is replicated each time it is copied from one DC to another. Active Directory is built to make replication efficient so that it transports as little as possible over a network, saving network resources. For example, Active Directory in Windows Server 2008 can:

- Replicate individual properties instead of entire accounts, which means that a single property can be changed without replicating information for the whole account

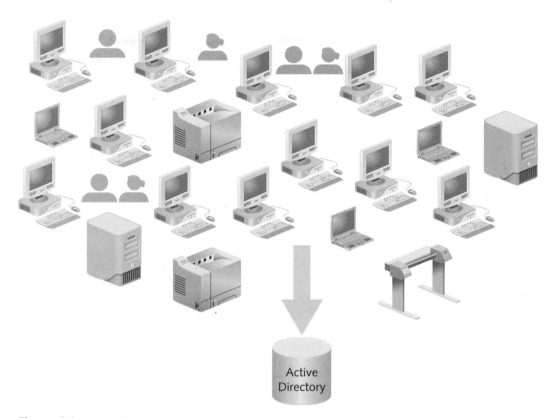

Figure 4-1 Active Directory domain objects include servers, workstations, printers, users, user groups, and other resources.

- Replicate Active Directory on the basis of the speed of the network link, such as replicating more frequently over a local area network link than over a wide area network link

Three general concepts are important as a starting place for understanding Active Directory: schema, global catalog, and namespace. These concepts are described in the next sections.

 For all of the activities in this chapter, you'll need an account with Administrator privileges. Also, all of these activities can be completed on a virtual server or computer, such as in Hyper-V.

 Some steps in the activities in this book include bulleted questions with space for you to record your responses/answers.

Activity 4-1: Installing Active Directory

Time Required: Approximately 20–30 minutes
Objective: Install Active Directory.

Description: To make a Windows Server 2008 server a domain controller, you must install the Active Directory Domain Services role. In this activity, you learn how to install the role. You'll need to log on to Windows Server 2008 as Administrator, and a DNS server should already be set up on your network. Before you begin, consult with your instructor about what domain name to use. Additionally, make sure that all other programs and windows are closed before you start (because the computer will reboot when you finish the installation).

1. Click **Start,** point to **Administrative Tools,** and click **Server Manager.**

2. Scroll to the Roles Summary section in the right pane.

3. Click **Add Roles.**

4. If you see the Before You Begin dialog box, click **Next.**

5. Click the box for **Active Directory Domain Services.** Click **Next.**

6. Read the information about Active Directory Domain Services.

   • What other services are installed when you install this role?

7. Click **Next.**

8. Click **Install.**

9. Review the Installation Results window and ensure that you see Active Directory Domain Controller is an installed service and that the installation succeeded, as shown in Figure 4-2.

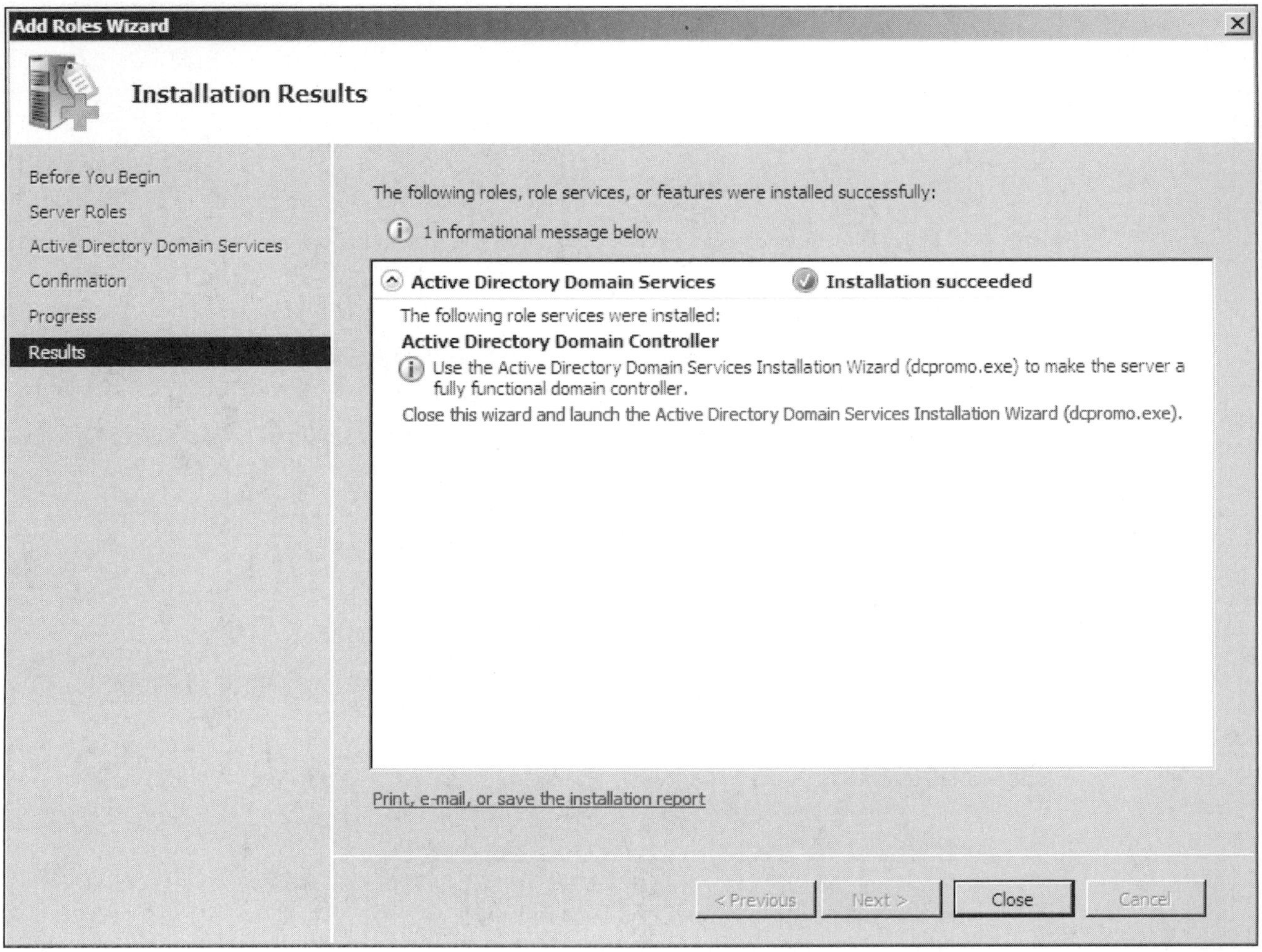

Figure 4-2 Installation Results window

10. Click **Close**.

11. Click **Start** and click **Run**.

12. Type **dcpromo** in the Open text box to run the Active Directory Domain Services Installation Wizard. You use this wizard to finish the steps to make this computer a domain controller. Click **OK**.

 The *dcpromo* tool is one of the newly reconfigured tools in Windows Server 2008. It not only offers more capabilities, but it also helps ensure that you set up Active Directory following what Microsoft calls "best practices" for security and effectiveness.

13. After the wizard starts, click **Next**.

14. If you see a screen with information about improved security settings, read the information and click **Next**.

15. Click the option button to **Create a new domain in a new forest**, and then click **Next**.

16. Enter the domain name, such as *jp***comp.com** (where *jp* are your initials), and click **Next**.

17. Click the **Forest functional level** drop-down list arrow. Notice that you can select from three forest functional levels: Windows 2000, Windows Server 2003, and Windows Server 2008. For this activity, select **Windows Server 2008**, unless your instructor specifies otherwise (you learn more about forest functional levels in the section, "Forest"). Click **Next** (see Figure 4-3).

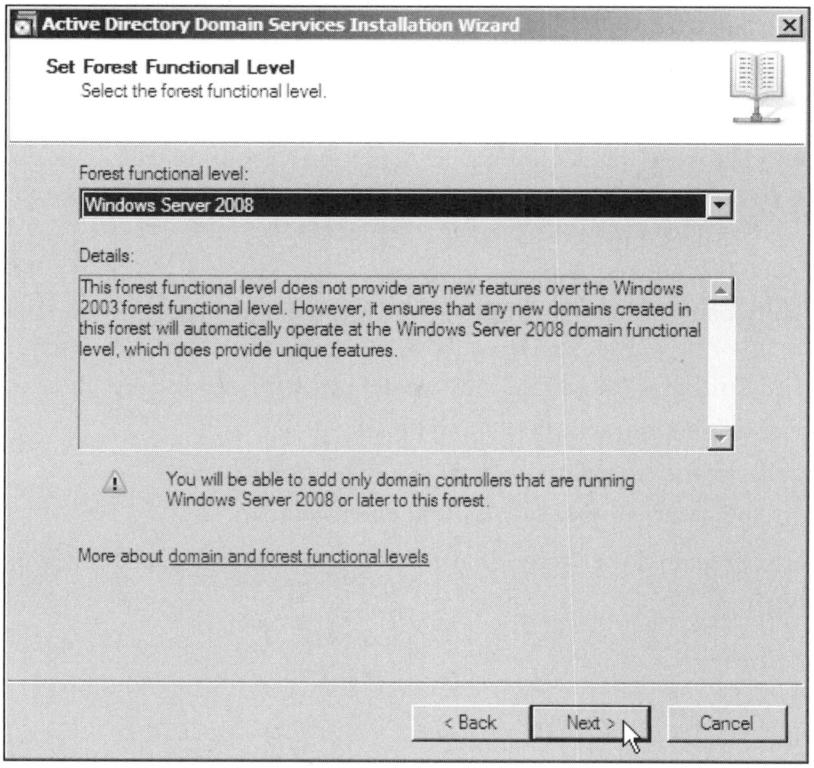

Active Directory Domain Services Installation Wizard ☒

Set Forest Functional Level
Select the forest functional level.

Forest functional level:

Windows Server 2008	▼

Details:

This forest functional level does not provide any new features over the Windows 2003 forest functional level. However, it ensures that any new domains created in this forest will automatically operate at the Windows Server 2008 domain functional level, which does provide unique features.

⚠ You will be able to add only domain controllers that are running Windows Server 2008 or later to this forest.

More about domain and forest functional levels

< Back	Next >	Cancel

Figure 4-3 Configuring the forest functional level

18. Click **Next** in the Additional Domain Controller Options window. If you see a warning box that this computer has a dynamically assigned IP address, click **Yes** so that you can proceed. This means your IPv4 or IPv6 address is dynamically configured (the IP address is assigned automatically), which you can reconfigure later. If you see this message, plan to go back

and reconfigure your network connection to have a manually (static) assigned IPv4 and IPv6 address—see your instructor for a specific address to use.

- Record the location of the database, log files, and SYSVOL.

19. Click **Next**.
20. Assign a password to use in case the domain controller needs to be started in the Directory Services Restore Mode, and confirm the password (you can use the Administrator account password for this activity). Click **Next**.
21. Review the selections you have made and click **Next**.
22. As the wizard works to configure the services, check the box for **Reboot on completion**.
23. Log on after the computer has rebooted.

Schema

The Active Directory **schema** defines the objects and the information pertaining to those objects that can be stored in Active Directory. Each kind of object in Active Directory is defined through the schema, which is like a small database of information associated with that object, including the object class and its attributes. Schema information for objects in a domain is replicated on every DC. To help you understand a schema, consider the characteristics associated with a vehicle. First, there are different classes of vehicles, including automobiles, trucks, tractors, and motorcycles. Further, each class has a set of attributes. For automobiles those attributes include engine, headlights, seats, steering wheel, dashboard, wheels, windshield, CD player, cup holder, and many others. Some of those attributes must be present in every automobile, such as an engine and wheels. Other attributes are optional—whether there is a CD player or cup holder, for instance.

A user account is one class of object in Active Directory that is defined through schema elements unique to that class. The user account class as a whole has the following schema characteristics (see Figure 4-4):

- A unique object name
- A **globally unique identifier (GUID)**, which is a unique number associated with the object name
- Required attributes (those that must be defined with each object)
- Optional attributes (those that are optionally defined)
- A syntax (format) to determine how attributes are defined
- Pointers to parent entities, such as to a parent domain

Examples of required user account attributes that must be defined for each account are:

- Logon name
- User's full name
- Password
- Domain

Optional attributes for a user account include:

- Account description
- Account holder's office number or address
- Account holder's telephone number
- Account holder's e-mail address
- Web page

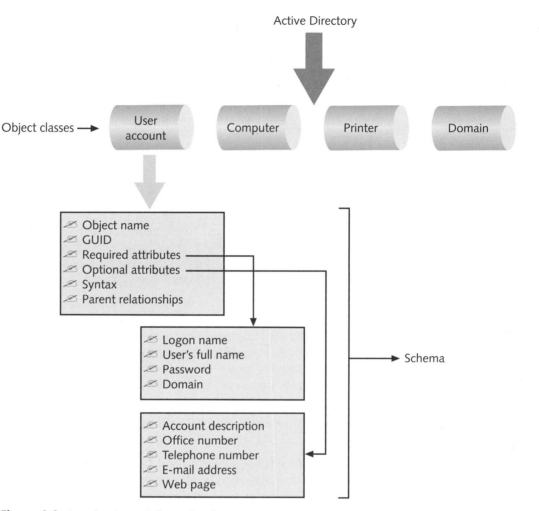

Figure 4-4 Sample schema information for user accounts

Providing an account description or specifying if the account holder has a Web page are examples of optional attributes that do not have to be completed when you create an account. In some instances, the attributes that are required and those that are optional can be influenced by the security policies that the server administrator sets in Active Directory for a class of objects (see Chapter 10, "Securing Windows Server 2008" for more about security policies). This is true, for example, with account password restrictions because it is possible (but not recommended) for you to have a security policy that does not require account password restrictions.

Each attribute is automatically given a version number and date when it is created or changed. This information enables Active Directory to know when an attribute value, such as a password, is changed, and update only that value on all DCs. When you install Windows Server 2008 for the first time on a network server, designating it as a domain controller, you also create several object classes automatically. The default object classes include domain, user account, group, shared drive, shared folder, computer, and printer.

Global Catalog

The **global catalog** stores information about every object within a forest (you learn more about forests later in this chapter). The first DC configured in a forest becomes the global catalog server. The global catalog server will store a full replica of every object within its own domain and a partial replica of each object within every domain in the forest. The partial replica for each object contains those attributes most commonly used to search for objects. The global catalog serves the following purposes:

- Authenticating users when they log on
- Providing lookup and access to all resources in all domains
- Providing replication of key Active Directory elements
- Keeping a copy of the most used attributes for each object for quick access

The global catalog server enables forest-wide searches of data. Because it contains attributes pertaining to every object within a forest, users can query this server to locate an object, as opposed to having to perform an extensive search. The global catalog server also can be used for network logons. When a user logs on to the network, the global catalog server is contacted for universal group membership information pertaining to the user's account (universal groups are discussed in this chapter in the section "Implementing Universal Groups"). In a Windows 2000 domain, if the global catalog was unavailable, the user could only log on to the local computer. In Windows Server 2003 and 2008, if the global catalog is unavailable for group membership information, the user can log on to the network with cached credentials.

Cached credentials means that a record is kept in server cache if a user has successfully logged on previously. Thus, authentication when the user logs off and then logs on again can be performed by checking the cached credentials, instead of the global catalog. However, when a user is logging on for the first time and there is no cached credential for that user, if the global catalog is unavailable, access is provided only to the local computer.

By default, the first DC in the forest is automatically designated as the global catalog server. You have the option of configuring another DC to be a global catalog server as well as designating multiple DCs as global catalog servers.

There must be at least one global catalog server in a forest. Also, in most cases it makes sense to place one global catalog server in every site (you learn about sites in the section of this chapter called "Sites"). If you use e-mail servers, such as for Microsoft Exchange, consider having one global catalog server for every four mailbox servers. Global catalog servers can create quite a lot of traffic, so configuring every DC to be a global catalog server is generally too much.

Namespace

Active Directory uses Domain Name System (DNS), which means there must be a DNS server on the network that Active Directory can access. As you learned in Chapter 1, "Introduction to Windows Server 2008," DNS is a TCP/IP-based name service that converts computer and domain host names to dotted decimal addresses and vice versa, through a process called **name resolution**. A computer running Windows Server 2008 can be set up to act as a DNS server on a network. For example, when a Windows Vista client sends a TCP/IP-based request to connect to a specific server on the same network, such as a server named Research, a DNS server on the network can be used to translate Research into its dotted decimal address, 142.78.14.4.

A DNS server does more than provide name resolution. It also provides services such as registration of hosts, contains service (SRV) records to identify servers providing particular TCP/IP services, enables transfers of DNS information for redundancy, and provides other services. You learn more about DNS servers in Chapter 8, "Managing Windows Server 2008 Network Services."

A **namespace** is a logical area on a network that contains directory services and named objects, and that has the ability to perform name resolution. Active Directory depends on one or more DNS servers to resolve names in a designated logical DNS namespace. Within Active Directory is another namespace that contains named objects, such as accounts and printers, but which Active Directory coordinates with information in the DNS namespace. Both namespaces (DNS and Active Directory) can be on a single computer, such as a Windows Server 2008 server set up as a DC and a DNS server in a small network. Or, they can be distributed across several servers on a large network, which might have two servers set up as DNS servers and 22 servers set up as DCs.

Active Directory employs two kinds of namespaces: contiguous and disjointed. A **contiguous namespace** is one in which every child object contains the name of the parent object, such as in the example of the child object *msdn2.microsoft.com* and its parent object *microsoft.com*. When the child name does not resemble the name of its parent object, this is called a **disjointed namespace**, such as when the parent for a university is *uni.edu*, and a child is *bio.ethicsresearch.com*.

Containers in Active Directory

Active Directory has a treelike structure that is similar to the hierarchy of folders and subfolders in a directory structure. For example, in a directory structure information is stored in a root folder, which is at the highest level. The root folder may contain several main folders, 15 or 20, for instance. Under each folder are subfolders, and within subfolders there can be more subfolders. Subfolders can have a nearly infinite depth, but typically do not go more than five or ten layers deep. Just as files are the basic elements that are grouped in a hierarchy of folders and subfolders, objects are the basic elements of Active Directory and are grouped in a hierarchy of larger containers. Also, just as the folder structure affects how you can set up security on a server, Active Directory structure affects how you can manage security in an enterprise. The hierarchical elements, or **containers**, of Active Directory include forests, trees, domains, organizational units (OUs), and sites (see Figure 4-5).

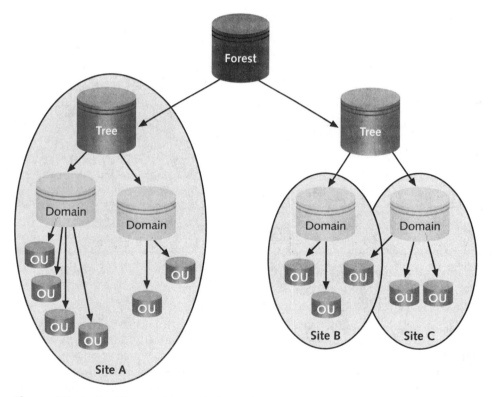

Figure 4-5   Active Directory hierarchical containers

Forest

At the highest level in an Active Directory design is the **forest**. A forest consists of one or more Active Directory trees that are in a common relationship and that have the following characteristics:

- The trees can use a disjointed namespace.
- All trees use the same schema.
- All trees use the same global catalog.
- Domains enable administration of commonly associated objects, such as accounts and other resources, within a forest.
- Two-way transitive trusts (resources shared equally) are automatically configured between domains within a single forest.

A forest provides a means to relate trees that use a contiguous namespace in domains within each tree but that have disjointed namespaces in relationship to each other. Consider, for example, an international automotive parts company that is really a conglomerate of separate companies, each having a different brand name. The parent company is PartsPlus, located in Toronto. PartsPlus manufactures alternators, coils, and other electrical parts at plants in Toronto, Montreal, and Detroit, and has a tree structure for domains that are part of partsplus.com. Another company owned by PartsPlus, Marty and Mike's (2m.com), makes radiators in two South Carolina cities, Florence and Greenville, and radiator fluid in Atlanta. A third member company, Chelos (chelos.com), makes engine parts and starters in Mexico City, Corsica, Monterrey, and Puebla, all in Mexico—and also has a manufacturing site in Valencia, Venezuela. In this situation, it makes sense to have a contiguous tree structure for each of the three related companies and to join the trees in a forest of disjointed name spaces, as shown in Figure 4-6.

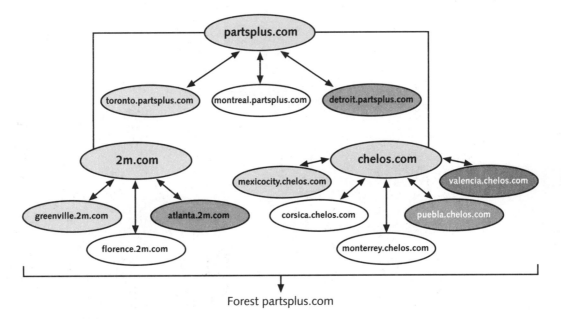

Forest partsplus.com

Figure 4-6 A forest

The advantage of joining trees into a forest is that all domains share the same schema and global catalog. A schema is set up in the root domain, which is partsplus.com in our example, and the root domain is home to the master schema server. At least one DC functions as a global catalog server, but in our example, it is likely that you would plan to have a global catalog server located at each geographic location (domain).

Windows Server 2008 Active Directory recognizes three types of forest functional levels. The **forest functional level** refers to the Active Directory functions supported forest-wide. The functional levels are as follows:

- *Windows 2000 Native forest functional level*—Provides Active Directory functions compatible with a network that has a combination of Windows 2000 Server, Windows Server 2003, and Windows Server 2008 domain controllers.

- *Windows Server 2003 forest functional level*—Intended for Windows Server 2003 and 2008 domain controllers only and enables more forest management functions, such as more options for creating trust relationships between forests, domain renaming, Read-Only Domain Controllers, and enhanced replication of Active Directory. (You'll learn more about trust relationships in the next section.)

- *Windows Server 2008 forest functional level*—Contains only Windows Server 2008 domain controllers. Currently this level has no more functional features than in the Windows Server 2003 forest functional level, although there is room for new features that can be added later. This level is also included for compatibility with the domain functional levels discussed in the section, "Domains."

After Active Directory is installed, the general steps for raising the forest functional level are as follows:

1. Click Start, point to Administrative Tools, and click Active Directory Domains and Trusts.

2. In the tree in the left pane, right-click Active Directory Domains and Trusts (*server and domain name*).

3. Click Raise Forest Functional Level.

4. Select a functional level. (The options depend on which functional level is currently set. You cannot roll back to a lower functional level. If no options are displayed, this is because you are currently in the Windows Server 2008 forest functional level and all you can do is click OK and go to Step 8.)

5. Select the appropriate forest functional level and click Raise.

6. Read the message box and click OK.

7. Read the acknowledgement box and click OK.

8. Close the Active Directory Domains and Trusts window.

Tree

A **tree** contains one or more domains that are in a common relationship, and has the following characteristics:

- Domains are represented in a contiguous namespace and can be in a hierarchy.

- Two-way trust relationships exist between parent domains and child domains, essentially creating a trust path.

- All domains in a single tree use the same schema for all types of common objects.

- All domains use the same global catalog.

The domains in a tree typically have a hierarchical structure, such as a root domain at the top and other domains under the root (similar to a parent-child relationship). Using tracksport.org as an example, tracksport.org might be the root domain and have four domains under the root to form one tree: east.tracksport.org, west.tracksport.org, north.tracksport.org, and south .tracksport.org, as shown in Figure 4-7. These domains use the contiguous namespace format in that the child domains each inherit a portion of their namespace from the parent domain.

The domains within a tree are in what is called a **Kerberos transitive trust relationship**, which consists of **two-way trusts** between parent domains and child domains (see Figure 4-7). A **transitive trust** means that if A and B have a trust and B and C have a trust, A and C

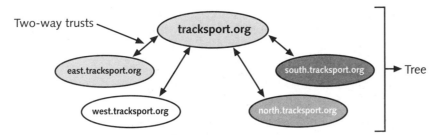

Figure 4-7   Tree with hierarchical domains

automatically have a trust as well. In a two-way trust, each domain is trusting and trusted. A trusted domain is one that is granted access to resources, whereas a trusting domain is the one granting access. In a two-way trust, members of each domain can have access to the resources of the other.

 Windows Server 2003 and 2008 also have a forest trust. In a forest trust, a Kerberos transitive trust relationship exists between the root domains in Windows Server 2003 and 2008 forests, resulting in trust relationships between all domains in the forests.

Because of the trust relationship between parent and child domains, any one domain can have access to the resources of all others. The security in the two-way trust relationships is based on Kerberos techniques, using a combination of protocol-based and encryption-based security techniques between clients and servers. A new domain joining a tree has an instant trust relationship with all other member domains through the trust relationship that is established with its parent domain, which makes all objects in the other domains available to the new one.

All domains within a single tree (as well as all trees in single forest) share the same schema defining all the object types that can be stored within Active Directory. Further, all domains in a tree also share the same global catalog and a portion of their namespace. In addition, a child domain contains part of the name of the parent domain.

Domain

Microsoft views a domain as a logical partition within an Active Directory forest. A domain is a grouping of objects that typically exists as a primary container within Active Directory. The basic functions of a domain are as follows:

- To provide an Active Directory "partition" in which to house objects, such as accounts and groups, that have a common relationship, particularly in terms of management and security
- To establish a set of information to be replicated from one DC to another
- To expedite management of a set of objects

When you use the server-based networking model described in Chapter 1 to verify users who log on to the network, there is at least one domain. For example, if you are planning Active Directory for a small business of 34 employees who have workstations connected to a network that has one or two Windows Server 2008 servers, then one domain is sufficient for that business.

The domain functions as a partition within which to group all of the network resource objects consisting of servers, user accounts, shared printers, and shared folders and files.

In a midsized or large business, you might use more than one domain—for instance, when business units are separated by long distances and you want to limit the amount of DC replication over expensive wide area network links or to manage objects differently between locations, such as through different account or security policies. For example, consider a company that builds tractors in South Carolina and has a parts manufacturing division in Japan. Each site has a large enterprise network of Windows Server 2008 servers, and the sites are linked together in a wide area network by an expensive satellite connection. When you calculate the cost of replicating DCs over the satellite link, you cannot justify it in terms of the increased traffic that will delay other vital daily business communications. In this situation, it makes sense to create two separate domains, one for each site, as shown in Figure 4-8.

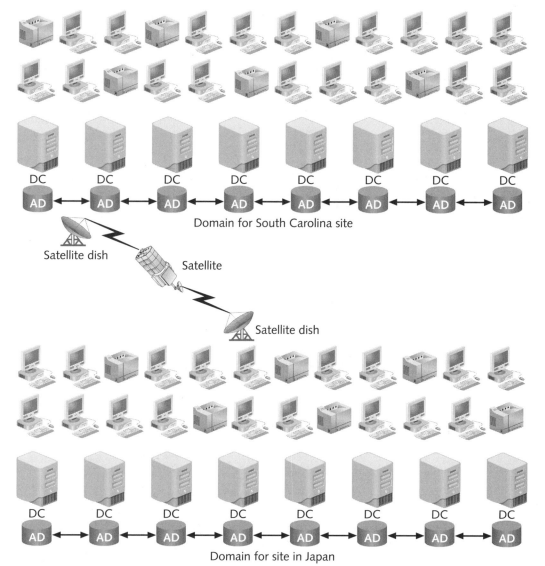

Figure 4-8 Using multiple domains

Windows Server 2008 Active Directory recognizes three **domain functional levels,** which refers to the Windows Server operating systems on domain controllers and the domain-specific functions they support. The domain functional levels are as follows:

- *Windows 2000 domain functional level*—Provides Active Directory functions compatible with a network that has a combination of Windows 2000 Server, Windows Server 2003, and Windows Server 2008 domain controllers. This level supports universal groups, which were not previously available in Windows NT Server, converting types of groups, and nesting groups (see the section in this chapter, "Security Group Management").

- *Windows Server 2003 domain functional level*—Intended for Windows Server 2003 and 2008 domain controllers only and enables more domain management functions, such as delegating management of Active Directory objects, time stamps for logons, use of

Authorization Manager policies in Active Directory, and other features not available in Windows 2000 Server domain controllers.

- *Windows Server 2008 domain functional level*—Contains only Windows Server 2008 domain controllers, and offers new features such as default incorporation of the Distributed File System (with better security), enhanced security for Kerberos authentication, and enhanced user account password policies.

As is true for forest functional levels, you cannot go back to an earlier domain functional level. For example, if you are at the Windows Server 2008 domain functional level, you cannot go back to the Windows Server 2003 or Windows 2000 domain functional levels. If you are at the Windows Server 2003 domain functional level, you cannot go back to the Windows 2000 Server level, but you can convert to the Windows Server 2008 level.

Activity 4-2: Managing Domains

Time Required: Approximately 10 minutes
Objective: Learn where to manage domains and domain trust relationships.

Description: After Active Directory is installed, you might need to customize the properties of a domain or its trust relationships. In this activity, you learn about the tool used to manage domains and trust relationships.

1. Click **Start**, point to **Administrative Tools**, and click **Active Directory Domains and Trusts**.

2. In the left pane, right-click the domain you created in the last project (or an existing domain).

3. Click **Properties**.

4. Click each of the **General**, **Trusts**, and **Managed By** tabs to view their contents.

   - Make notes about their contents here:

5. Click **Cancel**.

6. Right-click the domain again and click **Raise Domain Functional Level**. Notice that if you are currently at the Windows 2000 domain functional level, you can raise to either the Windows Server 2003 or Windows Server 2008 domain functional level. If you are currently at the Windows Server 2003 domain functional level, you can raise to the Windows Server 2008 domain functional level only. Or, if you are at the Windows Server 2008 functional level, there are no options to implement a different functional level. You can only raise to a higher functional level; you cannot go back to a lower level. Depending on the options available to you, click either **Cancel** or **Close**.

7. Close the Active Directory Domains and Trusts window.

Organizational Unit

An **organizational unit** (OU) offers a way to achieve more flexibility in managing the resources associated with a business unit, department, or division than is possible through domain administration alone. An OU is a grouping of related objects within a domain, similar to the idea of having subfolders within a folder. OUs can be used to reflect the structure of the organization without having to completely restructure the domain(s) when that structure changes.

OUs allow the grouping of objects so that they can be administered using the same group policies, such as security and desktop setup. OUs also make it possible for server administration to be delegated or decentralized. For example, in a software company in which the employees are divided into 15 project teams, the user accounts, shared files, shared printers, and other shared resources of each team can be defined as objects in separate OUs. There would be one domain for the entire company and 15 OUs within that domain, all defined in Active Directory. With this arrangement, file and folder objects can be defined to specific OUs for security, and the management of user accounts, account setup policies, and file and folder permissions (access privileges) can be delegated to each group leader (OU administrator).

OUs can be nested within OUs, as subfolders are nested in subfolders, so that you can create them several layers deep. In the grocery chain example, you might have one OU under the Retail OU for the Accounting Department, an OU under the Accounting OU for the Accounts Receivable Group, and an OU under Accounts Receivable for the cashiers—creating four layers of OUs. The problem with this approach is that creating OUs many layers deep can get as confusing as creating subfolders several layers deep. It is confusing for the server administrator to track layered OUs, and it is laborious for Active Directory to search through each layer.

When you plan to create OUs, keep three concerns in mind:

- Microsoft recommends that you limit OUs to 10 levels or fewer.

- Active Directory works more efficiently (using less CPU resources) when OUs are set up horizontally instead of vertically. Using the grocery chain example, it is more efficient to create the Accounting, Accounts Receivable, and Cashier OUs directly under the Retail OU, resulting in two levels instead of four.

- The creation of OUs involves more processing resources because each request through an OU (for example, to determine permission on a folder) requires CPU time. When that request must go several layers deep through nested OUs, even more CPU time is needed.

Activity 4-3: Managing OUs

Time Required: Approximately 10 minutes
Objective: Create an OU and delegate control over it.

Description: One advantage of an OU is that it enables a server administrator to delegate some server management tasks, such as managing user accounts. For example, some organizations prefer to have OUs that reflect the department structure. In this way, accounts for a particular department are created within an OU, and a department administrator who has authority over an OU can create and manage user accounts for her or his department within the OU. In this activity, you learn how to create an OU and delegate authority for account management within that OU.

1. Click **Start**, point to **Administrative Tools**, and click **Active Directory Users and Computers**.

2. Right-click the top domain in the tree in the left pane, such as jpcomp.com, point to **New**, and click **Organizational Unit**.

3. Enter **SalesOU** and your initials, such as SalesOUJP. Click **OK**.

4. Click the **plus sign** in front of the domain in the left pane so that you can see the OU you created listed under the domain.

5. Right-click the OU, such as SalesOUJP.

   - What options are available on the shortcut menu?

6. Click **Delegate Control**.

7. Click **Next** when the Delegation of Control Wizard starts.

8. Click **Add**.

9. Click the **Advanced** button.

10. Click **Find Now**.

11. Because you have not yet defined user accounts, click **Administrator** for this activity. Notice that names with a single head icon represent accounts and names with a double head icon represent groups of accounts. Click **OK**.

12. Click **OK** in the Select Users, Computers, or Groups dialog box.

13. Click **Next** in the Delegation of Control Wizard.

14. Click the box for **Create, delete, and manage user accounts**, as shown in Figure 4-9.

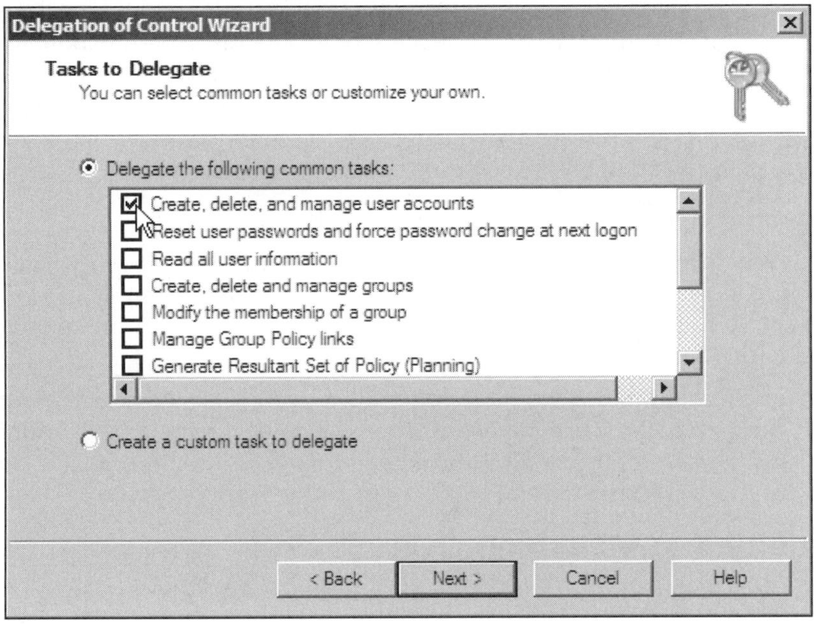

![Delegation of Control Wizard dialog box. Title bar reads "Delegation of Control Wizard" with a close (X) button. Heading "Tasks to Delegate — You can select common tasks or customize your own." with a keys icon. Radio button "Delegate the following common tasks:" is selected. A list contains checkboxes: Create, delete, and manage user accounts (checked); Reset user passwords and force password change at next logon; Read all user information; Create, delete and manage groups; Modify the membership of a group; Manage Group Policy links; Generate Resultant Set of Policy (Planning). Radio button "Create a custom task to delegate" below. Buttons at bottom: Back, Next >, Cancel, Help.]

Figure 4-9   Delegating authority over accounts in an OU

15. Click **Next**.

16. Review the tasks that you have completed and then click **Finish**.

17. Close the Active Directory Users and Computers window.

 In addition to delegating control of an OU, it is possible to delegate control of a domain. Some large organizations, for example, have different server administrators manage different domains. You can delegate control over a domain by right-clicking the domain in the Active Directory Users and Computers window and clicking Delegate Control. Then, follow the instructions in the Delegation of Control Wizard.

Site

A **site** is a TCP/IP-based concept (container) within Active Directory that is linked to IP subnets and has the following functions:

- Reflects one or more interconnected subnets, usually having good network connectivity
- Reflects the physical aspect of the network
- Is used for DC replication
- Is used to enable a client to access the DC that is physically closest
- Is composed of only two types of objects, servers and configuration objects

Sites are based on connectivity and replication functions. You might think of sites as a way of grouping Active Directory objects by physical location so Active Directory can identify the fastest communications paths between clients and servers and between DCs. The physical representation of the network to Active Directory is accomplished by defining subnets that are interconnected. For this reason, one site may be contained within a single OU or a single domain, or a site may span multiple OUs and domains, depending on how subnets are set up. The most typical boundary for a site consists of the local area network topology and subnet boundaries rather than the OU and domain boundaries.

There are two important reasons to define a site. First, by defining site locations based on IP subnets, you enable a client to access network servers using the most efficient physical route. In the PartsPlus example (discussed in the "Forest" section), it is faster for a client in Toronto to be authenticated by a Toronto global catalog server than for the client to go through Detroit or Mexico City. Second, DC replication is most efficient when Active Directory has information about which DCs are in which locations.

Within a site, each DC replicates forest, tree, domain, and OU naming structures, configuration naming elements, such as computers and printers, and schema information. One advantage of creating a site is that it sets up redundant paths between DCs so that if one path is down, there is a second path that can be used for replication. This redundancy is in a logical ring format, which means that replication goes from DC to DC around a ring until each DC is replicated. If a DC is down along the main route, then Active Directory uses site information to send replication information in the opposite direction around the ring. Whenever a new DC is added or an old one removed, Active Directory reconfigures the ring to make sure there are two replication paths available from each DC. Also, between sites, replication is coordinated through one server, called a bridgehead server, located at each site (see Figure 4-10).

When you replicate between sites, the replication occurs only between two bridgehead servers. The **bridgehead server** is a DC that is designated to have the role of exchanging replication information. Only one bridgehead server is set up per site, so the network traffic per site is kept to a minimum. Otherwise, having multiple DCs replicating with partners across sites could take up considerable bandwidth.

Consider a state university network that might take advantage of sites. The university has three domains—students.uni.edu, faculty.uni.edu, and staffadmin.uni.edu—organized into a single tree. Also, the university has three campuses in different cities. The domains span each campus location. Thus students.uni.edu contains accounts and printers on DCs at all locations, for example. Each domain contains OUs that are appropriate to that domain. For instance, students.uni.edu has an OU for students at each campus—for a total of three OUs all at the same level. The campuses are relatively large with 7000 students, 10,000 students, and 18,000 students, and have networks that are physically divided into subnets. In this situation, you can designate each campus network as a site in Active Directory, which enables it to find the fastest routes for traffic that is on-campus and for traffic that goes between campuses. For example, when a student logs on to students.uni.edu, Active Directory can help that student find the nearest DC and avoid the chance that the logon authentication is performed over a wide area network link at a different campus location. Another advantage is that the DC replication for each domain between sites (over wide area network links) can be set to occur less frequently than replication within a site.

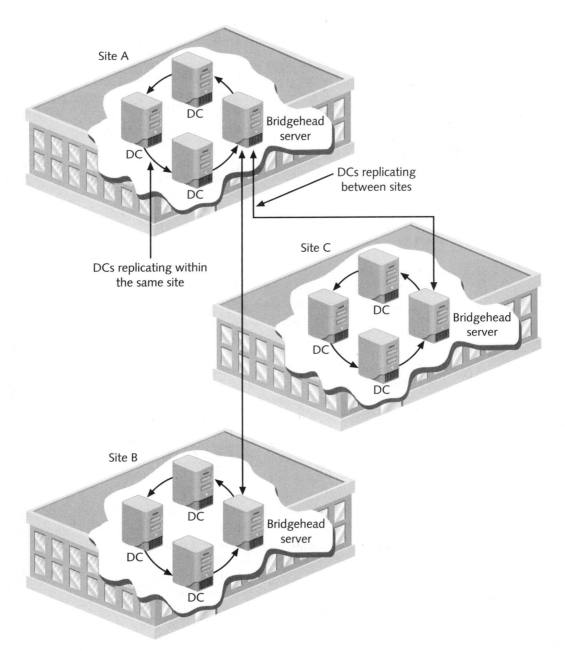

Figure 4-10   DCs replicating within and between sites

Active Directory Guidelines

Planning the Active Directory structure of forests, trees, domains, and OUs is a potentially complex process. The following guidelines summarize the most important aspects of the Active Directory planning process that you have learned in the previous sections for the forest, tree, domain, OU, and site containers:

- Above all, keep Active Directory as simple as possible and plan its structure before you implement it.
- Implement the least number of domains possible, with one domain being the ideal and building from there.
- Implement only one domain on most small networks.

- When you are planning for an organization that is likely to reorganize in the future, use OUs to reflect the organization's structure.

- Create only the number of OUs that are absolutely necessary.

- Do not build an Active Directory with more than 10 levels of OUs (optimally, no more than one or two levels).

- Use domains as partitions in forests to demarcate commonly associated accounts and resources governed by group and security policies.

- Implement multiple trees and forests only as necessary.

- Use sites in situations where there are multiple IP subnets and multiple geographic locations, as a means to improve logon and DC replication performance.

User Account Management

Once Active Directory is installed and configured, you enable users to access network servers and resources through user accounts. Several accounts might be set up by default, depending on which Windows components you install, but including two primary accounts: Administrator and Guest (Guest is disabled as a security measure).

Accounts can be set up in two general environments:

- Accounts that are set up through a stand-alone server that does not have Active Directory installed

- Accounts that are set up in a domain when Active Directory is installed

When accounts are created in the domain through Active Directory, then those accounts can be used to access any domain server or resource.

Creating Accounts when Active Directory Is Not Installed

New accounts are created by first installing the Local Users and Groups MMC snap-in for stand-alone servers that do not use Active Directory. The general steps for creating a local user account on a server that is not a DC are as follows:

1. Click Start, click Run, enter mmc, and click OK.

2. Click the File menu, and click Add/Remove Snap-in.

3. Under Available snap-ins, find and click Local Users and Groups, as shown in Figure 4-11.

4. Click the Add button to make this a selected snap-in.

5. In the Choose Target Machine dialog box, leave Local computer (the computer on which this console is running) selected and click Finish.

6. Click OK. Expand the console windows, if necessary.

7. Double-click Local Users and Groups in the tree in the left pane.

8. Click the Users folder in the tree and then click the Action menu.

9. Click New User and complete the information to create the user account, as shown in Figure 4-12.

NOTE

Symbols that cannot be used in an account name in Windows Server 2008 are: [ ] ; : < > = , + / \ | . Also, each account name must be unique, so that there are no duplicates. Finally, when you specify a password, it needs to meet the password policy requirements on the local computer. The password requirements include a minimum password length, complexity, and whether the password has been used recently (password history). You learn about setting up password requirements in Chapter 10.

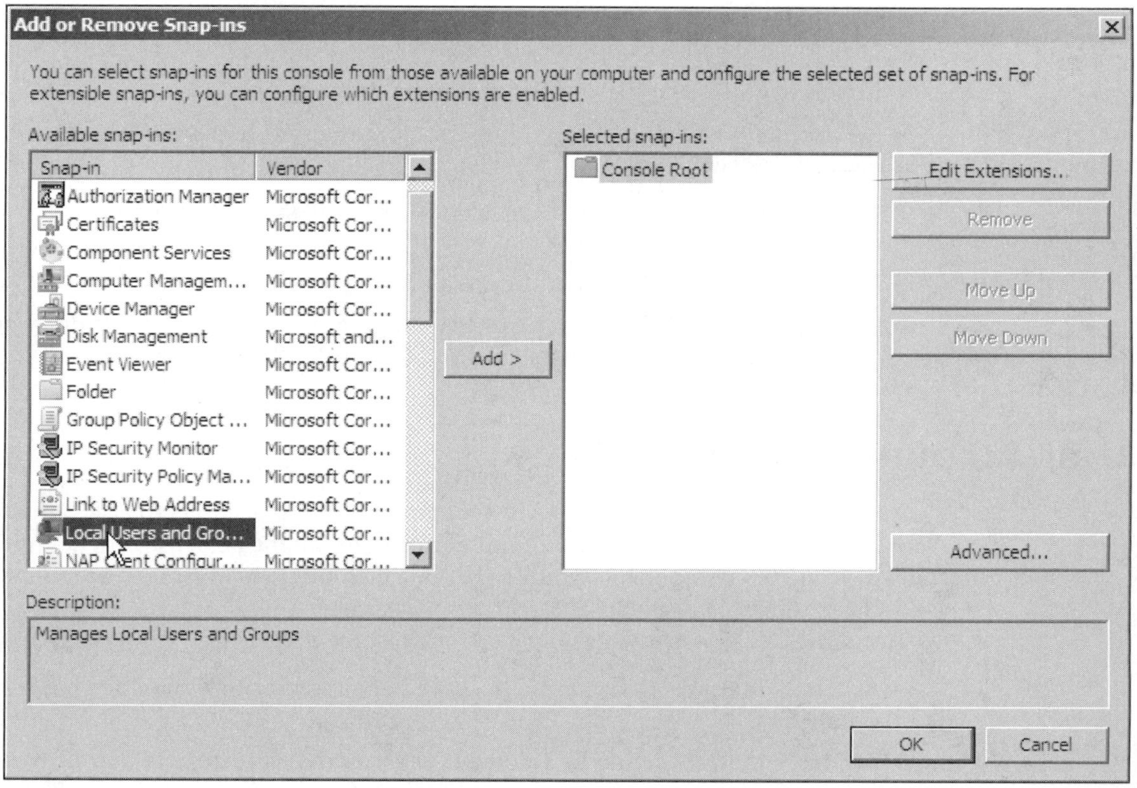

Figure 4-11   Selecting the Local Users and Groups MMC snap-in

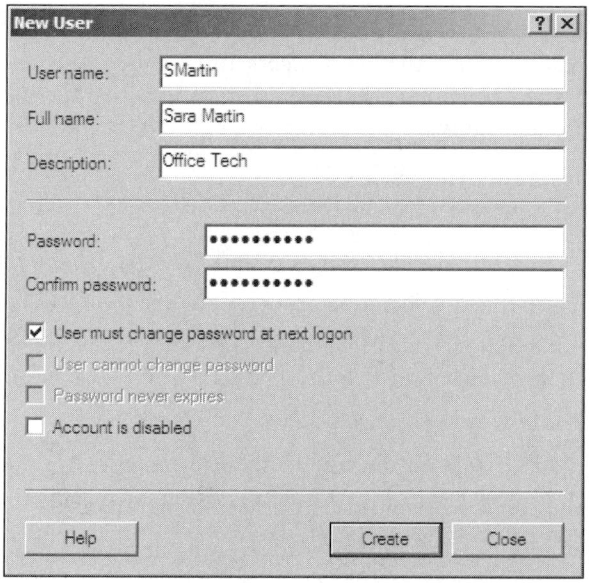

Figure 4-12   Creating a user account without Active Directory installed

10. Click Create. If you see a warning message that the password does not meet the password requirements, click OK and enter a new password that does meet the requirements, such as one that is over six characters long and that contains a combination of uppercase and lowercase letters and numbers.

11. Create another account, or click Close if you're finished creating accounts.

12. Close the MMC and click Yes to save the console settings. Enter a name for the console, such as Manage Accounts, and click Save.

The console will now appear as a tool in the menu when you click Start, point to All Programs, and click Administrative Tools. However, it does not appear when you click Start and point to Administrative Tools. This is true when you save a customized MMC regardless of whether Active Directory is installed.

Creating Accounts when Active Directory Is Installed

When Active Directory is installed and the server is a domain controller, use the Active Directory Users and Computers tool either from the Administrative Tools menu or as an MMC snap-in. You create each new account by entering account information and password controls.

If you are using Active Directory and are working on a DC, Windows Server 2008 will not allow you to install the Local Users and Groups snap-in, because you must use the Active Directory Users and Computers snap-in instead.

Activity 4-4: Creating User Accounts in Active Directory

Time Required: Approximately 15 minutes
Objective: Learn how to create a user account in Active Directory.

Description: Management and access to resources through Active Directory begins through user accounts. In this activity, you learn how to set up a new account.

1. Click **Start**, click **Run**, type **mmc**, and click **OK**. Maximize the console windows, if necessary. Click the **File** menu and click **Add/Remove Snap-in**. Under the Available snap-ins, click **Active Directory Users and Computers** and click **Add**. Click **OK**.

2. In the left pane, click the **plus sign** in front of **Active Directory Users and Computers**, if necessary, to display the elements under it. Click the **plus sign** in front of the domain name, such as jpcomp.com, to display the folders and OUs under it.

3. Click the **Users** folder in the left pane.
   - Are any accounts already created? What groups are shown along with the accounts?

4. Click the **Action** menu or right-click **Users** in the left pane, point to **New**, and click **User**.

5. Type your first name in the First name box, type your middle initial (no period), and type your last name with the word "Test" appended to it in the Last name box (for example, RyanTest). Enter your initials with Test appended to them in the User logon name box (for example, JRTest), as shown in Figure 4-13.
   - What options are automatically completed for you?

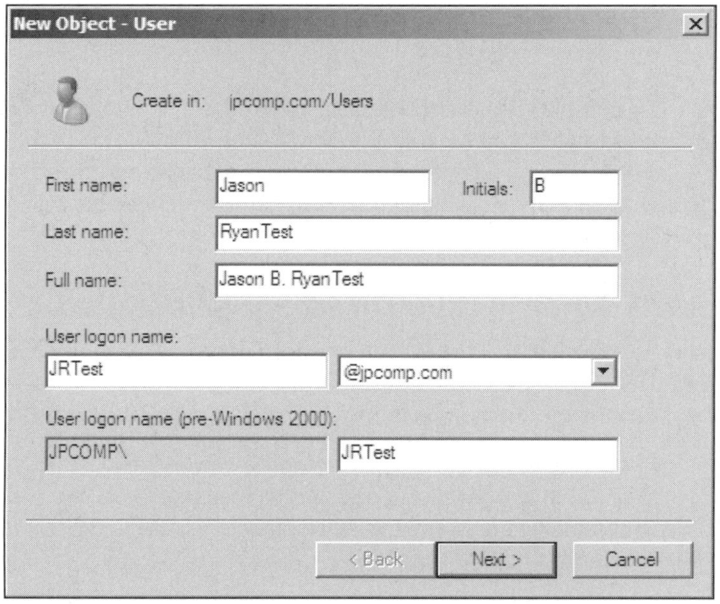

Figure 4-13   Creating a user account

 Many organizations follow a user account naming scheme. For example, some organizations prefer to use account names that consist of the first name initial and the user's last name. Others prefer to use the last name followed by the first name initial. Still others prefer to use a name that matches the job title. The advantage of using last name first is that reports of users' logon names can be printed in alphabetical order. Also, it is easier to find a particular user's account by last name.

6. Click **Next**.

7. Enter a password and enter the password confirmation. Ensure the box is checked for **User must change password at next logon**. This option forces users to enter a new password the first time they log on, so that the account creator will not know their password. The other options include:

   - *User cannot change password*, which means that only the account administrator can change the user's password

   - *Password never expires*, which is used in situations in which an account must always be accessed, such as when a program accesses an account to run a special process

   - *Account is disabled*, which provides a way to prevent access to an account without deleting it

 The Windows Server 2008 default password requirements are enabled when you create an account. A password must be six characters or longer and cannot contain the account name or portions of the user's full name (beyond two characters of the name). Also, a minimum of three of the following four rules apply: includes numbers, includes uppercase letters, includes lowercase letters, includes characters such as $, #, and !.

8. Click **Next**.

9. Verify the information you have entered and click **Finish**.

10. To continue configuring the account, in the right pane, double-click the account you just created, such as RyanTest (alternatively, you can right-click the account and click Properties).

11. Notice the tabs that are displayed for the account properties.

12. Click the **General** tab, if it is not already displayed, and enter a description of the account, such as Test account.

13. Click the **Account** tab to view the information you can enter on it.

14. Click the tabs you have not yet viewed to find out what information can be configured through each one.

15. Click **OK**.

16. Leave the Active Directory Users and Computers window open for the next activity.

 If you need to close the MMC after a project in this chapter, close it and click Yes to save the console settings. Enter a name for the console, such as Manage Accounts, and click Save. You can later open the console by clicking Start, pointing to All Programs, clicking Administrative Tools, and clicking the saved console name.

The following is a brief summary of the account properties that can be set by right-clicking an account and clicking Properties in the Active Directory Users and Computers window (see Figure 4-14).

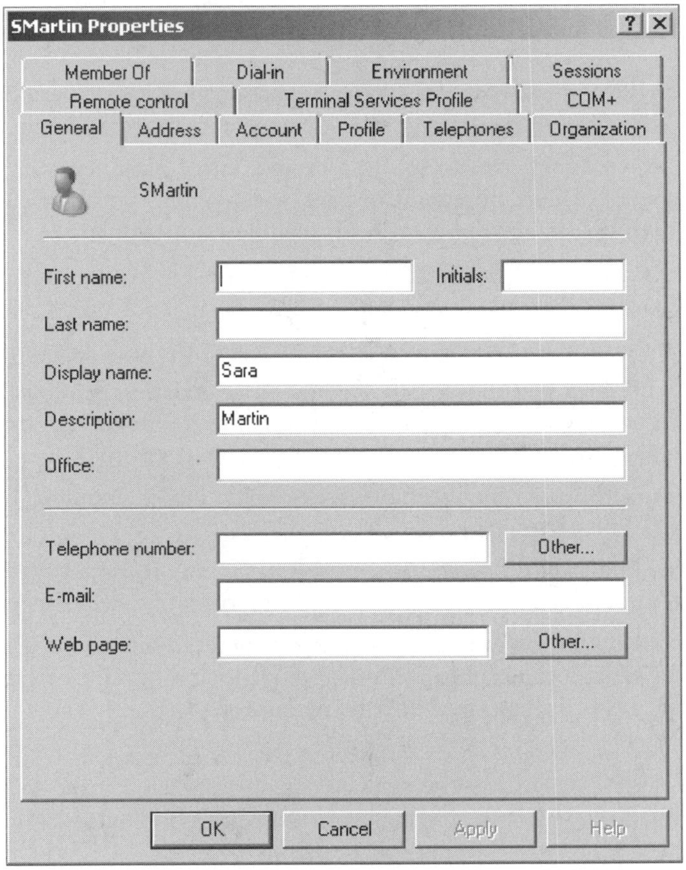

SMartin Properties

| Member Of | Dial-in | Environment | Sessions |

| Remote control | Terminal Services Profile | COM+ |

| General | Address | Account | Profile | Telephones | Organization |

SMartin

First name: | Initials: |

Last name:

Display name: Sara

Description: Martin

Office:

Telephone number: | Other... |

E-mail:

Web page: | Other... |

OK | Cancel | Apply | Help

Figure 4-14 User account properties

- *General tab*—Enables you to enter or modify personal information about the account holder that includes the first name, last name, and name as it is displayed in the console, description of the user or account, office location, telephone number, e-mail address, and Web page. There are also buttons to enter additional telephone numbers and Web page addresses for the account holder.

- *Address tab*—Provides information about the account holder's street address, post office box, city, state or province, postal code, and country or region.

- *Account tab*—Provides information about the logon name, domain name, and account options, such as requiring the user to change her or his password at next logon, and account expiration date, if one applies. A Logon Hours button on this tab enables you to set up an account so that the user only logs on to the domain at designated times, such as only from 8:00 a.m. to 7:00 p.m. Monday through Friday. Also, the Log On To button enables you to limit from which computer a user can log on to the server or domain.

- *Profile tab*—Enables you to associate a particular profile with a user or set of users, such as a common desktop (profiles are discussed later in this chapter). This tab also is used to associate a logon script and a home folder (directory) with an account. A logon script is a file of commands that are executed at logon, and a home folder is disk space on a particular server given to a user to store his or her files.

 You can use the %username% variable to automatically create a user's home folder with her or his logon name. For example, to automatically create a home folder for the user Rkurkowski, simply enter the universal naming convention name and the variable (\\servername\sharename\%username%).

- *Telephones tab*—Enables you to associate specific types of telephone contact numbers for an account holder, which include one or more numbers for home, pager, mobile, fax, and IP phones.

- *Organization tab*—Provides a place to enter the account holder's title, department, company name, and the name of the person who manages the account holder.

- *Remote control tab*—Enables you to set up remote control parameters for a client that uses Terminal Services. The remote control capability enables you to view and manipulate the client session while it is active, in order to troubleshoot problems.

- *Terminal Services Profile tab*—Enables you to set up a user profile for a client that uses Terminal Services.

- *COM+ tab*—Specifies the COM+ partition set of which the user is a member.

- *Member Of tab*—Enables you to add the account to an existing group of users that has the same security and access requirements (you'll learn more about groups later in this chapter). The tab also is used to remove the account from a group.

- *Dial-in tab*—Permits you to control remote access from dial-in modems or from virtual private networks (VPNs).

- *Environment tab*—Enables you to configure the startup environment for clients that access one or more servers using Terminal Services (for running programs on the server).

- *Sessions tab*—Enables you to configure session parameters for a client using Terminal Services, such as a session time limit, a limit on how long a session can be idle, what to do when a connection is broken, and how to reconnect.

 The information on some of these tabs can be extra work to maintain, such as when telephone numbers and office locations change. Keep this in mind as you enter information, so that you don't introduce more work than is necessary or required by your organization.

Disabling, Enabling, and Renaming Accounts

When a user takes a leave of absence, you have the option to disable his or her account. Your organization might also have the practice of disabling accounts when someone leaves, and then later renaming and enabling the account for that person's replacement (this is easier than deleting the account and creating a new one).

Activity 4-5: Disabling, Renaming, and Enabling an Account

Time Required: Approximately 5 minutes

Objective: Practice disabling, renaming, and then enabling an account.

Description: In this activity, you learn how to disable an account, rename the account, and then enable that account.

1. Access the Active Directory Users and Computers window, or if it is closed, open it.

2. Browse to find the account, such as the one for Jason B. RyanTest, you created in Activity 4-4 under the Users folder within the domain that you created.

3. Right-click the account and click **Disable Account** on the shortcut menu, as shown in Figure 4-15.

Figure 4-15 Disabling an account

4. Click **OK** when you see the informational dialog box that verifies you have disabled the account. The account icon will have a down arrow inside a white circle to show that it is disabled. No one can use the account until you enable it.

5. To rename the account, right-click it and click **Rename** (see Figure 4-15). Enter a new name, such as Martin Sanchez, and then press **Enter**.

6. When you see the Rename User dialog box, change the First name and the Last name boxes to reflect the new name. Change the User logon name, such as to MSTest. Click **OK**.

7. Make sure the account is now listed as Martin Sanchez in the Users folder.

8. Right-click the account you renamed and click **Enable Account**. Click **OK**.

   • What happens to the display of the account in the Users folder?

9. Leave the Active Directory Users and Computers window open for the next activity.

Moving an Account

When an employee moves from one department to another, for example from the Payroll Department to the budget office, you might need to move that person's account from one container to another—between OUs, for example.

Activity 4-6: Moving an Account

Time Required: Approximately 5 minutes
Objective: Practice moving an account.

Description: If your organization uses OUs to reflect different departments, then you might need to move accounts between OUs as people are transferred to different departments. In this activity, you move the account you renamed in Activity 4-5 to the OU that you created in Activity 4-3.

1. Access the Active Directory Users and Computers window, or if it is closed, open it.

2. Right-click the account you renamed, such as Martin Sanchez.

3. Click **Move** (refer to Figure 4-15).

4. Find the OU that you created in Activity 4-3, such as SalesOUJP, and click it (see Figure 4-16). Click **OK**.

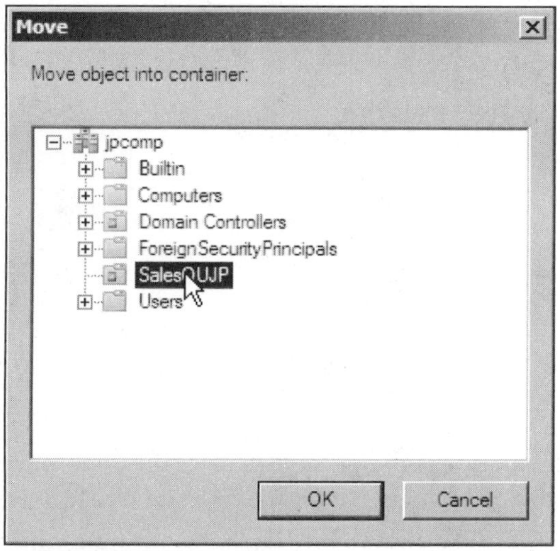

Figure 4-16   Moving an account

5. In the tree of the left pane, double-click the OU to which you moved the account and verify that it is moved.

6. Leave the Active Directory Users and Computers window open for the next activity.

Resetting a Password

Sometimes users change their passwords or go several weeks without logging on—and forget their passwords. You do not have the option to look up a password, but you can reset it for the user. For organizations that have accounts that manage sensitive information, particularly financial information, it is advisable to have specific guidelines that govern the circumstances under which an account password is reset. For example, an organization might require that the account holder physically visit his or her account manager, rather than placing a telephone call—because there is no way to verify the authenticity of the request by telephone.

Accounts that handle financial information are typically audited by independent financial auditors. These auditors might require that you keep records of each time a password is reset, so that they can examine them along with other financial information.

Activity 4-7: Changing an Account's Password

Time Required: Approximately 5 minutes

Objective: Practice changing an account's password.

Description: One of the most common account management tasks is resetting passwords. In this activity, you learn how to reset the password for a user.

1. Access the Active Directory Users and Computers window, or open it if it is closed.

2. Open the OU that you created in Activity 4-3, if it is not already open, so that you can see the account you created and renamed.

3. Right-click the account for which you want to reset the password, such as Martin Sanchez.

4. Click **Reset Password** (refer to Figure 4-15).

5. Enter the new password and then confirm it.

6. Ensure that the box is checked for **User must change password at next logon** (see Figure 4-17). Checking this box enables you to force the user to change the password you set, so that you will not know the new password, which is a best practice endorsed by Microsoft and often a requirement of financial auditors who scrutinize networks that handle financial information.

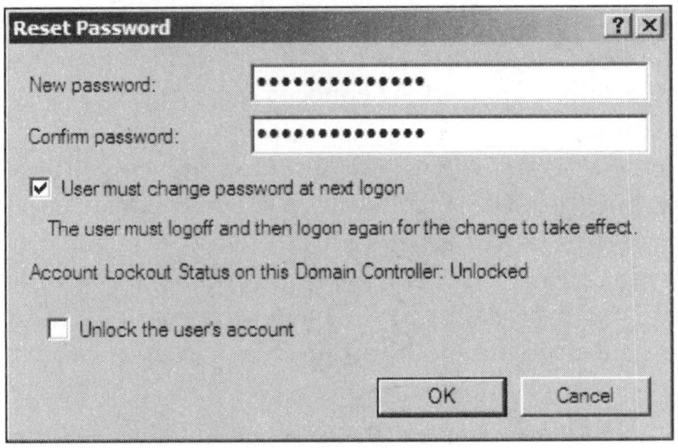

Figure 4-17   Resetting a password

Notice in Figure 4-17 that you can also unlock an account that has been locked. You might need to unlock an account when a user has unsuccessfully tried to log on too many times and the account goes into a locked status for a prespecified interval.

7. Click **OK** in the Reset Password dialog box. Click **OK** in the information message box.

8. Leave the Active Directory Users and Computers window open for the next activity.

Deleting an Account

Plan to practice good account management by deleting accounts that are no longer in use. If you don't, the number of dormant accounts might grow into a confused tangle of accounts, and you expose your company to security risks. When you delete an account, its globally unique identifier (GUID) is also deleted and will not be reused even if you create another account using the same name.

Activity 4-8: Deleting an Account

Time Required: Approximately 5 minutes
Objective: Practice deleting an account.

Description: In this project, you delete the account that you renamed in Activity 4-5.

1. Access the Active Directory Users and Computers window, or open it if it is closed.

2. Open the OU that you created in Activity 4-3, if it is not already open, so that you can see the account you created and renamed.

3. Right-click the account you want to delete, such as Martin Sanchez, and click **Delete** (refer to Figure 4-15).

4. Click **Yes** to verify that you want to delete this account.

5. Close the Active Directory Users and Computers window. Click **Yes** when asked to save the console settings, enter a name for the console (such as Manage Accounts) if you haven't previously, and click Save.

Security Group Management

One of the best ways to manage accounts is by grouping accounts that have similar characteristics, such as those that are in a single department, in a specific project group, or that access the same folders and printers. The group management concept saves time by eliminating repetitive steps in managing user and resource access.

Windows 2000 Server, Windows Server 2003, and Windows Server 2008 expand on the concept of groups from the one originally used in Windows NT Server. The two types of groups in Windows NT Server are local groups used to manage resources on a single workstation or on domain controllers in one domain and global groups used to manage resources across multiple domains. With the introduction of Active Directory, newer versions of Windows Server expand the use of groups through the concept of **scope of influence** (or **scope**), which is the reach of a group for gaining access to resources in Active Directory. When Active Directory is not implemented, the scope of a group is limited to the stand-alone server, and only local groups are created. In contrast, the implementation of Active Directory increases the scope from a local server or domain to all domains in a forest. The types of groups and their associated scopes are as follows:

- *Local*—Used on stand-alone servers that are not part of a domain; scope of this type of group does not go beyond the local server on which it is defined

- *Domain local*—Used when there is a single domain or to manage resources in a particular domain so that global and universal groups can access those resources

- *Global*—Used to manage group accounts from the same domain so that those accounts can access resources in the same and in other domains

- *Universal*—Used to provide access to resources in any domain within a forest

All of these groups can be used for security or distribution groups. **Security groups** are used to enable access to resources on a stand-alone server or in Active Directory. **Distribution groups** are used for e-mail or telephone lists, to provide quick, mass distribution of information. In this section, the focus is on security groups.

Implementing Local Groups

A **local security group** is used to manage resources on a stand-alone computer that is not part of a domain and on member servers in a domain (non-DCs). For example, you might use a local group in a small office situation with only 5, 15, or 30 users. Consider an office of mineral resource consultants in which there are 18 user accounts on the server. Four of these accounts are used by the founding partners of the consulting firm, who manage employee hiring, payroll, schedules, and general accounting. Seven accounts are for consultants who specialize in coal-bed methane extraction, and the seven remaining accounts belong to consultants who work with oil extraction. In this situation, the company might decide not to install Active Directory, and divide these accounts into three local groups. One group would be called Managers and consist of the four founding partners. Another group would be called CBM for the coal-bed methane consultants, and the third group would be called Oil and be used for the oil consultants. Each group would be given different security access based on the resources at the server, which would include access to folders and to printers.

You create local groups by using the Local Users and Groups MMC snap-in.

Implementing Domain Local Groups

A **domain local security group** is used when Active Directory is deployed. This type of group is typically used to manage resources in a domain and to give global groups from the same and other domains access to those resources. As shown in Table 4-1, a domain local group can contain user accounts, global groups, and universal groups.

Table 4-1 Membership capabilities of a domain local group

Active Directory objects that can be members of a domain local group	Active Directory objects that a domain local group can join as a member
User accounts in the same domain	Access control (security) lists for objects in the same domain, such as permissions to access a folder, shared folder, or printer
Domain local groups in the same domain	Domain local groups in the same domain
Global groups in any domain in a tree or forest (as long as there are transitive or two-way trust relationships maintained)	
Universal groups in any domain in a tree or forest (as long as there are transitive or two-way trust relationships maintained)	

The scope of a domain local group is the domain in which the group exists, but you can convert a domain local group to a universal group as long as the domain local group does not contain any other domain local groups. Also, to convert any group, the domain must be in the Windows Server 2003 or Windows Server 2008 domain functional level.

Although a domain local group can contain any combination of accounts, global, and universal groups, the typical purpose of a domain local group is to provide access to resources, which means that you grant access to servers, folders, shared folders, and printers to a domain local group. Under most circumstances, you should plan to put domain local groups in access control lists only, and the members of domain local groups should be mainly global groups. An **access control list (ACL)** is a list of security descriptors (privileges) that have been set up for a particular object, such as a shared folder or shared printer. Generally, a domain local group does not contain accounts, because account management is more efficient when you handle it through global groups. Examples of using domain local groups with global groups are presented in the next section.

You'll learn more about how ACLs are configured as you learn about permissions in Chapter 5, "Configuring, Managing, and Troubleshooting Resource Access."

Implementing Global Groups

A **global security group** is intended to contain user accounts from a single domain and can also be set up as a member of a domain local group in the same or another domain. This capability gives global groups a broader scope than domain local groups, because their members can access resources in other domains. A global group can contain user accounts and other global groups from the domain in which it was created.

Nesting global groups to reflect the structure of OUs means that global groups can be layered. For example, your organization might consist of an OU for management, an OU under the management OU for the Finance Department, and an OU under the Finance Department for the Budget office—resulting in three levels of OUs. Also, you might have a global group composed of the accounts of vice presidents in the management OU, a global group of accounts for supervisors in the Finance Department OU, and a global group of all members of the Budget office in the budget OU. The global group membership can be set up to reflect the structure of OUs, as shown in Figure 4-18.

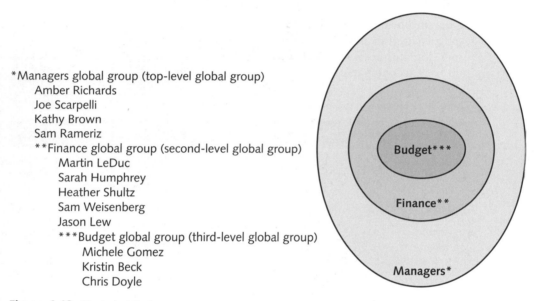

```
*Managers global group (top-level global group)
    Amber Richards
    Joe Scarpelli
    Kathy Brown
    Sam Rameriz
    **Finance global group (second-level global group)
        Martin LeDuc
        Sarah Humphrey
        Heather Shultz
        Sam Weisenberg
        Jason Lew
        ***Budget global group (third-level global group)
            Michele Gomez
            Kristin Beck
            Chris Doyle
```

Figure 4-18 Nested global groups

 Plan nesting of global groups carefully. You can convert a global group to a universal group at a later time, but only if it is not a member of another global group.

A global group can be converted to a universal group as long as it is not nested in another global group or in a universal group. In the example shown in Figure 4-18, the Finance and Budget global groups cannot be converted to universal groups because they already are members of the Managers and Finance groups, respectively.

A typical use for a global group is to build it with accounts that need access to resources in the same or in another domain, and then to make the global group in one domain a member of a domain local group in the same or another domain. This model enables you to manage user accounts and their access to resources through one or more global groups, while reducing the complexity of managing accounts.

For example, consider a college that has a domain for students, a domain for faculty and staff, and a domain for research organizations that are associated with the college. The college's executive council, consisting of the college president and vice presidents, needs access to resources in all three domains. One way to enable the executive council to have access is to create a domain local group called LocalExec in each domain that provides the appropriate access to folders, files, and other resources. Next, create a GlobalExec global group in the faculty and staff domain that has the president's and vice presidents' user accounts as members (see Figure 4-19). These steps enable you to manage security for all of their accounts at one time from one global group. If the president or a vice president leaves to take another job, you simply delete (or disable) that person's account from the global group and later add an account (or rename and enable the old account) for her or his replacement. You also can manage access to resources in each domain one time through each domain local group, resulting in much less management work. If a new printer is added to a domain, for example, you can give the domain local group full privileges to the printer.

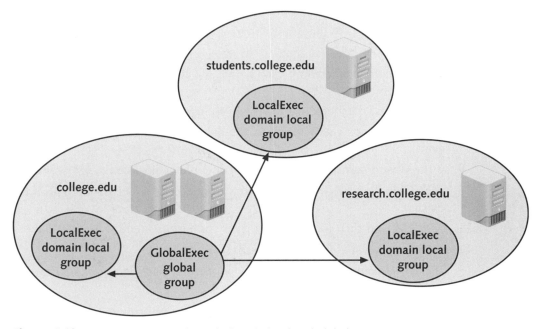

Figure 4-19   Managing security through domain local and global groups

When the Active Directory structure becomes complex enough in a large organization so that many domains, trees, and forests are in use, global groups are used as members of universal groups to manage accounts, as described in the next section, "Implementing Universal Groups."

Activity 4-9: Creating Domain Local and Global Security Groups

Time Required: Approximately 15 minutes
Objective: Create a domain local and a global security group and make the global group a member of the domain local group.

Description: In this activity, assume that you have been asked to set up groups to manage access for the managers in an Active Directory that has four domains. You will practice beginning the setup by creating a domain local group that will be used to manage resources and a global group of accounts. Last, you will add the global group to the domain local group. To complete the activity, you will first need an environment in which Active Directory is installed, and two accounts that are already set up by your instructor (or that you create in advance). You'll also need to have an account that has Administrator privileges.

1. Open the MMC you have previously saved for accessing the Active Directory Users and Computers tool. For example, if you saved the MMC using the name Manage Accounts, then click **Start**, point to **All Programs**, click **Administrative Tools**, and click **Manage Accounts**. Expand the windows, if necessary. (Another way to access the Active Directory

Users and Computers tool is to click **Start**, point to **Administrative Tools**, and click **Active Directory Users and Computers**.)

2. In the tree in the left pane, double-click **Active Directory Users and Computers**, and the domain, such as jpcomp.com, if the contents of these are not displayed in the tree.

3. Click **Users** in the tree.

4. Click the **Action** menu, point to **New**, and click **Group**.

   • What defaults are already selected in the New Object–Group dialog box?

5. In the Group name box, enter **DomainMgrs** plus your initials, for example DomainMgrsJP.

   • What is the pre-Windows 2000 group name?

6. Click **Domain local** under Group scope, and click **Security** (if it is not already selected) under Group type.

7. Click **OK** and then look for the group you just created in the right pane within the Users folder.

8. Click the **Create a new group in the current container** icon on the button bar (with two heads).

9. In the Group name box, type **GlobalMgrs** plus your initials, for example GlobalMgrsJP.

10. Click **Global** under Group scope, and click **Security** under Group type, if they are not already selected.

11. Click **OK** and then look for the group you just created in the right pane.

12. Double-click the global group you created.

13. Click the **Members** tab. Notice that no members are currently associated with this group.

14. Click the **Add** button.

15. Click the **Advanced** button in the Select Users, Contacts, Computers, or Groups dialog box.

16. Click **Find Now**.

17. Click the first user provided by your instructor, press and hold down the **CTRL** key and click the second user provided by your instructor. Click **OK** (see Figure 4-20).

18. Make sure that the users you selected are shown in the Select Users, Contacts, Computers, or Groups dialog box. Click **OK**.

19. Again, be sure that both accounts are shown in the Members box on the Members tab. Click **OK**.

20. Double-click the domain local group, such as DomainMgrsJP, and then click the **Members** tab.

   • What members are shown?

21. Click **Add**.

22. Click **Advanced** in the Select Users, Contacts, Computers, or Groups dialog box.

23. Click **Find Now**.

24. Locate the global group you created, such as **GlobalMgrsJP**. Click that global group and click **OK**.

25. Verify that the global group is displayed in the Select Users, Contacts, Computers, or Groups dialog box, and then click **OK**.

26. Make sure the global group is listed under Members on the Members tab. Click **OK**.

27. Close the MMC and click **Yes** to save the console settings. If you haven't already given the console a name, enter a name for it, such as Manage Accounts, and click **Save**.

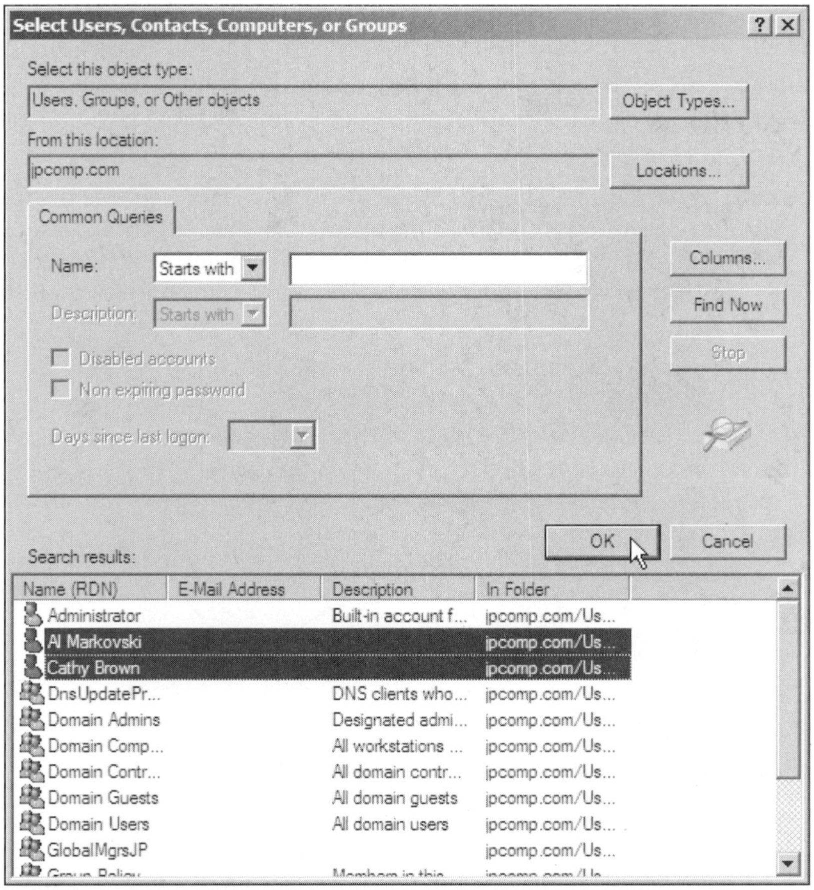

Figure 4-20   Adding user accounts as global group members

Implementing Universal Groups

In an Active Directory context in which there are multiple hierarchies of domains, trees, and forests, **universal security groups** provide a means to span domains and trees. Universal group membership can include user accounts from any domain, global groups from any domain, and other universal groups from any domain.

    Universal groups are offered to provide an easy means to access any resource in a tree or among trees in a forest. If you carefully plan the use of universal groups, then you can manage security for single accounts with a minimum of effort. Planning is done in relation to the scope of access required for a group of accounts. Here are some guidelines to help simplify how you plan to use groups:

- Use global groups to hold accounts as members—and keep the nesting of global groups to a minimum (or do not use nesting) to avoid confusion. Give accounts access to resources by making the global groups to which they belong members of domain local groups or universal groups or both.

- Use domain local groups to provide access to resources in a specific domain. Avoid placing accounts in domain local groups—but do make domain local groups members of access control lists for specific resources in the domain, such as shared folders and printers.

- Use universal groups to provide extensive access to resources, particularly when Active Directory contains trees and forests, or to simplify access when there are multiple domains. Make universal groups members of access control lists for objects in any domain, tree, or forest. Manage user account access by placing accounts in global groups and joining global groups to domain local or universal groups, depending on which is most appropriate to the scope required for access.

If you attempt to create a new universal group, but find that the radio button in the Create New Object – (Group) dialog box is deactivated, this means that the domain is set up in Windows 2000 domain functional level and you must convert the domain to the Windows Server 2003 or Windows Server 2008 domain functional level.

In the example of setting up access for the executive council in a college that has three domains, an alternative is to create one universal group that has access to all resources in the three domains—create one global group containing the president and vice presidents, and make that global group a member of the universal group. This model has only two groups to manage, as shown in Figure 4-21.

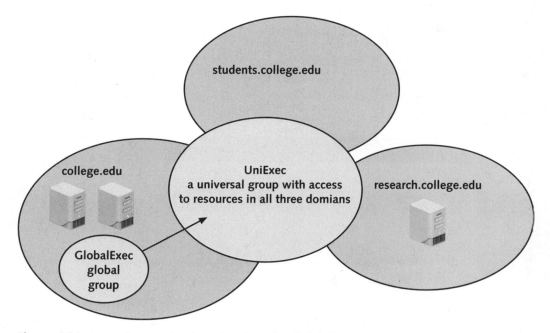

Figure 4-21 Managing security through universal and global groups

Properties of Groups

All of the groups that you can create in Windows Server 2008 have a set of properties that can be configured. As you probably noticed in Activity 4-9, you can configure the properties of a specific group by double-clicking that group in the Local Users and Groups tool for a stand-alone (non-domain) or member server, or in the Active Directory Users and Computers tool for DC servers in a domain. The properties are configured using the following tabs:

- *General*—Used to enter a description of the group, change the scope and type of group, and provide e-mail addresses for a distribution group
- *Members*—Used to add members to a group, such as adding user accounts to a global group, and enables members to be removed
- *Member Of*—Used to make the group a member of another group, or to remove the group's membership
- *Managed By*—Used to establish an account or group that will manage the group, if the manager is other than the server administrator; also, the location, telephone number, and fax number of the manager can be provided

Implementing User Profiles

Client access to Windows Server 2008 can be customized through user profiles. A **local user profile** is automatically created at the local computer when you log on with an account for the first time, and the profile can be modified to consist of desktop settings that are customized for one or more clients who log on locally.

User profiles provide the following advantages:

- Multiple users can use the same computer and maintain their own customized settings. When users log on, they receive their own personalized settings that were saved when they last logged off.

- Profiles can be stored on a network server so they are available to users regardless of the computer they use to log on.

- Profiles can be made mandatory so users have the same settings each time they log on. When a user logs on, she can modify the settings but the changes are never saved when the user logs off.

 Profiles are used in Microsoft operating systems to provide a consistent working environment for one or more users. A local user profile is a particular desktop setup that always starts in the same way and is stored on the local computer. A roaming profile is a desktop setup that starts in the same way from any computer used to access an account, including remote connections from home or on the road. In a network environment where users are moving between computers, a roaming profile is ideal so the users' settings are available from any computer.

For example, if there are two server administrators and two backup operators who primarily run backups, you might create one profile for the administrators and a different one for the backup operators. That can be useful if each type of account needs to have certain program icons, startup programs, or some other prearranged desktop settings. Also, a user profile can be set up on a server so it is downloaded to the client workstation each time a specific account is logged on. This is a **roaming profile**, which enables a user to start off with the same desktop setup, no matter which computer she or he uses. In some circumstances, you need to set up profiles so that certain users cannot change their profiles. This is done by creating a **mandatory user profile** in which the user does not have permission to update the folder containing his profile. A mandatory user profile overrides the user's locally stored profile if it has been changed from the version stored on the server. This means that when a user logs on, he can make changes to the profile and customize it, but when the user logs off the changes are not saved. To make a server profile (either local or roaming) mandatory, you can rename the user's Ntuser.dat file to Ntuser.man. A specific user's profile can be placed under the /User/*Accountname* folder in Windows Server 2008, for instance.

One way to set up a profile is to first set up a generic account on the server or use the Guest account as a model with the desired desktop configuration, including desktop icons, shortcut folders, and programs in the Startup folder to start when the client workstation starts. Then copy the Ntuser.dat file to the \Users\Default folder in Windows Server 2008. This step makes that profile the default for new users. You can also create a profile to use as a roaming profile for specific users. To create the roaming profile, set up a generic account and customize the desktop. For example, you might create an account called BUDGET for users in the budget office and customize the desktop, Start menu, and network and printer connections. After you create that account, set up those users to access that profile by opening the Profile tab in each user's account properties (see Figure 4-22) and entering the path to that profile. You can also use the System applet in the Control Panel Classic View to copy profiles from one location to another.

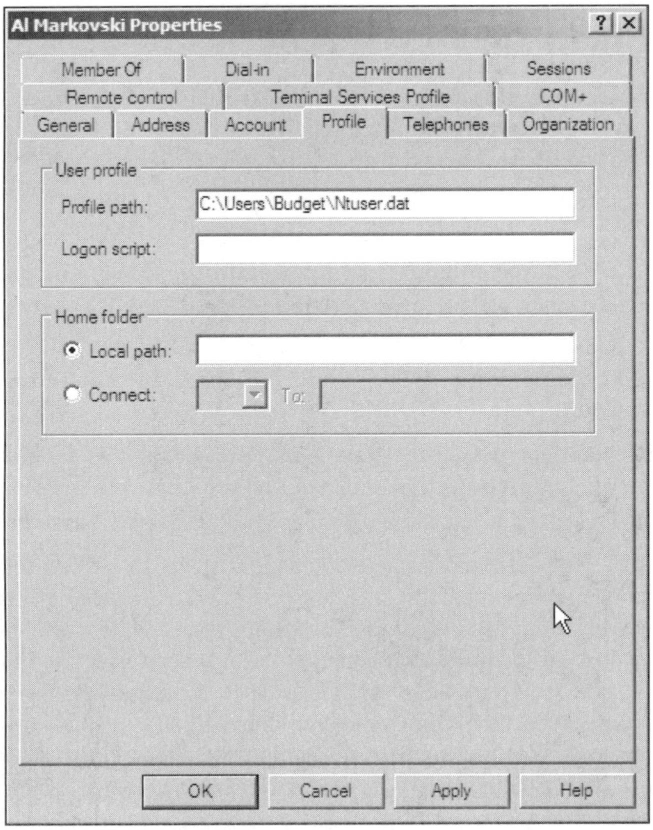

Figure 4-22   Setting a roaming profile in an account's properties

 **CAUTION**   Windows Server 2008 and Windows Vista use the version 2 format for user profiles, while earlier Windows operating systems use version 1. Version 1 and version 2 user profiles are not compatible. If you want to migrate user profiles from an earlier operating system to Windows Server 2008 or to Windows Vista, use the User State Migration Tool (USMT) from Microsoft. For more information, visit: *http://support.microsoft.com/kb/947025*.

What's New in Windows Server 2008 Active Directory

Windows Server 2008 Active Directory offers many new features. Five new features deserve particular mention:

- Restart capability
- Read-Only Domain Controller
- Auditing improvements
- Multiple password and account lockout policies in a single domain
- Active Directory Lightweight Directory Services role

Restart Capability

In Windows Server 2000 and 2003, if you need to service Active Directory on a particular domain controller, such as to defragment its database, you need to follow these steps:

1. Take down the server.

2. Restart in Directory Services Restore Mode.

3. Log on using the special administrator account for Active Directory.

4. Perform the servicing task.

5. Reboot the server.

This older method can involve considerable downtime. Windows Server 2008 provides the option to stop Active Directory Domain Services without taking down the computer. After your work is done on Active Directory, you simply restart Active Directory Domain Services. The general steps to stop and restart Active Directory Domain Services are as follows:

1. Click Start, point to Administrative Tools, and click Server Manager.

2. Under the tree in the left pane, click the plus sign next to Configuration.

3. Click Services in the tree.

4. Click Active Directory Domain Services.

5. Click Stop the service, as shown in Figure 4-23.

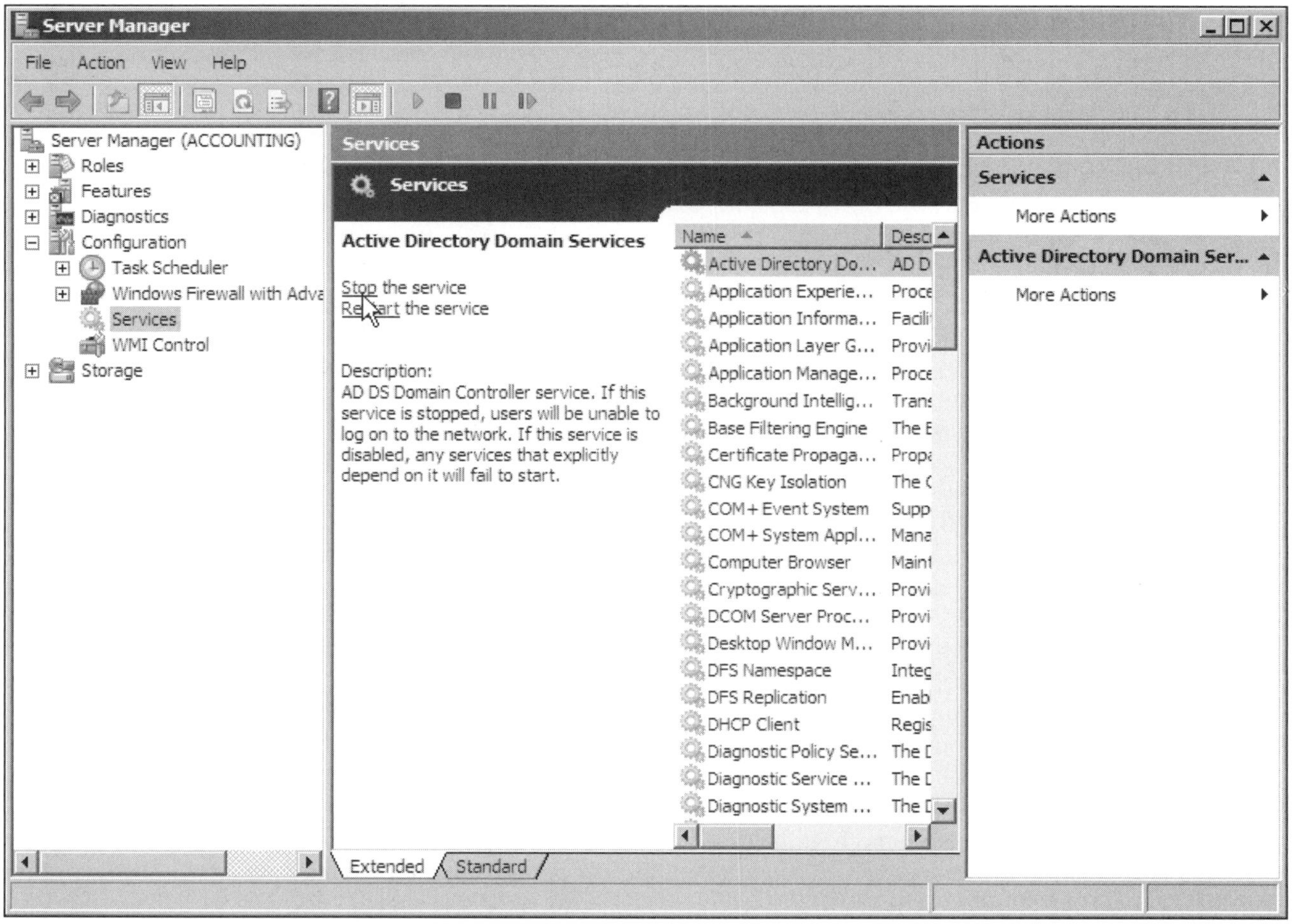

Figure 4-23 Stopping Active Directory Domain Services

6. Click Yes to confirm the other services that will be stopped along with Active Directory Domain Services.

7. Complete your work on Active Directory.

8. Go back into Server Manager and repeat Steps 2 through 4, if necessary.

9. Click Start the service.

10. Close Server Manager.

Read-Only Domain Controller

The most advertised update to Active Directory is the implementation of the Read-Only Domain Controller. As you learned earlier in this chapter, normal DCs replicate information to one another. If a new account is created or a password is changed, this information is replicated to all DCs on a network. A **Read-Only Domain Controller (RODC)** is different in that you cannot use it to update information in Active Directory and it does not replicate to regular DCs. If a company uses Distributed File System (DFS, see Chapter 2, "Installing Windows Server 2008"), shared files in DFS are only updated to the RODC, but the RODC cannot update DFS files to the entire network.

An RODC can still function as a Key Distribution Center for the Kerberos authentication method that is the default authentication in Windows Server 2008 (see Chapter 10 to learn about Kerberos). It acts as a Key Distribution Center contacting a DC (all DCs are Key Distribution Centers) when a user first requests to log on. The user's account credentials are then loaded into cache (memory) on the RODC so the credentials can be verified from the RODC for future logons by that user.

An RODC can only function as a Key Distribution Center for user credentials if you first configure the Password Replication Policy in Active Directory to allow it. You learn about configuring policies in Chapter 10.

At this point, you're probably wondering why this is an important addition to Active Directory. The purpose of having an RODC is for better security at branch locations, where physical security measures might not be as strong as at a central office. Take, for example, a national investment company that invests in mutual funds, stocks, and other securities for its clients. The company has a home office in Chicago and branch offices throughout the United States. Each branch office has a server that is configured as an RODC. Some branch offices keep the server in a locked room, but some have only open office locations and the server is not physically secured from theft. Also, there is no trained server administrator at each branch office, only a regular employee who is given general responsibility for the server.

In this example, the central office can delegate authority over the RODC to a relatively untrained person at the branch office, who would not have access to change Active Directory at the local RODC in any significant way. Additionally, that employee could make no changes to Active Directory that would affect the entire company. If an unauthorized person, such as a night cleaning person, attempts to create an account or make a change to Active Directory, he can't do it. He also can't upload a bogus or virus-infected file via DFS to all DCs on the network. This protects the entire network from Active Directory intrusions coming from a less secure branch office, and also reduces the risk of spreading viruses. If the branch office server is stolen, the thieves only have access to the Key Distribution Center credentials stored in the RODC's cache, and not the credentials of everyone in the company. In the event of a theft, the account credentials of users at one branch are much easier to change on a moment's notice than the credentials for all users in the company.

In the past, some organizations chose not to have DCs at branch offices, even though this makes logon credential authentication slower because it has to go over a busy wide area network (WAN) connection to a central office DC. Also, access to shared files through DFS is slower for the same reason. With Windows Server 2008 Active Directory, the security concerns of these companies are addressed by using an RODC, which also raises user productivity through faster network access.

Another advantage of having an RODC at the branch site is that it can be configured as a DNS server. This means DNS translations can be performed locally, which reduces WAN traffic and provides users with faster response.

To further enhance the security on an RODC, you can combine it with the new BitLocker Drive Encryption, which enables data encryption and protected data deletion in Windows Server 2008 data volumes, including Active Directory data. With this protection enabled, even if your server is stolen, thieves won't be able to get much valuable information from it. You learn about BitLocker Drive Encryption in Chapter 10.

Auditing Improvements

New auditing capabilities were introduced for Active Directory in the Windows Server 2003 R2 version of the operating system and have been continued in Active Directory. Server administrators can now create an audit trail of many types of changes that might be made in Active Directory, including when:

- There are attribute changes to the schema (auditing saves information on both the old and new values)
- Objects are moved, such as user accounts moved from one OU to a different one
- New objects are created, such as a new OU
- A container or object is deleted and then brought back, even if it is moved to a different location than where it was originally located

All of these actions can be recorded in terms of successful completion or if they fail for some reason. You can track the audited actions by regularly viewing the security log. The security log can be accessed by clicking Start, pointing to Administrative Tools, selecting Server Manager, expanding Diagnostics in the tree, double-clicking Event Viewer, and opening the Security Log in the middle pane. (You learn more about examining logs in Chapter 12, "Managing System Reliability and Availability.")

The reason for tracking Active Directory changes is that many organizations now include this as part of their written security policy. Also, financial and computer system auditors expect this kind of tracking information. Active Directory is central to many Windows Server networks, and tracking changes to it is a sound security practice.

You must set up Active Directory auditing in two places:

1. Enable a Domain Controllers (global) Policy to audit successful or failed Active Directory change actions.
2. Configure successful or failed change actions on specific Active Directory objects or containers.

The general steps to configure the global audit policy are as follows:

1. Click Start, point to Administrative Tools, and click Group Policy Management.
2. If necessary, click the plus sign in front of the forest, such as *Forest: jpcomp.com*, in the left pane under Group Policy Management.
3. If necessary, click the plus sign in front of Domains.
4. Double-click the domain name.
5. Click the plus sign in front of Domain Controllers.
6. Right-click Default Domain Controllers Policy, and click Edit in the shortcut menu.
7. In the right pane, double-click Computer Configuration.
8. Double-click the Policies folder (in some editions you might not see this folder).
9. Double-click Windows Settings.
10. Double-click Security Settings.
11. Double-click Local Policies.
12. Double-click Audit Policy.
13. Double-click Audit directory service access (see Figure 4-24).
14. Click Define these policy settings.

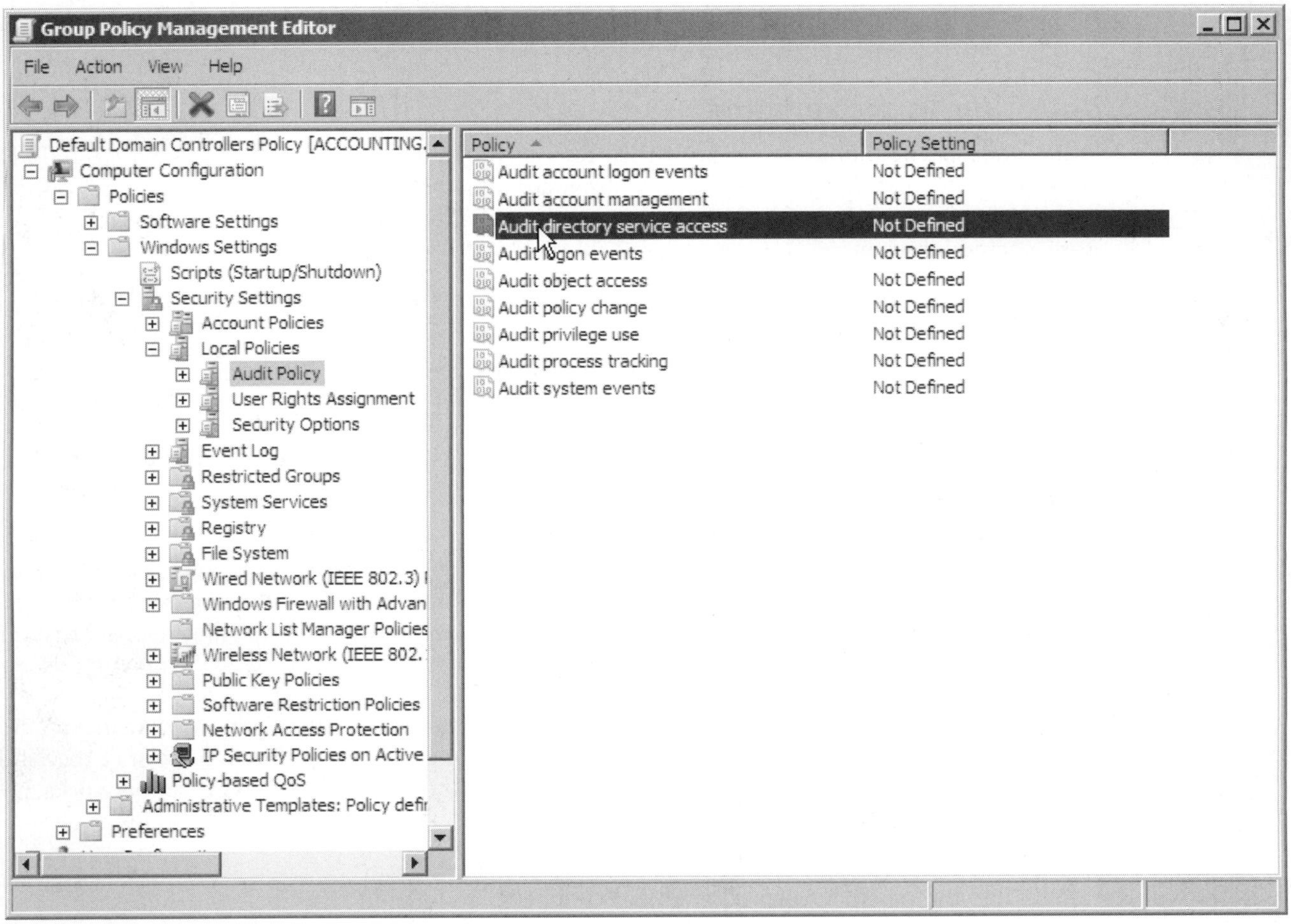

Figure 4-24   Setting up directory service access auditing

15. Click Success, Failure, or both (it is recommended that you click both to enable them for the domain controllers policy). Click OK.

16. Close the Group Policy Management Editor.

After you have configured the domain controller policy to enable Active Directory auditing, you can configure auditing on an individual object in Active Directory. For example, to audit events associated with a domain, follow these general steps:

1. Click Start, point to Administrative Tools, and click Active Directory Users and Computers.

2. Click the domain in the tree.

3. Click the View menu and click Advanced Features.

4. Right-click the domain in the tree and click Properties.

5. Click the Security tab in the domain Properties dialog box.

6. Click the Advanced button on the Security tab.

7. Click the Auditing tab.

8. In the Advanced Security Settings dialog box, click the Administrators (*domainname*\Administrators) group.

9. Click the Edit button.

10. In the Auditing Entry dialog box (see Figure 4-25), select the domain objects and actions that you want to audit for Successful and Failed modifications, such as Delete actions or actions to Create User objects (accounts) or Create Shared Folder objects.

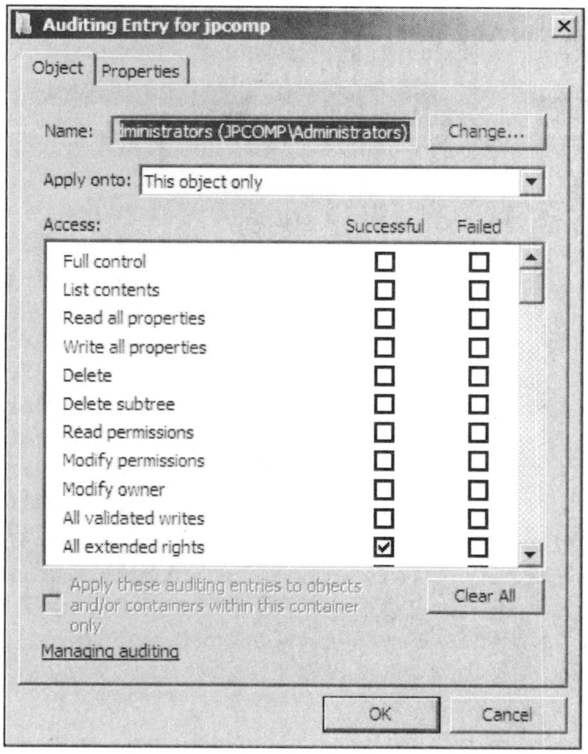

Figure 4-25 Configuring object auditing for a domain

11. Click OK.

12. Click OK in the Advanced Security Settings dialog box.

13. Click OK in the domain Properties dialog box.

14. Close the Active Directory Users and Computers window.

Multiple Password and Account Lockout Policies in a Single Domain

Before Windows Server 2008, Active Directory administrators could not establish different account lockout policies in the same domain. An account lockout policy is one that locks a user account in certain situations. For example, you can set up a policy that protects an account from intruders by locking it after five unsuccessful logon attempts. This discourages an intruder from trying all kinds of password combinations until the right one is found to break into an account. Also, an administrator could require that a password be a certain length or have other characteristics to make it hard to guess.

In the past, an administrator could set only one password and lockout policy to apply to all accounts. That policy, for example, might require a minimum of seven characters in a password and would lock accounts for 30 minutes after four wrong passwords are entered. (The only way to unlock the account before 30 minutes in this example is for the administrator to do this manually.) With this policy governing every account, there might be some accounts for which the security policy is too severe or too lenient. For example, an organization might want to make access more secure for accounts with Administrator privileges by setting account lockout to go into effect for one hour after only three unsuccessful logon attempts. Also, the organization might want such accounts to be required to have longer, hard-to-guess passwords. Additionally, for accounts that have little access to resources, such as guest accounts for visitors that are only allowed to access the Internet, the account lockout policy might be to never lock out the account and have the same short password for each account.

In Windows Server 2008, you can set up multiple password and account lockout security requirements and associate them with a security group or user. There is also a way to associate them with an OU by creating a "global shadow security group," which is a group that can be mapped to an OU. This process is called setting up "fine-grained password policies." You learn how to configure password and lockout policies in Chapter 10.

Active Directory Lightweight Directory Services Role

As you learned in Chapter 2, the Active Directory Lightweight Directory Services (AD LDS) role is targeted for servers that manage user applications. This enables the applications to store configuration and vital data in a central database. AD LDS is a skeleton version of Active Directory Domain Services, housing only those elements needed for central configuration and data management required by applications, including directory replication and security services. No services are provided for managing domains and domain resources, such as user accounts and computers. AD LDS is more forgiving than AD DS, because if you make a mistake in a modification the mistake in most circumstances does not affect how users access their accounts and resources in a domain.

AD LDS is installed as a server role via Server Manager. After the installation, you can use the Active Directory Lightweight Directory Services Setup Wizard to create an "instance" or application directory. The new instance is separate from AD DS. This means that AD LDS can be installed on a server that either has or does not have AD DS installed. To start the wizard, click Start, point to Administrative Tools, and click Active Directory Lightweight Directory Services Setup Wizard.

Chapter Summary

- Active Directory (or AD DS) is a directory service to house information about network resources including servers, computers, user accounts, printers, and management and security policies. AD DS is like a central management center for a Windows Server network.

- Servers housing Active Directory are called domain controllers (DCs), and the same Active Directory information is replicated to every DC.

- The most basic component of Active Directory is an object. Each object is defined through an information set called a schema.

- The global catalog stores information about every object, replicates key Active Directory elements, and is used to authenticate user accounts when they log on.

- A namespace consists of using the Domain Name System for resolving computer and domain names to IP addresses and vice versa. Named objects in Active Directory also exist in a namespace. Active Directory requires a Domain Name System server to help with the management of network resources.

- Active Directory is a hierarchy of logical containers: forests, trees, domains, and organizational units. Forests are the highest-level containers; organizational units are the lowest level. Another important container is the site, which is created out of IP subnets.

- You can delegate management of many Active Directory containers to specific types of administrators to match the structure of your organization.

- User accounts enable individual users to access specific resources, such as folders and files. You can customize account properties as well as manage accounts to disable, enable, rename, move, and delete them. Another common management function is to change user account passwords.

- On a stand-alone or member server, you can create local security groups to help manage user accounts. When Active Directory is installed, you can use domain local, global, and universal security groups for managing access to resources through accounts.

- User profiles are tools for customizing accounts, such as customizing desktop and other user features.

- The ability to stop and restart Active Directory without taking down a DC is new to Windows Server 2008. The implementation of Read-Only Domain Controllers (RODCs) is another new feature for using and securing Active Directory in branch office and remote locations.

- Three additional new features include new Active Directory auditing capabilities, fine-grained password policies, and the Active Directory Lightweight Directory Services role.

Key Terms

access control list (ACL) A list of all security descriptors that have been set up for a particular object, such as for a shared folder or a shared printer.

bridgehead server A domain controller at each Active Directory site with access to a site network link, which is designated as the DC to exchange replication information. There is only one bridgehead server per site. *See* site.

container An Active Directory object that houses other objects, such as a tree that houses domains or a domain that houses organizational units.

contiguous namespace A namespace in which every child object has a portion of its name from its parent object.

directory service A large container (database) of network data and resources, such as computers, printers, user accounts, and user groups, that enables management and fast access to those resources.

disjointed namespace A namespace in which the child object name does not resemble the parent object name.

distribution group A list of users that enables one e-mail message to be sent to all users on the list. A distribution group is not used for security and thus cannot appear in an access control list (ACL).

domain controller (DC) A Windows Server 2003 or 2008 server that contains a full copy of the Active Directory information, is used to add a new object to Active Directory, and replicates all changes made to it so the changes are updated on every DC in the same domain.

domain functional level Refers to the Windows Server operating systems on domain controllers and the domain-specific functions they support. Depending on the functional level, one, two, or all of the following operating systems are supported: Windows 2000 Server, Windows Server 2003, and Windows Server 2008.

domain local security group A group that is used to manage resources—shared folders and printers, for example—in its home domain, and that is primarily used to give global groups access to those resources.

forest A grouping of Active Directory trees that each have contiguous namespaces within their own domain structure, but that have disjointed namespaces between trees. The trees and their domains use the same schema and global catalog.

forest functional level A forest-wide setting that refers to the types of domain controllers in a forest, which can be any combination of Windows 2000 Server, Windows Server 2003, or Windows Server 2008. The level also reflects the types of Active Directory services and functions supported.

global catalog A repository for all objects and the most frequently used attributes for each object in all domains. Each forest has a single global catalog that can be replicated onto multiple servers.

global security group A group that typically contains user accounts from its home domain, and that is a member of domain local groups in the same or other domains, so as to give that global group's member accounts access to the resources defined to the domain local groups.

globally unique identifier (GUID)   A unique number, up to 16 characters long, that is associated with an Active Directory object.

Kerberos transitive trust relationship   A set of two-way trusts between two or more domains (or forests in a forest trust) in which Kerberos security is used.

local security group   A group of user accounts that is used to manage resources on a stand-alone computer.

local user profile   A desktop setup that is associated with one or more accounts to determine what startup programs are used, additional desktop icons, and other customizations. A user profile is local to the computer in which it is stored.

mandatory user profile   A user profile set up by the server administrator that is loaded from the server to the client each time the user logs on; changes that the user makes to the profile are not saved.

member server   A server on an Active Directory managed network that is not installed to have Active Directory.

multimaster replication   Windows Server 2003 and 2008 networks can have multiple servers called DCs that store Active Directory information and replicate it to each other. Because each DC acts as a master, replication does not stop when one DC is down, and updates to Active Directory continue, for example creating a new account.

name resolution   A process used to translate a computer's logical or host name into a network address, such as to a dotted decimal address associated with a computer—and vice versa.

namespace   A logical area on a network that contains directory services and named objects, and that has the ability to perform name resolution.

object   A network resource, such as a server or a user account, that has distinct attributes or properties, is defined in a domain, and exists in Active Directory.

organizational unit (OU)   A grouping of objects within a domain that provides a means to establish specific policies for governing those objects, and that enables object management to be delegated.

Read-Only Domain Controller (RODC)   A domain controller that houses Active Directory information, but cannot be updated, such as to create a new account. This specialized domain controller receives updates from regular DCs, but does not replicate to any DCs because it is read-only by design. *See* domain controller (DC).

roaming profile   Desktop settings that are associated with an account so that the same settings are employed no matter which computer is used to access the account (the profile is downloaded to the client from a server).

schema   Elements used in the definition of each object contained in Active Directory, including the object class and its attributes.

scope of influence (scope)   The reach of a type of group, such as access to resources in a single domain or access to all resources in all domains in a forest (see domain local, global, and universal security groups). (Another meaning for the term scope is the beginning through ending IP addresses defined in a DHCP server for use by DHCP clients; see Chapter 8).

security group   Used to assign a group of users permission to access network resources.

site   An option in Active Directory to interconnect IP subnets so that the server can determine the fastest route to connect clients for authentication and to connect DCs for replication of Active Directory. Site information also enables Active Directory to create redundant routes for DC replication.

transitive trust   A trust relationship between two or more domains in a tree, in which each domain has access to objects in the others.

tree   Related domains that use a contiguous namespace, share the same schema, and have two-way transitive trust relationships.

two-way trust A domain relationship in which both domains are trusted and trusting, enabling one to have access to objects in the other.

universal security group A group that is used to provide access to resources in any domain within a forest. A common implementation is to make global groups that contain accounts members of a universal group that has access to resources.

Review Questions

1. Your company has four departments: Marketing and Sales, Manufacturing, Product Research, and Business. Which of the following Active Directory container design plans might you use to best manage the user accounts and network access needs of each department?

   a. Create four trees.

   b. Create four parent domains in one site.

   c. Create four OUs in one domain.

   d. Create four trees and map them to four domains.

2. Using the example in Question 1, what Active Directory capability can you use to establish different account lockout policies for each of the four departments?

   a. fine-grained password policies

   b. lightweight group policies

   c. password distribution groups

   d. shadow password files

3. Your colleague is trying to create a universal security group for the three administrators of the single stand-alone server in his company. The problem is that he can't find an option to create a universal security group. What is the problem?

   a. He must first create the administrators' personal accounts before it is possible to create a universal group.

   b. He needs to put the account creation tool into the Advanced Features mode.

   c. He must create a universal distribution group first and then create the universal security group.

   d. He cannot create a universal security group on a stand-alone server and must instead create a local security group.

4. One of the DCs in your company reports that it has an Active Directory error. You need to fix it as quickly as possible to reduce downtime. Which of the following tools can you use to stop and restart AD DS on that server? (Choose all that apply.)

   a. Active Directory Domains and Trusts

   b. Server Manager

   c. Device Manager

   d. Active Directory Users and Computers

5. Which of the following server operating systems can be used when the domains in Windows Server 2008 Active Directory are set at the Windows Server 2003 domain functional level? (Choose all that apply.)

   a. Windows NT 4.0 Server with 2008 Domain Services installed

   b. Windows 2000 Server with Service Pack 4

   c. Windows Server 2003

   d. Windows Server 2008

6. Domains in a tree are in a _____ relationship.

7. You've installed the AD DS server role, but find that Active Directory is not fully implemented. What should you do next?

    a. Use Server Manager to create an AD DS partition.

    b. Use Server Manager to create an AD DS security database.

    c. Run *dcpromo*.

    d. Designate a global AD DS server.

8. A _____ is a unique number associated with each object in AD DS.

9. Your school has a parent object named straton.edu and the child object names stratonalum.org and studentarts.org. What kind of namespace is this?

    a. disjointed

    b. distributed

    c. contiguous

    d. coordinated

10. Your company's management has decided that the accounts in all OUs should be set up and managed by the Information Technology Department's security specialist. As the AD DS administrator, how can you best give this capability to the security specialist?

    a. Give her Full Control rights to AD DS.

    b. Make her user account a member of the AD DS Admins local security group.

    c. Use the delegate control feature to give her control of all OUs that contain user accounts.

    d. Give her Accounts Management permissions in AD DS.

11. Name three optional attributes associated with a user account.

12. Which of the following are actions performed by the global catalog? (Choose all that apply.)

    a. provides lookup and access to all resources in all domains

    b. caches IP addresses for all computers in a forest for faster logon

    c. stores shared DFS folders and files for centralized shared file access

    d. authenticates users when they log on

13. The business manager in your organization is leaving, but she has been training the new business manager who will take over the day after she leaves. What AD DS capability can you use to transfer the old business manager's account to the new business manager? Note that in this organization, accounts reflect the actual names of users.

    a. Use the delete and re-create user account feature in AD DS on the day the new business manager takes over.

    b. The only option is to create a new account and then transfer the old business manager's files to the new account on the day the new business manager takes over.

    c. Use the transfer account option in AD DS on the day the new business manager takes over.

    d. Disable the old business manager's account when she leaves work. As soon as the new business manager takes over, rename the account for the new business manager and then enable the account.

14. Your company builds roads and bridges. The home office is located in Ohio. For each construction project, the company establishes a temporary office at the construction site. The project manager for each project takes along a server set up for the AD DS role to connect remotely to the home office. For the sake of security, what should the remote server be?

    a. a DC

    b. an RODC

    c. an AD LDS

    d. an ACL

15. Which of the following is true about all trees in a forest? (Choose all that apply.)

    a. They all use the same schema.

    b. They all use the same OUs.

    c. They all use the same global catalog.

    d. They all use the same groups.

16. You have set up auditing for modifications to Active Directory. Now you want to monitor the results of the auditing. How do you do this?

    a. Set up an audit filter in Device Manager.

    b. Use the Windows Messaging Service to create a constant audit display on your monitor.

    c. Periodically view the security log.

    d. View the audit results in the Active Directory Domains and Trusts MMC snap-in.

17. A site reflects interconnected _____ and is used for DC _____.

18. When you create user accounts, you want to set them up so that users do not have access to use their accounts after 7:00 p.m. on workdays and on weekends as a security measure. From where can you set up these logon restrictions?

    a. You set these restrictions up when you create trust relationships.

    b. These are the default restrictions already set up in AD DS.

    c. You set up these restrictions from the Account tab in the user account properties.

    d. These are properties you can set up when you create a global security group.

19. To reset a password, you use the _____ tool.

20. What is the scope of a domain local security group?

    a. the domain in which the group is created

    b. the OU in which the group is created

    c. the share that the group controls access to

    d. A domain local group does not have a scope, instead it has a range of control.

Case Projects

Advanced Sounds makes audio systems for home entertainment centers, computers, industry, and motor vehicles. Over the past 10 years, this company has pioneered new technologies in audio systems, which have spurred rapid growth. The company has one large office, research, and manufacturing complex in New York City. This complex is divided into the following divisions: Business, Research and Development, Manufacturing, and Distribution. Parts manufacturing centers are located in Quebec City and in Montreal. Advanced Sounds also has seven outlet stores in New York City, four outlets in Quebec

City, and two in Montreal. Each outlet store has a WAN connection to the central office computer center in New York City.

Advanced Sounds is engaging in a full upgrade of its Windows Server 2003 network to Windows Server 2008. The upgrade includes using Windows Server 2008 Active Directory. Advanced Sounds has pioneered many technological innovations and is very concerned about keeping its network and computer systems secure. Their Information Technology (IT) Department hires you to help them implement Windows Server 2008 Active Directory.

Case Project 4-1: Active Directory Installation Planning

Advanced Sounds IT Department has formed a small installation planning committee consisting of the IT server operations manager, two system programmers, the current Active Directory administrator, and you. After the first meeting, they have asked you to prepare a small report to address the following questions:

- What tools are used in Windows Server 2008 to install Active Directory?
- What information is needed for the initial installation involving these tools?
- What special considerations exist in terms of having both Windows Server 2003 and Windows Server 2008 servers as DCs?

Case Project 4-2: Active Directory Design

Due to a political decision several years ago, there is only one forest and domain for this company. Given what you know about the company's basic structure, how many forests, trees, and domains do you recommend? Do you recommend any sites? Note that there are four IP subnets at the New York City complex and two IP subnets at each of the Quebec City and Montreal locations. Create a report and if you have access to drawing software, create a diagram of your proposed design.

Case Project 4-3: Creating OUs

Until now, user accounts have been stored in only three OUs in the single domain. There is currently one OU for each of the New York City, Quebec City, and Montreal locations. The Advanced Sounds installation planning committee has decided to adopt your Active Directory structure proposed in Case Project 4-2, and now they want to also create OUs for each division in the company and place these under the domains that you have proposed. Further, the committee wants to have a computer technical specialist in each division to manage its OU and the user accounts under it. To help accomplish this, the committee asks you to create an instructional document that shows how to create an OU and delegate authority.

Case Project 4-4: Installing Servers at the Outlet Stores

All of the outlet stores have grown and have their own networks with 10 or more workstations. In the past, these stores have not had network connectivity to the home complex. However, this has created many problems due to extra paperwork and outdated handling of data. The installation committee would like to install WAN links to each outlet store and place servers in them. For efficiency, they would like to have the servers installed with Active Directory. Create a short report of your recommendations for installing a server at these outlet stores, and include the reasoning behind your recommendations.

chapter 5

Configuring, Managing, and Troubleshooting Resource Access

After reading this chapter and completing the exercises, you will be able to:

- Set up security for folders and files
- Configure shared folders and shared folder security
- Install and set up the Distributed File System
- Configure disk quotas
- Implement UNIX compatibility

Resource sharing is a bread-and-butter function for a Windows Server 2008 network because it empowers users to be productive. The most frequently used resources on a server are folders and files, which include written documents, spreadsheets, data files and databases, and multimedia files. Some of these resources need to be kept secure because they contain sensitive information. Other resources are to be shared with limited groups to far-reaching audiences. Windows Server 2008 can securely protect folders and files or open them up to wide-scale sharing, depending on the need.

You begin this chapter by learning how to use attributes and permissions to manage who accesses folders and files. You learn how to use the Encrypting File System to guard important resources, and how to customize access through special permissions and ownership. You also learn how to create an audit trail for historical data about who has accessed information. You explore the steps for configuring information to be shared over the network and publish it in Active Directory. You additionally find out how to install and set up the Distributed File System for coordinating and backing up a system of shared information. You also examine how to avoid overloaded disks by setting up disk quotas. Finally, you learn to use the Subsystem for UNIX-based Applications to support a network of UNIX, Linux, and Windows computers.

Managing Folder and File Security

Creating accounts and groups are the initial steps for sharing resources, such as folders, files, and printers. The next steps are to create access control lists (ACLs) to secure these objects and then to set them up for sharing. As you learned in Chapter 4, "Introduction to Active Directory and Account Management," an ACL is a list of privileges given to an account or security group granting access to an object, such as a shared folder or shared printer.

Windows Server 2008 uses two types of ACLs: discretionary and system control. A **discretionary ACL (DACL)** is an ACL that is configured by a server administrator or owner of an object. For example, the server administrator can configure who can access a company-wide shared folder containing personnel policies. Additionally, the human resources director may have her own folder of confidential information on the server that she makes available only to members of the Human Resources Department. Because she owns the folder, she can configure the folder's ACL to permit access only to members of her department.

A **system control ACL (SACL)** contains information used to audit the access to an object. For example, a soft drink company decides to audit files that contain the secret recipes for their products. By configuring an SACL for each file containing a recipe, the company monitors who has successfully viewed the file's contents and who has tried to view the contents, but failed because of DACL restrictions. When an SACL is not configured, this means an object is not audited. The server administrator and object owners can configure DACLs and SACLs.

Good security practices mean using DACLs and SACLs to protect the resources on your Windows Server 2008 network. The ACL-based object security techniques that you learn in the next sections include the following DACL and SACL controls for folders and files:

- Attributes
- Permissions
- Auditing
- Ownership

Configuring Folder and File Attributes

Use of **attributes** is retained in the NT file system (NTFS) from its predecessor File Allocation Table (FAT) file system. Attributes are stored as header information with each folder and file, along with other characteristics including volume label, designation as a subfolder, date of creation, and time of creation.

Two basic attributes remain in NTFS that are still compatible with FAT in older Windows operating systems: read-only and hidden. Both of these attributes are accessed from the

General tab when you right-click a folder or file and click Properties, such as from Windows Explorer.

When you check read-only for a folder, the folder is read-only, but not the files in the folder. This means the folder cannot be deleted from the command prompt (even though the folder attribute says "Only applies to files in a folder"). When a file is checked as read-only, it also cannot be deleted from the command prompt. Most Windows Server 2008 server administrators ignore the read-only attribute box and set the equivalent protection in permissions instead, because the read-only permissions apply to the folder and can be inherited by its files.

Folders and files can be marked as hidden to prevent users from viewing their contents, which is a carryover from MS-DOS operating systems. The hidden attribute can be defeated by any Windows 98 and above client using My Computer or Windows Explorer, if the user makes a selection in the operating system Control Panel Folder Options to view hidden files and folders.

The read-only and hidden attributes are on the General tab in an NTFS folder's or file's properties dialog box. In addition to these attributes, NTFS offers advanced or extended attributes, which are accessed by clicking the General tab's Advanced button (see Figure 5-1).

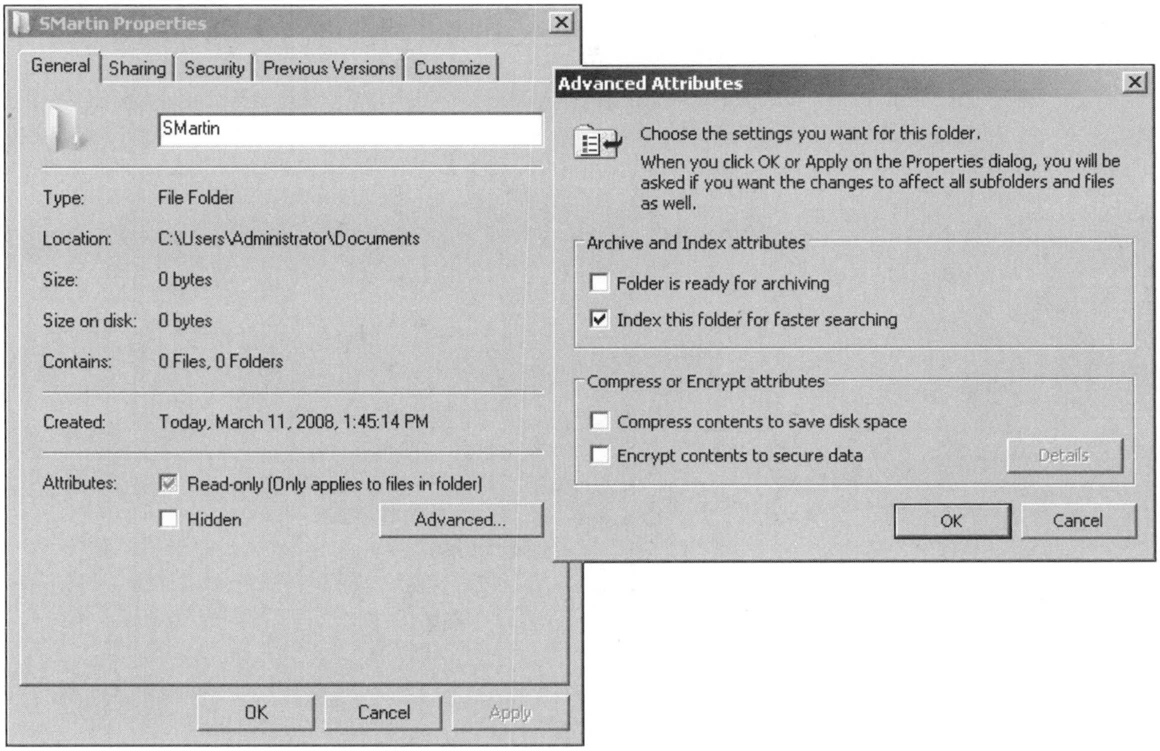

Figure 5-1   Attributes of a folder on an NTFS formatted disk

The advanced attributes are archive, index, compress, and encrypt. When you make a change to an attribute in the Advanced Attributes dialog box in a folder's properties, you see a message box with the option to apply that change to only the folder and the files in that folder or to apply the change to the folder, its files, and all subfolders and files within the folder. After the message box appears, make your selection about how to apply the change and click OK (as in Activity 5-1).

Archive Attribute   The archive attribute (Folder is ready for archiving; see Figure 5-1) is checked to indicate that the folder or file needs to be backed up because it is new or changed. Most network administrators ignore the folder archive attribute, but instead rely on it for files. Files, but not folders, are automatically flagged to archive when they are changed. File server backup systems can be set to detect files with the archive attribute to ensure those files are backed up. The backup system ensures each file is saved following the same folder or subfolder scheme as on the server.

Index Attribute vs. Windows Search Service The index attribute and accompanying
Indexing Service are legacy features for continuity with earlier operating systems, such as Windows Server 2003 and Windows 2000 Server. The NTFS index attribute (Index this folder for
faster searching; see Figure 5-1) is used to index the folder and file contents so that file name,
text, creation or modification date, author, and other properties can be quickly searched in Windows Server 2008. The index attribute marks a folder's contents or a specific file to be indexed
through the Indexing Service. The Indexing Service creates a catalog of documents to be tracked
and searched.

Windows Server 2008 offers a newer, faster search service called the Windows Search Service.
This service is meant to replace using the index attribute and the Indexing Service, and it is recommended that you use this replacement—you can't use both the Windows Search Service and
the Indexing Service at the same time. When you try Windows Search Service, you'll be impressed
by its speed compared with the old Indexing Service.

To use the Windows Search Service, you must install the File Services role via Server Manager
(see Chapter 3, "Configuring the Windows Server 2008 Environment"). When you install the File
Services role, be sure to do the following:

1. Select the box for Windows Search Service in the Select Role Services window, as shown in
   Figure 5-2.

2. Select the volume or volumes to index, such as Local Disk (C:), in the Select Volumes to
   Index for Windows Search Service window.

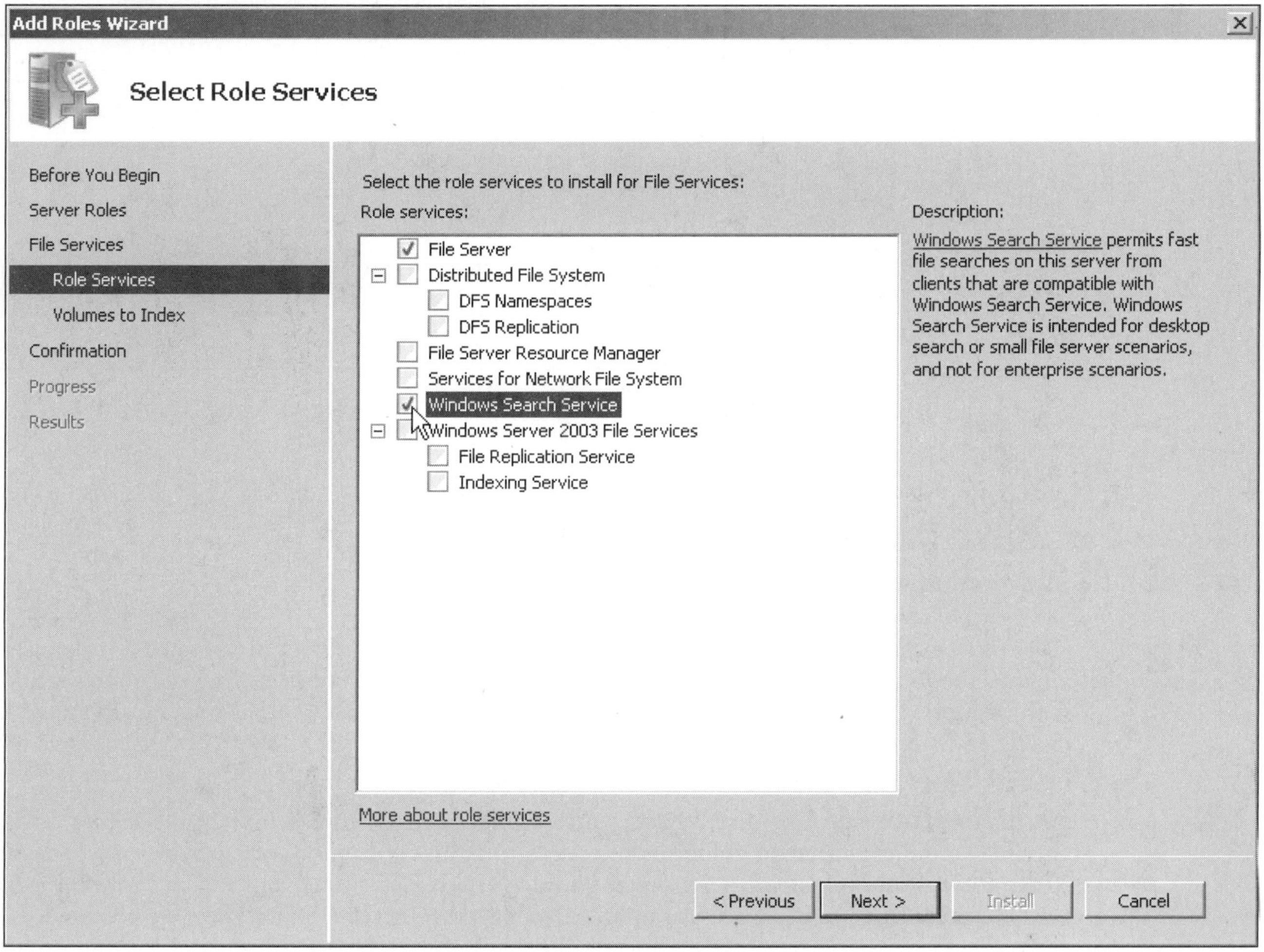

Figure 5-2 Installing the Windows Search Service with the File Services role

Once Windows Search Service is installed with the File Services role, Windows Server 2008 automatically creates an index of files. The indexed files include files in the Documents folder for an account, e-mail files, photos, multimedia files, and any files that are commonly accessed. Some files that are not conducive to searches, such as system files, are not included. These files are excluded to help reduce the size of the index catalog as a way to keep searches as fast as possible.

Whenever you open a window, such as Windows Explorer, that has a Search box with a magnifying glass, you can use that box to perform a fast search using the Windows Search Service. Also, when a Windows XP or Vista client searches for a file on Windows Server 2008, the Windows Search Service is used. Having fast client searches is a compelling reason alone for installing the File Services role in Windows Server 2008. This makes users more productive and reduces time using the network that connects to a server.

You can maintain the Windows Search Service through Control Panel as follows:

1. Click Start and click Control Panel.

2. In the Control Panel Home View, click System and Maintenance and click Indexing Options. Or in Classic View, double-click Indexing Options.

3. To select a new volume to index (or stop indexing a volume), click the Modify button, and select or deselect the appropriate volume(s) and click OK.

4. Click the Advanced button to configure advanced indexing options from the Index Settings and File Types tabs (see Figure 5-3). For example, you can index encrypted files, rebuild the index, change where the index is stored, or select certain file types to index. Click OK after making your selections.

5. Close the Indexing Options dialog box and Control Panel when you are finished.

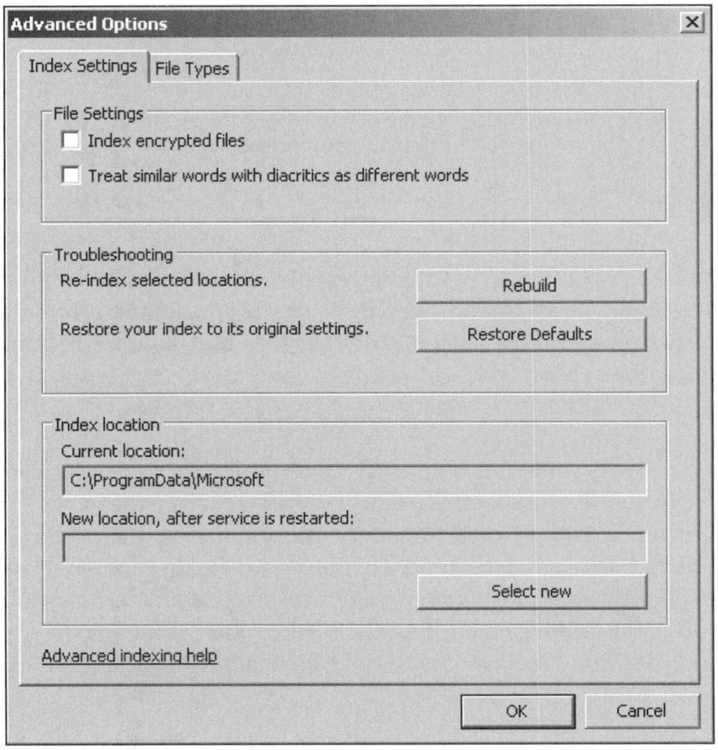

Figure 5-3 Configuring advanced indexing options

Windows Search Service by default is installed to start automatically each time the server is booted. If your searches are slow or not working, you can stop and restart the service. To do this, open Server Manager, expand Configuration in the tree, click Services in the tree, and check the middle pane to see if the Windows Search Service is stopped. To reset the service, it is best to click *Stop the service* to fully stop it. Next, click *Start the service*.

Compress Attribute A folder and its contents can be stored on the disk in compressed format, which is an option that enables you to reduce the amount of disk space used for files, particularly in situations in which disk space is limited or for folders that are accessed infrequently, such as those used to store accounting data from a previous fiscal year. Compression saves space and you can work on compressed files in the same way as on uncompressed files. The disadvantage of compressed files is increased CPU overhead to open the files and to copy them. On a busy server, this might be an important consideration. Further, you can't execute a compressed program file.

When you compress a folder, you have the option to compress the folder, its subfolders, and files in the folder. Also, when you add new files to a folder marked with the compress attribute, the new files are compressed automatically. By default, compressed files and folders are displayed in colored font, such as blue. If they are not displayed in color, you can turn on this feature using the following steps:

1. Click Start and click Control Panel.

2. In the Control Panel Home View, click Appearance and Personalization and click Folder Options. Or in Classic View, double-click Folder Options.

3. Click the View tab.

4. Click Show encrypted or compressed NTFS files in color.

5. Close the Folder Options dialog box and the Control Panel window.

If you are concerned about security and want to use the encrypt attribute, do not compress files because compressed files cannot be encrypted.

Encrypt Attribute The NTFS encrypt attribute protects folders and files so that only the user who encrypts the folder or file is able to read it. As a server administrator, you might use this option to protect certain system files or new software files that you are not yet ready to release for general use. In an organization with sensitive file contents, encryption can be an essential security measure. It's also good business practice to encrypt stored files vital to a business strategy or containing company secrets.

An encrypted folder or file uses the Microsoft **Encrypting File System (EFS)**, which sets up a unique, private encryption key associated with the user account that encrypted the folder or file. The file is protected from network intruders and in situations in which a server or hard drive is stolen. EFS uses both symmetric and asymmetric encryption techniques. The symmetric portion uses a single key to encrypt the file or folder. In the asymmetric portion, two encryption keys are used to protect the key for encrypting the file or folder. Because the asymmetric portion is connected to a user account, the account should have a strong password to help ensure that attackers can't guess it easily.

File encryption and decryption involve some CPU overhead, which might be a consideration on a busy server.

When you view them in Windows Explorer, encrypted folders and files are displayed in color by default (but not the same color as compressed files), such as green. If they are not in color, you can configure the Folder Options using the same steps as for compressed files.

For the sake of security and disaster recovery, backing up EFS keys is as important as backing up EFS files. If EFS keys are not backed up, you have no access to EFS files when they are restored after a recovery. To make sure the keys are backed up, ensure that you back up the full OS, not just the EFS files. You can also back up EFS keys using the Certificate MMC snap-in and exporting the keys to removable media, such as a CD/DVD, for each account that uses EFS. Once you are in the Certificate MMC, expand the Personal folder in the tree and click Certificates. In the middle pane, right-click the user account, point to All Tasks, click Export, and follow the steps in the Certificate Export Wizard.

When you move an encrypted file to another folder on the same computer, that file remains encrypted, even if you rename it. No prompt is given to retain the Encrypt attribute when you move the file. The same holds true for copying the file to a different Windows Server 2008 (or 2003) server. If the folder or file is moved to a Windows 2000 Server or Windows XP/Vista computer, however, there should be a prompt to determine whether the Encrypt attribute is retained.

If you are the owner or have appropriate permissions, you can decrypt a folder or file by using Windows Explorer (click Start and click Computer) to remove the Encrypt attribute and then apply the change. Folders and files can also be encrypted or decrypted by using the *cipher* command in the Command Prompt window (type *cipher /?* to view the command's switch options).

For all of the activities in this chapter, you'll need an account with Administrator privileges. Also, most of these activities can be completed on a virtual server or computer, such as in Hyper-V.

Some steps in the activities in this book include bulleted questions with space for you to record your responses/answers.

Activity 5-1: Encrypting Files

Time Required: Approximately 10 minutes
Objective: Encrypt files in a folder.

Description: The news media have reported on cases about theft in organizations in which a computer's drive has been stolen because of its valuable contents, such as business secrets or information crucial to national security. One way to provide security in these situations is to use the Encrypting File System to protect files. In this activity, you practice encrypting the contents of a folder.

1. Use Windows Explorer to create a new folder. For example, click **Start**, click **Computer**, double-click a local drive, such as *Local Disk C:*, click **File**, point to **New**, click **Folder**, and enter a folder name that is a combination of your first initial and last name, such as *JRyan*, and press **Enter**. Find a file to copy into the folder, such as a text-based document or another file already in the root of drive C. To copy the file, right-click it, drag it to the folder you created, and click **Copy Here**.

2. Right-click your new folder, such as *JRyan*, and click **Properties**. Make sure that the **General** tab is displayed, and if it is not, then click it.

   • What attributes are already checked?

3. Click the **Advanced** button.

- Which attributes are already checked in the Advanced Attributes dialog box?

4. Check **Encrypt contents to secure data**, and then click **OK**.
5. Click **Apply**.
6. Be certain that **Apply changes to this folder, subfolders and files** is selected, and click **OK**.

- Make a note of how you would verify that the file you copied into the folder is now encrypted. How would you decrypt the entire folder contents?

7. Click **OK** again to exit the Properties dialog box. Move the pointer to a blank area and click so that your folder is no longer highlighted. Now notice that the folder name appears in green.
8. Decrypt the folder so that you can use it for another activity.
9. Close the folder's Properties dialog box and close the Local Disk (C:) (or other appropriate disk) window.

Configuring Folder and File Permissions

Permissions control access to an object, such as a folder or file. For example, when you configure a folder so that a domain local group has access to only read the contents of that folder, you are configuring permissions. At the same time, you are configuring that folder's discretionary access control list (DACL) of security descriptors.

Use the Edit button on the folder properties Security tab to change which groups and users have permissions to a folder. To add a group, for example, click the Edit button, as shown in Figure 5-4. Activity 5-2 enables you to configure permissions and add a group. (As you learn shortly, in some cases you must remove inherited permissions before you can make changes.)

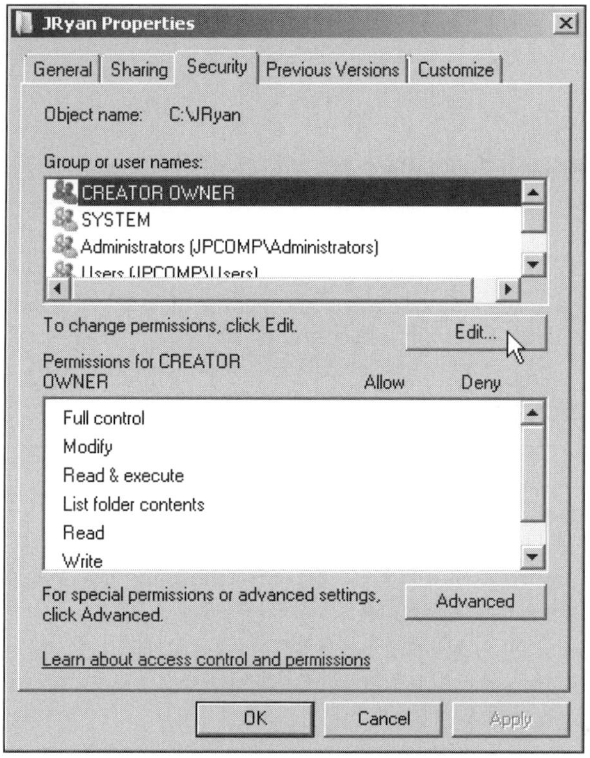

Figure 5-4   Configuring folder permissions

Table 5-1 lists the folder and file permissions supported by NTFS.

Table 5-1 NTFS folder and file permissions

Permission	Description	Applies to
Full control	Can read, add, delete, execute, and modify files plus change permissions and attributes, and take ownership	Folders and files
Modify	Can read, add, delete, execute, and modify files; cannot delete subfolders and their file contents, change permissions, or take ownership	Folders and files
Read & execute	Implies the capabilities of both List folder contents and Read (traverse folders, view file contents, view attributes and permissions, and execute files)	Folders and files
List folder contents	Can list (traverse) files in the folder or switch to a subfolder, view folder attributes and permissions, and execute files, but cannot view file contents	Folders only
Read	Can view file contents, view folder attributes and permissions, but cannot traverse folders or execute files	Folders and files
Write	Can create files, write data to files, append data to files, create folders, delete files (but not subfolders and their files), and modify folder and file attributes	Folders and files
Special permissions	Special permissions apply (see Table 5-2)	Folders and files

If none of the Allow or Deny boxes are checked, then the associated group or user has no access to the folder. Also, when a new folder or file is created, it typically inherits permissions from the parent folder or from the root. Finally, if the Deny box is checked, this overrides any other access. For instance, if an account in a group has Allow checked for a specific permission, but the group to which the account belongs has Deny checked—Deny prevails, even for the account with Allow checked.

Activity 5-2: Configuring Folder Permissions

Time Required: Approximately 10 minutes
Objective: Configure permissions on a folder so that users can modify its contents.

Description: Some organizations employ a group of server operators who perform the day-to-day management of servers. Assume that you need to create a Utilities folder for the server operators so that they can place new utilities in the folder, plus list the folder's contents and execute utilities out of that folder.

1. Use Windows Explorer (click **Start** and click **Computer**) to create a folder called Utilities plus your initials, such as *UtilitiesJR*. Create this folder inside another folder, such as under the folder Test (that you create now) that is under the Users folder (\Users\Test) or in another location specified by your instructor.

2. Right-click the new folder, click **Properties,** and then click the **Security** tab.

   • What users and groups already have permissions to access the folder? Click each group and user to determine what permissions they have and record your results.

3. Click the **Edit** button. Click each group and user again, and notice that some boxes are checked and deactivated because they represent inherited permissions.

4. Click the **Add** button.

5. Click the **Advanced** button in the Select Users, Computers, or Groups dialog box. Click **Find Now**. Double-click **Server Operators** in the list at the bottom of the box. Click **OK**.

6. Click **Server Operators** to highlight this group.

   - What permissions do they have by default?

7. Click the **Allow** box for **Modify**.

8. Click **OK** in the folder's Permissions dialog box and click **OK** in the Properties dialog box.

9. Leave Windows Explorer (the window with the folder containing the Utilities folder you have been working on) open for the next activity, unless you need to stop working now.

As you noticed in Step 3 of Activity 5-2, some of the Allow boxes for permissions are checked and deactivated. These are **inherited permissions,** which means that the same permissions on a parent object, such as the root folder in this case, apply to the child objects such as files and sub-folders within the parent folder. If you want to change inherited permissions that cause Allow or Deny boxes to be deactivated (and checked), you can do this by removing the inherited permissions.

Activity 5-3: Removing Inherited Permissions

Time Required: Approximately 10 minutes
Objective: Remove inherited permissions on a folder.

Description: Often you want to remove inherited permissions for specific situations. In this activity, you reconfigure the inherited permissions so that you can remove the Users group from those who can access the Utilities folder you created earlier.

1. Using Windows Explorer (click **Start** and click **Computer**), find the Utilities folder that you created in the last activity. Right-click the folder, and click **Properties**.

2. Click the **Security** tab.

3. Click the **Advanced** button.

4. Click the **Edit** button to see the Advanced Security Settings dialog box (see Figure 5-5).

5. Remove the check mark from the box for **Include inheritable permissions from this object's parent.**

6. In the Windows Security message box, notice that there are three options from which to select. One is to copy back the inherited permissions (if you have removed them already), one is to remove the inherited permissions, and one is to cancel this operation. Click **Remove.**

7. Click **OK** in the Advanced Security Settings dialog box. Click **OK** again.

   - Compare the groups that now remain with those you recorded in Step 2 of Activity 5-2. What group or groups remain? (Notice that the Users group is no longer on the list for access.)

8. Click **OK** in the folder's Properties dialog box.

9. Leave Windows Explorer open for the next activity, unless you need to stop working now.

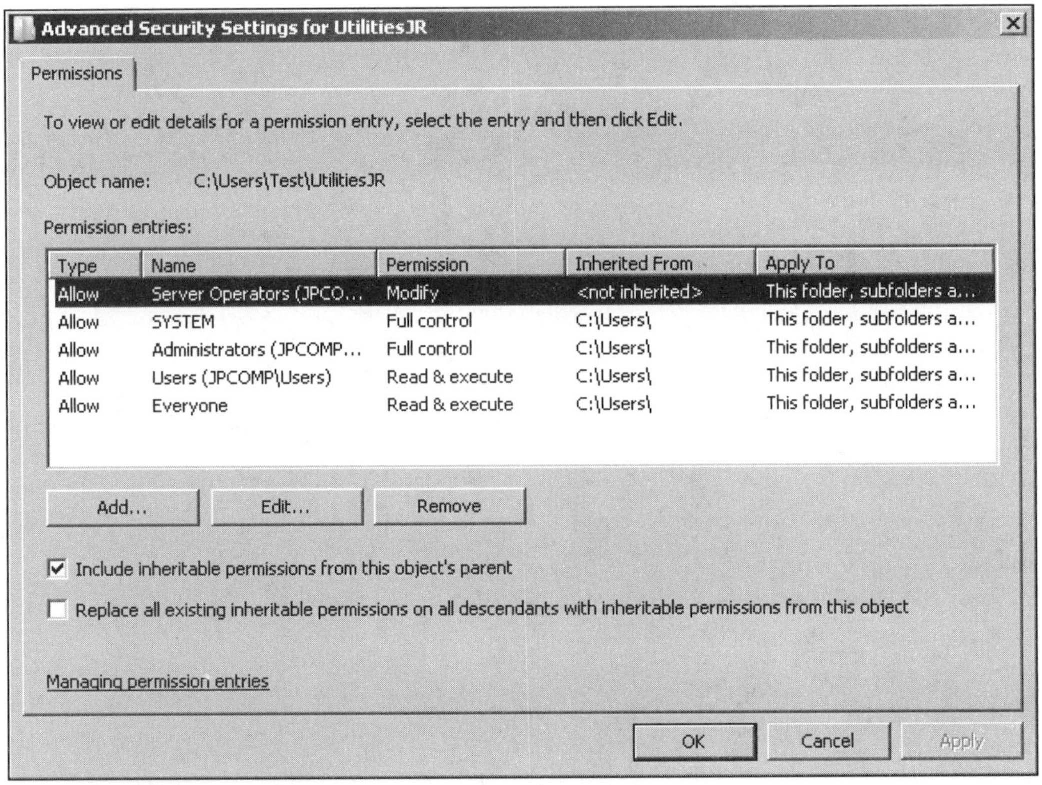

Figure 5-5 Advanced Security Settings dialog box

If you need to customize permissions, you have the option to set up special permissions for a particular group or user. Figure 5-6 illustrates the special permissions that you can set up, and Table 5-2 explains each of the special permissions.

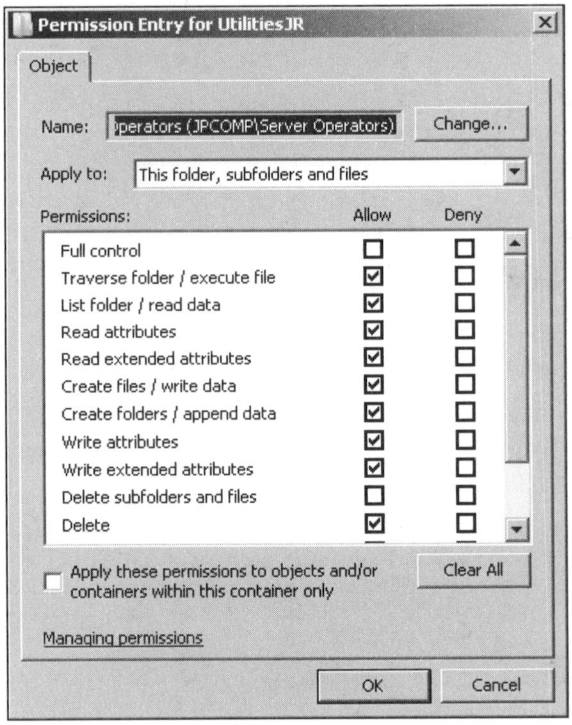

Figure 5-6 Special permissions

Table 5-2 NTFS folder and file special permissions

Permission	Description	Applies to
Full control	Can read, add, delete, execute, and modify files, plus change permissions and attributes, and take ownership	Folders and files
Traverse folder/execute file	Can list the contents of a folder and run program files in that folder; keep in mind that all users are automatically granted this permission via the Everyone and Users groups, unless it is removed or denied by you	Folders and files
List folder / read data	Can list the contents of folders and subfolders and read the contents of files	Folders and files
Read attributes	Can view folder and file attributes (read-only and hidden)	Folders and files
Read extended attributes	Enables the viewing of extended attributes (archive, index, compress, and encrypt)	Folders and files
Create files / write data	Can add new files to a folder and modify, append to, or write over file contents	Folders and files
Create folders / append data	Can add new folders and add new data at the end of files, but otherwise cannot delete, write over, or modify data	Folders and files
Write attributes	Can add or remove the read-only and hidden attributes	Folders and files
Write extended attributes	Can add or remove the archive, index, compress, and encrypt attributes	Folders and files
Delete subfolders and files	Can delete subfolders and files (the following Delete permission is not required)	Folders and files
Delete	Can delete the specific subfolder or file to which this permission is attached	Folders and files
Read permissions	Can view the permissions (ACL information) associated with a folder or file (but does not imply you can change them)	Folders and files
Change permissions	Can change the permissions associated with a folder or file	Folders and files
Take ownership	Can take ownership of the folder or file (read permissions and change permissions automatically accompany this permission)	Folders and files

Activity 5-4: Configuring Special Permissions

Time Required: Approximately 15 minutes
Objective: Configure special permissions for a folder to grant a group expanded access.

Description: Sometimes the regular NTFS permissions do not enable you to create exactly the type of access you want on a folder. In this activity, you set up special permissions on a new folder for use by all users in your organization.

1. Using Windows Explorer, create a new folder (under the \Users\Test folder or in another location specified by your instructor) called Documentation plus your initials, such as *DocumentationJR*.

2. Right-click the new folder, and click **Properties**.

3. Click the **Security** tab.

4. Click **Edit**.

5. Click **Add**.

6. Click **Advanced** in the Select Users, Computers, or Groups dialog box.

7. Click **Find Now** as in Figure 5-7.

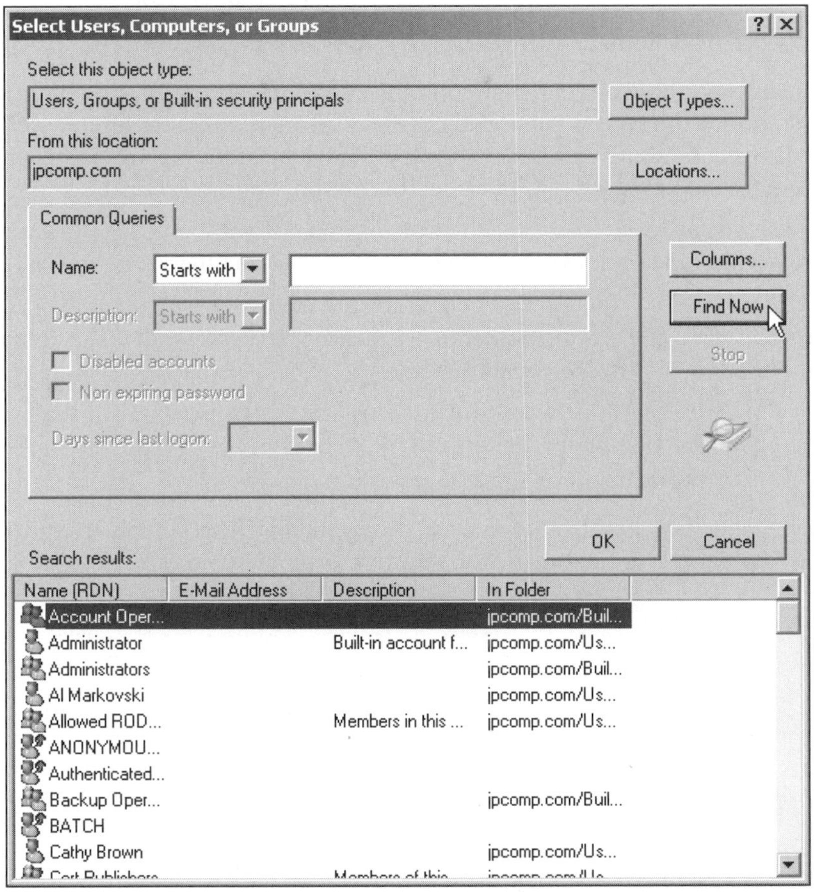

Figure 5-7 Click the Find Now button to access the list of users, computers, and groups

8. Double-click the **Domain Users** group under *Search results*.

9. Click **OK** in the Select Users, Computers, or Groups dialog box.

10. Click **OK** in the Permissions dialog box.

11. Click **Domain Users** under *Group or user names* in the Properties dialog box.

12. Click the **Advanced** button.

13. Ensure that **Domain Users** is selected under *Permission entries*, and click the **Edit** button.

14. Again make sure that the **Domain Users** group is still highlighted and click the **Edit** button in the Advanced Security Settings dialog box.

    • Record the permissions that are selected by default for the Domain Users group.

15. Click the **Allow** box for each of the following special permissions entries: **Create files / write data, Create folders / append data, Delete subfolders and files**, and **Delete**.

16. Click the box for **Apply these permissions to objects and / or containers within this container only.**

17. Click **OK** in the Permission Entry dialog box.

18. Click **OK** in the Advanced Security Settings dialog box.

19. Click **OK** in the next Advanced Security Settings dialog box.

20. Click **OK** in the Properties dialog box.

21. Leave Windows Explorer open for the next activity (unless you need to stop working).

Microsoft provides guidelines for setting permissions as follows:

- Protect the \Windows folder that contains operating system files on Windows Server 2008 servers and its subfolders from general users through allowing limited access, such as Read & execute and List folder contents or by just using the special permission to Traverse folder / execute file, but give the Administrators group Full control access.

- Protect server utility folders, such as for backup software and network management, with access permissions only for the Administrators, Server Operators, and Backup Operators groups.

- Protect software application folders with Read & execute and Write to enable users to run applications and write temporary files.

- Create publicly used folders to have Modify access, so users have broad access except to Take ownership, Change permissions, and Delete subfolders and files.

- Provide users Full control of their own home folders.

- Remove general access groups, such as Everyone and Users, from confidential folders, as in those used for personal mail, for sensitive files, or for software development projects.

 Always err on the side of too much security. It is easier, in terms of human relations, to give users permissions later than it is to take away permissions.

 When removing groups and users from confidential folders, make sure you do not remove all access. Remember to keep administrator access (but have audit controls on such folders to protect the administrator from questions about accessing confidential material).

Configuring Folder and File Auditing

Accessing folders and files can be tracked by setting up **auditing**, which in Windows Server 2008 enables you to track activity on a folder or file, such as read or write activity. Some organizations choose to implement auditing on folders and files that involve financially sensitive information, such as those involving accounting and payroll. Other organizations monitor access to see which users access information, such as a folder containing files of employee guidelines and announcements, to determine if it is being used. Windows Server 2008 NTFS folders and files enable you to audit a combination of any or all of the activities listed as special permissions in Table 5-2. When you set up auditing, the options for each type of access are to track successful and failed attempts.

For example, consider a situation in which your organization's financial auditors specify that all accounting files in the Accounting folder must create an "audit trail" for each time a person who has access changes the contents of a file in the folder. Further, the financial auditors might want to verify that only groups that have access to write to files are those in the Accounting and Administrators groups. You would set up auditing by configuring the folder's security to audit each successful type of write event, such as Create files / write data and Create folders / append data. For extra information, you might track permission, attribute, and ownership changes by monitoring successful attempts to Write attributes, Write extended attributes, Change permissions, and Take ownership. Audited events are recorded in the Windows Server 2008 Security log that is accessed from Event Viewer. You learn to use the Event Viewer in Chapter 11, "Server and Network Monitoring."

Activity 5-5: Auditing a Folder

Time Required: Approximately 10 minutes

Objective: Configure auditing on a folder to monitor how it is accessed and who is making changes to the folder.

Description: Now that you have created the Documentation folder, you decide to monitor how people are using the folder as well as the frequency of use. To do this, you set up auditing on that folder.

1. From the Windows Explorer window you have been using, right-click the Documentation folder you created in Activity 5-4, and click **Properties**.

2. Click the **Security** tab.

3. Click the **Advanced** button.

4. Click the **Auditing** tab.

5. Click the **Edit** button.

6. Click **Add**.

7. Click the **Advanced** button in the Select User, Computer, or Group dialog box.

8. Click **Find Now**.

9. Double-click the **Everyone** group.

10. Click **OK**.

11. Notice in the Auditing Entry dialog box (see Figure 5-8) the Successful and Failed boxes that you can check for each special permission.

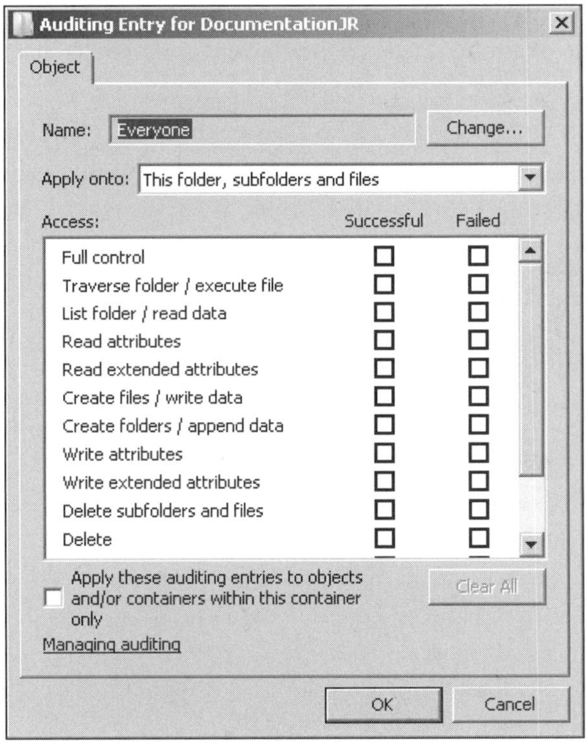

Figure 5-8 Folder auditing selections

12. Click the **Successful** box for each of the following: **Traverse folder / execute file, List folder / read data, Create files / write data, Create folders / append data,** and **Delete subfolders and files.**

13. Click **OK.**

14. Click **OK** in the Advanced Security Settings dialog box.

15. Click **OK** again.

16. Click **OK** in the Properties dialog box.

17. Close any open windows.

 Before these auditing measures will be tracked in the Security log, you must have previously set up a global audit policy as you learned in Chapter 4, "Introduction to Active Directory and Account Management." Also, you can view the Security log by opening Server Manager, expanding Diagnostics in the tree, expanding Event Viewer, expanding Windows Logs, and clicking Security.

Configuring Folder and File Ownership

With permissions and auditing set up, you might want to verify the **ownership** of a folder. Folders are first owned by the account that creates them, such as the Administrator account. Folder owners have the ability to change permissions for the folders they create. Also, ownership can be transferred only by having the Take ownership special permission or Full control permission (which includes Take ownership). These permissions enable a user to take control of a folder or file and become its owner. Taking ownership is the only way to shift control from one account to another. The Administrators group always has the ability to take control of any folder, regardless of the permissions, particularly because there are instances in which the server administrator needs to take ownership of a folder, such as when someone leaves an organization. The general steps you use to take ownership of a folder, using your account with Administrator privileges, are as follows:

1. Right-click the folder for which you want to take ownership, and click Properties.

2. Click the Security tab.

3. Click the Advanced button.

4. Click the Owner tab.

5. Click the Edit button in the Advanced Security Settings dialog box.

6. Under *Change owner to*, click the Administrators (*domainname*\Administrators) group, as shown in Figure 5-9.

7. Click OK.

8. Click OK in the Advanced Security Settings dialog box.

9. Click OK in the folder's Properties dialog box.

10. Close any other open windows.

```
┌─────────────────────────────────────────────────────────────────────────┐
│ ▌ Advanced Security Settings for DocumentationJR                    [×] │
├─────────────────────────────────────────────────────────────────────────┤
│ Owner │                                                                   │
│                                                                           │
│  You can take or assign ownership of this object if you have the required permissions or privileges. │
│                                                                           │
│                                                                           │
│  Object name:      C:\Users\Test\DocumentationJR                          │
│                                                                           │
│  Current owner:                                                           │
│  ┌──────────────────────────────────────────────────────────────────┐   │
│  │ Administrators (JPCOMP\Administrators)                            │   │
│  └──────────────────────────────────────────────────────────────────┘   │
│                                                                           │
│  Change owner to:                                                         │
│  ┌──────────────────────────────────────────────────────────────────┐   │
│  │ Name                                                              │   │
│  │ 👤 Administrator                                                  │   │
│  │ 👥 Administrators (JPCOMP\Administrators)                         │   │
│  │                                                                   │   │
│  │                                                                   │   │
│  │                                                                   │   │
│  │                                                                   │   │
│  └──────────────────────────────────────────────────────────────────┘   │
│                                                                           │
│  ┌─────────────────────────┐                                             │
│  │ Other users or groups... │                                            │
│  └─────────────────────────┘                                             │
│                                                                           │
│  ☐ Replace owner on subcontainers and objects                            │
│                                                                           │
│  Learn about object ownership                                            │
│                                                                           │
│                          ┌──────┐ ┌────────┐ ┌───────┐                   │
│                          │  OK  │ │ Cancel │ │ Apply │                   │
│                          └──────┘ └────────┘ └───────┘                   │
└─────────────────────────────────────────────────────────────────────────┘
```

Figure 5-9   Taking ownership of a folder

Configuring Shared Folders and Shared Folder Permissions

Along with establishing folder permissions, auditing, and ownership, a folder can be set up as a shared folder for users to access over the network. Configuring a shared folder is changed in Windows Server 2008 from previous versions to help make the person offering the shared folder more aware of security options. For example, when you select to share a folder, you now go into the File Sharing dialog box, which has a new format to encourage selecting specific users with which to share a folder (although you can still select to share with the Everyone or other general population groups).

The first step for sharing a folder over the network is to turn on file sharing. This is a simple but important action you can take from the Network window, as you learn in Activity 5-6.

Activity 5-6: Enabling Sharing a Folder

Time Required: Approximately 5 minutes
Objective: Turn on file sharing and public folder sharing.

Description: Before you can share files over a network, you have to configure Windows Server 2008 to enable file sharing. In this activity, you turn on network file sharing and public folder sharing. Your computer must be connected to a network to configure sharing options.

1. Click **Start** and click **Network**.

2. Click **Network and Sharing Center** in the Network window.

3. Under Sharing and Discovery, check to see if Network discovery is turned on. If it is not, click its **down arrow**, click **Turn on network discovery,** and click **Apply**.

4. Next, check to see if File sharing is turned on. If it is not, click its **down arrow**. Click **Turn on file sharing** and click **Apply**. Notice the green On button is now displayed for File sharing.

5. Click the **down arrow** for Public folder sharing.

6. Click **Turn on sharing so anyone with network access can open files**. This enables network clients to access the Public folder in Windows Server 2008 over the network to read or copy files. Click **Apply**.

7. Close the Network and Sharing Center window. Also, close the Network window.

The Public folder is similar to the same folder in other Windows operating systems. It offers a convenient way to share files over a network. You simply drag the files you want to share into this folder. By default, the Public folder cannot be accessed by network clients unless you configure to share it.

Network discovery must be enabled so that clients can find and access a shared folder. If you try to turn on network discovery, but it goes back to the off state, configure the Firewall exceptions to allow this type of network access. Click the Windows Firewall link in the Network and Sharing Center, click Change settings, click the Exceptions tab, and check exceptions such as Network Discovery and Netlogon Service. The Windows Firewall also needs to be configured to enable incoming and outgoing access.

To share a server folder, access the Sharing tab in the folder properties dialog box and click the Share button (or from the Windows Explorer, right-click the folder and click Share). Figure 5-10 shows the new File Sharing dialog box from which to configure file sharing.

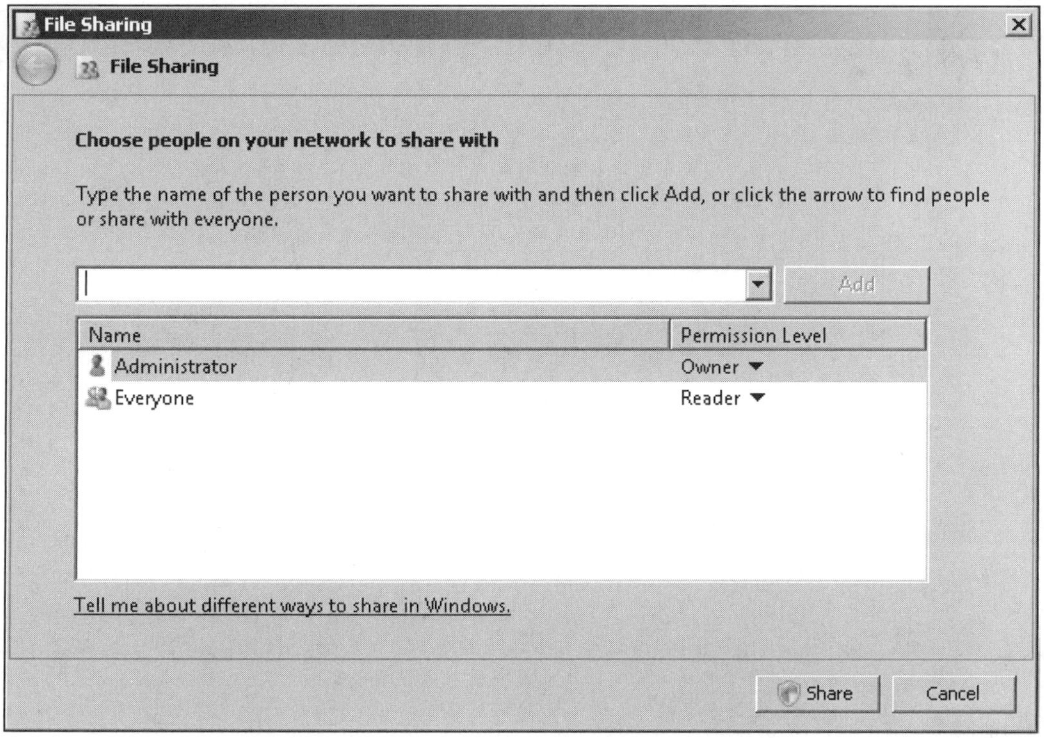

Figure 5-10   File Sharing dialog box

To share the folder, click the down arrow in the drop-down box next to the Add button, click Find, click Advanced, click Find Now, and select the groups and users with whom to share the folder. After the groups and users are selected, click OK twice, and click the Share button. Next, you can e-mail the link to the shared folder to those who have access. You can also copy the link to the Windows Clipboard and then paste it into a program. Click Done and you go back to the Sharing tab in the Properties dialog box for the shared folder. From the Sharing tab, you can now turn off sharing or configure the share permissions by clicking the Share button, or configure custom permissions by selecting the Advanced Sharing button (see Figure 5-11).

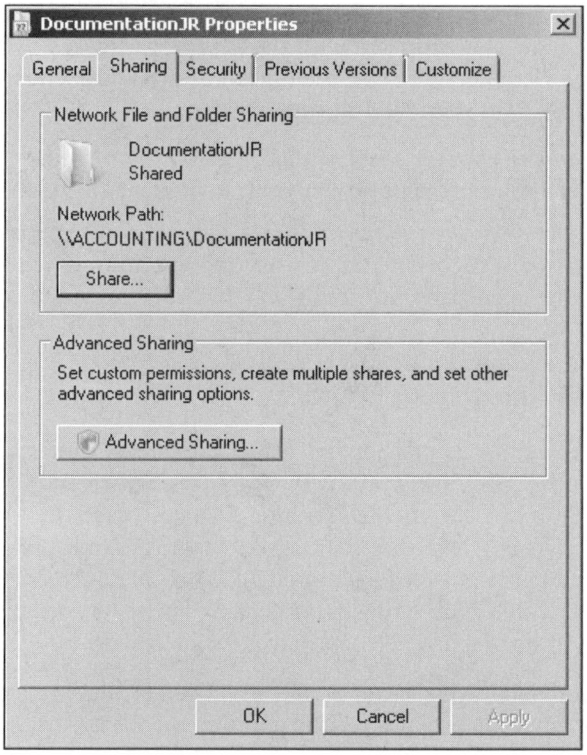

Figure 5-11   Sharing tab

Share permissions for an object differ from the NTFS access permissions set through the Security tab, and the NTFS and share permissions are cumulative, with the exception of permissions that are denied (denied permissions take precedence). Four share permissions (these are new in Windows Server 2008 and Windows Vista) are associated with a folder:

- *Reader*—(same as Read) Permits groups or users to read and execute files, but cannot add or delete files and folders and cannot modify files

- *Contributor*—(same as Change) Enables groups and users to read, execute, and add files, but can only modify and delete files provided by them

- *Co-owner*—(same as Full control) Permits groups or users to read, execute, add, delete, and modify files, and to create and delete subfolders and manage share permissions

- *Owner*—Assigned to the original owner of the folder, such as the folder's creator, and enables the owner to read, execute, add, delete, and modify files in the shared folder as well as create and delete subfolders and manage the share permissions

Before setting the share permissions, first make sure you have selected the appropriate groups and users, such as by specifying the Everyone, Domain Users, or Users groups for a publicly accessed folder. Use the Add button in the Permissions dialog box to set up additional groups and the Remove button to delete a group's access to a shared folder. For example, you can remove a group by highlighting it in the list box in the Group or user names dialog box and clicking Remove. To set the share permissions, highlight a group, and click the appropriate Allow and Deny boxes for the permissions.

From the Advanced Sharing button shown in Figure 5-11, you can click the Caching button to make the contents of a shared folder available offline. This step enables you to set up a folder so that it can be accessed by a client even when the client computer is not connected to the network, such as when the network connection is lost or when a user disconnects a laptop computer to take home. Offline in this situation means that the folder is cached on the client computer's hard drive for continued access after losing the network connection and that the folder location remains unchanged in Windows Explorer. When the network connection is resumed, any offline files that have been modified can be synchronized with the network versions of the files. If two or more users attempt to synchronize a file, they have the option of choosing whose version to use or of saving both versions. A folder can be cached in three ways:

- *Only the files and programs that users specify will be available offline*—Files and programs are cached only per the user's request per each document (the default option).

- *All files and programs that users open from the share will be automatically available offline*—Files and programs are cached without user intervention, which means that all files in the folder which are opened by the client or which are executed by the client are cached automatically.

- *Files or programs from the share will not be available offline*—Files and programs are not cached on the computer's hard drive.

When you share a folder, an option is provided to hide that shared folder so that it does not appear on a browser list, as in the Network window in Windows Server 2008 and Vista and My Network Places in Windows 2000 or XP clients. To hide a share, place the $ sign just after its name. For instance, if the *Share name* text box contains the share name Budget, you can hide the share by entering Budget$. (This is an actual example of what one university does to discourage general scanning of a folder containing budget worksheets. However, department accounting technicians who know of the folder's existence can map it to help with budget planning.)

When you right-click a folder to view its properties, the Share option on the shortcut menu might be missing or you might not see the Sharing tab. You can troubleshoot this problem by making sure that the Server service is started, and even if it is, you can restart it in case the service is hung (make sure no users are on if you restart it). To start or restart the Server service, open Server Manager, expand Configuration in the right pane, click Services, double-click Server, and check for "Started" for the Server status. If it is stopped, click Start; if it is Paused, click Resume.

Activity 5-7: Configuring a Shared Folder

Time Required: Approximately 15 minutes
Objective: Configure a shared folder, share permissions, and offline access.

Description: As a server administrator, one of the most important tasks you perform is to enable folder sharing. In this activity, you configure a folder to be shared over the network.

1. Use Windows Explorer (click **Start** and click **Computer**) to locate the Documentation folder you created in Activity 5-4, such as *DocumentationJR*.

2. Right-click the folder and click **Share** to see the File Sharing window (refer to Figure 5-10).

3. Click the **down arrow** next to the Add button and click **Find**.

4. Click the **Advanced** button in the Select Users or Groups dialog box.

5. Click **Find Now**.

6. Double-click the DomainMgrs group you created in Activity 4-9 in Chapter 4, such as *DomainMgrsJP* (DomainMgrs with your initials). Click **OK**.

7. Click the **down arrow** for the Permission Level for the DomainMgrs group and click **Co-owner**.

8. Click the **Share** button at the bottom of the File Sharing dialog box.

9. Notice the File Sharing dialog box now indicates the folder is shared. Click **Done**.

10. Right-click the folder you just shared and click **Properties**.

11. Click the **Sharing** tab (refer to Figure 5-11).

12. Click the **Share** button.

- What activities can you now complete from the File Sharing dialog box?

13. Click **Cancel**.

14. Click the **Advanced Sharing** button in the Properties dialog box.

15. In the Advanced Sharing dialog box (see Figure 5-12), notice that the Share name is the same name as the shared folder.

- How can you change the name of the share? How could you set the limit of users who can access the share at the same time?

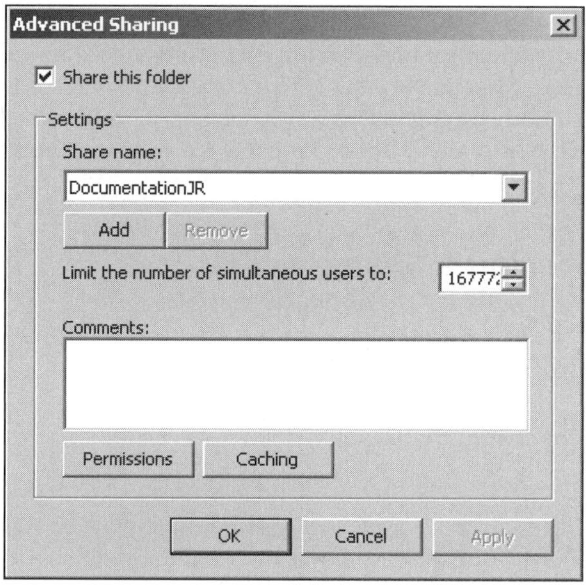

Figure 5-12 Advanced Sharing dialog box

16. Click the **Permissions** button in the Advanced Sharing dialog box. Notice that the permissions are now displayed as Full control (same as Owner or Co-Owner), Change (same as Contributor), and Read (same as Reader). Also, you can select the Allow or Deny boxes for any of the permissions. Click **Cancel**.

17. In the Advanced Sharing dialog box, click **Caching**.

18. To configure offline use, click **All files and programs that users open from the share will be automatically available offline**. Notice that *Optimized for performance* is enabled by default. Click **OK**.

19. Click **OK** in the Advanced Sharing dialog box.

20. Click **Close** in the Properties dialog box. Close Windows Explorer.

Client computers can now access the shared folder through the network. In Windows 2000 and XP, clients can access a shared folder or map it as a network drive using My Network Places; in Windows Vista, they can use the Network window (click Start and click Network).

Publishing a Shared Folder in Active Directory

One reason for having Active Directory is to enable certain objects to be "published" so that users can find and access them quickly. To **publish** an object means to make it available for users to access when they view Active Directory contents. For example, a shared folder or a shared printer can be published in Active Directory for clients to access. Publishing an object also makes it easier to find when a user searches for that object, such as by using My Network Places in Windows XP or the Network (Windows Explorer) window in Windows Vista. Once an object is published, information associated with it is replicated in copies of Active Directory that are kept when multiple domain controllers are present on a network, enabling a published object to be accessed even when one domain controller is down.

Active Directory search capabilities are automatically built into all Windows 2000/XP Professional clients and Windows Vista clients. Earlier Windows-based operating systems, such as Windows 98, are able to search Active Directory when the **Directory Service Client (DSClient)** software is installed on those systems. The Directory Service Client software is available from Microsoft as the program, Dsclient.exe.

The Directory Service Client software installs Active Directory search features at the client, even if the client does not know the specific name of a printer. To search Active Directory for a printer using Windows 98 for example, click Start, point to Find, and click Printers (Printers is a new option added by the Directory Service Client).

When you publish an object, you can publish it to be shared for domain-wide access or to be shared and managed through an organizational unit (OU). A shared folder, for example, might be used only by a department in a company. If you publish the shared folder in that department's OU, then the accounts (users) that manage that OU can also manage the shared folder and how it is accessed.

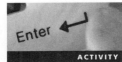

Activity 5-8: Publishing a Shared Folder

Time Required: Approximately 5 minutes
Objective: Publish a shared folder in Active Directory.

Description: In this activity, you learn how to use the Active Directory Users and Computers tool to publish the shared folder you configured in Activity 5-7.

1. Click **Start**, point to **Administrative Tools**, and click **Active Directory Users and Computers**.

2. Double-click the **Users** folder in the tree (or you could double-click an OU at this point to control administration of the published folder from an OU by delegating authority over the OU).

3. Right-click the **Users** folder and point to **New**.
   - What are two objects that you can publish using this menu?

4. Click **Shared Folder**.

5. Enter the name for the published shared folder, such as *DocumentationJR*. Enter the network path to the share, such as *servername**Users**DocumentationJR*. Click **OK**. Notice that the shared folder is now one of the objects listed in the right pane within the Users (or OU) folder.

6. To find the published folder in Active Directory, click **Start** and click **Network**.

7. Click the **Search Active Directory** button.

8. Click the **down arrow** in the Find text box within the Find Users, Contacts, and Groups dialog box.

   • What elements can you search for?

9. Click **Shared Folders**.

10. In the Name text box, enter the name of your published folder and click **Find Now**. You should see the folder listed under Search results.

11. Close the Find Shared Folders dialog box.

12. Close the Network window and close the Active Directory Users and Computers window.

 Windows Vista clients that are members of a domain also can use Steps 6–10 to find a published folder.

Troubleshooting a Security Conflict

Sometimes you will set up access for a user but find that the user does not actually have the type of access you set up. Consider the example of Cleo Jackson, an English professor who maintains a shared subfolder called Assignments for his students from the account CJackson. Assignments is a subfolder under the parent folder English, which contains folders used by all English professors. CJackson needs to update files, copy in new files, and delete files. As Administrator, you have granted CJackson Modify access permissions to Assignments. However, you omitted the step of reviewing the groups to which CJackson belongs, such as the Paper group, which consists of Cleo Jackson and the student newspaper staff. The Paper group has been denied all access to the English folder and all of its subfolders. When Cleo Jackson attempts to copy a file to the Assignments folder, he receives an access denied message.

To troubleshoot the problem, you should review the folder permissions and share permissions for the CJackson account and for all of the groups to which CJackson belongs. In this case, because the Paper group is denied access, CJackson is also denied. The easiest solution is to remove CJackson from the Paper group and perhaps create a group of English professors, such as Eng-Profs, who all have access to the same resources as the Paper group.

Windows Server 2008 offers the Effective Permissions tab in the properties of a folder or file as a tool to help troubleshoot permissions conflicts. To access this tab, right-click a folder or file, click Properties, click the Security tab, click the Advanced button, and click the Effective Permissions tab. Using the Effective Permissions tab, you can view the effective permissions assigned to a user or group. The calculation will take into account group membership as well as permission inheritance. After the calculation is complete, a user's or group's effective permissions are indicated with a check mark beside them.

When you troubleshoot permissions, also take into account what happens when a folder or files in a folder are copied or moved. When a file is copied, the original file remains intact and a copy is made in another folder. Moving a file causes it to be deleted from the original location and placed in a different folder on the same or on a different volume. Copying and moving works the same for a folder, but the entire folder contents (files and subfolders) is copied or moved. When a file or folder is created, copied, or moved, the file and folder permissions can be affected in the following ways (depending on how inheritance is set up in the target location):

• A newly created file inherits the permissions already set up in a folder.

• A file that is copied from one folder to another on the same volume inherits the permissions of the folder to which it is copied.

- A file or folder that is moved from one folder to another on the same volume takes with it the permissions it had in the original folder. For example, if the original folder had Read permissions for the Users domain local group and the folder to which it is transplanted has Modify permissions for Users, that file (or folder) will still only have Read permissions.

- A file or folder that is moved or copied to a folder on a different volume inherits the permissions of the folder to which it is moved or copied.

- A file or folder that is moved or copied from an NTFS volume to a folder in a FAT volume, such as on a Windows 2000 Server or Windows Server 2003 server, is not protected by NTFS permissions, but it does inherit share permissions if they are assigned to the FAT folder.

- A file or folder that is moved or copied from a FAT volume to a folder in an NTFS volume inherits the permissions already assigned in the NTFS folder.

Activity 5-9: Troubleshooting Permissions

Time Required: Approximately 10 minutes
Objective: View the effective permissions on a folder.

Description: The Effective Permissions tab in a folder's properties is an excellent place to start when you are troubleshooting a security conflict, such as when you think someone should be able to access a folder, but the system prevents them from accessing it. In this activity, you use the Effective Permissions tab.

1. Find the Documentation folder that you created in Activity 5-4, such as DocumentationJR, via Windows Explorer.

2. Right-click the folder and click **Properties**.

3. Click the **Security** tab.

4. Click the **Advanced** button.

5. Click the **Effective Permissions** tab.

6. Click the **Select** button, click **Advanced**, click **Find Now**, and double-click **Administrators**. Click **OK**.

7. Scroll through the Effective permissions box (see Figure 5-13).

8. Click **Select**, click **Advanced**, click **Find Now**, and double-click the **Everyone** group. Click **OK**.

   - What are the effective permissions for the Everyone group?

9. Click **OK** and click **OK** again. Close any other open windows.

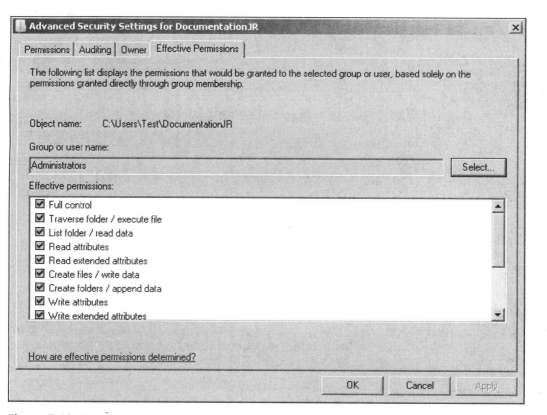

Figure 5-13 Examining effective permissions as a troubleshooting aid

Implementing a Distributed File System

The **Distributed File System (DFS)** enables you to simplify access to the shared folders on a network by setting up folders to appear as though they are accessed from only one place. If the network, for example, has eight Windows Server 2008 servers that make a variety of shared folders available to network users, DFS can be set up so that users do not have to know what server offers which shared folder. All of the folders can be set up to appear as though they are on one server and under one broad folder structure. DFS also makes managing folder access easier for server administrators. After the DFS role is installed, DFS is configured using the DFS Management tool in the Administrative Tools menu (click Start, and point to Administrative Tools) or the DFS Management MMC snap-in.

If DFS is used in a domain, then shared folder contents can be replicated to one or more DCs or member servers, which means that if the original server goes offline then its shared folders are still available to users through the replica servers. Also, from the server administrator's perspective, he or she can update software in a shared folder without having to make the folder temporarily inaccessible during the update. DFS offers the following advantages:

- Shared folders can be set up so that they appear in one hierarchy of folders, enabling users to save time when searching for information.

- NTFS access permissions fully apply to DFS on NTFS-formatted volumes.

- Fault tolerance is an option by replicating shared folders on multiple servers resulting in uninterrupted access for users.

- Access to shared folders can be distributed across many servers, resulting in the ability to perform **load balancing**, so that one server does not experience more load than others.

- Access is improved to resources for Web-based Internet and intranet sites.
- Vital shared folders on multiple computers can be backed up from one set of master folders.

In addition to enabling users to be more productive, server administrators are also immediately more productive because DFS reduces the number of calls to server administrators asking where to find a particular resource. Another advantage of DFS in a domain is that folders can be replicated automatically or manually through Microsoft File Replication Service. When you set up DFS so that shared folders are replicated on two or more servers (called targets), the Microsoft File Replication Service performs the copying to the target servers. Each time the contents of a DFS folder are changed, the Microsoft File Replication Service goes into action. Shared folders in DFS are copied to each designated target computer, which yields two significant advantages:

- Important information is not lost when a disk drive on one server fails.
- Users always have access to shared folders even in the event of a disk failure.

DFS Models

The two models for implementing DFS are stand-alone and domain-based. The stand-alone DFS model offers more limited capabilities than the domain-based model. In the **stand-alone DFS model,** no Active Directory implementation is available to help manage the shared folders, and this model provides only a single or flat level share, which means that the main DFS shared folder does not contain a hierarchy of other shared folders. Also, the stand-alone model does not have DFS folders that are linked to other computers through a DFS container that has a main root and a deep, multilevel hierarchical structure.

 Windows Server 2008 Stand-alone Edition supports only one stand-alone DFS root. Also, the File Services role with DFS is not currently available in the Itanium and Web Editions.

The **domain-based DFS model** has more features than the stand-alone approach. Most important, the domain-based model takes full advantage of Active Directory and is available only to servers and workstations that are members of a domain. The domain-based model enables a deep, root-based, hierarchical arrangement of shared folders that is published in Active Directory. DFS shared folders in the domain-based model are replicated for fault tolerance and load balancing, whereas the stand-alone DFS model does not implement these features.

DFS Topology

The hierarchical structure of DFS in the domain-based model is called the **DFS topology.** The three elements to the DFS topology are namespace root, folder, and replication group.

A **namespace root** is a main container (top-level folder) in Active Directory that holds links to shared folders that can be accessed from the root. The server that maintains the namespace root is called the namespace server. When a network client views the shared folders under the namespace root, all of the folders appear as though they are in one main folder on the same computer, which is the Windows Server 2008 server containing the namespace root—even though the folders might actually reside on many different computers in the domain. Consider, for example, a plant biology research group that has shared folders on four different servers. Those folders can be associated with a namespace root so that all of the folders appear as though they are available from one place, with the namespace BioResearch, through the published information in Active Directory. Importantly, the namespace can also exist on more than one computer to distribute the access load and increase availability of the shared information.

After the namespace root is created, it is populated by shared folders for users to access. Folders are established in a level hierarchy and appear to be in one server location, although they can be on many servers.

 Prior to Windows Server 2003 R2, folders were called links.

A **replication group** is a set of shared folders that is replicated or copied to one or more servers in a domain. In the plant biology example, the replica set would consist of all shared folders under the DFS namespace root that are designated to be replicated to other network servers. Part of this process means that links are established to each server that participates in the replication. Another part of the process is to set up synchronization so that replication takes place among all servers at a specified interval, such as every 15 minutes.

Installing DFS

DFS is installed as a service within the File Services role. In Chapter 3, "Configuring the Windows Server 2008 Environment," you learned how to install server roles. When you install the File Services role, select to install Distributed File System including DFS Namespaces and DFS Replication in the Select Role Services window.

If the File Services role is already installed, but you don't see the DFS Management tool on the Administrative Tools menu, this means you didn't install Distributed File System when you installed the File Services role. If this is the case, you can install DFS using the following general steps (from Step 4 on, these are the same steps you would follow if you are installing DFS while installing the File Services role from scratch):

1. Open Server Manager.

2. Scroll to the Roles Summary section in the right pane and click the link for File Services.

3. In the right pane, scroll to the Role Services section and click the link for Add Role Services.

4. In the Select Role Services window, click the box for Distributed File System (see Figure 5-14). When you click this box, the boxes for DFS Namespaces and DFS Replication are automatically checked.

5. Click Next.

6. Enter a name for the namespace, such as the name of a server to hold DFS, the name of the organization, or a description of the file contents such as Research Data.

7. Click Next.

8. If you see the Create a DFS Namespace dialog box, click Create a namespace now, using this wizard. Click Next.

9. Select whether to install a Domain-based namespace or a Stand-alone namespace, as shown in Figure 5-15.

10. Click Next.

11. In the Configure Namespace window, you can add shared folders to appear in the namespace by using the Add button. Add any folders at this time (you can add more later), and click Next.

12. Click Install.

13. Click Close and close Server Manager.

If you choose not to configure a namespace when you install the DFS services, you can configure it later by using the DFS Management tool from the Administrative Tools menu. You can also create additional namespaces.

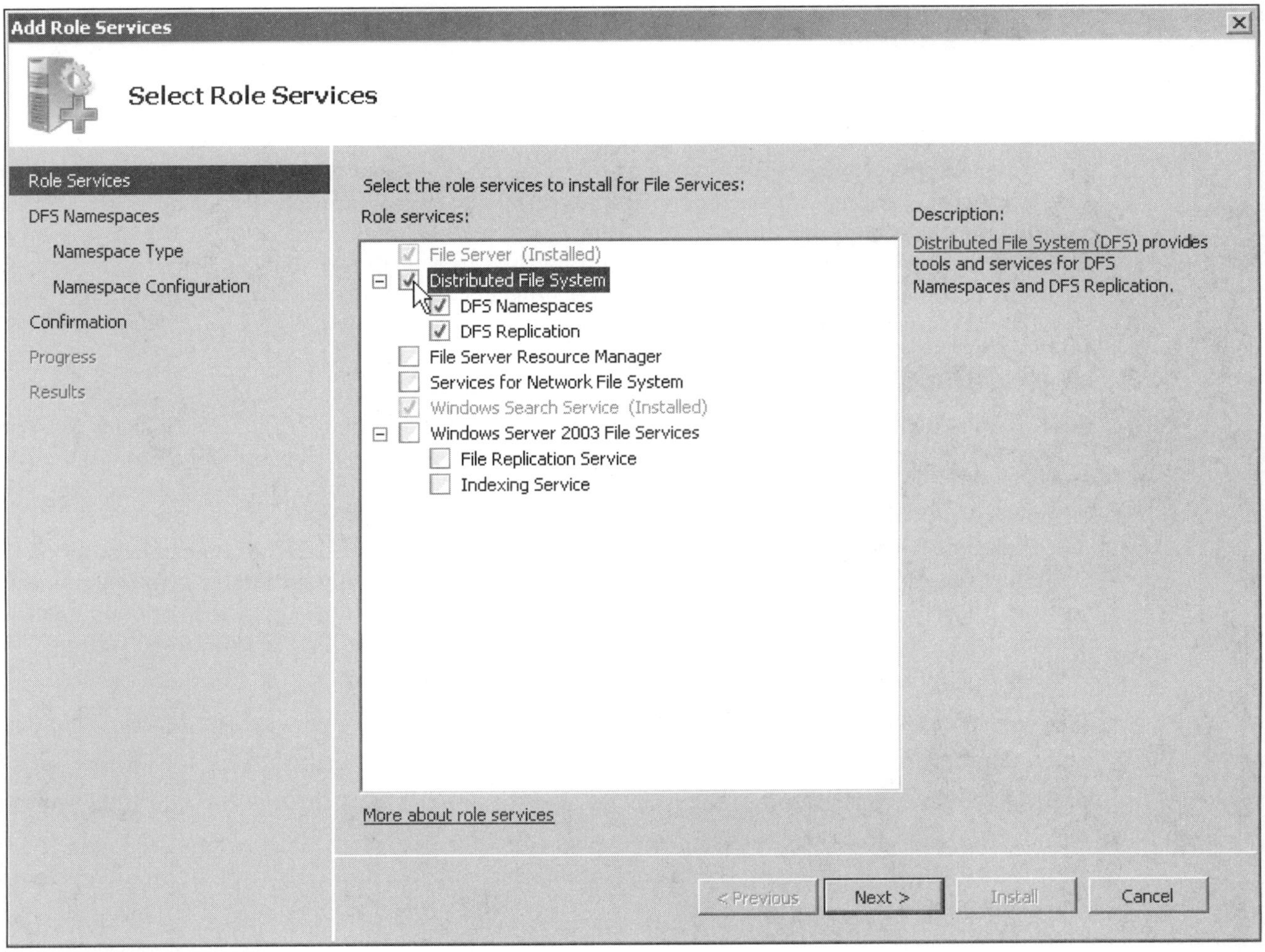

Add Role Services   ✕

Select Role Services

Role Services	Select the role services to install for File Services:
DFS Namespaces	Role services:
Namespace Type	
Namespace Configuration	
Confirmation	
Progress	
Results	

Role services:

- ☑ File Server (Installed)
- ☐ ☑ Distributed File System
  - ☑ DFS Namespaces
  - ☑ DFS Replication
- ☐ File Server Resource Manager
- ☐ Services for Network File System
- ☑ Windows Search Service (Installed)
- ☐ ☐ Windows Server 2003 File Services
  - ☐ File Replication Service
  - ☐ Indexing Service

Description:

Distributed File System (DFS) provides tools and services for DFS Namespaces and DFS Replication.

More about role services

[< Previous]   [Next >]   [Install]   [Cancel]

Figure 5-14   Selecting to install DFS

Activity 5-10: Creating a Namespace Root

Time Required: Approximately 10 minutes
Objective: Configure a namespace root.

Description: Creating a namespace root is an important configuration step for DFS. In this activity, you create a new namespace root. Don't worry whether a namespace root already exists, because you use the same steps to install the first namespace root and additional ones. The File Services role with DFS should already be installed. Also, have in mind a name for the namespace, such as Data plus your initials.

1. Click **Start**.
2. Point to **Administrative Tools** and click **DFS Management**.

As an alternative, you can also open the DFS Management snap-in using the MMC.

3. In the DFS Management window, click the **Action** menu at the top of the window or right-click **DFS Management** in the tree.
4. Click **New Namespace** to start the New Namespace Wizard.

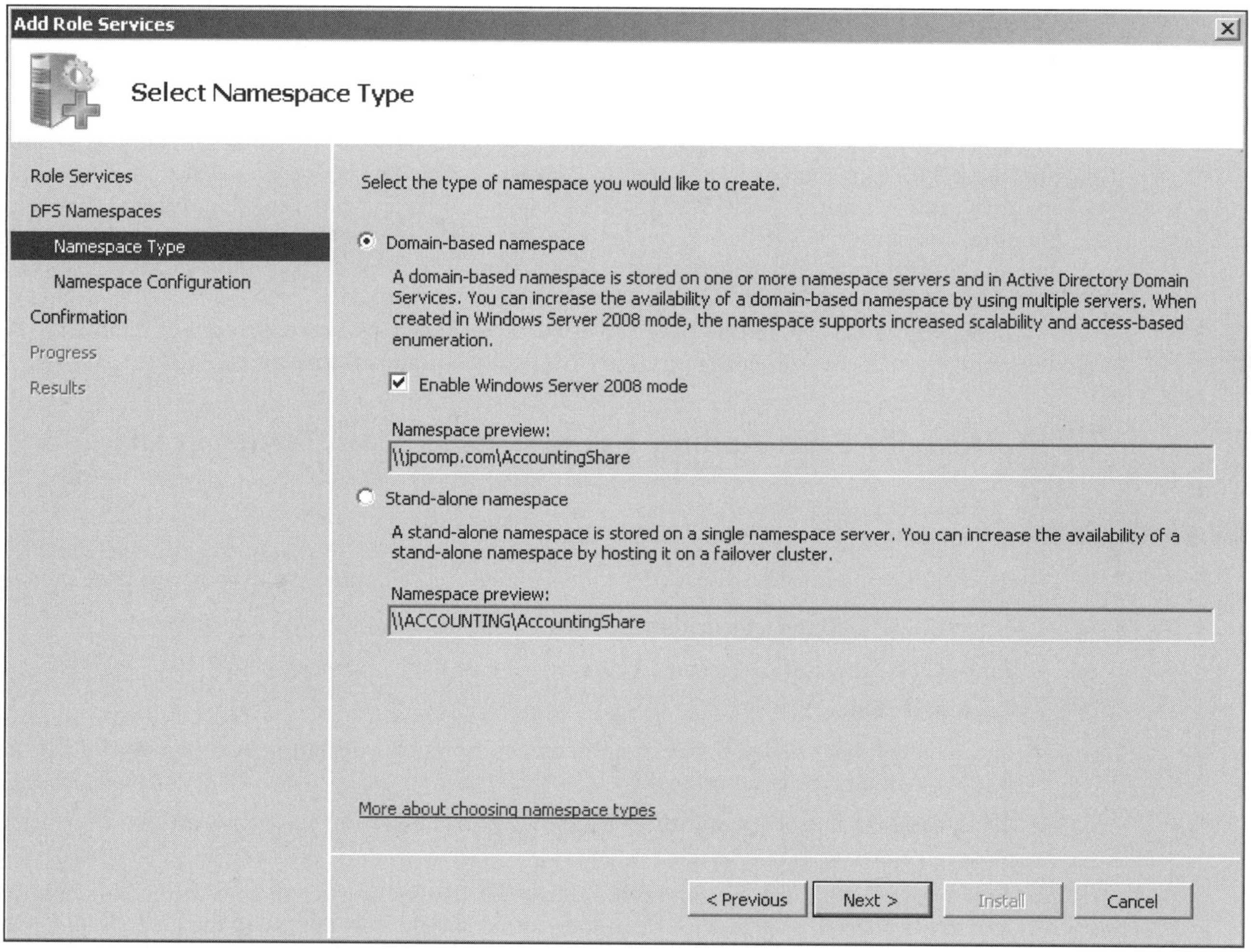

Add Role Services   ⊠

Select Namespace Type

Role Services

DFS Namespaces

   Namespace Type

   Namespace Configuration

Confirmation

Progress

Results

Select the type of namespace you would like to create.

◉ Domain-based namespace

A domain-based namespace is stored on one or more namespace servers and in Active Directory Domain Services. You can increase the availability of a domain-based namespace by using multiple servers. When created in Windows Server 2008 mode, the namespace supports increased scalability and access-based enumeration.

   ☑ Enable Windows Server 2008 mode

   Namespace preview:

   \\jpcomp.com\AccountingShare

○ Stand-alone namespace

A stand-alone namespace is stored on a single namespace server. You can increase the availability of a stand-alone namespace by hosting it on a failover cluster.

   Namespace preview:

   \\ACCOUNTING\AccountingShare

More about choosing namespace types

< Previous   Next >   Install   Cancel

Figure 5-15 Configuring the namespace type

5. Enter the name of the server to hold the namespace (the name of the server you are using) and click **Next**.

6. Enter the namespace name and click **Next**.

7. Leave **Domain-based namespace** as the default selection and click **Next**.

8. Click **Create**.

9. Click **Close**.

10. Leave the DFS Management window open for the next activity.

Managing a Domain-Based Namespace Root System

After the namespace root system is set up, several tasks are involved in managing the namespace root. These tasks can include:

- Creating a folder in a namespace
- Delegating management
- Tuning a namespace
- Deleting a namespace root
- Using DFS replication

Each of these tasks is described in the following sections.

Creating a Folder in a Namespace After the namespace root is created, the next step is to add folders and folder targets. A folder is simply a shared folder that you add to (or link to) the namespace root. However, you cannot add a folder that already contains other DFS folders under it.

You can also create folder targets. A **folder target** is a path in the Universal Naming Convention (UNC) format, such as to a shared folder or to a different DFS path—for example, a namespace for another folder (including a shared folder you have created outside of DFS). **Universal Naming Convention (UNC)** is a naming convention that designates network servers, computers, and shared resources. The format for a UNC name is, for example, \\servername\namespace\folder\file.

Clients who access the namespace can see a list of folder targets ordered in a hierarchy. The hierarchy is called the target priority, which the DFS administrator can configure.

Activity 5-11: Adding a Folder and Folder Target in DFS

Time Required: Approximately 5 minutes
Objective: Add a folder in DFS.

Description: In this activity, you add a folder under the DFS namespace root you have created.

1. Open the DFS Management tool if it is not already open.

2. Right-click the namespace you created in the tree under Namespaces.

3. Click **New Folder**.

4. In the New Folder dialog box, enter **Documentation** plus your initials as the name of the new folder, such as DocumentationJR.

5. Click the **Add** button to add the path to the Documentation folder you set up as a shared folder in Activity 5-7.

6. In the Add Folder Target dialog box, click the **Browse** button to find the Documentation folder you shared, double-click the folder, and it should now appear in the *Path to folder target* text box, as shown in Figure 5-16.

Add Folder Target	✕
Path to folder target:	
\\ACCOUNTING\DocumentationJR Browse...	
Example: \\Server\Shared Folder\Folder	
	OK Cancel

Figure 5-16   Adding a folder target

7. Click **OK**.

8. Notice that the folder target you configured now appears in the *Folder targets* box. Click **OK** in the New Folder dialog box. You'll see the new folder listed under the namespace in the tree.

9. Close the DFS Management tool.

Delegating Management You can delegate management of a DFS namespace so that the day-to-day activities can be managed by an assistant or by another person who oversees the management of the DFS shared folders. Delegating management simply involves right-clicking the namespace and clicking Delegate Management Permissions. Even if you are the main person to manage the DFS shared folders, it is still a good idea to have a backup person who is trained to work with the namespace root while you are out of the office.

Tuning a Namespace After you configure a DFS namespace, you can tune it to match the needs of your organization. The tuning options include the following:

- *Configure the order for referrals*—When a client accesses the namespace domain controller, she receives a list of targets in a specified order. This is called a referral. Targets on the same Active Directory site are listed before those on remote sites. To configure the order of referrals via the DFS Management tool, right-click the namespace root, click Properties, and click the Referrals tab (see Figure 5-17). The possible ordering methods are: Random order, Lowest cost, and Exclude targets outside of the client's site. Lowest cost refers to accessing the DFS server that is closest or on the least-cost network link.

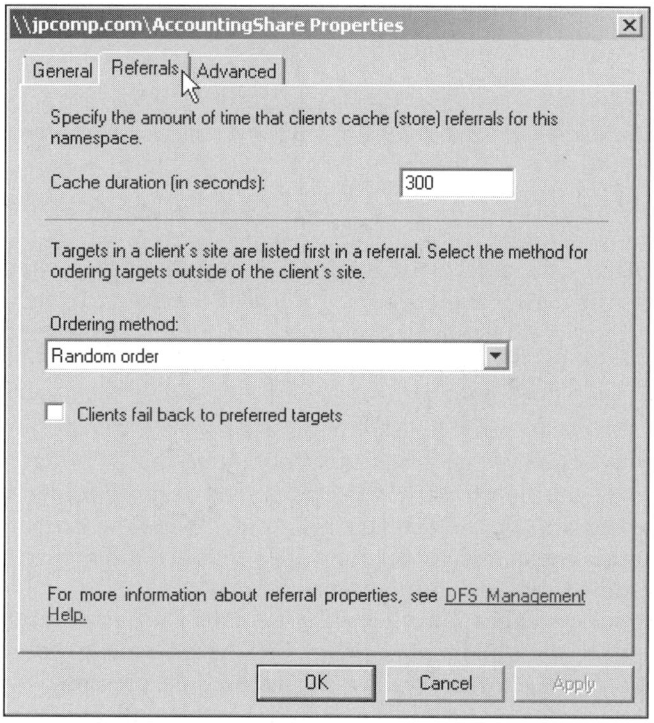

Figure 5-17 Referrals tab

- *Configure cache duration for a namespace*—A client can cache in memory a referral so that the referral is faster to access on later attempts. The cache duration is configured in seconds, with 300 seconds as the default. You can reconfigure the cache duration from the Referrals tab in the properties of the namespace root (the same tab used to configure the order of referrals).

- *Configure cache duration for a folder*—You can also configure the cache duration for a folder, such as one you access often. To do this, right-click the folder in the DFS Management tool and click the Referrals tab. The default setting for a folder is 1800 seconds.

- *Configure namespace polling*—If more than one namespace server exists, the servers check or poll other namespace servers in case there are changes to the namespace, such as the addition of a folder or target folder. In this way, all namespace servers stay current when there are changes. You can tune the poll method. One method is to optimize for consistency, which means that the namespace servers poll the primary domain controller for each change. Another option is to optimize for scalability. This means a namespace server polls its nearest namespace controller for any changes. The polling method is changed by right-clicking the namespace root in the DFS Management tool, clicking Properties, and clicking the Advanced tab.

- *Configure folder targets as enabled or disabled*—You can configure a folder target so that it is enabled or disabled. You might disable a folder target, for example, while you are working on the folder or adding many new files and then enable it when you are done. To do this from the DFS Management tool, click the folder with folder targets in the tree, ensuring that the Folder Targets tab is displayed in the middle pane. Right-click the folder and click Disable Folder Target (this option toggles between Disable and Enable). When you are ready to enable it, right-click the folder in the middle pane and click Enable Folder Target.

Deleting a Namespace Root If you find there is no longer a need to have a namespace root, you can delete it. You might do this, for example, because the namespace root was for a special project that is now finished. You can delete the namespace root via the DFS Management tool by clicking the namespace root and clicking Delete.

 If you want to leave the namespace intact for a while, but not displayed, you can right-click the namespace root and click *Remove Namespace from Display*.

Using DFS Replication DFS folders in a namespace root can be replicated on servers other than the one that contains the master folders (which is called the primary member). The replication capability is what enables you to provide fault tolerance and to create load balancing. On a network in which there are multiple servers, replication can prove to be a vital service to provide uninterrupted access for users, in case the computer with the master folder is inaccessible. Load balancing also is vital as a way to provide users with faster service and better network performance by enabling them to access the nearest server containing the DFS shared folders.

To configure replication, you first must have defined two or more folder targets. Also, you need to decide which server is to be the primary group member. The primary group member should be the server containing shared folders and files that are most current. Other servers that you replicate to are called replication group members.

When you are ready to set up replication, click a folder under the namespace root in the tree of the DFS Management tool. In the middle pane of the DFS Management tool, click the Replication tab, click Replicate Folder Wizard, and follow the instructions presented in the wizard. After a replication group is established, you can add a new folder to the replication group by expanding Replication in the tree, right-clicking a replication group, and clicking New Replicated Folders to start the New Replicated Folders Wizard. Replication is handled by the File Replication Service.

Windows Server 2008 includes some important improvements to DFS replication:

- It enables faster and more reliable recovery of changes to folders in DFS when a server crashes or goes down unexpectedly, such as during a power loss.

- Replication is faster for all sizes of files.

- DFS replication is more efficient over LANs and WANs to help reduce its overhead on networks.

Configuring Disk Quotas

One reason why setting up shared folders and DFS shared folders using NTFS-formatted volumes works well is that NTFS offers the ability to establish **disk quotas**. Using disk quotas has the following advantages:

- Preventing users from filling the disk capacity
- Encouraging users to help manage disk space by deleting old files when they receive a warning that their quota limit is approaching
- Tracking disk capacity needs on a per-user basis for future planning
- Providing server administrators with information about when users are nearing or have reached their quota limits

Disk quotas can be set on any local or shared volume. By simply enabling the disk quota feature on a volume, you can determine how much disk capacity is occupied by each user, without specifically setting quotas on those users. Another option is to set default quotas for all users, particularly on volumes that house user home folders. For example, many organizations establish a specific quota per user on home folder volumes. The default quota prevents a few users from occupying disk space needed by all users. Disk quotas also can be established on a per-user basis, or special exceptions can be made for users who need additional space, such as a newspaper publishing group on a college campus that requires a large amount of space for text and graphics files.

The general parameters that can be configured for disk quota management include the following:

- *Enable quota management*—Starts tracking disk quotas and sets up quota management
- *Deny disk space to users exceeding quota limit*—Prevents users from writing new information to disk after they have exceeded their quotas
- *Do not limit disk usage*—Tracks disk usage without establishing quotas on users, such as to gather statistics for disk capacity planning
- *Limit disk space to*—Sets the default amount of disk space that users can use
- *Set warning level to*—Sets the default amount of disk space users can occupy to trigger a warning message to users that they are reaching their quota
- *Log event when a user exceeds their quota limit*—Causes an event to be entered in the System log to notify the administrator that the user has reached his or her quota
- *Log event when the user exceeds their warning level*—Causes an event to be entered in the System log to notify the administrator that the user is approaching his or her quota

Activity 5-12: Configuring Disk Quotas

Time Required: Approximately 10 minutes
Objective: Enable disk quotas and then set a disk quota for a specific group of users.

Description: In this activity, you begin by enabling default disk quotas on the C: volume of a server for all users. Next, you set a special disk quota exception for a user account.

1. Click **Start** and click **Computer**.
2. Right-click **Local Disk (C:)** and click **Properties**.
3. Click the **Quota** tab.
4. Click the box to **Enable quota management**.
5. Click the box for **Deny disk space to users exceeding quota limit**.
6. Click the option button to **Limit disk space to**, and enter the limitation value, such as **800 MB**.

7. Enter a value in the *Set warning level to* boxes, such as **780 MB**.

8. If necessary, place a check in front of **Log event when a user exceeds their quota limit**.

9. Place a check in front of **Log event when a user exceeds their warning level** (see Figure 5-18).

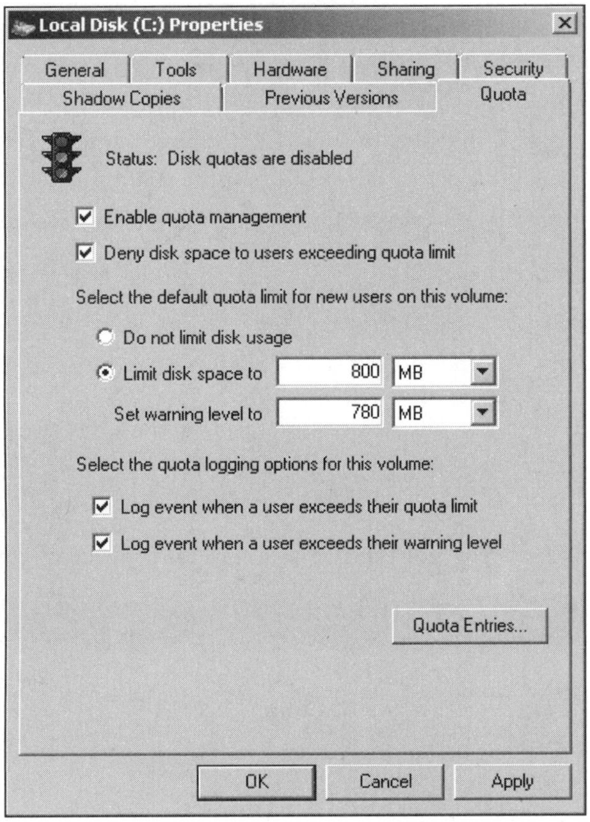

Local Disk (C:) Properties

| General | Tools | Hardware | Sharing | Security |

| Shadow Copies | Previous Versions | Quota |

Status: Disk quotas are disabled

☑ Enable quota management

☑ Deny disk space to users exceeding quota limit

Select the default quota limit for new users on this volume:

○ Do not limit disk usage

● Limit disk space to   800   MB ▼

Set warning level to   780   MB ▼

Select the quota logging options for this volume:

☑ Log event when a user exceeds their quota limit

☑ Log event when a user exceeds their warning level

[Quota Entries...]

[OK]   [Cancel]   [Apply]

Figure 5-18 Setting default disk quotas

---

10. Disk quotas for specific user accounts that are exceptions to the default quotas are set by clicking the Quota Entries button. Click **Quota Entries.**

11. Click the **Quota** menu and click **New Quota Entry.**

12. Click the **Advanced** button, click **Find Now,** and double-click an account in the list that you or your instructor have created previously (do not use the Administrator account). Click **OK.**

13. Click **Limit disk space to** and enter **500 MB**.

14. Click in the **Set warning level to** text box and enter **450 MB**.

15. Click **OK**.

16. Close the Quota Entries for (C:) window.

17. Remove the check mark from the box for **Enable quota management**. (This will ensure disk quotas are turned off so they do not interfere with future activities in this book. Make sure you have the disk quotas turned off before going on to the next activity.)

18. Click **OK** in the Properties dialog box. Close the Computer window.

CAUTION

Be careful that you don't set general disk quotas too low (see Steps 6 and 7), because this could restrict activities for the administrator and others. For example, if general quotas are set too low, Server Manager cannot survey information for roles and features because it needs disk space in a temporary folder for its work.

Using UNIX Interoperability in Windows Server 2008

Windows Server 2008 offers the **Subsystem for UNIX-based Applications (SUA)** for compatibility with UNIX and Linux systems. This subsystem provides interoperability between Windows Server 2008 and UNIX and Linux systems. Microsoft recognizes that many IT operations include both UNIX/Linux and Windows Server 2008 computers. The UNIX/Linux computers run a wide range of UNIX/Linux applications that represent a considerable investment in terms of time and expense to develop and install. Also, an environment with both UNIX/Linux and Windows computers requires extra work in administering two sets of user accounts, one for UNIX/Linux computers and one for Windows Servers.

SUA removes many of the barriers between these two systems so that it is easier to integrate them and eases the management load of server administrators. When you install SUA in Windows Server 2008, you can do the following:

- Run UNIX/Linux applications with few or no changes to the program source code.
- Run UNIX/Linux scripts.
- Use popular UNIX/Linux shells.
- Run most UNIX/Linux commands.
- Run the popular vi UNIX/Linux editor.

Most UNIX/Linux applications can be moved over to Windows Server 2008 SUA with only minor program code modifications that would be typical for moving an application from one distribution of UNIX/Linux to a different distribution, such as from Red Hat Enterprise Linux to SUSE Linux or to BSD UNIX. However, whether or not modifications are needed, all applications must be recompiled in SUA, such as by using the included C or C++ compiler in SUA. A **compiler** is a program that reads lines of program code in a source file and converts the code into machine-language instructions the computer can execute.

A UNIX/Linux script consists of lines of commands that are executed when you run the script, similar to the use of scripts in Windows Server 2008. Scripts can be moved over to Windows Server 2008 SUA and run with no or few modifications. Typical modifications might be for different locations of directories and files or for commands that are specific to a particular UNIX/Linux shell.

A **shell** is an interface between the user and the operating system. The Command Prompt window in Windows Server 2008 is an example of a shell as a UNIX/Linux administrator might experience it when writing computer code or administering a computer from the command line. SUA supports two commonly used UNIX/Linux shells: the Korn shell and the C shell.

When you are in the Korn or C shell hosted by SUA, you can run most of the same commands as in those shells on a native UNIX/Linux system. This includes common commands such as the *ls* command to list the contents of a directory, the *mkdir* command to create a directory, and the *cat* command to create a file or view its contents. You can also use the *man* command to view online documentation for a UNIX/Linux command. SUA supports more than 300 native UNIX/Linux commands and utilities.

SUA offers the vi (also called the vim) editor, which can be used from either the Korn or C shells. UNIX/Linux server administrators and programmers rely on the popular UNIX/Linux vi editor for creating scripts, writing program source code, editing data files, and many more functions. The vi editor comes with virtually all UNIX/Linux distributions and so is an old friend to UNIX/Linux pros.

SUA can be set up to run in "mixed mode," which further removes the barriers between UNIX/Linux and Windows Server 2008. In mixed mode, every process that is run is treated as a Windows process. This means that UNIX/Linux processes can link to Windows dynamic-link library files. **Dynamic-link library (DLL) files** contain program code that can be called and run by Windows applications (and with SUA, also used by UNIX/Linux applications). DLL files have the .dll extension and are a standardized library of functions used by applications.

DLL files can be loaded into memory for fast response while also reducing the overhead on a computer when multiple applications are running.

Another advantage of using SUA is the inclusion of **Server for Network Information Services**. Network Information Services (NIS) provides a naming system for shared resources on a UNIX/Linux network. Typically, one UNIX/Linux network server acts as the NIS server on a UNIX/Linux network. Through the NIS server, a user can access shared resources, such as a shared partition containing shared files. In SUA, Server for NIS can be loaded as part of Active Directory and used on domain controllers. This enables the server administrator to combine management of user accounts, groups, and shared resources through Active Directory. This reduces the need to maintain separate user accounts and groups on Windows and UNIX/Linux systems, which halves the work for the administrator. Server for NIS also ensures the synchronization of account passwords. This means that if a UNIX/Linux user changes the account password on her UNIX/Linux workstation, the password change is also made automatically for the same account name in Windows Servers via Active Directory.

Windows Server 2008 offers several important new features for SUA:

- More transparent ability for UNIX/Linux applications to connect to Oracle and SQL Server databases—made possible through the implementation of two database access standards, Open Database Connectivity (ODBC) and Oracle Call Interface (OCI)

- Inclusion of true 64-bit libraries for support of 64-bit applications and utilities for high-performance response

- New utilities to support both the major UNIX versions: BSD UNIX and SVR-5 UNIX (which also includes support for most Linux utilities)

- Ability for application developers to use Microsoft Visual Studio for designing UNIX/Linux applications

You can install SUA from Server Manager by following these general steps:

1. Click Start, point to Administrative Tools, and click Server Manager.

2. Scroll to the Features Summary section and open it if necessary.

3. Click Add Features.

4. Click Subsystem for UNIX-based Applications and click Next.

5. Click Install.

6. Click Close.

7. Close Server Manager.

8. Ensure you are connected to the Internet.

9. Click Start and click All Programs.

10. Click Subsystem for UNIX-based Applications and click Download Utilities for Subsystem for UNIX-based Applications.

11. Follow the instructions for proceeding with the download and installation of utilities (from Microsoft's Web site). Ensure that you install both the utilities and the software development kit (SDK). (You might need to register with Microsoft, and you also will need to select the appropriate download for an x86 or x64 computer.)

12. Follow the instructions for installing the utilities and SDK.

When you are finished installing the utilities and SDK, you can open a command-line window for either the Korn shell or the C shell. For example, to open the window for the Korn shell, do the following (see Figure 5-19, which also shows the use of the UNIX/Linux *pwd* command to display the current path):

1. Click Start.

2. Point to All Programs.

3. Click Subsystem for UNIX-based Applications.

4. Click Korn Shell.

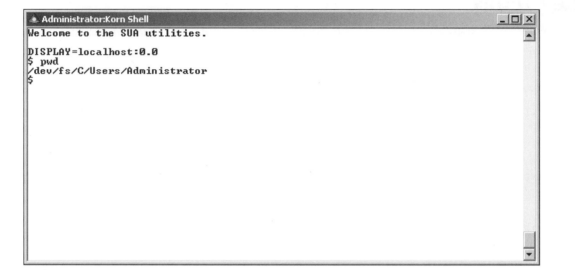

Figure 5-19 Window for using the Korn shell

Chapter Summary

- Windows Server 2008 uses discretionary access control lists for managing access to resources.

- NTFS uses folder and file attributes for one level of security. The basic attributes are read-only and hidden. Extended or enhanced attributes are archive, index, compress, and encrypt.

- When you use the encrypt attribute, this employs the Microsoft Encrypting File System to protect files and folders.

- Permissions provide another level of security for files and folders. The types of permissions depend on the type of resource that is to be secured, such as a folder, file, printer, or other resource. Groups and users are granted permissions.

- Special permissions provide the option to further customize security at a more granular level than basic permissions.

- Folder and file auditing enable you to track who has accessed resources.

- Folder and file owners have Full control permissions, including the ability to change permissions.

- Folders can be shared for users to access over a network, and shared folder security is configured through share permissions. After a folder has been shared, it can be published in Active Directory for better management.

- Use the Effective Permissions capability to troubleshoot a security conflict.

- The Distributed File System (DFS) enables you to set up shared folders that are easier for users to access and can be replicated for backup and load distribution.
- Use disk quotas to manage the resources put on a server disk volume so you do not prematurely or unexpectedly run out of disk space.
- If you have a network that uses a combination of Windows Servers and UNIX/Linux computers, you can install the Subsystem for UNIX-based Applications so that UNIX/Linux applications and scripts work on a Windows Server 2008 server.

Key Terms

attribute   A characteristic associated with a folder or file used to help manage access.

auditing   In Windows Server 2008, a security capability that tracks activity on an object, such as reading, writing, creating, or deleting a file in a folder.

compiler   A program that reads lines of program code in a source file and converts the code into machine-language instructions the computer can execute.

DFS topology   Applies to a domain-based DFS model and encompasses the DFS namespace root, shared folders, and replication folders.

Directory Service Client (DSClient)   Microsoft software for pre-Windows 2000 clients that connect to Windows 2000 Server, Windows Server 2003, and Windows Server 2008 and enables those clients to view information published in Active Directory.

discretionary access control list (DACL)   An access control list that manages access to an object, such as a folder, and that is configured by a server administrator or owner of the object.

disk quota   Allocating a specific amount of disk space to a user or application with the ability to ensure that the user or application cannot use more disk space than is specified in the allocation.

Distributed File System (DFS)   A system that enables folders shared from multiple computers to appear as though they exist in one centralized hierarchy of folders instead of on many different computers.

domain-based DFS model   A DFS model that uses Active Directory and is available only to servers and workstations that are members of a particular domain. The domain-based model enables a deep, root-based, hierarchical arrangement of shared folders that is published in Active Directory. DFS shared folders in the domain-based model can be replicated for fault tolerance and load balancing.

dynamic-link library (DLL) files   A library of files containing program code that can be called and run by Windows applications (and with SUA, also used by UNIX/Linux applications). *See* Subsystem for UNIX-based Applications.

Encrypting File System (EFS)   Set by an attribute of NTFS, this file system enables a user to encrypt the contents of a folder or a file so that it can only be accessed via private key code by the user who encrypted it. EFS adheres to the Data Encryption Standard's expanded version for data protection.

folder target   A path in the Universal Naming Convention (UNC) format, such as to a DFS shared folder or to a different DFS path.

inherited permissions   Permissions of a parent object that also apply to child objects of the parent, such as to subfolders within a folder.

load balancing   On a single server, distributing resources across multiple server disk drives and paths for better server response; and on multiple network servers, distributing resources across two or more servers for better server and network performance.

namespace root   The main container that holds DFS links to shared folders in a domain.

ownership   Having the privilege to change permissions and to fully manipulate an object. The account that creates an object, such as a folder or printer, initially has ownership.

permissions   In Windows Server 2008, privileges to access and manipulate resource objects, such as folders and printers; for example, the privilege to read a file or to create a new file.

publish   Making an object, such as a printer or shared folder, available for users to access when they view Active Directory contents and so that the data associated with the object can be replicated.

replication group   A grouping of shared folders in a DFS namespace root that are replicated or copied to all servers that participate in DFS replication. When changes are made to DFS shared folders, all of the participating servers are automatically or manually synchronized so that they have the same copy.

Server for Network Information Services   A service that Subsystem for UNIX-based Applications (SUA) can add to Active Directory to make a Windows Server 2008 server a Network Information Services server for coordinating management of user acccounts and groups between UNIX/ Linux computers and Windows Server 2008 servers on the same network. *See* Subsystem for UNIX-based Applications.

share permissions   Permissions that apply to a particular object that is shared over a network, such as a shared folder or printer.

shell   An interface between the user and the operating system.

stand-alone DFS model   A DFS model in which no Active Directory implementation is available to help manage the shared folders. This model provides only a single or flat level share.

Subsystem for UNIX-based Applications (SUA)   A subsystem that can be installed in Windows Server 2008 for using UNIX and Linux commands, applications, and scripts.

system control ACL (SACL)   An access control list that contains settings to audit the access to an object, such as a folder.

Universal Naming Convention (UNC)   A naming convention that designates network servers, computers, and shared resources. The format for a UNC name is, for example, \\servername \namespace\folder\file.

Review Questions

1. Your company writes software for voting machines and needs to ensure that the software and documentation is carefully protected on its servers. Last week, one of the servers was stolen from its machine room, but fortunately that server did not contain sensitive voting machine files. What folder and file security can your company use to protect its information in the future, so that even if a server is stolen its files cannot be accessed?

   a.   Microsoft Encrypting File System

   b.   the Verify permission

   c.   scramble key authentication for folders and files

   d.   Microsoft Distributed Security

2. A fellow programmer has set up a shared folder of programs he is working on, but the problem is that several users have discovered the folder and have been trying out the programs. What steps can the programmer take to ensure that only he can view and access the folder? (Choose all that apply.)

   a.   Use permissions to secure the shared folder.

   b.   Remove all attributes to the shared folder.

   c.   Place a dollar sign after the name of the shared folder to hide it.

   d.   Create a logon list for the shared folder.

3. Your company has salespeople who use laptop computers for travel. When they go out they need to access marketing files stored on the server. What capability enables them to access these files while they are on the road and cannot connect to the network?

   a. sync files

   b. file refresh

   c. Clipboard

   d. offline files

4. The water resources group in your organization asked you to create a shared folder to hold research data. Ten people are in the group; two of them cannot access the file but the other eight can. What can you do to easily determine why two people cannot access it?

   a. Check every group on the server to determine its members.

   b. Re-create the accounts for the two users.

   c. Check the effective permissions for that folder.

   d. Use the Security Configuration Wizard to create new security.

5. You have configured a folder for sharing, but users do not see the server on the network. What might be the problem? (Choose all that apply.)

   a. You did not configure the sharing as network wide on the Sharing tab.

   b. Network discovery is disabled.

   c. The Windows Firewall is blocking incoming and outgoing access.

   d. Folder reciprocation is not turned on.

6. The _____ can change permissions on a folder.

7. You've published a folder in Active Directory and now want to test your work by finding it in Active Directory from Windows Server 2008. What steps do you take?

   a. Click Start, click Computer, and click the Search Active Directory button.

   b. Click Start, click Network, and click the Search Active Directory button.

   c. Click Start, point to All Programs, and click Search Network.

   d. Click Start, click Run, type adsearch, and click OK.

8. Use the _____ tool to publish a shared folder in Active Directory.

9. Your college uses shared folders to make class information and assignments available to students. The shared folders are currently on three different computers, and finding the right folder can be confusing. What is a possible solution to make the folders easier for students to find and use?

   a. Move the servers to specific student lab locations.

   b. Use UNC for naming the servers.

   c. Create a contiguous sharing space.

   d. Set up the shared folders in DFS.

10. The Computer Advisory Committee in your company has been concerned that users store many files on the servers, but aren't good about deleting old files. This has resulted in less free space on the servers' disks. What solution do you propose?

    a. Only store files on member computers and not DCs.

    b. Configure the file space attribute on user folders.

    c. Use DFS to allocate limited space for users.

    d. Set up disk quotas for user accounts.

11. What are the two DFS models?

12. Your company has installed Subsystem for UNIX-based Applications (SUA) on a Windows Server 2008 server. You have copied over a test program from a UNIX computer and try to run it in the SUA environment, but it won't run. What might be the cause of the problem?

    a. You have to first configure SUA for the program mode.

    b. UNIX programs will only run if you link them to .dll files first.

    c. UNIX programs only run from the Windows shell.

    d. You have to recompile the program source file in the SUA environment.

13. Several of your DFS clients complain that it can take some time to access a DFS shared folder, even though they just recently accessed it. They are expecting faster response. What can you do?

    a. Tune the cache duration for the folder.

    b. Disable polling.

    c. Limit the size of shared folders in DFS.

    d. Configure a DFS site link.

14. You have a series of older files that you don't access often, but you do need them occasionally. Some of these folders take up large quantities of disk space. What NTFS feature can you use to reduce the disk space they occupy?

    a. Use the virtual indexing attribute.

    b. Use the compress attribute.

    c. Use the zip permission.

    d. Use the size control permission.

15. As the server administrator, you currently own a folder but want to transfer ownership to the user who will now manage that folder's contents. How can ownership be transferred to the user?

    a. Transfer ownership to the user.

    b. Give the user Modify permissions and then transfer ownership to that user.

    c. Give the user Full control permissions and then have the user take ownership.

    d. Give the user the special permissions, read extended attributes, and full ownership.

16. Subsystem for UNIX-based Applications is installed as which of the following?

    a. a DFS component

    b. a role

    c. a kernel DLL

    d. a feature

17. Your network has Linux, Windows Vista, and Windows Server 2008 computers. Active Directory is also in use through Windows Server 2008. You are tired of managing accounts and groups for both the Linux computers and the Windows computers. To reduce your account and group management workload, you can _____.

18. Which of the following can you accomplish using the DFS Management tool? (Choose all that apply.)

    a. Create a namespace root.

    b. Delegate management over a namespace root.

    c. Create a folder in a namespace root.

    d. Tune a namespace root.

19. A set of shared folders copied in DFS to one or more servers is called a _____.

20. You have created a shared folder for the management team at your company. You need to give each member of the team the ability to add files to the shared folder, but also to only change and delete files that the member has placed in the shared folder. Which of the following share permissions should you allow for the members of the management team?

a. Co-owner

b. Reader

c. Contributor

d. Co-author

Case Projects

Rocky Mountain College in Colorado is a fast-growing community college. It offers typical college programs and combines these with special classes for certificate and two-year programs such as fisheries management, wildlife studies and management, mountain geology, and ski and snowboard technologies. The college is located in the foothills below Rocky Mountain National Park and is both a residential and commuter campus.

The college's Information Technology Department manages the servers used for academic and administrative computing. Some departments, such as Engineering Studies, Computer Science, and English have servers located in the departments, with some administrative server tasks delegated to each department's computer specialist. The Engineering Studies Department has two Linux servers, and its faculty use a combination of UNIX and Linux computers. The college's Development Department also has a Linux server for specialized alumni and development software. All other academic and administrative servers are in the process of being upgraded from Windows Server 2003 to Windows Server 2008. Active Directory is installed and used for the servers. The college has 10 walk-in computer labs for students and faculty. Also, many faculty use laptop computers that they can connect to the college computer network. The IT Department has hired you to consult on improving use of the servers and to advise on the upgrades.

Case Project 5-1: Enabling Fast Searches

The servers that have been upgraded to Windows Server 2008 have shown no improvement in performing searches for folders and files. One of the reasons the college has decided to upgrade was for faster search response. After you have analyzed the situation, you realize that they are using the older Indexing Service. Create a short report of your recommendations for using a faster search alternative, including the general steps for implementing this alternative.

Case Project 5-2: Planning Folder Permissions

Up to this point, the college has used a relatively unplanned approach to planning folder permissions, sometimes using the default permissions on newly created folders. Now they have created a new committee to review security on the servers, and the committee is working to develop a specific policy for setting up NTFS folder permissions and share permissions. They have asked for your recommendations on the following types of folders:

• The \Windows folder (which is not shared)

• Software application folders (which are not shared)

• Home folders for faculty and staff (which are not shared)

• Folders containing the college's financial accounting databases (which are not shared and are used only by members of the Administrative Business Department)

- A shared folder containing electronic pages from the faculty and staff handbook (which is shared for faculty and staff use only)
- Shared folders used by instructors to provide students with class information and assignments

Case Project 5-3: Using DFS

Each Windows Server 2008 server contains shared folders that are accessed by students, faculty, and staff. The problem is that many users are still very confused about which folders are on which servers. As a result, they waste a lot of time trying to find the specific shared folder that they need. The college asks you to help them develop a way to make the folders easier to find and access. Create a report that explains how DFS works and how it can be of value in their situation. Design a very general DFS folder structure that they might implement. For example, you might base the folder structure on academic and administrative departments in the college.

Case Project 5-4: Integrating the UNIX and Linux Computers

The IT Department is interested in trying to better integrate the college's UNIX and Linux computers with the Windows Server 2008 computers. For example, they want to look into reducing user account management headaches. They also want to be able to run some of the alumni and development programs on Windows Server 2008, particularly programs that use an Oracle database. The IT director asks you to create a short report that discusses how they can achieve this integration.

chapter 6

Configuring Windows Server 2008 Printing

After reading this chapter and completing the exercises, you will be able to:

- Understand how Windows Server 2008 printing works
- Use the XPS Print Path
- Use the XML Paper Specification (XPS)
- Install the Print Services role
- Use the Printers window to configure printing properties
- Install local and shared printers
- Configure printer properties
- Configure a nonlocal or Internet printer
- Manage print jobs
- Use the Print Management tool
- Troubleshoot common printing problems

If you have ever needed to print a file, but didn't have access to a printer or found your printer not working, then you know how important printing can be. It's something people take for granted until the printer is down or not available. Networks and servers have helped to revolutionize printing by enabling shared printers. Sharing printers can save dollars, because not everyone needs a printer physically connected to his or her computer. Sharing printers also can save time by ensuring there is a group of printers that are reliably set up and available.

In this chapter, you learn how printing works in Windows Server 2008, including Internet printing. You install the Print Services role to help coordinate printing functions on a server. Also, you learn how to install a printer and manage its properties. You set up a shared printer and configure security for that printer. With your printer set up, you learn to manage print jobs and print queues. Finally, you learn how to use the Print Management tool to centralize printer control for easier management of multiple printers.

An Overview of Windows Server 2008 Printing

The network printing process on Windows Server 2008 LANs begins when a client decides to print a file, either on a printer locally connected to the client's computer (a **local print device**), on a shared network printer (a **network print device**), or through Internet printing (a type of network print device). A shared network printer can be connected to a workstation sharing a printer, a printer attached to a server, or a printer attached to a print server device. The workstation or application that initially generates the print job is the network **print client,** and the computer or print server device offering the printer share is the network **print server.** A **print job** is a document or items to be printed.

A shared network printer device is an object, like a folder, that is made available to network users for print services. When the printout goes to a printer share, it is temporarily spooled in specially designated disk storage or memory and held until it is sent to be printed. **Spooling** frees the server CPU to handle other processing requests in addition to print requests.

When its turn comes, the print file is sent to the printer along with formatting instructions. A **printer driver** that holds configuration information for the given printer provides the formatting instructions. The formatting and configuration information includes instructions to reset the printer before starting, information about printing fonts, and special printer control codes.

The printer driver resides on the computer offering the printer services (for local and network print jobs) and also can reside on the workstation client sending the print job. For example, when you send a print job to be printed on a Windows Server 2008 print share, your printout is formatted using the printer driver at your workstation and then further interpreted by print services software on the print server. The printer driver is either contained on the Windows Server 2008 installation DVD or obtained from the printer manufacturer.

How Network Printing Works

In technical terms, both the network print client and the network print server run specific processes to deliver a print job to a printer. The following steps outline the printing process.

1. The first stage in the process is when the software application at the client generates a print file.

2. As it creates the print file, the application communicates with the Windows **graphics device interface (GDI).** The GDI integrates information about the print file—such as word-processing codes for fonts, colors, and embedded graphics objects—with information obtained from the printer driver installed at the client for the target printer, in a process that Microsoft calls rendering.

3. When the GDI is finished, the print file is formatted with control codes to implement the special graphics, font, and color characteristics of the file. At the same time, the software application places the print file in the client's spooler by writing the file, called the **spool file,** to a

subfolder used for spooling. In the Windows environment, a **spooler** is a group of DLLs, information files, and programs that processes print jobs for printing.

Large print files cannot be processed if there is inadequate disk space on which to store spooled files. Make sure clients and the server have sufficient disk space to handle the largest print requests, particularly for huge graphics and color files that are targeted for a color printer or plotter.

4. The remote print provider at the client makes a remote procedure call to the network print server to which the print file is targeted, such as a Windows Server 2008 server. If the print server is responding and ready to accept the print file, the remote printer transmits that file from the client's spooler folder to the Server service on Windows Server 2008.

5. The network print server uses four processes to receive and process a print file: router, print provider, print processor, and print monitor. The router, print provider, and print processor all are pieces of the network print server's spooler.

6. Once it is contacted by the remote print provider on the print client, the Server service calls its router, the Print Spooler service. The router directs the print file to the print provider, which stores it in a spool file until it can be sent to the printer.

7. While the file is spooled, the print provider works with the print processor to ensure that the file is formatted to use the right data type, such as TEXT or RAW.

8. When the spool file is fully formatted for transmission to the printer, the print monitor pulls it from the spooler's disk storage and sends it off to the printer.

For all of the activities in this chapter, you'll need an account with Administrator privileges. Also, these activities can be completed on a virtual server or computer, such as in Hyper-V.

Some steps in the activities in this book include bulleted questions with space for you to record your responses/answers.

Activity 6-1: Print Spooler Service

Time Required: Approximately 5 minutes
Objective: Learn about the Print Spooler service and the services upon which it depends.

Description: The Print Spooler service works in conjunction with the Remote Procedure Call service to help make Windows Server 2008 printing possible. In this activity, you use the Computer Management tool to view the Print Spooler service as well as services upon which it depends.

1. Click **Start**, point to **Administrative Tools**, and click **Computer Management**.

In previous activities, you have used Server Manager to view services. In this activity, you use the Computer Management tool so you are familiar with it as an alternative.

2. Click **Services and Applications** in the tree under Computer Management.
3. Double-click **Services** in the middle pane.
4. Scroll the middle pane to find the Print Spooler service. Click **Print Spooler**. Notice the description of the Print Spooler service, as shown in Figure 6-1.

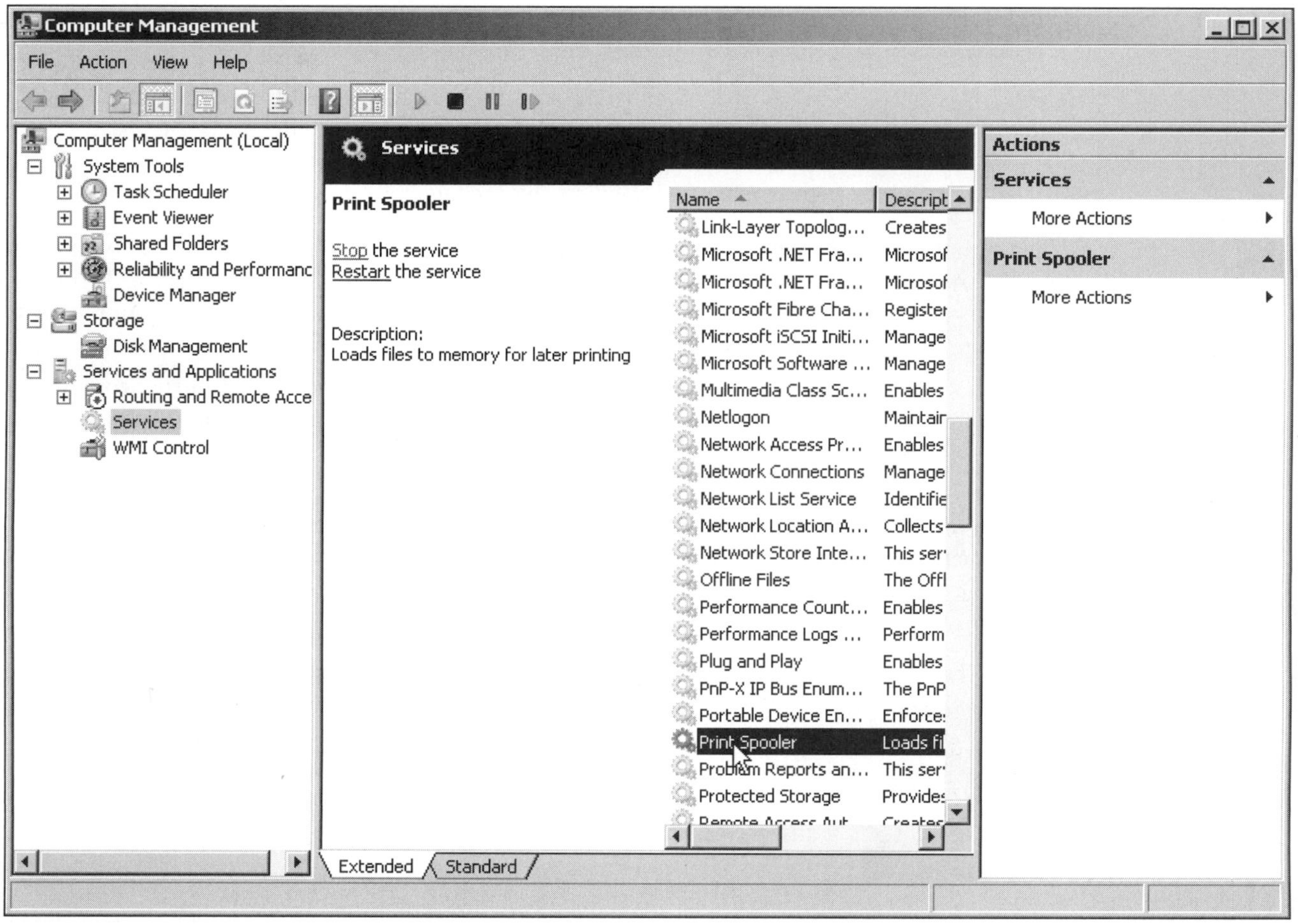

Figure 6-1 Viewing the description of the Print Spooler service

    5. Double-click **Print Spooler** to view its properties.

    6. Click the **Dependencies** tab.

       • What service(s) depend on the Print Spooler service? On what service(s) does the Print Spooler depend?

    7. Click **Cancel**.

    8. Close the **Computer Management** window.

How Internet Printing Works

When a print job is processed over the Internet or an intranet, Internet Information Services (IIS) must be installed and running in Windows Server 2008, and the client must connect to the Windows Server 2008 IIS using a Web browser such as Microsoft Internet Explorer. The print process on the client is nearly the same as for network printing, with a couple of exceptions. One exception is that the browser, instead of a software application such as Microsoft Word, sends the print file to the GDI. Another exception is that the remote print provider at the client makes a remote procedure call to IIS on the Windows Server 2008 server. The remote procedure call is made through the TCP/IP-based Hypertext Transfer Protocol (HTTP) protocol, which transports another protocol, called the **Internet Printing Protocol (IPP)**. The IPP encapsulates the remote procedure call and print process information and is transported in HTTP just as a human passenger is transported inside a bus along a highway. IIS sends the IPP encapsulated information to its HTTP print server. The HTTP print server works with the regular Windows Server 2008 spooler services—the print provider, print processor, and print monitor processes—to prepare the print file for transmission to the target printer.

For the sake of security, server clients who are using the Internet printing capability through IPP should set their local Web browsers to have a high security setting. For example, Internet Explorer users should have security set at medium or higher. To configure Internet Explorer security, open Internet Explorer, click the Tools menu, click Internet Options, click the Security tab, and set the appropriate security level.

Activity 6-2: Installing the Internet Printing Client

Time Required: Approximately 5 minutes

Objective: Install the Internet Printing Client so that clients can use IPP.

Description: Windows Server 2008 comes with the Internet Printing Client that enables clients connecting to Windows Server 2008 for print services to use IPP for network and Internet printing. In this activity, you install the Internet Printing Client.

1. Click **Start**, point to **Administrative Tools**, and click **Server Manager**.
2. Scroll to the Features Summary section of Server Manager and click **Add Features**.
3. Under *Features*, click the box for **Internet Printing Client**.
4. Click **Next**.
5. Click **Install**.
6. Click **Close**.
7. Leave Server Manager open for the next activity.

Using the XPS Print Path

Windows Server 2008 printing comes with support for **XML Paper Specification (XPS)**. XPS is an advanced way of printing documents for multiple purposes, including viewing electronic pages and printing pages in a polished format. XPS is a concept similar to using PDF files. When you print to this option, the document can be opened to view in XPS document format, which is an electronic view of the document as though it has been printed.

The XPS print path in Windows Server 2008 is offered as an alternative to the GDI print path used by conventional documents. The XPS print path offers these enhancements to printing:

- Customized print path for documents using XPS
- Advanced color support for sophisticated color printers
- Faster performance for printouts generated by .NET Framework applications
- Full WYSIWYG (What You See Is What You Get, which means documents viewed in the creation/editing stage are rendered in a similar format in a printout)

The XPS drive path uses the XPSDrv Driver Model. This driver can print to an XPS-enabled printer or a file. It brings more efficiency to print spooling by eliminating intermediate spool files for formatting and by using smaller spool files in final printing. One technique it uses to produce smaller spool files is Zip compression. Smaller spool files means less network traffic and faster network transmission from print server to printer.

Installing the Print Services Role

To take full advantage of Windows Server 2008 to manage shared printers for one location, install the Print Services role. This enables you to use the Print Management tool to manage shared printers (see the section in this chapter, "Using the Print Management Tool"). It also enables you to track printing events through a log you can view using the Event Viewer. Another advantage is that you can configure a group policy for standardized management of printer connections.

When you install the Print Services role, you can use the following services within the role:

- *Print Server*—A service that is mandatory when you install the Print Services role and that installs the Print Management tool. This service also creates an exception in the Windows Firewall to permit file and printer sharing.

- *Internet Printing*—Creates a Web site through IIS (IIS must also be installed as a server role) for managing print jobs and for connecting to shared printers using IPP.

- *LPD Service*—Line Printer Daemon (LPD) enables UNIX and Linux computers to print to shared printers managed through Windows Server 2008. This installs and uses the TCP/IP Print Server service, and when installed it configures the Windows Firewall to allow the TCP communications port (port 515) for network spooler communications to be used for print processing between the client and the server.

Activity 6-3: Installing the Print Services Role

Time Required: Approximately 10 minutes
Objective: Install the Print Services role using Windows Server 2008.

Description: Windows Server 2008 can be made a full-featured print server by installing the Print Services role. In this activity, you use Server Manager to install the role.

1. Ensure that Server Manager is open, or open Server Manager from the Administrative Tools menu.

2. Scroll to the Roles Summary section and click **Add Roles**.

3. If you see the Before You Begin dialog box, click **Next**.

4. Click the box for **Print Services** and click **Next**.

5. Read the information about Print Services.

   - What role services can you select from the Select Role Services window?

6. Click **Next**.

7. Click **Next**.

8. Click **Install**.

9. Click **Close**.

10. Close Server Manager.

Using the Printers Window

The Windows Server 2008 Printers window (see Figure 6-2) is enhanced from previous versions to enable more versatility. In its native mode, it offers two panes. The left pane lists Favorite Links to folders, such as to the Documents folder, which is the default folder for storing documents, including those created from Microsoft Office software. Below the Favorite Links is a listing of folders on the server.

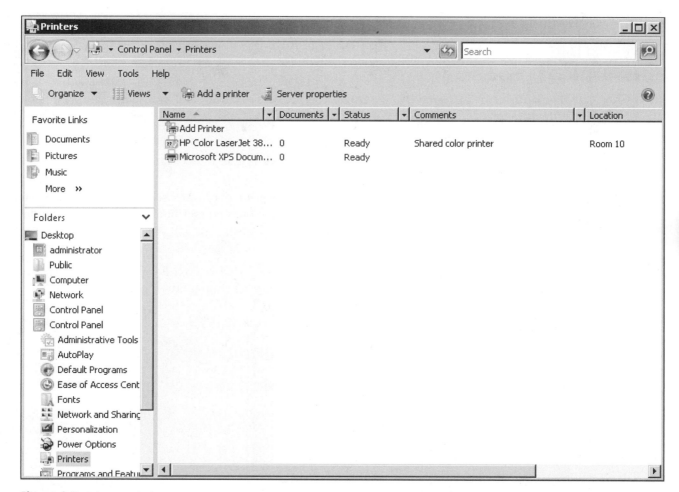

Figure 6-2 Printers window

The right pane in the Printers window shows the following information:

- *Name*—Shows the names of printers managed through the Printers window (with the exception of the Add Printer Wizard and the Microsoft XPS Document Writer, which shows and manages documents processed through the XPS print path)

- *Documents*—Shows the number of documents currently in the print queue for a printer

- *Status*—Shows at a glance if a printer is ready to accept print jobs

- *Comments*—Shows descriptions of printers or other information about printers (which users see as well)

- *Location*—Shows where a printer is located

When you click a printer in the right pane, options are added above in the button bar under the menu bar to enable you to *See what's printing*, *Select printing preferences*, and *Delete this printer* so you can manage the printer more easily. If the printer you select in the right pane is not the default printer for the server, you also see a button that enables you to set that printer as the default.

In the menu bar, you can use the File menu to add a printer, configure a shared printer, use a printer offline, configure a printer's properties, and more.

Also, you can configure the properties of the Windows Server 2008 print server from the button bar when no printer is selected in the right pane. Configure the print server properties by clicking the Server properties button.

Activity 6-4: Configuring the Print Server Properties

Time Required: Approximately 10 minutes
Objective: Configure the print server properties from the Printers window.

Description: In this activity, you open the Printers window and configure the print server properties.

1. Click **Start** and click **Control Panel**.

2. If you are in the Control Panel Home View, click **Printer** under Hardware and Sound. If you are in the Classic View, double-click **Printers**.

3. In the Printers window, ensure that none of the printers or other selections in the right pane are highlighted. If any are highlighted, click the mouse pointer in an open space in the right pane.

4. Click the **Server properties** button.

5. Four tabs are shown in the Print Server Properties dialog box: Forms, Ports, Drivers, and Advanced (see Figure 6-3). Click each tab to view its configuration options.

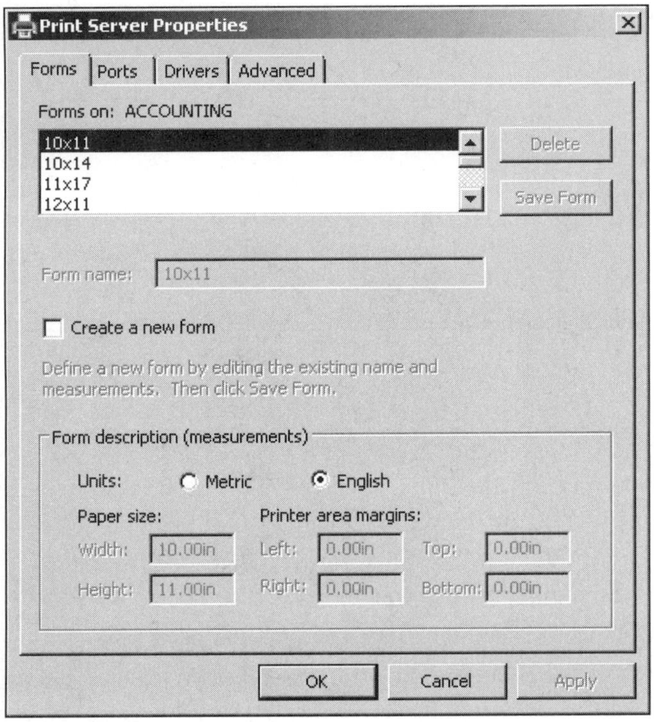

Figure 6-3 Print Server Properties dialog box

6. Click the **Advanced** tab.

   • What spooler management options are already selected? What is the folder and its path where spooler files can be written?

7. Click **Cancel**.

8. Leave the Printers window open for the next activity.

Installing Local and Shared Printers

On a Microsoft network, any server or workstation running Windows Server 2008 or 2003, Windows Vista, Windows XP, Windows 2000, or Windows 98 can host a shared printer for others to use through the network. In Windows Server 2008, you can configure a printer that is attached to the server computer as a local printer and then enable it as a shared printer. When you share a printer, the Windows Server 2008 server becomes a true print server. Figure 6-4 is a simplified representation of how shared printers are connected to a network, including printers connected to servers, workstations, and print server devices.

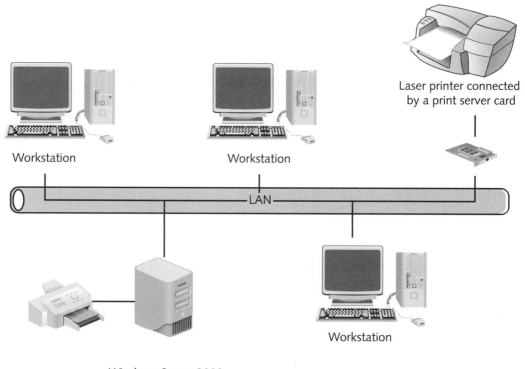

Figure 6-4 Shared network printers

If you are setting up a computer as a print server, make sure it has sufficient RAM to process the documents and sufficient disk space to store the spooled documents.

In the sections that follow, you learn how to install a shared printer and then you learn how to enable network printer sharing.

Installing a Printer

The steps for installing a printer in Windows Server 2008 depend on the type of printer you are adding. If you are installing a Plug and Play compatible printer, Windows Server 2008 will automatically detect and install the new hardware. If the printer is not automatically detected, you can use the Add Printer Wizard to install it. Printers that are added using the Add Printer Wizard are shared by default. Printers installed using Plug and Play technology are not automatically shared and must be configured for sharing after installation.

Activity 6-5: Installing a Printer

Time Required: Approximately 15 minutes
Objective: Install a printer using the Add Printer Wizard.

Description: In this activity, you install a printer using the Add Printer Wizard. This activity does not require a printer to be attached to the computer, because you practice a manual configuration without automatic detection.

1. Open the Printers window, if it is not already open. Or to open it, click **Start** and click **Control Panel**. If you are in the Control Panel Home View, click **Printer** under Hardware and Sound. If you are in the Classic View, double-click **Printers**.

2. In the Printers window, double-click **Add Printer**.

3. Notice the options to install a local or a network printer (see Figure 6-5). A local printer is one that is physically attached to the computer, and a network printer is one that is connected to a different computer or to a dedicated print server device and that is shared over the network. For this activity, click **Add a local printer**.

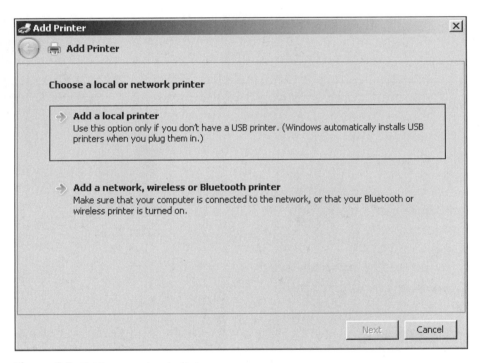

Figure 6-5 Setting up a local printer

4. Click the **down arrow** for **Use an existing port**.

   • What options are available?

5. Use the default selection for the printer port (port to which the printer is connected), such as LPT1: (Printer Port), and click **Next**.

6. If you have a printer connected, select the printer manufacturer and model. If no printer is connected, select **HP** under Manufacturer, and select **HP Color LaserJet3800**. (Notice that you can use the Windows Update button to obtain newer printer driver files, or you can use the Have Disk button to obtain printer drivers from the manufacturer's disk.)

7. Click **Next**.

8. For the name, leave HP Color LaserJet 3800 (or the name of your connected printer) but add your initials, such as HP Color LaserJet 3800 JR. Click **Next**.

9. In the Printer Sharing dialog box, leave the option button selected for **Share this printer so that others on your network can find and use it**. In the *Share name* text box, leave the default name of the printer. This is the name that users on the network will see. In the *Location* text box, enter a theoretical room number, such as **Room 10**. Also, enter a comment, such as **Shared color printer** (see Figure 6-6). Click **Next**.

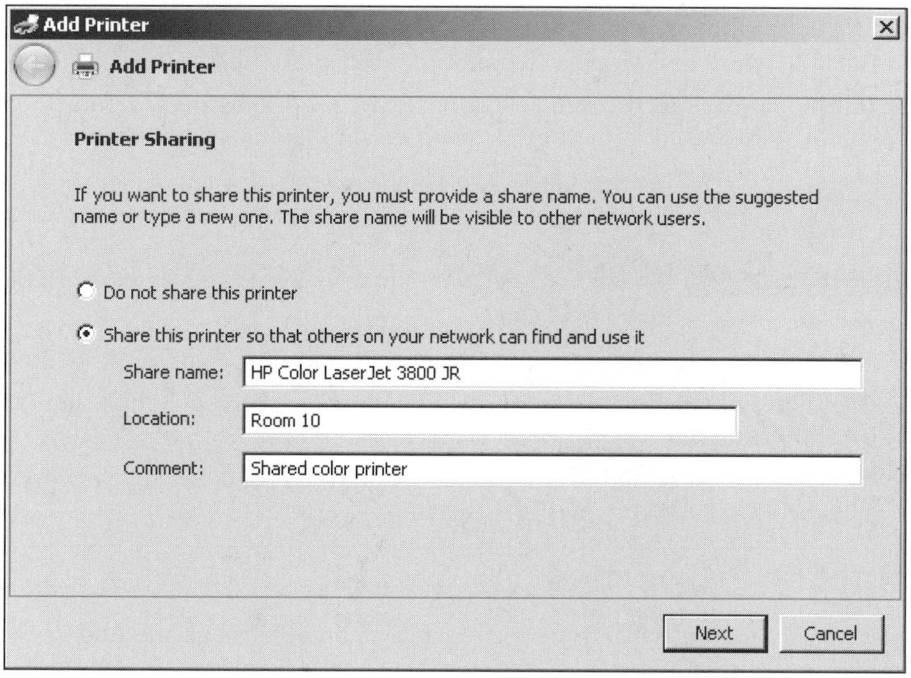

Figure 6-6 Sharing a printer

10. Notice that you could now print a test page as a way to test your installation. Click **Finish**.

11. Leave the Printers window open for Activity 6-7.

Use the following guidelines when choosing a share name:

- Compose names that are easily understood and spelled by those who will use the printer.
- Include a room number, floor, or workstation name to help identify where the printer is located.
- Include descriptive information about the printer, such as the type, manufacturer, or model.

Enabling Printer Sharing on a Network

After you install a printer on a network to be shared, turn on network printer sharing. This step enables printer sharing through the Windows Firewall so that shared printers appear when users view network resources and so that communications are permitted between the shared printers and the users who want to access them.

Activity 6-6: Enabling Printer Sharing

Time Required: Approximately 5 minutes
Objective: Turn on printer sharing over the network.

Description: To enable sharing printers over a network, you have to configure Windows Server 2008 to allow this through the Windows Firewall. In this activity, you turn on network printer sharing. Your computer must be connected to a network to configure sharing options.

1. Click **Start** and click **Network**.

2. Click **Network and Sharing Center** in the Network window.

3. Under Sharing and Discovery, check to see if Network discovery is turned on. If it is not, click its **down arrow**, click **Turn on network discovery**, and click **Apply**.

Network discovery may also be displayed as *Custom* instead of as *On*. This means that some network discovery access is enabled and some is blocked, such as through Windows Firewall. You can open Windows Firewall via Control Panel to verify that there is an exception checked for Network Discovery.

4. Next, check to see if Printer sharing is turned on. If it is not, click its **down arrow**.

5. Click **Turn on printer sharing** and click **Apply**. The green On button should now be displayed for Printer sharing.

6. Close the Network and Sharing Center window. Also, close the Network window.

Configure Printer Properties

The setup information that you specify while stepping through the Add Printer Wizard can be modified and further tuned by accessing the Properties dialog box for a printer. Printer properties are available by opening Control Panel, then clicking Printer in the Control Panel Home View or the Printers applet in the Classic View to access the Printers window. You can manage the following functions associated with a printer from the tabs in the Properties dialog box:

- General printer information
- Printer sharing
- Printer port setup
- Printer scheduling and advanced options
- Security
- Device settings

These are the main printer properties available after a printer is installed. Other properties and tabs might be available, depending on the printer and its driver, such as a Color Management tab for printers that support color printing.

General Printer Specifications

The title bar and top portion of the General tab in a printer's properties show the name of the printer (see Figure 6-7). The Location and Comment boxes are used to store special notes about the printer that can help distinguish it from other printers, particularly for the sake of users if the printer is shared on the network. The printer model name is shown below the Comment box, and below the name is an area that describes features of the printer, such as its speed and resolution. The Printing Preferences button is used to specify additional information such as

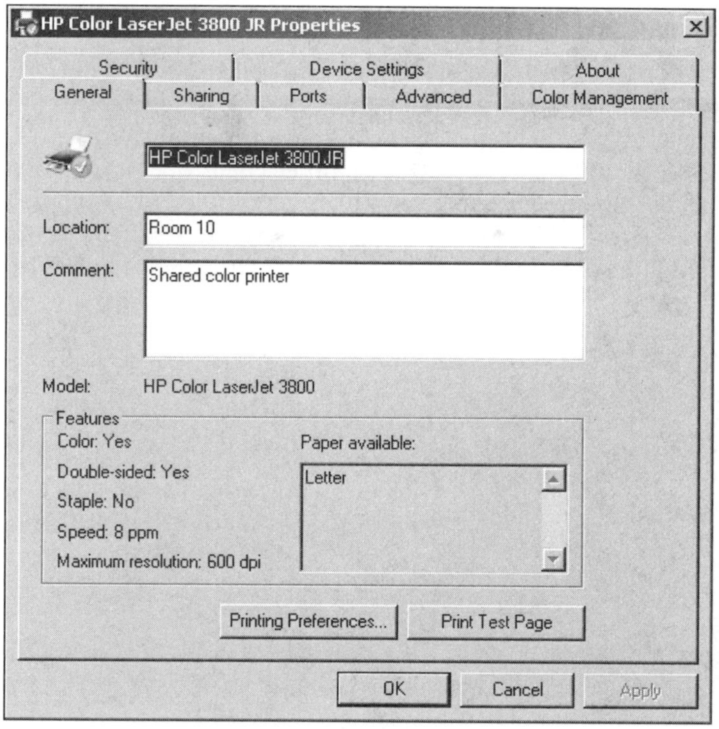

![HP Color LaserJet 3800 JR Properties dialog box showing the General tab with fields for printer name "HP Color LaserJet 3800 JR", Location "Room 10", Comment "Shared color printer", Model "HP Color LaserJet 3800", and Features section listing Color: Yes, Double-sided: Yes, Staple: No, Speed: 8 ppm, Maximum resolution: 600 dpi, with Paper available: Letter. Buttons shown are Printing Preferences, Print Test Page, OK, Cancel, and Apply.]

Figure 6-7 Printer Properties General tab

the default paper size, paper source, print resizing options, and more. Also, the Print Test Page button enables you to print a test page as a way to verify that the printer is working.

Activity 6-7: Viewing Printing Preferences

Time Required: Approximately 10 minutes
Objective: Determine the default setup for printing preferences on a printer.

Description: After you install a printer, it is a good idea to verify the printing preferences to make certain they match the intended use of the printer. In this activity, you view the printing preferences for the printer you installed in Activity 6-5.

1. Ensure the Printers window is open. If it is not, open it from Control Panel (see Activity 6-5, Step 1).

2. Right-click the printer you installed in Activity 6-5, such as HP Color LaserJet 3800 JR. Click **Properties**.

3. Make sure the General tab is displayed. Click the **Printing Preferences** button near the bottom of the dialog box.

   • What tabs are shown? What are the options on the tabs that can be configured?

4. Click **Cancel**. Leave the Properties dialog box open for the next activity.

Sharing Printers

The Sharing tab is used to enable or disable a printer for sharing as well as to specify the name of the share (see Figure 6-8). If you enable sharing, provide a name for the shared printer and check *List in the directory* to publish the printer through Active Directory. When you publish a printer, Windows Vista, XP, and 2000 clients as well as other client operating systems that have the Directory Service Client software installed can easily find it using the Search function. The option to *Render print jobs on client computers* means that the print job is first prepared by software on the client and submitted to the spooler on the client (which is the default setting).

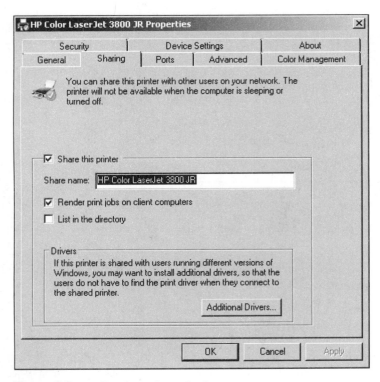

Figure 6-8 Configuring printer sharing

Another way to publish a printer in Active Directory is to open the Active Directory Users and Computers tool, right-click the domain (or an OU in the domain), point to New, click Printer, and enter the UNC (Universal Naming Convention) path to the shared printer.

The Additional Drivers button on a printer's properties Sharing tab is used to add new types of clients. For example, if the server is an x64 computer you might add drivers for x86 clients. Another option is to add drivers for Itanium clients. When you check these boxes, the appropriate printer drivers are installed so users can automatically download them when they connect to the print server for the first time. You might need the Windows Server 2008 installation DVD to install the drivers.

Clients check the printer driver each time they connect to the printer. If the driver on a client is not current, the driver will automatically be updated.

Windows 98 does not automatically update the driver. If the Windows 98 client driver is updated by the manufacturer, the new driver must be manually installed.

Activity 6-8: Configuring the Domain Group Policy to Enable Publishing a Printer

Time Required: Approximately 10 minutes
Objective: Learn how to enable printer publishing in the domain's group policy.

Description: Publishing a printer for domain-wide access must be enabled in a domain's group policy within Active Directory. In this activity, you make certain that the domain's group policy for publishing printers is enabled.

1. Click **Start** and click **Run**.

2. Type **mmc** in the Open text box and click **OK**.

3. Click the **File** menu and click **Add/Remove Snap-in**.

4. In the Add or Remove Snap-ins window, select the **Group Policy Management Editor** and click the **Add** button.

5. After the Group Policy Wizard starts, click the **Browse** button.

6. Double-click **Default Domain Policy**.

7. Click **Finish**.

8. Click **OK**.

9. Expand the console windows, if necessary.

10. In the tree, click **Default Domain Policy [*computername.domainname*] Policy**.

11. In the tree, double-click the following, if necessary, to open these folders: **Computer Configuration**, **Policies**, **Administrative Templates**, and **Printers** (you might or might not see the Policies folder depending on your version of Windows Server 2008).

12. Click **Standard** at the bottom of the middle pane for better viewing of the settings that can be configured.

13. Notice the policies that can be configured.

14. Double-click **Allow printers to be published**.

    • How is this policy currently configured?

15. Make sure the option button for **Enabled** is selected.

16. Click **OK**.

17. In addition to enabling printer publishing, you might want to enable the ability for browse master servers to include published printers as users browse for network printers when installing them through their operating system's version of the Add Printer Wizard. To enable printer browsing, double-click **Printer browsing**, select **Enabled** (if it is not already selected), and click **OK**.

18. Review the middle pane to ensure your changes have been made, as shown in Figure 6-9.

19. Close the console window. Click **No** to not save the console settings.

Port Specifications

The Ports tab has options to specify which server port, such as LPT1, is used for the printer, and options to set up bidirectional printing and printer pooling (see Figure 6-10). **Bidirectional printing** is used with printers that have bidirectional capability. A bidirectional printer can engage in two-way communications with the print server and with software applications. These allow the

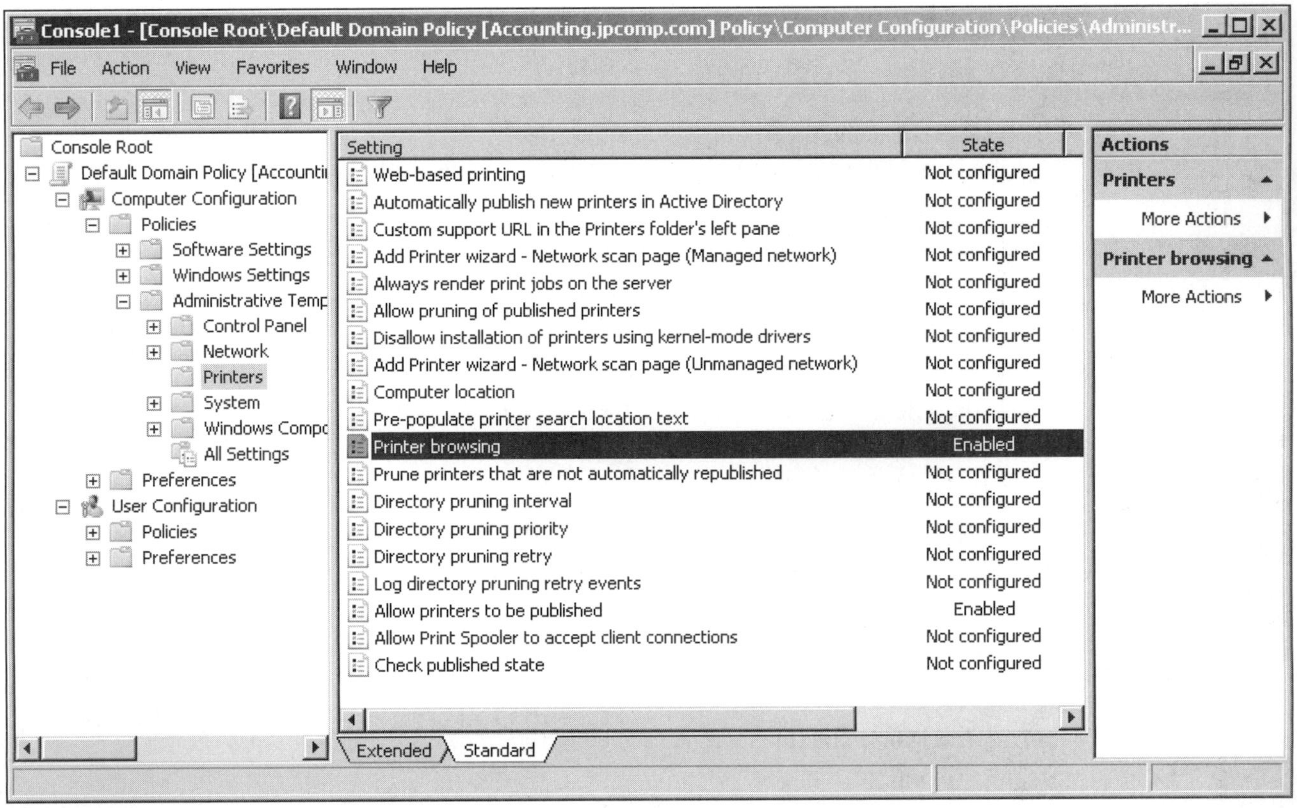

Figure 6-9 Configuring printer policies

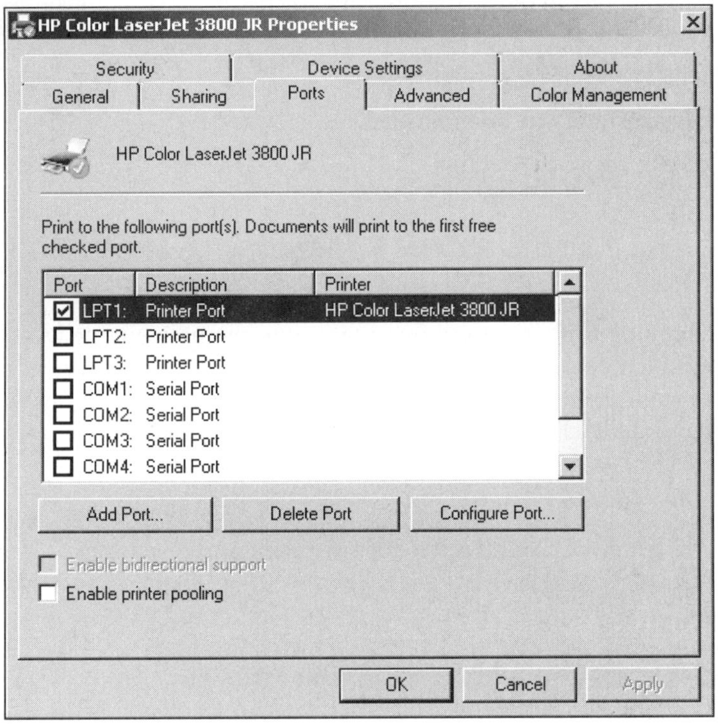

Figure 6-10 Configuring printer ports

printer driver to determine how much memory is installed in the printer, or other print capabilities. The printer also might be equipped with the ability to communicate that it is out of paper in a particular drawer or that it has a paper jam.

Before you connect a printer, consult the manual to determine whether the printer is bidirectional. If so, the printer requires a special bidirectional cable labeled as an IEEE 1284 cable, and the printer port might need to be designated as bidirectional in the computer's BIOS setup program. Check both of these contingencies if you have a bidirectional printer, but the bidirectional box is deactivated on the Ports tab as in Figure 6-10.

Printer pooling involves configuring two or more identical printers connected to one print server. For example, you might connect three identical laser printers (except for port access) to one parallel port and two USB or serial ports on a Windows Server 2008 server. On the Ports tab, check the Enable printer pooling box, and then check all of the ports to which printers are attached, such as LPT1, COM2, and COM3.

All of the printers in a pool must be identical so that they use the same printer driver and handle print files in the same way. The advantage of having a printer pool is that the Windows Server 2008 print monitor can send print files to any of the three printers (or however many you set up). If two of the printers are busy, it can send an incoming file to the third printer. Printer pooling can significantly increase the print volume in a busy office, without the need to configure network printing for different kinds of printers.

It is wise to locate pooled printers in close physical proximity, because users are not able to tell to which pooled printer a print job may be sent.

The Add Port button enables you to add a new port, such as a new print monitor or a fax port. Click this button if you need to configure print monitors for specialized printing needs. The default options are shown in Figure 6-11 and described below.

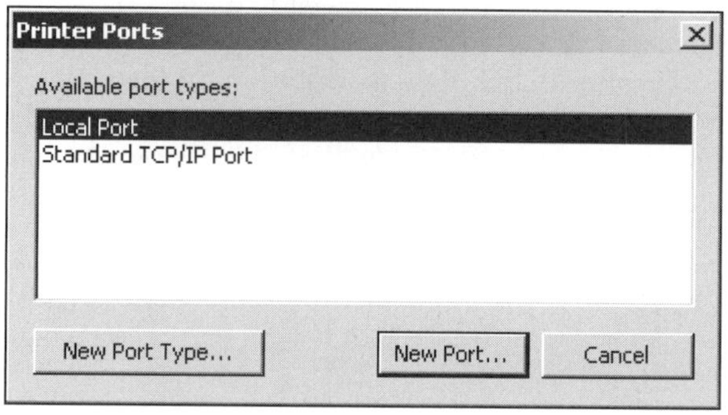

Figure 6-11 Port options

- *Local Port*—The Local Port print monitor handles print jobs sent to a local physical port on the server, such as an LPT or COM port. It also sends print jobs to a file, if you specify FILE as the port. When a print job is sent to FILE, a prompt appears to supply a file name. XPS users have an option to print to XPS using the XPS print path.

- *Standard TCP/IP Port*—This print monitor is used for TCP/IP-based printers that are connected to the network through print server cards or print servers.

The Delete Port button is used to remove a port option from the list of ports. The Configure Port button is used to tune the configuration parameters that are appropriate to the type of port. On an LPT port, click the Configure Port button to check the port timeout setting. This setting is the amount of time the server will continue to try sending a print file to a printer while the printer is not responding. The default setting is normally 90 seconds. Consider increasing the setting to 120 seconds or more if you are installing a printer to handle large print files, such as files for combined graphics and color printing. On a COM port, the Configure Port button is used to set the serial port speed in bits per second, data bits, parity, stop bits, and flow control.

Activity 6-9: Configuring Printer Pooling

Time Required: Approximately 10 minutes
Objective: Learn how to configure printer pooling.

Description: Printer pooling can enable users in a busy office to be more productive, so they are not waiting on printouts. In this activity, you practice configuring printer pooling (you do not need an additional printer for this activity, but you would, of course, in an actual office situation).

1. The printer Properties dialog box should still be open from Activity 6-7; if not, open it.
2. Click the **Ports** tab.
3. Click **Enable printer pooling**.
4. Click **COM3** or another port that is not in use.
5. Click **Apply**.

   • How has that port's printer assignment changed? How could you print a test page?

6. Leave the Properties dialog box open for the next activity.

Activity 6-10: Transferring Print Jobs

Time Required: Approximately 15 minutes
Objective: Learn how to transfer print jobs from a malfunctioning printer.

Description: Assume that you have a small network in which a printer is connected to the server, the printer has failed, but an identical printer shared by a workstation on the network is working. You practice configuring the print monitor associated with the Local Port option and, at the same time, learn how to transfer print jobs to another printer. You will need a printer set up in Windows Server 2008. Obtain from your instructor the name of a workstation (or server) that has a shared printer.

1. Make sure the Ports tab is still displayed for the printer you installed in Activity 6-5.
2. Click the **Add Port** button.

   • What port types are available?

3. Click **Local Port** and click the **New Port** button (do not click the New Port Type button). Enter the UNC name of the workstation and printer provided by your instructor, such as **\\Lab1\HPLaser** and click **OK**.

If your server has two printers connected, you can also enter the server name and the name of the other printer.

4. Click **Close**.

 • Is the new port added to the list of ports? What is the Port name and description?

5. Click **Close**.

Printer Scheduling and Advanced Options

The Advanced tab allows you to have a printer available at all times or to limit the time to a range of hours (see Figure 6-12). To have a printer available at all times, click *Always available*; to limit printer use to only certain times, click *Available from* and enter the range of times when the printer can be used, such as from 8:00 a.m. to 10:00 p.m.

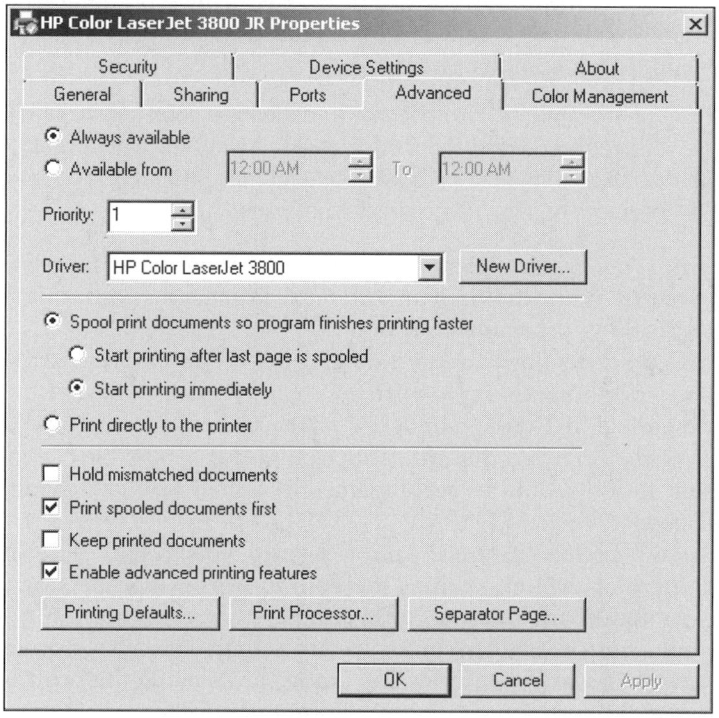

Figure 6-12 Advanced printer properties

You can set the priority higher to give a particular printer or printer pool priority over other printers attached to the server, which applies only if there are two or more printer icons set up in the Printers folder. The priority can be set from 1 to 99. For example, if the server is managing several printer shares, one may be set for higher priority because it prints payroll checks or is used by the company president.

Printer scheduling can be useful when there is one printer and two printer objects (shares) for that printer. One object can be set up for immediate printing, and the other can be used for long print jobs that are not immediately needed. The object for the longer jobs that can wait might be set up so those print jobs are scheduled to print between 6:00 p.m. and midnight. Another way to handle the longer jobs is to pause that printer object and resume printing when the printer has a light load, such as at noon or during slow times of the day.

The Advanced tab provides the option to use spooled printing or to bypass the spooler and send print files directly to the printer. It works best to spool print jobs so they are printed on a first-come, first-served basis and to enable background printing so the CPU can work on other tasks. Printing directly to the printer is not recommended, unless there is an emergency need to focus all resources on a specific printout. Print spooling also helps ensure that jobs are printed together, so a long Word document is not interrupted by a one-page print job. Without spooling, such an interruption can occur if the one-page job is ready to print at the time the Word job is pausing to read the disk. The spool option is selected by default, with the instruction to start printing before all the pages are spooled. This is an appropriate option in a small office in which most print files are not resource-intensive and there is infrequent contention for printers, reducing the odds of intermixing printouts.

 If a busy office has a problem with pages intermixing from printouts, for example, click the option to *Start printing after last page is spooled*.

The *Hold mismatched documents* option causes the system to compare the setup of the printer with the setup in the document. For example, if the printer is set up in a print share as a laser printer but the document is formatted for a plotter, the print job is placed on hold. The job does not print until the document is released by the user, a member of the Print Operators or Server Operators group, or an administrator.

 The *Hold mismatched documents* option is a good way to save paper in a heterogeneous situation, such as a student lab, where users have very different formatted print jobs. One mismatch situation can use hundreds of pages printing one character per page.

The option to *Print spooled documents first* enables jobs that have completed spooling to be printed, no matter what their priority. In high-volume printing situations, this speeds the process by reducing the wait for long print jobs to spool.

The *Keep printed documents* option retains documents in the spooler after they have printed, which enables the network administrator to re-create a printout damaged by a printer jam or other problem. For example, if a large number of paychecks are printing and a printer problem strikes in the middle of the printout, this critical option makes it possible to reprint the damaged checks. However, this option should be accompanied by a maintenance schedule to delete documents no longer needed.

The *Enable advanced printing features* option permits you to make use of special features associated with a particular printer, such as the ability to print booklets or to vary the order in which pages are printed—back to front, for example.

The Printing Defaults button enables you to specify default settings for print jobs, unless they are overridden by control codes in the print file. These can include the print layout, page print order (front to back), and paper source, depending on the printer.

Use the Print Processor button to specify one of the print processors and data types, for example using the WinPrint print processor (the default) and the EMF data type for Windows-based clients. The **data type** is the way in which information is formatted in a print file. Data types include the following:

- *RAW*—A print file formatted as the **RAW** data type is often used for files sent from legacy MS-DOS and Windows 3.x operating systems, and from UNIX and Linux clients. It is also the default setting for a PostScript printer. A RAW print file is intended to be printed by the print server with no additional formatting.

- *RAW (FF appended)*—In this data type, the FF is a form-feed code placed at the end of the print file. Some non-Windows and old 16-bit Windows software do not place a form feed at the end of a print file. The form feed is used to make sure the last page of the file is printed.

- *RAW (FF auto)*—In this data type, the print processor checks the print file for a form feed as the last character set, before appending a form feed at the end. If a form feed is already present, it does not add anything to the file.

- *NT EMF (different versions)*—Windows 95, 98, Me, NT, 2000, XP, Vista, Server 2003, and Server 2008 clients use the **enhanced metafile (EMF)** data type. This data type is created when a print file is prepared by the GDI at the client. EMF print files offer a distinct advantage in Windows operating system environments because they are very portable from computer to computer.

- *TEXT*—The **TEXT** data type is used for printing text files formatted according to the ANSI standard that uses values between 0 and 255 to represent characters, numbers, and symbols. You would use the TEXT data type for printing many types of legacy MS-DOS print files, such as text files printed from older word processors or MS-DOS text editors.

 A **PostScript** printer is one that has special firmware or cartridges to print using a page-description language (PDL). Most non-PostScript laser printers use a version of the **Printer Control Language (PCL)**, which was developed by Hewlett-Packard.

The Separator Page button is used to place a blank page at the beginning of each printed document. This helps designate the end of one printout and the beginning of another, so that printouts do not get mixed together, or so that someone does not take the wrong printout in a medium-size or large office setting in which many people share the same printer. Another advantage to using a separator page is that it sends control codes to the printer to make sure that special formatting set for the last printout is reset prior to the next one. In small offices, a separator page might not be needed, because print formatting might not vary, and users can quickly identify their own printouts. Windows Server 2008 has four separator page files from which to choose, located in the \Windows\System32 folder:

- *Pcl.sep*—Used to print a Printer Control Language (PCL) separator page on a printer that handles PCL and PostScript

- *Pscript.sep*—Used to print a PostScript separator page on a printer that handles PCL and PostScript

- *Sysprint.sep*—Used with PostScript-only printers and prints a separator page at the beginning of each document

- *Sysprtj.sep*—Used in the same way as Sysprint.sep, but for documents printed in the Japanese language

Consider the cost of paper before you set up separator pages. If you set up a separator page for each document, and each user also specifies a banner page from the client, the resulting paper costs quickly mount in an office. For example, depending on the setup, one or more extra pages will print per document, turning a one-page original document into two, three, or more printed pages. Many offices sharing a printer simply decide to forgo separator and banner pages, because each person usually knows what he or she printed.

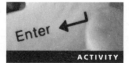

Activity 6-11: Changing Data Types

Time Required: Approximately 10 minutes
Objective: Learn how to change the data type when printing problems occur.

Description: In this activity, you practice changing the data type to accommodate UNIX and Linux clients that print to a printer connected to Windows Server 2008. Assume you have been experiencing garbled printouts using the TEXT setup and a problem with getting the first page to print. To solve the problem, you change the data type to RAW with FF appended.

1. Click **Start** and click **Control Panel**.
2. In the Control Panel Home View, click **Printer**, or in the Classic View double-click **Printers**.

3. Right-click the printer you installed in Activity 6-5, such as HP Color LaserJet 3800 JR. Click **Properties.**

4. Click the **Advanced** tab and click the **Print Processor** button.

   • What print processors and data types are listed?

5. Click **WinPrint** (if it is not already selected) and click **RAW [FF appended]**.

6. Click **OK**.

   • What other parameters can you set on the Advanced tab?

7. Leave the Properties dialog box open for the next activity.

Configuring Security

As an object, a shared printer can be set up to use security features such as share permissions, auditing, and ownership. To configure security for a printer, you must have Manage printers permissions for that printer. Use the Security tab to set up printer share permissions (see Figure 6-13).

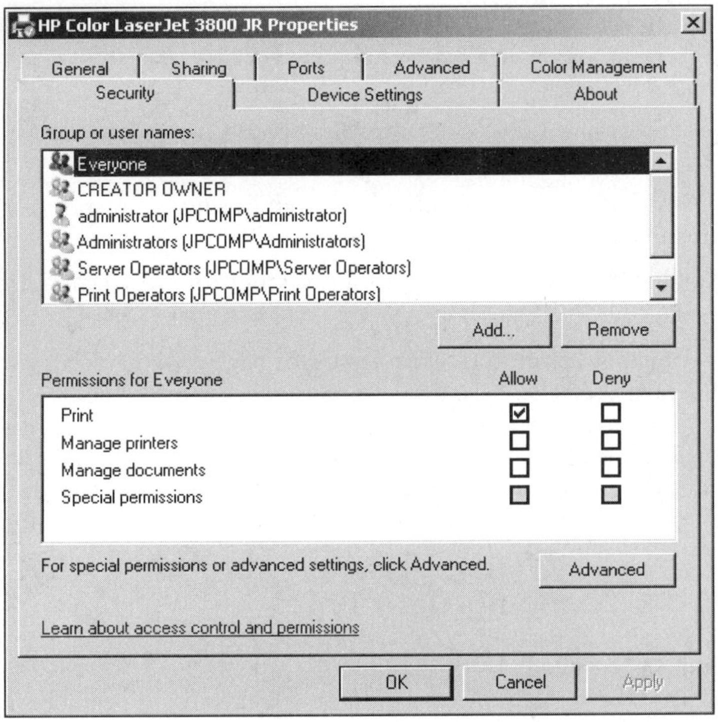

Figure 6-13 Configuring security

Once a printer is shared, the default permissions are as follows:

• *Everyone group*—Print

• *Creator Owner*—Manage documents

• *Administrator account*—Print, Manage printers, and Manage documents

- *Administrators, Server Operators, Print Operators groups*—Print, Manage printers, and Manage documents

Click an existing group to modify its permissions, and use the Add button to add new groups or the Remove button to delete a group from accessing the printer. Table 6-1 lists the printer share permissions that can be set.

Table 6-1   Printer share permissions

Share permission	Access capability
Print	Users can connect to the shared printer, send print jobs, and manage their own print requests (such as to pause, restart, resume, or cancel a print job)
Manage documents	Users can connect to the shared printer, send print jobs, and manage any print job sent (including jobs sent by other users)
Manage printers	Users have complete access to a printer share, including the ability to change permissions, turn off sharing, configure printer properties, and delete the share
Special permissions	Similar to configuring special permissions for a folder, special permissions can be set up for a printer from the Advanced tab

By clicking the Advanced button on the Security tab, you can:

- Set up special printer permissions for a specific group or user (click the Permissions tab, click the group or user, and click Edit).
- Add or remove a group or user for security access or denial (click the Permissions tab).
- Set up printer auditing (click the Auditing tab).
- Take ownership of a printer (click the Owner tab).
- View the effective permissions for a user or group (click the Effective Permissions tab).

Special permissions enable you to fine-tune shared printer permissions, for instance to configure a group that has *Manage printers* permissions so that group can perform all functions except taking ownership.

Any user account or group can be set up for auditing, by clicking the Auditing tab and the Add button. Before you set up printer auditing, make sure that there is a group policy or default domain security policy that enables object auditing on the basis of successful and failed activity attempts. For a shared printer you can track successful or failed attempts to:

- Print jobs
- Manage printers
- Manage documents
- Read printer share permissions
- Change printer share permissions
- Take ownership of the printer

Activity 6-12: Configuring Printer Security

Time Required: Approximately 10 minutes
Objective: Learn how to set up security on a shared printer.

Description: Configuring security is very important on a shared printer, so that you can control who has access and ensure the productivity of the printer's users. In this activity, you remove the Everyone group from access to a printer, and provide access to the domain local group that you created in Chapter 4, "Introduction to Active Directory and Account Management." You also set up auditing of failed printing attempts for the domain local group you created.

1. Access the printer Properties dialog box still open from Activity 6-11.
2. Click the **Security** tab.
   - What security is set up already?

3. Click the **Everyone** group and click **Remove**. Notice that the *Group or user names* box is updated to reflect the change.
4. Click the **Add** button.
5. In the Select Users, Computers, or Groups dialog box, click the **Advanced** button, click **Find Now**, double-click the domain local group you created in Chapter 4, such as DomainMgrsJP, and click **OK**.
   - What permissions are given to this group by default?

6. Make sure that **Print** is checked for **Allow**.
7. Click the **Advanced** button.
8. In the Advanced Security Settings dialog box, click the **Auditing** tab.
9. Click **Add**.
10. In the Select User, Computer, or Group dialog box, click the **Advanced** button, click **Find Now**, double-click the domain local group you created in Chapter 4, such as DomainMgrsJP, and click **OK**.
11. Click the **Failed** box for **Print** (notice that Read permissions is also checked automatically) and click **OK** (see Figure 6-14).
    - What information now appears in the *Auditing entries* box?

12. Click **OK**.
    - If there is a message that auditing is not turned on as a group policy, how would you turn it on?

13. Click **OK**.
14. Leave the Printers window open for the next activity.

Configuring Device Settings

The Device Settings tab enables you to specify printer settings that are specific to the printer you have installed, such as printer trays, memory, paper size, fonts, duplexing, and installable options (see Figure 6-15). For example, in many cases if you have a multiple-tray printer you will leave the paper tray assignment on Auto Select (not shown in Figure 6-15, but available on some printers) and let the software application at the client specify the printer tray. However, if your organization uses special forms such as paychecks, you can specify use of a designated paper tray when checks are printing.

The printer memory is usually automatically detected in bidirectional printers, but if it is not, you can specify the amount of memory in the Printer Memory option under Installable Options. In the client operating systems, such as Windows 2000 Professional, Windows XP Professional, and Windows Vista, the workstation printer setup also can have information about how much memory is installed in a shared printer.

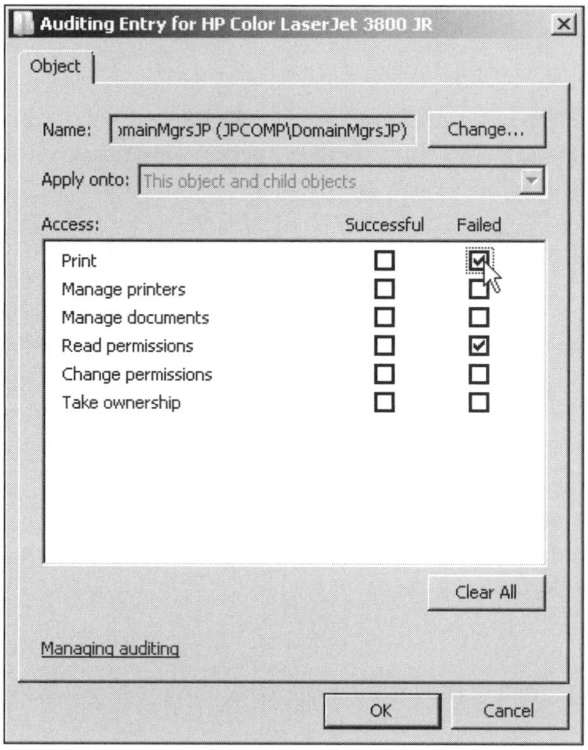

Figure 6-14   Configuring shared printer auditing

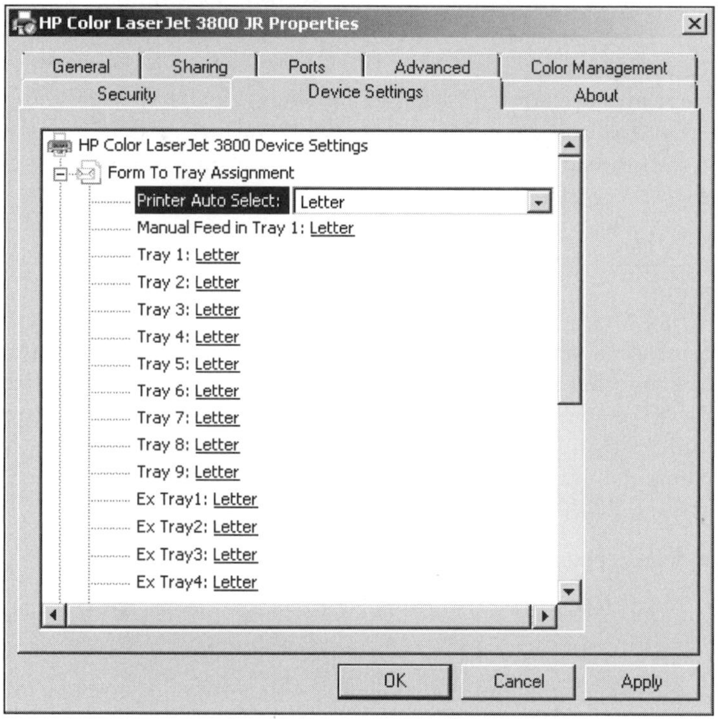

Figure 6-15   Configuring printer device settings

Make sure the memory reported in the device settings matches the memory installed in the printer, because this enables the print server to off-load more work to the printer, improving the speed at which print jobs are completed as well as server performance. Most other settings are better left to the software at the client end to handle. For example, a client printing in

Microsoft Word can specify font and paper tray instructions inside the document and by using the Printer Setup.

Configuring a Nonlocal Printer or an Internet Printer

There are times when you want to enable a Windows Server 2008 server to connect to a printer that is not directly connected to one of its ports, for example a printer shared from a workstation, another server, the Internet or an intranet, or one that is connected to the network through a print server card or device. You can connect to a network printer by using the Add Printer Wizard and following these general steps:

1. Open the Printers window, if it is not already open.

2. Double-click Add Printer.

3. Click *Add a network, wireless or Bluetooth printer* (see Figure 6-5).

4. Select a printer from the list of printers found by the Add Printer Wizard; or click the button *The printer that I want isn't listed.* (If you click the button to specify a printer, you can select among *Find a printer in the directory, based on location or feature*; *Select a shared printer by name*; or *Add a printer using a TCP/IP address or hostname.* If you select one of these options, you will see additional dialog boxes to complete the tasks for the particular option you selected.)

5. Follow the instructions to complete the installation, which in most cases involves providing a printer name and clicking Next, clicking Yes to print a test page, and clicking Finish.

When the remote printer is installed on a domain controller, you can change the properties of the shared printer you just installed, even though you are not logged on to its host computer. This means you can manage any remote shared network printer, even though it is not connected to a port on the server. For example, open Control Panel, click Printer from the Control Panel Home View or double-click Printers from the Classic View, and right-click the remote printer you installed. Click the Properties selection and make any changes you desire. This capability is very useful when you manage a large network with network printers located in distant buildings. If you need to change the print processor used by a shared printer that is a block away, you can do so without leaving your office.

Managing Print Jobs

In the time after a print job is sent and before it is fully transmitted to the printer, several options are available for managing that job. Users with print permissions can print and manage their own jobs. Also, members of the Printer Operators, Server Operators, and Administrators groups can manage the jobs of others through the Manage documents and Manage printers permissions. To manage printed documents, open the Printers window from Control Panel and double-click the appropriate printer. Users with Print permissions can:

- Send print jobs to the printer
- Pause, resume, and restart their own print jobs
- Cancel their own print jobs

Print Operators, Server Operators, and other groups having Manage documents permissions can:

- Send print jobs to the printer
- Pause, resume, and restart any user's print jobs
- Cancel any user's print jobs

Administrators, Print Operators, Server Operators, and any other groups having Manage printers permissions can do all of the same things as those with Manage documents permissions, but they also can pause and restart the printer and change the properties of the printer. For example, in terms of changing properties, those with Manage printers permissions can start and stop sharing, configure printer properties, take ownership, change permissions, and set the default printer for the Windows Server 2008 server.

Controlling the Status of Printing

In Windows Server 2008, printer control and setup information for a particular printer is associated with that printer's properties. For example, if you have two printers installed, HPLaser_Rm20 and InkJet_Rm8, a set of properties and printer control information applies for each printer. If you want to pause a print job on the HPLaser_Rm20 printer, open the Printers window from Control Panel and double-click HPLaser_Rm20. If you want to delete a print job on the InkJet_Rm8 printer, find that printer in the Printers window and double-click it.

Sometimes you need to pause a printer to fix a problem, for example to reattach a loose cable or to power the printer off and on to reset it. You can pause printing to that printer by opening the Printers window, double-clicking the printer, clicking the Printer menu, and clicking the Pause Printing option so there is a check mark beside it (see Figure 6-16). Remember that you need to uncheck Pause Printing before print jobs can continue printing. The Pause Printing capability is particularly important if a user sends an improperly formatted document to the printer, such as a PostScript-formatted document to a non-PostScript printer. If you do not have *Hold mismatched documents* enabled, the printer might print tens or hundreds of pages with a single control code on each page. By pausing printing, you have time to identify and delete the document before too much paper is used.

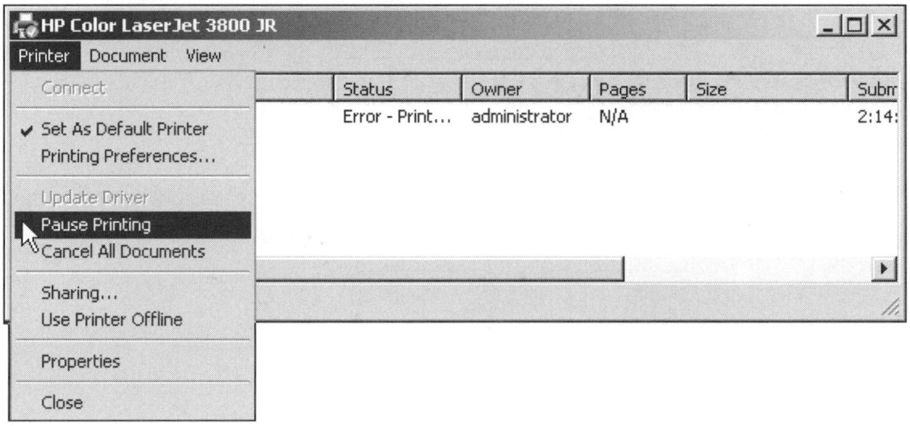

Figure 6-16 Pausing printing

Controlling Specific Print Jobs

You can pause, resume, restart, or view the properties of one or more documents in the print queue of a printer. A **print queue** is like a stack of print jobs, with the first job submitted at the top of the stack and the last job submitted at the bottom, and all of the jobs waiting to be sent from the spooler to the printer.

In Windows Server 2008, to pause a print job, open the Printers window from Control Panel and double-click the appropriate printer. The resulting window shows a list of jobs to be printed, the status of each job, the owner, the number of pages to be printed, the size of the print file, and when the print job was submitted. Click the document you want to pause, click the Document menu, and then click Pause. The print job will stop printing until you highlight the document and click Resume or Restart on the Document menu. Resume starts printing at the point in the document where the printing was paused. Restart prints from the beginning of the document. You also can use the Document menu to cancel a print job. First click the job in the status window, click the Document menu, and click Cancel.

 Depending on the amount of memory in your printer, a print job might not stop printing right away after you cancel it.

Jobs print in the order they are received, unless the administrator changes their priority. Jobs come in with a priority of 1, but can be assigned a priority as high as 99. For example, if you work for a university, the president might need to quickly print a last-minute report before going to a meeting with the trustees. You can give the president a 99 priority by clicking her print job in the window listing the print jobs. Next, click the Document menu, click Properties, and access the General tab. The Priority box is in the middle of the General tab. Move the slider from Lowest (1) to Highest (99), depending on your requirements, and click OK (see Figure 6-17).

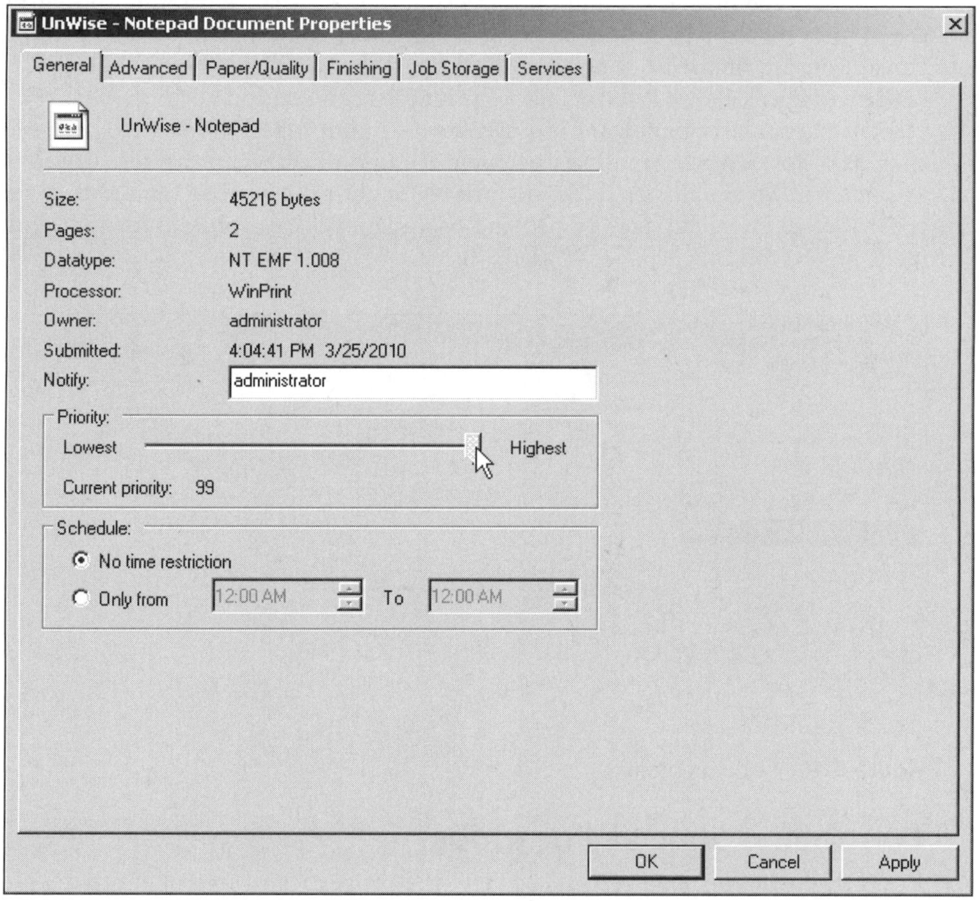

UnWise - Notepad Document Properties

General | Advanced | Paper/Quality | Finishing | Job Storage | Services

UnWise - Notepad

Size:	45216 bytes
Pages:	2
Datatype:	NT EMF 1.008
Processor:	WinPrint
Owner:	administrator
Submitted:	4:04:41 PM 3/25/2010
Notify:	administrator

Priority:

Lowest ——————————————— Highest

Current priority: 99

Schedule:

⦿ No time restriction

○ Only from   12:00 AM   To   12:00 AM

[OK]   [Cancel]   [Apply]

Figure 6-17 Changing the print priority

You also can use the General tab to set a time for selected jobs to print on a printer. For example, if the server is very busy during the day, you can ease the load by setting jobs to print at a certain time of day, such as from noon to 1:00 p.m. The General tab also provides basic information about the file, such as the size, owner, data type used, print processor used, and when the job was submitted.

Activity 6-13: Pausing a Printer and Canceling a Document

Time Required: Approximately 10 minutes
Objective: Learn how to pause a printer and then cancel a document.

Description: Assume that your office has a printer that is printing sheet after sheet of garbled text. This activity enables you to pause printing to that printer until you can cancel the print job.

1. Open the Printers window, if it is not still open.
2. Double-click the printer you installed in Activity 6-5, such as HP Color LaserJet 3800 JR.
3. Click the **Printer** menu and ensure that **Set As Default Printer** is checked.
4. Click the **Printer** menu again and click **Pause Printing**.

   • Has the title bar of the Printers window changed, and if so how?

5. Create a document using a word processor or Notepad that contains only one or two words, such as **Test**. (To use Notepad, click Start, point to All Programs, click Accessories, and click Notepad.) Print the document to the printer that you have paused. Close the document you created and do not save it.
6. When the document appears in the printer window, click it.
7. Click the **Document** menu and leave it open.

   • What options are available to you to control a print job?

8. Close the Document menu.
9. Double-click the document you sent to the print queue.

   • How would you reset the priority of this print job?

10. Click the **Cancel** button to close the Document Properties dialog box.
11. Right-click the document that you sent to the printer and click **Cancel**. Click **Yes** to cancel the document.
12. Click the **Printer** menu and click **Pause Printing** to remove the check.
13. Close the window you have been using to manage print jobs and close the Printers window.

Using the Print Management Tool

The Print Management tool (also called the Print Management Console or PMC) centralizes shared printer control in one place, enabling printer administrators and operators to manage the print functions of some or all of the shared printers on a network. Because printers can be a labor-intensive part of managing a network, the Windows Server 2008 Print Management tool is a welcome addition. For example, if a remote printer is hung or jammed, you can use the Print Management tool to identify which printer has the problem. If you receive a call that a printer seems overloaded with print jobs, you can verify the number of jobs in that printer's queue and change the priority of jobs as needed. You can open this tool from the Administrative Tools menu or as an MMC snap-in. Figure 6-18 shows the Print Management tool.

Using the Print Management tool, you can do the following:

• Start the Network Printer Installation Wizard to set up network printers for sharing.
• View and manage installed printers.
• View and manage printer drivers for installed printers.

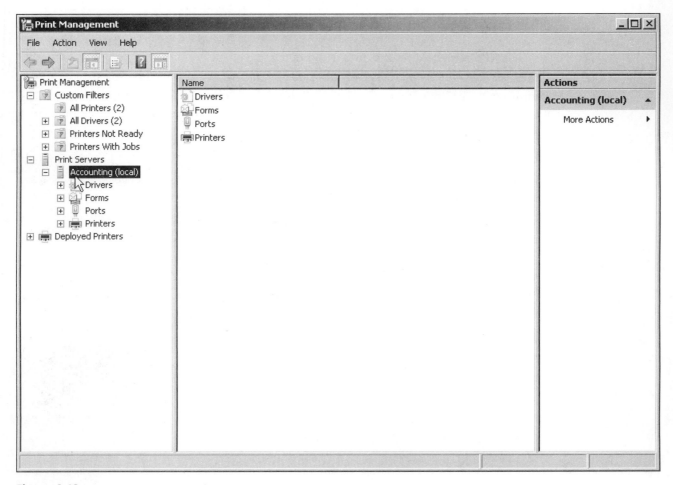

Figure 6-18   Print Management tool

- Determine if any printers are not ready to print.
- Determine which printers have print jobs in the print queue.
- Manage the use of printer forms.
- Manage which printers are associated with which printer ports.
- Pause and restart printing on a particular shared printer.
- Manage print jobs.
- Manage printer sharing.
- Configure printer pooling.
- Add Windows Server 2008 print server for central printer management.
- Manage from one place shared printers set up on Windows 2000, Windows Vista, Windows Server 2003, and Windows Server 2008.
- Export preconfigured settings to a network printer using the Printer Migration Wizard.

As you can see, the Print Management tool offers many of the printer control features of the Printers window and adds new features for consolidated shared printer management. The best way to understand the features of this tool is to use it, as in Activity 6-14.

Activity 6-14: Using the Print Management Tool

Time Required: Approximately 15 minutes
Objective: Learn how to use the Print Management tool.

Description: The Print Management tool uses a management concept similar to the Server Manager in that it houses many printer management features in one location. In this activity, you explore the features of the Print Management tool.

1. Click **Start**, point to **Administrative Tools**, and click **Print Management**.

2. If necessary, click the **plus sign** in the tree next to **Custom Filters** to view the items under it.

3. Click **All Printers** in the tree. This enables you to see in the middle pane the printers already under the management control of the Print Management tool.

4. Click the **plus sign** next to **Print Servers** in the tree, if this is not expanded.

5. In the tree, click the **plus sign** in front of your server's name, if the items under it are not shown.

6. Click **Printers** under the server name.

7. Right-click the printer you installed in Activity 6-5.

   • What selections appear on the menu?

8. With the menu still open, click **Properties**. Notice that you can configure the properties of the printer using the same tabs as in previous activities in this chapter.

9. Click **Cancel** to close the Properties dialog box.

10. In the middle pane, again right-click the printer you installed in Activity 6-5 and click **Pause Printing**. In the middle pane, notice that the Queue Status for that printer is Paused.

11. Next, create a document in Notepad to send to the print queue. Click **Start**, point to **All Programs**, and click **Accessories**.

12. Click **Notepad**.

13. In Notepad, type **This is a test printout**.

14. While still in Notepad, click **File**, click **Print**, and click the **Print** button.

15. Close **Notepad** and click **Don't Save**.

16. In the Print Management tool's tree, click **Printers Not Ready**. You should see your printer in the middle pane and 1 in the Jobs In Queue column (not all of the column head may be visible).

17. In the tree, click **Printers With Jobs**. Notice that your printer is displayed in the middle pane with 1 in the Jobs In Queue column.

18. Click **Printers** under the server in the tree.

19. Right-click the printer you created in Activity 6-5 and click **Open Printer Queue**. You see the same window to manage print jobs and printers as you used in Activity 6-13.

20. Click the print job you sent to the printer, click the **Document** menu, click **Cancel**, and click **Yes** to delete the print job.

21. Close the window you used to cancel the print job.

22. In the middle pane, right-click the printer you paused and click **Resume Printing**.

23. Click the server in the tree.

24. Click the **Action** menu and click **Add Printer**. This action opens the Network Printer Installation Wizard from which you can install a network printer.

25. Click **Cancel** to close the wizard.

26. Right-click **Print Servers** in the tree. Notice the menu item, *Add/Remove Servers*. You can use this capability to add another Windows Server on your network so you can manage its shared printers from the Print Management tool.

27. Click the pointer in a blank area to close the shortcut menu you opened in Step 26.

28. Close the Print Management window.

Troubleshooting Common Printing Problems

One printing problem can occur when the Windows Server 2008 Print Spooler service experiences a temporary difficulty, gets out of synchronization, or hangs. Because the spooler contains several complex pieces, it is a possible source of printer problems. The result is that print jobs are not processed until the problem is solved. If a print job is not going through, and you determine that one or more printers are not paused, and that the cable connection is good, then stop and restart the Print Spooler service by using the following general steps:

1. Click Start, point to Administrative Tools, and click Computer Management.

You can alternatively stop and restart the Print Spooler service from Server Manager by opening this tool, expanding Configuration in the tree, and clicking Services in the tree.

2. Click Services and Applications in the tree under Computer Management.

3. Double-click Services in the middle pane.

4. Scroll through the middle pane to find the Print Spooler service and then double-click this service.

5. Check the status to determine if the Print Spooler service is started, and make sure that it is set to start automatically. If you need to start the service, click Start. If you need to set it to start automatically, set this option in the *Startup type box* to stop and restart the service, click Stop, and then click Start. Make sure that the service status is Started and that the startup type is Automatic. Click OK.

6. Because the Print Spooler service is dependent on the Remote Procedure Call (RPC) service, check to make sure that the Remote Procedure Call service is also started and set to start automatically. Further, make sure that the Server service is working.

7. Close the Computer Management window.

Warn users before you stop and restart the Print Spooler service, because queued print jobs will be deleted.

Several other common problems and their solutions are summarized in Table 6-2.

Table 6-2 Troubleshooting printing problems

Network printing problem	Solutions
Only one character prints per page	If only one workstation experiences this problem, reinstall the printer driver on that workstation using the Add Printer Wizard.
	If all workstations are experiencing the problem, first turn off the printer, wait 30 seconds, and turn on the printer. If this doesn't work, reinstall the printer and printer driver at the computer or print server offering the printer share (using the Add Printer Wizard).
	Check the print monitor and data type setup.
Some users get a no-access message when trying to access the printer share	Check the share permissions. Make certain the clients belong to a group for which at least Print permission has been granted, and that none of the groups to which these users belong are denied Print permission. The fast way to check this is by using the effective permissions capability on the Security tab of that printer's properties.
Printer control codes are on the printout	Sometimes this is caused by the formatting of a previous printout; all you need to do is turn the printer off, wait for 30 seconds, and turn it back on. This action resets the printer.
	If only one workstation experiences the problem, reinstall the printer driver on that workstation using the Add Printer Wizard. Also, make sure the software generating the printout is installed correctly.
	If all workstations are experiencing the problem, reinstall the printer and printer driver at the computer or print server offering the printer share (using the Add Printer Wizard).
	Make sure the share is set up for all operating systems that access it, that the correct print monitor is installed, and that the appropriate data type is used.
A print job shows it is printing, the printer looks fine, but nothing is printing	Open Control Panel, click Printer from the Control Panel Home View or double-click Printers from the Classic View, and double-click the printer in the Printers window (or use the Print Management tool). Check for a problem with the print job at the top of the queue. If it shows the job is printing but nothing is happening, delete the print job because it might be hung (and resubmit the print job).
	Also, try stopping and restarting the Print Spooler service (warn users first).
Some clients find that the ending pages are not printed for large print jobs	Check the disk space on the server or workstation in which the job is spooled. It might not have enough space to fully spool all jobs.
On some long print jobs, pages from other print jobs are found in the printout	Set the printer's properties so that the printer starts printing only after all pages are spooled. To do this, right-click the printer in the Print Management tool or the Printers window, click Properties on the shortcut menu, click the Advanced tab, click the radio button for *Spool print documents so program finishes printing faster*, click the radio button for *Start printing after last page is spooled*, and click OK.
Extra separator pages are printed, or print jobs seem to get stuck in the printer for all users	Check the print processor in use by accessing the printer's Properties dialog box, click the Advanced tab, click the Print Processor button, and check the print processor in use. Also check the data type. If the problem continues, try a different data type.
Clients send documents that print garbage on hundreds of pages before anyone can stop the printing	Have the spooler automatically hold print jobs that contain the wrong printer setup information. To do this, access the printer's Properties dialog box, click the Advanced tab, click the check box to *Hold mismatched documents*, and click OK in the Properties dialog box.
No documents are printing from the printer	Look for warning lights on the printer indicating a printer jam. If you see them, clear the printer jam.
	Turn off the printer, wait 30 seconds, and restart the printer. Also, check the printer's connection to a computer or the network (both ends). Unplug the connection and plug it back in.

Chapter Summary

- Windows Server 2008 printing uses the graphics device interface (GDI) to integrate print file information with the printer driver. It also involves using the spooler and spool files for printing via the Print Spooler services.

- Internet printing enables users to print files through an Internet connection using HTTP and Internet Printing Protocol (IPP).

- Windows Server 2008 supports using XML Paper Specification (XPS) for polished print documents.

- You can turn Windows Server 2008 into a full-featured print server by installing the Print Services role.

- Use the Add Printers Wizard to install local and shared printers.

- The properties of an installed printer enable you to configure printer sharing, printer port setup, scheduling, security, and specialized device settings.

- Through the Add Printer Wizard, you can install a nonlocal printer or an Internet printer. When these are configured through Windows Server 2008, it is possible to manage their properties configurations from the server.

- Managing a printer involves actions such as pausing and unpausing printing and setting the default printer. Specific print jobs can be canceled, paused, started, and resumed. Also, each print job has associated properties, such as the priority setting for the print job.

- The Print Management tool consolidates printer control and management features in one place. Through this tool, you can manage shared printers, configure printer properties, manage print jobs, install a printer, and more.

- Printer problems can occur at any time. In many cases, you have several actions to try to solve printer problems. Some approaches are as simple as turning the printer off and back on. Others are more complex, such as reinstalling a printer driver or restarting the Print Spooler service.

Key Terms

bidirectional printing Ability of a parallel printer to conduct two-way communication between the printer and the computer, such as to provide out-of-paper information; also, bidirectional printing supports Plug and Play and enables an operating system to query a printer about its capabilities.

data type Way in which information is formatted in a print file.

enhanced metafile (EMF) A data type for printing used by Windows 95, 98, Me, NT, 2000, XP, Vista, Server 2003, and Server 2008 operating systems. EMF print files offer a distinct advantage in Windows operating system environments because they are very portable from computer to computer.

graphics device interface (GDI) An interface on a Windows network print client that works with a local software application, such as Microsoft Word, and a local printer driver to format a file to be sent to a local printer or a network print server.

Internet Printing Protocol (IPP) A protocol that is encapsulated in HTTP and that is used to print files over the Internet.

local print device A printer, such as a laser printer, physically attached to a port on the local computer.

network print device A printing device, such as a laser printer, connected to a print server through a network.

PostScript printer   A printer that has special firmware or cartridges to print using a page-description language (PDL).

print client   Client computer or application that generates a print job.

print job   A document or items to be printed.

print queue   A stack or lineup of print jobs, with the first job submitted at the top of the stack and the last job submitted at the bottom, and all of the jobs waiting to be sent from the spooler to the printer.

print server   Network computer or server device that connects printers to the network for sharing and that receives and processes print requests from print clients.

Printer Control Language (PCL)   A printer language used by non-PostScript Hewlett-Packard and compatible laser printers.

printer driver   Contains the device-specific information that Windows Server 2008 requires to control a particular print device, implementing customized printer control codes, font, and style information so that documents are converted into a printer-specific language.

printer pooling   Linking two or more identical printers with one printer setup or printer share.

RAW   A data type often used for printing MS-DOS, Windows 3.x, and UNIX and Linux print files.

spool file   A print file written to disk until it can be transmitted to a printer.

spooler   In the Windows environment, a group of DLLs, information files, and programs that process print jobs for printing.

spooling   A process working in the background to enable several print files to go to a single printer. Each file is placed in temporary storage until its turn comes to be printed.

TEXT   A data type used for printing text files formatted using the ANSI standard that employs values between 0 and 255 to represent characters, numbers, and symbols.

XML Paper Specification (XPS)   An advanced way of printing documents for multiple purposes, including viewing electronic pages and printing pages in a polished format.

Review Questions

1. One of the users on your network has called to report that a shared printer on your Windows Server 2008 print server is not printing. Which of the following tools can you use to check the status of the printer?

   a. Server Manager

   b. Print Queue Supervisor

   c. Print Management tool

   d. Shared Printer tool in Control Panel

2. You have a printer that is primarily used to handle large graphics print files. When you configure the port for this printer, which of the following port timeout settings should you use?

   a. 10 seconds

   b. 40 seconds

   c. 75 seconds

   d. 120 seconds

3. You own an architectural firm that has two plotters and four laser printers. Your paper costs are very high because people often send print jobs intended for a plotter to a laser printer and vice versa. These errors typically result in page after page of printing with strange characters, wasting money and time. What can you do to address this problem?

    a. Use smaller spooling files.

    b. Configure the printers to hold mismatched documents.

    c. Configure printers to print spooled documents after nonspooled documents.

    d. Enable the advanced printing features in the properties of all of the printers.

4. You have set up a shared printer for UNIX and Linux clients, but when you test the setup the printer produces strings of control codes or simply hangs up. Which of the following might be the problem?

    a. The data type is set to NT EMF and should be RAW.

    b. You have not set up a GDI client processor for the print queue.

    c. The data configuration is set to ASCII instead of to binary.

    d. The port setup is using port 80, which is for HTTP-based printing instead of UNIX and Linux printing.

5. Your company's programmers use one shared printer to print out lines of program code for analysis. They complain that often when they retrieve a printout, ending pages from the last printout or the beginning pages of the next printout are mixed in. This is because many of the printed pages appear very similar at first glance and it's hard to know where one printout ends and the next begins. What do you propose as a solution?

    a. Set up the grayscale colors in the printer's properties so that one printout is printed lighter and the next is printed darker, the next lighter, and so on.

    b. Configure a different spooler for each programmer to use.

    c. Configure the printer properties to use a separator page.

    d. Use a different print processor for each programmer.

6. You can install the _____, _____, and _____ services when installing the Print Services role.

7. Which of the following can you accomplish from the Printers window, which is opened through Control Panel? (Choose all that apply.)

    a. Install a printer.

    b. View what is printing on a printer.

    c. Access the printer's properties.

    d. Determine how fast pages are printing on a printer.

8. You can publish a shared printer in Active Directory by accessing the printer's properties and using the _____ tab.

9. You are configuring a serial printer on a COM port. Which of the following can you configure by using the Configure Port button? (Choose all that apply.)

    a. port timeout

    b. port speed

    c. flow control

    d. port cable type

10. Your associate has configured five shared printers so that print files are sent directly to the printer and printing is done in the foreground. However, when the printers are busy this slows down the CPU on the server managing the print jobs. What should be done to address this problem?

    a. Deactivate one of the printers because a Windows Server 2008 print server is only intended to manage four printers maximum.

    b. In the printers' properties, configure printing to cycle CPU use.

    c. Configure the printers to use zipped spool files.

    d. Configure every printer to spool the print jobs and to print in the background.

11. Briefly explain the purpose of the graphics device interface (GDI).

12. You have just set up two shared printers from Windows Server 2008, and you also plan to manage four other network printers from the server. Your plan is to manage all of these printers using the Print Management tool, but the tool does not appear on the Administrative Tools menu. What is the problem?

    a. The Print Management tool is only available as an MMC snap-in and is not listed on the Administrative Tools menu until you save it as a console with a customized name.

    b. You must first enable use of the Print Management tool in the default domain policy.

    c. You need to install the Print Services role.

    d. The Print Management tool is only a command-line tool, and you must start it from the Command Prompt window using the command *prnmnt*.

13. Which of the following can you accomplish using the Print Management tool? (Choose all that apply.)

    a. Consolidate Windows Server 2008 print servers in one place for management.

    b. Find out how many jobs are in the print queue of a printer.

    c. Set up to use special forms for printing.

    d. Reconfigure printer ports used with printers.

14. You have set up a shared printer on a Windows Server 2008 server. Also, you have given Mat Chen's user account Manage documents permission so that Mat can delete the print jobs of any user. However, when Mat tries to delete someone else's print job, he doesn't have permission. Mat is a member of two global groups, Supervisors and Marketing. Also, the Supervisors group is a member of the Managers domain local group, and the Marketing group is a member of the Business domain local group. Which of the following might be a problem?

    a. Global groups cannot be given printer permissions and so they are automatically denied use of printers.

    b. The Business domain local group is denied Manage documents permission on that printer.

    c. One of the domain local groups to which Mat belongs must be given Print permissions to that printer.

    d. The Supervisors global group must also be a member of the Business domain local group.

15. You have purchased a printer that has the capability to print in duplex mode so that users can print on both sides of a sheet of paper. However, when users try to use this capability when they send a print job, documents are still printed on only one side. Which of the following might be the problem?

    a. The print timeout is set too low in the printer's properties Advanced tab, which does not allow enough time for duplexing.

    b. No printer driver is installed for the printer, and Windows Server 2008 is using the Generic Print Mode Driver.

    c. The duplex button is not turned to on in the Printers window.

    d. The duplex mode needs to be enabled on the Device Settings tab in the printer's properties.

16. From where can you stop and restart the Print Spooler service? (Choose all that apply.)

    a. Computer Management tool

    b. Spooler MMC snap-in

    c. Properties dialog box for any printer

    d. Server Manager

17. A _____ printer can engage in two-way communications between the printer and the print server and requires a(n) _____ cable.

18. Your committee has created a 290-page report for management and you decide to print one copy initially. You send the copy to the printer and then remember that you might not have made a correction to the footer material that prints at the bottom of each page. You pause the printout to check. After you determine all is OK, you decide to continue printing. Which of the following options should you use from the Document menu on the printer window for that printer to continue from where you left off?

    a. Continue

    b. Resume

    c. Restart

    d. Rerun

19. WinPrint is a _____.

20. Your department head is in a hurry to print his report for the managers meeting that starts in 20 minutes, but the printer he uses is currently backed up with 32 print jobs that might take more than 20 minutes to print. You are the print server administrator. How can you help your department head?

    a. Delete the 32 print jobs and send a message to users to resubmit them.

    b. Pause the printer and then use the Pause option to print a single document by ID number while the other documents are paused.

    c. Open that printer's print window and drag the print job to the top of the print queue.

    d. Open that printer's print window and change the priority of the print job to 99 in that print job's properties.

Case Projects

Capital Financial Planning offers accounting and other financial and legal services for small businesses. This firm consists of 28 accountants, one attorney, two bookkeepers, and 20 support staff including two computer support persons. They have been in the process of upgrading their two servers from Windows Server 2003 to Windows Server 2008. Windows Server 2008 is now installed on both servers, but there are continuing configuration tasks as they modernize how they use the servers.

Because computer users in the firm have aging printers, the firm is also upgrading printers and working to centralize printers and printing functions. Their goal is to have more consistency among printers and to reduce printer support time spent by the computer support staff. In terms of client computers, about half of the users have Windows XP and the other half have Windows Vista. The firm has been upgrading users to Windows Vista gradually to ensure that the support staff is not further overloaded. Capital Financial Planning has hired you through Aspen Consulting to consult on the server upgrade process and now they are relying on you to help with the printer upgrades.

Case Project 6-1: Installing a Print Server

After a history of nearly anyone configuring and reconfiguring printers throughout the firm, the management has decided to centralize coordination of five new centrally located printers in the hands of the two computer support staff. The computer support staff wants to turn one of the servers into a print server from which to manage the five new printers. Create a short report that describes the basic steps for installing a Windows Server 2008 print server. In your report, also discuss two tools that can be used to set up and manage printers that the support staff will be able to use with the print server.

Case Project 6-2: Configuring Printer Security

The computer support staff is not sure what permissions should be configured on each printer for themselves and what permissions to configure for the users of the printers. They ask you to create a short report that explains:

- What permissions to use for the computer support people
- What permissions to give to average users of the printers
- How to set up permissions on shared printers

Case Project 6-3: Configuring Printers for Special Needs

As you are working with the computer support staff, they have some questions about specific printing needs for the firm. Their questions are the following:

- During tax season, there is a need to print out completed limited partnership and corporate tax returns in bulk after most of the staff has gone home by 9:00 p.m. Each tax return can involve many pages of forms. Is there a way to set up a printer to print these tax returns after 9:00 p.m.?
- How can a printer be stopped from printing while it is being maintained?
- Is there a way to retain print files, such as completed tax returns, so that they can be reprinted? And if so, how are they deleted when no longer needed?

Case Project 6-4: Using the Print Management Tool

The computer support staff has heard about the new Windows Server 2008 Print Management tool and has questions for you about how to do certain tasks. Create a short report explaining how to use this tool to:

- Install a network printer.
- Pause a printer.
- View the driver files for a printer.
- Determine which printers are currently printing jobs.

chapter 7

Configuring and Managing Data Storage

After reading this chapter and completing the exercises, you will be able to:

- Understand storage options for Windows Server 2008
- Use the Disk Management tool to configure and manage storage
- Explain and configure RAID disk storage fault tolerance
- Understand storage enhancements in Windows Server 2008
- Back up disk storage

Storing information on a computer is important to users, so server administrators spend considerable time ensuring the integrity of disk drives. Everyone who uses a computer sleeps better when they know that disk storage is set up properly, carefully managed, and regularly backed up. With good disk management practices comes the assurance that data is there when you need it and that your work can continue even when a disk drive fails.

This chapter begins by explaining disk storage options in Windows Server 2008, including the use of basic and dynamic disks. You learn how to set up different disk configurations, starting with simple volumes and advancing to more complex disk configurations. You learn to configure and manage disks using the Disk Management tool. For times when you encounter disk problems, you learn to use the Disk Defragmenter and the tools for finding and fixing disk problems. Next, you learn about using RAID alternatives to help ensure high availability of data, even when a disk fails. You also learn about two important storage enhancements and ways to back up and restore data.

Windows Server 2008 Storage Options

Windows Server 2008 supports two data storage types: basic disks and dynamic disks. A **basic disk** is one that uses traditional disk management techniques and contains primary partitions, extended partitions, and logical drives. A **dynamic disk** is one that does not use traditional partitioning. Dynamic disk architecture provides more flexibility than basic disks so there is virtually no restriction on the number of volumes that can be on one disk. Both types of data storage are discussed in the next sections.

Basic Disks

Because a basic disk uses traditional disk management techniques, it is partitioned and formatted, and can be set up to employ disk sets. **Partitioning** is a process that blocks a group of tracks and sectors to be used by a particular file system, such as NTFS. **Formatting** is a process that creates a table containing file and folder information for a specific file system in a partition. Formatting also creates a root directory (folder) and a volume label.

Another concept important to introduce is volume. A **volume** is a logical designation of disk storage that is created out of one or more physical disks. It is partitioned and formatted with one file system, such as NTFS. A volume can also be identified to users through a unique drive letter, such as C:. One volume contains at least one partition, but can encompass more than one.

The terms volume and partition are sometimes used interchangeably, but this is not technically accurate in part because a volume may consist of more than one partition. Also, a volume is a logical designation and a partition is a physical designation. For example, you might have a server that houses two operating systems, Windows Server 2008 and Linux. When you are in Windows Server 2008, this operating system recognizes the NTFS-formatted partition as a volume with a drive letter (a logical designation)—but it only recognizes the Linux file system portion of a disk as a partition (physical designation) it cannot access. However, because a volume often has one formatted partition on a physical disk, volume and partition are sometimes mistakenly said to be the same thing.

Basic disks recognize primary and extended partitions, which are discussed in the next section. Basic disks also can be configured for any of three RAID levels: disk striping (RAID level 0), disk mirroring (RAID level 1), and disk striping with parity (RAID level 5). **RAID** stands for **redundant array of inexpensive** (or **independent**) **disks**—a set of standards for lengthening disk life and preventing data loss. Disk **striping** is the ability to spread data over multiple disks or volumes. For example, part of a large file may be written to one disk and part to another. The goal is to spread disk activity equally across all disks, preventing wear from being focused on a single disk in a set. **Disk mirroring** is the practice of creating a mirror image of all data on an original disk, so that the data is fully copied or mirrored to a backup disk. The sole purpose of the backup disk is to go into live production if the original disk fails.

When you install Windows Server 2008, the existing disks are configured as basic disks by default. Any disks that are added later are automatically configured as basic disks. Also, if you upgrade Windows Server 2003 with basic disks to Windows Server 2008, the basic disks remain.

MBR and GPT Support
When a drive is partitioned, a **Master Boot Record (MBR)** and a **partition table** are created at the beginning track and sectors on the disk. The MBR is located in the first sector and track of the hard disk and has startup information about partitions and how to access the disk. The partition table contains information about each partition created, such as the type of partition on MBR Disks, size, and location. Also, the partition table provides information to the computer about which partition to access first. As you learn in the next section, "Primary and Extended Partitions on MBR Disks," the MBR limits the number of partitions per disk.

Globally Unique Identifier (GUID) Partition Table or **GPT** is a newer way to partition disks, without imposing the same type of limits on the number of partitions as with MBR. GPT is one element of the **Extensible Firmware Interface (EFI)** approach that is offered by the Unified EFI Forum. EFI is an alternative to using BIOS firmware (see Chapter 2, "Installing Windows Server 2008"). Some computers that you work on might have EFI instead of the traditional BIOS firmware, and along with EFI they will have GPT disks. GPT disks can also be used in computers that use BIOS firmware.

 EFI was initiated by Intel for new-generation computers. You can find out more about it at www.*intel.com/technology/efi*.

Instead of storing partition information in an MBR and a partition table at the beginning of the disk, GPT disks store partition information in each partition using main and backup tables. Also, each partition is identified by a different GUID or reference number. One reason why GPT disks have been developed is that GPT disk partitions can be very large, with size limited by the operating system rather than by the actual physical limit of the GPT disk. In Windows Server 2008 x64 systems, a GPT partition can theoretically be up to 18 exabytes, which is considerably larger than the 2 terabyte limit of a traditional MBR disk in Windows Server 2008. Also, in Windows Server 2008, a GPT disk can hold up to 128 partitions (a limit imposed by the operating system). In Windows Server 2008, you can convert an MBR disk to GPT and vice versa. You might convert an MBR disk, for example, if it is GPT compatible, very large in size, and you want to have many basic disk partitions, such as 10, 20, or more. You can also convert a GPT disk to MBR, which you might consider if you have other MBR disks you want to use with it.

The general steps for converting an MBR disk to GPT are as follows:

1. Back up any data on the MBR disk before you do the conversion (see the section "Disk Backup" later in this chapter).

2. Click Start, point to Administrative Tools, click Computer Management, double-click Storage under the tree (if necessary to expand the tree), and click Disk Management.

3. Use the Disk Management tool to delete any volumes on the MBR disk. To do this, right-click each volume and click Delete Volume.

4. In the Disk Management tool, right-click the disk to convert, such as Disk 1, and click Convert to GPT Disk.

The steps for converting a GPT disk to MBR are as follows:

1. Back up the data on the disk prior to the conversion.

2. Open the Disk Management tool, click each volume on the GPT disk, and click Delete Volume.

3. Right-click the MBR disk, such as Disk 1, and click Convert to MBR Disk.

Primary and Extended Partitions on MBR Disks   An MBR disk partition can be set up as primary or extended. A basic disk must contain at least one primary partition and can contain up to a maximum of four partitions per disk. A **primary partition** is one from which you can boot an operating system, such as Windows Server 2008. Or a primary partition can simply hold files in a different file system format. When you boot from a primary partition, it contains the operating system startup files in a location at the beginning of the partition. At least one primary partition must be marked as active, and only one primary partition can be active at a given time. The **active partition** is the partition where your computer will look for the hardware-specific files to start the operating system (system partition).

An **extended partition** is created from space that is not yet partitioned. The purpose of an extended partition is to enable you to exceed the four-partition limit of a basic disk. Only one extended partition can exist on a single basic disk. An extended partition is not actually formatted and assigned a drive letter. Once an extended partition is created, it is further divided into logical drives. The logical drives are then formatted and assigned drive letters. Figure 7-1 illustrates two disks in a server. Disk 0 has four partitions, including the active partition, and Disk 1 has two regular partitions and one extended partition.

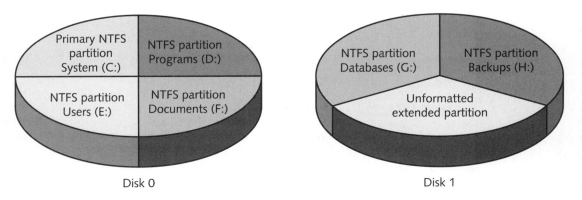

Figure 7-1   Partitions on two disk drives

A computer with multiple partitions boots from the partition that is designated as the active partition, which must also be the system partition containing the startup files. To determine which partition is designated as active, look for the "(System)" designation in the Disk Management tool pane that gives information about the disk's size and file system.

Two other references to partitioning used by Microsoft are important to understand. The **system partition** is the partition that contains the hardware-specific files needed to load the operating system. In Windows Server 2008, the system partition may use the FAT file system for faster booting. (However, you cannot configure a FAT partition.) The **boot partition** is the partition that contains the operating system files located in the \Windows folder. The system partition has to be on a primary partition, but the boot partition can be installed on either a primary or extended partition.

For all of the activities in this chapter, you'll need an account with Administrator privileges. Also, most of these activities can be completed on a virtual server or computer, such as in Hyper-V.

Some steps in the activities in this book include bulleted questions with space for you to record your responses/answers.

Activity 7-1: Viewing the Active Partition

Time Required: Approximately 10 minutes
Objective: Verify which partition is marked as active.

Description: In this activity, you use the Computer Management window to access the Disk Management tool and verify which is the active partition, along with other information about the disks on your system. Also, you learn how to mark a partition as active.

1. Click **Start**, point to **Administrative Tools**, and click **Computer Management**.

2. Double-click **Storage** under the tree, if the tools under it are not displayed.

3. Click **Disk Management** in the tree. Notice the listing of partitions at the top of the middle pane (see Figure 7-2).

    • What is the disk type for each of your partitions? Also, look under the Status column. Which partition is marked as active? Which are shown as the Boot and System partitions?

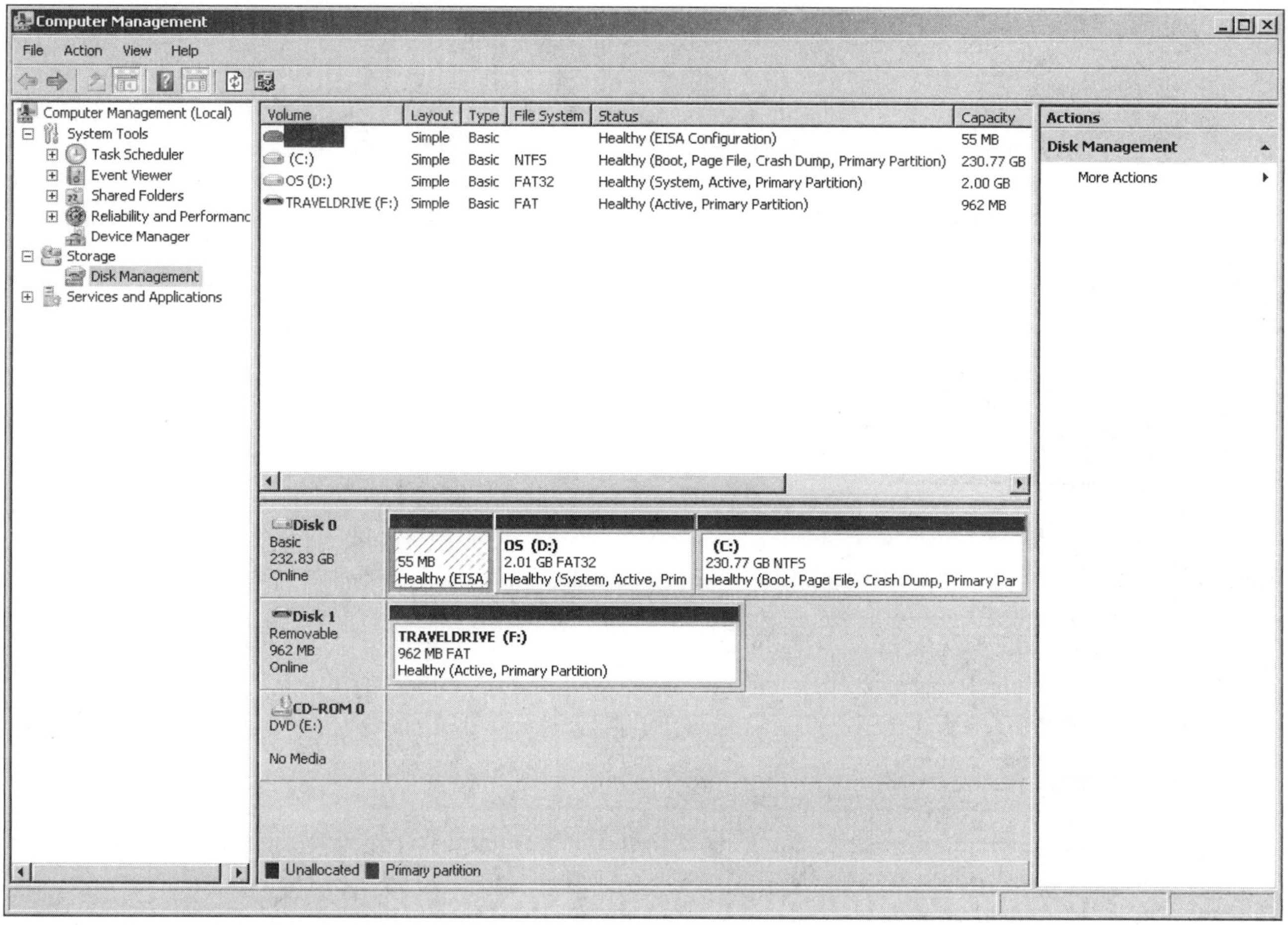

Figure 7-2 Viewing disk information in the Computer Management tool

4. In the middle pane, find a partition that is not the system partition and right-click it (do not click in the area that says Disk 0 or Disk 1, but do click in the area labeled as (C:) or (D:), for example).

5. Notice the Mark Partition as Active option on the shortcut menu (see Figure 7-3). This is the option you would click to mark a partition as active. (Do not mark the partition active in this practice session, unless your instructor gives you permission.)

```
Open
Explore

Mark Partition as Active
Change Drive Letter and Paths...
Format...

Extend Volume...
Shrink Volume...
Add Mirror...
Delete Volume...

Properties

Help
```

Figure 7-3 Shortcut menu

6. Close the Computer Management window.

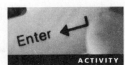

Activity 7-2: Customizing the MMC to Access Disk Management Tools

Time Required: Approximately 10 minutes
Objective: Create a customized console from which to perform disk management and disk defragmentation.

Description: Some server managers prefer to customize an MMC window from which to access disk management tools. Also, by default no Disk Management console is available from the Administrative Tools menu, so it is handy to add one. In this activity, you customize an MMC window to contain the Disk Management tool and save the MMC console.

1. Click **Start** and click **Run**. Enter **mmc** in the *Open* text box and click **OK**.

2. Maximize the console windows, if necessary. Click the **File** menu and click **Add/Remove Snap-in**.

3. Under *Available snap-ins*, click **Disk Management**.

4. Click the **Add** button.

5. Leave *This computer* as the default selection and click **Finish**.

6. Click **OK**.

7. Notice the title bar of the window is titled Console1 – [Console Root].

8. Click the **File** menu and click **Save As**. Enter **Disk Management.msc** (or if you are sharing a server with other students, enter Disk Management plus your initials, such as Disk Management JR.msc) as the name for this console setup and click **Save**.

9. Notice that the title bar now displays a new title that matches the filename you used to save the console.

10. Close the console window.

11. Click **Start**, point to **All Programs**, and click **Administrative Tools**. Notice that your customized console is listed in the menu.

12. Click **Disk Management** and leave the window open.

Volume and Stripe Sets Under Windows NT 4.0, you could create multidisk volumes known as volume sets and stripe sets. A **volume set** consists of two or more partitions that are combined to look like one volume with a single drive letter. A **stripe set** is two or more disks that are combined like a volume set, but that are striped for RAID level 0 or RAID level 5 (RAID is discussed later in this chapter). Windows 2000 Server, Windows Server 2003, and Windows Server 2008 provide backward compatibility with basic disk volume and stripe sets that have previously been created through legacy Windows NT systems. If you have any of these legacy multidisk volumes on a Windows Server 2003 server, you can still use them after you upgrade to Windows Server 2008, but you cannot create new volume or stripe sets should the disks fail. For this reason, after a Windows Server 2003 server is upgraded to Windows Server 2008, you should plan to convert basic disks to dynamic disks in order to implement any new multidisk volumes.

Dynamic Disks

A dynamic disk does not use traditional partitioning, which makes it possible to set up a large number of volumes on one disk and provides the ability to extend volumes onto additional physical disks. The number of disks that can be incorporated into one spanned volume is limited to 32. In addition to volume extensions and spanned volumes, dynamic disks support RAID levels 0, 1, and 5. Dynamic disks can be formatted for NTFS and are used when you do not implement a dual-boot system. Also, dynamic disks can be reactivated should they go offline because they have been powered down or disconnected.

When you upgrade from a Windows Server 2003 system with basic disks or when you install Windows Server 2008 from scratch, you end up with basic disks. Plan to convert basic disks to dynamic disks after you install Windows Server 2008 so that you can take advantage of the richer set of options associated with dynamic disks. The five types of dynamic disk configurations are simple volumes, spanned volumes, mirrored volumes, striped volumes, and RAID-5 volumes. The functional concepts of these disk configurations are similar to those originally used for Windows NT 4.0-compatible basic disks, but the Windows Server 2008 dynamic disks have better disk management options and do not use partitioning. For example, the dynamic disk equivalent of a simple or regular basic disk is a simple dynamic disk volume, and the equivalent of a basic disk stripe set is called striped volumes.

On dynamic disks, instead of using the basic disk terminology of boot partition and system partition, the volume that contains the \Windows folder of system files is called the boot volume, and the volume that contains the files used to boot the computer is called the system volume.

In the next sections, you learn more about simple, spanned, and striped volumes. Later, in the section titled "Introduction to Fault Tolerance," you learn about dynamic disk mirrored volumes and RAID-5 volumes, plus additional information about using striped volumes.

Simple Volume A **simple volume** is a portion of a disk or an entire disk that is set up as a dynamic disk. If you do not allocate all of a disk as a simple volume, you have the option to later take all or a portion of the unallocated space and add it to an existing simple volume, which is called extending the volume. A simple volume can be extended onto multiple sections of the same disk (up to 32 sections). A simple volume does not provide fault tolerance because it cannot be set up for any RAID level (see the section "Introduction to Fault Tolerance" later in the chapter).

Spanned Volume A **spanned volume** is stored on 2 to 32 dynamic disks that are treated as one volume. For example, you might create a spanned volume if you have four separate small hard disks (80 GB, 80 GB, 100 GB, and 120 GB), as shown in Figure 7-4. Another reason to use a spanned volume is if you have several small free portions of disk space scattered throughout the server's disk drives. You might have 600 MB of free space on one drive, 750 MB on another, and 424 MB on a third. All of these free areas can be combined into a single 1774 MB spanned volume with its own drive letter, with the advantage that you reduce the number of drive letters needed to make use of the space.

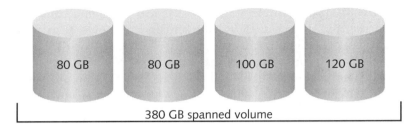

Figure 7-4 Creating one spanned volume from four disks

As you add new disks, the spanned volume can be extended to include each disk. The advantage of creating spanned volumes is the ability to more easily manage several small disk drives or to maximize the use of scattered pockets of disk space across several disks.

The disadvantage of using a spanned volume is that if one disk fails, the entire volume is inaccessible. Also, if a portion of a spanned volume is deleted, the entire disk set is deleted. For these reasons, avoid placing mission-critical data and applications on a spanned volume.

Striped Volume Striped volumes are often referred to as RAID-0. The main purpose for striping disks in a volume is to extend the life of hard disk drives by spreading data equally over two or more drives. Spreading the data divides the drive load so that one drive is not working more than any other. Another advantage of striping is that it increases disk performance. Contention among disks is equalized and data is accessed faster for both reads and writes than when it is on a single drive, because Windows Server 2008 can write to all drives at the same time.

In Windows Server 2008, striping requires at least two disks and can be performed over as many as 32. The total of striped disks is called a striped volume. Equal portions of data are written in 64 KB blocks in rows or stripes on each disk. For example, consider that you have set up striping across five hard disks and are working with a 720 KB data file. The first 64 KB portion of the file is written to disk 1, the next 64 KB portion is written to disk 2, the third portion is written to disk 3, and so on. After 320 KB are spread in the first data row across disks 1 through 5, the next 320 KB are written in 64 KB blocks in the second row across the disks. Finally, 64 KB will be written to the third row on disk 1 and 16 KB in the third row on disk 2 (see Figure 7-5).

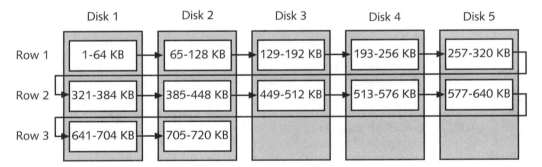

Figure 7-5 Disks in a striped volume

Because of its high performance, striping is useful for volumes that store large databases or for data replication from one volume to another. Striping is not a benefit when most of the data files on a server are very small, such as under 64 KB.

Data can be lost when one or more disks in the striped volume fail because the system has no automated way to rebuild data. If you use striping to increase disk performance for a critical database, consider frequently backing up that database (backups are discussed later in this chapter).

You also can create mirrored volumes and RAID-5 volumes on a dynamic disk for fault tolerance. Fault-tolerant volumes are covered later in this chapter.

Shrinking a Volume Windows Server 2008 comes with the ability to shrink a basic or dynamic disk volume. Shrinking a volume enables you to create a new partition when one is needed and you don't have extra disks. For example, you might need a partition for a new database as a way to better secure, manage, and back up that database. Another example is to create a new partition for an additional server system, such as Linux, that you install as a virtual server in Hyper-V.

When you shrink a volume, Windows Server 2008 starts from the end of that volume and works its way back through contiguous space to create unallocated disk space. You can specify the amount of space to recover. If files on the space are being recovered, Windows Server 2008 moves those files to the original partition so the move is transparent to the user. If the shrinking process encounters a file that cannot be moved, it stops shrinking at that point. Examples of files that cannot be moved include the paging file and shadow backup files.

If you need to recover more space, but cannot because of the paging file, you can move the paging file to another volume (see Chapter 3, "Configuring the Windows Server 2008 Environment"). Also, disks that have a high number of bad clusters cannot be shrunk.

The general steps for shrinking a volume are as follows:

1. Open the Disk Management tool or snap-in.
2. Right-click the blue bar above the volume you want to shrink.
3. Click Shrink Volume.
4. Specify the amount of space you need for the unallocated space in the box, *Enter the amount of space to shrink in MB* (see Figure 7-6).

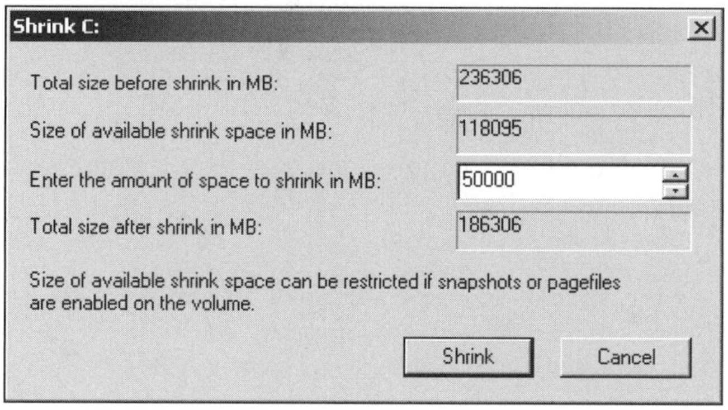

Shrink C:	
Total size before shrink in MB:	236306
Size of available shrink space in MB:	118095
Enter the amount of space to shrink in MB:	50000
Total size after shrink in MB:	186306

Size of available shrink space can be restricted if snapshots or pagefiles are enabled on the volume.

[Shrink] [Cancel]

Figure 7-6 Shrinking a volume

5. Click Shrink.
6. After a few minutes, you'll see the newly unallocated space in the Disk Management tool.

Disk Management

Disk Management tasks can be performed using the Disk Management tool. This tool provides a central location for viewing disk information and performing tasks such as creating and deleting partitions and volumes. The following sections introduce you to the different tasks you can perform using the Disk Management tool: creating a partition and simple volume, converting to dynamic disks, and mounting a drive. Also in the next sections, you learn how to manage and troubleshoot disks using the Disk Defragmenter, Disk Check, and *chkdsk* tools.

Creating a Partition and Simple Volume

When you partition a disk, leave 1 MB or more of the disk space free. This is the amount of workspace that Windows Server 2008 needs to convert a basic disk to a dynamic disk, in case you want to upgrade later.

Partitions operate as separate storage units on a hard disk. This allows you to better organize your data and make better use of your hard disk space. For example, you can create one partition on which to install the operating system and another partition for user data. The most basic way to create a partition is to take unallocated disk space and use the New Simple Volume Wizard to create a simple volume. In this process, you can specify the size of the volume, whether or not to format the volume, the file system (NTFS), and a volume label.

In terms of configuring your server, it's always a good idea to keep the operating system on a partition separate from user data. This way, if you need to reinstall the operating system, all your data still remains intact (unless you format the partition the data is stored on during the reinstall).

Activity 7-3: Creating a Simple Volume

Time Required: Approximately 10–30 minutes
Objective: Create a new partition from unpartitioned disk space.

Description: This activity enables you to create a new partition. You'll need access to a server that has some amount of unpartitioned disk space or free space. If a server is not available with unpartitioned space, remember the location of this activity so you can refer to these steps before partitioning disk space in a live work situation.

1. If the customized MMC you created in Activity 7-2 is closed, open it by clicking **Start**, pointing to **All Programs**, clicking **Administrative Tools**, and clicking **Disk Management**. Maximize the console windows and also click **Disk Management (Local)**, if necessary.

2. If you have unallocated disk space, right-click that space and click **New Simple Volume**.

3. Click **Next** in the New Simple Volume Wizard.

4. For *Simple volume size in MB*, enter an appropriate size for the volume you are creating or use the default entry (see Figure 7-7).

5. Click **Next**.

6. Use the default drive letter, such as F, and click **Next**. (If you see a message that the drive letter is already mapped, change the current mapping or go back and select a different drive letter.)

7. In the Format Partition dialog box, the default is to format the volume using NTFS and use the Default allocation unit size. You can also specify a volume label (see Figure 7-8). Additionally, you have the option to perform a quick format, which is not advised because this doesn't check the integrity of the partition. Another option is to permit folders and files to be compressed. Click **Next**.

The only available file system to select for the new simple volume is NTFS. FAT is not an option, although when you install Windows Server 2008, the installation process can create a FAT32 partition (usually on EFI-based x64 and Itanium computers) for the system partition because FAT enables faster booting from the boot file.

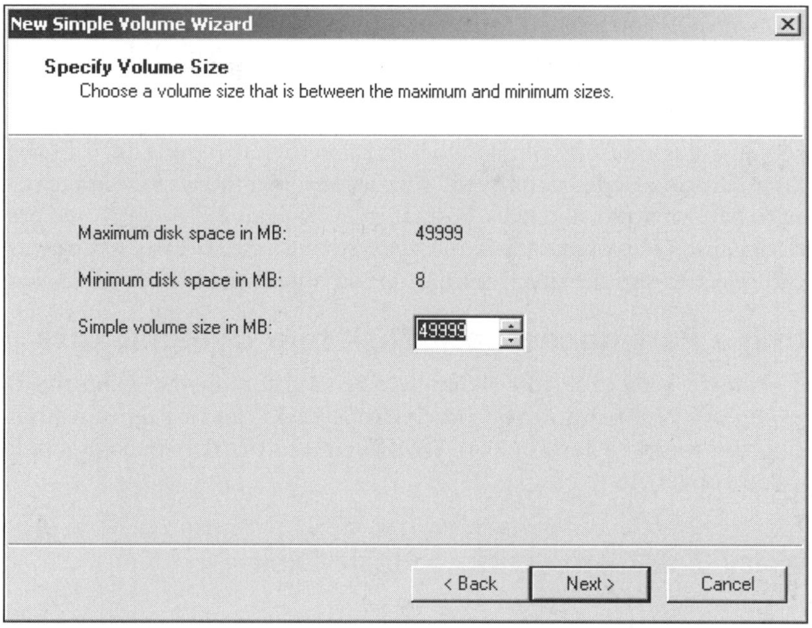

Figure 7-7 Specifying the volume size

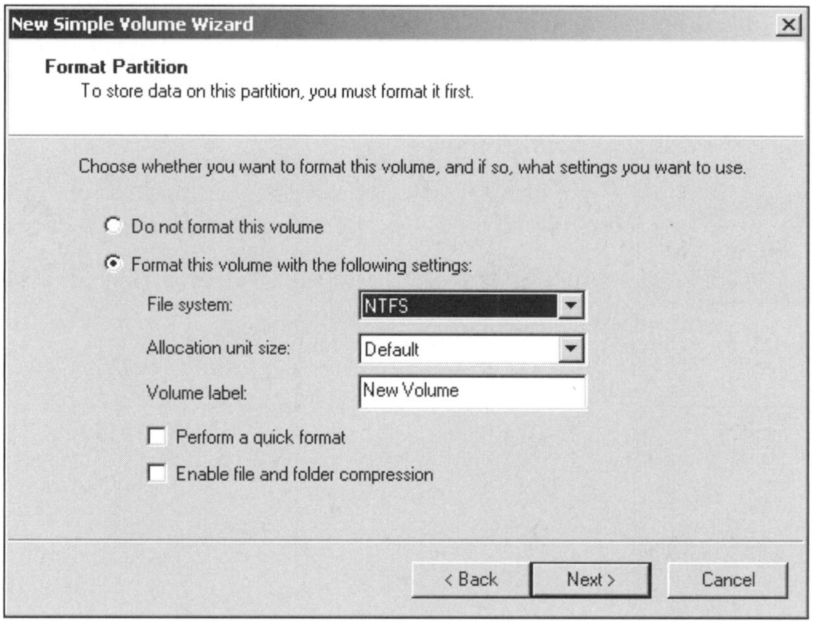

Figure 7-8 Format instructions for creating a partition

8. Review the selections you have made and click **Finish**. (It may take a few minutes to create the new simple volume. The Disk Management tool displays its progress as it is working.)

9. Leave the Disk Management tool open for the next activity.

You can also delete a partition using the Disk Management tool. To delete a partition, right-click the partition you want to delete. The partition will have a dark gray border and shading to indicate that you have selected it. Click Delete Volume on the shortcut menu. The Disk Management tool gives you a warning that data will be lost. Click Yes to continue the delete process.

When you step through the New Simple Volume Wizard, you have the option of not formatting the partition. If you do not format a partition when it is created, it still needs to be formatted before it can be used. You may, for example, format it later with a different operating system, such as Linux, when you install Linux as a virtual server in Hyper-V.

Once a partition is formatted, it is called a volume and can be assigned a drive letter. Assigning a drive letter makes it easier to refer to the volume, for example assigning it drive letter C:. You can also provide a customized volume label to reflect what is contained in the volume.

To format a partition that is not already formatted, open the Disk Management tool, right-click the partition to be formatted, and click Format (refer to Figure 7-3, only the Format option will be active). You can specify a volume label, the file system to use (NTFS), and the allocation unit size. Also, you can select to use the quick format option and to enable file and folder compression.

Converting a Partitioned Basic Disk to a Dynamic Disk

Converting a simple basic disk to a dynamic disk is accomplished from the Disk Management tool. When you convert from a basic to dynamic disk, the process does not damage data in any way, but you must be certain that 1 MB or more of free space is available on the basic disk before you convert it.

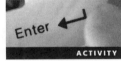

Activity 7-4: Converting a Basic Disk

Time Required: Approximately 10 minutes
Objective: Convert a simple basic disk to a dynamic disk.

Description: In this activity, you convert a simple basic disk, such as the one you created in Activity 7-3, to a dynamic disk. Before you start, make sure you have permission from your instructor to convert the disk. If you do not have permission to convert the disk, click Cancel at Step 5.

1. Open the Disk Management tool if it is closed.

2. Right-click the disk you want to convert.

 Make sure that you right-click the disk, for example Disk 0, and not the volume, for example (C:), or else the upgrade option will not be displayed.

3. Click **Convert to Dynamic Disk**, as shown in Figure 7-9.

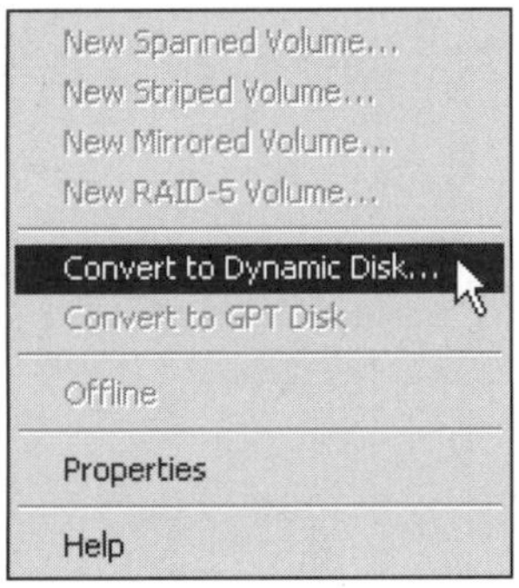

New Spanned Volume...
New Striped Volume...
New Mirrored Volume...
New RAID-5 Volume...

Convert to Dynamic Disk...
Convert to GPT Disk

Offline

Properties

Help

Figure 7-9 Converting a disk

4. Make sure that the correct disk is selected, such as Disk 0 or Disk 1 (check all that apply), in the Convert to Dynamic Disk dialog box. Click **OK**.

5. Verify the disk or disks to convert in the Disks to Convert dialog box and click **Convert**. Or, if you do not have permission to convert the disk, click **Cancel**.

6. Click **Yes** in the Disk Management information box.

7. If necessary, click **Yes** to acknowledge that the file systems on the disk will be dismounted.

8. Notice under the Type column that the basic disk has now been converted to a dynamic disk.

9. Leave the Disk Management tool open for the next activity.

In some circumstances, you might need to change a dynamic disk back to a basic disk, such as when you want to implement a dual-boot setup with an operating system that doesn't support dynamic disks, or when you want to remove Windows Server 2008 from the computer so that a different operating system can be loaded. Before reverting back to a basic disk, the disk must be empty—so data must be backed up or moved to another disk. A dynamic disk can be converted back to a basic disk by using the following general steps:

1. Back up all data on the dynamic disk volume before you start.

2. Delete all of the dynamic disk volumes on the disk, using the Disk Management tool, by right-clicking the volume, such as (D:), and clicking **Delete Volume**.

3. The disk should convert back to a basic disk automatically.

Mounting a Drive

Windows Server 2008 enables you to mount a drive as an alternative to giving it a drive letter. A **mounted drive** is one that appears as a folder and is accessed through a path like any other folder. You can mount a basic or dynamic disk drive, a CD/DVD drive, or a removable drive. Only an empty folder on a volume formatted for NTFS can be used for mounting a drive. Once a drive is mounted, other drives can be added to the same folder to appear as one drive. There are several reasons for using mounted drives. The most apparent reason is that Windows operating systems are limited to 26 drive letters, and mounting drives enables you to reduce the number of drive letters in use because they are not associated with letters. Another reason for creating a mounted drive is for user home directories that are stored on the server. A **home directory** or **home folder** is a server folder that is associated with a user's account and that is a designated workspace for the user to store files. (Microsoft sometimes uses the term home directory instead of home folder for consistency with terminology used by legacy server systems.) As server administrator, you might allocate one drive for all user home directories and mount that drive in a folder called Users. The path to the drive might be C:\Home or C:\Users. In another situation, you might have a database that you want to manage as a mounted drive so that it is easier for users to access. Also, by mounting the drive, you can set up special backups for that database by simply backing up its folder.

Activity 7-5: Configuring a Mounted Drive

Time Required: Approximately 10–15 minutes
Objective: Learn how to set up a mounted drive.

Description: This activity enables you to create a mounted volume. In the first series of steps, you create a folder on an NTFS-formatted volume or disk that will hold the mounted drive. After those steps, you mount the drive into the folder. You will need an available disk drive to mount into the folder (or stop at Step 9).

1. Click **Start**, click **Computer**, and double-click a main volume that is formatted for NTFS, such as *Local Disk C:*.

2. Click the **File** menu, point to **New**, and click **Folder**. Enter your initials appended to Mount for the folder name, such as *MountJR*. Press **Enter**. Leave the window open.

3. Access the Disk Management tool.

4. Right-click the disk drive, such as *D:*, that you want to mount into the folder and click **Change Drive Letter and Paths**.

5. Click the existing drive letter for the drive, such as *D:*, in the Name box and click the **Add** button.

6. Click **Mount in the following empty NTFS folder.**

7. Click the **Browse** button and navigate to the folder you created, then click that folder, such as *MountJR*.

8. Click **OK** in the Browse for Drive Path dialog box.

9. Click **OK** in the Add Drive Letter or Path dialog box (or click Cancel if you do not want to complete mounting the drive).

10. Go back to the window containing the folder you created, such as the Local Disk (C:) window. Find the mounted volume you created.

    • What icon is used to represent the mounted volume?

11. Right-click the mounted volume and click **Properties.**

    • What tabs are available? What is entered for *Type* on the General tab?

12. Close the mounted volume's properties dialog box and close the window, such as Local Disk (C:). Close the Disk Management tool. Click **Yes** to save the console settings.

Managing Disks

Once you have your physical disks partitioned and formatted, they are ready to be used as storage mediums. To ensure system performance, the disks must still be maintained. Windows Server 2008 includes several tools, such as Disk Defragmenter, Disk Check, and *chkdsk*, that can be used to diagnose disk problems and maintain disk performance.

Using Disk Defragmenter   When you save a file to a disk, Windows Server 2008 saves the file to the first area of available space. The file might not be saved to a contiguous area of free space and the disk gradually becomes **fragmented**, particularly as more and more files are created and deleted. When your computer attempts to access the file, it might have to be read from different areas on a disk, slowing access time and creating disk wear. The process of **defragmenting** locates fragmented folders and files and moves them to a location on the physical disk so they are in contiguous order.

On a busy server, drives should be defragmented every week to two weeks. On less busy servers, defragment the drives at least once a month.

Activity 7-6: Using the Disk Defragmenter

Time Required: Approximately 15 minutes
Objective: Practice using Disk Defragmenter.

Description: One of the best ways to keep your server running quickly is to defragment its disk drives. This activity enables you to use the Windows Server 2008 Disk Defragmenter.

1. Click **Start,** point to **All Programs,** and click **Accessories.**

2. Click **System Tools.**

3. Click **Disk Defragmenter.**

4. The Disk Defragmenter will begin to analyze your volumes to determine if they need to be defragmented. If your system is in good health, you'll see the following two lines:

   Your file system performance is good.
   You do not need to defragment at this time.

5. Click **Run on a schedule (recommended)**.

6. Click the **Modify schedule** button.

7. In the Disk Defragmenter: Modify Schedule dialog box, click the **down arrow** for the How often box and select **Weekly**.

8. In the What day box, select **Friday**.

9. In the What time box, select **11:00 PM** (see Figure 7-10).

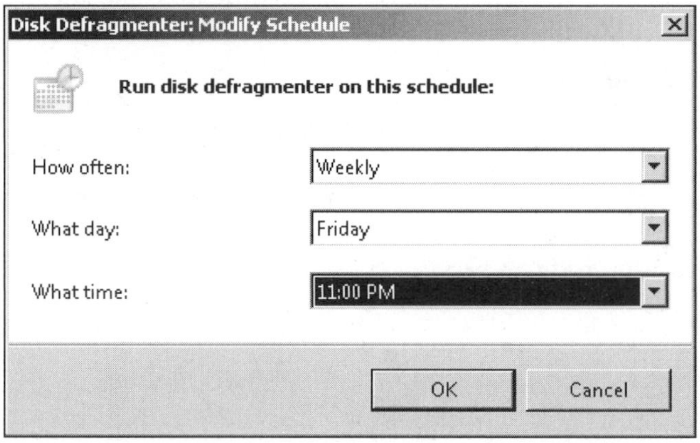

Figure 7-10   Configuring the Disk Defragmenter schedule

10. Click **OK**.

11. Regardless of whether your disk needs to be defragmented, click the **Defragment now** button to start defragmenting.

   • What disks can you select to defragment?

12. Click **Cancel** (or click OK if you want to try out the defragmenting process, which can take anywhere from several minutes to several hours, depending on the size of your disk).

13. Close the Disk Defragmenter.

Using Disk Check   The Disk Check tool allows you to scan your disk for bad sectors and file system errors. This tool is meant for use when no users need to access the files on the disk you want to check because the disk is made unavailable during the scan for problems. The Disk Check tool is started from the Properties dialog box for a disk.

When you start the Disk Check tool, two options are available:

   • *Automatically fix file system errors*—Select this option to have Windows repair any file system errors it finds during the disk checking process. To use this option, all programs must be closed.

   • *Scan for and attempt recovery of bad sectors*—Select this option to have the system find and fix bad sectors and file errors, recovering any information that it can read. Choosing this option also includes the file system fixes that are performed by the selection *Automatically fix file system errors*.

Activity 7-7: Using Disk Check

Time Required: Depends on the size of the disk and number of files (10 to over 40 minutes)

Objective: Learn how to use Disk Check.

Description: In this activity, you practice using the Disk Check utility to scan your disk. If you are using a multiple disk system, ask your instructor which disk to scan. Also, if you have a large disk with many files, you might want to stop at Step 6 because the disk check can take a long time. When you do this activity, you really defer Disk Check to run the next time you boot the server.

1. Click **Start** and click **Computer**.
2. Right-click the disk you want to scan, such as **Local Disk (C:)**.
3. Click **Properties**.
4. Click the **Tools** tab.
   - What tools can you use on this tab?

5. Click **Check Now**.
6. Leave the **Automatically fix file system errors** box checked by default, and click the box for **Scan for and attempt recovery of bad sectors** so that it is checked, as shown in Figure 7-11.

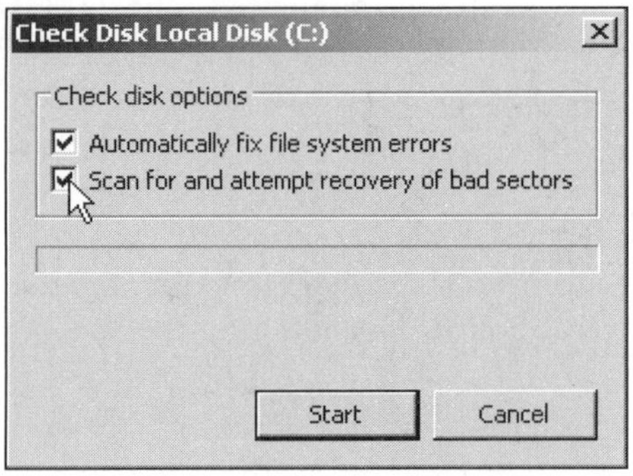

Figure 7-11 Selecting a Disk Check option

7. Click **Start**.
8. Click **Schedule disk check** to have Disk Check run when you reboot the computer.
9. Close the disk's **Properties** dialog box.
10. Close any open windows and save any work.
11. Click **Start**, and click the **right pointing arrow** at the bottom of the Start menu.
12. Click **Restart**.
13. Select an option, such as *Hardware: Maintenance (Planned)* and click **OK**.
14. When the computer reboots, you'll see the disk checking processes start.

Using *chkdsk* You can also check your disk for errors by running the *chkdsk* utility from the Command Prompt window. *chkdsk* also starts automatically when you boot Windows Server 2008, and the boot process detects file allocation table or file corruption, such as in the system files. In NTFS, *chkdsk* checks files, folders, indexes, security descriptors, user files, sectors, and disk allocation units. Table 7-1 summarizes the different switches that can be used with the *chkdsk* command.

Table 7-1 *chkdsk* switch and parameter options

Switch/Parameter	Purpose
[*volume*] (such as C:)	Specifies that *chkdsk* only check the designated volume
[*filename*] (such as *.dll)	Enables a check of the specified file or files only
/c	Uses an abbreviated check of the folder structure
/f	Instructs *chkdsk* to fix errors that it finds
/i	Uses an abbreviated check of indexes
/L:size	Enables you to specify the size of the log file created by the disk check
/r	Searches for bad sectors, fixes problems, and recovers information (when not possible; use the Recover command on separate files)
/x	Dismounts or locks a volume before starting

Allow plenty of time for *chkdsk* to run on large disk systems, such as a system having over 80 GB. If you have multiple disks, you might want to stagger running *chkdsk* on different disks for each week. Also, the presence of some bad sectors is normal. Many disks have a few bad sectors that are marked by the manufacturer during the low-level format and on which data cannot be written.

When *chkdsk* finds lost allocation units or chains, it prompts you with the Yes or No question: *Convert lost chains to files?*. Answer Yes to the question so that you can save the lost information to files. The files that *chkdsk* creates for each lost chain are labeled Filexxx.chk and can be edited with a text editor to determine their contents.

Activity 7-8: Using *chkdsk* from the Command Line

Time Required: Depends on the size of the disk and number of files (10 to over 40 minutes)
Objective: Learn how to use *chkdsk* from the command line.

Description: You run the *chkdsk* command-line utility to examine a disk for errors.

1. Click **Start**, point to **All Programs**, click **Accessories**, and click **Command Prompt**.

2. Type **chkdsk** and press **Enter**. Figure 7-12 shows the sample results of this tool.

   • What happens when you run *chkdsk* without the /f option?

3. Close the Command Prompt window.

```
Administrator: Command Prompt                                          _ □ ×
   183892 index entries processed.
Index verification completed.
   0 unindexed files processed.
CHKDSK is verifying security descriptors (stage 3 of 3)...
   136832 security descriptors processed.
Security descriptor verification completed.
   23531 data files processed.
CHKDSK is verifying Usn Journal...
   391056280 USN bytes processed.
Usn Journal verification completed.
Windows has checked the file system and found no problems.

  190777339 KB total disk space.
   39486424 KB in 113120 files.
      68524 KB in 23532 indexes.
          0 KB in bad sectors.
     592751 KB in use by the system.
      65536 KB occupied by the log file.
  150629640 KB available on disk.

       4096 bytes in each allocation unit.
   47694334 total allocation units on disk.
   37657410 allocation units available on disk.

C:\Users\Administrator>
```

Figure 7-12 *chkdsk* results

Introduction to Fault Tolerance

Fault tolerance is the ability of a system to gracefully recover from hardware or software failure. Servers often store critical data that must have high availability. Windows Server 2008 provides a level of fault tolerance through software-level RAID. RAID is not meant as a replacement for performing regular backups of data, but it increases the availability of disk storage. For example, if a hard disk fails and you have not implemented fault tolerance, any data stored on that disk is lost and unavailable until the drive is replaced and data is restored from backup. With fault tolerance, data is written to more than one drive so in the event one drive fails, data can still be accessed from one of the remaining drives.

RAID Volumes

Because hard disk drives are prone to failure, one of the best data security measures is to plan for disk redundancy in servers and host computers. This is accomplished in two ways: by performing regular backups and by installing RAID drives.

RAID is a set of standards for lengthening disk life, preventing data loss, and enabling relatively uninterrupted access to data. There are six basic levels of RAID (other RAID levels exist beyond the basic levels), beginning with the use of disk striping.

The six basic RAID levels are as follows:

- *RAID level 0*—Striping with no other redundancy features is RAID level 0. Striping is used to extend disk life and improve performance. Data access on striped volumes is fast because of the way the data is divided into blocks that are quickly accessed through multiple disk reads and data paths. A significant disadvantage to using level 0 striping is that if one disk fails, you can expect a large data loss on all volumes. Windows Server 2008 supports RAID level 0, using 2 to 32 disks in a set. In Windows Server 2008, this is called striped volumes, as you learned earlier in this chapter.

- *RAID level 1*—This level employs simple disk mirroring and provides a means to duplicate the operating system files in the event of a disk failure. Disk mirroring is a fault-tolerance method that prevents data loss by duplicating data from a main disk to a backup disk (see Figure 7-13). **Disk duplexing** is the same as disk mirroring, with the exception that it places the backup disk on a different controller or adapter than is used by the main disk (see Figure 7-14). Windows Server 2008 supports level 1, but includes disk duplexing as well as mirroring. If three or more volumes will be mirrored or duplexed, this solution is more expensive than the other RAID levels. On modern operating systems

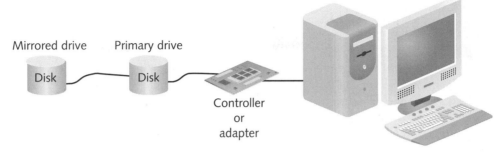

Figure 7-13 Disk mirroring

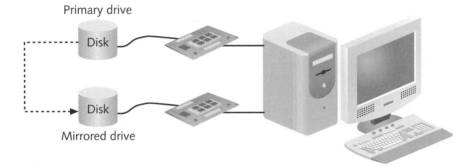

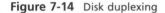

Figure 7-14 Disk duplexing

including Windows Server 2008, data is written simultaneously on both disks for the sake of performance (instead of writing on the primary disk and then on the mirrored disk). Some server administrators consider disk mirroring and disk duplexing to offer one of the best guarantees of data recovery when a disk failure occurs.

- *RAID level 2*—This uses an array of disks whereby the data is striped across all disks in the array. Also, in this method all disks store error-correction information that enables the array to reconstruct data from a failed disk. The advantages of level 2 are that disk wear is reduced and data can be reconstructed if a disk fails.

- *RAID level 3*—Like level 2, RAID level 3 uses disk striping and stores error-correcting information, but the information is only written to one disk in the array. If that disk fails, the array cannot rebuild its contents.

- *RAID level 4*—This level stripes data and stores error-correcting information on all drives, in a manner similar to level 2. An added feature is its ability to perform checksum verification. The checksum is a sum of bits in a file. When a file is re-created after a disk failure, the checksum previously stored for that file is checked against the actual file after it is reconstructed. If the two do not match, you will know that the file might be corrupted. Windows Server 2008 does not support RAID levels 2 through 4.

- *RAID level 5*—Level 5 combines the best features of RAID, including striping, error correction, and checksum verification. Windows Server 2008 supports level 5, calling it "stripe set with parity on basic disks" or a RAID-5 volume (for dynamic disks), depending on the disk architecture. Whereas level 4 stores checksum data on only one disk, level 5 spreads both error-correction and checksum data over all of the disks, so there is no single point of failure. This level uses more memory than other RAID levels, with at least 16 MB recommended as additional memory for system functions. In addition, level 5 requires at least three disks in the RAID array. Recovery from a failed disk provides roughly the same guarantee as with disk mirroring, but takes longer with level 5. RAID 5 can recover from a single disk failure. However, if more than one drive in the array fails, all data is lost and must be restored from backup.

None of these RAID techniques mean that you no longer have to do backups. A solid backup, for example, is the only way to recover an important file or set of files that are inadvertently deleted.

Windows Server 2008 supports RAID levels 0, 1, and 5 for disk fault tolerance (each of these levels is discussed further in the sections that follow), with levels 1 and 5 recommended. RAID level 0 is not recommended in many situations because it does not really provide fault tolerance, except to help extend the life of disks while providing relatively fast access. When you decide upon using RAID level 1 or RAID level 5, consider the following:

- The boot and system files can be placed on RAID level 1, but not on RAID level 5. Thus, if you use RAID level 5, these files must be on a separate disk or a separate RAID level 1 disk set.

- RAID level 1 uses two hard disks, and RAID level 5 uses from 3 to 32.

- RAID level 1 is more expensive to implement than RAID level 5, when you consider the cost on the basis of each megabyte of storage. Keep in mind that in RAID level 1, half of your total disk space is used for redundancy, whereas that value is one-third (for three disks) or less (for more disks) for RAID level 5. The amount of RAID level 5 used for parity is $1/n$ where n is the number of disk drives in the array.

- RAID level 5 requires more memory than RAID level 1.

- Disk read access is faster in RAID level 1 and RAID level 5 than is write access, with read access for RAID level 1 identical to that of a disk that does not have RAID.

- Because RAID level 5 involves more disks and because the read/write heads can acquire data simultaneously across striped volumes, it has much faster read access than RAID level 1.

RAID levels 0, 1, and 5 are used most commonly in server operating systems because they address most disk fault-tolerance needs.

Using a Striped Volume (RAID-0)

As you learned earlier in this chapter, the reasons for using a RAID level 0 or a striped volume in Windows Server 2008 are to:

- Reduce the wear on multiple disk drives by equally spreading the load

- Increase disk performance compared with other methods for configuring dynamic disk volumes

Although striped volumes do not provide fault tolerance, other than to extend the life of the disks, they are acceptable for use in some situations. Consider, for example, an organization that maintains a "data warehouse" in which the vital data is stored and updated on a large server or mainframe, and a copy is downloaded at regular intervals to a server housing the data warehouse. The purpose of the data on the server is to create reports and to provide fast lookup of certain kinds of data, without slowing down the server or mainframe. In this instance, the goal is to provide the fastest possible access to the data and not fault tolerance, because the original data and primary data services are on the mainframe. For this application, you might create a striped volume on the server used for the data warehouse, because it yields the fastest data access.

To create a striped volume, right-click the unallocated space for the volume and click New Striped Volume. Only dynamic disks can be striped volumes.

Using a Mirrored Volume (RAID-1)

Disk mirroring involves creating a shadow copy of data on a backup disk and is RAID level 1. Only dynamic disks can be set up as a **mirrored volume** in Windows Server 2008. It is one of the most guaranteed forms of disk fault tolerance because the data on a failed drive is still available on the mirrored drive (with a short downtime to make the mirrored drive accessible). Also, disk read performance is the same as reading data from any single disk drive. Depending on the hardware and system configuration, in some cases there can be a slight performance degradation for disk writes, but this is likely to go unnoticed. However, a disk write in mirroring is normally faster than writing to disk when you use RAID-5. A mirrored volume cannot be striped and requires two dynamic disks.

A mirrored volume is particularly well suited for situations in which data is mission-critical and must not be lost under any circumstances, such as customer files at a bank. It also is valuable for situations in which computer systems must not be down for long, such as for medical applications or in 24-hour manufacturing. The increased expense of having duplicate disks is offset by the assurance that data will not be lost and that the system will quickly be back online after a disk failure.

The Windows Server 2008 system and boot volumes can be in a mirrored volume, but they cannot be in a striped or RAID-5 volume.

A mirrored volume is created through the Disk Management tool. To create the volume, right-click unallocated space on one disk and click New Mirrored Volume.

Using a RAID-5 Volume

Fault tolerance is better for a RAID-5 volume than for a simple striped volume. A **RAID-5 volume** requires a minimum of three disk drives. Parity information is distributed on each disk so that if one disk fails, the information on that disk can be reconstructed. The parity used by Microsoft is Boolean (true/false, one/zero) logic, with information about the data contained in each row of 64 KB data blocks on the striped disks. Using the example of storing a 720 KB file across five disks, one 64 KB parity block is written on each disk. The first parity block is always written in row 1 of disk 1, the second is in row 2 of disk 2, and so on, as illustrated in Figure 7-15 (compare this figure with Figure 7-5 for a striped volume).

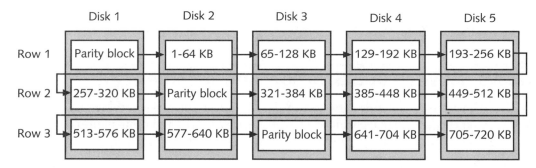

Figure 7-15 Disks in a RAID-5 volume

When you set up a RAID-5 volume, the performance is not as fast as with a striped volume because it takes longer to write the data and calculate the parity block for each row. However, accessing data through disk reads is as fast as a striped volume. RAID-5 is a viable fault-tolerance choice for mission-critical data and for applications when full mirroring is not feasible due to the expense. It works well with disk arrays that are compatible with RAID-5. A RAID-5 volume is particularly useful in a client/server system that uses a separate database for queries and creating reports because disk read performance is fast for obtaining data. In applications such as a customer service database that is constantly updated with new orders, disk read performance will be slower than with striping without parity.

 If you create a RAID-5 volume, keep in mind that it uses 16 MB or more of RAM because RAID-5 uses more memory than mirroring or simple striping. Also, RAID-5 takes up disk space for the parity information.

The amount of storage space used is based on the formula $1/n$ where n is the number of physical disks in the volume. For example, with four disks, the amount of space taken for parity information is 1/4 of the total space of all disk drives in the volume. This means you get more usable disk storage if there are more disks in the volume. A set of eight 100 GB disks yields more usable storage than a set of four 200 GB disks in RAID-5.

Use the Disk Management tool to create a RAID-5 volume. To start, right-click the unallocated or free space on a disk that is to be part of the volume, then click New RAID-5 Volume. RAID-5 can only be configured on dynamic disks.

Software RAID vs. Hardware RAID

Two approaches to RAID can be implemented on a server: software RAID and hardware RAID. Software RAID implements fault tolerance through the server's operating system, such as using RAID levels 0, 1, or 5 through the Windows Server 2008 Disk Management tool. Hardware RAID is implemented through the server hardware and is independent of the operating system. Many manufacturers implement hardware RAID on the adapter, such as a SCSI adapter, to which the disk drives are connected. The RAID logic is contained in a chip on the adapter. Also, a battery is often connected to the chip to ensure that the chip never loses power and has fault tolerance to retain the RAID setup even when a power outage occurs. Hardware RAID is more expensive than software RAID, but offers many advantages over software RAID:

- Faster read and write response
- The ability to place boot and system files on different RAID levels, such as RAID levels 1 and 5
- The ability to "hot-swap" a failed disk with one that works or is new, thus replacing the disk without shutting down the server (this option can vary by manufacturer)
- More setup options to retrieve damaged data and to combine different RAID levels within one array of disks, such as mirroring two disks using RAID level 1 and setting up five disks for RAID level 5 in a seven disk array (the RAID options depend on what the manufacturer offers)

Windows Server 2008 Storage Enhancements

For medium to large networks, Windows Server 2008 offers storage enhancements in two important realms: management of Storage Area Networks and using multiple paths to storage for fault tolerance. The next two sections describe these enhancements.

Storage Manager for SANs

Windows Server 2008 offers an enhanced version of the Storage Manager for SANs for organizations that use Storage Area Networks. A **Storage Area Network (SAN)** is a grouping of storage devices that forms a subnet. The storage devices are available to any server on the main network and appear to the user as though they are attached to the server they are accessing. Typically, the subnet containing the storage devices uses Fibre Channel or iSCSI technology. **Fibre Channel** is a subnetwork technology originally developed for mainframes but now is used primarily for SANs and enables gigabit high-speed data transfers. **Internet Small Computer System Interface (iSCSI)** is another high-speed technology used in SANs that employs TCP/IP communications and SCSI disk drives.

Storage Manager for SANs is used to manage the logical unit numbers for Small Computer System Interface drives. **Small Computer System Interface (SCSI)** is a 32- or 64-bit computer adapter that transports data between one or more attached devices, such as hard disks, and the computer. A **logical unit number (LUN)** is a number that identifies a physical SCSI drive or logical SCSI targets (which can be volumes, IP addresses, adapter ports, and other connections depending on the SAN technology). A SAN containing multiple drives configured for RAID will have many LUNs to manage. Although there is not space here to fully explain SANs, as you have probably guessed, there can be many LUNs that need to be created and managed for connections between disks and computers through SANs. This is why Storage Manager for SANs is included in Windows Server 2008.

Storage Manager for SANs is used for SANs that employ Virtual Disk Service. **Virtual Disk Service (VDS)** is used to enable management of disk volumes in SANs through one interface at a server. If your organization uses SANs, plan to install Storage Manager for SANs. It is one of the features that you can install through Server Manager.

In terms of planning a new SAN architecture for your network, it is important to know that Microsoft seems particularly interested in providing capabilities for iSCSI. This is because Microsoft recognizes the following advantages of iSCSI compared with Fibre Channel:

- More options for configuring topologies
- Less cost
- Fewer distance limitations
- Compatible with existing IPv4 and IPv6 networks over Ethernet
- Enables dynamic expansion
- Easier to configure
- More scalable
- More storage capacity
- Supports IPSec for security
- Easier to expand using equipment from different vendors

 For faster response when you plan a SAN, Microsoft recommends using more disks with less disk space instead of fewer disks with more disk space (to increase the number of spindles). Also, use fast high-performance disks, particularly for data-intense software applications.

Another enhancement to Windows Server 2008 is that the iSCSI initiator is now built into the operating system. The iSCSI initiator is a driver that enables Windows Server 2008 to communicate with an iSCSI SAN. On Windows Server systems prior to Windows Server 2008, you had to manually install the iSCSI initiator.

Multipath Input/Output Enhancements

Even though you have RAID or a SAN (or both), you still do not have complete fault tolerance if a server has just one path to reach the disks in your storage setup, such as having one adapter and one cable to a RAID array. One approach already discussed for establishing redundant paths is to use disk duplexing. Another approach in Windows Server 2008 is to use Multipath I/O.

Multipath I/O provides a means to establish multiple paths between a server and its disk storage. The first step in this process is to create the multiple paths between the storage and the server or servers, depending on the type of disk storage setup you are using. For example, on a server with one RAID array, establishing multiple paths would be connecting two cables and adapter cards between the RAID array and the server. For a SAN, creating multiple paths might involve establishing two or more network paths through two or more network switches to the SAN.

Once the multiple paths are physically set up, the next step is to install Multipath I/O, which is a feature installed through Server Manager. When you install Multipath I/O, you also install the **Device Specific Module (DSM)**, which is compatible with the following disk storage array controller technologies:

- *Asymmetric logical unit access (ALUA)*, which provides multiple ports to arrays and different levels of access per port
- *Active/Active controller model*, which means that the contents of one controller's cache is shadowed to another controller in an array, creating a backup path to the array

Windows Server 2008 DSM enables you to choose between the following configuration models:

- *Dynamic Least Queue Depth*—Tracks current traffic on all paths and transmits the newest traffic to the least busy path.
- *Failback*—Sends current traffic to disks on a path that is preselected as the main path to use. If that path is down, then an alternate path is used.
- *Failover*—Uses a main path and secondary paths. The main path is used unless it is down. Next, the secondary path marked with the highest priority is used, and so on. All secondary paths are ranked in terms of priority.
- *Round Robin*—Each functional path is used in a round-robin order, such as path 1 first, path 2 next, and so on.
- *Round Robin with a subset of paths*—Sets of primary paths and secondary paths are established. Each primary path is used in round-robin order. If all of the primary paths are down, then the secondary paths are used in round-robin order.
- *Weighted Path*—Each path is given a priority. For example, if there are five paths, then the path to use first is designated as 1, and the path weighted as 2 is used next in priority if the path weighted as 1 is down. If the paths weighted as 1, 2, and 3 are down, then the path weighted as 4 is used, and so on.

Disk Backup

RAID is one of the ways that you can provide fault tolerance for your server's hard disks. Most software implementations of RAID can only recover from single disk failure, so it is still no substitute for performing regular, scheduled backups. One of the best ways to make sure you do not lose valuable information on a hard disk is to fully back up information on a regular basis, using backup media such as DVDs, removable hard drives, and tapes. These backups can be performed from the server or from a workstation on the network.

Performing backups from a backup device installed on the server has several advantages:

- No extra load is produced on the network from traffic caused by transferring files over the network.
- Equipping each server with its own backup capability gives you a way to perform backups on a multiple-server network, even if a backup device fails on one of the servers. Backups can be performed from backup media on one of the other servers.
- Backing up from backup media on a server provides more assurance that the Registry is backed up because access to the Registry is limited to backups performed at the server. The Registry contains vital information about a server's setup.

The advantages of performing a network backup are that backup jobs can be stored on a single backup media and one administrator can be responsible for backing up multiple servers. The main disadvantages are the increase in network traffic and the Registry cannot be backed up from across the network.

Windows Server Backup

Windows Server 2008 comes with the Windows Server Backup tool. To use this tool, you need to install it using Server Manager. The Windows Server Backup tool offers the ability to back up all server files or files that have changed. It is particularly targeted for use by new server administrators, small to medium organizations, and server administrators who like to use a tool specifically designed to work for Windows Server 2008.

The Windows Server Backup tool in Windows Server 2008 contains the following enhanced features:

- Is easier to recover from a backup with better options to recover specific files, folders, and from partial backups, such as incremental backups.

- Has more backup options, including using the **Volume Shadow Copy Service (VSS)**, which is created to make stable images of files and folders on servers based on the point-in-time when the image is made. It also includes facilities so that programmers can write applications to enhance backing up application pieces and data created by those applications, such as SQL Server database applications and Microsoft Exchange Server for e-mail. VSS runs faster in Windows Server 2008.

- Is more reliable in recovering applications.

- Provides information about disk use to help ensure you do not prematurely run out of disk space.

- Offers the *wbadmin* command-line tool for server administrators who prefer command-line control of backups.

- Has full support to back up to optical media, such as DVDs.

Microsoft lists the following considerations for using the Windows Server Backup tool, which has been upgraded from the similar tool used in previous versions of Windows Server operating systems:

- The Windows Server Backup tool only backs up NTFS volumes, so if you are configuring to remotely back up a Windows Server 2003 server that has FAT-formatted volumes, for example, it cannot back up the FAT volumes.

- Unlike previous versions, Windows Server Backup does not back up to tape.

- The backup tool in Windows Server 2003 runs the program Ntbackup.exe. If you have backup media made from Windows Server 2003 using Ntbackup.exe, you cannot restore from that media using the Windows Server Backup tool in Windows Server 2008. You can, however, download Ntbackup.exe from Microsoft's Web site (*www.microsoft.com*) and run it in Windows Server 2008 to restore files from backups made from Windows Server 2003.

 Do not try to use Ntbackup.exe to make backups from your Windows Server 2008 server.

Activity 7-9: Installing the Windows Server Backup Tool

Time Required: Approximately 10 minutes
Objective: Install the Windows Server Backup tool.

Description: Performing regular backups is a critical task for ensuring your organization's working environment. Even if you lose a disk drive, you still have your important files if you have backed them up. You probably won't need to restore from backups often, but when you need to, there is no better feeling than having sound backups. In this activity, you install the Windows Server Backup tool that some server administrators prefer using for backups, because it is native to Windows Server 2008. Also, you add this tool as a snap-in to the Disk Management MMC console you set up in Activity 7-2.

1. Click **Start**, point to **Administrative Tools**, and click **Server Manager**.

2. Scroll to the Features Summary section.

3. Click **Add Features**.

4. Click the **plus sign** in front of **Windows Server Backup Features**.

5. Click the boxes for **Windows Server Backup** and **Command-line Tools**. (If you see the Add Features Wizard to add Windows PowerShell and/or Windows Recovery Disc, click Add Required Features.)

6. Click **Next**.

7. Click **Install**.

8. Click **Close**.

9. Open the Disk Management console that you created in Activity 7-2. For example, click **Start**, point to **All Programs**, click **Administrative Tools**, and click **Disk Management**.

10. After the console is open, click the **File** menu and click **Add/Remove Snap-in**.

11. Under *Available snap-ins*, click **Windows Server Backup** and click the **Add** button.

12. Use the default selection **Local computer: (the computer this console is running on)** and click **Finish**.

13. Click **OK** in the Add or Remove Snap-ins dialog box.

14. Windows Server Backup (Local) should now appear in the tree.

15. Leave the Disk Management console open for the next activity.

Backup Options

The three types of backups that can be performed using the Windows Server Backup tool are:

- Full backup
- Incremental backup
- Custom backup

A **full backup** is a backup of an entire system, including all system files, programs, and data files. The full backup changes each file's archive attribute to show that it has been backed up. As you will recall from Chapter 5, "Configuring, Managing, and Troubleshooting Resource Access," each NTFS folder or file has an archive attribute that can be set to show whether that folder or file has been backed up since the last change to it. A full backup is performed the first time you back up a server, and afterwards once a night, once a week, or at a regular interval depending on the number of files on your server and your organization's particular needs.

An **incremental backup** only backs up files that are new or that have been updated. The Windows Server 2008 incremental option backs up only files that have the archive attribute marked. When it backs up a file, the incremental backup removes the archive attribute to show that the file has been backed up. Using incremental backups enables you to save time backing up a server when there are large numbers of files to back up. Many files don't change on a server and so don't have to be backed up every time. Your organization might, for example, perform a full backup once a week, such as at the end of the work week or on Saturdays. On all other work days, it might perform incremental backups.

A **custom backup** enables you to configure backups differently for each volume, such as doing an incremental backup every time you back up the C drive and a full backup each time you back up the D drive. You might do this, for example, if the C drive mainly contains files that do not change often, such as operating system files and files for software applications. On the D drive files might change regularly, such as database files, documents, spreadsheets, and others.

Activity 7-10: Backing Up a Server

Time Required: Approximately 10 to 30 minutes
Objective: Perform a full backup.

Description: In this activity, you practice starting a manual full backup. You will need a computer with a DVD drive loaded with blank DVD media on which to make the backup. You won't need to write on the DVD because you'll stop before instructing the program to start the backup.

1. Open the Disk Management console if it is not already open.
2. Click **Windows Server Backup (Local)** in the tree.
3. Click **Backup Once** in the right pane, as shown in Figure 7-16.

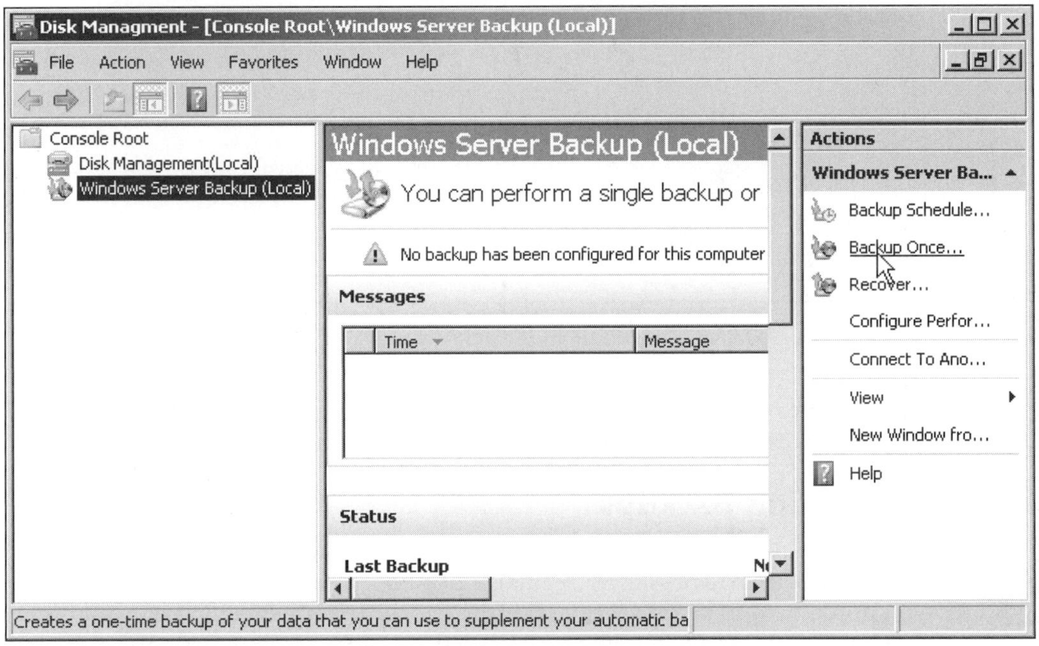

Figure 7-16 Selecting the Backup Once option

4. Click **Next** in the Backup options window.

5. If you see the Windows Server Backup warning box, click **Yes**.

6. Leave **Full server (recommended)** selected as the default in the Select backup configuration window.

   - What other option(s) can you select?

7. Click **Next**. If a FAT volume is configured for the x partition, you'll see a warning message that FAT is an unsupported file system. Click **OK** if you see this message box.

8. Leave the default **Local drives** selected for the type of storage for the backup (see Figure 7-17). Click **Next**. (If you select to back up a dynamic disk, you will need to discontinue after clicking Next.)

9. In the Select backup destination window, notice that *Backup item size* shows the amount of data to be backed up. Click **Next**. (You may see a message box saying that the backup destination is included in the list of items to back up, along with the option to *Exclude this volume from list of volumes to back up or add another disk and retry*. Click **Yes** in the message box.)

10. Select **VSS full backup** and click **Next**.

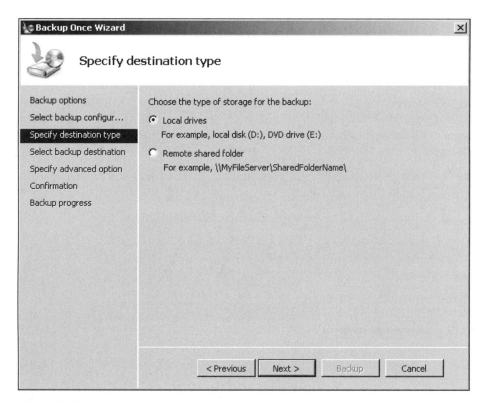

Figure 7-17 Specifying the destination type

11. In the Confirmation window, you'll see a review of the parameters you have selected. Click **Cancel** at this point so you don't start the backup.

Scheduling Backups

Windows Server Backup includes a scheduling capability so that you can have the server automatically start backups after regular work hours or at a specific time of day. This means that you don't have to be present to start the backups. For example, you could schedule full backups to start at 7:00 p.m. after everyone has left work. In another example, an accounting office in an organization might perform a daily closing routine in which they stop processing by 4:20 p.m. and back up accounting files at 4:30 p.m.

The scheduling process requires a disk to back up to, such as a removable hard drive.

The following general steps illustrate how to create and schedule a backup:

1. Open the Windows Server Backup MMC snap-in.
2. Click Backup Schedule.
3. Click Next after the Backup Schedule Wizard starts.
4. Select the type of backup, Full Server or Custom (see Figure 7-18). Click Next. If you select the Custom backup, choose which volumes to back up. Click Next. (If you have a FAT volume configured, you'll see a warning that FAT is an unsupported file system and cannot be backed up. Click OK to continue.)
5. If you choose to back up once a day, specify the time to start the backup (see Figure 7-19). If you choose more than once a day, specify the times to schedule the backup. Click Next.

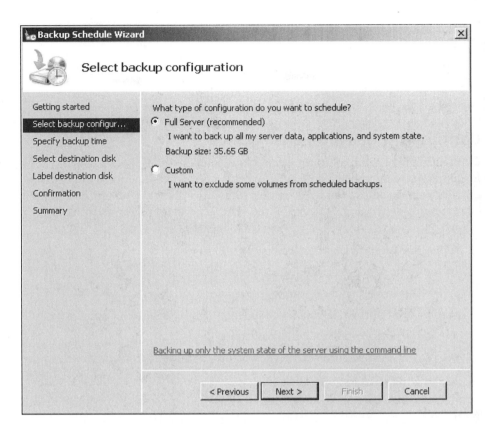

Figure 7-18 Selecting the backup configuration

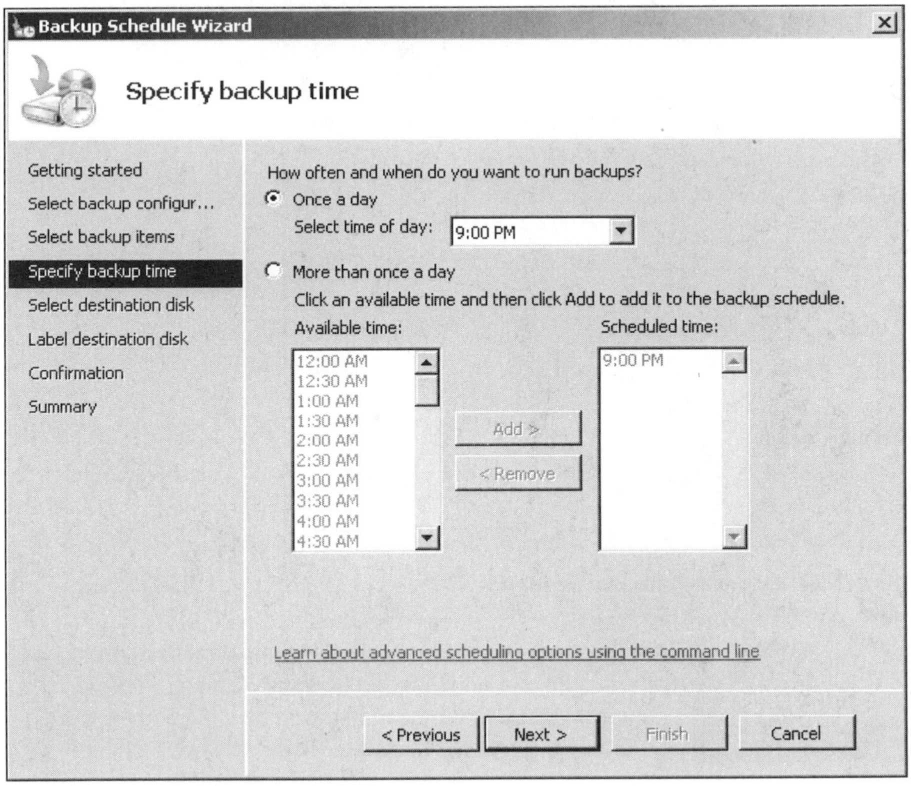

Figure 7-19 Specifying the backup time

6. Select the destination for the backup. Note that the Windows Server Backup tool will format the disk if it is not formatted for the backup. Click Next.

7. Provide a label for the destination disk and click Next.

8. Review your selections and click Next.

9. Click Finish.

Configuring Backup Performance

Configuring the backup performance options enables you to specify which types of backups to perform: full, incremental, and custom. The default is to always perform full backups; however, to save time on your backups, you might prefer to use incremental backups or a combination of full and incremental, depending on the volume. The general steps for selecting your preference are as follows:

1. Open the Windows Server Backup MMC snap-in.

2. In the right pane, click Configure Performance Settings.

3. As shown in Figure 7-20, three options are available:

   • Always perform full backup

   • Always perform incremental backup

   • Custom (to configure whether to perform a full or incremental backup on specific volumes)

4. Make your selection and click OK.

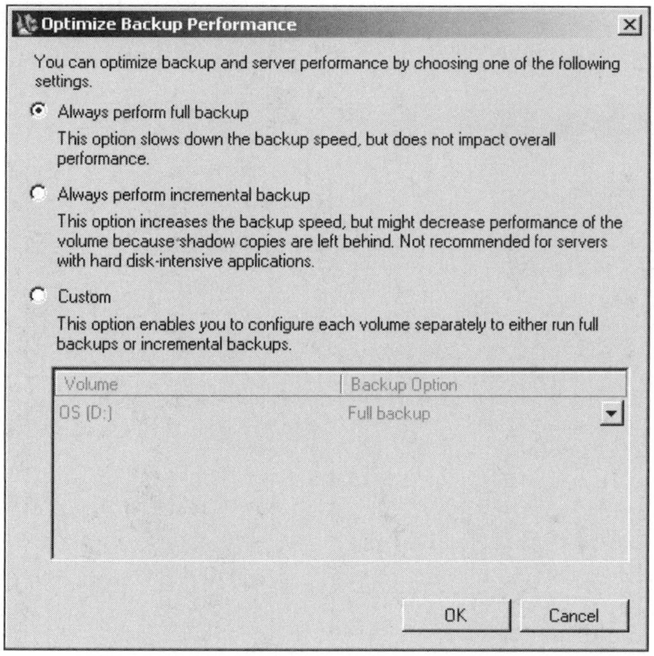

Figure 7-20 Optimizing backup performance

As part of a disaster recovery plan, it is important to store a copy of a backup off-site. This is a good precaution in case of fire, flooding, or some other natural disaster. Many organizations are now fulfilling this need by using off-site backup services or software. Some examples of these providers are eBackitUp.com (*www.ebackitup.com*), Double-Take Software (*www.doubletake.com*), EVault (*www.evault.com*), IBackup (*www.ibackup.com*), and U.S.DataTrust (*www.usdatatrust.com*).

Performing a Recovery

Use the Windows Server Backup tool to perform a recovery from removable media. The Recovery Wizard in the Backup utility steps you through a restore. The Windows Server Backup tool enables you to recover any of the following (if it is in the backup):

- Files
- Folders
- Volumes
- Applications and application data
- The backup catalog (of information in the backup)
- The operating system (to the same computer or to another computer using identical hardware)

Before you start, determine the following information:

- Date of the backup from which to recover
- Type of recovery, such as files and folders or applications
- What to recover
- Where to recover, such as in the original location or another location

To start a recovery, first insert or attach the media with the backup files. Open the Windows Server Backup MMC snap-in, click Recover in the right pane, and follow the steps as presented in the Recovery Wizard (which will vary depending on what you are recovering).

Chapter 12, "Managing System Reliability and Availability," explains backing up and using system state data for recovering the operating system.

Chapter Summary

- Windows Server 2008 uses basic and dynamic disks. Basic disks are backward compatible with earlier Windows server and workstation operating systems. Dynamic disks offer more flexibility for configuration.
- Dynamic disks can be configured as simple, spanned, striped, mirrored, and RAID-5 volumes.
- If you need to recover space from a basic or dynamic disk, you can shrink the disk so that the recovered space can be configured as a separate volume.
- The Disk Management tool enables you to create basic and dynamic disks. It performs disk configurations from simple volumes to RAID-5. You can also use it to convert a basic disk to a dynamic disk or vice versa.
- For optimum disk performance, plan to set up a schedule to regularly defragment disks on a server.
- Use the Disk Check and *chkdsk* tools to find and repair disk problems.
- RAID provides fault tolerance for hard disks. Windows Server 2008 supports RAID levels 0, 1, and 5.
- RAID level 0 is disk striping. It provides no actual fault tolerance other than to help extend the life of the disks.
- With disk mirroring or duplexing (RAID level 1), the same data is written to a partition on each of the two disks included in the mirror.

- With RAID level 5, data is written across a minimum of three disks. Parity information is added to achieve fault tolerance.

- Two important enhancements for Windows Server 2008 include new features for Storage Manager for SANs and features for Multipath I/O. Storage Manager for SANs supports both Fibre Channel and iSCSI. Multipath I/O extends your options for creating fault tolerance for storage through using redundant paths.

- Windows Server Backup offers features to schedule backups, perform full or incremental backups (or a combination of both), and recover data from backups.

Key Terms

active partition   The partition from which a computer boots.

basic disk   In Windows Server 2008, a partitioned disk that can have up to four partitions and that uses logical drive designations. This type of disk is compatible with MS-DOS, Windows 3.x, Windows 95, Windows 98, Windows NT, Windows 2000, Windows XP, Windows Vista, Windows Server 2003, and Windows Server 2008.

boot partition   Holds the Windows Server 2008 \Windows folder containing the system files.

custom backup   Enables you to configure backups differently for each volume, using either a full backup or an incremental backup.

defragmenting   A software process that rearranges data to fill in the empty spaces that develop on disks and makes data easier to obtain.

Device Specific Module (DSM)   A software interface between the Multipath I/O capability in Windows Server 2008 and the hard disk hardware.

disk duplexing   A fault-tolerance method similar to disk mirroring in that it prevents data loss by duplicating data from a main disk to a backup disk; but disk duplexing places the backup disk on a different controller or adapter than is used by the main disk.

disk mirroring   A fault-tolerance method that prevents data loss by duplicating data from a main disk to a backup disk. Some operating systems also refer to this as disk shadowing.

dynamic disk   In Windows Server 2008, a disk that does not use traditional partitioning, which means that there is no restriction to the number of volumes that can be set up on one disk or to the ability to extend volumes onto additional physical disks. Dynamic disks are only compatible with Windows Server 2008, Windows Server 2003, and Windows 2000 Server platforms.

extended partition   A partition that is created from unpartitioned free disk space and is linked to a primary partition in order to increase the available disk space.

Extensible Firmware Interface (EFI)   A firmware alternative to BIOS that includes the use of GPT disks. *See* Globally Unique Identifier (GUID) Partition Table or GPT.

fault tolerance   Techniques that employ hardware and software to provide assurance against equipment failures, computer service interruptions, and data loss.

Fibre Channel   A subnetwork technology used primarily for SANs that enables gigabit high-speed data transfers. *See* Storage Area Network (SAN).

formatting   A process that prepares a hard disk partition for a specific file system.

fragmented   Having files spread throughout a disk with empty pockets of space between files; a normal and gradual process in the functioning of an operating system, addressed by using a defragmentation utility.

full backup   A backup of an entire system, including all system files, programs, and data files.

Globally Unique Identifier (GUID) Partition Table or **GPT**   A method for partitioning disks that allows for theoretically unlimited partitions and use of larger disks. In Windows Server 2008, the maximum number of partitions on a GPT disk is 128, and the maximum partition size is up to 18 exabtyes.

home directory or home folder A server folder that is associated with a user's account and that is a designated workspace for the user to store files.

incremental backup Backs up only files that are new or that have been updated.

Internet Small Computer System Interface (iSCSI) A high-speed technology used in SANs that employs TCP/IP communications and SCSI disk drives. *See* Storage Area Network (SAN).

logical unit number (LUN) A number that identifies a physical SCSI drive or logical SCSI targets (which can be volumes, IP addresses, adapter ports, and other connections depending on the SAN technology). *See* Small Computer System Interface (SCSI).

Master Boot Record (MBR) Data created in the first sector of a disk, containing startup information and information about disk partitions.

mirrored volume Two dynamic disks that are set up for RAID level 1 so that data on one disk is stored on a redundant disk.

mounted drive A physical disk, CD/DVD, removable drive, or other drive that appears as a folder and that is accessed through a path like any other folder.

Multipath I/O A set of drivers in Windows Server 2008 that can be used with device and network architecture to set up multiple paths between a server and its disk storage to achieve fault tolerance.

partition table Table containing information about each partition on a disk, such as the type of partition, size, and location. Also, the partition table provides information to the computer about how to access the disk.

partitioning Blocking a group of tracks and sectors to be used by a particular file system, such as NTFS.

primary partition Partition or portion of a hard disk that is bootable.

RAID (redundant array of inexpensive [or independent] disks) A set of standards designed to extend the life of hard disk drives and to prevent data loss from a hard disk failure.

RAID-5 volume Three or more dynamic disks that use RAID level 5 fault tolerance through disk striping and creating parity blocks for data recovery.

simple volume A portion of a disk or an entire disk that is set up as a dynamic disk.

Small Computer System Interface (SCSI) A 32- or 64-bit computer adapter that transports data between one or more attached devices, such as hard disks, and the computer.

spanned volume Two or more Windows Server dynamic disks that are combined to appear as one disk.

Storage Area Network (SAN) A grouping of storage devices that forms a subnet. The storage devices are available to any server on the main network and appear to the user as though they are attached to the server they are accessing.

stripe set Two or more basic disks set up so that files are spread in blocks across the disks.

striped volume Two or more dynamic disks that use striping so that files are spread in blocks across the disks.

striping A data storage method that breaks up data files across all volumes of a disk set to minimize wear on a single volume.

system partition Partition that contains boot files.

Virtual Disk Service (VDS) Used to enable management of disk volumes in SANs through one interface at a server.

volume A logical designation of one or more physical disks partitioned and formatted with one file system. One volume can be composed of one or more partitions. In Windows Server 2008, a volume can be a basic disk partition that has been formatted for a particular file system, a primary partition, a volume set, an extended volume, a stripe set, a stripe set with parity, or a mirror set. A volume can also be a dynamic disk that is set up as a simple volume, spanned volume, striped volume, RAID-5 volume, or mirrored volume.

volume set Two or more formatted basic disk partitions (volumes) that are combined to look like one volume with a single drive letter.

Volume Shadow Copy Service (VSS)   Backup service used in Windows Server 2003 and Windows Server 2008 to create stable images of files and folders on servers based on the point in time when the image is made.

Review Questions

1. You have just installed a new disk on a Windows Server 2008 server. Which of the following do you do first to prepare the disk for use?

   a. partition the disk

   b. format the disk

   c. block release the disk

   d. block stripe the disk

2. The _____ partition or volume contains the operating system files, such as the files in the \Windows folder.

3. You have just upgraded from Windows Server 2003 to Windows Server 2008. Now you are trying to recover a set of databases that you backed up on DVDs in Windows Server 2003 before you started the upgrade, but the Windows Server Backup tool gives you an error message. What is the problem?

   a. You must start the Windows Server Backup tool from the command line using the /2003 switch.

   b. The Windows Server Backup tool only supports recovering Windows Server 2003 files from flash drives or tape backups.

   c. The Windows Server Backup tool is not compatible with backups made from the Windows Server 2003 Backup tool.

   d. You must first initialize the DVD in the Windows Server Backup tool before you start the recovery.

4. Your company is considering installing an iSCSI SAN, but one of the department heads mentions that he has heard Windows Server 2008 does not have a management tool for an iSCSI SAN. What is your response?

   a. This is true because Windows Server 2008 is only compatible with Fibre Channel.

   b. This is true, but you can purchase third-party tools to use an iSCSI SAN with Windows Server 2008.

   c. This is not true because Disk Manager has the NtSCSI.exe plug-in you can download from Microsoft.

   d. This is not true because you can install Storage Manager for SANs.

5. You are consulting for a company that has been performing full backups every night for its Windows Server 2008 servers. A problem they have been experiencing is that the backups are taking longer and longer. What is your recommendation for this company?

   a. Perform the full backups in zip mode, which cuts the backup time in half.

   b. Use a custom backup that enables you to use a combination of full and incremental backups.

   c. Use a copy backup, which copies every other folder each time it runs.

   d. Purchase disk drives with smaller spindles for faster rotation.

6. Dynamic disks support RAID levels _____, _____, and _____.

7. You are consulting for an organization that has chosen to use disk striping as a way to extend the life of their four hard disks. Now one of the disks has failed and they call you for help. What do you advise them?

    a. Take the failed disk offline and let the other three disks rebuild the data from the failed disk automatically.

    b. Download the failed disk's folder header information to the second disk in the series and let it rebuild the data that was on the failed disk.

    c. Install a new disk and download the backup cache from the failed disk to restore files to the new disk.

    d. Install a new disk and perform a full restore on all four disks.

8. RAID level 5 requires a minimum of _____ hard disks.

9. As the IT director for a large investment company, you are always looking for ways to build in better fault tolerance for your computer systems. As you consider your present hard disk storage situation, you have a large SAN connected to the main network through a high-speed switch. What else can you do to ensure fault tolerance for your SAN?

    a. Create additional paths to the SAN, such as through one or more additional switches, and take advantage of Multipath I/O.

    b. Use X-on/X-off flow control for protection against viruses at the SAN and on the Windows Server 2008 servers connecting to the SAN.

    c. Create phantom LUNs for the SAN and on Windows Server 2008 so these can be activated if the currently active LUNs are corrupted.

    d. Replace the optical interface at the switch with a wireless fault-tolerant interface containing its own battery backup.

10. Which of the following can you restore from the Windows Server Backup tool? (Choose all that apply.)

    a. the backup catalog

    b. volumes

    c. folders

    d. the operating system

11. How much free space must you have on a basic disk to convert it to a dynamic disk?

12. You have decided to shrink a 250 GB disk to change 130 GB of that disk to unallocated space. However, the shrinking process only results in 98 GB of unallocated space. What would have caused the smaller portion of unallocated space?

    a. You cannot shrink more than half of a disk.

    b. The shrinking process encountered a full disk cluster and had to stop early.

    c. The shrinking process encountered a file that cannot be moved and had to stop early.

    d. You cannot shrink more than 100 GB on any size disk.

13. You have spent the morning archiving old files to DVDs and then deleting those files as a way to get back some disk space. Also, you've recovered some archived financial files to prepare for the auditor's visit. After you finish, you notice that the server seems to run slower. What should you do?

    a. Perform a full backup. Reformat the disk and then perform a recovery from your backup.

    b. Start the Disk Defragmenter to defrag your disks.

    c. Use the Disk Check tool to retrieve contiguous disk space.

    d. Use Device Manager to perform a disk verification.

14. Which of the following can you accomplish with the Disk Management tool? (Choose all that apply.)

    a. set up LUNs

    b. reacquire a SAN after it has been taken offline

    c. create a simple volume

    d. convert a basic disk to a dynamic disk

15. Your new IT colleague is trying to determine the location of a mounted drive on the server because he is not sure what a mounted drive is. Which of the following do you tell him?

    a. A mounted drive is always a DVD mounted in the DVD drive.

    b. A mounted drive is located in a folder.

    c. Because Windows Server 2008 does not support floppy drives, a mounted drive is always drive A.

    d. A mounted drive is always a drive used by UNIX and Linux clients for sharing folders and files on Windows Server 2008 and is designated as drive U.

16. Which of the following must be true to boot from a basic disk in Windows Server 2008? (Choose all that apply.)

    a. It is an active partition.

    b. It does not have a disk quota set for users.

    c. It is a RAID-0 volume.

    d. It is a primary partition.

17. Briefly explain the concept of a spanned volume.

18. Which of the following is checked by the *chkdsk* utility? (Choose all that apply.)

    a. indexes

    b. disk allocation units

    c. log markers

    d. sectors

19. Explain disk duplexing.

20. You have configured a RAID-5 volume using five 250 GB disks. How much disk space is actually available for storage of folders and files?

    a. 875 GB

    b. 934.5 GB

    c. 1000 GB

    d. 1993.75 GB

Case Projects

Fresh Recipes started over 50 years ago producing different varieties of soups. Today the company is a well-recognized brand name that offers soups, chili, stews, and other canned foods. Fresh Recipes is divided into the following departments: Business, Research and Recipes, Canning, Distribution, and IT. The company has over 450 employees and is employee owned. Two employees from each department make up the Management Council, which additionally includes the company president, vice president, operations manager, and the managers of each department.

Five Windows Server 2008 servers are located in the Business Department. The Research and Recipes Department has three Windows Server 2008 servers at its location. The Canning and Distribution departments have four Windows Server 2008 servers each, including servers that are used to control machinery. The IT Department has three servers. The company makes extensive use of databases, and each department has at least one Datacenter Edition server to house its databases.

The IT Department has been working with the Management Council on storage capacity issues because many of the company's servers will soon need more disk storage. The IT Department has retained you through Aspen Consulting to help with storage setup and planning issues.

Case Project 7-1: Planning for Basic or Dynamic Disks

Because the company started with Windows NT 4.0 servers, they have continued to use basic disks in the form of stripe sets even as the servers have been upgraded through the years to Windows 2000 Server, Windows Server 2003, and now Windows Server 2008. They like the speed of the stripe sets, but now want to investigate if there are advantages to using dynamic disks. The IT Department asks you to create a report or slide presentation that addresses the following:

- Advantages of dynamic disks
- Sample steps for converting from basic to dynamic disks

Case Project 7-2: Fault Tolerance for the Canning Department

The Canning Department uses one server to run the canning conveyor machinery, which operates 24 hours a day. The server has some built-in fault tolerance, such as two network interface cards and battery backup for its power supply. However, no fault tolerance is provided for the single hard drive in the server, which is configured as a basic disk. Fault tolerance is important for this server because the company loses over $15,000 an hour when the conveyor machinery is down. Create a short report with your recommendations for fault tolerance, including general guidelines for setting it up.

Case Project 7-3: Planning Disk Storage for the Databases

The databases used by the Datacenter Edition servers are experiencing rapid growth in terms of use and size. Many of the databases are now used across departments. These databases are considered by the Management Council to be one of the company's best strategic assets. The Management Council wants to consolidate physical management of the databases and the Datacenter Edition servers in the IT Department's computer room as a way to secure them in one place. Also, they want to consolidate the disk storage used for these databases and provide for fault tolerance. Create a report or slide show for the Management Council with your recommendations, including the advantages of what you recommend.

Case Project 7-4: Changing the Backups to Accommodate Growth

Because they have used basic disk stripe sets, the server administrators at Fresh Recipes have been performing nightly full backups for years. They have also chosen to manually start the backups. Now that the company has grown and the amount of data to back up has increased, the backups are taking much longer, which is causing the server administrators to put in extra hours. Create a short report with some suggestions for changing how they do backups to correspond with the company's growth.

chapter 8

Managing Windows Server 2008 Network Services

After reading this chapter and completing the exercises, you will be able to:

- Install, configure, and troubleshoot DNS
- Implement Microsoft WINS
- Install, configure, and troubleshoot DHCP
- Install, configure, and troubleshoot Microsoft Internet Information Services

When users communicate through a network, a variety of activities go on behind the scenes. Many of these activities involve managing IP communications. Users don't want to have to remember IP addresses of a server or another user; it's easier to remember a name of a user or server. Users don't want the responsibility of configuring their own IP addresses. Also, network administrators don't want users configuring their IP addresses, because mistakes can mean network chaos. Fortunately, services such as Domain Name System and Dynamic Host Configuration Protocol have automated network IP communications and removed a large burden from users and network administrators.

Accessing Web sites is another aspect of network communications. Microsoft offers Internet Information Services as Web site software for Windows Server 2008 servers. Internet Information Services turns Windows Server 2008 into a multifeatured Web server and comes with versatile management tools.

This chapter gives you a foundation for understanding both Domain Name System and Dynamic Host Configuration Protocol. You learn how to install, configure, and troubleshoot these services for automated IP communications. At the end of the chapter, you learn to install and manage Internet Information Services to round out your network communications expertise.

Implementing Microsoft DNS

As you learned in Chapter 1, "Introduction to Windows Server 2008," Domain Name System (DNS) is a TCP/IP application protocol that enables a DNS server to resolve (translate) domain and computer names to IP addresses, or IP addresses to domain and computer names. For example, your server might have the name Banker and be in the domain bankingcorp.com. Also, its address might be 134.175.10.77. When a request is placed by another computer to contact Banker in the domain bankingcorp.com, DNS resolves this name to the IP address 134.175.10.77 so network communications can use this IP address.

DNS servers provide the DNS namespace for an enterprise (see Chapter 4, "Introduction to Active Directory and Account Management"), which includes resolving computer names and IP addresses as well as many other services.

 Microsoft recommends that DNS servers have a static IP address, which is an IP address that is manually configured and not automatically leased by DHCP (you learn more about DHCP later in this chapter). Also, before installing DNS on a server when Active Directory is in use on a network, make sure that the server is a DC. Use Server Manager to install the AD Domain Services role and the *dcpromo* tool to complete making the server a DC (see Chapter 4).

One of the requirements for using Active Directory on a Windows Server 2008 network is to have a DNS server on the network. When you set up a Windows Server 2008 network, if no DNS servers have been implemented, plan to use Windows Server 2008 DNS, because it is most compatible with Active Directory. Non-Microsoft DNS servers can be used, but then it is necessary to make sure they are compatible with Active Directory. Also, non-Microsoft versions of DNS do not offer the DNS replication advantages through Active Directory.

In the following sections, you learn how to install DNS, how to set up zones and services in DNS, and you learn about DNS replication.

Installing DNS Services

DNS is installed as a server role in Windows Server 2008. The installation steps for DNS are similar to those for DHCP, because both are installed as Windows components. Also, if you want to use Active Directory on a network, plan to install DNS before you install Active Directory.

For all of the activities in this chapter, you'll need an account with Administrator privileges. Also, most of these activities can be completed on a virtual server or computer, such as in Hyper-V.

Some steps in the activities in this book include bulleted questions with space for you to record your responses/answers.

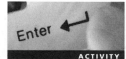

Activity 8-1: Installing DNS

Time Required: Approximately 10 minutes
Objective: Learn how to install DNS.

Description: DNS works behind the scenes to help automate network access. In this activity, you use Server Manager to install the DNS role.

If DNS has been installed previously to enable you to install Active Directory, you can remove it now without removing Active Directory. To remove it, click Start, point to Administrative Tools, click Server Manager, click Remove Roles, select to remove DNS, and follow the Remove Roles Wizard steps.

1. Click **Start**, point to **Administrative Tools**, and click **Server Manager.**
2. Scroll to the Roles Summary section and click **Add Roles.**
3. If you see the Before You Begin dialog box, click **Next.**
4. Click the check box for **DNS Server** and click **Next.**
5. Take a few moments to review the information about DNS Server (see Figure 8-1). Click **Next.**
6. Click **Install.**
7. Click **Close.**
8. Close Server Manager.

DNS Zones

DNS name resolution is enabled through the use of tables of information that link computer names and IP addresses. The tables are associated with partitions in a DNS server that are called **zones** and that contain resource records. Each zone houses tables, called the zone file or zone database, of different types of resource records, such as records that link a computer name to an IP address.

The zone that links computer names to IP addresses is called the **forward lookup zone,** which holds host name records called address records. Each IP-based server and client should have a host record so that it can be found through DNS. For example, if the DNS server name is Accounting, with the IP address 129.70.10.1, then the forward lookup zone maps Accounting to 129.70.10.1. In IP version 4, a host record is called a **host address (A) resource record.** IP version 6 (IPv6), the newer version of IP that is used primarily on educational and experimental networks, consists of a 128-bit address (instead of the 32-bit address used with IPv4). An IPv6 record is called an **IPv6 host address (AAAA) resource record.** Microsoft, along with other major network software and hardware vendors, has made a commitment to implement IPv6. When you install DNS on a domain controller (DC) in a domain, a forward lookup zone is automatically created for the domain with the DNS server's address record already entered. You must enter the records of other hosts or configure Dynamic Host Configuration Protocol (DHCP) to

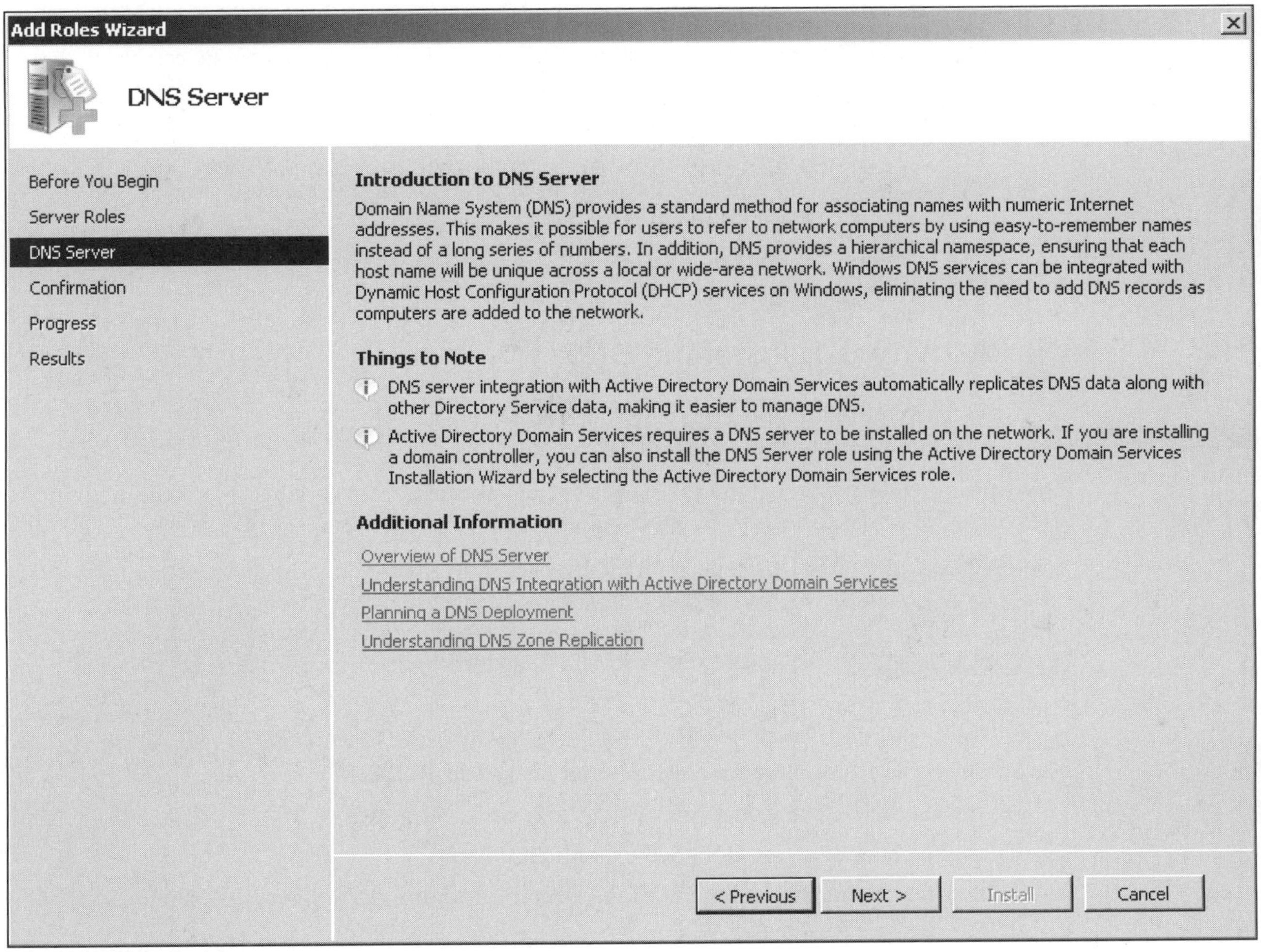

Figure 8-1 DNS Server information window

automatically update the DNS forward lookup zone each time it leases an IP address (you learn more about DHCP in the section of this chapter, "Implementing Microsoft DHCP").

Depending on the domain structure and Internet connectivity, a DNS server can have several forward lookup zones, but there should be at least one for the parent domain, such as jpcomp. com. Another zone, called the **reverse lookup zone**, holds the **pointer (PTR) resource record**, which contains the IP address-to-host name. The reverse lookup zone is not used as commonly as the forward lookup zone, but can be important to create for those instances when a network communication requires associating an IP address to a computer name, such as for monitoring a network using IP address information. Because it is less commonly used, the reverse lookup zone is not automatically configured when DNS is installed. If you anticipate that there will be users who access your network off-site, such as over the Internet, however, plan to implement information in a reverse lookup zone. Table 8-1 summarizes the commonly used resource records in DNS.

Activity 8-2: Creating a Reverse Lookup Zone

Time Required: Approximately 10 minutes
Objective: Learn how to create a reverse lookup zone.

Description: If you plan to use a reverse lookup zone, create it before DNS forward lookup zone records are created. The reason for this is that when a DNS forward lookup zone record is created, either manually or through dynamic updating, an associated reverse lookup zone PTR

Table 8-1 DNS resource records

Resource record	Description
Host (A)	Links a computer or network host name to its IP address
Canonical name (CNAME)	Links an alias to a computer name; sometimes also called common name
Load sharing	Spreads the load of DNS lookup requests among multiple DNS servers as a way to provide faster resolution for clients and better network response
Mail exchanger (MX)	Provides the IP addresses for Simple Mail Transfer Protocol (SMTP) servers that can accept e-mail for users in a domain
Name server (NS)	Provides information in response to queries about secondary DNS servers for an authoritative server (described later in this section) and information about off-site primary servers that are not authoritative for the domain
Pointer record (PTR)	Associates an IP address to a computer or network host name
Service (SRV) locator	Associates a particular TCP/IP service to a server along with the domain of the server and its protocol
Start of authority (SOA)	Is the first record in a zone and also indicates if this server is authoritative for the current zone
Windows Internet Naming Service (WINS)	Forwards a lookup request for a NetBIOS name to a Windows Internet Naming Service (WINS; see the section "Implementing Microsoft WINS") server when the host name cannot be found in DNS
Windows Internet Naming Service Reverse (WINS-R)	Forwards a reverse lookup (IP address to computer name) request to a WINS server

record can be created automatically. You create a reverse lookup zone in this activity, and in Activity 8-3 you create a forward lookup zone.

1. Click **Start**, point to **Administrative Tools**, and click **DNS**.
2. If necessary, click the plus sign in front of your server's name to expand the elements under it.
3. Click the **plus sign** in front of **Reverse Lookup Zones**, right-click the **Reverse Lookup Zones** folder in the tree under the DNS server, and click **New Zone** (see Figure 8-2).
4. Click **Next** after the New Zone Wizard starts.
5. Notice the zone options that are available (see Figure 8-3) and then click **Primary zone**. Also, ensure the box is checked for **Store the zone in Active Directory (available only if DNS server is a writeable domain controller)**. This last option enables the DNS server contents to be replicated to other DNS servers on the network (you learn more about this later in the chapter).
6. Click **Next**.
7. In the Active Directory Zone Replication Scope window, you can select how the DNS server is replicated through Active Directory. Make sure that **To all DNS servers in this domain:** *domainname* is selected.
   - What other options are available?

8. Click **Next**.
9. In the next window, you can select whether to create the reverse lookup zone for IPv4 or IPv6. Because most networks still use IPv4, click (if necessary) **IPv4 Reverse Lookup Zone**. Click **Next**.
10. Enter the network ID of the reverse lookup zone (which is the first two or three octets that identify the network, depending on the subnet mask that you use). This information is used

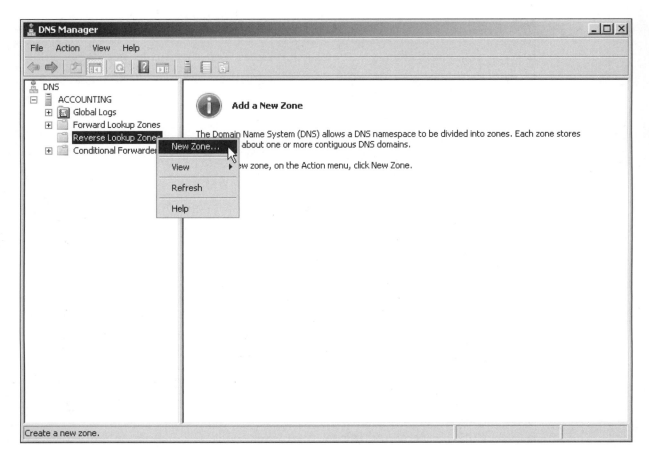

Figure 8-2 Creating a reverse lookup zone

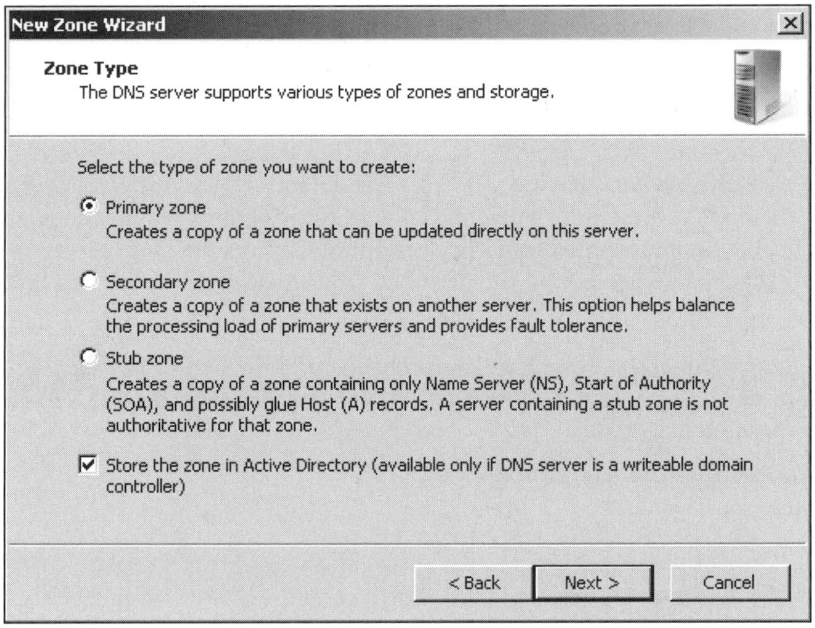

Figure 8-3 Selecting the zone type

to build the "in-addr.arpa" reverse lookup zone name. For example, if your zone network address is 129.70 then the in-addr.arpa reverse lookup zone is named 70.129.in-addr.arpa. The wizard automatically builds the in-addr.arpa name format when you enter the network address (see Figure 8-4). Click **Next**.

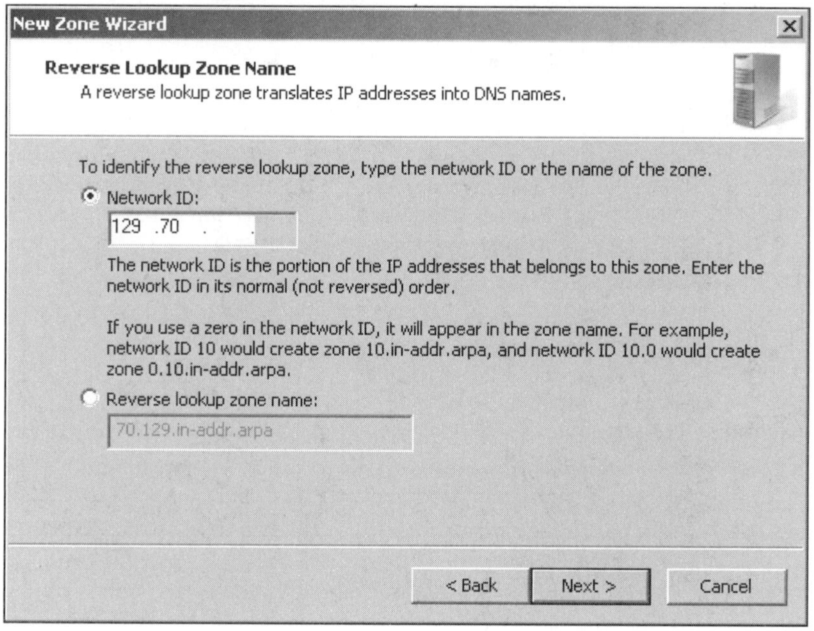

New Zone Wizard   [x]

Reverse Lookup Zone Name
A reverse lookup zone translates IP addresses into DNS names.

To identify the reverse lookup zone, type the network ID or the name of the zone.

(•) Network ID:

| 129 | .70 | . | . |

The network ID is the portion of the IP addresses that belongs to this zone. Enter the network ID in its normal (not reversed) order.

If you use a zero in the network ID, it will appear in the zone name. For example, network ID 10 would create zone 10.in-addr.arpa, and network ID 10.0 would create zone 0.10.in-addr.arpa.

( ) Reverse lookup zone name:

| 70.129.in-addr.arpa |

                                    [< Back] [Next >] [Cancel]

Figure 8-4 Configuring the in-addr.arpa reverse lookup zone name

11. Configure the security of updates made through DHCP by making sure that **Allow only secure dynamic updates (recommended for Active Directory)** is selected.

   • What other options are available and which option is least secure?

12. Click **Next**.

13. Review the information you have entered and click **Finish**. You should see the new reverse lookup zone displayed in the right pane.

14. Leave the DNS tool open for the next activity.

Activity 8-3: Manually Creating DNS Host Address A Resource Records

Time Required: Approximately 15 minutes
Objective: Create a Host Address A Resource Record.

Description: In this activity, you learn how to configure a Host Address A Resource Record in a forward lookup zone. Obtain the name of a host computer and its IP address from your instructor.

1. Open the DNS tool, if it is not still open.

2. Double-click **Forward Lookup Zones** in the tree under the server's name.

3. Double-click the domain name, such as jpcomp.com (see Figure 8-5). Notice there is already a Host (A) record for your server in the right pane.

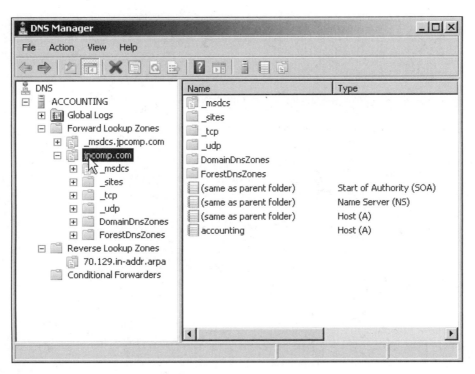

Figure 8-5   Opening the DNS tree

4. Click the **Action** menu.

   • What are the options in this menu? Record your answers.

5. Click **New Host (A or AAAA)**.

6. Enter the name of the host computer, such as **Computer1,** and its IP address, such as **129.70.10.50,** in the New Host dialog box.

7. Check the box to **Create associated pointer (PTR) record** (note that the reverse lookup zone must be created first, as in Activity 8-2).

8. Check the box to **Allow any authenticated user to update DNS records with the same owner name** (for computers running Windows 2000, XP, Vista, Server 2003, and Server 2008 that can update in coordination with DHCP, and this option also ensures security, because it associates an ACL with the record).

9. Click **Add Host** (see Figure 8-6).

10. Click **OK** when you see the message box that your host record was successfully created.

11. Click **Done.**

12. Leave the DNS tool open for the next activity.

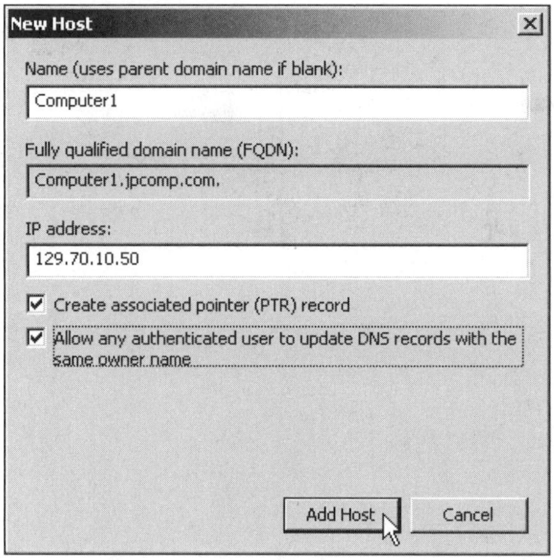

![New Host dialog box. Title bar reads "New Host" with an X close button. Name (uses parent domain name if blank): Computer1. Fully qualified domain name (FQDN): Computer1.jpcomp.com. IP address: 129.70.10.50. Checked: Create associated pointer (PTR) record. Checked: Allow any authenticated user to update DNS records with the same owner name. Buttons: Add Host, Cancel.]

Figure 8-6 Configuring a new host record

Using the DNS Dynamic Update Protocol

Microsoft DNS is also called **Dynamic DNS (DDNS)**, which is a modern form of DNS that enables client computers and DHCP servers to automatically register IP addresses. The **DNS dynamic update protocol** enables information in a DNS server to be automatically updated in coordination with DHCP. Using the DNS dynamic update protocol can save network administrators a great deal of time, because they no longer have to manually register each new workstation or to register a workstation each time its IP lease is up and a new IP address is issued. After you configure DNS, always make sure that it is configured to use the DNS dynamic update protocol.

Activity 8-4: Verifying the DNS Dynamic Update Configuration

Time Required: Approximately 5 minutes
Objective: Verify that DNS is configured to be dynamically updated using the DNS dynamic update protocol.

Description: In this activity, you make certain that dynamic DNS updating is properly configured. This step is important in two respects. One is to ensure that the workload for the DNS server administrator is reduced and the other is to be sure security is set on dynamic updating.

1. Open the DNS tool, if it is not still open.

2. In the left pane under Forward Lookup Zones, right-click the domain and click **Properties**.

3. Make sure that the **General** tab is displayed. In the *Data is stored in Active Directory* section of the dialog box, check the setting for *Dynamic updates*. The best practice, as shown in Figure 8-7, is for this parameter to be configured as *Secure only*, so that an ACL is associated with a host record (only an authorized client can perform an update). Click the down arrow in the list box to view the other options.

   • What are the other options?

4. Click **OK**.

5. Close the DNS management tool.

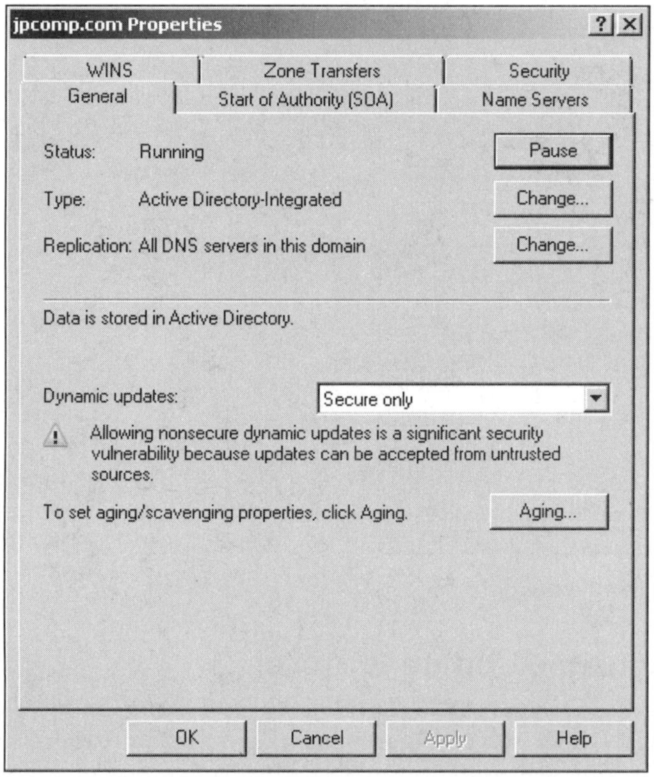

Figure 8-7 Dynamic updates configuration

Keep in mind that the DHCP server must also be configured to perform automatic DNS registration, as you will learn in Activity 8-10.

DNS Replication

DNS servers on a network fall into two broad categories: primary and secondary. A **primary DNS server** is the DNS server that is the main administrative server for a zone and thus is also the *authoritative* server for that zone. For example, when you first create a forward lookup zone on a DNS server for the york.com domain, you create an SOA resource record that identifies that DNS server as authoritative for the domain. This means that all changes to the zone, the creation of address (A) resource records, new SRV resource records, and so on must be made on that DNS server.

You have the option to create one or more backup DNS servers, called **secondary DNS servers,** for a primary DNS server. A secondary DNS server contains a copy of the primary DNS server's zone database, but is not used for administration (is not authoritative). It obtains that copy through a zone transfer over the network. The three vital services performed by secondary DNS servers are:

- To make sure that there is a copy of the primary DNS server's data, in case the primary server fails.

- To enable DNS load balancing (via the load sharing resource records) among a primary DNS server and its secondary servers. Load balancing means that if the DNS primary server is busy performing a name resolution, a different request for a name resolution that is received at the same time can be fielded by a secondary DNS server for faster response to users.

- To reduce congestion in one part of the network by spreading secondary servers to different geographic locations and to different Active Directory sites, yielding faster network response.

 One DNS server can be authoritative for multiple domains because it can have multiple zones. Also, because one server can have multiple zones, a single DNS server can be a secondary server for more than one primary server. Plus, one DNS server can be a primary server for one zone and a secondary server for another zone.

If you use Active Directory and have two or more DCs, plan to set up Microsoft DNS services on at least two of the DCs, because the multimaster replication model (see Chapter 4) enables you to replicate DNS information on each DC. The advantage of replicating DNS information is that if one DC that hosts DNS services fails, another DC is available to provide uninterrupted DNS services for the network. This is especially critical on a network that provides Internet access and Web-based e-mail services. Whenever you create a zone, as you practiced in Activity 8-2, select the option to *Store the zone in Active Directory (available only if DNS server is a writeable domain controller)*, which enables you to take advantage of multimaster replication.

Stub Zone

With Windows Server 2003, Microsoft introduced the concept of a stub zone. A **stub zone** has only the bare necessities for DNS functions, which are copies of the following:

- SOA record zone
- Name server (NS) records to identify authoritative servers
- A record for name servers that are authoritative

One common use for a stub zone is to help quickly resolve computer names between two different namespaces by enabling clients in one namespace to instantly find an authoritative server in a different namespace. For example, when two companies with different namespaces such as compA.com and compB.com merge, creating stub zones on DNS servers in each namespace can help clients in one namespace quickly find an authoritative DNS server in the other namespace. This is faster and creates less network traffic than if the client has to query a root name server (one of just a few master servers that look up namespaces) on the Internet, for example. Also, because stub zones are so small, replicating them between DNS servers within a namespace creates negligible network traffic.

You can create a stub zone using the same steps as when you create a primary or secondary zone. The general steps for creating a stub zone are:

1. Open the DNS tool.
2. Right-click the server.
3. Click New Zone to start the New Zone Wizard.
4. Click Next.
5. Click Stub zone (refer to Figure 8-3).
6. Follow the guided steps in the New Zone Wizard.

Additional DNS Server Roles

DNS servers can play several specialized roles in addition to or other than those of authoritative/ primary or secondary DNS server. For instance, when there are multiple sites (see Chapter 4) or when there is Internet connectivity, it is common to designate one DNS server to forward name resolution requests to a specific remote DNS server. One example of how forwarding works is a set of state community colleges that operate under a community college commission. Each college maintains DNS servers for resolution of addresses within its own namespace. Each college also has designated one on-site DNS server to automatically forward name resolution requests involving another college or the commission. For a name resolution request that involves finding a server at the community college commission, the DNS forwarder server on the college network forwards the resolution request to a DNS server on the commission's network (see Figure 8-8). For example, if a professor at one college needs to access a shared folder offered by a professor at another college, the DNS forwarder server at the first college transfers the resolution request to a DNS server at the other college.

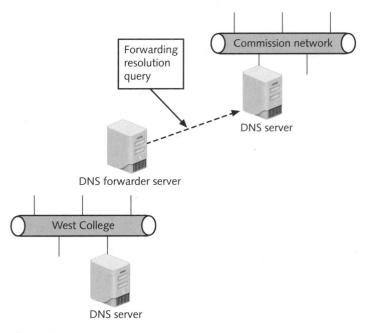

Figure 8-8   DNS forwarder server

 When one DNS server is set up as the forwarder, then all other DNS servers that have queries to send to an off-site DNS server send those queries to the single DNS forwarder server. By designating only one DNS forwarder server, you ensure that only one server is sending queries over a site link, instead of having multiple servers sending queries and creating extra traffic over the site link.

DNS forwarding can be set up so that if the DNS server that receives the forwarded request cannot resolve the name, then the server that originally forwarded the request attempts to resolve it. This is called *nonexclusive forwarding*. When DNS forwarding is set so that only the DNS server receiving the request attempts resolution (and not the server that forwarded the request), this is called *exclusive forwarding*. In exclusive forwarding, the DNS server that initially forwards the request is called a *slave DNS server*.

A DNS server can function as as a *caching server*. A caching server is used to provide fast queries because the results of each query are stored in RAM. As more resolution queries are performed, a large set of information is stored in RAM for fast response to users. Usually a caching server does not contain zone databases, but queries a primary or secondary DNS server and caches the results to provide a fast response for the next identical query. Caching servers are used as a way to reduce the number of secondary DNS servers and, therefore, reduce the extra network traffic that results because of replicating zones from the primary to the secondary servers. One limitation of using caching servers is that it takes time for each one to build up a comprehensive set of resolved names to IP addresses; every time a caching server goes down, it must rebuild its information from scratch.

Creating a DNS Implementation Plan

When you plan DNS implementation, consider the following recommendations:

- Implement Windows Server 2008 DNS servers instead of other versions of DNS, if possible, and use Active Directory. The advantage is that the DNS servers, like the DCs, exist in a multimaster relationship. The multimaster relationship reduces the need to use caching servers because DNS zone transfers from DNS server to DNS server occur as a built-in process along with normal DC replication. Also, when you use Windows Server 2008 DNS server, you can take advantage of dynamic DNS updating, which will save you time as an administrator and make your DNS A and PTR resource records more accurate.

- Plan to locate a DNS server across most site links (see Chapter 4), just as you would locate DCs. The exceptions may be when there are not enough users across certain site links or when the site links are very reliable, high-speed links.

- Just as you should create two or more DCs per domain, also create two or more DNS servers to take advantage of the load balancing, the multimaster relationships, and the fault tolerance.

- When you have off-site links between different domains, designate one DNS server as a forwarder to reduce traffic over those links.

- The number of DNS servers that you set up can be related to your analysis of an organization. For example, an organization that is centralized will typically have fewer domains and, therefore, fewer DNS servers and DNS server administrators. An organization that is decentralized will likely have more domains, DNS servers, and DNS server administrators.

DNS Enhancements

Microsoft DNS servers now include support for IPv6. You can set up forward and reverse lookup zones to use IPv6 on a network. Another DNS improvement is called background zone loading. This means that a DNS server that has a large number of entries in its zones can load those entries as a background process. DNS queries can be going on as the zones are loading, instead of waiting until all zone loading is finished as in previous versions of Microsoft DNS.

Yet another enhancement is that a DNS server can be housed on a Read-Only Domain Controller (RODC; see Chapter 4) for branch offices. This means that if the RODC at the branch site is disconnected from the main site, branch site users still have fast DNS lookup services because they use their local RODC for DNS lookups.

Troubleshooting DNS

If DNS is installed, but is not resolving names or does not seem to be working, there are many steps you can take to troubleshoot the problem, such as restarting the DNS Server and DNS Client services. Another step is to check for the most recent log errors relating to DNS. Activity 8-5 shows you how to restart the DNS Server and Client services, and Activity 8-6 shows you how to check for DNS errors in the log information kept by Windows Server 2008. Also, Table 8-2 presents a full range of troubleshooting tips.

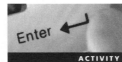

Activity 8-5: Checking the DNS Server and Client Services

Time Required: Approximately 5 minutes
Objective: Verify that the DNS Server and Client services are started.

Description: One troubleshooting tool for DNS is to ensure that the DNS Client and Server services are started. The DNS Client service enables DNS name queries to be cached. The DNS Server service enables name queries to be resolved and it enables dynamic DNS updating. You learn how to verify these services in this activity.

1. Click **Start**, point to **Administrative Tools**, and click **Server Manager**.
2. Click the **plus sign** in front of **Configuration** in the tree.

3. Click **Services** in the **Tree**.

4. Click the **Standard** tab at the bottom of the middle pane.

5. Scroll to find DNS Client and DNS Server in the tree.

6. Look under the Status column and determine if the DNS Client and DNS Server services are started (see Figure 8-9).

7. Double-click **DNS Client** in the middle pane.

8. Ensure that *Startup type* is set to **Automatic**.

9. To stop and restart the service, click the **Stop** button, as shown in Figure 8-10 (unless the service is already stopped).

10. Click the **Start** button.

11. Click **OK**.

12. Double-click **DNS Server** in the middle pane.

13. Make sure that *Startup type* is set to **Automatic**.

14. To stop and restart the service, click the **Stop** button (unless the service is already stopped).

15. Click the **Start** button.

16. Click **OK**.

17. Click **Server Manager** (*servername*) in the tree to return the right pane to the default display.

18. Leave the Server Manager window open for the next activity.

Table 8-2 Troubleshooting DNS server problems

DNS server problem	Solutions
DNS server is not responding with the correct information to DNS queries from clients.	Ensure that Dynamic DNS is enabled and configured correctly. Check manually added DNS host address records for accuracy. If the errors are related to one client, check the DNS client computer to ensure it is working correctly, including that the NIC and its driver are working correctly.
Users can contact the DNS server, but receive a permission denied message when trying to read DNS records.	Ensure that users have permission to read the DNS records, open the DNS Manager, right-click the domain in the tree, click Properties, click the Security tab, and ensure that the Everyone group (and other general user groups) has *Allow* checked for the Read permission.
Users cannot access the DNS server.	Check the DNS server's connection to the network to ensure it is live on the network.
Users can access the DNS server, but DNS record information is not being processed.	Ensure that the DNS Server and DNS Client services are started and set to start automatically when the server is booted.
You have installed an update to the DNS server, but DNS response to clients is experiencing errors.	Reload the DNS server database, open DNS Manager, click the domain in the tree, click the Action menu, and click Reload to reload the database.

Activity 8-6: Checking Log Entries for DNS

Time Required: Approximately 10 minutes
Objective: Check the log information about possible DNS errors.

Description: You can use Server Manager to check the log information for any of the roles you have installed, including the DNS server role. In this activity, you check the most recent log entries for DNS services.

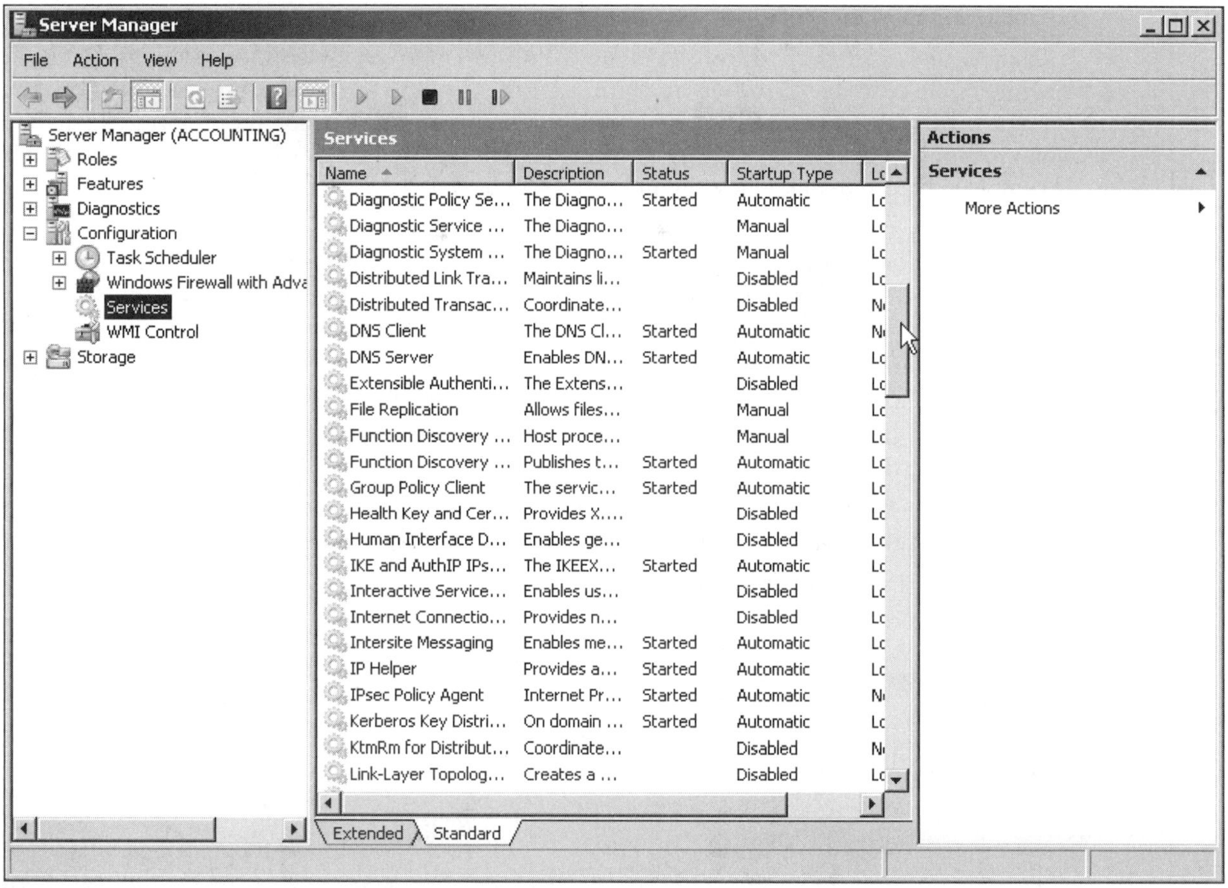

Figure 8-9 Viewing the status of the DNS Client and DNS Server services

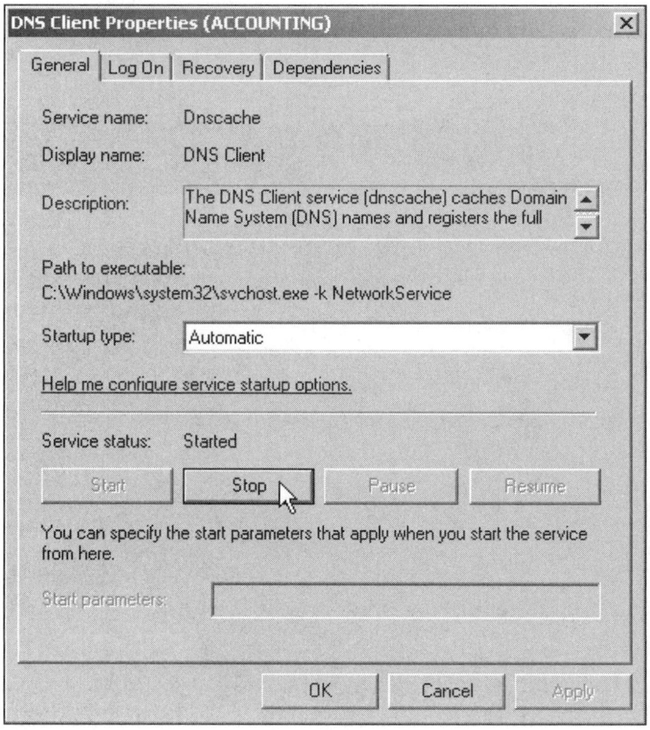

Figure 8-10 Stopping the DNS Client service

1. Open Server Manager if it is not already open.

2. In the Roles Summary section, look for a link to DNS Server with any of the following: a white circle with an "i" inside (for information), a yellow caution sign with an exclamation point inside (for a caution), or a red circle with a white "x" inside representing an error. If any of these symbols appears in front of DNS Server, it means there is log information to view (see Figure 8-11). Click the link for **DNS Server**.

3. In the right pane, you see the events logged for DNS Server in the last 24 hours. In most cases, you should look for error (red circle) or caution (yellow caution sign) events first so you can investigate these. For this activity, however, double-click any event listed under *Events*, because at this point they are likely to be only information events. In the Event Properties dialog box, you'll see a description of the event on the General tab. In a troubleshooting situation, you can use this description for information about the problem. Click **Close**.

4. Scroll down in the right pane to see the *System Services* section. Notice that here you can check to see that the DNS Server service is running.

5. Scroll down further in the right pane and you'll find the Resources and Support section, which contains additional resources for using and troubleshooting the DNS Server role.

6. In the left pane, click **Server Manager (*servername*)** and leave Server Manager open for the next activity.

In Chapter 12, "Managing System Reliability and Availability," you learn about using the Event Viewer to see the information in the Windows Server 2008 logs for troubleshooting and monitoring the status of a server.

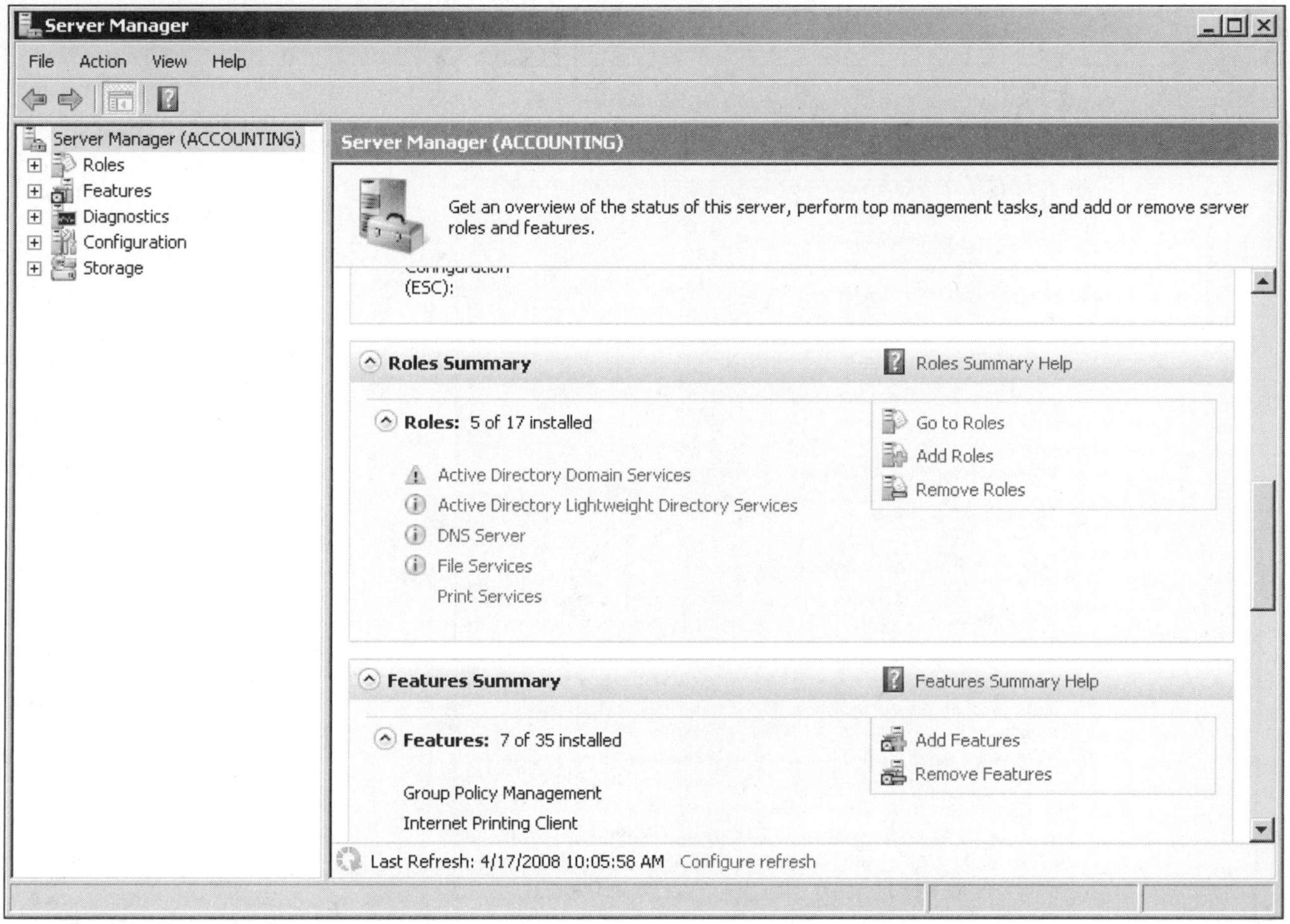

Figure 8-11   Accessing log information about DNS Server

Implementing Microsoft WINS

Windows Internet Naming Service (WINS) is used to register NetBIOS computer names and map them to IP addresses for any systems that use NetBIOS name resolution (pre-Windows 2000 servers and pre-Windows 2000 clients often use NetBIOS names). As you learned in Chapter 1, WINS automatically registers network clients that use NetBIOS and builds a database that other network clients can query in order to locate a computer. For example, if a Windows 98 network computer called Eggplant offers a shared folder for other network clients, those other clients can query WINS to find Eggplant.

An important advantage of WINS is its dynamic nature. When a WINS client computer is connected to the network and turned on, it automatically registers its name and IP address with the WINS server. Then, any other WINS client can query the WINS server for the IP address using the computer name.

WINS consists of two main parts: the WINS server and the WINS database. The WINS server registers the IP addresses and names of its client computers by writing them to the WINS database. The WINS database stores the IP addresses, names, and mapping information for name-to-IP address lookups. The database can be configured to copy or push its contents to a partner server for fault tolerance.

If your network uses early Windows systems, such as Windows NT, Windows 95, Windows 98, or Windows Me, you can install WINS in Windows Server 2008 for NetBIOS name and IP lookup. One disadvantage is that WINS does not have the same security as DDNS in terms of the option to accept information only from secure clients. If security is a concern on your network, consider upgrading network clients to avoid using legacy Windows systems. WINS is installed as a feature through Server Manager.

Activity 8-7: Installing WINS

Time Required: Approximately 10 minutes
Objective: Learn how to install WINS.

Description: WINS is a backward-compatible feature in Windows Server 2008 to accommodate legacy Windows clients. In this activity, you use Server Manager to install the WINS feature in Windows Server 2008.

1. Open Server Manager if it is not already open.
2. Scroll to the Features Summary section and click **Add Features**.
3. Click **WINS Server** (see Figure 8-12) and click **Next**.
4. Click **Install**.
5. Click **Close**.
6. You can now use the WINS management tool. Click **Start**, point to **Administrative Tools**, and click **WINS**.
7. Click the name of your computer in the tree to display the elements under it, if necessary.
8. Click **Active Registrations** in the tree. When there are registered NetBIOS names and IP addresses, the right pane will display the records in the WINS database for these registrations (if your network does not presently have any registrations, you won't see any data listed).
9. Right-click **Replication Partners** in the tree to see the shortcut menu.
   - What would you click to create a replication partner? Also, how can you have the WINS database replicate its contents to a replication partner after it has been created?

10. Click in a blank area of the window to close the shortcut menu.

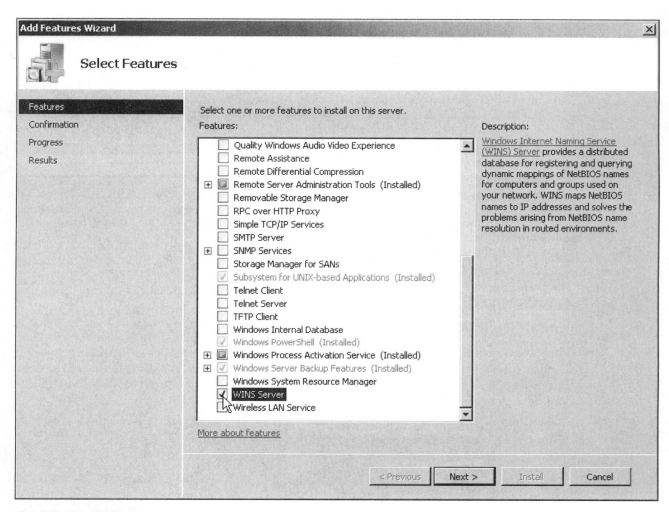

Figure 8-12 Installing WINS Server

11. Click **Server Status** in the tree. This is a simple troubleshooting measure you can take to ensure the WINS Server is responding (notice the Status column in the right pane).

12. Close the WINS window.

13. In the Server Manager window, click the **plus sign** in front of **Configuration**, if necessary, to see the elements under it in the tree.

14. Click **Services** in the tree.

15. Scroll to **WINS** and double-click it.

16. You can use the WINS Properties dialog box to ensure the *Startup type* is Automatic. You can also use this dialog box to start and stop the WINS service if it is not responding. Click **Cancel**.

17. Click **Server Manager (*servername*)** in the tree to return the right pane to its default display.

18. Leave Server Manager open for the next activity.

Implementing Microsoft DHCP

Dynamic Host Configuration Protocol (DHCP) enables a Windows Server 2008 server with DHCP services to detect the presence of a new workstation and assign an IP address to that workstation. This capability enables a network or server administrator to save hours of time by not having to keep track of IP addresses on a network and assign specific addresses to users and network devices. As you learned in Chapter 1, DHCP also saves users time because they don't have to configure their own IP addresses—DHCP can do this for them. When you set up a Windows 98, Me, NT, 2000, XP, or Vista client to automatically obtain an IP address, the client contacts a DHCP server to obtain that address. The DHCP server has a preassigned range of IP addresses that it can give to a new client. Each address is assigned for a specific period of time, such as eight hours, two weeks, a month, a year, or even permanently. A range of contiguous addresses is called the **scope**. A single Microsoft DHCP server can support the following:

- Dynamic configuration of DNS server forward and reverse lookup zone records
- Up to 1000 different scopes (not the theoretical upward limit, but a Microsoft recommendation)
- Up to 10,000 DHCP clients (also not the theoretical upward limit, but a Microsoft recommendation)

A Windows Server 2008 server can be configured in the role of a DHCP server using Microsoft DHCP services. When you set up a Microsoft DHCP server, you have the option to set it up to automatically register forward and reverse lookup zone records with a Microsoft DNS server (you learn about these later in this chapter). The DHCP server automatically updates the DNS server at the time it assigns an IP address. Using dynamic DNS updates can significantly save time in creating DNS lookup zone records. A Microsoft DHCP server can also:

- Reserve an IP address for a specific computer, such as for a server (servers should always use the same IP address to avoid network confusion)
- Update all computers on a network for a particular change in DHCP settings, which eliminates the need to manually update the computers
- Provide DHCP services to multiple subnetworks (subnets), as long as the DHCP server is connected to each subnet
- Omit certain IP addresses from a scope, so that these addresses can be used manually or statically set up on a particular computer or device, such as a server or network printer

Multiple scopes are supported in a single Microsoft DHCP server because it is often necessary to assign different address ranges, such as one range that is 129.70.10.1 to 129.70.10.122 and another that is 129.71.20.10 to 129.71.20.182. As this example illustrates, you can assign address ranges to reflect the network subnet structure or other network divisions (see Figure 8-13).

 If your network has Internet connectivity, make sure you obtain IP address ranges from your Internet service provider, so that you use addresses that are specifically assigned to your organization and recognized as valid by the Internet community.

Activity 8-8: Installing DHCP

Time Required: Approximately 15 minutes
Objective: Learn how to install DHCP.

Description: DHCP is installed as a server role in Windows Server 2008 using Server Manager. In this activity, you install DHCP.

1. Open Server Manager, if necessary.
2. Scroll to the Roles Summary section and click **Add Roles**.
3. If you see the Before You Begin dialog box, click **Next**.

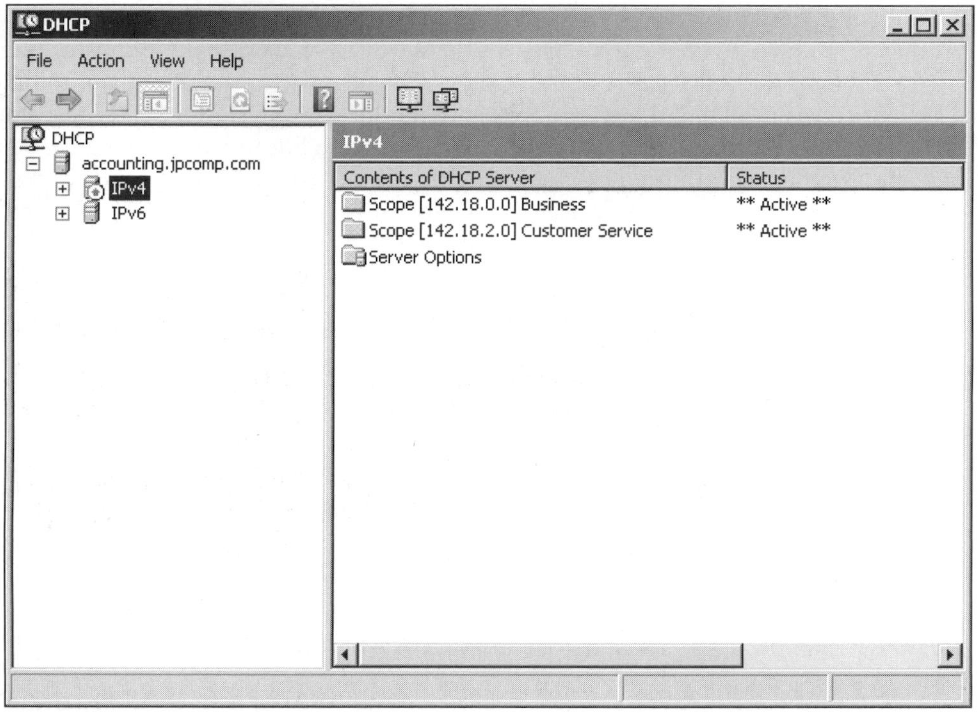

Figure 8-13 Using multiple scopes

4. Under *Roles,* click the check box for **DHCP Server.** (If you see a warning that your server does not have a static IP address, make a note to configure a static IP address soon and click Install DHCP Server anyway (not recommended)). Click **Next.**

5. Review the information about DHCP Server and click **Next.**

6. You might see the Select Network Connection Bindings window. If you see this window, it means that the installation process has identified network servers that have automatically or statically assigned IP addresses. If necessary, select the IP address for the computer you are using and click **Next.**

7. In the Specify IPv4 DNS Server Settings window, if necessary specify the name of the parent domain, such as jpcomp.com, and specify the IPv4 address of the DNS server on your network (see Figure 8-14). (If no DNS server is set up yet, specify the address of the computer that will have DNS services. Also, the DNS server should have a statically assigned IP address.) If there is an alternate DNS server, you can also specify its address as well. Click **Next.**

8. Because you have already configured WINS, click **WINS is required for applications on this network.** In the box *Preferred WINS Server IP Address,* enter the IP address of the WINS server you created in Activity 8-7. (You can also select not to require WINS if you do not plan to use it even though you have already installed it. Consult with your instructor if you have a question about this.) Click **Next.**

9. Notice that you can now configure one or more scopes. Leave scopes undefined for now so you can come back to this step later. Click **Next.**

10. Use the default option to **Enable DHCPv6 stateless mode for this server** (so that IPv6 clients are configured without using the DHCP server). Click **Next.**

11. Review the IPv6 setting provided by the installation program and click **Next.**

12. Leave the default setting to **Use current credentials** of the current user (which is you) and click **Next.**

13. Review your configuration settings and click **Install.**

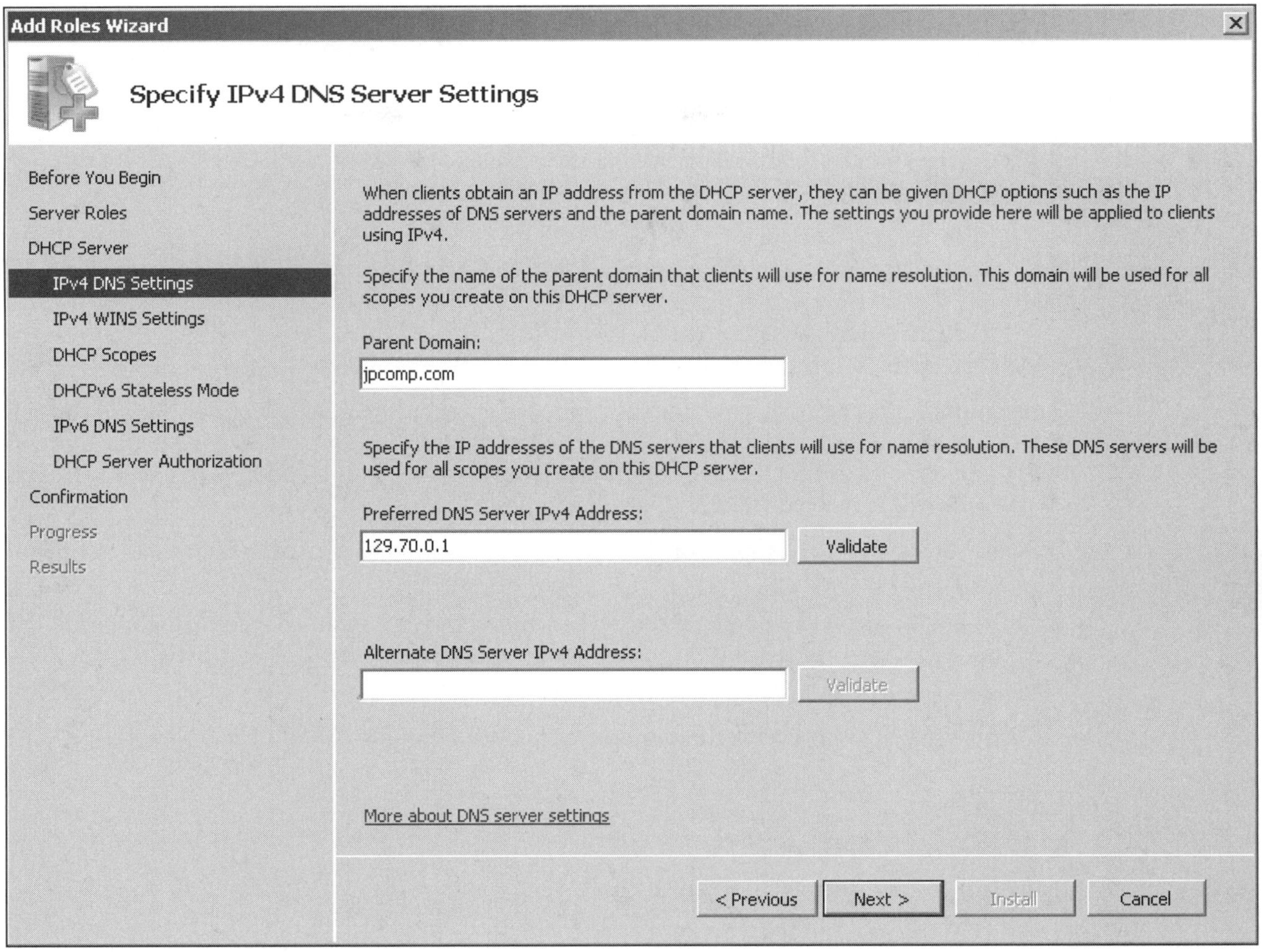

Figure 8-14 Specifying the IPv4 DNS Server settings

14. Click **Close**.

15. Close Server Manager.

Configuring a DHCP Server

After DHCP is installed, it is necessary to configure the DHCP server. First, set up one or more scopes of contiguous address ranges and activate each scope. Configuring a scope includes the following:

- Obtain the range of addresses to be used.
- Determine the subnet mask for the range of addresses.
- Decide on a name for the scope, such as naming it to reflect the name of a department or division in your organization.
- Decide how long to lease IP addresses.
- Determine whether to exclude specific addresses.

Second, authorize the DHCP server. The process of authorizing the server is a security precaution to make sure IP addresses are only assigned by DHCP servers that are managed by network and server administrators. The security is needed because it is critical for IP address leasing to be carefully managed through ensuring that only valid IP addresses are used and that there is no possibility that duplicate IP addresses can be leased. DHCP servers that are not authorized are prevented from running on a network.

Third, a step that is not required, but that saves time in managing DNS, is to configure the DHCP server and its clients to automatically update DNS records.

Only domain controllers and member servers can be authorized as DHCP servers when Active Directory is in use on the network. If Active Directory is not implemented, a stand-alone server can be authorized.

Activity 8-9: Configuring DHCP Scopes

Time Required: Approximately 15 minutes
Objective: Learn how to configure a DHCP scope.

Description: In this activity, you practice configuring a scope on a DHCP server. Before you start, obtain the address or computer name of a DNS server from your instructor (or use the address of this computer) and ask for a range of addresses for the scope, plus an address to exclude from the scope. You will also need to know the subnet mask.

1. Click **Start**, point to **Administrative Tools**, and click **DHCP**. (An alternative is to open the DHCP MMC snap-in.)

2. In the tree, click the name of the server under DHCP, such as accounting.jpcomp.com. Notice that two folders are displayed under the server name: IPv4 and IPv6.

3. Double-click **IPv4** in the tree to select it.

4. Right-click **IPv4** to access the shortcut menu (see Figure 8-15) and click **New Scope**.

```
Display Statistics...

New Scope...
New Multicast Scope...

Define User Classes...
Define Vendor Classes...

Reconcile All Scopes...

Set Predefined Options...

View                          ▶

Refresh

Properties

Help
```

Figure 8-15 Configuring a new scope

5. Click **Next** after the New Scope Wizard starts.

6. Enter a name for the scope so it is easy for you to identify as you maintain it, such as Administration plus your initials (AdministrationJR), and enter a description for the scope, such as Admin area subnet. Click **Next**.

7. Enter the start and end IP addresses, such as 129.70.19.51 and 129.70.19.99. To go from field to field, press the period key (when you enter fewer than three numbers). Further, enter the subnet mask, such as 255.255.255.0, and then click the entry area in the Length box (see Figure 8-16).

   - What happens when you click the box?

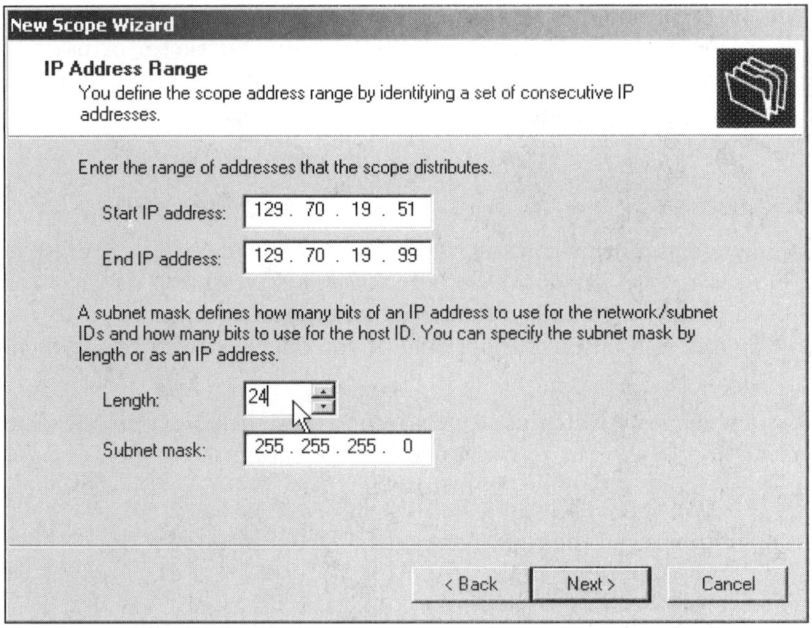

New Scope Wizard

IP Address Range
You define the scope address range by identifying a set of consecutive IP addresses.

Enter the range of addresses that the scope distributes.

Start IP address: 129 . 70 . 19 . 51

End IP address: 129 . 70 . 19 . 99

A subnet mask defines how many bits of an IP address to use for the network/subnet IDs and how many bits to use for the host ID. You can specify the subnet mask by length or as an IP address.

Length: 24

Subnet mask: 255 . 255 . 255 . 0

< Back   Next >   Cancel

Figure 8-16   Configuring the scope

8. Click **Next**.

9. Enter an address, such as 129.70.19.70, in the Start IP address box and click **Add**.

   • What happens after you click Add? Do you need to enter an ending address?

 When you statically assign IP addresses to servers on a network, use this feature to exclude those addresses from the DHCP address pool.

10. Click **Next**.

11. You can now configure the lease duration.

    • What is the default lease time? For what types of situations would this default be appropriate?

12. Change the default lease time to **5 days**. Click **Next**.

 Set the duration of a DHCP lease on the basis of the type of connection. For desktop computers that are connected on a more permanent basis, set leases to expire after a longer period, such as from three days to a couple of weeks. Particularly use a longer lease period on medium and large networks in which you have a large number of IP addresses that can be used. For laptop and portable computers that are less permanent on the network, set leases to expire after the duration of the communication session, such as 8–24 hours.

13. Click **Yes, I want to configure these options now** and click **Next**.

14. The next dialog box offers the ability to enter an IP address for a router (default gateway). You would configure this information if access to the addresses in this scope is through a router (default gateway). Click **Next**.

15. Enter the parent domain in which DNS name resolution will occur, such as jpcomp.com. Enter the name of the DNS server (check with your instructor or use the DNS server you have already set up) and click **Resolve**, or enter the DNS server's IP address. Click **Add**.

    • How would you enter more than one DNS server?

16. Click **Next**.

17. In the next dialog box, you can enter the names and IP addresses of WINS servers, such as for the WINS server you set up in Activity 8-7. This would be used on networks in which NetBIOS naming is used and so that these names can be mapped to IP addresses. (Entering the name of your WINS server is optional. If you do, click Resolve and then click Add.) Click **Next**.

18. Click **Yes, I want to activate this scope now** and then click **Next** (or click **Cancel** if you do not have permission from your instructor to finish creating the scope).

19. Click **Finish**.

    • What now appears in the right pane of the DHCP window?

20. Your server should be authorized by default. You can verify this by right-clicking the server name in the tree. If you see the menu option *Unauthorize,* this means your server is already authorized and you should click an open space to close the menu. If instead you see *Authorize* in the menu, click this option to authorize the server.

21. Leave the DHCP window open for the next activity.

When it is installed, a DHCP server is automatically configured to register IP addresses at the DNS server, but you must also provide the DNS server's IP addresses when you configure each scope. Also, you can manually configure automatic DNS registration through a DHCP server, as you learn in the next activity.

Activity 8-10: Configuring Automatic DNS Registration

Time Required: Approximately 10 minutes
Objective: Verify that a DHCP server is configured to automatically register IP addresses with a DNS server.

Description: In this activity, you verify that the DHCP server you have configured is set up to automatically register with a DNS server the IP addresses that it leases and that it is configured for the types of clients on your network.

1. Open the DHCP tool, if it is not still open.

2. Ensure the server is expanded to show the elements under it.

3. Double-click **IPv4** to select it.

4. Right-click **IPv4** and then click **Properties**.

5. Click the **DNS** tab (see Figure 8-17) and make sure that the box for **Enable DNS dynamic updates according to the settings below** is checked. Clients running Windows 2000, Windows XP, Windows Vista, Windows Server 2003, or Windows Server 2008 operating systems can request to update a DNS server. If you have only these clients, click the box for **Dynamically update DNS A and PTR records only if requested by the DHCP clients**. If other operating systems are connecting to the network, such as Windows 98 or Windows NT, which do not request to update a DNS server, click instead **Always dynamically update DNS A and PTR records**—which means that the DHCP server takes the responsibility to update the DNS server's records every time a client obtains the IP address. Also, make sure that **Discard A and PTR records when lease is deleted** is checked, so that the DHCP server alerts

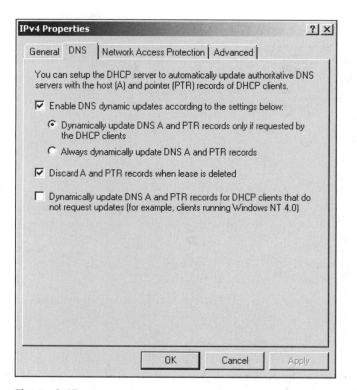

Figure 8-17 Configuring automatic updates for DNS servers

the DNS server to delete a record each time a lease is up. If some clients are running Windows 95, 98, and NT, also check **Dynamically update DNS A and PTR records for DHCP clients that do not request updates (for example, clients running Windows NT 4.0)**.

6. Click **OK**.

7. Close the DHCP window.

DHCPv6 Support

Windows Server 2008 and Windows Vista both enable a network to use **Dynamic Host Configuration Protocol for IPv6 (DHCPv6)** for networks that are working to implement IPv6. The Windows Server 2008 and Windows Vista implementation of DHCPv6 follows the official standard for DHCPv6 (as defined in Request for Comment 3315). The Microsoft implementation of DHCPv6 supports both stateful and stateless autoconfiguration.

Stateful autoconfiguration means that the computer or network device using IPv6 contacts a DHCP server for a leased address. In stateless autoconfiguration, the computer or network device assigns its own IPv6 address, which is constructed from the MAC address of its NIC (see Chapter 1) combined with the subnet designation obtained from communication with a router. Stateless autoconfiguration of an IPv6 address does not require a DHCP server, but is included in the DHCPv6 standard for compliance with IPv6 capabilities.

Troubleshooting DHCP

When you set up a DHCP server, some problems may occur, such as the server stopping or not working, creating extra network traffic, or not automatically registering with DNS servers. Table 8-3 presents several typical problems and their resolutions.

Table 8-3 Troubleshooting a DHCP server

Problem	Solution
The DHCP server will not start.	Use Server Manager or the Computer Management tool to make sure that the DHCP Client and DHCP Server services are started and set to start automatically. If the DHCP Server service will not start, make sure that the COM+ Event System, Remote Procedure Call (RPC), Security Accounts Manager, TCP/IP Protocol Driver, and Windows Event Log services are already started, because the DHCP Server service depends on these services. Make sure that the DHCP server is authorized.
	Use Server Manager or Event Viewer to check the System log (see Chapter 12, "Managing System Reliability and Availability").
The DHCP server creates extra or excessive network traffic (as determined by using the Performance Monitor as discussed in Chapter 11, "Server and Network Monitoring").	Increase the lease period in each scope, so there is less traffic due to allocating new leases when the old ones expire.
The DNS lookup zone records are not automatically updated.	Make sure that DNS servers and IP addresses are set up in each DHCP scope. Make sure that the IPv4 properties are set up to automatically update the DNS server. Also, have the DHCP server do the updating instead of clients, when there are pre-Windows 2000 clients. Finally, enable DNS updating for clients that do not dynamically support it.
One of the leased IP addresses is conflicting with a permanent IP address leased to a computer, such as a server.	Exclude that IP address from the scope.
Your network has a large number of portable and laptop computers and is in short supply of IP addresses.	Reduce the lease duration so that leases expire sooner and can be reassigned.
The System log is reporting Jet database error messages.	The DHCP database is corrupted. Have users log off from the network and disable the server's connection (click Start, click Network, click Network Sharing Center, click Manage network connections, right-click the connection, and click Disable). Use the DHCP management tool to reconcile the scopes (right-click the IPv4 folder and click Reconcile All Scopes). Another option is to open the Command Prompt window and use the Jetpack.exe program to repair the database. A third option is to use the Nesh.exe command to dump the database and then reinitialize it.
The DHCP server is not responding.	Click Start, click Network, click Network and Sharing Center, and make sure that the server is connected to the network.
	Use Server Manager or the Computer Management tool to make sure that the DHCP Client and DHCP Server services are started and set to start automatically.
	Also, ensure that the DHCP server has a static IP address and not a dynamic IP address. Click Start, click Network, click Network and Sharing Center, click Manage network connections, right-click the network connection, click Properties, and double-click Internet Protocol Version 4 (TCP/IPv4).

Implementing Microsoft Internet Information Services

Microsoft **Internet Information Services (IIS)** is software included with Windows Server 2008 that enables you to offer a complete Web site. Your Web site might fulfill any number of functions. On a college campus you might use it to enable applicants to apply for admission or to allow currently enrolled students to view their progress toward completing degree requirements. Many companies use their Web sites for multiple purposes, such as to announce new products, provide product support, take product orders, and advertise job openings. Another use is to provide training to company employees on using software, such as an inventory or order entry system.

IIS benchmarks prove these services are fast, and the software design enables the use of software applications to coordinate with an IIS server, such as a distributed client/server system that implements Web-based features. One reason why IIS services are fast and can be integrated with other programs is the built-in **Internet Server Application Programming Interface (ISAPI)**. ISAPI is a group of DLL (dynamic link library) files that are applications and filters. The applications files enable developers to link customized programs into IIS and to speed program execution. IIS filters are used to automatically trigger programs, such as a Microsoft Access database lookup or a security program to authorize a user to access specific Web functions. The Web Server (IIS) role contains the World Wide Web services, which are vital for a Web site. Another service that can be employed through IIS is the **File Transfer Protocol (FTP)** service. FTP is a TCP/IP-based application protocol that handles file transfers over a network. Additional services allow you to make an IIS server function as an e-mail server using the **Simple Mail Transfer Protocol (SMTP)**. An SMTP server acts as an Internet gateway and in partnership with e-mail services, such as Microsoft Exchange, to accept incoming e-mail from the Internet and forward it to the recipient. It also forwards outgoing e-mail from a network's e-mail service to the Internet.

Windows Server 2008 is a good candidate for a Web server for several reasons. One reason is that Windows Server 2008's privileged-mode architecture (see Chapter 1) and fault-tolerance capabilities make it a reliable server platform. Another is that Windows Server 2008 is compatible with small databases, such as Microsoft Access, and large databases, such as SQL Server and Oracle. Also, users can log in to a database through the IIS **Open Database Connectivity (ODBC)** drivers. ODBC is a set of database access rules used by Microsoft in its ODBC application programming interface (API) for accessing databases and providing a standard doorway to database data. This makes IIS very compatible with Web-based client/server applications. IIS also is compatible with Microsoft Point-to-Point Encryption (MPPE) security, IP Security (IPsec), and the Secure Sockets Layer (SSL) encryption technique. SSL is a dual-key encryption standard for communication between a server and a client and is also used by Microsoft Internet Explorer. IIS enables security control on the basis of username and password, IP address, and folder and file access controls.

IIS is newly designed for Windows Server 2008 and is broken into modules or features so that you can install only the features you need. This presents a smaller attack surface and makes IIS more efficient. Also, you can install IIS and many features in Windows Server Core as well as in the full version of Windows Server 2008. Table 8-4 shows some of the features that can be used with IIS.

Installing a Web Server

Installing and using IIS on the Internet requires the following:

- Windows Server 2008 installed on the computer to host IIS
- TCP/IP installed on the IIS host
- Access to an Internet service provider (ISP); ask the ISP for your IP address, subnet mask, and default gateway IP address
- Sufficient disk space for IIS and for Web site files (the required space depends on the number of Web files that you publish)
- A method for resolving IP addresses to computer or domain names, such as DNS and WINS

Table 8-4 Internet Information Services features (modules)

IIS features	Feature modules
Common HTTP features	Modules for publishing using common Web document environments, such as HTML, designating a default Web page, enabling directory browsing, and enabling redirection to another URL
Application development features	Modules for Web application development tools including Common Gateway Interface (CGI) scripting, Active Server Pages (ASP), Internet Server Application Programming Interface (ISAPI) extensions and filters, Server Side Includes (SSI), ASP.NET, and .NET Extensibility
Health and diagnostics features	Modules for HTTP logging, tracing, tools for Web server logs, ODBC logging for databases, and ability to create customized logging for specific needs
Security features	Modules to support multiple authentication techniques for public and private network use, including IIS Client Certificate Mapping Authentication, Client Certificate Mapping Authentication, Digest Authentication, Windows Authentication, and Basic Authentication; also includes request filtering and access limitations based on IP addresses and domain names
Performance features	Module for static content compression for content that does not change and that can be cached; also a module for dynamic content compression for content that changes—both forms of compression are intended to reduce the bandwidth load
IIS management features	Module to install the IIS Management console, IIS management scripts and tools, and management service; you can also install tools used in IIS version 6.0 (the previous version of IIS)
File Transfer Protocol (FTP) publishing features	Module to install FTP Server (for creation of an FTP site from which to upload and download files using FTP); and a module to install the FTP Management tool

Activity 8-11: Installing IIS

Time Required: Approximately 15 minutes
Objective: Learn how to install IIS.

Description: The Web Server (IIS) role is used to turn your Windows Server 2008 server into a Web site hosting server. In this activity, you use Server Manager to install the Web Server (IIS) role. (The Web Server (IIS) role should not already be installed on your server. If it is already installed, check with your instructor about removing it.)

1. Click **Start**, point to **Administrative Tools**, and click **Server Manager**.

2. Find the Roles Summary section and click **Add Roles**.

3. If you see the Before You Begin dialog box, click **Next**.

4. Click **Web Server (IIS)**. (If you are asked about enabling Windows (Process) Activation Service, click **Add Required Features**.) Click **Next**.

5. Review the information window about Web Server (IIS) and then click **Next**.

6. Review the modules that are installed by default in the Select Role Services window.

   • Record the modules checked by default.

7. Click the box for **IIS Client Certificate Mapping Authentication** and read its description on the right side of the window. This selection enables you to use digital IDs for security.

Don't worry if you think you might need more modules. You can always install them later through Server Manager.

8. Click **Next**.

9. Review your selections and click **Install**.

10. Click **Close**.

Internet Information Services (IIS) Manager

The Internet Information Services (IIS) Manager is a redesigned tool for managing IIS (see Figure 8-18). Through this tool, you can do the following:

- Connect to a Web server on your computer or remotely connect to a Web server, an application, or site.
- Have connections to multiple Web servers, applications, and sites.
- Manage a Web server.
- Manage ASP.NET.
- Manage authorization for users and for specific Web server roles.
- Manage Web server logging.
- Compress Web server files.
- Manage code modules and worker processes.
- Manage server certificates.
- Troubleshoot a Web server.

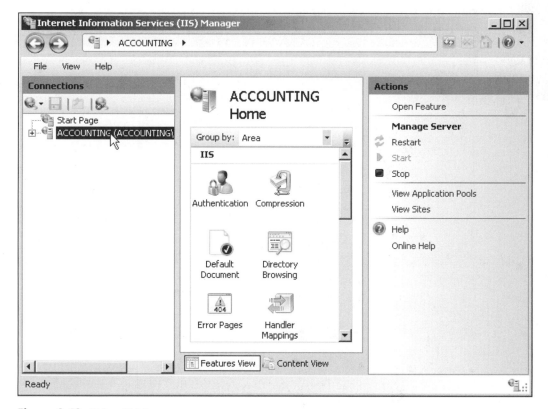

Figure 8-18 Using IIS Manager

This book is not intended to teach you how to fully implement and manage the Web Server role. However, through the use of IIS Manager in the next sections, you get a small taste of this tool and how to manage a few Web server tasks.

For more information and FAQs about IIS 7, visit: *oforums.iis.net/1069.aspx*.

Creating a Virtual Directory

A **virtual directory** is really a physical folder or a redirection to a **Uniform Resource Locator (URL)** that points to a folder, so that it can be accessed over the Internet, an intranet, or VPN. This means that the virtual folder can reside on the same computer that hosts IIS, or it can be on another computer. A URL is a special addressing format used to find, for example, particular Web locations or FTP sites.

The reason for creating a virtual directory is to provide a shortcut path to specific IIS server content. For example, one reason for creating a virtual directory is to provide an easy way for multiple users to publish on the Web site, by modifying and uploading files to the virtual directory. In an organization with many departments or divisions that manage portions of a Web site, you might create a virtual directory for each one.

When you set up a virtual directory, you give it an alias, which is a name to identify it to a Web browser. The URL format for accessing a file in a virtual directory entails providing the server name, the virtual directory alias, and the filename, such as \\Accounting\Webpub\Mypage.html. In this example, Accounting is the server name, Webpub is the alias of the virtual directory, and Mypage.html is the filename.

When you create a virtual directory, you can choose the permissions you want to apply, which are the same as permissions for a regular NTFS folder and files in the folder, as shown in Table 8-5.

Table 8-5 Virtual directory security options

Permission	Description	Applies to
Full control	Can read, add, delete, execute, and modify files plus change permissions and attributes, and take ownership	Folders and files
Modify	Can read, add, delete, execute, and modify files; cannot delete subfolders and their file contents, change permissions, or take ownership	Folders and files
Read & execute	Implies the capabilities of both List Folder Contents and Read (traverse folders, view file contents, view attributes and permissions, and execute files)	Folders and files
List folder contents	Can list (traverse) files in the folder or switch to a subfolder, view folder attributes and permissions, and execute files, but cannot view file contents	Folders only
Read	Can view file contents, view folder attributes and permissions, but cannot traverse folders or execute files	Folders and files
Write	Can create files, write data to files, append data to files, create folders, delete files (but not subfolders and their files), and modify folder and file attributes	Folders and files
Special permissions	Special permissions apply (same as for a regular folder)	Folders and files

After a virtual directory is created, you can modify its properties in IIS Manager by clicking Default Web Site in the tree under the server, right-clicking the virtual directory's alias, such as WebPub, and then clicking Edit Permissions (see Figure 8-19; also, you perform these steps in Activity 8-11). Notice in Figure 8-19 that the folder's properties are the same as those for a regular folder.

![Web DocumentsJR Properties dialog box]

Web DocumentsJR Properties	×

General | Sharing | Security | Previous Versions | Customize

Web DocumentsJR

Type:	File Folder
Location:	C:\Users\Administrator
Size:	0 bytes
Size on disk:	0 bytes
Contains:	0 Files, 0 Folders
Created:	Today, April 20, 2008, 31 minutes ago
Attributes:	☑ Read-only (Only applies to files in folder) ☐ Hidden Advanced...

OK   Cancel   Apply

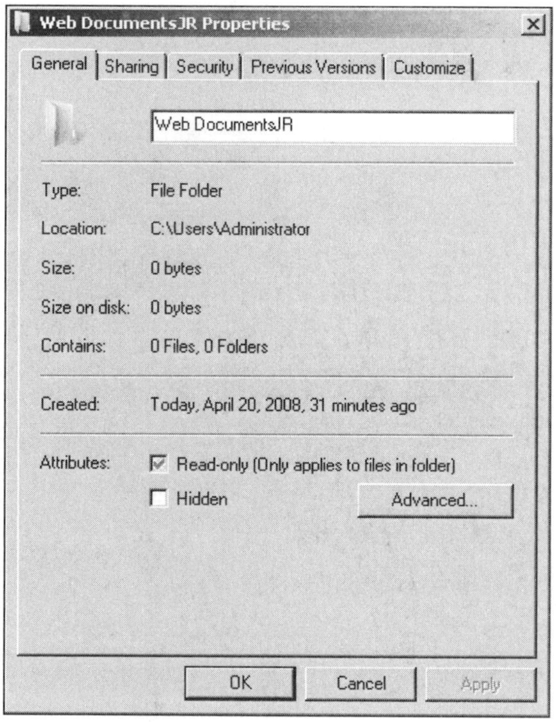

Figure 8-19 Properties of a virtual directory

You can set up the virtual directory to be shared so that users who need access to add contents to the directory can do this over the network. The share permissions are the same as those for a regular folder, as shown in Table 8-6.

Table 8-6 Virtual directory share permissions

Share permission	Description
Reader	Permits groups or users to read and execute files, but cannot add or delete files and folders and cannot modify files (same as Read)
Contributor	Enables groups and users to read, execute, and add files, but can only modify and delete files provided by them (same as Change)
Co-owner	Permits groups or users to read, execute, add, delete, and modify files, as well as create and delete subfolders and manage share permissions (same as Full Control)
Owner	Assigned to the original owner of the folder, such as the folder's creator, and enables the owner to read, execute, add, delete, and modify files in the shared folder as well as create and delete subfolders and manage the share permissions (same as Full Control)

Activity 8-12: Creating a Virtual Directory

Time Required: Approximately 10 minutes
Objective: Set up a virtual directory.

Description: In this activity, you set up a virtual directory from which to publish documents for the IIS Web server that you installed in Activity 8-11. Before you start, create a folder such as under the \inetpub\wwwroot or \Users folder under Local Disk (C:) called Web Documents with your initials at the end of the folder name, such as Web DocumentsJR.

1. Click **Start,** point to **Administrative Tools,** and click **Internet Information Services (IIS) Manager.**

2. In the tree, click the **plus sign** in front of the server name.

3. Also in the tree, click the **plus sign** in front of the **Sites** folder.

4. Right-click **Default Web Site** in the tree and click **Add Virtual Directory,** as shown in Figure 8-20.

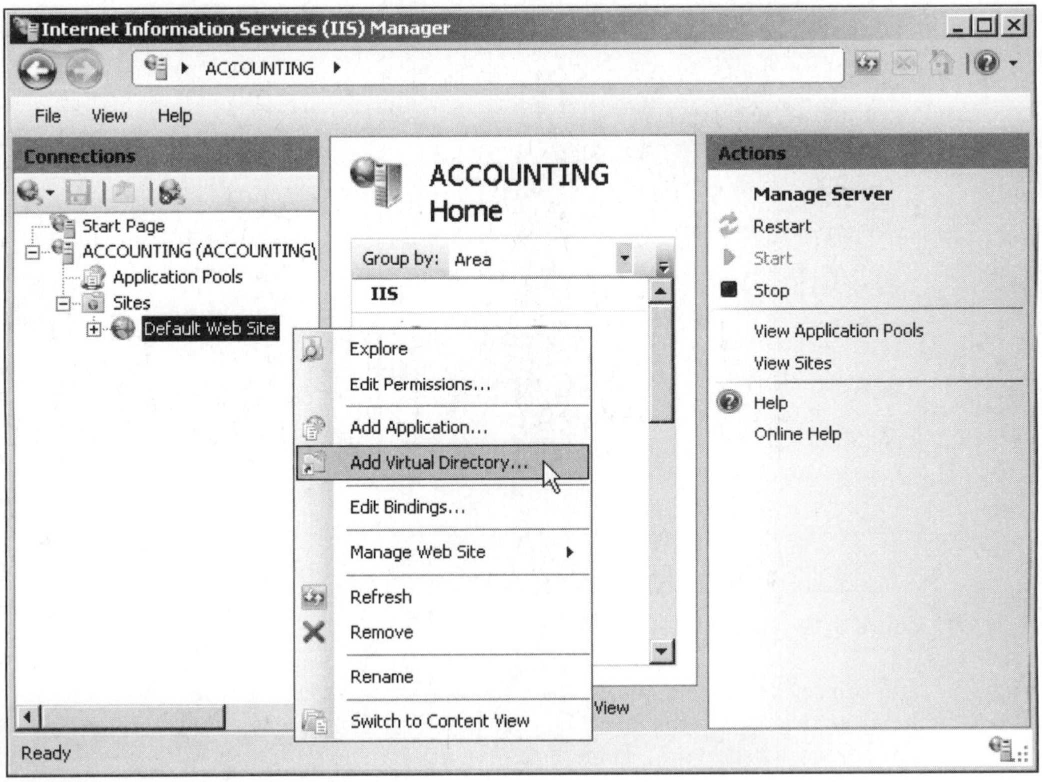

Figure 8-20 Creating a virtual directory

5. Enter an alias for the virtual directory, which users will employ to access it, such as *Webdoc* plus your initials at the end, such as *WebdocJR*. Also, enter the path to the physical folder you created before starting this assignment, such as *C:\Users\Administrator\Web Documents JR* (or use the Browse button to find it). Your entries should look similar to those in Figure 8-21. Click **OK.**

6. In the tree under Default Web Site, right-click the virtual directory you created and click **Edit Permissions.**

7. Click the **Security** tab to view the current permissions.

8. Click the **Sharing** tab.

   • How can you set up this folder for sharing?

9. Click **Cancel** in the Properties dialog box.

10. Leave the Internet Information Services (IIS) Manager window open for the next activity.

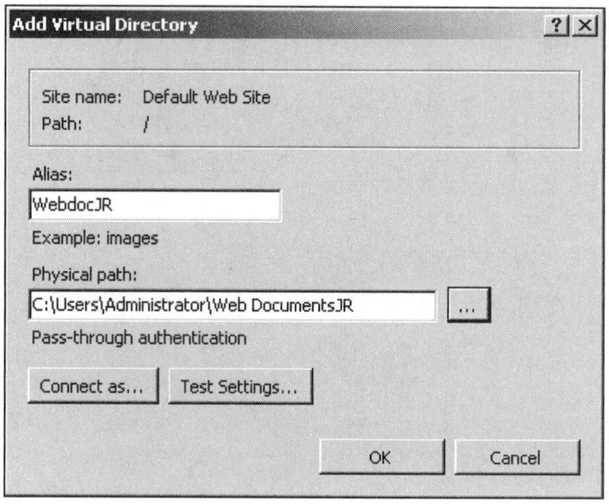

Figure 8-21   Providing the alias and path for the virtual directory

Managing and Configuring an IIS Web Server

After it is installed, you can manage a Web server using IIS Manager, described in the previous section. The Internet Information Services tool enables you to manage IIS components including the following the following:

- Application pools
- Sites
- SMTP e-mail
- Certificates

Application pools enable you to group similar Web applications into pools or groups for management, such as for common settings and for common worker processes. (A worker process is an ASP.NET process that runs on its own without using the same memory space as IIS.) Using application pools also ensures isolation between applications, so that a problem with one application does not affect another one. One application pool, called DefaultAppPool, is created automatically when you install the Web Server role. To configure this capability, click Application Pools in the tree under the server name (see Figure 8-22).

Sites is a folder used to manage multiple Web sites from one administrative Web server, and the Default Web Site, which you worked with in Activity 8-12, is automatically set up within the Web sites folder. You can choose to rename Default Web Site by right-clicking it in the tree and clicking Rename.

The SMTP E-mail Page feature is used to manage Internet e-mail via e-mail programs that take advantage of the application programming interface, system.net.mail. This feature can be used to configure the following:

- Reception of e-mail
- The SMTP Server to receive e-mail
- Authentication settings
- Storage of e-mail messages
- Other e-mail elements

Through the certificates feature, you can configure and monitor certificate security that is used with other Web sites. You can configure certificates and view certificate information including certificate names, to whom and by whom certificates are issued, and expiration date.

A Web site can be configured in many ways, but the best advice is to start by setting the basic properties and features, such as configuring performance to match the number of users, and a

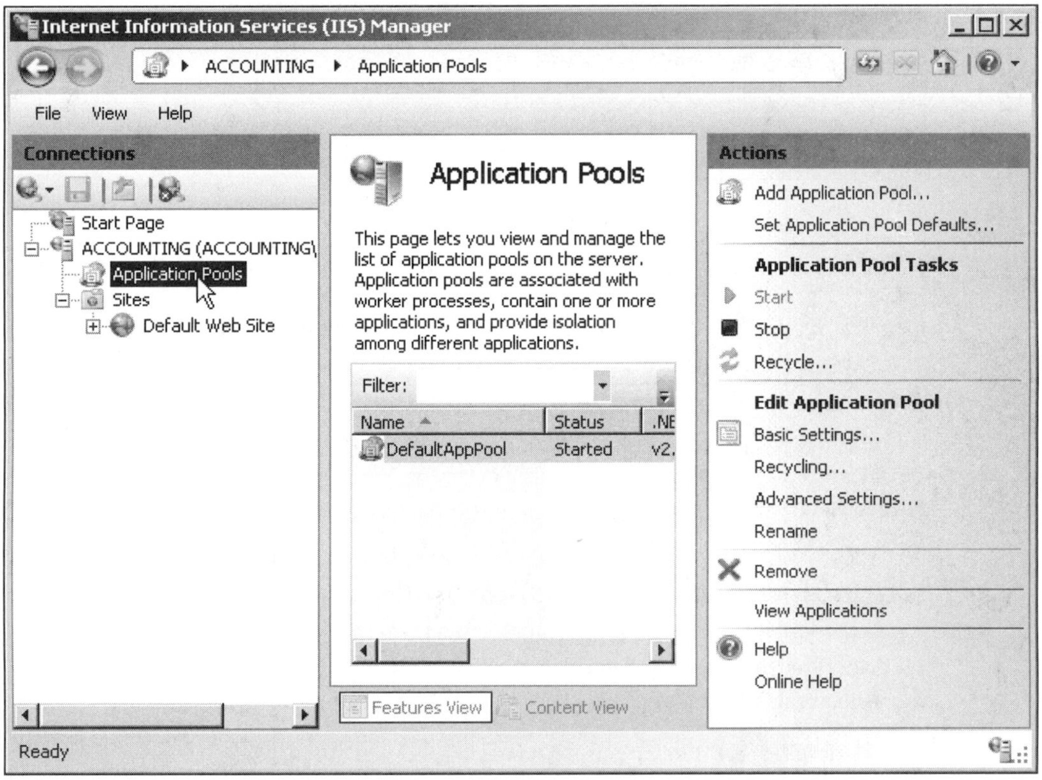

Figure 8-22   Application Pools in IIS Manger

default Web page. Table 8-7 lists many of the features you can configure through icons displayed in IIS Manager (refer to the middle pane in Figure 8-18).

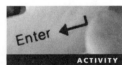

Activity 8-13: Configuring a Web Site

Time Required: Approximately 15 minutes
Objective: Learn basic Web site configuration.

Description: In this activity, you practice configuring some basic parameters for the Web site you have installed.

1. Open IIS Manager, if you have closed it.

2. Click **Default Web Site** in the tree under the Sites folder.

3. Right-click **Default Web Site** to see the shortcut menu and review its contents. Point to **Manage Web Site**.

   • How can you rename the Web site? Also, how can you restart the Web site if it is stopped?

4. Click the pointer in a blank area to close the open menus.

5. Double-click **Default Document** in the middle pane. Notice that Default.htm is set up to display first when the client connects to the Web site without specifying a file to access. Follow the instruction in the window and make iistart.htm display first. Click **iistart.htm** and click **Move Up** (click **Yes**, if prompted). Continue clicking **Move Up** to move **iistart.htm** to the top of the list.

6. Click the **back arrow** in the upper-left side of the Internet Information Services (IIS) Manager window.

Table 8-7 Web site features to configure

Feature	Purpose
Authentication	Configures the authentication required of Web clients, with anonymous authentication configured as the default
Compression	Configures dynamic content (content that changes) or static content (content that does not change) compression
Default Document	Specifies the default Web page or pages that a client views, including, for example, default.htm, default.asp, indext.htm, index.html, and iistart.htm
Directory Browsing	Specifies information displayed when listing a folder's contents
Error Pages	Sets up error messages that are displayed in a client's browser when specific errors occur while accessing the Web server
Handler Mappings	Configures the .DLL files, code files, and other files used to fulfill client requests
HTTP Response Headers	Sets an expiration date on the directory contents, to set properties of headers that are returned to the client's browser, to set content ratings (such as for content limited to adults), and to specify Multipurpose Internet Mail Extensions (MIME)
Logging	Configures IIS logging of Web site access requests, including the location of the log file
MIME Types	Configures the accepted file extensions for files that don't change (static files)
Modules	Configures modules of code used when a client requests a specific Web site action
Output Caching	Configures how the output cache is used
SSL Settings	Configures Secure Sockets Layer (SSL) options, which enables data encryption between the server and the client over the Internet

7. Double-click **Directory Browsing** in the middle pane.

8. In the right pane, click **Enable** to enable directory browsing (see Figure 8-23).

9. Click the **back arrow** in the upper-left side of the Internet Information Services (IIS) Manager window.

10. Right-click **Default Web Site** in the tree, click **Edit Permissions**, and click the **Security** tab.

11. Click **Users** (*domainname*\Users) under *Group or user names:* to view the security given to general users.

12. Click **Cancel** in the Properties dialog box.

13. In the right pane, find the Configure section and click **Limits**.

14. Enter **240** in the *Connection time-out (in seconds)* box to increase the amount of time a user can be connected without taking action.

15. Click the box for **Limit number of connections.** Enter **500** as the number for simultaneous connections so you can control the load on the server. This is a number you should monitor in the future. If the server is frequently overloaded with users and performing slowly, you can reduce this number, for example by 50 at a time, as needed. Click **OK**.

16. Close the Internet Information Services (IIS) Manager window.

Troubleshooting a Web Server

Occasionally a Web server can experience problems, such as users not being able to connect to the server. Table 8-8 lists possible problems and their solutions.

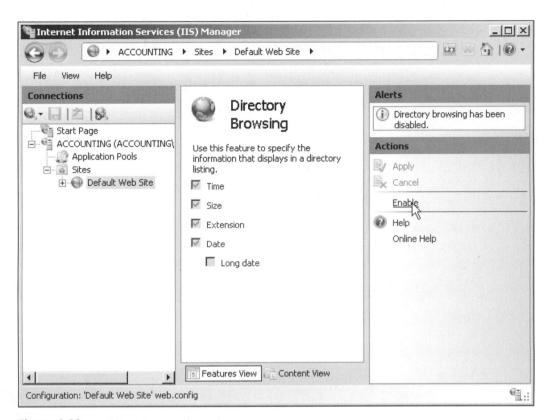

Figure 8-23 Enabling directory browsing

Table 8-8 Troubleshooting IIS

Problem	Solution
The Web server is not responding.	Use Control Panel or the network connection icon in the taskbar to make sure that the server's connection to the network or Internet is enabled.
	Use Device Manager to ensure the NIC is connected and working.
	Right-click the Web server in the tree of IIS Manager, click Manage Web Site, and click Start or Restart to start the IIS service.
	Use Server Manager or the Computer Management tool to make sure that the Server service is started and set to start automatically.
No one can access the Web server, but the server is booted and its network and Internet connections are enabled.	Make sure that the DNS server(s) is (are) connected and working on the network.
	Use a Web browser from different computers and locations to test the connection, and determine if the problem is due to a network segment location, the Internet connection, or a specific client that cannot access the server.
Clients can connect to the Web server, but cannot access its contents.	Make sure that the authentication and encryption set at the server matches the authentication and encryption properties that the client computers can support.
	Check the NTFS and share permissions on the Web server and on virtual directories to make sure that they enable the appropriate client access, such as permissions to Allow for Read & Execute.
	Make sure that no NTFS permissions on Web folders are set to Deny.
	Make sure that the \Inetpub\wwwroot folder is intact and contains all of the necessary HTML files (open IIS Manager, right-click Default Web Site, and click Explore to view the files).
	Make sure that the startup HTML file name is spelled correctly and is in the correct folder.

Chapter Summary

- DNS is used to resolve domain and computer names to IP addresses and vice versa.
- Before you install DNS, ensure that the server to house this role has a static address. (All servers and other network devices that users regularly access should have a static IP address.)
- After you install DNS as a server role, the next step is to configure forward and reverse lookup zones, as well as DNS resource records.
- When you configure Dynamic DNS, you enable automated IP address registration in a coordinated way with a DHCP server.
- Plan to set up two or more DNS servers on most networks to integrate DNS with Active Directory for DNS replication and load balancing.
- DNS enhancements in Windows Server 2008 include IPv6 support, background zone loading, and DNS on Read-Only Domain Controllers.
- For networks that use NetBIOS naming, Windows Server 2008 provides WINS for NetBIOS name and IP address lookup.
- DHCP dynamically leases IP addresses to client computers, which saves the network administrator time and helps ensure reliable IP address assignment and configuration.
- Configuring DHCP involves configuring scopes that are IP address ranges from which addresses are leased to clients.
- Windows Server 2008 includes an enhancement to DHCP that supports DHCPv6.
- To create a Windows Server 2008 Web server, implement Internet Information Services.
- Create IIS virtual directories to enable multiple users to publish information on a Web site.
- Use standard NTFS and share permissions to protect virtual directories so that only authorized users can publish in them.
- After you install a Web server, configure it to customize features such as application pools, authentication, compression, default Web pages, error pages, logging, and SSL security.

Key Terms

DNS dynamic update protocol   A protocol that enables information in a DNS server to be automatically updated in coordination with DHCP.

Dynamic DNS (DDNS)   A form of DNS that enables client computers to update DNS registration information so that this does not have to be done manually. DDNS is often used with DHCP servers to automatically register IP addresses on a DNS server.

Dynamic Host Configuration Protocol for IPv6 (DHCPv6)   A version of DHCP that can be used with IPv6 implementation on a network.

File Transfer Protocol (FTP)   Available through the TCP/IP protocol suite, FTP enables files to be transferred across a network or the Internet between computers or servers.

forward lookup zone   A DNS zone or table that maps computer names to IP addresses.

host address (A) resource record   A record in a DNS forward lookup zone that consists of a computer or domain name correlated to an IP version 4 (or 32-bit) address.

Internet Information Services (IIS)   A Microsoft Windows Server 2008 role that provides Internet Web, FTP, mail, and other services, and that is particularly offered to set up a Web server.

Internet Server Application Programming Interface (ISAPI) A group of dynamic link library (DLL) files that consists of applications and filters to enable user-customized programs to interface with IIS and to trigger particular programs, such as a specialized security check or a database lookup.

IPv6 host address (AAAA) resource record A record in a DNS forward lookup zone that consists of a computer or domain name mapped to an IP version 6 (or 128-bit) address.

Open Database Connectivity (ODBC) A set of database access rules used by Microsoft in its ODBC application programming interface for accessing databases and providing a standard doorway to database data.

pointer (PTR) resource record A record in a DNS reverse lookup zone that consists of an IP (version 4 or 6) address correlated to a computer or domain name.

primary DNS server A DNS server that is used as the main server from which to administer a zone, such as updating records in a forward lookup zone for a domain. A primary DNS server is also called the authoritative server for that zone.

reverse lookup zone A DNS server zone or table that maps IP addresses to computer or domain names.

scope A range of IP addresses that a DHCP server can lease to clients.

secondary DNS server A DNS server that is a backup to a primary DNS server and therefore is not authoritative.

Simple Mail Transfer Protocol (SMTP) An e-mail protocol used by systems having TCP/IP network communications.

stub zone A DNS zone that contains only the SOA record zone, name server (NS) records for authoritative servers, and A records for authoritative servers.

Uniform Resource Locator (URL) An addressing format used to find an Internet Web site or page.

virtual directory A URL-formatted address that provides an Internet location (virtual location) for an actual physical folder on a Web server that is used to publish Web documents.

zone A partition or subtree in a DNS server that contains specific kinds of records in a lookup table, such as a forward lookup zone that contains records in a table for looking up computer and domain names in order to find their associated IP addresses.

Review Questions

1. What step can you take when you install a DHCP server to ensure that IP addresses are only assigned by a DHCP server managed by a server administrator in your company?

    a. Certify the server as a managed container.

    b. Put a manager lock on the server.

    c. Authorize the server.

    d. Duplicate the server's key.

2. What is DHCPv6?

3. Your company has Microsoft Windows Server 2008 servers functioning as DCs. The IT Department is debating whether to use Microsoft DNS or a free open source version of DNS that one of the system programmers likes. What are some reasons for using Microsoft DNS? (Choose all that apply.)

    a. Microsoft DNS is automatically installed when you install a Windows Server 2008 server.

    b. Microsoft DNS is backed up to Microsoft's IIS Web site to enable an off-site backup.

    c. Microsoft DNS is fully compatible with Active Directory.

    d. Microsoft DNS can be replicated through Active Directory.

4. Your colleague at another company has installed DNS, but it is not mapping computer names to IP addresses. Which of the following might be the problem? (Choose all that apply.)

    a. DNS lookup zone records are not set up to update automatically, and your colleague has not manually created any records.

    b. There is no WINS-R zone.

    c. The INIT record is missing.

    d. A single zone database can hold only 100 lookup records and there are over 100 records, so DNS has locked the zone.

5. Your school has a Web site with links for each department, such as for English, Math, Biology, and so on. Each department wants to maintain its own portion of the site. Which of the following can you set up for each department to maintain its own Web files?

    a. a Web zone

    b. a Web partition

    c. a Web server for each department

    d. a virtual directory for each department

6. On a DNS server, the _____ record maps a computer name to an IPv4 address.

7. You work for an environmental consulting company in which most employees work in the field and then come back to the office for a day at a time. Consequently, the company only purchases laptop computers for its employees to accommodate their travel. When you set up the lease duration in DHCP, which of the following should you use?

    a. 24 hours

    b. 7 days

    c. 14 days

    d. 30 days

8. A Web server that handles e-mail coming in through the Internet must be compatible with the _____ Protocol.

9. You work for a nonprofit organization that still uses many Windows 98 workstations because it doesn't have the budget to upgrade computer equipment. However, the organization did receive a donation to sponsor the purchase of a new Windows Server 2008 server. What naming service should you configure to register computer names and IP addresses on the network?

    a. DNSS

    b. WINS

    c. NetBIOS

    d. NetBEUI

10. What tool is used to configure a DHCP scope?

    a. Computer Management tool

    b. Device Manager

    c. DHCP tool

    d. DNS tool

11. You are setting up a scope of addresses on a DHCP server between 138.90.10.2 through 138.90.10.99. However, you don't want to have addresses 138.90.10.7 and 138.90.10.10 in the range of addresses to assign because these addresses are currently used for Web servers. Which of the following is the best solution?

    a. Set up three separate scopes.

    b. Set up a static address zone.

    c. Use the ability to exclude specific IP addresses when you set up the scope.

    d. Don't worry because DHCP will survey existing IP addresses on network servers and automatically omit them from the scope.

12. Which of the following are DNS resource records? (Choose all that apply.)

    a. mail exchanger (MX)

    b. name server (NS)

    c. master browser (MB)

    d. service locator (SRV)

13. Name three reasons to have a secondary DNS server.

14. Your assistant reports that users cannot access the DHCP server to lease addresses. What troubleshooting measures do you take? (Choose all that apply.)

    a. Ensure that the DHCP Client and DHCP Server services are started.

    b. Make sure the DHCP server is connected to the network.

    c. Use Device Manager to restart the DHCP server.

    d. Ensure DHCP is configured with a NIC binding.

15. Your Web site contains pages of special events. You don't always remember to deactivate these Web pages and some remain available after the event has occurred. How can you prevent the display of Web pages that are no longer current?

    a. Use the IIS scheduler to deactivate these pages.

    b. Configure the HTTP response headers function to expire specific documents.

    c. Configure the Web alert feature in IIS to send you a reminder message to remove these pages.

    d. Use the IIS permission timeout setting to automatically deny the Read permission for a Web document to be effective on a specified date.

16. Which of the following can you accomplish with IIS Manager? (Choose all that apply.)

    a. manage streaming media speed

    b. manage ASP.NET

    c. manage logging of Web server activities

    d. manage server certificates

17. What are the names of DNS host records for IPv4 and IPv6?

18. You work for a university that has about 7800 students, faculty, and staff. In an IT managers meeting discussing the implementation of new Windows Server 2008 servers, one of the managers questions if this number of computer users is beyond the maximum that a single Windows Server 2008 DHCP server can handle. What is your response?

    a. This exceeds the maximum for one DHCP server by 2000 connections.

    b. This exceeds the maximum for one DHCP server by 3500 connections.

    c. This is within the capacity of a single DHCP server.

    d. This is within the capacity of a single DHCP server, but only when there are fewer than 100 scopes.

19. You have installed a DNS server and now you want to check log information to make sure it is running properly before you release the server into live production. What tool or tools can you use to access log entries? (Choose all that apply.)

    a. DNS Server Updates Log

    b. Server Manager

    c. Event Viewer

    d. Network Sharing Center

20. Users complain that when an error occurs on your Web site, confusing messages are displayed. What IIS feature enables you to address this problem?

Case Projects

D'Amico Guitars manufactures acoustic and electric guitars along with guitar equipment such as cases, strings, and tuners. They are currently moving to new facilities that offer more space for production. The added space means they will be hiring new people, installing a new network, and purchasing new Windows Server 2008 servers. The company is anticipating growth to 428 employees and there will be over 300 client computers on the new network. They also will have 12 Windows Server 2008 servers by the time the move is completed.

The company has previously sold many guitars through third-party Internet distributors and has not had its own Web site. Online sales have been phenomenal, which has led them to decide to implement their own Web site to sell guitars and guitar equipment. As they transition to the new facilities, they regard their network and particularly the proposed Web site as essential to their business strategy.

D'Amico recently lost two server administrators who were hired by other companies. The loss of these administrators means they are shorthanded on people who know server and network administration, which is why they have contacted Aspen Consulting for your help. Your assignment is to assist with the setup of crucial network services.

Case Project 8-1: Planning Network Services

The Information Services Department director asks you to develop a report explaining how to plan the implementation of Web, DNS, and DHCP services. In your report, address the following issues:

- In what order should the Web, DHCP, and DNS services be implemented? Should all of these services be implemented on one server or on different servers?

- What setup elements should be planned in advance, such as DHCP scopes and other elements?

- What security issues should be addressed in the setup of these services?

Case Project 8-2: Configuring a DNS Server

As you are demonstrating how to configure a DNS server to the new server administrators, one of them asks the following questions:

- What is the purpose of the reverse lookup zone and how is it configured?

- Can more than one DNS server be configured using Active Directory on the network, and if so, what is the advantage?

- What is the most efficient way to update DNS records?

Case Project 8-3: Troubleshooting Network Services Problems

After the network has been set up and an initial 250 users are on the network, you discover a unique problem. Each Monday morning when the users come to work at 8:00 a.m. there are delays in logging in to the network. Your analysis shows that the server housing DHCP is experiencing intense traffic at that time. What steps do you take to solve this problem?

Also, as you are considering the problem, one of the Information Services Department employees calls to let you know that the DHCP server no longer seems to be issuing IP addresses, causing error messages. What do you do to solve this problem?

Case Project 8-4: Setting Up a Web Server

The D'Amico Guitar management team is considering options for the Web server. They have asked you to write a report or create a slide show covering the following:

- What IIS features can benefit the company's plan to sell guitars and guitar equipment online?

- Is there an effective tool to manage the Web server after it is installed? If so, what are its advantages?

- Does IIS provide security to protect the Web-based assets, such as Web documents, after they are set up?

chapter 9

Configuring Remote Access Services

After reading this chapter and completing the exercises, you will be able to:

- Understand Windows Server 2008 remote access services
- Implement and manage a virtual private network
- Configure a VPN server
- Configure a dial-up remote access server
- Troubleshoot virtual private network and dial-up remote access installations
- Install and configure Terminal Services

Using a network no longer means being tied down to a desk in an office or always using your computer from the same place. Many network users telecommute from home or while on the road. If you visit an airport, coffee shop, or stay in a motel, you'll likely see people with computers who are connected to a wireless network. Students connect while in a cafeteria or library. Home users connect through a high-speed network adapter or modem. Many of these users are accessing servers at their place of business or school, either through the Internet or a dial-up connection. Windows Server 2008 makes remote access possible by offering virtual private network and dial-up networking servers.

In addition to remote access, Windows Server 2008 offers Terminal Services, which enables organizations to save money on client computers and control how users run software applications. Terminal Services can be accessed through a local network or remotely.

In this chapter, you learn to use Windows Server 2008 remote access services. You begin by learning the forms of remote access available in Windows Server 2008. You learn to install and configure a virtual private network for highly secure remote networking, and to install and use dial-up access for dial-up clients. This chapter describes a range of hardware and software troubleshooting techniques for both virtual private networks and dial-up remote networking. Finally, you learn how to install, configure, and use Terminal Services for running applications on a server.

Introduction to Remote Access

People are often on the go and expect to use networks and servers anywhere there is access to the Internet. A college recruiter who travels throughout the country wants a way to remotely connect to servers on his main campus to obtain information for prospective students and update recruiting data. A traveling sales rep who sells tools to auto repair shops needs to access the home company's server to record sales information. A commuter student wants remote access to campus computers to obtain and turn in assignments, register for classes, and view her personal student information. These are examples of how remote access capabilities can put all kinds of people in touch with their home-base networks.

Windows Server 2008 meets this need with **Routing and Remote Access Services (RRAS)**, which enable routing and remote access through two means: virtual private networking and dial-up networking. A **virtual private network (VPN)** is like a tunnel through a larger network—such as the Internet, an enterprise network, or both—that is restricted to designated member clients only.

Dial-up networking, which has been around since before the Internet, means using a telecommunications line and a modem (or other telephony device) to dial into a network or specific computers on a network. A **modem** is a modulator/demodulator that converts a transmitted digital signal to an analog signal for a telephone line. It also converts a received analog signal to a digital signal for use by a computer. Many computers come with a modem built in or as a separate card inside the computer.

A computer running Windows Server 2008 can have RRAS installed to turn it into a dial-up Remote Access Services (RAS) server capable of handling hundreds of simultaneous connections. Performing a variety of roles, Windows Server 2008 executes its normal functions as a server, but serves remote access needs at the same time.

A VPN user may remotely access the server through a network, the Internet, or a private intranet. A dial-up user uses a modem to dial another modem or bank of modems connected to a Windows Server 2008 server. Figure 9-1 illustrates a VPN connection with four VPN tunnels, two through the outside Internet connections and two through the internal network. These tunnels connect to the Windows Server 2008 combined VPN and IIS server. Figure 9-2 shows a RAS (pronounced "rass") dial-up network.

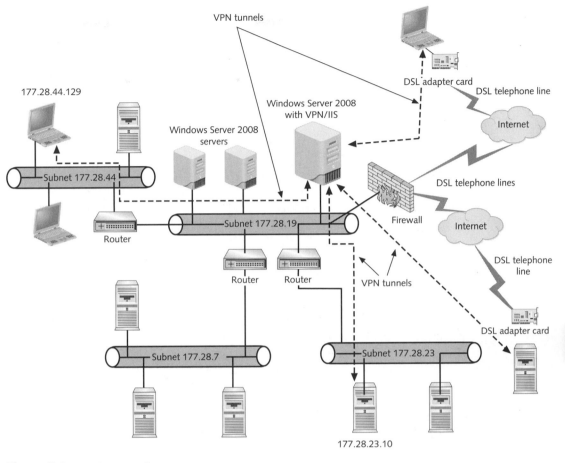

Figure 9-1 A VPN network

Implementing a Virtual Private Network

A VPN can use an Internet connection or an internal network connection as a transport medium to establish a connection with a VPN server. A VPN uses LAN protocols as well as tunneling protocols to encapsulate the data as it is sent across a public network such as the Internet. One of the benefits of using a VPN for remote access is that users can connect to a local ISP and connect through the ISP to the local network, avoiding any long-distance charges of dialing in to a server. A VPN is used to ensure that any data sent across a public network, such as the Internet, is secure. Security is achieved by having the VPN create an encrypted tunnel between the client and the RAS server.

To create this tunnel, the client first connects to the Internet by establishing a connection using a remote access protocol. Once connected to the Internet, the client establishes a second connection with the VPN server. The client and the VPN server agree on how the data will be encapsulated and encrypted across the virtual tunnel. Information can then be sent securely between the two computers because outsiders can't see into the tunnel.

Using Remote Access Protocols

The workhorse of a VPN connection is the remote access protocol because it carries the network packets over a wide area network (WAN) link. One function of the remote access protocol is to encapsulate a packet, usually TCP/IP, so that it can be transmitted from a point at one end of a WAN to another point—such as between two computers with DSL adapters connected by a telecommunications line. TCP/IP is the most commonly used transport protocol, and so it is most typically encapsulated in a remote access protocol for transport over a WAN. Two other legacy

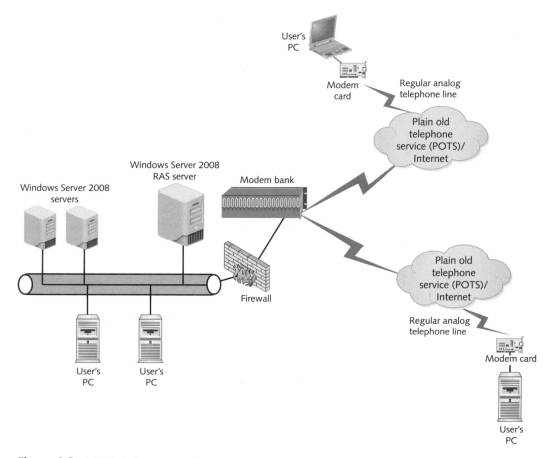

Figure 9-2   A RAS dial-up network

transport protocols that are sometimes encapsulated in a remote access protocol are IPX for legacy NetWare networks and NetBEUI for legacy Microsoft networks. Windows Server 2008 does not support IPX or NetBEUI.

 NetWare was the first commercially available server operating system offered by Novell. NetWare is widely used today and can now be combined with SUSE Linux in an integrated server environment. Recent versions of NetWare use TCP/IP by default. SUSE Linux also uses TCP/IP.

Several remote access protocols are used by Windows Server 2008 and its remote clients. For simple dial-up connections, the two main remote access protocols used are Serial Line Internet Protocol and Point-to-Point Protocol.

Serial Line Internet Protocol (SLIP) was originally designed for UNIX environments for point-to-point communications among computers, servers, and hosts using TCP/IP. SLIP is an older remote communications protocol with relatively high overhead (larger packet header and more network traffic). **Compressed Serial Line Internet Protocol (CSLIP)** is a newer version of SLIP that compresses header information in each packet sent across a remote link. CSLIP, now usually referred to as SLIP, reduces the overhead of a connection so that it is less than that of PPP, by decreasing the header size and thus increasing the speed of communications. However, the header still must be decompressed at the receiving end. The original SLIP and the newer SLIP (CSLIP) are limited in that they do not support network connection authentication to prevent someone from intercepting a communication. They also do not support automatic negotiation of the network connection through multiple network connection layers at the same time. Another disadvantage of both versions of SLIP is that they are intended only for asynchronous communications, such as through a modem-to-modem type of connection. If you are working with an older version of UNIX or Linux that uses SLIP, consider converting to PPP.

Point-to-Point Protocol (PPP) is used more commonly than either version of SLIP for remote communications because it has more capability. PPP also supports more network protocols, not only TCP/IP but also IPX and NetBEUI. It can automatically negotiate communications with several network communications layers at once, and it supports connection authentication.

When you implement a Windows Server 2008 VPN server, one of three remote access protocols are used: Point-to-Point Tunneling Protocol, Layer Two Tunneling Protocol, and Secure Socket Tunneling Protocol.

Developed by a consortium of vendors including Microsoft, **Point-to-Point Tunneling Protocol (PPTP)** offers PPP-based authentication techniques and encrypts data carried by PPTP through using Microsoft Point-to-Point Encryption. **Microsoft Point-to-Point Encryption (MPPE)** is a starting-to-ending-point encryption technique that uses special encryption keys varying in length from 40 to 128 bits.

The specification for PPTP does not include mandatory encryption. Microsoft uses its own implementation of PPTP that follows the specification, but includes MPPE encryption as well.

PPTP can transport data encapsulated in TCP/IP, IPX, or NetBEUI, which is one reason why PPTP has historically been used by Windows Server systems. Many earlier users of Windows systems used NetBEUI instead of TCP/IP because it worked well on small networks that did not have routers. The Windows Server 2008 and Windows Vista implementations of PPTP disable the use of MPPE 40- and 56-bit encryption keys through a Registry setting. This enforces the stronger 128-bit encryption. It is possible to reconfigure this Registry setting, but it is not recommended.

Layer Two Tunneling Protocol (L2TP) works similarly to PPTP. Both protocols use PPP authentication techniques and create special tunnels over a public network, such as the Internet, that reflect intranets and VPNs. Unlike PPTP, L2TP uses an additional network communications standard, called Layer Two Forwarding, that enables forwarding on the basis of MAC addressing (which is the physical address of the network interface) in addition to IP addressing. Also, L2TP uses IP Security for additional authentication and for data encryption. **IP Security (IPSec)** is a set of IP-based secure communications and encryption standards created through the Internet Engineering Task Force (IETF). IPSec is more secure in Windows Server 2008 and Windows Vista because it uses Triple Data Encryption Standard (3DES). **Data Encryption Standard (DES)** was developed by IBM and the National Security Agency in cooperation with the National Bureau of Standards (now called the National Institute of Standards and Technology) as an encryption technique using a secret key between the communicating stations. Triple DES employs three secret keys combined into one long key.

Secure Socket Tunneling Protocol (SSTP) employs PPP authentication techniques. Also, it encapsulates the data packet in the Hypertext Transfer Protocol (HTTP) used through Web communications. This gives VPN communications more versatility over all kinds of mobile connections and through firewalls. In some mobile situations the remote access network communications may be too locked down to permit PPTP or L2TP remote access, but they still allow Web access through HTTP. SSTP additionally uses a Secure Sockets Layer channel for secure communications. **Secure Sockets Layer (SSL)** is a data encryption technique employed between a server and a client, such as between a client's browser and an Internet server. SSL is a commonly used form of security for communications and transactions over the Web and can be used by all Web browsers.

PPP, PPTP, L2TP, and SSTP all support the additional remote access and VPN authentication measures described later in this chapter when you configure remote access communications. They also support synchronous and asynchronous communications, enabling connectivity through synchronous and asynchronous modems, cable modems, dial-up and high-speed leased telecommunication lines, T-carrier lines, DSL, ISDN, frame relay, and X.25 lines. See Table 9-1 for more information about these forms of connectivity.

Table 9-1 Communications technologies

Technology	Description
Asynchronous modem	A modem from which communications occur in discrete units, and in which the start of a unit is signaled by a start bit at the front, and a stop bit at the back signals the end of the unit
Cable modem	A digital modem device designed for use with the cable TV system, providing high-speed data transfer
Dial-up and high-speed **leased lines**	Telecommunications lines or bandwidth on telecommunications lines that can be leased from a telecommunications company
Digital subscriber line (DSL)	A technology that uses advanced modulation techniques on regular telephone lines for high-speed networking at speeds of up to about 52 Mbps between subscribers and a telecommunications company
Frame relay	A WAN communications technology that relies on packet switching and virtual connection techniques to transmit at rates from 56 Kbps to 45 Mbps
Integrated Services Digital Network (ISDN)	A telecommunications standard for delivering data services over digital telephone lines with a current practical limit of 1.536 Mbps and a theoretical limit of 622 Mbps
Synchronous modem	A modem that communicates using continuous bursts of data controlled by a clock signal that starts each burst
T-carrier	A dedicated leased telephone line that can be used for data communications over multiple channels for speeds of up to 400.352 Mbps
X.25	An older packet-switching protocol for connecting remote networks at speeds up to 2.048 Mbps

On the client side, PPP, PPTP, and L2TP are available in Windows 2000, Windows XP, Windows Vista, Windows 2000 Server, Windows Server 2003, and Windows Server 2008. SSTP is available in Windows Server 2008 and Windows Vista.

Configuring a VPN Server

Configuring a VPN server on a Windows Server 2008 network requires several general steps:

1. Installing the Network Policy and Access Services role
2. Configuring a Microsoft Windows Server 2008 server as a network's VPN server, including configuring the right protocols to provide VPN access to clients
3. Configuring a VPN server as a DHCP Relay Agent for TCP/IP communications
4. Configuring the VPN server properties
5. Configuring a remote access policy for security

When you configure a VPN server, Windows Server 2008 requires at least two network interfaces in the computer, one for the connection to the LAN and one for a connection to the physical VPN network.

For all of the activities in this chapter, you'll need an account with Administrator privileges. Also, these activities can be completed on a virtual server or computer, such as in Hyper-V.

Some steps in the activities in this book include bulleted questions with space for you to record your responses/answers.

Activity 9-1: Installing Network Policy and Access Services

Time Required: Approximately 10 minutes

Objective: Learn how to install Routing and Remote Access Services.

Description: VPN servers enable remote users to access a Windows Server 2008 server through using secure tunneling protocols. In this activity, you install the Network Policy and Access Services role as a first step in implementing a VPN server.

1. Click **Start**, point to **Administrative Tools**, and click **Server Manager**.

2. In the Roles Summary section, click **Add Roles**.

3. If you see the Before You Begin dialog box, click **Next**.

4. Click the check box for **Network Policy and Access Services** and click **Next**.

5. Read the introductory information in the Network Policy and Access Services window.

6. Click **Next**.

7. Click the boxes for **Network Policy Server** and **Routing and Remote Access Services**. When you click Routing and Remote Access Services, the boxes are automatically checked for **Remote Access Service** and **Routing**, as shown in Figure 9-3. Click **Next**.

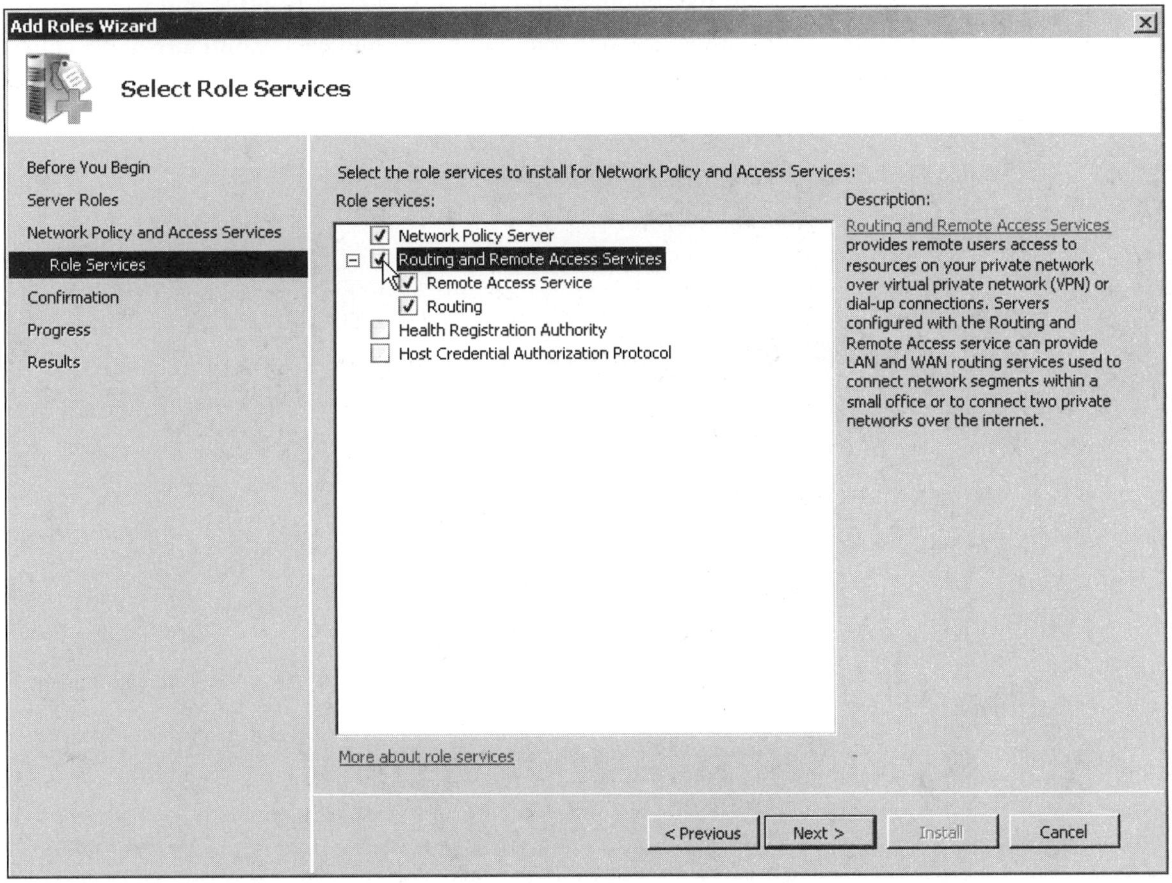

9

Add Roles Wizard   ×

Select Role Services

Before You Begin	Select the role services to install for Network Policy and Access Services:
Server Roles	Role services:
Network Policy and Access Services	☑ Network Policy Server
Role Services	⊟ ☑ Routing and Remote Access Services
Confirmation	☑ Remote Access Service
Progress	☑ Routing
Results	☐ Health Registration Authority
	☐ Host Credential Authorization Protocol

Description:

Routing and Remote Access Services provides remote users access to resources on your private network over virtual private network (VPN) or dial-up connections. Servers configured with the Routing and Remote Access service can provide LAN and WAN routing services used to connect network segments within a small office or to connect two private networks over the internet.

More about role services

[< Previous] [Next >]   [Install]   [Cancel]

Figure 9-3 Selecting the services to install

8. Click **Install**.

9. Click **Close**.

When you install the Network Policy and Access Services role in Activity 9-1, you also install two key elements needed for implementing a VPN:

- Routing and Remote Access Services
- The Routing and Remote Access tool

The next step in the process is to use the Routing and Remote Access tool to set up a VPN.

Activity 9-2: Setting Up a VPN Server

Time Required: Approximately 15 minutes
Objective: Set up a VPN server.

Description: In this activity, you configure a VPN server for remote users to access. You will need a server that has two or more network interfaces to complete this activity.

> **NOTE**
> If your computer does not have two NICs or is configured as a virtual server, install a dial-up RAS instead. You can do this by selecting Dial-up in Step 6. For a virtual server, you might see a message in Step 9 that there is no network interface. Click OK and proceed to the next step to install the dial-up server anyway. Also, see the section later in this chapter, "Configuring a Dial-Up Remote Access Server." Then do Activities 9-3 through 9-6, but with minor modifications for a dial-up RAS server.

1. Click **Start**, point to **Administrative Tools**, and click **Routing and Remote Access**.

2. Right-click the name of your server in the tree and click **Configure and Enable Routing and Remote Access**, as shown in Figure 9-4. (If you see a message that ICS is enabled, choose to disable it so that you can continue.)

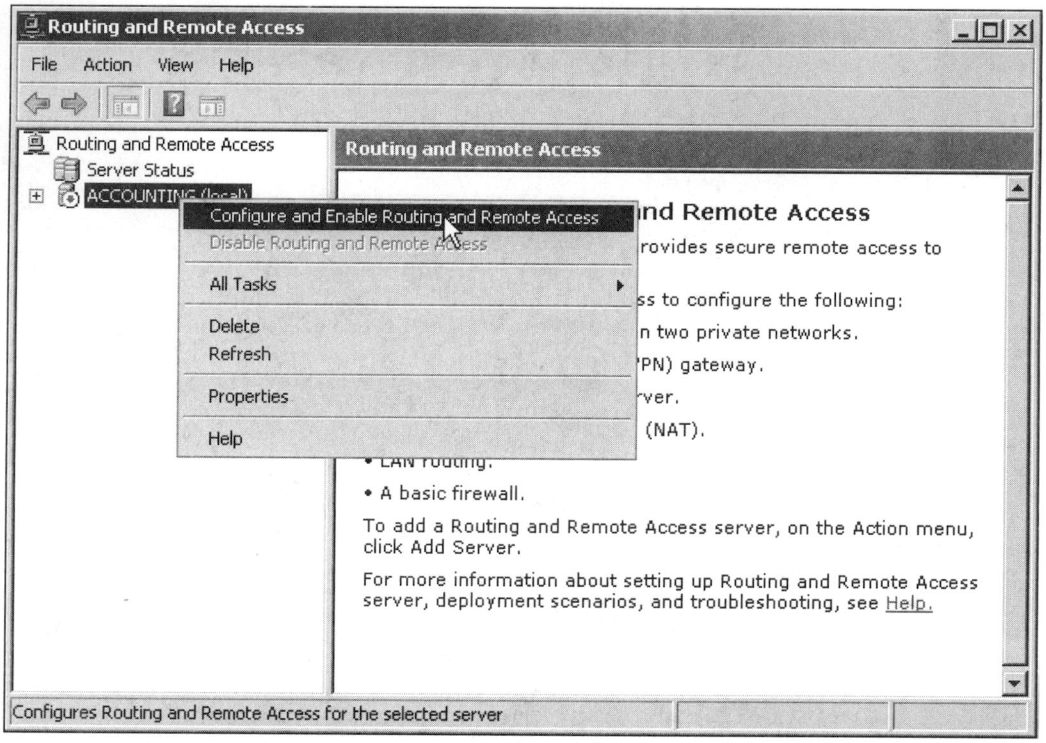

Routing and Remote Access

File   Action   View   Help

⬅ ➡ | ▦ | ? ▦

- Routing and Remote Access
  - Server Status
  - ⊞ ACCOUNTING (local)

Routing and Remote Access

Configure and Enable Routing and Remote Access
Disable Routing and Remote Access

All Tasks ▶

Delete
Refresh

Properties

Help

nd Remote Access

rovides secure remote access to

ss to configure the following:

n two private networks.

PN) gateway.

ver.

(NAT).

• LAN routing.

• A basic firewall.

To add a Routing and Remote Access server, on the Action menu, click Add Server.

For more information about setting up Routing and Remote Access server, deployment scenarios, and troubleshooting, see Help.

Configures Routing and Remote Access for the selected server

Figure 9-4   Selecting to configure and enable remote access

3. Click **Next** after the Routing and Remote Access Server Setup Wizard starts.

4. You can select from five options. Table 9-2 summarizes the available options. Click **Remote access (dial-up or VPN)** to make this a dial-up or VPN server (in this case, a VPN server), if it is not already selected.

Table 9-2 Routing and remote access options

Option	Description
Remote access (dial-up or VPN)	Use this option to set up remote access services to the network through a Windows Server 2008 server, using either dial-up modems or a VPN network connection.
Network Address Translation (NAT)	Use this option to enable Internet access by employing **Network Address Translation (NAT)**. Used by Microsoft Routing and Remote Access Services and by firewalls, NAT translates IP addresses on an internal network so that the actual IP addresses cannot be determined on the Internet, because each address is seen externally on the Internet as one or more decoy addresses. The advantages of using NAT include (1) addresses on the internal network do not have to be registered on the Internet, because they are only seen on the local internal network and (2) users on the internal network gain some measure of protection from Internet intruders.
Virtual private network (VPN) access and NAT	Use this option when you want to configure the server so that users can access it using a VPN and so that internal network VPN users take advantage of NAT.
Secure connection between two private networks	Use this option for secure communications between two servers over the Internet, such as one server at a branch location in St. Louis and another at the headquarters in Chicago (both servers must be configured with this option).
Custom configuration	Use this option when you want to customize the routing and remote access capabilities.

5. Click **Next**.

6. Click **VPN** (see Figure 9-5).

7. Click **Next**.

8. In the VPN Connection window, click the network interface to be used for the VPN connection. Also, make sure that **Enable security on the selected interface by setting up static packet filters** is selected. This option ensures that the interface is only used for the VPN, which is important for security and for the efficiency of the VPN server. Click **Next**.

9. In the IP Address Assignment window, you can specify how IP addresses are assigned to VPN clients. One option is to assign IP addresses through a DHCP server, and another option is to have the VPN server assign the IP address from a predefined pool. Ensure that **Automatically** is selected (to have the DHCP server assign IP addresses) and click **Next**.

10. The Managing Multiple Remote Access Servers dialog box offers the option to have this server work with a **Remote Authentication Dial-in User Service (RADIUS)** server. A RADIUS server is typically used on a large network. To use a RADIUS server, one must already be set up. A **RADIUS** server might be used if you plan to set up two or more RAS servers and want to standardize access policies and authentication, or if you want to use a RADIUS server's access accounting features. For this activity, click **No, use Routing and Remote Access to authenticate connection requests**. (If you were to click *Yes, set up this server to work with a RADIUS server*, then the next dialog box would request the names of the primary and alternate RADIUS servers and a shared secret —a password— to use for communications with those servers.)

11. Click **Next**.

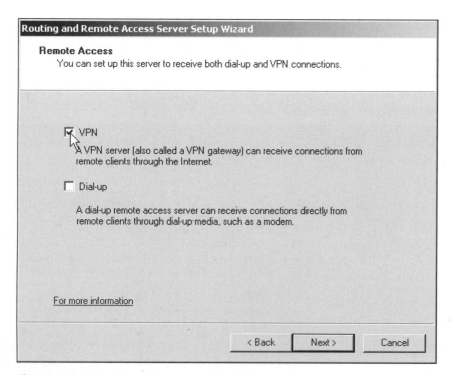

Figure 9-5 Selecting to configure a VPN

12. Review the summary of your selections and click **Finish**.

13. You are likely to see a warning message that the port for Routing and Remote Access is closed through the Windows Firewall. Several TCP and UDP ports may be affected. Click **OK** (you might have to click OK twice). To configure the firewall, click **Start** and click **Control Panel**. In the Control Panel Home View, click **Allow a program through Windows Firewall**, or in Classic View double-click **Windows Firewall** and click **Allow a program through Windows Firewall**. Ensure the **Exceptions** tab is displayed. Use the *Add port* button to add the necessary ports for the VPN protocol or protocols and services you plan to use. For example, if you are planning to use PPTP, click **Add port**. Enter **PPTP VPN port** in the Name box and enter **1723** in the Port number box. Leave **TCP** selected. Click **OK** in the Add a Port dialog box to save your change. Repeat this process to ensure all of the ports you need are opened. Table 9-3 lists the protocols/services and the ports you need to open for each one. When you are finished adding ports, click **OK** in the Windows Firewall Settings dialog box and close Control Panel.

Table 9-3 Ports to open in the Windows Firewall for a VPN

Remote access protocol or service	Port(s)	Transport protocol
PPTP	1723	TCP
L2TP	500 , 1701, and 4500 (4500 if you are using NAT)	UDP
SSTP	443	TCP
VPN	1194	TCP and UDP
DHCPv4 Relay Agent	67 and 68	UDP
DHCPv6 Relay Agent	547	UDP
Radius Server	1812	UDP

14. After you click Finish, you might also see a message box that a DHCP Relay Agent needs to be configured for networks using DHCP. You configure the DHCP Relay Agent in the next activity. Click **OK**.

15. Double-click the server in the tree in the Routing and Remote Access window to view the VPN features that can be configured or reconfigured (see Figure 9-6).

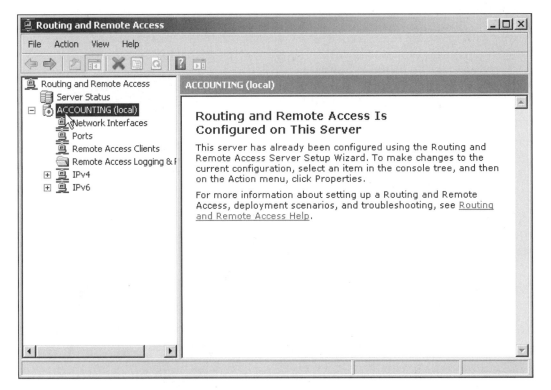

Figure 9-6 VPN configuration features

16. Leave the Routing and Remote Access window open for the next activity.

A VPN or dial-up RAS connection requires the following services: Routing and Remote Access, Remote Access Auto Connection Manager, and the Remote Access Connection Manager. Further, these services are dependent on several other services. In most cases, you will need to use Server Manager or the Computer Management tool to make sure all of the necessary services are started and set to start automatically.

The next steps in the process of setting up a VPN are to configure the DHCP Relay Agent and to configure the VPN properties.

Configuring a DHCP Relay Agent

When a VPN server is configured so that the IP addresses of clients are obtained automatically via a DHCP server, as you did in Step 9 in Activity 9-2, the VPN server must be designated as a DHCP Relay Agent. A DHCP Relay Agent broadcasts IP configuration information between the DHCP server on a network and the client acquiring an address. In basic terms:

1. The client contacts the VPN server to make a connection.

2. The VPN server, as a DHCP Relay Agent, contacts the DHCP server for an IP address for the client.

3. The DHCP server notifies the VPN server of the IP address.

4. The VPN server relays this IP address assignment to the client.

You can use the Routing and Remote Access tool to configure the VPN server as a DHCP Relay Agent.

Activity 9-3: Configuring a DHCP Relay Agent

Time Required: Approximately 5 minutes
Objective: Set up a DHCP Relay Agent.

Description: In this activity, you configure the VPN server you set up to be a DHCP Relay Agent. Because you have already set up your server as a DHCP server in Activity 8-8 in Chapter 8, you can use the IP address of your server. Or ask your instructor what address to use for the DHCP server. (If you don't know the address of your server, click Start, point to All Programs, click Accessories, click Command Prompt, type *ipconfig*, and record the IPv4 address.)

1. Open the **Routing and Remote Access** tool, if it is not still open.

2. Double-click the name of the server in the tree, if the items under the name are not displayed.

3. Double-click **IPv4** in the tree.

4. In the right pane, right-click **DHCP Relay Agent**, and click **Properties** (see Figure 9-7).

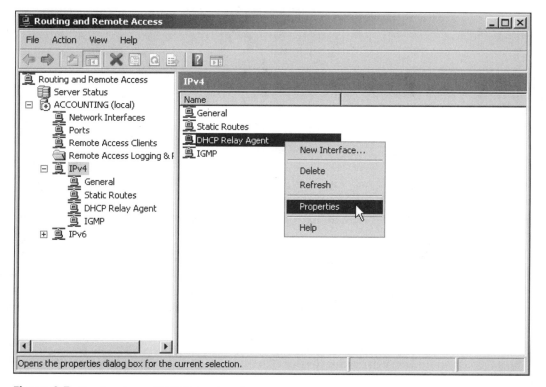

Figure 9-7   Configuring a DHCP Relay Agent

5. In the Server address box, enter the IP address of the DHCP server and click **Add**, as shown in Figure 9-8. (If the DHCP server's address has already been added automatically, you don't need to put it in.)

6. Click **OK**.

7. Leave the Routing and Remote Access tool open for the next activity.

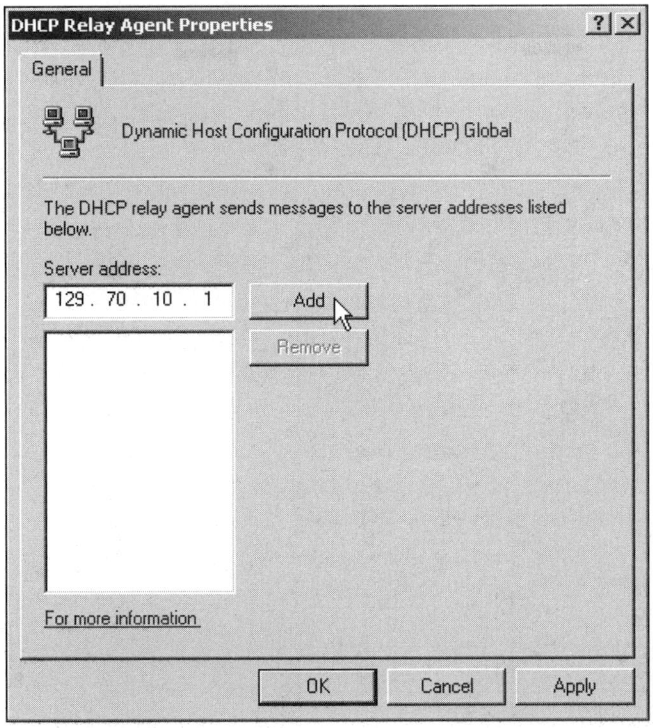

DHCP Relay Agent Properties   ? X

General

Dynamic Host Configuration Protocol (DHCP) Global

The DHCP relay agent sends messages to the server addresses listed below.

Server address:

| 129 . 70 . 10 . 1 | Add

                        Remove

For more information

                    OK   Cancel   Apply

Figure 9-8   Entering the IP address of the DHCP server

You can further configure the DHCP Relay Agent by specifying the maximum number of DHCP servers that can be reached through routers, which in this case Microsoft calls the hop count. You do this by configuring the network interface on the VPN server, such as the internal NIC.

Activity 9-4: Additional DHCP Relay Agent Configuration

Time Required: Approximately 5 minutes
Objective: Configure the DHCP Relay Agent hop count.

Description: In this activity, you configure hop count routing information for the DHCP Relay Agent.

1. Make sure the **Routing and Remote Access** tool is open and that you see DHCP Relay Agent in the tree under IPv4.

2. Click **DHCP Relay Agent** in the tree.

3. In the right pane, right-click the interface, such as **Internal**.

4. Click **Properties**.

5. Be certain that the **Relay DHCP packets** box is checked.

6. In the Hop-count threshold text box, enter **1** for this activity. Note that the maximum number you can enter is 16.

7. Set the Boot threshold (seconds) value at **4** (the default). This parameter is used to give the DHCP server on the local network time to respond (in this case, four seconds) before a DHCP server on a remote network is contacted.

8. Click **OK**, as shown in Figure 9-9.

9. Leave the Routing and Remote Access tool open for another activity.

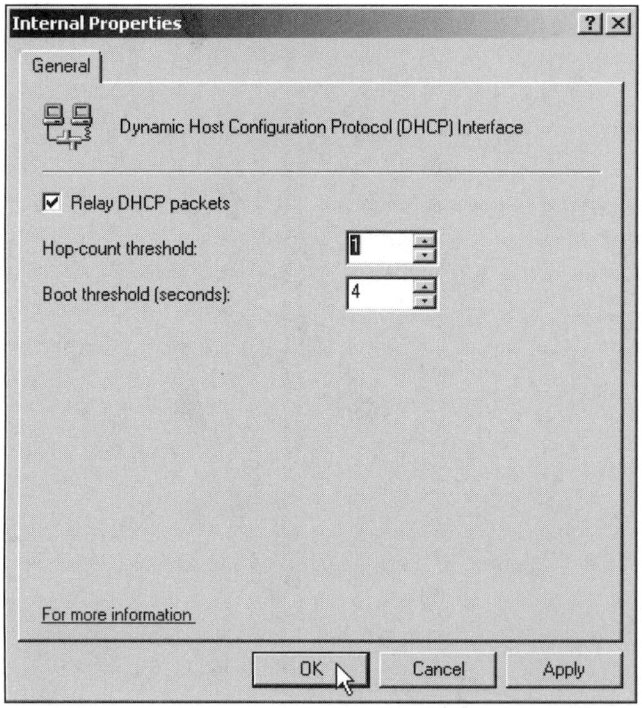

Figure 9-9   Configuring the interface properties

Configuring VPN Properties

After the VPN server is set up, you can further configure it from the Routing and Remote Access tool by right-clicking the VPN server in the tree and clicking Properties (see Figure 9-10). Table 9-4 summarizes the different property tabs available.

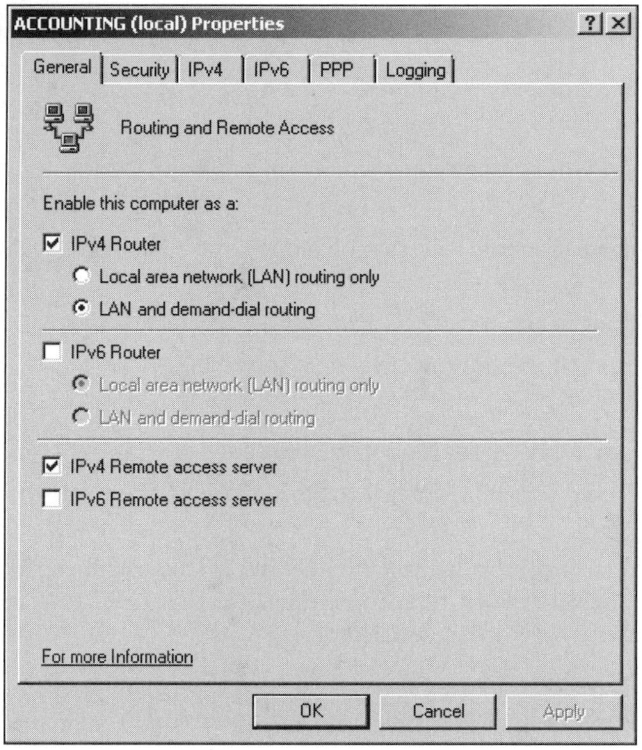

Figure 9-10   VPN server properties

Table 9-4 VPN server properties tabs

Property tab	Description
General	Allows you to enable the server as a router and/or a remote access server (by default, it is set up as an IPv4 router and remote access server)
Security	If Network Policy Server (NPS) is not installed, this tab allows you to configure an authentication provider and accounting provider (such as a RADIUS server); selecting the Authentication Methods button allows you to enable authentication protocols on the RAS server or enable unauthenticated access
IPv4	Allows you to enable IPv4 forwarding; from this tab, you can also change how IP addresses are assigned to clients using either a DHCP server or a static address pool
IPv6	Allows you to enable IPv6 forwarding and default route advertisement; also enables you to assign the IPv6 prefix
PPP	Allows you to enable PPP options such as **Multilink** or **Multilink PPP (MPPP)** connections; Multilink enables you to aggregate multiple incoming lines, such as ISDN lines into one logical connection (if Multilink is used, the lines must be aggregated at the server and at the remote connection or device)
Logging	Allows you to enable PPP logging and specify what type of events to log

The General tab in Figure 9-10 enables you to configure the server as a router. Some network and server administrators prefer to avoid using a server as a router, because handling routing can create an extra burden on the server, slowing other services. Also, generally it is better to purchase a dedicated router that is connected between the VPN server and the network, Internet, WAN, or telecommunications connection. A dedicated router has an operating system designed for routing, including a full range of routing features and sophisticated firewall protection. However, if there is no router between your server and the Internet or WAN, for example, consider using the routing option in Figure 9-10. You would do this if your server directly connects to the Internet or WAN using a DSL adapter or an ISDN terminal adapter, for instance, and has a regular NIC to connect to the local network. A **DSL adapter** is a digital communications device that links a computer (or sometimes a router) to a DSL telecommunications line; and a **terminal adapter** (**TA**), popularly called a digital modem, links a computer or a fax to an ISDN line.

Configuring Multilink and Bandwidth Allocation Protocol

A VPN or dial-up RAS server can be configured to support Multilink (also called Multilink PPP). If your VPN/RAS server has more than one connection that can be used for remote access, Multilink can be enabled to combine or aggregate two or more communications channels so they appear as one large channel. For example, Multilink can combine two 64 Kbps ISDN channels and one 16 Kbps signaling channel in the ISDN basic rate interface service to appear as one 144 Kbps channel, or multiple 64 Kbps primary rate interface channels and one 64 Kbps signaling channel are aggregated into 1.536 Mbps. Another example is combining two 56 Kbps modems into an aggregate speed of 112 Kbps. The limitation of using Multilink is that it must be implemented in the client as well as in the server, so that the client can take full advantage of the **aggregated links**. For instance, if you use Multilink to aggregate two 56 Kbps modems for one 112 Kbps link at the server, then the client, such as Windows Vista, must have a communications link set up using Multilink to aggregate the two links.

This is an older connection technology compared with DSL or wireless metropolitan area networks (also called WiMAX), for example, but in some areas it may be the only feasible remote-connection technology available. Consider a family-owned rural company that makes agricultural products for farmers and that is located next to railroad lines for shipping. They have looked into satellite communications and found the delays due to latency to be unacceptable. They use ISDN and aggregated links to achieve reliable and fast remote access communications for employees.

Some companies prefer to locate in rural areas and may not know that ISDN is available. In fact, a consultation with a telephone company sales person may indicate that ISDN is not available. However, when telephone companies upgraded a few years ago to provide call forwarding, call waiting, and other similar services, these capabilities require ISDN capable network equipment, which means ISDN is actually available. Check with your local telephone company technicians and line installers instead of non local sale agents to determine if ISDN is truly available.

On its own, Multilink cannot change the bandwidth, or drop or add a connection as needed. This is why it is often used with **Bandwidth Allocation Protocol (BAP)** to ensure that a client's connection has enough speed or bandwidth for a particular application. BAP helps ensure that the amount of bandwidth increases to the maximum needed for the aggregated channels and reciprocally contracts as the need becomes less. Links are dynamically dropped or added as needed. For example, consider a connection in which the remote client begins by accessing a relatively low-bandwidth application such as e-mail over an aggregated link of two 56 Kbps modems. BAP might determine that only 56 Kbps is needed for the application. However, when the client accesses a voice and video presentation in a multimedia application, such as a physics lesson or a movie clip, BAP can increase the bandwidth to the full aggregated speed of 112 Kbps by adding the line to the second modem for the duration of the multimedia presentation. BAP matches bandwidth utilization to the need, so that unused bandwidth can be given to another client whenever possible. Besides adding a line for use by a client, BAP can hang up a line so that another client can use it. The Windows Server 2008 version of Multilink PPP also supports **Bandwidth Allocation Control Protocol (BACP)**, which is similar to BAP, but it selects a preferred client when two or more clients vie for the same bandwidth.

To configure Multilink and BAP, right-click the VPN/RAS server in the Routing and Remote Access tool, click Properties, and then click the PPP tab (shown in the next activity). After you enable Multilink, the option to use *Link control protocol (LCP) extensions* should be selected when you want to use callback security (discussed later in this chapter). Also, select the *Software compression* option to compress data over a remote link for faster transport. This option enables the use of the Microsoft Point-to-Point Compression Protocol.

Activity 9-5: Using Multilink

Time Required: Approximately 5 minutes
Objective: Configure a VPN (or RAS) server to use Multilink.

Description: This activity enables you to configure a VPN (or RAS) server to use Multilink. (You do not need two modems or multiple ISDN terminal adapters to practice Multilink configuration.)

1. Open the Routing and Remote Access tool, if it is not already open.

2. Right-click the RAS server in the tree in the left pane.

3. Click **Properties**.

4. Click the **PPP** tab.

5. Ensure that all of the following are selected (these should be selected by default): **Multilink connections, Dynamic bandwidth control using BAP or BACP, Link control protocol (LCP) extensions,** and **Software compression** (see Figure 9-11).

6. Click **OK**.

7. Leave the Routing and Remote Access window open to perform more configuration activities.

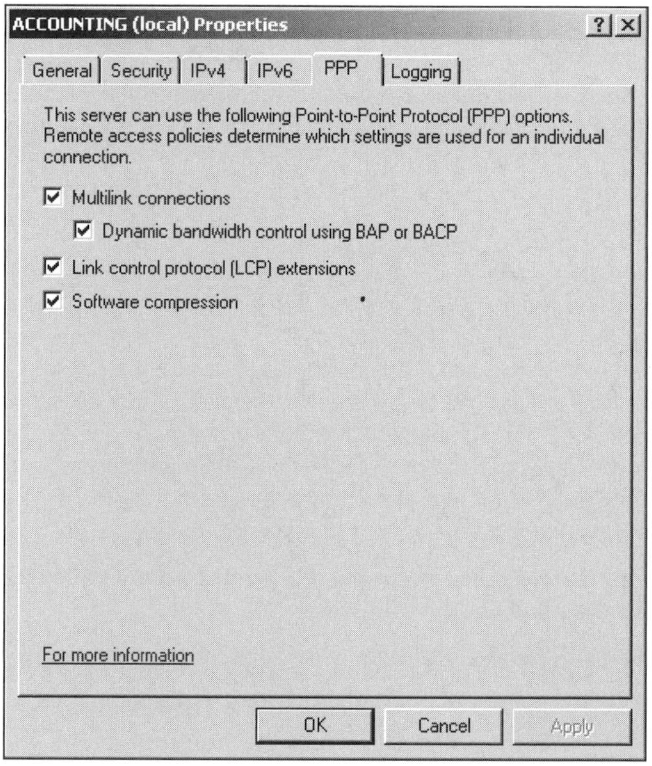

Figure 9-11 Configuring Multilink and BAP

Configuring VPN Security

When a user accesses a VPN server through his or her account, that access is protected by the account access security that already applies, such as through a group policy or the default domain security policy. For instance, if account lockout is set up in a group policy, the same account lockout settings apply when a VPN user enters her or his account name and password (see Chapter 10, "Securing Windows Server 2008" for more about security policies). In addition to the security policies already in place, you can set up VPN security through a remote access policy.

Prior to Windows 2000 Server, remote access was controlled through the properties of user accounts by enabling the Grant Dial-in permission option. One of the main problems with this is that each user account needed to be manually configured and if there were a large number of user accounts, administrative overhead was drastically increased. The Grant Dial-in permission option also did not offer much flexibility in controlling remote access. Windows Server 2008 uses a remote access policy, which greatly reduces administrative overhead and offers more flexibility and control for authorizing connection attempts.

Elements of a Remote Access Policy Once Routing and Remote Access is enabled via setting up a VPN or dial-up RAS server, a default remote access policy is created. You need to examine and change the policy to match your organization's needs. A remote access policy consists of several elements that must be evaluated before a user is granted remote access, as follows:

- Access permission
- Conditions
- Constraints
- Settings

The first step in evaluating access is to determine if access permission is enabled at the VPN (or dial-up RAS) server. The default permission for this policy is set to *Deny access*. Make sure you change the default permission to *Grant access* (see Activity 9-6).

The conditions of a remote access policy are a set of attributes that are compared with the attributes of the connection attempt. Conditions can include the vendor identification number of the network access server, for example. Each connection attempt is evaluated against the conditions of the remote access policy. The connection attempt must match all of the conditions of the policy or it will be rejected. If multiple policies are configured, the conditions of each policy are evaluated until a match is found. If no remote access policy is established, the connection attempt is rejected.

One way to manage users' access to VPN and dial-up RAS servers (you learn about dial-up RAS servers later in this chapter) is to set up only specific user accounts to grant dial-in access or to control access through the remote access policies. If you control access through the remote access policies, consider fine-tuning the management of user account access by creating groups. For example, create a universal or domain local group that has access to one or more VPN or dial-up RAS servers, and create a global group of the user accounts that you want to have the access. Make the global group a member of the universal or domain local group.

If the connection attempt matches the conditions of a remote access policy, the constraints are then evaluated. The constraints include the following:

- *Authentication methods*—The type of logon access, including access through a smart card
- *Idle Timeout*—How long a session can be idle before it is disconnected
- *Session Timeout*—Maximum time a user can be logged on during one session
- *Called Station ID*—Telephone number for the access server when a dial-up connection is used
- *Day and time restrictions*—Days of the week and times of day when the remote access server is open to users
- *NAS Port Type*—Type of connection to the remote access server

Next, the settings in the remote access policy are examined. The settings include elements such as IP filters, encryption, IP settings, and others. The IP filters setting enables you to control which IP addresses can access the VPN, for example. Encryption is for setting a common encryption method for data sent between the server and the client. IP settings govern how an IP address is assigned to a connection.

Establishing a Remote Access Policy Once Routing and Remote Access is enabled, plan to create a remote access policy. You can use the Routing and Remote Access tool (accessed via Administrative Tools or as an MMC snap-in) to create and configure a remote access policy. To create a new remote access policy, right-click the Remote Access Logging & Policies folder in the tree under the VPN or dial-up RAS server and click Launch NPS to launch the Network Policy Server tool.

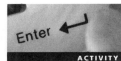

Activity 9-6: Configuring a Remote Access Policy

Time Required: Approximately 15 minutes
Objective: Configure a remote access policy.

Description: In this activity, you configure a remote access policy for the VPN server you have installed.

1. Open the Routing and Remote Access tool, if it is not already open.
2. Make sure that the tree is expanded to show the elements under the server.

3. First click and then right-click the folder for **Remote Access Logging & Policies** and click **Launch NPS**. (NPS is the Network Policy Server, which is used in Windows Server 2008 to centralize management of security and other policies for network access servers.)

4. Be sure that the **Network Policies** folder in the left pane is highlighted, or click it if it is not.

5. In the right pane, right-click **Connections to Microsoft Routing and Remote Access server** and click Properties, as shown in Figure 9-12.

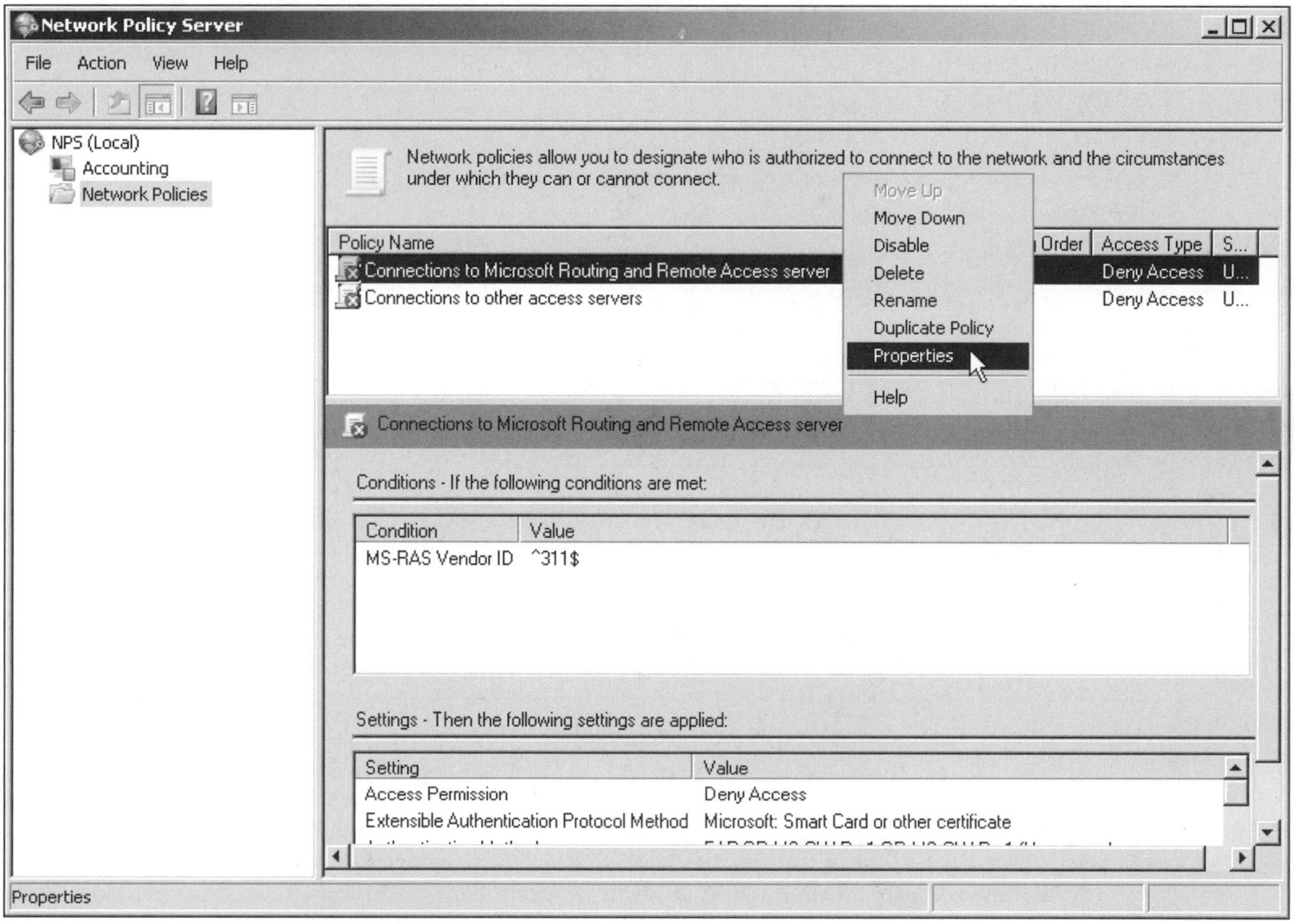

Figure 9-12 Configuring the remote access policy

6. Click the **Overview** tab, if it is not displayed. In the Access Permission section, notice that access to the VPN server is denied by default. Click **Grant access. Grant access if the connection request matches this policy.**

7. Under the Network connection method section, make sure that **Type of network access server** is selected. Click the down arrow for the box associated with this option and click **Remote Access Server (VPN-Dial up)**, as shown in Figure 9-13.

8. Click the **Constraints** tab.

9. In the left pane under Constraints, if necessary click **Authentication Methods**.

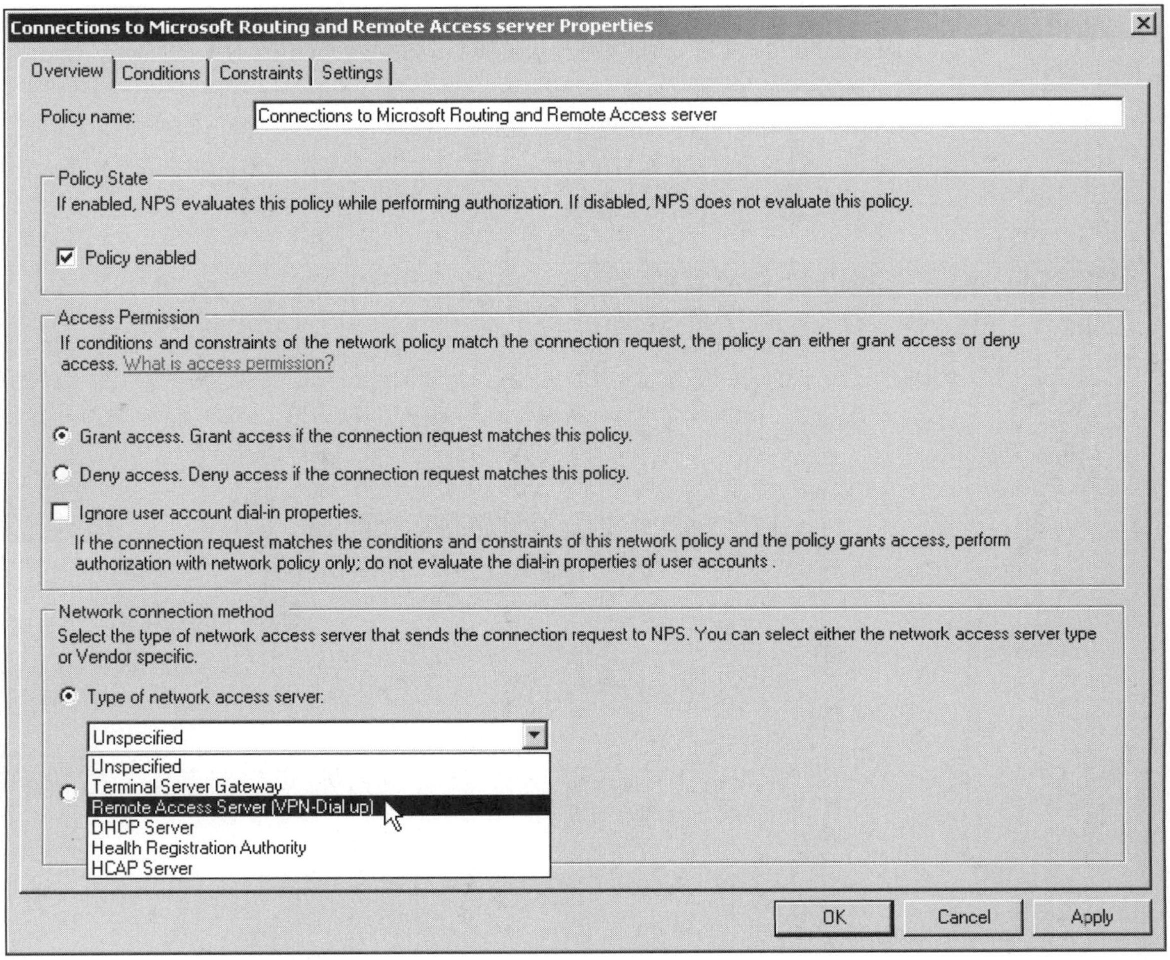

Figure 9-13 Selecting the type of network access server

10. Under *EAP Types*, notice that the default selection is *Microsoft: Smart Card or other certificate*. EAP is a strong form of authentication that is used with smart cards or certificates. A smart card is about the size of a credit card and is plugged into the computer to identify an authorized user. Also, under *Less secure authentication methods*, you can select from several authentication protocols: MS-CHAP-v2, MS-CHAP, CHAP, and PAP, SPAP. Table 9-5 describes these authentication protocols along with EAP.

    • What options are selected by default under *Less secure authentication methods*?

11. In the left pane, click **Idle Timeout**. In the right pane, click **Disconnect after the maximum idle time**. Enter **30** in the box to configure this for 30 minutes. This action disconnects users who have been idle and helps reduce the connection load on the server.

12. Click **Day and time restrictions** in the left pane. In the right pane, click **Allow access only on these days and at these times**.

13. Click the **Edit** button in the right pane. Notice that all of the times are blocked out as Permitted. Click the left most block under 12 for the Sunday row of times and drag your pointing device to block all of Sunday. Click **Denied**. Next, click the left most block for the Saturday row of times and drag the cursor to highlight the entire row. Click **Denied** (see Figure 9-14). This action secures the VPN server so that it cannot be accessed on the weekends. Click **OK**.

Table 9-5 Authentication types

Authentication protocol	Description
Challenge Handshake Authentication Protocol (CHAP)	CHAP requires encrypted authentication between the server and the client, but uses a generic form of password encryption that enables UNIX computers and other non-Microsoft operating systems to connect to a RAS server.
Extensible Authentication Protocol (EAP)	EAP is used for clients who access RAS through special devices such as smart cards, token cards, and others that use certificate authentication. If you click this option, then the Active Directory Certificate Services role should be installed so that you can configure it for a particular device or certificate type. The Active Directory Certificate Services role is installed through Server Manager.
MS-CHAP (also called CHAP with Microsoft extensions version 1)	MS-CHAP v1 and MS-CHAP v2 are set as the defaults when you install a VPN or RAS server, which means that clients must use MS-CHAP with PPP. MS-CHAP is a version of CHAP that uses a challenge-and-response form of authentication along with encryption. Windows 95, 98, NT, 2000, XP, Vista, Server 2003, and Server 2008 support MS-CHAP v1.
MS-CHAP v2 (also called CHAP with Microsoft extensions version 2)	Developed especially for VPNs, MS-CHAP v2 provides better authentication than MS-CHAP v1, because it requires the server and the client to authenticate mutually. It also provides more sophisticated encryption by using a different encryption key for receiving than for sending. Windows 2000, Windows XP, Windows Vista, Windows Server 2003, and Windows Server 2008 support MS-CHAP v2; and earlier Windows operating systems, such as Windows 98 can be updated to support this protocol. VPNs attempt to use MS-CHAP v2 with a client and then use MS-CHAP v1 if the client does not support version 2.
Password Authentication Protocol (PAP) and **Shiva PAP (SPAP)**	PAP can perform authentication, but does not require it, which means that operating systems without password encryption capabilities, such as MS-DOS, are able to connect to RAS. SPAP is a proprietary protocol used by Shiva remote access servers, such as Shiva LanRover.

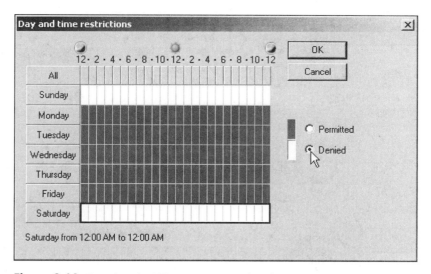

Figure 9-14 Securing the VPN server on weekends

14. Click **NAS Port Type** in the left pane. Under *Common dial-up and VPN tunnel types,* click **Virtual (VPN)**. Also, under *Common 802.1X connection tunnel types,* make the selection appropriate to your type of network. For example, a typical selection to make is *Ethernet,* for a wired network, or *Wireless – IEEE 802.11* for a wireless network.

15. Click the **Settings** tab.

   • What options can be configured via the left pane under Routing and Remote Access?

16. Click each of the settings under Routing and Remote Access in the left pane, and view their configuration options in the right pane.

17. Click **Encryption** in the left pane.

18. You can select from three forms of MPPE encryption; all of them are selected by default (see Figure 9-15). If your organization needs the strongest level of encryption and has primarily Windows XP and Windows Vista clients that support this, then remove the check marks from **Basic encryption (MPPE 40-bit)** and **Strong encryption (MPPE 56-bit)**. Table 9-6 describes the encryption options.

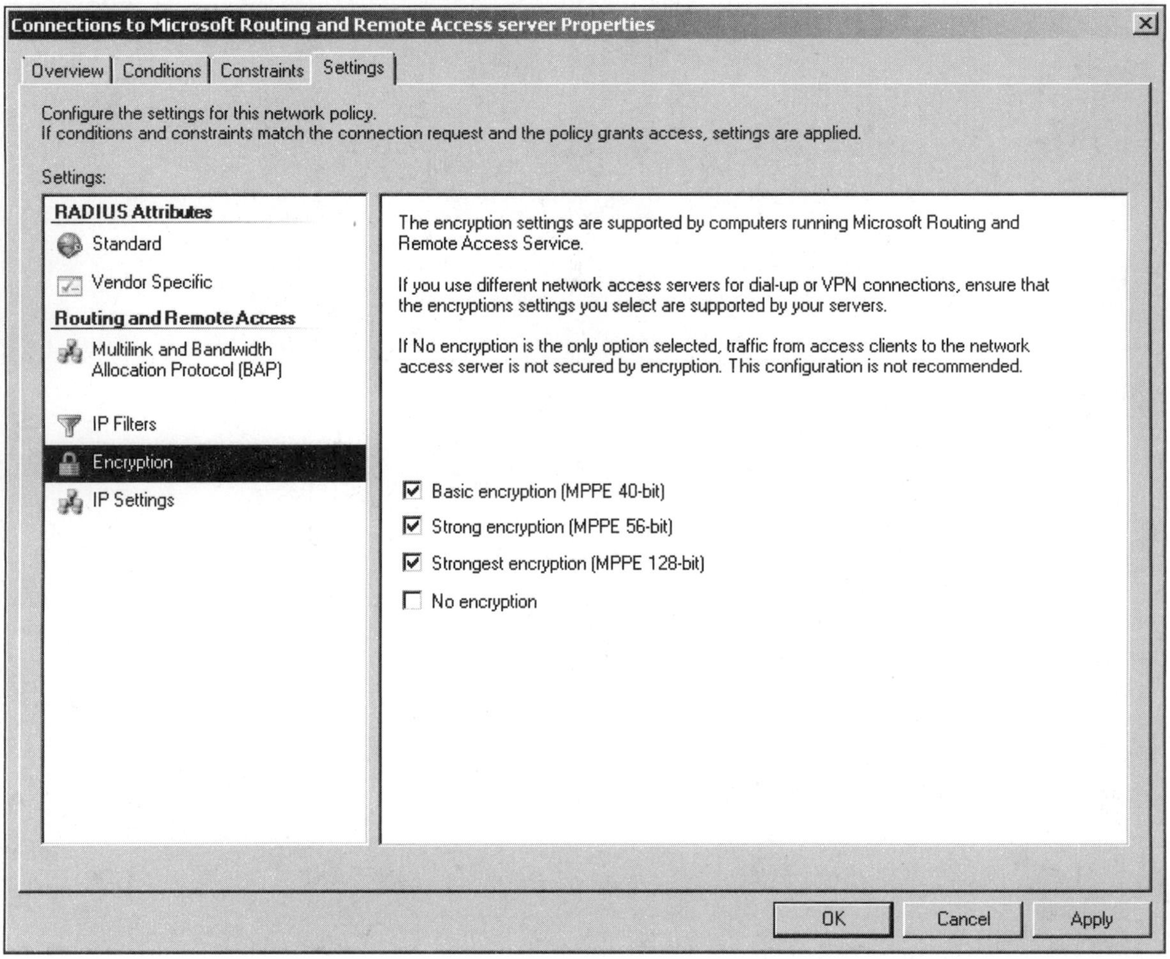

Figure 9-15 Encryption options

19. Click **OK** in the Connections to Microsoft Routing and Remote Access server Properties window to save your changes.

20. Close the Network Policy Server window.

Table 9-6 RAS encryption options

Encryption Option	Description
Basic encryption (MPPE 40 bit)	Enables clients using 40-bit encryption key MPPE (available in Windows operating systems sold throughout the world), or clients can use 56-bit IPSec or DES encryption
Strong encryption (MPPE 56 bit)	Enables clients using 56-bit encryption key MPPE, 56-bit IPSec encryption, or DES
Strongest (MPPE 128 bit)	Enables clients using 56-bit IPSec, Triple DES, or MPPE 128-bit encryption
No encryption	Enables clients to connect and not employ data encryption (not recommended)

21. Close the Routing and Remote Access window.

Steps 9 – 18 in the configuration in Activity 9-6 have traditionally been referred to by Microsoft as creating a remote access profile.

After a remote access policy is created, you can always change it by using the Network Policy Server tool, which you can access in the following ways:

- From the Routing and Remote Access tool (as in Step 3 of Activity 9-6)
- From the Administrative Tools menu
- As an MMC snap-in

Configuring a Dial-Up Remote Access Server

For many years, users have been able to connect to remote access networks through modems and modem banks via dial-up telephone lines. On a very small network, you might need to install only one or two modems directly into an existing networked computer running Windows Server 2008. For a larger network, you can install an **access server,** which is a single network device that can house multiple modems, ISDN connections, T-carrier line connections, and other types of connections. Refer back to Figure 9-2 that shows a modem bank. This illustrates an access server containing multiple modems.

Choose an access server that is designed to be compatible with Windows Server 2008. A compatible access server will include software and drivers that can be used to coordinate communications between the Windows server and the access server, including IP routing capabilities.

A dial-up remote access server is compatible with the following types of connections:

- Asynchronous modems (such as the modem you may already use in your PC)
- Synchronous modems through an access or communications server
- Null modem communications
- Regular dial-up telephone lines
- Leased telecommunication lines, such as T-carrier
- ISDN lines (and digital "modems")
- X.25 lines
- DSL lines

- Cable modem lines
- Frame relay lines

You install RAS using the Routing and Remote Access tool following steps very similar to installing a VPN server. Here are the general steps for installing a dial-up RAS server:

1. Install the Network Policy and Access Services role using Server Manager as in Activity 9-1.

2. Open the Routing and Remote Access tool from the Administrative Tools menu (or as an MMC snap-in).

3. Right-click the server in the tree in the left pane and click Configure and Enable Routing and Remote Access (refer to Figure 9-4).

4. Click Next after the Routing and Remote Access Server Setup Wizard starts.

5. Click Remote Access (dial-up or VPN), if it is not already selected. Click Next.

6. Click Dial-up (refer to Figure 9-5) and click Next.

7. If you see the window from which to select the network interface, click the interface to use for the connection and click Next.

8. Click Automatically to use IP addresses assigned by a DHCP server. Click Next.

9. If you see the Managing and Multiple Remote Access Services dialog box, select whether or not to use a RADIUS server. If you select to use a RADIUS server, you'll see another dialog box in which to provide the names of the primary and alternate RADIUS servers and a shared secret.

10. Click Finish.

11. If you see a message that Routing and Remote Access has created a default remote access policy, click OK.

12. Configure the Windows Firewall to allow remote access (see Activity 9-2, Step 13).

13. Use the Routing and Remote Access tool to create and configure a DHCP Relay Agent (see Activities 9-3 and 9-4).

14. If you are using aggregated connections, configure Multilink as in Activity 9-5.

15. Configure a remote access policy as in Activity 9-6.

You can configure a combined VPN and dial-up RAS server by clicking both boxes for VPN and Dial-up in Step 6 (refer to Figure 9-5). This enables access to the VPN through a dial-up connection.

Configuring Dial-Up Security

After you have configured the remote access policy, you can also configure dial-up security at the user account, which enables you to employ callback security. This security is set on each user's Windows Server 2008 account. With callback security set up, the server calls back the remote computer to verify its telephone number in order to discourage a hacker from trying to access the server. The callback options available in Windows Server 2008 are as follows:

- *No Callback*—The server allows access on the first call attempt.
- *Set by Caller (Routing and Remote Access Service only)*—The number used for the callback is provided by the remote computer.
- *Always Callback to*—The number to call back is already permanently entered into Windows Server 2008. (This option provides the most security.)

You can configure these and other properties for an individual account by finding the specific user account in the Active Directory Users and Computers tool, right-clicking the account, clicking Properties, and clicking the Dial-in tab (see Figure 9-16).

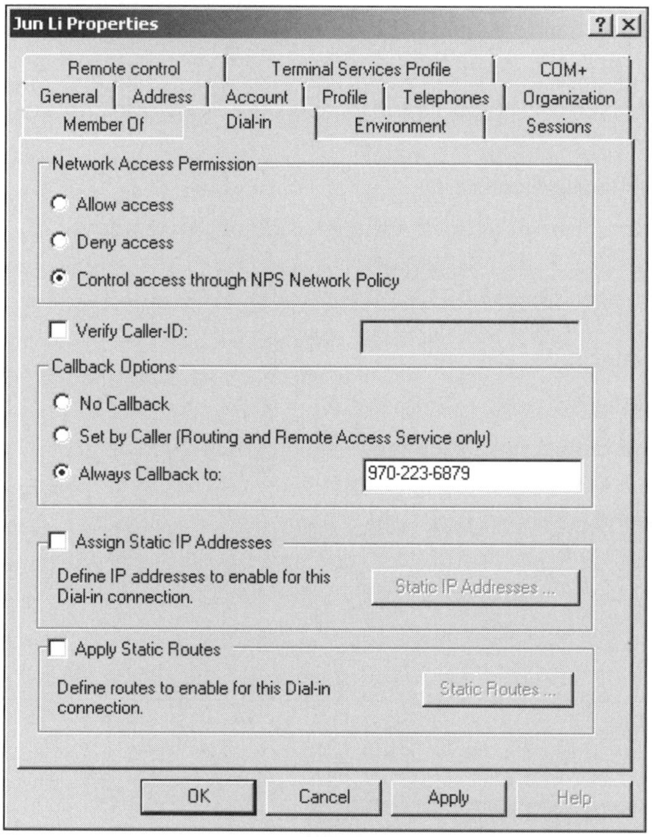

Figure 9-16   User account properties Dial-in tab

Another feature of the Dial-in tab in Figure 9-16 is the ability to control network access permission. Through this tab, you can set one of the following:

- Allow access
- Deny access
- Control access through NPS Network Policy (which is the default selection)

If you have configured a remote access policy on a VPN or dial-up server, also select *Control access through NPS Network Policy* for all users who will access the server. If you want to keep specific accounts from accessing the server at all, select *Deny access*. These represent good security practices for a VPN/dial-up server.

Configuring a Dial-Up Connection for a RAS Server

After RAS is installed and configured, and you have created a remote access policy, you might need to create one or more ways for the RAS server to connect to the network so clients can access it. In addition to the Local Area Connection that you set up when installing Windows Server 2008, you can also create other connections to match your particular connectivity needs, by configuring a dial-up connection to a private network or ISP through a phone line, for example, or by enabling clients to connect through a telecommunications line or the Internet. You can create any of these connections through the Network and Sharing Center.

Activity 9-7: Configuring a Dial-Up Network Connection

Time Required: Approximately 10 minutes

Objective: Configure a dial-up connection for a dial-up RAS server.

Description: In this activity, you configure a dial-up connection for a RAS server that is connected through a modem and telephone line.

1. Click **Start** and click **Network** (you can also open the Network and Sharing Center from Control Panel).

2. Click **Network and Sharing Center**.

3. Click **Set up a connection or network** on the left side of the window.

4. Notice the following connection setup options:

   • Connect to the Internet

   • Set up a dial-up connection

   • Connect to a workplace

5. Click **Set up a dial-up connection** (see Figure 9-17). Click **Next**.

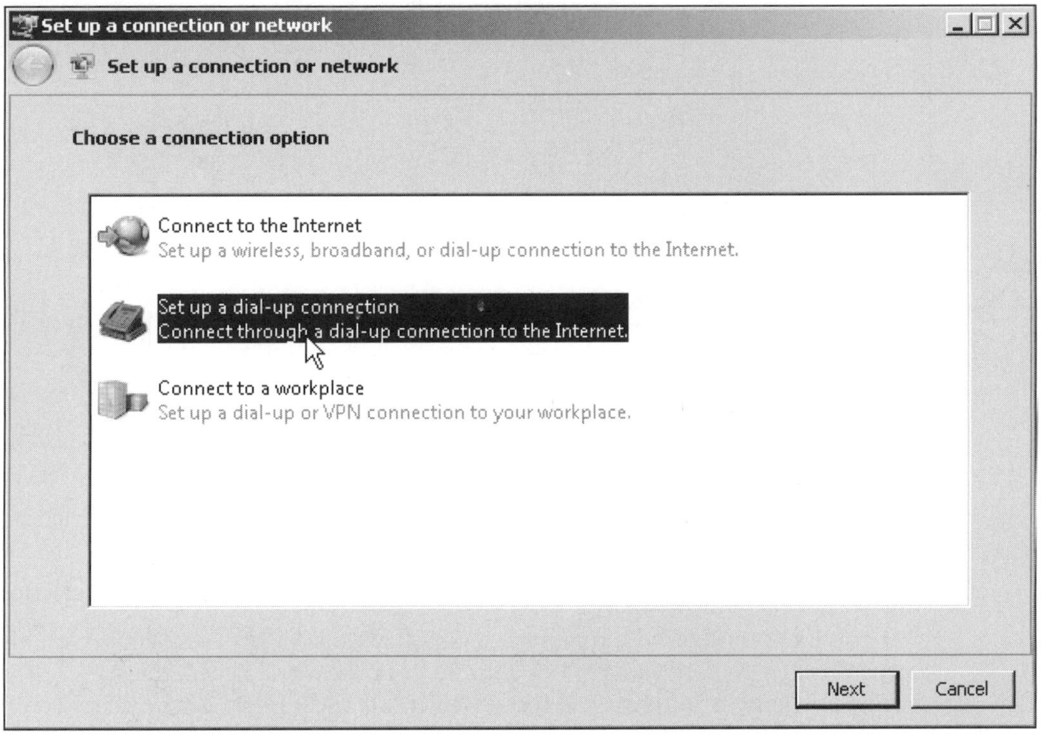

Figure 9-17 Configuring a dial-up connection

6. Type in the telephone number of the connecting ISP. Also, enter the user name for the connection and password (you can make these up for this activity).

7. Click **Connect** (or you might see **Create**).

8. Click **Cancel**.

9. Close the Network and Sharing Center window.

To use your connection, open the Network and Sharing Center, click Connect to a network, click Dial-up Connection, and click Connect.

Configuring Clients to Connect to RAS Through Dial-Up Access

Common dial-up RAS clients include Windows 98, 2000, XP, and Vista. You have already learned how to install dial-up RAS in Windows Server 2008 and how to set up a dial-up connection. To access a dial-up RAS server from other operating systems, you must configure a dial-up connection on those clients. For example, the steps for creating a dial-up connection in Windows Vista are the same as those in Activity 9-7.

For Windows XP users, use the following general steps to set up a dial-up connection as a client:

1. Click Start and click Control Panel.
2. In the Control Panel Category View, click Network and Internet Connections.
3. Click Create a connection to the network at your workplace.
4. Click Next when the New Connection Wizard starts.
5. Choose Dial-up connection. Click Next.
6. Enter the name of your company, such as JR's Company, and click Next.
7. Type the telephone number of the ISP to which to connect, and click Next.
8. Click Finish.

Troubleshooting VPN and Dial-Up RAS Installations

Troubleshooting a VPN or dial-up RAS server communications problem can be divided into hardware and software troubleshooting tips.

Hardware Solutions

If no one can connect to the VPN or dial-up RAS server, try these hardware solutions:

- Use Device Manager to make sure network adapters, WAN adapters, and modems are working properly. Also, use Device Manager to make sure that an adapter or modem has no resource conflicts (see Chapter 3, "Configuring the Windows Server 2008 Environment"). If a conflict exists, fix it immediately.
- If you are using one or more internal or external modems connected to the server, make sure the telephone line(s) is (are) connected to the modem(s) and to the wall outlet(s).
- For external modems, make sure the modem cable is properly attached, that you are using the right kind of cable (do not use a null modem cable), and that the modem has power.
- For internal modems or adapter cards (such as DSL or ISDN), make sure they have a good connection inside the computer. Reseat a card, if necessary.
- For a modem connection, test the telephone wall connection and cable by temporarily attaching a telephone to the cable instead of the modem and making a call.
- For an external DSL adapter or a combined DSL adapter and router, make sure the device is properly configured and connected, and check its monitor lights for problems. Sometimes the easiest way to troubleshoot an external DSL adapter/router is to just unplug it, wait 30 seconds, and plug it back in.
- Call your ISP to determine if problems are present on the ISP's WAN.

Software Solutions

Try the following software solutions if no one can access the VPN or dial-up RAS server:

- Use the Computer Management tool or Server Manager to make sure the Routing and Remote Access, Remote Access Auto Connection Manager, and the Remote Access Connection Manager services are started. All of these services are dependent on other services, which you might need to start first.

- Ensure that the Windows Firewall is set up to allow remote access.

- Make sure that the VPN or dial-up RAS server is enabled. To check, right-click the server in the Routing and Remote Access tool, then click Properties and make sure that the *IPv4* (or *IPv6*) *Remote access server* box is checked on the General tab (for a VPN or dial-up RAS server).

- Check the remote access policy to be sure that access permission is granted (see Activity 9-6, Step 6).

- Be certain that the VPN or dial-up RAS server is started. To check, right-click the server in the Routing and Remote Access tool, click All Tasks, and click Start or Restart.

- In the Routing and Remote Access tool, check the network interface. Under the server in the left pane, click Network Interfaces and make sure the network interface is enabled and connected. If not, right-click the interface and click Enable or Connect.

- If TCP/IP connectivity is used, make sure that the IP parameters are correctly configured to provide an address pool for either a VPN or dial-up RAS server. If IP configuration depends on DHCP, make sure that the DHCP server is working on the network and that you have configured a DHCP Relay Agent (with the correct hop-count threshold).

- If you are using a RADIUS server, make sure that it is connected and working properly and that **Internet Authentication Service (IAS)** is installed. IAS is used to establish and maintain security for RAS, Internet, and VPN dial-in access, and can be employed with RADIUS. IAS can use certificates to authenticate client access.

- Check to be sure the remote access policy is consistent with the users' access needs. For example, users may not be able to access a VPN or dial-up RAS server because the server is set to prevent access at certain times, or because certain users are not in a group that has access to the server.

If only certain clients but not all are having connection problems, try these solutions:

- Check the dial-up networking setup on the clients.

- Make sure the clients are using the same communications protocol as the server, for example PPP and PPTP, and that they are using an authentication and encryption method that is supported by the VPN or dial-up RAS server.

- Make sure that each client has a server account and that each knows the correct account name and password. Also, make sure that accounts have the necessary rights and permissions to access files and folders on the server.

- If you manage access to a VPN or dial-up RAS server by using groups, make sure that each user account that needs access is in the appropriate group.

- Make sure the client accounts have been granted dial-up access capability and have the correct callback setup.

- For a dial-up RAS connection, determine if the clients' modems are compatible with the modems on the dial-up RAS server.

Connecting Through Terminal Services

In addition to using Windows Server 2008 as a VPN or dial-up RAS server, you can also use it as a terminal server. A **terminal server** enables clients to run services and software applications on Windows Server 2008 instead of at the client, which means nearly any type of operating system can access Windows Server 2008. The Windows Server 2008 Terminal Services are used for two broad purposes: to support thin clients and to centralize program access. One of the main reasons for using a terminal server is to enable **thin clients**, such as downsized PCs that have minimal Windows-based operating systems, to access a Windows Server 2008 so that most CPU-intensive operations, such as creating a spreadsheet, are performed on the server. Some examples of thin client computers are IO's ProlEdge, Maxspeed's MaxTerm, IGEL's Compact/Winestra/Elegance series, and Wyse Technologies Thin Clients. These function similarly to a basic **terminal** that has no CPU and that accesses a mainframe computer to perform all program execution and processing on the mainframe. Thin client network implementations are generally used to save money and reduce training and support requirements. Also, they are used for portable field or hand held remote devices, such as remote hotel reservation terminals and inventory counting devices. Thin client computers typically cost hundreds of dollars less than a full-featured PC, and because the operating system is simpler it is easier to train users. Thin client field devices can be made inexpensively and tailored for a particular use, such as taking inventory in warehouses.

Another reason for using a terminal server is to centralize control of how programs are used. Some organizations need to maintain tight control over certain program applications, such as sensitive financial applications, top-secret program development, word-processed documents, and spreadsheets. For example, a network equipment company that invents a switch that is 100 times faster than any other on the market can use a terminal server to closely guard access to design documents and programs. These are stored and modified only on the server, which can be configured to provide a high level of security.

Windows Server 2008 Terminal Services not only support thin clients, but other types of client operating systems including Windows 2000, Windows XP, Windows Vista, Windows Server 2003, Windows Server 2008, UNIX, UNIX-based X-terminals, Linux, and Macintosh. Four main components enable terminal server connectivity, as shown in Table 9-7.

Table 9-7   Terminal Services components

Component	Description
Windows Server 2008 multi-user Terminal Services	These services enable multiple users to simultaneously access and run standard Windows-based applications on a Windows Server 2008 server.
Terminal server client	This client software runs on Windows 2000, Windows XP, Windows Vista, Windows Server 2003, and Windows Server 2008 to enable the client to run the Windows graphical user interface, which looks like a regular 32-bit version of Windows.
Remote Desktop Protocol (RDP)	This protocol is used for specialized network communications between the client and the server running Terminal Services. RDP follows the International Telecommunications Union (ITU) T.120 standard to enable multiple communication channels over a single line.
Terminal Services administration tools	These tools are used to manage Terminal Services.

When you install Terminal Services, you can install different role services for specific purposes. For example, the Terminal Services role service is used for accessing a terminal server over a network. Another example is the Web Access role service for accessing a terminal server through a Web browser. Table 9-8 lists the role services that can be enabled.

Table 9-8 Role services available through Terminal Services

Role service	Description
Terminal Server	Enables basic Terminal Services over a network so that clients can run applications on a terminal server
TS Web Access	Enables clients to use a Web browser to view a list of and start RemoteApp programs on the terminal server; you need to install the Web Server (IIS) role with this and the Process Activation Service (WPAS) feature
TS Licensing	Handles Terminal Services licenses needed by clients to enable access to the terminal server
TS Gateway	Enables clients to establish an encrypted connection to a terminal server through the Internet using **Hypertext Transfer Protocol Secure (HTTPS)** for added security
TS Session Broker	Used when multiple terminal servers are on a network; (1) ensures that a client is connected or reconnected to the right terminal server and (2) that clients are load balanced across the terminal servers so that one or two servers do not bear most of the load

Two of these role services are new to Windows Server 2008: TS Web Access and TS Gateway. TS Web Access replaces Remote Desktop Connection in previous versions of Terminal Services. Remote Desktop Connection requires ActiveX controls, and so Remote Desktop Connection cannot be used in organizations that prohibit downloading and using ActiveX controls for the sake of security when using Web browsers. TS Web Access does not require downloading ActiveX controls and is more flexible in running Terminal Services applications.

TS Web Access also employs RemoteApp, a new feature that enables a client to run an application without loading a remote desktop on the client computer. Previously users had two interfaces, one for the remote desktop and one that they had to access to still run programs at the local computer. The user then had to remember which desktop he was in, the one for the terminal server or the one for the local computer. RemoteApp enables the user to run a program on the terminal server without having to load the remote desktop. The program appears to be just another program in a window running on the local computer, with no switching between the remote desktop and the local desktop.

A RemoteApp program is started by clients in the following ways:

- From an icon on the client's desktop
- From the client's Start menu
- As a link on a Web site via TS Web Access
- As an .rdp (remote desktop protocol) file

TS Gateway provides a secure way to use Terminal Services over the Internet, which is vital for security conscious organizations. TS Gateway is designed to work through firewall security and works on networks that use NAT. TS Gateway uses the time-tested HTTPS, which you have probably already used if you have purchased products over the Internet using your credit card. One of the reasons for offering TS Gateway is to provide an alternative to using a VPN. Microsoft considers both TS Web Access and TS Gateway to be significant additions to Terminal Services because they make the services easier to use and more secure in a Web-based and Web browser environment already familiar to the user.

Installing Terminal Services

When you install the Terminal Services role, you also need to install the TS Licensing role service to manage the number of terminal server user licenses you have obtained from Microsoft. If you have one or more terminal servers, there must be at least one TS Licensing server. The TS Licensing role server can be installed when you install the Terminal Services role. Licenses can be purchased either per user account or by client device. The type of licensing you use depends on how users will access the Terminal Services. If users access it through the Internet, then you'll want per-user licenses. If they access it through a local network, then licensing by device is often more suitable. You can initially install the TS Licensing role without having purchased the necessary licenses, but you'll need the licenses when Terminal Services are made available to users in the production environment.

It is best if no applications are installed on the terminal server until after the Terminal Services role is installed. If applications are installed first, they might not work properly after the role is implemented.

When you install the Terminal Services role, you can choose to implement the new Network Level Authentication option. **Network Level Authentication (NLA)** enables authentication to take place before the Terminal Services connection is established, which thwarts would-be attackers. NLA is particularly designed to eliminate man-in-the-middle attacks in which an attacker redirects a client connection through his computer and then on to the terminal server, which enables the attacker to view all traffic between the client and the server. The authentication performed by NLA includes verifying the user account, the client computer, and the security credentials of the terminal server. These steps are all completed prior to starting the Terminal Services network connection between the client and server. NLA can be used by Windows Server 2008 terminal servers and by Windows Vista and Windows XP clients.

Another element to consider before you install the Terminal Services role is who will be allowed to access the terminal server. Create groups of user accounts in advance so that you can add these groups during the installation (you can add more groups later). If you are operating in an Active Directory environment, consider creating a domain local group, such as TS Users. Next, create different global groups of users, such as a global group for each department that will access the Terminal Services. Next, add the appropriate user accounts for each department's global group. Finally, add the global groups to the single domain local group (you can probably use the global groups for other types of security access as well). See Chapter 4, "Introduction to Active Directory and Account Management," to review global and domain local security groups.

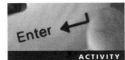

Activity 9-8: Installing Terminal Services

Time Required: Approximately 20 minutes
Objective: Learn how to install the Terminal Services role.

Description: Using Terminal Services can save a company money on client computer hardware, and it can be used for secure remote communications as an alternative to a VPN. In this activity, you install the Terminal Services role.

1. Click **Start**, point to **Administrative Tools**, and click **Server Manager**.

2. In the Roles Summary section, click **Add Roles**.

3. If you see the Before You Begin window, click **Next**.

4. Click the check box for **Terminal Services** and click **Next**.

5. Review the information about Terminal Services and click **Next**.

6. Click **Terminal Server**. If you have Active Directory loaded on this server, you'll see a warning box that having a terminal server on the same server as Active Directory Domain Services can pose a security risk and affect server performance. It is recommended that in a production environment, you should not load Terminal Services on a DC. However, for practice in this activity, click **Install Terminal Server anyway (not recommended)**.

7. Click the box for **TS Licensing**, as shown in Figure 9-18.

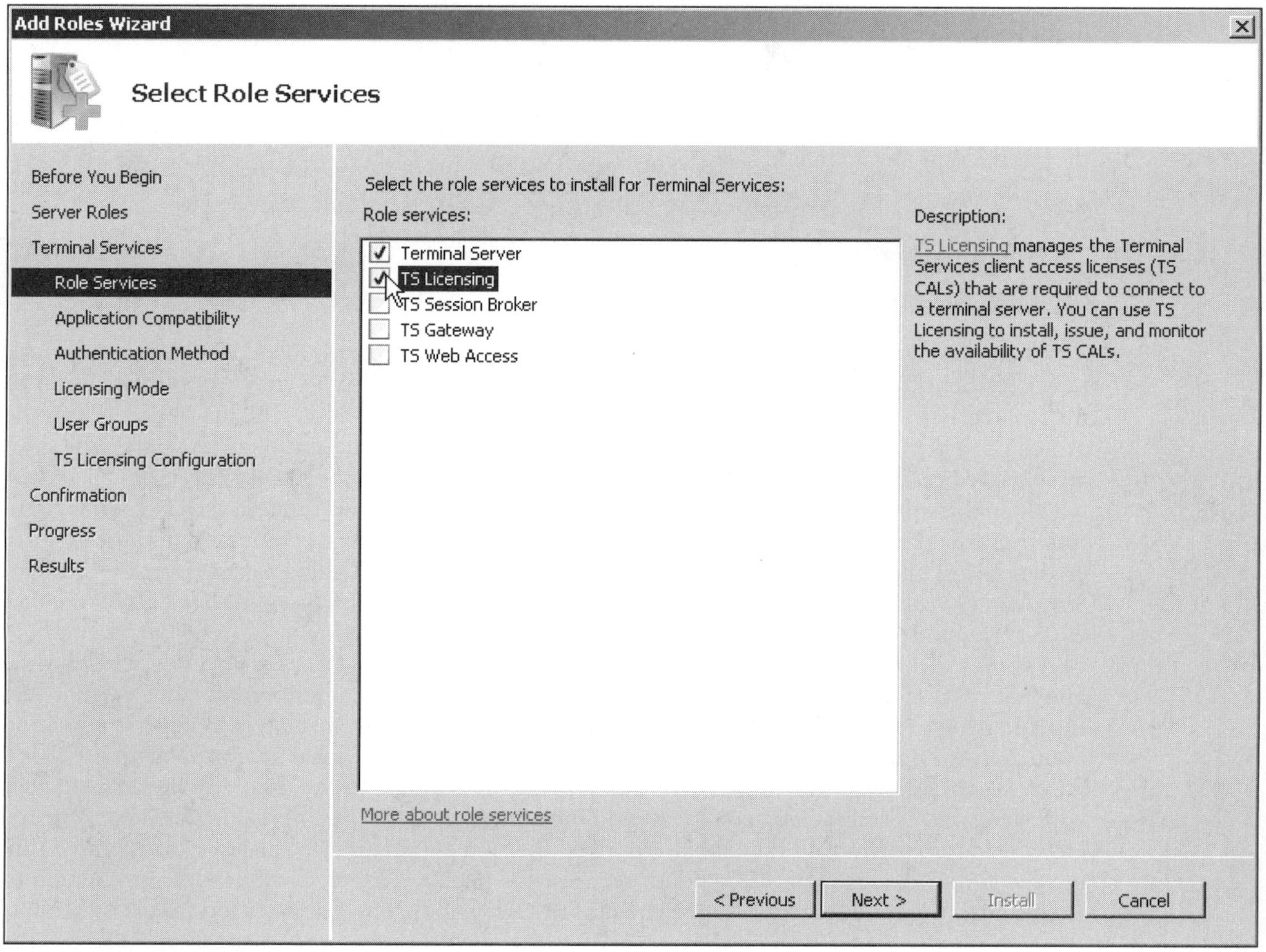

Figure 9-18 Selecting to install TS Licensing

8. Click **Next**.
   - What warning do you see about applications?

9. Click **Next**.

10. Click **Require Network Level Authentication** (assume you will have Windows Vista client computers) and click **Next**.

11. Leave **Configure later** as the licensing mode.
    - What other options can you select?

12. Click **Next**.

13. In the *Select User Groups Allowed Access To This Terminal Server* window, you can select users and groups that will have access to the terminal server. Click the **Add** button.

14. Click **Advanced** in the Select Users, Computers, or Groups dialog box and click **Find Now**. Scroll to find the domain local group that you created in Activity 4-9 of Chapter 4, such as DomainMgrsJP (see Figure 9-19). Double-click the group and click **OK** in the Select Users, Computers, or Groups dialog box.

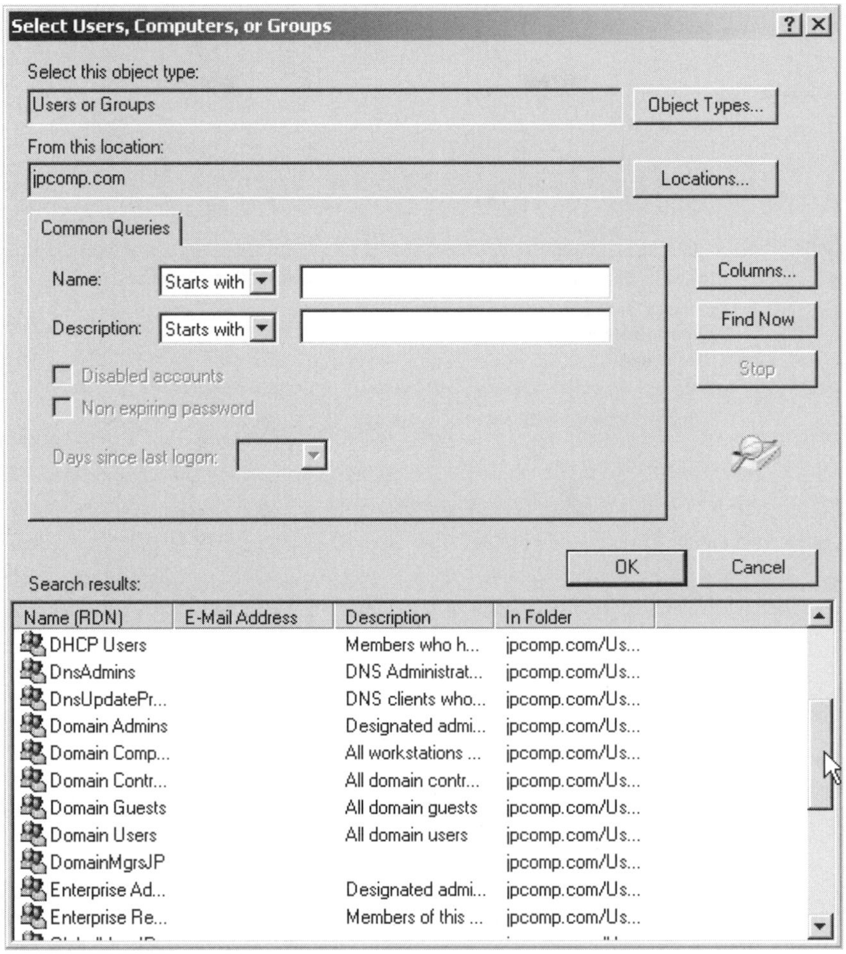

Select Users, Computers, or Groups   ? X

Select this object type:

Users or Groups   Object Types...

From this location:

jpcomp.com   Locations...

Common Queries |

Name: Starts with ▼   [   ]   Columns...

Description: Starts with ▼   [   ]   Find Now

☐ Disabled accounts   Stop

☐ Non expiring password

Days since last logon: [   ] ▼

                                        OK   Cancel

Search results:

Name (RDN)	E-Mail Address	Description	In Folder	
DHCP Users		Members who h...	jpcomp.com/Us...	
DnsAdmins		DNS Administrat...	jpcomp.com/Us...	
DnsUpdatePr...		DNS clients who...	jpcomp.com/Us...	
Domain Admins		Designated admi...	jpcomp.com/Us...	
Domain Comp...		All workstations ...	jpcomp.com/Us...	
Domain Contr...		All domain contr...	jpcomp.com/Us...	
Domain Guests		All domain guests	jpcomp.com/Us...	
Domain Users		All domain users	jpcomp.com/Us...	
DomainMgrsJP			jpcomp.com/Us...	
Enterprise Ad...		Designated admi...	jpcomp.com/Us...	
Enterprise Re...		Members of this ...	jpcomp.com/Us...	

Figure 9-19 Adding a group

15. Click **Next** in the *Select User Groups Allowed Access To This Terminal Server* window.

16. In the next window, you configure the scope of discovery for the use of TS Licensing. If Active Directory is not installed on your network, the only option will be *This workgroup*. If Active Directory is installed, the options are *This domain* and *The forest*. *This domain* means TS Licensing service will only allow licenses from the same domain as the one containing the terminal server. *The forest* means that licensed users may be from any of multiple domains in the forest. Leave **This domain** selected and click **Next**.

17. Review the information about your selections and notice that the server will need to be restarted and that it might be necessary to reinstall existing applications. Click **Install**.

18. Click **Close**.

19. Click **Yes** to restart the server (first ensure any open programs are closed and save any data).

20. After you reboot, you'll see the Resume Configuration Wizard, which means that the server is still configuring the installation of the Terminal Services role.

21. When the configuration is complete, you'll see the Installation Results window, as shown in Figure 9-20. (You might also see a message from the tray in the taskbar that Terminal Services licensing is not configured and you have 120 (or fewer) days until Terminal Services stop working. Close this warning message.)

22. Click **Close**.

23. Close Server Manager, if it is still open.

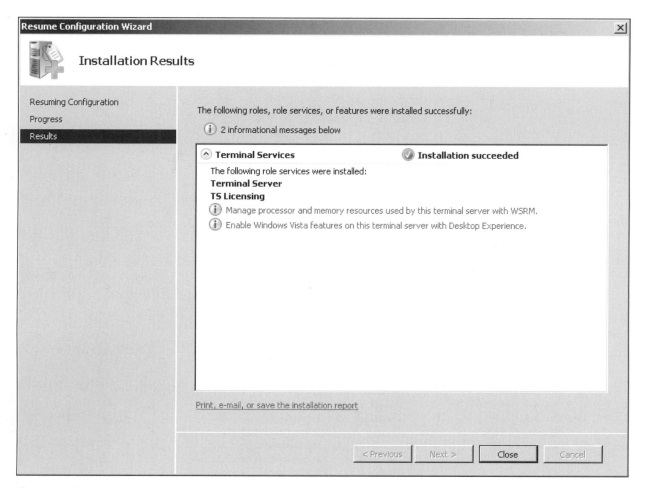

Figure 9-20   Installation Results window

After the Terminal Services are installed, five management tools are available in Windows Server 2008: Remote Desktops, Terminal Services Configuration, Terminal Services Manager, TS Licensing Manager, and TS RemoteApp Manager. Table 9-9 lists these tools, including a description of their functions and how to access them.

Table 9-9   Terminal Services management tools

Management tool	Function	Tool location
Remote Desktops	Used to manage remote desktop connections, such as adding a connection, starting a session, disconnecting from a session, changing a session, and deleting a connection	Administrative tools Terminal Services folder and as an MMC snap-in
Terminal Services Configuration	Used to configure terminal server settings and connections	Administrative tools Terminal Services folder and as an MMC snap-in
Terminal Services Manager	Used to control and monitor clients who are connected to Terminal Services on one or more servers; also monitors processes	Administrative tools Terminal Services folder and as an MMC snap-in
TS Licensing Manager	Used to administer client access licenses (CALs) for a terminal server in an enterprise or in a single domain	Administrative tools Terminal Services folder
TS RemoteApp Manager	Used to set up programs to be accessed remotely as RemoteApp programs	Administrative tools Terminal Services folder and as an MMC snap-in

Configuring Terminal Services

Begin by using the Terminal Services Configuration tool to configure the remote connection properties. Only one connection is configured for each NIC in the server, which is used to handle multiple clients.

Activity 9-9: Configuring Terminal Services

Time Required: Approximately 15 minutes
Objective: Configure a terminal server.

Description: In this activity, you configure your newly installed terminal server.

1. Click **Start,** point to **Administrative Tools,** point to **Terminal Services,** and click **Terminal Services Configuration.**

2. In the middle pane, you will see a default connection for the NIC installed in the server, such as RDP-Tcp, as shown in Figure 9-21. (If you install additional NICs later on, you can configure additional connections by clicking **Create New Connection** to start the Terminal Services Connection Wizard.)

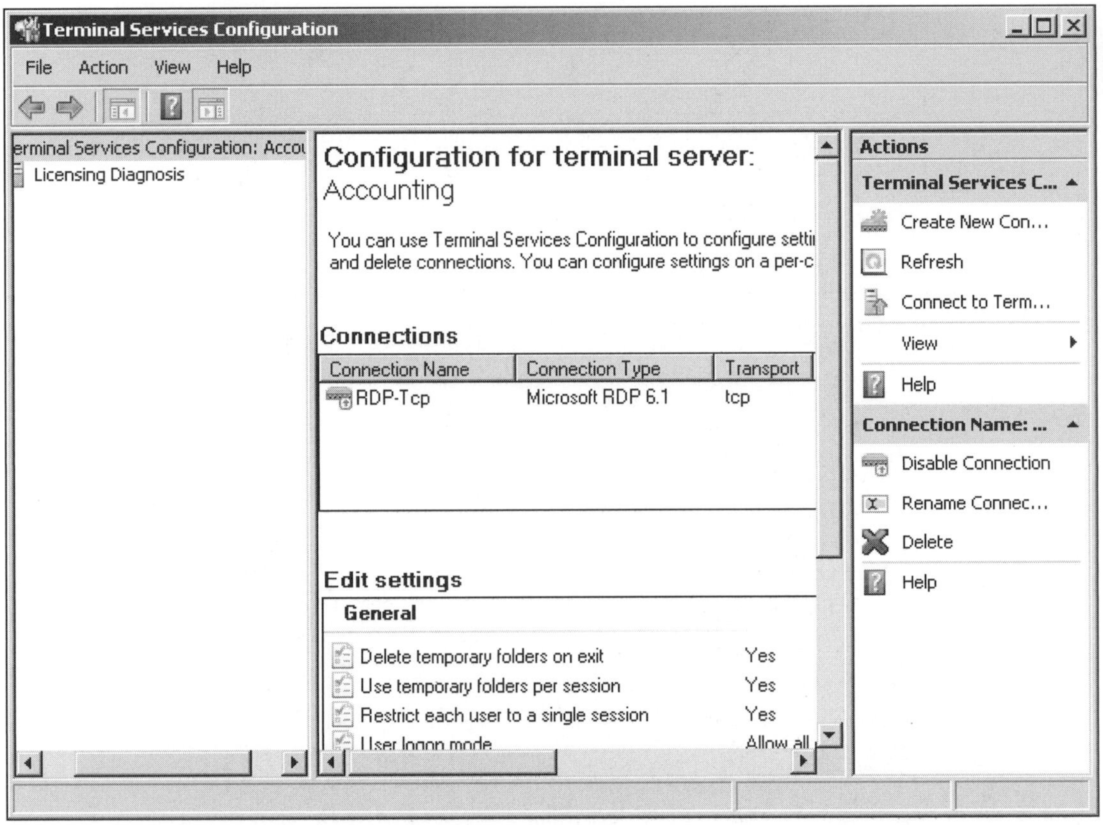

Figure 9-21 Default connection for the server

3. Right-click the connection in the middle pane, such as RDP-Tcp, and click **Properties.** You should see a dialog box similar to the one in Figure 9-22. Table 9-10 describes the properties that can be configured on each tab.

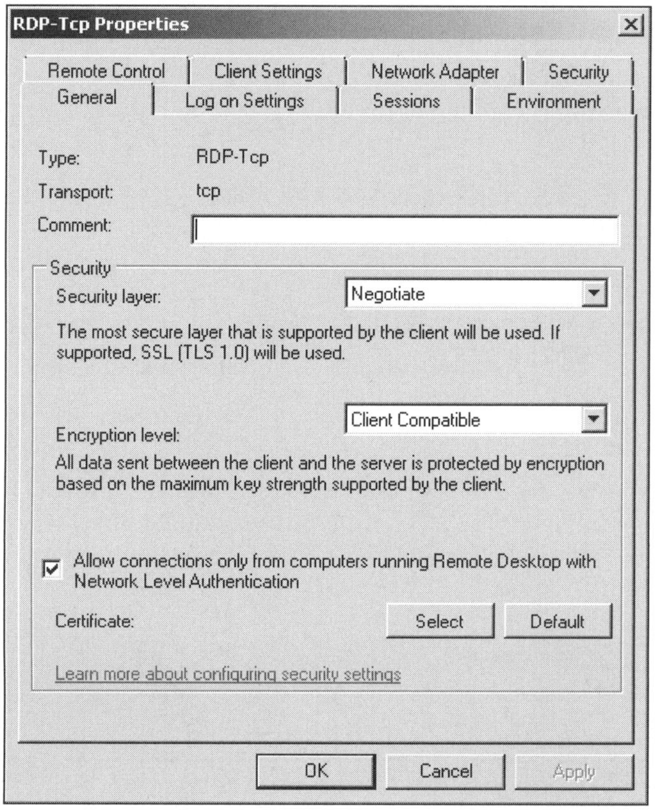

Figure 9-22 Connection properties

Table 9-10 Terminal Services connection properties

Tab	Description
Client Settings	Used to configure client connection settings such as color depth, and redirection options that include drive, Windows printer, LPT port, COM port, clipboard, audio, supported Plug and Play devices, and whether to default to the main client printer
Environment	Used to establish a program that runs automatically when the client logs on and override user profile, remote desktop, or Terminal Services client settings
General	Used to set up security (authentication) and encryption
Log on Settings	Used to determine how the client logs on, using information provided by the client or a preset logon account setup
Network Adapter	Used to specify a NIC to use and to control the number of simultaneous connections
Remote Control	Used to remotely control a client or to observe a client's session while that session is active, such as to watch the user's key and mouse strokes to help diagnose a problem without having to go to the client's site
Security	Used to set permissions for who can access the server
Sessions	Used to establish disconnect settings and how clients can reconnect to the server if a session is interrupted

4. Right after you have installed Terminal Services, make sure you examine the existing permissions and make any changes that are needed for your organization. Click the **Security** tab. You should see a message box to alert you to using the Remote Desktop Users group on which to set permissions. It is a good idea to use this default group for consistent security administration. Click **OK** (if you see the box). Table 9-11 lists the permissions used for Terminal Services.

   • What are the default permissions set up for each group on the Security tab?

Table 9-11 Terminal Services permissions

Permission	Description
Full control	Enables access that includes query, set information, remote control, logon, log-off, message, connect, disconnect, and virtual channel use
User access	Enables access to query, connect, and logon
Guest access	Enables access to logon
Special permissions	Indicates if any special permissions have been configured and is deactivated by default

5. Another set of properties that should be checked are security and encryption. Click the **General** tab to check these properties. Security is set by default to *Negotiate* so that the highest level of security that is supported by the client is used. You can also use SSL security and Remote Desktop Protocol (RDP) security, which is less secure and native to Terminal Services. RDP cannot be used if you set authentication to NLA when you installed the Terminal Services role. Also, click the **down arrow** in the **Encryption level** box to view the following options:

   • *Low*—No encryption is used for data sent from the server and 56-bit encryption is used from data sent via the client, which is used for older Windows client operating systems, such as Windows 98.

   • *Client Compatible*—Data sent from the client to the server and from the server to the client is encrypted using the highest encryption level that the client can employ.

   • *High*—Data sent from the client to the server and from the server to the client is encrypted using 128-bit encryption. Only clients that support this encryption level are permitted to connect.

   • *FIPS Compliant*—Data sent from the client to the server and from the server to the client is encrypted using the Federal Information Process Standard (FIPS) 140-1.

NOTE You can also select to *Allow connections only from computers running Remote Desktop with Network Level Authentication.* This box is checked because in Step 10 of Activity 9-8 you selected to *Require Network Level Authentication.*

6. Click each of the tabs you have not yet viewed to see their contents.

7. Click **OK** when you are finished examining the tabs.

8. Close the Terminal Services Configuration window.

Managing Terminal Services

The Terminal Services Manager enables you to manage user connections and other features of the terminal server. With this tool, you can do the following:

- Monitor the number of users connected to the terminal server.
- Add additional terminal servers to monitor (or remove servers).
- Determine if a user session is active.
- Determine which programs are running in a user's session.
- Disconnect a user's session or log off a user.
- Reset a connection that is having trouble.
- Send a message to a user.

After you make the terminal server available to users, you will often use the Terminal Services Manager tool. Consider using the tool to monitor the number of users at different times of day so you gain an idea of how busy the server is at those times and who is logged on. This enables you to establish a rough baseline to determine what is normal for your server. If use of the server grows, you'll have an idea of by how much and if you need to upgrade the hardware or add another network interface to accommodate the growth. Also, by getting an idea of who is normally logged on, you can quickly identify an intruder or if a particular user is having problems connecting. If a user's session is hung, you can disconnect it so the user can have a fresh start.

Activity 9-10: Using Terminal Services Manager

Time Required: Approximately 10 minutes
Objective: Use Terminal Services Manager.

Description: In this activity, you explore the capabilities of the Terminal Services Manager.

1. Click **Start**, point to **Administrative Tools**, point to **Terminal Services**, and click **Terminal Services Manager**.

2. If you see an informational message that certain features only run from a Terminal Services client session, click **OK**.

3. The middle pane shows a listing of the users who are currently logged on. You'll see a connection for the Administrator, which is your connection (see Figure 9-23).

4. Click the **Processes** tab in the middle pane to view the processes/programs in use. Look under the User column to see the processes in use by the Administrator account (or by your account name with Administrator privileges).

5. Click the **Users** tab.

6. Right-click the account listed, such as Administrator.

7. Click **Send Message** (an option you can use to send a message to a connected user).

8. In the Send Message dialog box, enter the practice message: **Please log off. This server will go down in 15 minutes for repairs.** Click **OK**.

9. You should see a message box containing the message you sent. Click **OK** in the message box.

10. Ensure the account in the middle pane is highlighted, or click it if it is not. In the right pane, notice that you can also send a message by clicking the Send Message option.

    - What are two ways to disconnect or log off a user?

11. Close the Terminal Services Manager window.

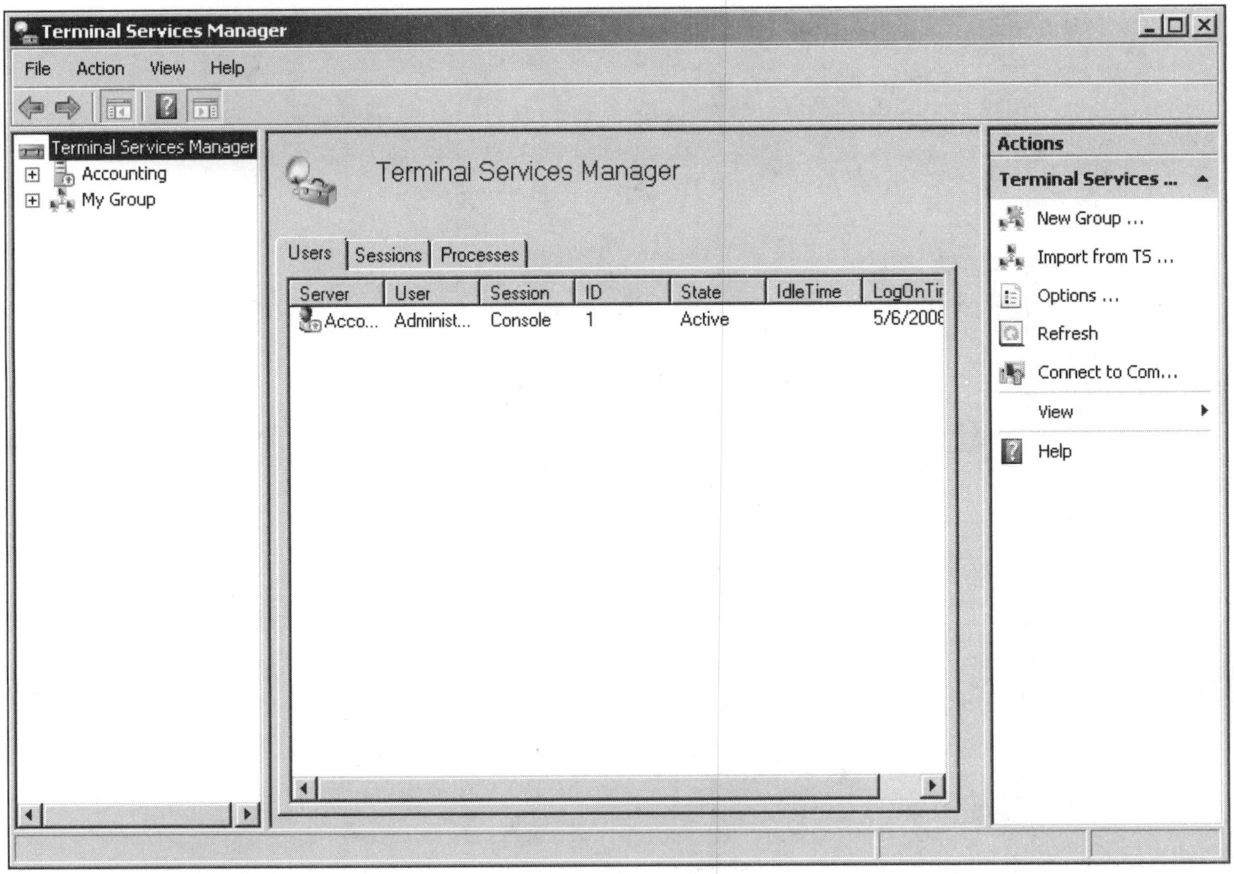

Figure 9-23 Terminal Services Manager

Configuring Licensing

When you set up a terminal server, you must activate the Terminal Services licensing server and configure the licensing by using the TS Licensing Manager that you installed in Activity 9-8. Also, until you configure licensing, you'll see a frequent reminder message from the tray in the right side of the taskbar.

Activity 9-11: Using the TS Licensing Manager

Time Required: Approximately 10 minutes
Objective: Use TS Licensing Manager.

Description: In this activity, you explore the TS Licensing Manager.

1. Click **Start,** point to **Administrative Tools,** point to **Terminal Services,** and click **TS Licensing Manager.**

2. Right-click the server in the right pane and click **Activate Server,** as shown in Figure 9-24.

3. When the Activate Server Wizard starts, click **Next.**

4. Click the **down arrow** for the **Connection method** box to view the options.

   • Record the connection method options.

5. Leave the recommended option as the one selected and click **Next.**

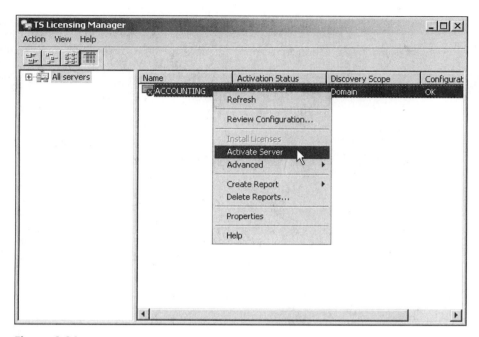

Figure 9-24 Activating a server

6. Enter your first and last name in the Company Information dialog box. Also enter your first initial and last name for the company. Enter the country or region and click Next.

7. Leave the optional information blank for this activity and click **Next**.

8. At this point, if you had licenses to install you could continue with the wizard to install them. Because you have no licenses to install now, remove the check mark from **Start Install Licenses Wizard now**. Click **Finish**.

9. Click the cursor on a blank area so that the server in the right pane is no longer highlighted. Notice that the server is activated.

10. Close the TS Licensing Manager window.

If users are unable to connect to the server, check to make sure that you have activated the server using the TS Licensing Manager.

Accessing a Terminal Server from a Client

Terminal Services client computers can log on using the **Remote Desktop Connection (RDC)** client. The RDC client is already installed in Windows Vista, Windows Server 2008, and Windows XP operating systems. In Windows XP clients, ensure that Service Pack 2 or higher is installed so that clients can use RDC 6.0 or higher. RDC 6.0 enables the use of Network Level Authentication (NLA).

The general steps to start RDC in Windows Vista or Windows Server 2008 are as follows:

1. Click Start, point to All Programs, and click Accessories.

2. Click Remote Desktop Connection.

3. Enter the name of the computer to access and click Connect.

4. Provide the username and password and proceed with the connection.

The steps for using RDC in Windows XP are as follows:

1. Click Start, point to All Programs, point to Accessories, and point to Communications.

2. Click Remote Desktop Connection.

3. Enter the name of the computer to access and click Connect.

4. Provide the username and password and proceed with the connection.

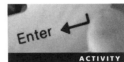

Activity 9-12 (optional): Configuring Authentication in Windows Vista

Time Required: Approximately 5 minutes
Objective: Configure NLA authentication in Windows Vista.

Description: NLA is the recommended level of authentication for a client accessing a terminal server. In this activity, you learn how to configure RDC to use this authentication level in Windows Vista. (You'll need a computer running Windows Vista for this project.)

1. Click **Start**, point to **All Programs**, and click **Accessories**.

2. Click **Remote Desktop Connection**.

3. In the Remote Desktop Connection box, click **Options >>** (see Figure 9-25).

Figure 9-25   RDC client in Windows Vista

4. Click the **Advanced** tab.

5. What you see next depends on your version of Vista. In some versions, ensure that **Do not connect** is selected in the *If the actual verification does not meet minimum policy requirements* box. In other Vista versions, make sure that **Do not connect if authentication fails** is selected in the *Authentication options* box.

6. Close the Remote Desktop Connection box.

If your network has pre-Windows XP clients, you can download remote connection software from Microsoft's Web site at *www.microsoft.com*.

Installing Applications on a Terminal Server

After you configure a terminal server, applications are installed to be compatible with this mode. For this reason, you might need to reinstall some applications that were installed before you installed the Terminal Services role. If you have already installed some programs, use Control Panel to uninstall them. To install a program, open Control Panel. In Control Panel Home view, click Programs, and click Install Application on Terminal Server. In Classic view, double-click Install Application on Terminal Server. Insert the first floppy disk, CD, or DVD for the application and follow the installation wizard instructions.

Chapter Summary

- Windows Server 2008 offers Routing and Remote Access Services to enable users to have remote access to a server.

- Routing and Remote Access Services includes virtual private network (VPN) and dial-up services that can be installed individually or together on a server.

- Remote access protocols include SLIP, CSLIP, PPP, PPTP, L2TP, and SSTP. PPP provides the foundation for modern remote networking. PPTP, L2TP, and SSTP are tunneling protocols used by VPNs for security through public networks, including the Internet.

- Use Server Manager to install the Network Policy and Access Services role in Windows Server 2008.

- To install and configure a VPN, use the Routing and Remote Access tool.

- After a VPN is installed, it should be configured to be a DHCP Relay Agent for IP address leasing to clients.

- A VPN has many properties that can be configured, including enabling the server, security, IPv4 and IPv6 properties, Multilink PPP, and logging.

- Plan to configure a remote access policy to govern how a VPN server is accessed, including using authentication and other restrictions to protect the server.

- A dial-up remote access server can be configured using the Routing and Remote Access tool.

- Dial-up remote access can be through a telephone line, ISDN line, T-carrier connection, and other telephony configurations.

- When you configure dial-up remote access, also configure a DHCP Relay Agent, Multilink (if used), and a remote access policy for security. Additionally, configure the dial-up access for the server, such as through a modem in the server or through an access server (box of modems) connected to the server.

- Many troubleshooting strategies can be used if your VPN or dial-up RAS server is having problems. A common hardware fix is to ensure that all communications links are working. A common software fix is to ensure the Windows Firewall is configured to allow remote communications and to make sure the services required by the VPN and dial-up remote access server are working.

- Use Server Manager to install the Terminal Services role.

- After a terminal server is installed, configure the connection properties and the access permissions.

- Configure Terminal Services client access licenses to enable users to access a terminal server.

- Terminal Services clients use the Remote Desktop Connection client to log onto a terminal server.

Key Terms

access server   A device that connects several different types of communications devices and telecommunications lines to a network, providing network routing for these types of communications.

aggregated links   Linking two or more communications channels, such as ISDN channels, so that they appear as one channel, but with the combined speed of all channels in the aggregate.

asynchronous modem   A modem from which communications occur in discrete units, and in which the start of a unit is signaled by a start bit at the front, and a stop bit at the back signals the end of the unit.

Bandwidth Allocation Control Protocol (BACP)   Similar to BAP, but is able to select a preferred client when two or more clients vie for the same bandwidth. *See* Bandwidth Allocation Protocol (BAP).

Bandwidth Allocation Protocol (BAP)   A protocol that works with Multilink in Windows Server 2008 to enable the bandwidth or speed of a remote connection to be allocated on the basis of the needs of an application, with the maximum allocation equal to the maximum speed of all channels aggregated via Multilink.

cable modem   A digital modem device designed for use with the cable TV system, providing high-speed data transfer.

Challenge Handshake Authentication Protocol (CHAP)   An encrypted handshake protocol designed for standard IP- or PPP-based exchange of passwords. It provides a reasonably secure, standard, cross-platform method for sender and receiver to negotiate a connection.

CHAP with Microsoft extensions (MS-CHAP)   A Microsoft-enhanced version of CHAP that can negotiate encryption levels and that uses the highly secure RSA RC4 encryption algorithm to encrypt communications between client and host.

CHAP with Microsoft extensions version 2 (MS-CHAP v2)   An enhancement of MS-CHAP that provides better authentication and data encryption and that is especially well suited for VPNs.

Compressed Serial Line Internet Protocol (CSLIP)   A newer version of SLIP that compresses header information in each packet sent across a remote link. *See* Serial Line Internet Protocol (SLIP).

Data Encryption Standard (DES)   A data encryption method developed by IBM and the National Security Agency in cooperation with the National Bureau of Standards (now called the National Institute of Standards and Technology) as an encryption technique using a secret key between the communicating stations. Triple DES (3DES) employs three secret keys combined into one long key.

dial-up networking   Using a telecommunications line and a modem to dial into a network or specific computers on a network via a modem at the other end.

digital subscriber line (DSL)   A technology that uses advanced modulation technniques on regular telephone lines for high-speed networking at speeds of up to about 52 Mbps between subscribers and a telecommunications company.

DSL adapter   A digital communications device that links a computer (or sometimes a router) to a DSL telecommunications line.

Extensible Authentication Protocol (EAP)   An authentication protocol employed by network clients that uses special security devices such as smart cards, token cards, and others that use certificate authentication.

frame relay   A WAN communications technology that relies on packet switching and virtual connection techniques to transmit at rates from 56 Kbps to 45 Mbps.

Hypertext Transfer Protocol Secure (HTTPS)   A secure form of HTTP that uses Secure Sockets Layer to implement security.

Integrated Services Digital Network (ISDN)   A telecommunications standard for delivering data services over digital telephone lines with a current practical limit of 1.536 Mbps and a theoretical limit of 622 Mbps.

Internet Authentication Service (IAS)   Used to establish and maintain security for RAS, Internet, and VPN dial-in access, and can be employed with RADIUS. IAS can use certificates to authenticate client access.

IP Security (IPSec)   A set of IP-based secure communications and encryption standards created through the Internet Engineering Task Force (IETF).

Layer Two Tunneling Protocol (L2TP)   A protocol that transports PPP over a VPN, an intranet, or the Internet. L2TP works similarly to PPTP, but uses an additional network communications standard, called Layer Two Forwarding, that enables forwarding on the basis of MAC addressing. *See* Point-to-Point Tunneling Protocol (PPTP).

leased lines   Telecommunications lines or bandwidth on telecommunications lines that can be leased from a telecommunications company.

9

Microsoft Point-to-Point Encryption (MPPE)   A starting-to-ending-point encryption technique that uses special encryption keys varying in length from 40 to 128 bits.

modem   A modulator/demodulator that converts a transmitted digital signal to an analog signal for a telephone line. It also converts a received analog signal to a digital signal for use by a computer.

Multilink or Multilink PPP (MPPP)   A capability of a remote access server to aggregate multiple data streams into one logical network connection for the purpose of using more than one modem, ISDN channel, or other communications line in a single logical connection.

Network Address Translation (NAT)   Used by Microsoft Routing and Remote Access Services and by firewalls, NAT translates IP addresses on an internal or local network so that the actual IP addresses cannot be determined on the Internet, because the address seen on the Internet is a decoy address.

Network Level Authentication (NLA)   A security method that enables authentication to take place before a Terminal Services connection is established and that involves verifying the user account, client computer, and network server.

Password Authentication Protocol (PAP)   A nonencrypted plaintext password authentication protocol. This represents the lowest level of security for exchanging passwords via PPP or TCP/IP.

Point-to-Point Protocol (PPP)   A widely used remote communications protocol that transports PPP as well as legacy protocols such as IPX and NetBEUI. PPP is used for dial-up connections between a client and Windows Server 2008.

Point-to-Point Tunneling Protocol (PPTP)   A remote communications protocol that enables connectivity to a network through the Internet and connectivity through intranets and VPNs.

Remote Authentication Dial-In User Service (RADIUS)   A protocol and service set up on one VPN or dial-up RAS server, for example in a domain, when there are multiple VPN or dial-up RAS servers to coordinate authentication and to track remote dial-in statistics for all VPN or dial-up RAS servers.

Remote Desktop Connection (RDC)   Software on a client computer that enables it to connect to a terminal server. This was originally called Terminal Services Client.

Routing and Remote Access Services (RRAS)   Microsoft software services that enable a Windows Server 2008 server to provide routing capabilities and remote access so that off-site workstations have access to a Windows Server 2008 network through telecommunications lines, the Internet, or intranets.

Secure Sockets Layer   A data encryption technique employed between a server and a client, such as between a client's browser and an Internet server. SSL is a commonly used form of security for communications and transactions over the Web and can be used by all Web browsers.

Secure Sockets Tunneling Protocol (SSTP)   A remote access communications protocol used in VPN communications and that employs PPP authentication techniques along with Web-based communications transport and encryption through Hypertext Transfer Protocol and Secure Sockets Layer. *See* Secure Sockets Layer (SSL).

Serial Line Internet Protocol (SLIP)   An older remote communications protocol that is used by some UNIX and Linux computers. The modern compressed SLIP (CSLIP) version uses header compression to reduce communications overhead. *See* Compressed Serial Line Internet Protocol (CSLIP).

Shiva Password Authentication Protocol (SPAP)   A proprietary version of Password Authentication Protocol used on Shiva systems. *See* Password Authentication Protocol (PAP).

synchronous modem   A modem that communicates using continuous bursts of data controlled by a clock signal that starts each burst.

T-carrier   A dedicated leased telephone line that can be used for data communications over multiple channels for speeds of up to 400.352 Mbps.

terminal   A device that consists of a monitor and keyboard to communicate with host computers that run the programs. The terminal does not have a processor to use for running programs locally.

terminal adapter (TA)   Popularly called a digital modem, links a computer or a fax to an ISDN line.

terminal server   A server configured to offer Terminal Services so that clients can run applications on the server, similar to having clients respond as terminals.

thin client   A specialized personal computer or terminal device that has a minimal Windows-based operating system. A thin client is designed to connect to a host computer that does most or all of the processing. The thin client is mainly responsible for providing a graphical user interface and network connectivity.

virtual private network (VPN)   A private network that is like a tunnel through a larger network—such as the Internet, an enterprise network, or both—that is restricted to designated member clients only.

X.25   An older packet-switching protocol for connecting remote networks at speeds up to 2.048 Mbps.

Review Questions

1. Your company's management wants to install a VPN server and use Web access to the VPN. They also want to use the same protocol as is used for secure transactions on the Web. Which of the following protocols can you install to provide this security?

   a. SSN

   b. SSTP

   c. PPP/HTTP

   d. 3DES

2. You have set up a VPN, but no one can access it on the network. Your analysis at the VPN server shows that all of the remote access connections are working and that the VPN is enabled. Which of the following might be the problem? (Choose all that apply.)

   a. Windows Firewall needs to be configured to allow the VPN communications.

   b. The Remote Access Connection Manager service is stopped.

   c. Dial-up Manager is hung.

   d. WAN sockets is not configured.

3. You have installed a dial-up remote access server to obtain IP addresses from a DHCP server that is connected to the network. No error messages were displayed during the installation, but for some reason IP addresses are not being automatically assigned to the dial-up clients. What step might you have omitted?

   a. disabling router communications that assign network numbers

   b. enabling static addressing in the client's dial-up manager

   c. configuring IP address piping

   d. configuring a DHCP Relay Agent

4. A thin client is typically used with a _____ server.

5. Your company is planning to set up a dial-up remote access server. Which of the following types of WAN networks can you use for your dial-up remote access server? (Choose all that apply.)

   a. ISDN

   b. T-carrier

   c. DSL

   d. cable modem

6. What are the three forms of MPPE encryption?

7. Your company works with classified government information and wants to use smart cards for accessing its secure VPN server. What authentication should be configured at the VPN server to enable smart card use?

    a. EAP

    b. S-CHAP

    c. VPNSecure

    d. SPAP

8. _____ on a terminal server enables clients to run applications without loading a remote desktop on the client computer.

9. Your company's network is in Chicago, but seven employees telecommute from a shared office in Kansas City. Each of the telecommuters has his or her own telephone line and dedicated number. How can you set up security so that the dial-up RAS server verifies each user by his or her telephone number?

    a. Assign a static IP address to each of the seven users and set up a telephone number in the dial-up RAS server that is assigned to each IP address.

    b. Insert the list of telephone numbers in the dial-up RAS server's Ports folder used to control access through telephone portals.

    c. Set up callback security on each user's account so that only a specific number is called back.

    d. Use an access server with the dial-up RAS server and dedicate seven modems in the access server for use with those telephone numbers.

10. The _____ tool enables you to view the users logged on to a terminal server.

11. Your company is planning to implement five VPN servers. Which of the following actions enables you to standardize access policies and authentication for the VPN servers?

    a. Create a VPN scope.

    b. Implement a RADIUS server.

    c. Install a proxy VPN server.

    d. Create a security pointer record in the network's DNS server.

12. Your VPN server is configured to enable Multilink as a way to aggregate frame relay channels when users need more bandwidth, such as for multimedia applications. However, when a user connects, the server does not seem to adjust for the amount of bandwidth needed by a user. How can you fix the problem?

    a. Configure the VPN server to dynamically use the Bandwidth Allocation Protocol along with Multilink.

    b. Restrict Multilink to increments of 128 Kbps per port.

    c. Configure the VPN server to limit the maximum number of ports to 1.

    d. Implement the IPSec protocol for security and bandwidth management.

13. The _____ protocol is used for specialized network communications between a client and a terminal server.

14. Which of the following is true of TS Gateway? (Choose all that apply.)

    a. It eliminates the need for ActiveX controls.

    b. It works for both VPN and Terminal Services servers when they are configured to use the PPP protocol.

    c. It uses HTTPS.

    d. It is compatible with networks that use firewalls and NAT.

15. Your colleague has just installed a VPN and now wants to establish a remote access policy. Where is the remote access policy configured?

    a. Active Directory organizational unit

    b. Remote Policy Log

    c. Network Policy Server

    d. Domain Registry

16. Layer Two Tunneling Protocol (L2TP) uses which of the following? (Choose all that apply.)

    a. MAC addressing

    b. IPSec

    c. TCP encryption

    d. IP addressing

17. What are the four basic elements of a remote access policy?

18. Users often load up the connections on your company's VPN server because many just leave their connections on all of the time, including overnight, on weekends, and while they are not doing work on the VPN. Your IT manager views this as a security risk, and it places an unnecessary load on the server and network. Which of the following remote access policy elements can you configure to address the problem? (Choose all that apply.)

    a. Change the NAS port duration time.

    b. Configure the idle timeout.

    c. Configure session timeout.

    d. Configure day and time restrictions.

19. Which of the following is the Terminal Services permission that grants query, connect, and logon access?

    a. Query access

    b. View & modify

    c. View & query

    d. User access

20. Your terminal server has fallen victim to man-in-the-middle attacks recently. Now that you've eliminated older Windows systems and have upgraded clients to Windows Vista, what can you implement to counter these attacks?

Case Projects

Cryp Code is a new firm that has recently been contracted by the FBI and CIA to write security programs for their computer systems. All of the programmers who work for Cryp Code must qualify for a security clearance before they can go to work. This means that Cryp Code is currently shorthanded as the company tries to find qualified programmers. The company staff works in a secure office area where they develop and test computer code and programs.

When programmers are working in the FBI and CIA headquarters, they need secure remote access to their company's servers on which they develop computer code. This enables them to view program design documents, research notes, program flow charts, and program source files.

Cryp Code uses Windows Server 2008 servers, and the programmers use Windows Vista client computers. Because they are short-staffed, Cryp Code has retained Aspen Consulting to implement remote access communications. As the only consultant who already has a security clearance, you have been chosen to work with Cryp Code.

Case Project 9-1: VPN Issues

The partners who own Cryp Code are interested in having you install a VPN, but first they want to know more about VPN structural elements. The partners are programmers and not operating system experts, and this is why they want to know more. Create a white paper, slide show, or both to discuss the following elements of a Windows Server 2008 VPN server that particularly apply to their company's needs:

- Remote access protocols
- IP addressing considerations
- Remote access policies
- Authentication
- Encryption

Case Project 9-2: VPN Tools and Installation

The partners are also interested in having you include in your presentation the following information about a Windows Server 2008 VPN:

- What tools are available for configuring and managing a VPN?
- What are the general steps required to install a VPN?

Case Project 9-3: Troubleshooting a VPN Problem

You have installed and configured the VPN without difficulty. However, when you test it remotely you cannot connect because no VPN server seems to be available. What steps do you take to troubleshoot the problem?

Case Project 9-4: Addressing a Security Need

The CIA has a very secret security program that nine Cryp Code programmers are working on. It is important that computer code and programs only be located on a secure server that is in a controlled and locked computer room with camera monitors. The programmers are not allowed to have any of the code on their own computers or to test the programs on their computers. At this point the programmers are taking turns working around the clock on the server console in the computer room. The Cryp Code partners ask if you have a recommendation to enable the programmers to work on this project from their own computers without having the code on their computers. What do you suggest and what are the advantages of your suggestion? Provide as much detail as you can.

chapter 10

Securing Windows Server 2008

After reading this chapter and completing the exercises, you will be able to:

- Understand the security enhancements included in Windows Server 2008
- Understand how Windows Server 2008 uses group policies
- Understand and configure security policies
- Implement Active Directory Rights Management Services
- Manage security using the Security Templates and Security Configuration and Analysis snap-ins
- Configure security policies for client computers
- Use the *cipher* command for encryption
- Use BitLocker Drive Encryption
- Configure Network Address Translation
- Configure Windows Firewall
- Implement Network Access Protection

No one wants confidential files and information to be stolen. No one wants his or her computer to be compromised by an attacker. No network administrator wants a network intrusion. For these reasons, Windows Server 2008 is equipped with an arsenal of security tools. The tools range from security policies to Windows Firewall to Network Access Protection. It doesn't matter if you work with a small office network or a multicampus corporate network; it pays to learn about and use the Windows Server 2008 security features.

In this chapter, you start by discovering the security enhancements in Windows Server 2008. You might think of these enhancements as ways in which Microsoft has learned from experience to bolster server defenses. You learn how to put security policies to work and how to implement Rights Management Services. You learn to use the Security Templates and Security Configuration and Analysis tools to create defenses and to analyze the defenses you have already set up.

Windows Server 2008 group policies can be configured to enforce security on client computers, and you learn how to use this feature for a more secure network. You learn to use the *cipher* command for encrypting files and folders and how to use BitLocker Drive Encryption to protect entire drives. You set up Network Address Translation to hide IP addresses from intruders, and you find out how to configure basic and advanced Windows Firewall features. The chapter ends by showing you how to use Network Access Protection, which is like covering your network with a sophisticated security canopy.

Security Enhancements in Windows Server 2008

Windows Server 2008 was created to emphasize security. In surveys of computer professionals about their interest in Windows Server 2008, security typically ranked as the number one feature. Many security enhancements are provided in this operating system, but the following are of particular interest:

- Reduced attack surface of the kernel through Server Core
- Expanded group policy
- Windows Firewall
- Network Access Protection
- Security Configuration Wizard
- User Account Control
- BitLocker Drive Encryption

Microsoft offers Server Core for organizations that want a Windows Server 2008 server, but with a much smaller attack surface. As you learned in Chapter 1, "Introduction to Windows Server 2008," Server Core eliminates most of the GUI portion of the operating system. This makes the Windows kernel much smaller, presenting a minimal attack surface. Server Core can be a good solution particularly for a server that handles critical network operations, such as DNS and DHCP. It is also a good solution for a Web or other server in the demilitarized zone of a network. The **demilitarized zone (DMZ)** is a portion of a network that is between two networks, such as between a private network and the Internet. Computers in the DMZ generally have fewer security defenses via routers and firewalls, for example. When an organization plans security, Server Core should be considered as a serious option. It addresses the previous criticism that Windows Server did not have the option to operate without the overhead in the kernel of code for a GUI environment, an option available in many Linux and UNIX servers. The smaller kernel in Server Core also offers better performance and leads to fewer problems.

The security value of a smaller attack surface is also the reason why Windows Server 2008 is redesigned to be role based. As a role-based operating system, you select only the server role modules, and portions of modules, that you need.

Group policy is a way to bring consistent security and other management to Windows Server 2008 and to clients connecting to a server. Microsoft introduced group policy with Windows 2000 Server and has been building more functionality with each new version of the Windows Server operating system. In Windows Server 2008, Microsoft adds new categories of group policy management and over 700 new policy settings. The new categories include the following:

- Power management
- Assigning printers by location (particularly for mobile users)
- Delegation of printer driver installation
- Security settings (such as who can access storage devices and who can install devices)
- Internet Explorer settings

One of the reasons for adding a new category for Internet Explorer settings is that prior to Windows Server 2008, a change to Internet Explorer policy settings might also change more general group policy settings. Windows Server 2008 and Vista group policy administration is redesigned so this conflict no longer occurs. You learn more about configuring group policy later in this chapter.

Until Windows Server 2008, security settings for Windows Firewall and policies for IPsec were configured separately. The separate configuration sometimes led to security conflicts or configuring the same security measures twice. In Windows Server 2008, Windows Firewall and IPsec settings are merged for more consistency. Also, Windows Firewall now protects incoming and outgoing communications, instead of just incoming communications, a feature also included with Windows Vista. You learn more about using Windows Firewall later in this chapter.

Windows Server 2008 introduces Network Access Protection (NAP). As you learned in Chapter 1, NAP is a comprehensive set of security features that monitors and manages a server and its clients. The philosophy of NAP is that a network is only as secure as its least secure member. For this reason, NAP monitors clients and servers to ensure that the desired level of security is maintained on all of them. For example, if a client computer does not have recent security updates from Microsoft, NAP can limit the client's network access and can even automatically enable updating on the client. NAP is covered in more detail later in this chapter.

The Security Configuration Wizard that you used in Chapter 3, "Configuring the Windows Server 2008 Environment," is not new to Windows Server 2008, but it includes more security features and is automatically installed when you install Windows Server 2008. Plan to use this tool early on and run it periodically to ensure your security settings are keeping pace with changes you make to a server.

User Account Control (UAC) is designed to keep the user running in the standard user mode as a way to more fully insulate the kernel, which runs in privileged mode (see Chapter 1), and to keep operating system and desktop files stabilized. Prior to Windows Server 2008 and Windows Vista, when devices and software were installed or changed, users could potentially negatively alter a system or introduce malware. This is because users performed these actions with extensive access to the system, going beyond standard user mode. UAC was first introduced in Windows Vista and later in Windows Server 2008 so that software and device drivers could be installed from an account running in standard user mode. Although the operating system allows this (with the right permissions), the installation still requires authorization from the server administrator. UAC means there is little chance that the installation can destabilize the operating system, because the installation takes place only with the proper authorization and in standard user mode.

Another element of UAC is the Administrator Approval Mode. For example, even though you are on the Administrator account when you run a typical program, Windows Server 2008 runs that program with standard user permissions in the standard user mode—insulating the operating system from extensive access. If the program needs to run in a mode as Administrator with more permissions and extensive access, the operating system displays a message box or prompt via

10

UAC and you must respond. This security measure helps prevent malware or an intruder from acquiring control through a back door without the administrator knowing.

BitLocker Drive Encryption prevents an intruder from bypassing ACL file and folder protections. If a drive is protected using BitLocker Drive Encryption, no one can access information without proper authentication even if the drive has been stolen. The data on the drive is encrypted and protected against tampering. You learn more about BitLocker Drive Encryption later in this chapter.

Introduction to Group Policy

The use of **group policy** in Windows Server 2008 enables you to standardize the working environment of clients and servers by setting policies in Active Directory. Hundreds of policies can be configured through group policy to help you manage desktop configurations, logon security, resource auditing, software availability, and many other functions.

Group policy is set for many environments, ranging from client desktops to account policies to remote installation of Windows Vista on clients. Group policies are secured so that they cannot be changed by individual users. The defining characteristics of group policy are as follows:

- *Group policy can be set for a site, domain, OU, or local computer*—Group policy can be linked to any site, domain, OU, or local computer. An OU is the smallest Active Directory container with which a group policy is linked. Group policy is not linked to security groups directly, but it can be filtered through these groups. Also, when the first domain is created, a default domain policy is automatically associated with that domain. The default domain policy is, by default, inherited by child domains, but can be changed so that a child domain has a different group policy than its parent domain.

- *Group policy cannot be set for non-OU folder containers*—Default containers that are folders instead of OUs, such as the Builtin, Computers, ForeignSecurityPrincipals, and Users folders, in the Active Directory Users and Computers tool are not truly OUs; therefore, you cannot link group policy with these containers.

- *Group policy settings are stored in group policy objects*—A **group policy object (GPO)** is an Active Directory object that contains group policy settings (a set of group policies) for a site, domain, OU, or local computer. Each GPO has a unique name and globally unique identifier (GUID). When Active Directory is installed, one local GPO is created for every Windows Server 2008 server. A server can also be governed by Active Directory GPOs for sites, domains, and OUs.

- *GPOs can be local and nonlocal*—The local GPO applies to the local computer. Nonlocal GPOs apply to sites, domains, and OUs. When multiple GPOs are present, their effect is incremental (local GPO first, default domain GPO next, domain controller GPO next, site GPO next, and the GPOs for OUs next).

- *Group policy can be set up to affect user accounts and computers*—Group policy is set up to affect user configuration, computer configuration, or both, as illustrated in the Default Domain Policy shown in Figure 10-1. If a policy is set up for users but is not the same as a policy set up for computers, then the policy set up for computers prevails over the policy for user accounts.

- *When group policy is updated, old policies are removed or updated for all clients*—Each time you update group policy, the new information is updated for clients and the old information that no longer applies is removed.

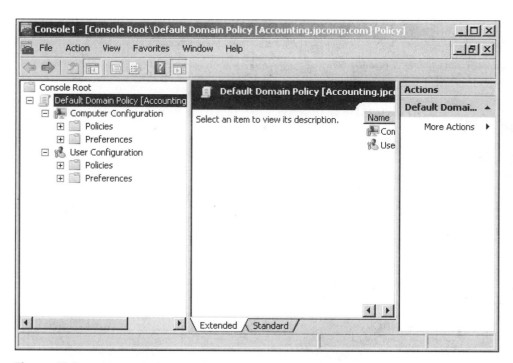

Figure 10-1 Default domain policy

Securing Windows Server 2008 Using Security Policies

Security policies are a subset of individual policies within a larger group policy for a site, domain, OU, or local computer. Windows Server 2008 has many individual security policies that you can configure; this chapter offers you a taste of some of the most important ones. In the next sections, you learn how to establish the following security policies:

- Account Policies
- Audit Policy
- User Rights
- Security Options
- IP Security Policies

Always make sure you configure the security policies on the local computer (the server as a computer on the network) and the default domain security policies prior to releasing a server for use.

Before learning about security policies, it is important to become familiar with the GPO Management MMC snap-in.

For all of the activities in this chapter, you'll need an account with Administrator privileges. Also, these activities can be completed on a virtual server or computer, such as in Hyper-V.

Some steps in the activities in this book include bulleted questions with space for you to record your responses/answers.

Activity 10-1: Using the Group Policy Management Snap-In

Time Required: Approximately 10 minutes
Objective: Learn how to use the Group Policy Management MMC snap-in.

Description: Group policy can be configured using the Group Policy Management MMC snap-in. In this activity, you set up a customized Group Policy Management console for managing the Default Domain Policy, and you save the console for later use.

1. Click **Start** and click **Run**.

2. Type **mmc** in the Open text box and click **OK**.

3. In the Console1 window, click **File** and click **Add/Remove Snap-in**.

4. Click the second **Group Policy Management** selection under Snap-in, as shown in Figure 10-2, and click **Add**.

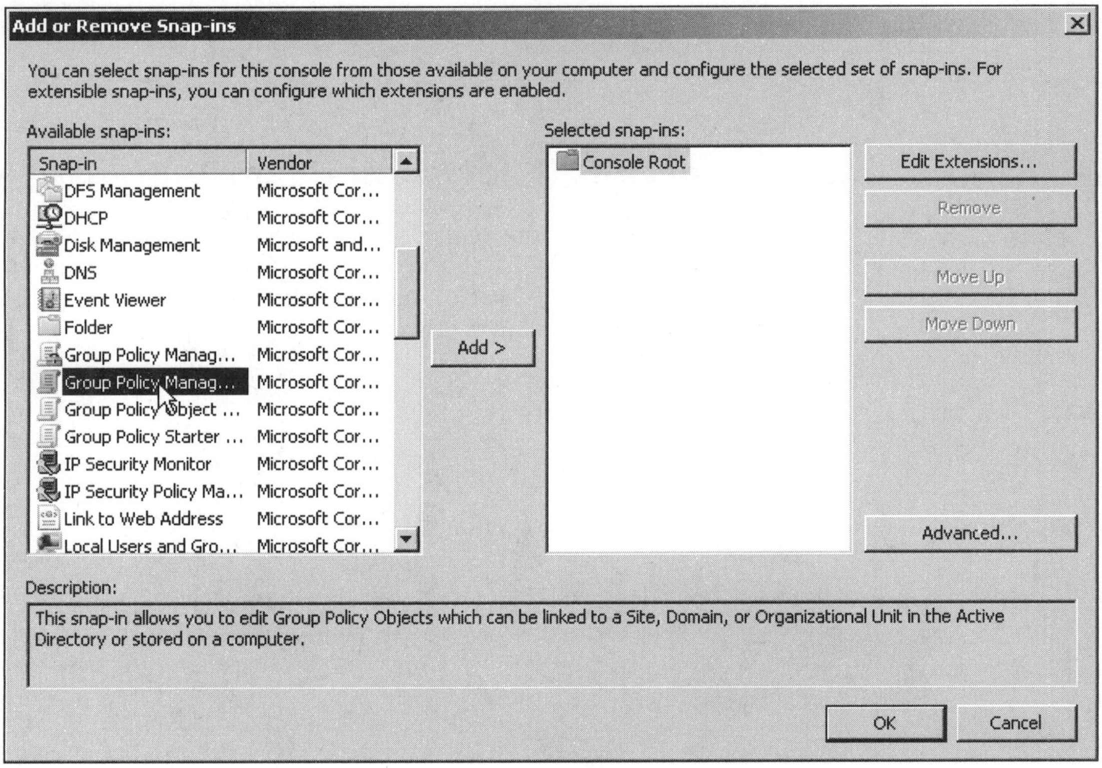

Figure 10-2 Selecting the Group Policy Management snap-in

5. In the Welcome to the Group Policy Wizard, click the **Browse** button.

6. Click **Default Domain Policy** in the Browse for a Group Policy Object box. Click **OK**.

7. Click **Finish** in the Select Group Policy Object dialog box.

8. Click **OK** in the Add or Remove Snap-ins dialog box.

9. Click **Default Domain Policy** in the tree in the left pane.

10. In the middle pane, double-click **Computer Configuration**.

11. Double-click the **Policies** folder in the middle pane.

    • What folders are listed for Policies?

12. Double-click **Windows Settings** in the middle pane.

    • What is listed within the Windows Settings folder?

13. Double-click **Security Settings** in the middle pane.

14. Click **User Configuration** in the tree in the left pane.

15. Double-click the **Policies** folder in the middle pane.

16. Double-click **Windows Settings** in the middle pane.

    • What is listed within the Windows Settings folder?

17. Close the Console1 window.

18. Click **Yes** to save the console settings.

19. Type **Default Domain Policy** plus your initials, such as *JR*. Click **Save**.

Establishing Account Policies

Account policies are security measures set up in a group policy that applies to all accounts or to all accounts in a container, such as a domain, when Active Directory is installed. The account policies are located in the following path in the tree of the Default Domain Policy: Computer Configuration, Policies, Windows Settings, Security Settings. This is what you will have observed in Step 13 of Activity 10-1, using the Group Policy Management tool. The account policy options that you can configure affect three main areas:

- Password security
- Account lockout
- Kerberos security

Each of these is described in the next sections.

Password Security The first line of defense in Windows Server 2008 is password security. One option is to set a password expiration period, requiring users to change passwords at regular intervals. Many organizations use this feature, for example requiring that users change their passwords every 45 to 90 days.

Server administrators should consider changing passwords every month or sooner for the Administrator account and other accounts that can access sensitive information.

Some organizations require that all passwords have a minimum length, such as seven characters (for a "strong password" Microsoft recommends a minimum of seven characters). This requirement makes passwords more difficult to guess. Another option is to have the operating system "remember" passwords that have been used previously. For example, the system might be set to recall the last five passwords, preventing a user from repeating one of these. Password recollection forces the user to change to a different password instead of reusing the same one when a new one is set. An account lockout option can also be configured. The specific password security options that you can configure are as follows:

- *Enforce password history*—Enables you to require users to choose new passwords when they make a password change, because the system can remember the previously used passwords

- *Maximum password age*—Permits you to set the maximum time allowed until a password expires

- *Minimum password age*—Permits you to specify that a password must be used for a minimum amount of time before it can be changed

- *Minimum password length*—Enables you to require that passwords are a minimum length

- *Passwords must meet complexity requirements*—Enables you to create a filter of customized password requirements that each account password must follow

- *Store password using reversible encryption*—Enables passwords to be stored in reversible encrypted format (similar to clear-text passwords) and used when applications or application processes must employ user passwords

Microsoft does not recommend enabling *Store password using reversible encryption* unless absolutely necessary for an application you must use. This setting weakens password security.

Activity 10-2: Configuring Password Security

Time Required: Approximately 10 minutes
Objective: Configure the password security in the default domain security policy.

Description: In this activity, you configure the password security for a domain.

1. Click **Start**, click **All Programs**, click **Administrative Tools**, and click **Default Domain Policy** plus your initials (if you used them in Activity 10-1).

2. Maximize the console windows, if necessary.

3. If necessary open the following in the tree in the left pane: **Computer Configuration, Policies, Windows Settings,** and **Security Settings** (see Figure 10-3).

4. Click **Account Policies** in the tree in the left pane.

5. Double-click **Password Policy** in the middle pane.

6. Double-click **Enforce password history** in the middle pane.

7. Ensure that **Define this policy setting** is checked. The default setting is **24** passwords remembered, which is the maximum. Assume you work for a company that has a policy to set this number at 15. Enter **15** in the box, as shown in Figure 10-4. Click **OK**.

8. Double-click **Maximum password age** and ensure that **Define this policy setting** is checked. Change the **days** text box to **60** and click **OK**.

9. Double-click **Minimum password length**. Be sure that **Define this policy setting** is checked and set the *characters* text box to **8**. Click **OK**. The Default Domain Security Settings window should now look similar to the one in Figure 10-5.

10. Leave the Default Domain Policy console window open for the next activity.

Account Lockout

The operating system can employ account lockout to bar access to an account (including the true account owner) after a number of unsuccessful tries. The lockout can be set to release after a specified period of time or by intervention from the server administrator.

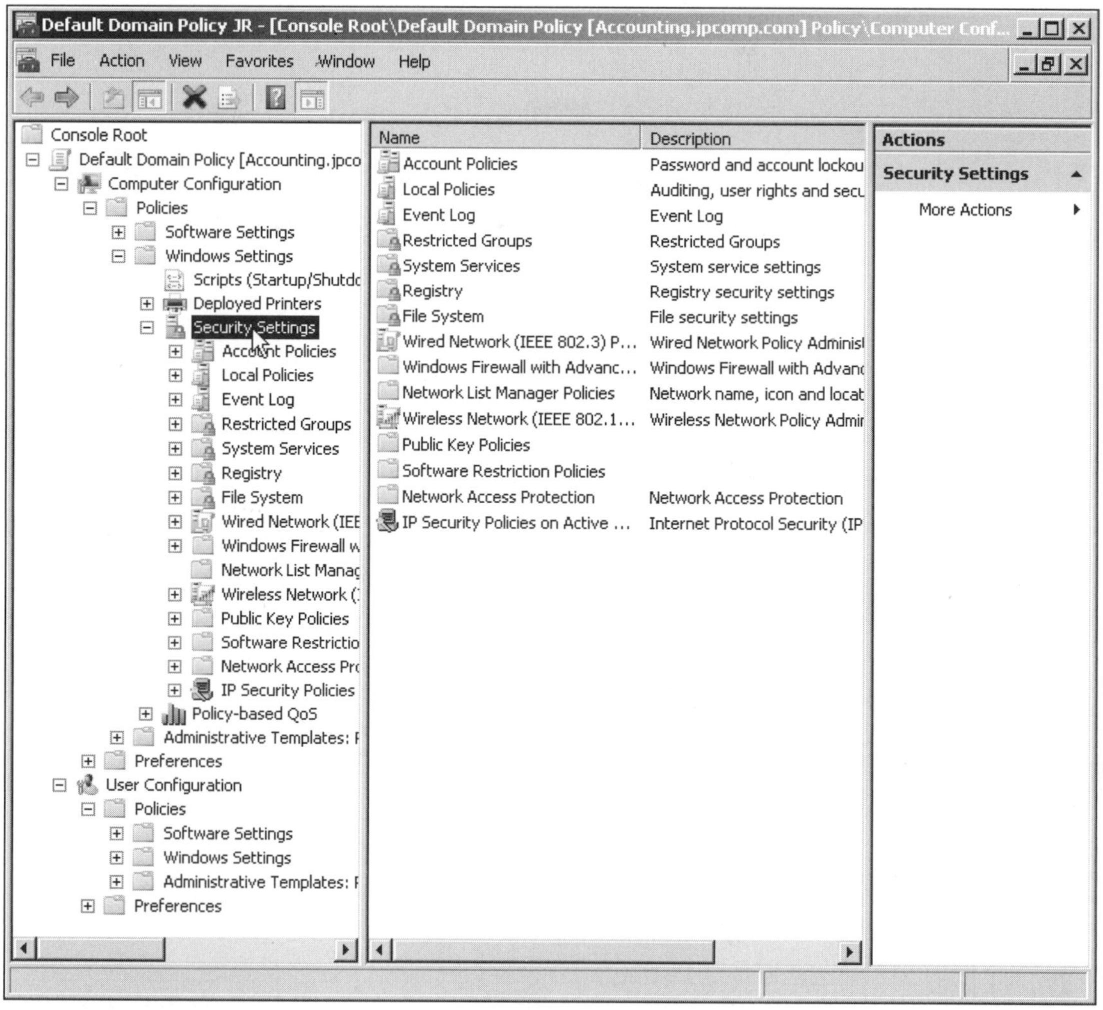

Figure 10-3 Viewing security settings for the default domain policy

A common policy is to have lockout go into effect after five to 10 unsuccessful logon attempts. Also, an administrator can set lockout to release after a designated time, such as 30 minutes. The 30 minutes creates enough delay to discourage intruders, while giving some leeway to a user who might have forgotten a recently changed password. The following are the account lockout parameters that you can configure in the account lockout policy:

- *Account lockout duration*—Permits you to specify in minutes how long the system will keep an account locked out after reaching the specified number of unsuccessful logon attempts

- *Account lockout threshold*—Enables you to set a limit to the number of unsuccessful attempts to log on to an account

- *Reset account lockout count after*—Enables you to specify the number of minutes to wait after a single unsuccessful logon attempt before the unsuccessful logon counter is reinitialized to 0

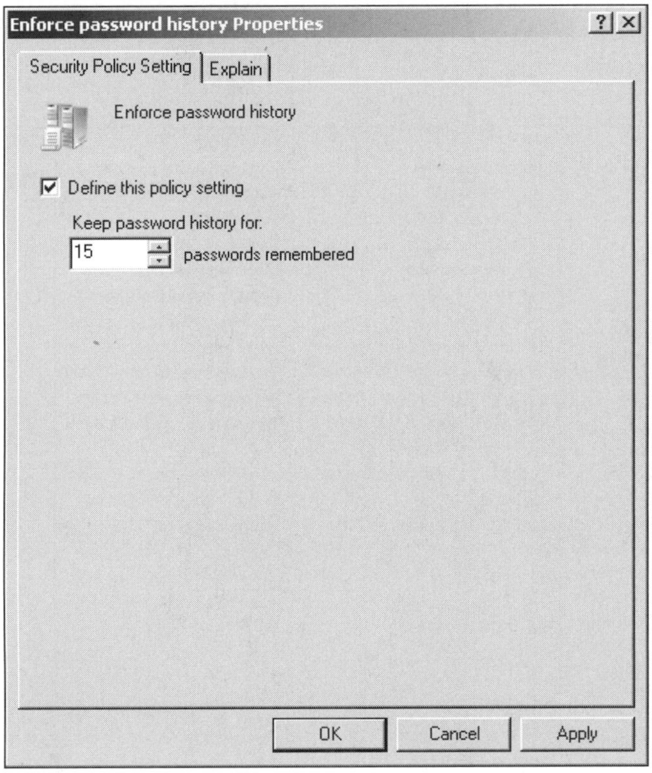

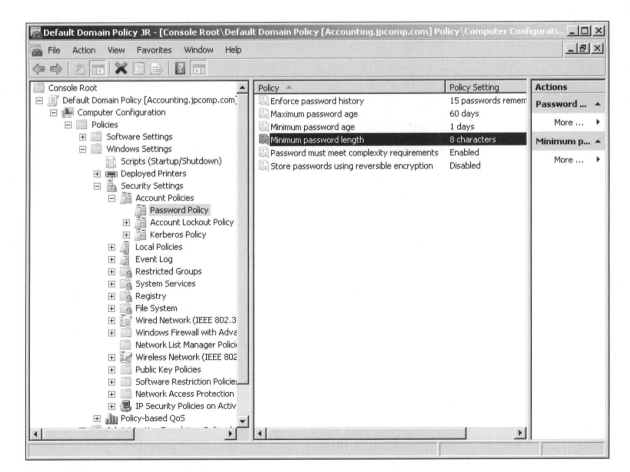

Figure 10-4 Configuring the password history

Figure 10-5 Password Policy configurations

Activity 10-3: Configuring Account Lockout Policy

Time Required: Approximately 10 minutes

Objective: Configure account lockout policy in the default domain security policy.

Description: In this activity, you configure the account lockout policy settings.

1. Open the Default Domain Policy console you created in Activity 10-1, if it is not already open.

2. Click **Account Lockout Policy** in the tree under Computer Configuration, Policies, Windows Settings, Security Settings, and Account Policies.

3. Double-click **Account lockout duration** in the right pane.

4. Check the box for **Define this policy setting**, if it is not already checked. Enter **40** in the minutes text box (see Figure 10-6), and click **OK**.

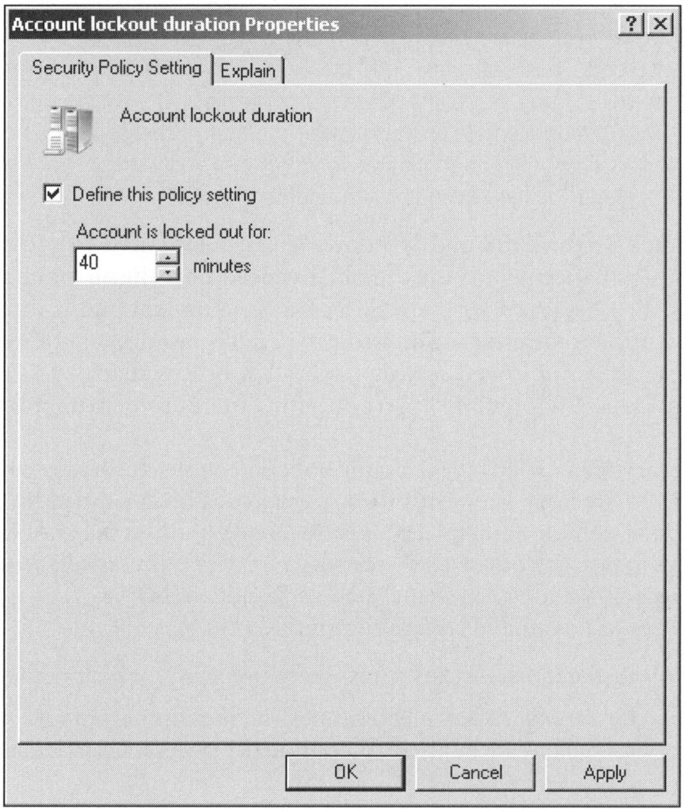

```
┌─────────────────────────────────────────────────────────┐
│ Account lockout duration Properties              ?│ X│   │
├─────────────────────────────────────────────────────────┤
│  Security Policy Setting │ Explain │                      │
│                                                           │
│     ▟▊      Account lockout duration                      │
│                                                           │
│   ☑ Define this policy setting                            │
│                                                           │
│      Account is locked out for:                           │
│      ┌────┬─┐                                             │
│      │40  │▲│  minutes                                    │
│      └────┴─┘                                             │
│                                                           │
│                                                           │
│                                                           │
│                                                           │
│                                                           │
│                                                           │
│                                                           │
│                           ┌──────┐ ┌──────┐ ┌──────┐      │
│                           │  OK  │ │Cancel│ │ Apply│      │
│                           └──────┘ └──────┘ └──────┘      │
└─────────────────────────────────────────────────────────┘
```

Figure 10-6 Configuring account lockout duration

5. You should see the Suggested Value Changes box.

   • What changes are suggested?

6. Click **OK** in the Suggested Value Changes box. In the middle pane, notice that your change plus the suggested changes have been implemented.

7. Leave the console windows open for the next activity.

Kerberos Security Kerberos security involves the use of tickets that are exchanged between the client who requests logon and network services access, and the server or Active Directory that grants access. On a network that does not use Active Directory, each stand-alone Windows Server 2008 server can be designated as a Kerberos key distribution center, which means that the server stores user accounts and passwords. When Active Directory is used, then each domain controller is a key distribution center. When a user logs on, the client computer sends an account name and password to the key distribution center. The key distribution center responds by issuing a temporary ticket that grants the user access to the Kerberos ticket-granting service on a domain controller (or stand-alone server), which then grants a permanent ticket to that computer. The permanent ticket, called a **service ticket**, is good for the duration of a logon session (or for another period of time specified by the server administrator in the account policies) and enables the computer to access network services beginning with the Logon service. The permanent ticket contains encrypted information such as a session key, an ID for the user account, IDs for services the user account can access, and the IP address of the user's computer. When the user seeks to access a service, the permanent ticket information is decrypted to validate the user and the services the user is permitted to use. You might think of a Kerberos ticket as similar to one you would purchase to enter a concert; the ticket is good for the duration of that event and for entry to refreshment and merchandise booths, but you must purchase a new ticket to attend a concert on another date.

Windows Server 2008 uses Kerberos version 5 (V5). This version of Kerberos authenticates both the user requesting server access and the server. Also, on every domain controller (DC), the Kerberos Key Distribution Center service must be running. If this service is not started, users cannot log on to the network. You can verify the service using Server Manager or the Computer Management tool.

Kerberos on Windows Server 2008 and Windows Vista is enhanced to provide even stronger security. One significant enhancement is the use of **Advanced Encryption Standard (AES)** encryption, which is the standard deployed by the U.S. federal government and is intended to be more secure than DES. In addition to offering strong security, AES is fast and uses a minimal amount of memory. Kerberos also offers improved security in branch offices that use RODCs (Read-Only Domain Controllers, see Chapter 4 "Introduction to Active Directory and Account Management").

When Active Directory is installed, the account policies enable Kerberos, which is the default authentication. If Active Directory is not installed, Kerberos is not included by default in the account policies because the default authentication is through **Windows NT LAN Manager version 2 (NTLMv2)**. NTLM is not as robust as Kerberos, but it is compatible with all versions of Windows, including legacy Windows systems such as Windows NT.

The following options are available for configuring Kerberos:

- *Enforce user logon restrictions*—Turns on Kerberos security, which is the default

- *Maximum lifetime for service ticket*—Determines the maximum amount of time in minutes that a service ticket can be used to continually access a particular service in one service session

- *Maximum lifetime for user ticket*—Determines the maximum amount of time in hours that a ticket can be used in one continuous session for access to a computer or domain

- *Maximum lifetime for user ticket renewal*—Determines the maximum number of days that the same Kerberos ticket can be renewed each time a user logs on

- *Maximum tolerance for computer clock synchronization*—Determines how long in minutes a client will wait until synchronizing its clock with that of the server or Active Directory it is accessing

If getting users to log off when they go home at night is a problem, limit the *maximum lifetime for service ticket* or *maximum lifetime for user ticket* values to a certain number of hours, such as 10 or 12.

Activity 10-4: Configuring Kerberos Security

Time Required: Approximately 10 minutes
Objective: Configure Kerberos in the default domain security policy.

Description: In this activity, you configure the Kerberos policy settings for a company in which people work 10- and 12-hour shifts (setting Kerberos for up to 12 hours).

1. Open the Default Domain Policy console, if it is not already open.

2. Click **Kerberos Policy** in the tree under Computer Configuration, Policies, Windows Settings, Security Settings, and Account Policies.

3. Double-click **Maximum lifetime for service ticket**. Ensure the box for **Define this policy setting** is checked. Enter **720** in the minutes text box. Click **OK**.

4. Click **OK** in the Suggested Value Changes dialog box to also set *Maximum lifetime for user ticket* to 12 hours. When you are finished, the right pane should look similar to Figure 10-7.

5. Leave the console window open for the next activity.

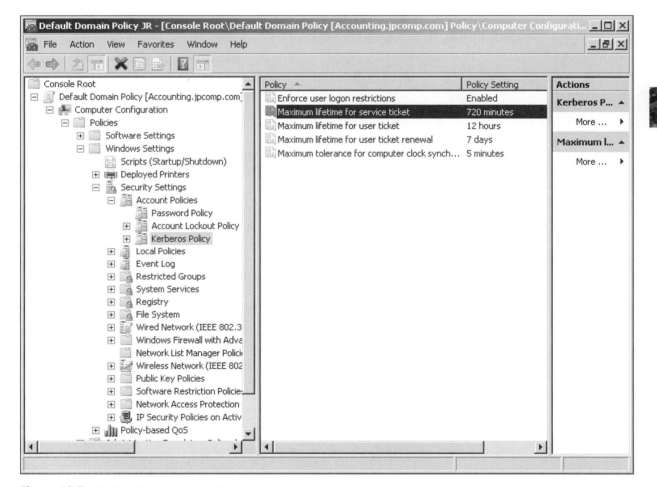

Figure 10-7 Configuring Kerberos Policy

Establishing Audit Policies

After accounts are set up, you can specify account auditing to track activity associated with those accounts. For example, some organizations need to track security changes to accounts, while others want to track failed logon attempts. Many server administrators track failed logon attempts for the Administrator account, to be sure an intruder is not attempting to access the server. Accounts that access an organization's financial information often are routinely audited to protect their users as well as the information they access. Examples of events that an organization can audit are as follows:

- Account logon (and logoff) events
- Account management
- Directory service access
- Logon (and logoff) events at the local computer
- Object access
- Policy change
- Privilege use
- Process tracking
- System events

Each listed activity is audited in terms of the success or failure of the event. For example, if account logon attempts are audited, a record is made each time someone logs on to an account successfully or tries to log on but fails.

Use auditing sparingly. Each audited event causes a record to be made in the Security event log. For example, if you audit all logon attempts of 200 domain accounts, the server log will quickly become loaded down just from auditing events. Reviewing all of the audit data can be time consuming, and the data can consume valuable disk space.

Activity 10-5: Configuring Auditing

Time Required: Approximately 10 minutes
Objective: Configure an audit policy.

Description: Assume that the IT manager in your organization wants to track the logon activity of all accounts in the domain over a 24-hour period. In this activity, you enable account logon auditing to facilitate that request.

1. Open the Default Domain Policy console, if it is not already open.
2. Click **Local Policies** in the tree under Computer Configuration, Policies, Windows Settings, and Security Settings.
3. Double-click **Audit Policy** in the middle pane.
4. Double-click **Audit account logon events** in the middle pane.
5. Click the box for **Define these policy settings**.
6. Ensure that both the **Success** and **Failure** boxes are checked, as shown in Figure 10-8.
7. Click **Apply** to have these take effect immediately and then click **OK**.
   - If you were concerned about tracking changes to group policy, what would you audit?

8. Leave the console window open for the next activity.

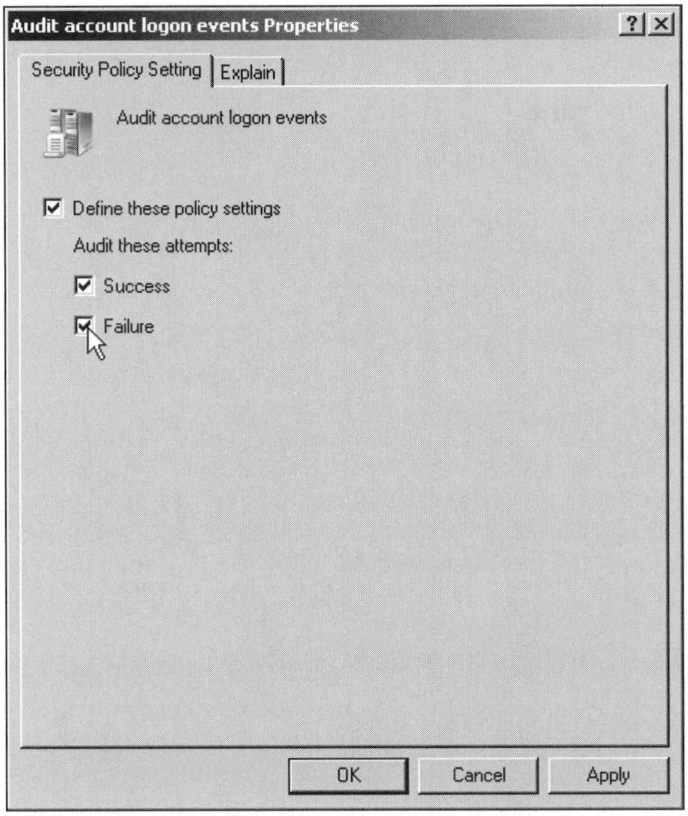

Audit account logon events Properties   ?| X|

Security Policy Setting | Explain |

    Audit account logon events

☑ Define these policy settings

Audit these attempts:

☑ Success

☑ Failure

| OK | Cancel | Apply |

Figure 10-8   Configuring account logon auditing

If you want to audit activity on a particular object, such as a folder, file, or printer, enable Audit object access. Next, in the object's properties, such as the properties for a folder, specify the accounts or groups you want to audit. For a folder, you would do this by right-clicking the folder in Windows Explorer and clicking Properties. Click the Security tab, the Advanced button, and the Auditing tab. (See Chapter 5 "Configuring, Managing, and Troubleshooting Resource Access.")

Configuring User Rights

User rights enable an account or group to perform predefined tasks. The most basic right is the ability to access a server. More advanced rights give privileges to create accounts and manage server functions. Although not specifically differentiated when you set them up, two general categories of rights are established: privileges and logon rights. Privileges generally relate to the ability to manage server or Active Directory functions, and logon rights are related to how accounts, computers, and services are accessed. Both types of rights are established through setting up the user rights assignment in a group policy.

Some examples of privileges include the following:

- Add workstations to domain
- Back up files and directories
- Change the system time
- Create permanent shared objects
- Generate security audits
- Load and unload device drivers

- Perform volume maintenance tasks
- Shut down the system

Examples of logon rights are as follows:

- Access this computer from the network
- Allow logon locally
- Allow logon through Terminal Services
- Deny access to this computer from the network
- Deny logon as a service
- Deny logon locally
- Deny logon through Terminal Services

 The most efficient way to assign user rights is to assign them to groups instead of to individual user accounts. When user rights are assigned to a group, then all user accounts (or groups) that are a member of that group inherit the user rights assigned to the group, making these **inherited rights**.

Activity 10-6: Configuring User Rights

Time Required: Approximately 15 minutes
Objective: Learn how to configure user rights.

Description: This activity enables you to view the existing user rights and restrict local logon access to this server to the Administrator account, the Administrators group, and the Server Operators group. Also, you restrict the ability to shut down the server to the Administrators group.

1. Open the Default Domain Policy console, if it is not already open.
2. Click **User Rights Assignment** in the tree under Computer Configuration, Policies, Windows Settings, Security Settings, and Local Policies.
3. Scroll through the middle pane to view the rights that can be configured, as shown in Figure 10-9.
4. Double-click **Allow log on locally**.
5. Check the box for **Define these policy settings**.
6. Click **Add User or Group**, as shown in Figure 10-10.
7. Click the **Browse** button in the Add User or Group box.
8. Click the **Advanced** button in the Select Users, Computers, or Groups dialog box.
9. Click the **Find Now** button in the Select Users, Computers, or Groups dialog box.
10. Hold down the **Ctrl** key and click **Administrator**, **Administrators**, and **Server Operators**. Ensure that Account Operators is not selected. If it is selected, continue holding down the **Ctrl** key and click **Account Operators** to deselect it. Click **OK**.
11. Click **OK** in the Select Users, Computers, or Groups dialog box.
12. Click **OK** in the Add User or Group box.
    - What now appears in the text box on the Allow log on locally Properties dialog box?

13. Notice that your changes are reflected in the text box. Click **OK** in the Allow log on locally Properties dialog box.
14. Double-click **Shut down the system**. Check **Define these policy settings**.
15. Click **Add User or Group**.

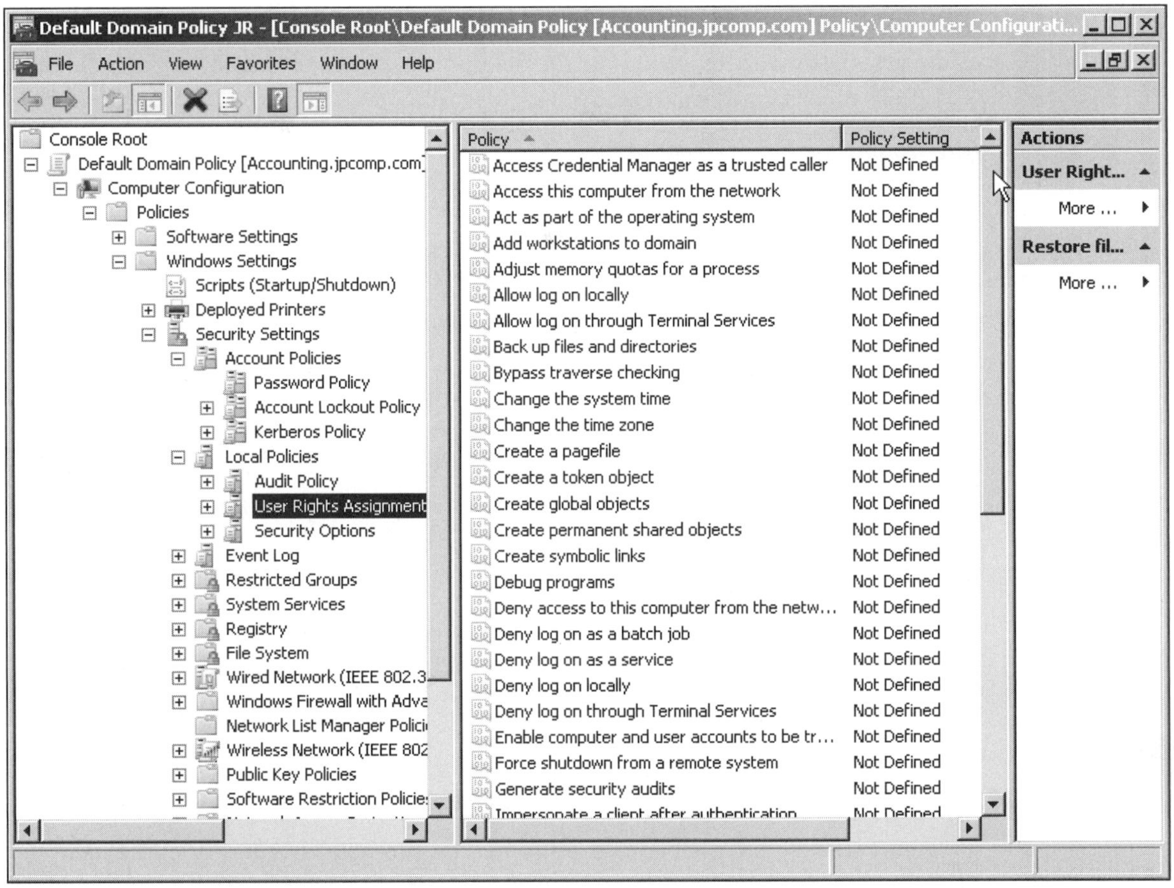

Figure 10-9 User Rights Assignment policy options

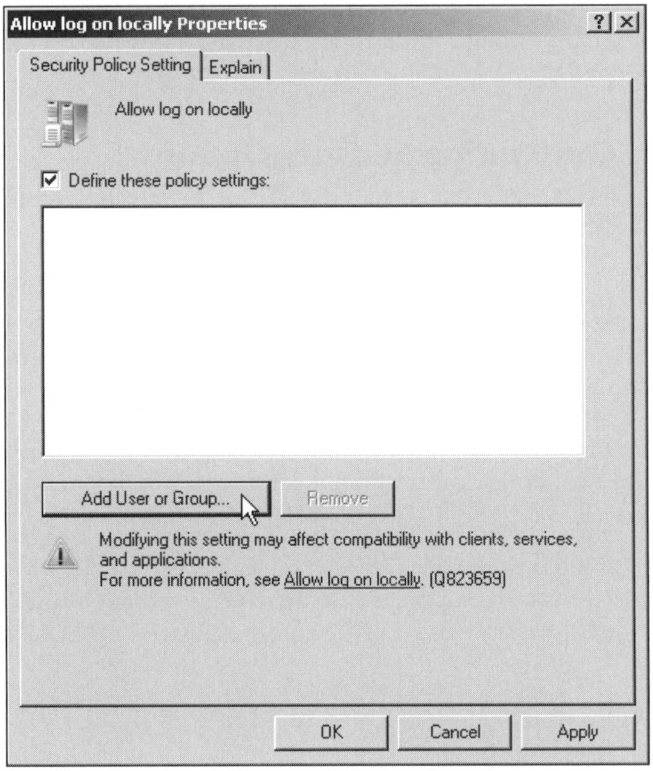

Figure 10-10 Adding a user or group to make a rights assignment

10

16. Click the **Browse** button in the Add User or Group box.

17. Click the **Advanced** button in the Select Users, Computers, or Groups dialog box.

18. Click **Find Now** in the Select Users, Computers, or Groups dialog box.

19. Double-click **Administrators**.

20. Click **OK** in the Select Users, Computers, or Groups dialog box.

21. Click **OK** in the Add User or Group box.

22. Click **OK** in the Shut down the system Properties box.

23. Leave the console window open for the next activity.

Configuring Security Options

Over 78 specialized security options, with many new ones added for Windows Server 2008, can be configured in the security policies. These options are divided into the following categories:

- Accounts
- Audit
- DCOM
- Devices
- Domain controller
- Interactive logon
- Microsoft network client
- Network access

- Network security
- Recovery console
- Shutdown
- System cryptography
- System objects
- System settings
- User Account Control

Each category has specialized options. For example, if you are concerned about intruders attempting to access the Administrator account, you can use the *Accounts: Rename administrator account* policy to disguise the Administrator account with another name. In another example, if you want only the Server Operators group to format and eject CDs and DVDs, configure *Devices: Allowed to format and eject removable media*. Or, if you have configured specific logon hour controls so that users cannot log on during certain times, then you can force off users who have not logged off after hours by configuring *Network security: Force logoff when logon hours expire*.

Activity 10-7: Configuring Security Options

Time Required: Approximately 10 minutes
Objective: Examine the Security Options and configure an option.

Description: In this activity, you view all of the Security Options that can be set up as policies. Next, you rename the Guest account to designate it for use by vendors who visit your organization, and then you create a message for users who log on to the server or network.

1. Open the Default Domain Policy console, if it is not already open.

2. Click **Security Options** in the tree under Computer Configuration, Policies, Windows Settings, Security Settings, and Local Policies. You should see a window similar to Figure 10-11.

3. Scroll through the options.

   - What option would you use to restrict access to the CD/DVD drive in the computer so that it can only be accessed by someone logged on locally? How can you set up the system so that it can be shut down without first having someone logged on locally?

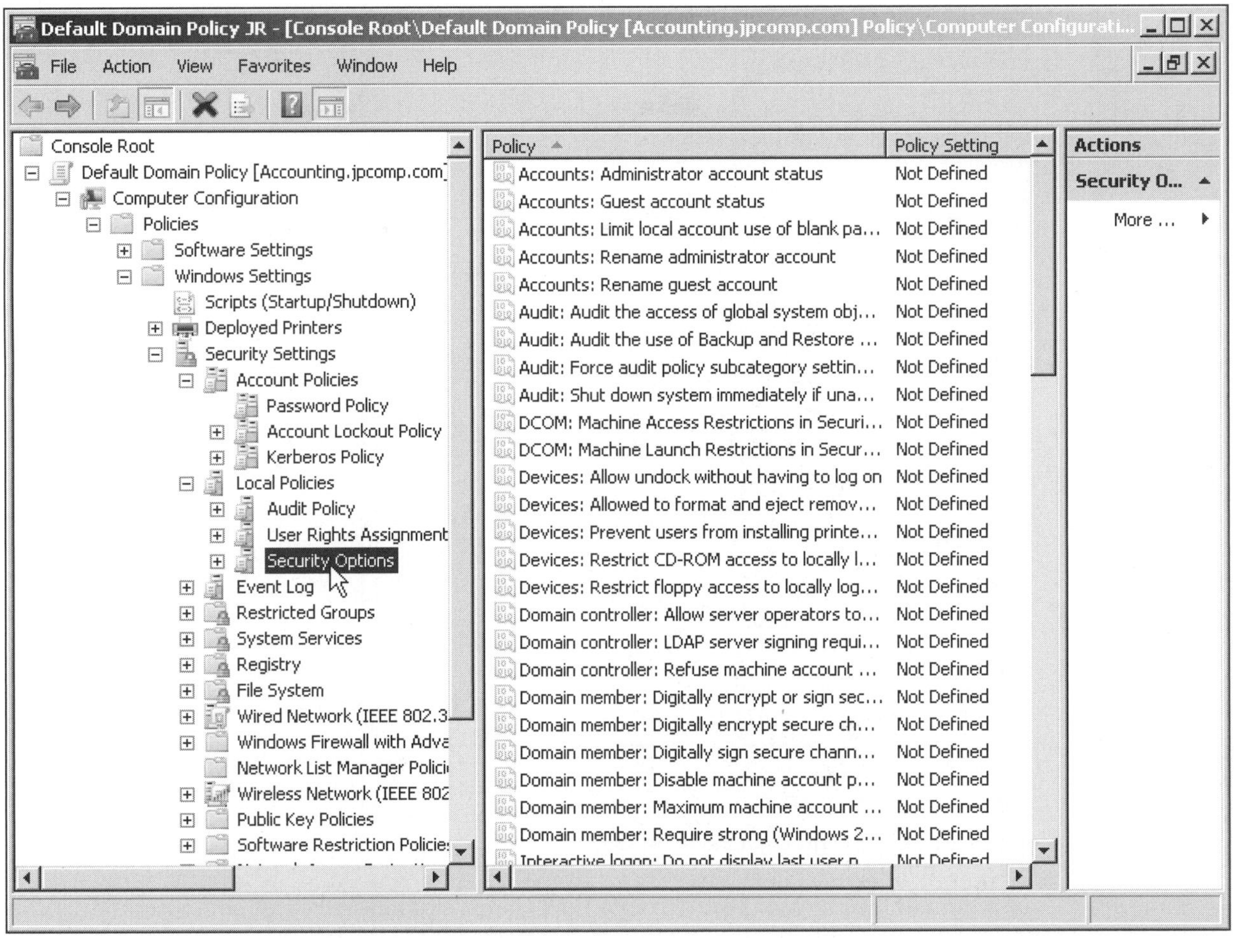

Figure 10-11 Accessing the Security Options

4. Double-click **Accounts: Rename guest account**.

5. Check the box for **Define this policy setting**.

6. Enter the name **Vendors** in the text box. Click **OK**.

7. Double-click **Interactive logon: Message text for users attempting to log on**.

8. Check the box for **Define this policy setting in the template**.

9. Click at the beginning of the text box and enter a message, such as **Welcome to our company network!** (see Figure 10-12).

10. Click **OK**. Notice how the Policy Setting column is changed for the policies you configured.

11. Leave the console window open for the next project.

Using IP Security Policies

Windows Server 2008 supports the implementation of **IP security (IPsec)**, which is a set of IP-based secure communications and encryption standards created through the Internet Engineering Task Force (IETF). When an IPsec communication begins between two computers, the computers first exchange certificates to authenticate the receiver and sender. Next, data is encrypted at the NIC of the sending computer as it is formatted into an IP packet, which consists of a header containing transmission control information, the actual data, and a footer with error-correction information. IPsec can provide security for all TCP/IP-based application and communications protocols, including FTP and HTTP, which are used in Internet transmissions. IPsec policies

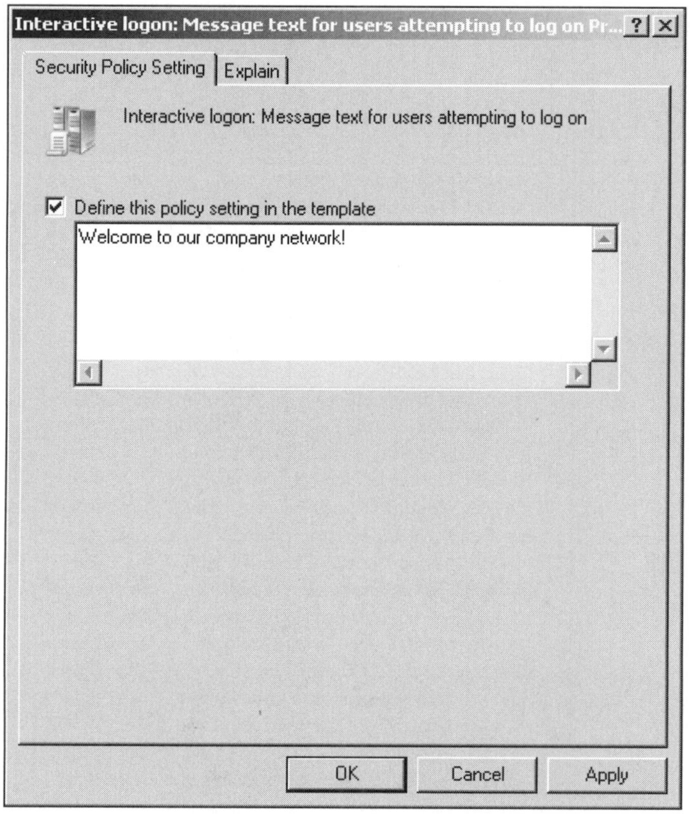

Figure 10-12 Configuring a logon message

for a domain can be managed through the Default Domain Policy. A computer that is configured to use IPsec communication can function in any of three roles:

- *Client (Respond Only)*—When Windows Server 2008 is contacted by a client using IPsec, it will respond by using IPsec communication.

- *Secure Server (Require Security)*—Windows Server 2008 will only respond using IPsec communication, which means that communication via any account and with any client is secured through strict IPsec enforcement.

- *Server (Request Security)*—When Windows Server 2008 is first contacted or when it initiates a communication, it will use IPsec by default. If the responding client does not support IPsec, Windows Server 2008 will switch to the clear mode, which does not employ IPsec.

IPsec security policies can be established through the Default Domain Policy. IPsec security policies can also be configured through the IP Security Policies Management MMC snap-in so that specific security standards apply to all computers that log on to a domain in Active Directory. (A more comprehensive security policy can be configured through the Security Configuration Wizard, as you learned in Chapter 3.)

Activity 10-8: Configuring IPsec in the Default Domain Policy

Time Required: Approximately 10 minutes
Objective: Configure IPsec group policy elements.

Description: In this activity, you learn how to configure a server to use IPsec.

1. Open the Default Domain Policy console, if it is not already open.

2. Click **IP Security Policies on Active Directory (*domainname*)** in the tree under Computer Configuration, Policies, Windows Settings, and Security Settings (see Figure 10-13).

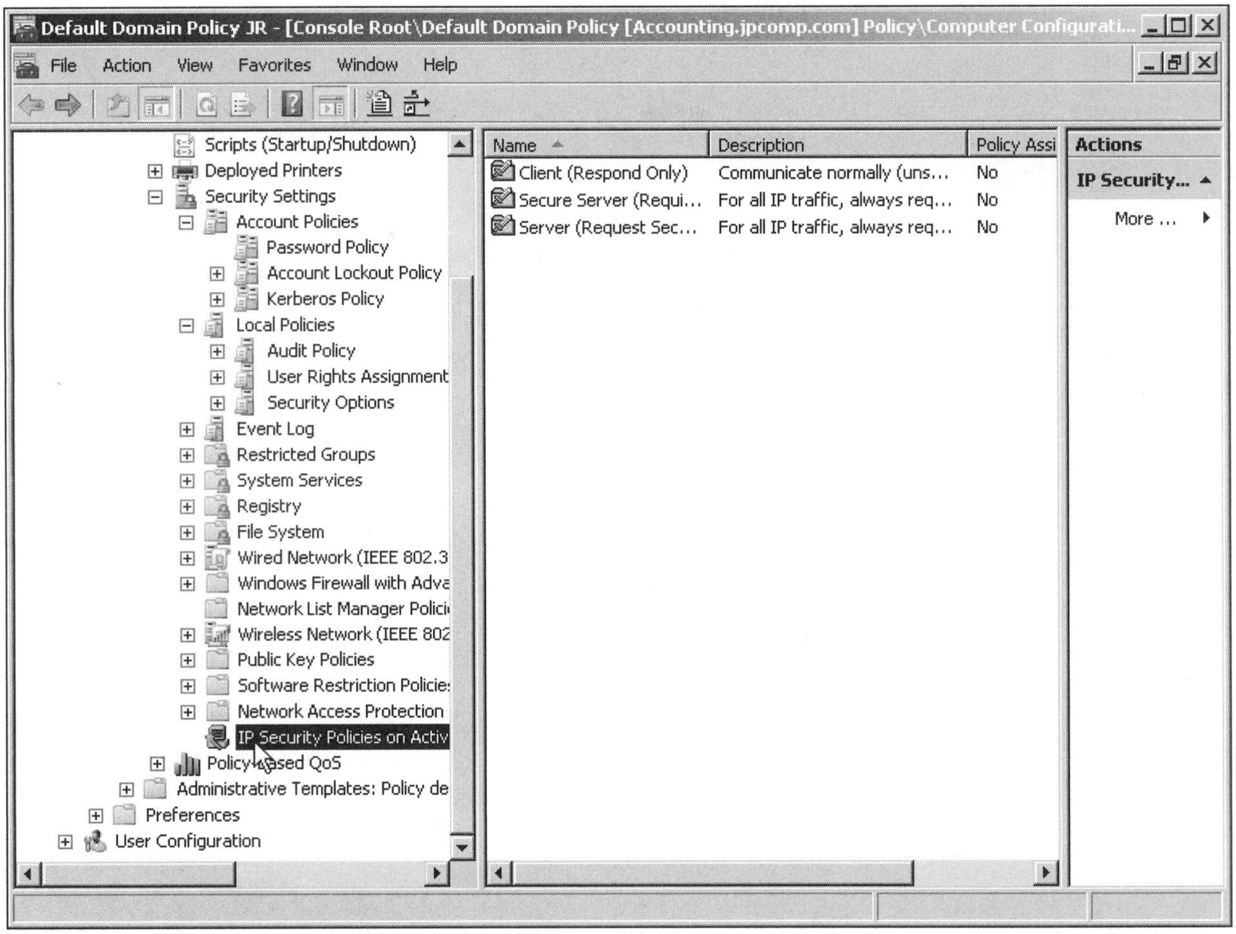

Figure 10-13 Configuring IPsec policies

3. Double-click **Server (Request Security)**. The Rules tab lists the IP Security rules already configured (see Figure 10-14). To create a new rule, you would click the Add button to start the Create IP Security Rule Wizard.

4. Double-click **All IP Traffic** to view the properties of a rule that is already created.

5. Click each tab to view the properties.

   • When you view the Filter Action tab, what Filter Action is selected? On the Connection Type tab, what connection types can be selected? What tab would you use to configure IPsec for tunneling, such as over a VPN? What Authentication Methods are used?

6. Click **Cancel**.

7. Click the **General** tab on the Server (Request Security) Properties dialog box. Review the contents of this tab.

8. Click **Cancel**.

9. In the console window, right-click **Server (Request Security)**, point to **All Tasks**, and click **Assign**. This policy is now assigned so that it will take effect for the server. (Check with your instructor about whether to leave it assigned. You can follow similar steps to unassign the policy.)

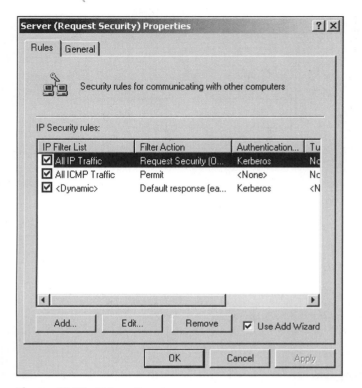

Figure 10-14 IP Security rules

10. Close the console window.

11. Click **Yes** to save the console settings.

Active Directory Rights Management Services

Active Directory Rights Management Services (AD RMS) is a server role to complement the client applications that can take advantage of Rights Management Services safeguards. **Rights Management Services (RMS)** are security rights developed by Microsoft to provide security for documents, spreadsheets, e-mail, and other types of files created by applications. Applications that can take advantage of RMS include Microsoft Word (including XPS documents), PowerPoint, Excel, SharePoint, Outlook, and Internet Explorer. Also, software developers can use Microsoft application development tools to implement RMS capabilities in the software they write.

RMS information protection goes beyond access control lists (ACLs) and the Windows Firewall. It uses security capabilities such as encryption, user authentication, and security certificates to help safeguard information. When used as a server role, AD RMS works with enabled programs to build in an extra layer of protection and offer multiple ways to control how information is used and distributed.

RMS works by implementing rights that manage who can read, modify, copy, save, print, forward, and manipulate a document, spreadsheet, e-mail, Web document, and other types of files. Rights are given to user accounts and groups. This means that an engineer working on a confidential company project can e-mail sensitive information to a boss or coworker and set security so that the e-mail cannot be printed or forwarded to anyone other than the intended recipient or recipients. The U.S. federal government uses RMS because it employs AES encryption and digital certificates. Even if Windows Firewall does not keep a sensitive e-mail from being forwarded without authorization, RMS can block the forwarding attempt. Even though an organization may not check printouts employees take home or pass on to someone else, RMS can block the information from even being printed.

Here are the general steps used in RMS security:

1. A user creates a Word document, for example, and uses RMS via Word to give a single user account on a Windows Server 2008 server access to read the document (but no other RMS access rights).

2. In the process of protecting the document with RMS, Word encrypts the document using an AES key and an additional RSA key. **RSA** (named after creators Rivest, Shamir, and Adleman) is an encryption technique that uses public and private keys along with a computer algorithm that relies on factoring large prime numbers. Also, Word provides a certificate-based identity license for the document to a Windows Server 2008 server that has the AD RMS role installed.

3. The AD RMS server issues an identity license to the client who can access the document.

4. When the authorized client attempts to read the document using Word, that client shows the AD RMS server its license to access the document.

5. The AD RMS server authenticates the client and determines the level of access. Next, the server issues a use license to the authorized client. Because the client has read access, the client can decrypt the document to read it using Word, but cannot copy, print, modify, or do other actions on the document.

If you work in an organization that needs RMS-based security and has applications to employ it, use Server Manager to install the AD RMS role in Windows Server 2008 to take advantage of RMS.

10

Managing Security Using the Security Templates and Security and Configuration Analysis Snap-Ins

Windows Server 2008 offers the Security Templates MMC snap-in that enables you to create one or more security templates to house in Active Directory. This snap-in enables you to set up security to govern the following:

- Account policies
- Local policies
- Event log tracking policies
- Group restrictions
- Service access security
- Registry security
- File system security

The Security Templates snap-in is particularly useful when you have multiple group policies to maintain or when you have multiple OUs, but many of those OUs share the same group policy. For example, if you have 20 OUs set up in a domain and use one security policy for eight OUs, a different one for eight OUs, and still another one for four OUs, then you would create three security templates.

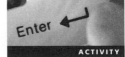

Activity 10-9: Using the Security Templates Snap-In

Time Required: Approximately 15 minutes
Objective: Learn to use the Security Templates Snap-In.

Description: In this activity, you learn how to use the Security Templates snap-in.

1. Click **Start**, click **Run**, type **mmc** in the *Open* text box and click **OK**.

2. Maximize the console window, if necessary.

3. Click the **File** menu and click **Add/Remove Snap-in**.

4. In the Add or Remove Snap-ins dialog box, click **Security Templates** and click the **Add** button. Now click **Security Configuration and Analysis** and click the **Add** button.

5. Click **OK**.

6. Click **Security Templates** in the tree.

7. In the middle pane, right-click the path to the Templates folder, such as **C:\Users\ Administrator\Documents\Security\Templates** and click **New Template** (see Figure 10-15).

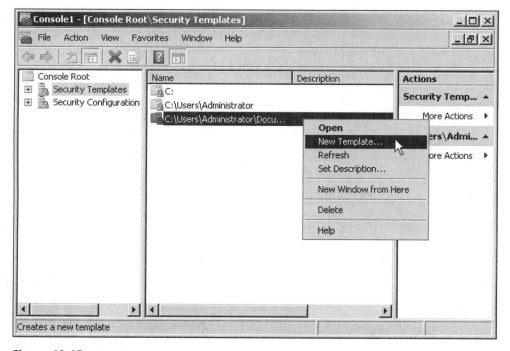

Figure 10-15   Creating a new security template

8. In the *Template name* box, enter the word **Template** plus your initials, such as *TemplateJR*. In the *Description* box, enter **Practice template**. Click **OK**.

9. Click the path to the template in the tree, such as **C:\Users\Administrator\Documents\ Security\Templates**, to ensure the new template is displayed in the middle pane.

10. Double-click the template name in the middle pane, such as *TemplateJR*.

   • What group policy elements are displayed in the middle pane that you can now configure?

11. Double-click **Account Policies** in the middle pane.

12. Double-click **Password Policy** in the middle pane.

13. Configure *Enforce password history* to **20** passwords remembered. Also, configure *Maximum password age* to **60** days, *Minimum password age* to **30** days (the suggested value), and *Minimum password length* to **8** characters (see Activity 10-2 if you want to review how to configure these).

14. Click **Account Lockout Policy** in the tree.

15. Configure *Account lockout duration* to **40** minutes and use the suggested values for *Account lockout threshold* and *Reset account lockout counter after* (see Activity 10-3).

16. Click the template in the tree, such as *TemplateJR*. Configure any other policies as desired in the middle pane.

17. Leave the console window open for the next activity; or if you have to close it now, save the console using the name **Security Tools** plus your initials, such as *Security Tools JR*, and click **Save**.

After you create a security template, you can install it using the Security Configuration and Analysis MMC snap-in. You can also use this snap-in to analyze your current security parameters. This tool offers another approach to analyzing security settings as an alternative to using the Security Configuration Wizard that you learned in Chapter 3.

Activity 10-10: Using the Security Configuration and Analysis Snap-In

Time Required: Approximately 20 minutes
Objective: Explore the features of the Security Configuration and Analysis snap-in.

Description: The Security Configuration and Analysis snap-in enables you to import a security template, apply the template, and analyze security. In this activity, you learn how to use this tool.

1. Open the Security Tools console you created in Activity 10-9, if it is closed.

2. Click **Security Configuration and Analysis** in the tree in the left pane.

3. Right-click **Security Configuration and Analysis** in the left pane and click **Open Database**.

4. In the *File name* text box, enter a database name consisting of **Domain** plus your initials, such as *Domain JR* (see Figure 10-16), and then click **Open**.

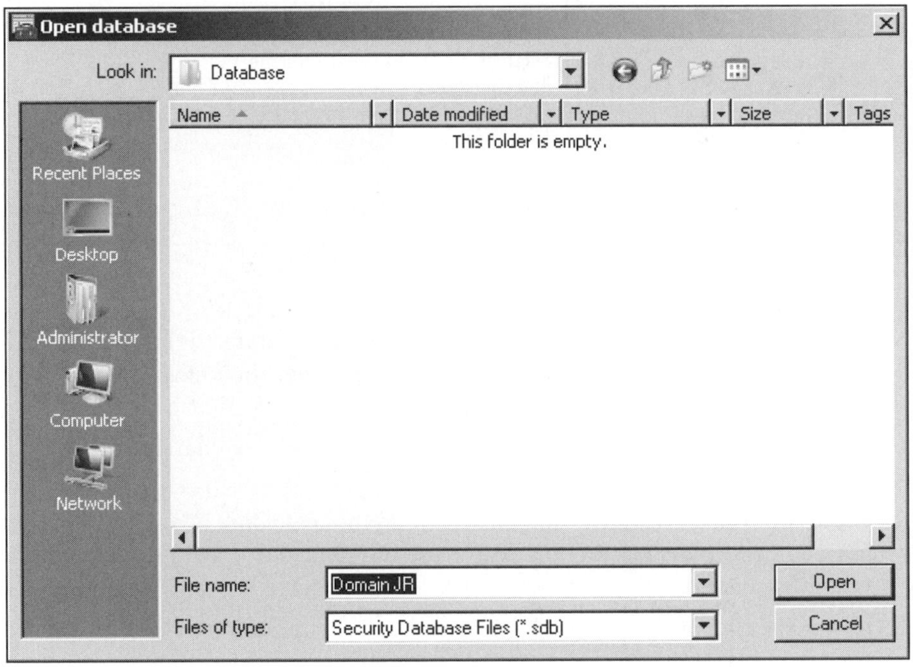

Figure 10-16 Creating a security database

5. In the Import Template dialog box, notice that the template you created in Activity 10-9 is listed. Click the template, such as *TemplateJR*, and click **Open**.

6. Right-click **Security Configuration and Analysis** in the left pane and click **Analyze Computer Now**.

7. In the Perform Analysis box, notice that the error log is created in the path \Users\ Administrator\Documents\Security\Logs and the log file name uses the name of your database, such as *Domain JR.log*. Click **OK**.

8. Right-click **Security Configuration and Analysis** in the left pane and click **View Log File**. You see the log file contents to review security analysis information. Use the scroll bar to view the contents, as shown in Figure 10-17. (Because you generated a sample database for demonstration purposes, your results don't necessarily reflect actual errors on your system.)

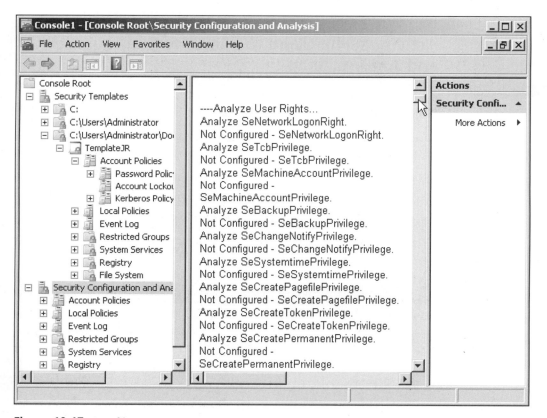

Figure 10-17 Log file contents

9. To configure your system using the imported template, right-click **Security Configuration and Analysis** and click **Configure Computer Now**, then click **OK** in the Configure System dialog box.

10. Notice that the log contents in the middle pane are now changed to show the successful configuration of security policies.

11. Close the console window and click **Yes**. In the *File name* box, enter **Security Tools** plus your initials, such as *Security Tools JR* (or use the same name as in the last step of Activity 10-9, if you already saved the console). Click **Save**.

12. If you see the Save Security Templates box, click **Yes**.

When you apply a security template, it incrementally updates the group policy object to which it is applied.

Configuring Client Security Using Policies in Windows Server 2008

You can customize desktop and other settings for client computers that access Windows Server 2008 networks. Customizing settings used by clients offers several advantages, including enhanced security and providing a consistent working environment in an organization. The settings are customized by configuring policies on the Windows Server 2008 servers that the clients access. When the client logs on to the server or the network, the policies are applied to the client.

For example, you can configure a policy that disables Control Panel or specific Control Panel options on particular clients or all clients. Another policy might be configured to ensure that all clients have an icon on their desktop that starts the same application in the same way. If a client inadvertently deletes the icon, it is reapplied the next time the client logs on. In some organizations, it is important to store sensitive information on a server to enhance security and conformity of use. If this is the case, you can use folder redirection, so that a folder appears on the clients' desktops that really points to a secure folder on the server. Windows Server 2008 offers literally hundreds of ways to configure clients through modifying group policies.

Manually Configuring Policies for Clients

You always have the option to manually configure policies that apply to clients, in order to accomplish specific purposes. For example, sometimes the management of an organization will make a decision to standardize a specific item, such as the use of certain printers or the implementation of specific software. In other cases, it might be necessary to prevent users from having access to specific functions because those functions are a security risk or a distraction.

You can manually configure one or more policies that apply to clients by using the Group Policy Object Editor snap-in or by using a customized snap-in, such as the Default Domain Policy console you configured in Activity 10-1. In either tool, you customize the desktop settings for client computers by using the Administrative Templates object under User Configuration and Policies in a group policy object (see Figure 10-18).

Table 10-1 presents very general descriptions of the Administrative Templates options under User Configuration.

Activity 10-11: Configuring Policies to Apply to Clients

Time Required: Approximately 10 minutes
Objective: Learn how to configure a group policy to apply to Windows Server 2008 clients.

Description: This activity gives you experience configuring policies to apply to clients. For this activity, assume that your organization has decided that its home page should appear in Internet Explorer for every user. Also, as a result of users configuring their own computers, the user support group has had to work overtime on unnecessary problems, and some security breaches have occurred. In response, the organization's management has decided to prohibit access to Control Panel on every client computer.

1. Click **Start,** click **All Programs,** click **Administrative Tools,** and click **Default Domain Policy** plus your initials (if you used them to save the Default Domain Policy console in Activity 10-1).

2. If necessary, click the **plus sign** in front of **User Configuration** in the tree to display the elements under it.

3. Click the **plus sign** in front of **Policies** under User Configuration.

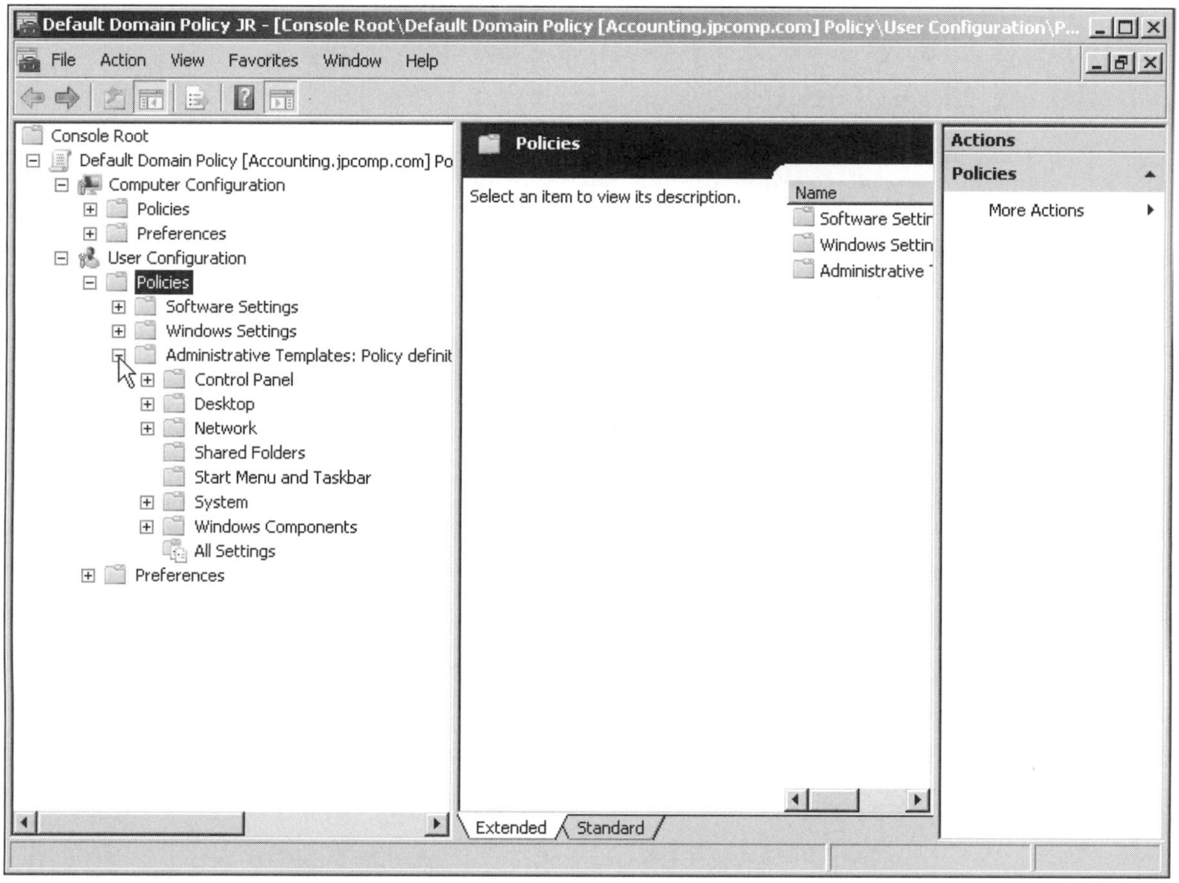

Figure 10-18 Group policies for clients

Table 10-1 Options for configuring administrative templates settings under User Configuration

Component	Description
Control Panel	Controls access to Control Panel functions such as Add or Remove Programs, Display, Printers, Programs, and Regional and Language Options; plus the ability to prohibit access to Control Panel, to hide or display only specific Control Panel icons, and force the classic Control Panel view
Desktop	Controls access to desktop functions, including specified desktop icons (such as Internet Explorer), the ability to adjust desktop toolbars, access to the My Documents icon on the desktop, use of the Desktop Cleanup Wizard, the ability to delete desktop items, and many others
Network	Controls access to many network access and configuration functions, such as the ability to configure TCP/IP, access to the New Connection Wizard, access to offline files, and many others
Shared Folders	Controls the ability to publish DFS roots and shared folders
Start Menu and Taskbar	Controls the ability to configure the Start menu and taskbar, the ability to access program groups from the Start menu, and the ability to use Start menu options including Run, Logoff, Documents, and others; also controls the ability to configure the taskbar
System	Controls access to Logon/Logoff capabilities, scripts, Task Manager functions, Change Password, group policy refresh rate, slow link detection, and other system functions
Windows Components	Controls access to installed software such as NetMeeting, Internet Explorer, Windows Explorer, MMC, Task Scheduler, Windows Installer, Windows Media Player, Windows Sidebar, and many others
All Settings	Controls a wide variety of settings, including processes, scripting, cut/copy/paste operations, file downloads, installation of desktop items, use of the screen saver, configuring Toolbar buttons, use of ActiveX controls, Internet Explorer use and maintenance, and many others

4. Double-click **Administrative Templates: Policy definitions (ADMX files) retrieved from the local machine** in the tree to display its contents.

5. Double-click **Windows Components** in the tree. Notice the range of folders that appear in the left and middle panes.

6. Double-click **Internet Explorer** in the left pane to view the settings you can configure (see Figure 10-19).

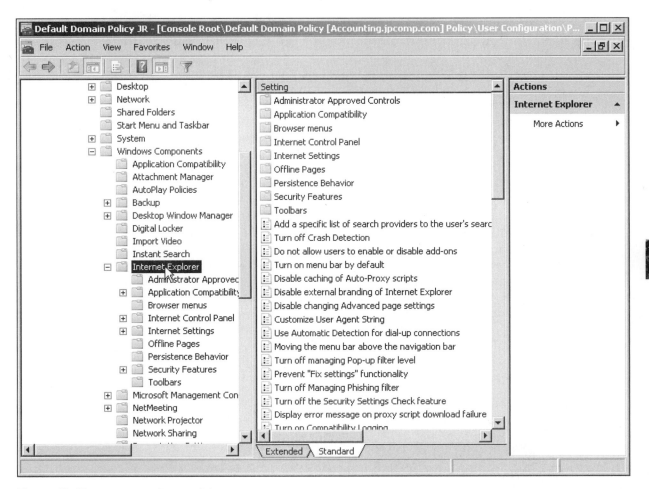

Figure 10-19 Internet Explorer policies

7. Double-click **Disable changing home page settings.** Click the **Explain** tab to see what this setting does. Click **Cancel.**

8. In the left pane under User Configuration and Administrative Templates, double-click **Control Panel.**

9. In the right pane, double-click **Prohibit access to the Control Panel.** Click the **Explain** tab to view what this does.

   • How would you enable this policy?

10. Click **Cancel.**

11. In the left pane, click each of the other folders under Administrative Templates that you have not yet opened to view their contents (**Desktop, Network, Shared Folders, Start Menu and Taskbar, System,** and **All Settings**).

12. Leave the console window open for the next activity.

Publishing and Assigning Software

For some organizations, one of the most important concerns is that their users employ the same software with the same software settings, for the sake of productivity and security. This can be particularly important for applications that have frequent version changes, such as Microsoft Word or Excel. Another important element is to make it possible for users to deploy this software without sending a user support professional to configure each workstation. This approach offers several advantages. One is that users can be more productive, because they use the same software in the same way, whether they are on their own computer or someone else's. Also, because all users have the same software setup, a large body of individuals is available to support their colleagues. These factors are great for ensuring user productivity. Another advantage is that data security weaknesses caused by users installing and configuring their own software are reduced. Further, the load on user support professionals is eased, because these professionals do not have to individually install software or troubleshoot problems created by users who install their own software.

Windows Server 2008 addresses all of these issues through the ability to configure policies for client software use. Two very effective ways to control client software use are by publishing applications and assigning applications. **Publishing applications** (or software) involves setting up software through a group policy so that the application is available for users to install from a central application distribution server, such as through the Add/Remove Programs capability via the user's desktop. An additional option is to automatically install an application on the client when a user opens a document formatted for that application, such as Microsoft Word for a .doc document. Technically, a published application is assigned to the user's account. **Assigning applications** means an application is automatically represented on the user's desktop, for example as a Start menu option or as an icon on the desktop, and which initially is really a link to the central application distribution server. The first time the user tries to open the application is the point at which it is fully installed from the distribution server and can be used from that point on. An assigned application can be assigned to either the computer or user account.

Windows Server 2008 does not monitor software licenses in either the publishing or assigning applications mode. The user is responsible for ensuring proper licensing for every application installation.

Activity 10-12: Configuring Software Installation

Time Required: Approximately 5 minutes
Objective: Learn where to set up software installation in a group policy.

Description: In this activity, you view where to configure software to be published or assigned.

1. Open your customized Default Domain Policy tool, if it is not open.

2. Under User Configuration and Policies in the tree, double-click **Software Settings**.

3. Right-click **Software installation**, and then click **Properties**.

4. Make sure that the **General** tab is displayed (see Figure 10-20). Notice that you can use the *Default package location* box to specify the location of the software that users will install, which can be on this server or on a different server in the network. Also, among the *New packages* parameters, there are options to *Publish* or *Assign* software.

5. Click each of the **Advanced, File Extensions**, and **Categories** tabs to view the properties that can be configured on those tabs.

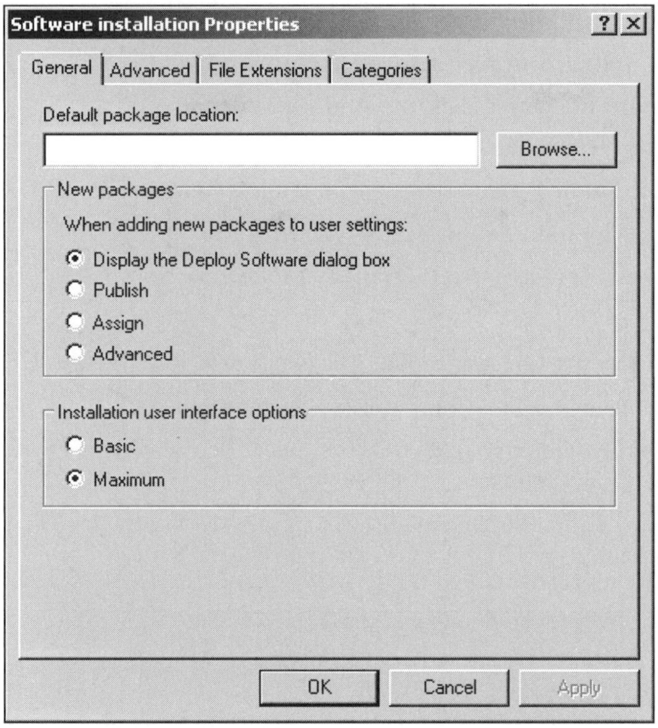

Figure 10-20 Software installation Properties dialog box

6. Click **Cancel**.

7. To view from where to set up published or assigned software, right-click **Software installation** (under User Configuration, Policies, Software Settings), point to **New**, and notice the Package option. If you were publishing or assigning software, from this point you would click Package, use the Open window to locate the installer package for the software, click Open, select Publish or Assigned, click OK, and complete the setup steps.

8. Click in an open location on your desktop to close the shortcut menus.

9. Close the console window and click **Yes** to save the settings.

Resultant Set of Policy

Resultant Set of Policy (RSoP) is used to make the implementation and troubleshooting of group policies much simpler for an administrator. When multiple group policies are applied, configuration settings and conflicts can be difficult to track. RSoP can query the existing policies that are in place and then provide reports and the results of policy changes.

RSoP supports two modes: planning and logging. Planning mode generates a report and provides the result of proposed policy changes. Logging mode generates a report based on the current policies in place and provides the resulting policy settings.

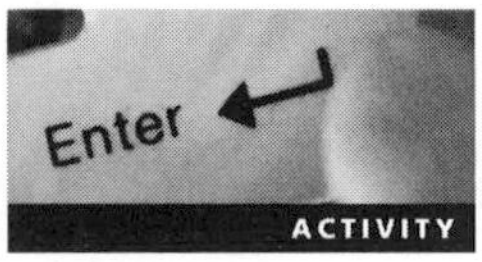

Activity 10-13: Using the Resultant Set of Policy Tool

Time Required: Approximately 10 minutes
Objective: Learn how to use the Resultant Set of Policy tool.

Description: In this activity, you create an RSoP report using the logging mode to review the policies you have set in this chapter.

1. Click **Start** and click **Run**.

2. Enter **mmc** in the *Open* text box and click **OK**.

3. Maximize the console windows, if necessary.

4. Click the **File** menu and click **Add/Remove Snap-in.**

5. Click **Resultant Set of Policy** and click the **Add** button.

6. Click **OK** in the Add or Remove Snap-ins window.

7. Right-click **Resultant Set of Policy** in the tree and click **Generate RSoP Data.**

8. Click **Next** after the Resultant Set of Policy Wizard starts.

   - What two modes can you select to use on the Mode Selection dialog box?

9. Click the option button for **Logging mode**, if it is not selected already. Click **Next.**

10. Ensure the option button for **This computer** is selected, and click **Next.**

11. For this activity, use the default settings for User Selection, which are **Display policy settings for** and **Current user.** Click **Next.**

12. Review the summary of the selections you have made (see Figure 10-21) and click **Next.** It will take a few moments for the tool to create the report.

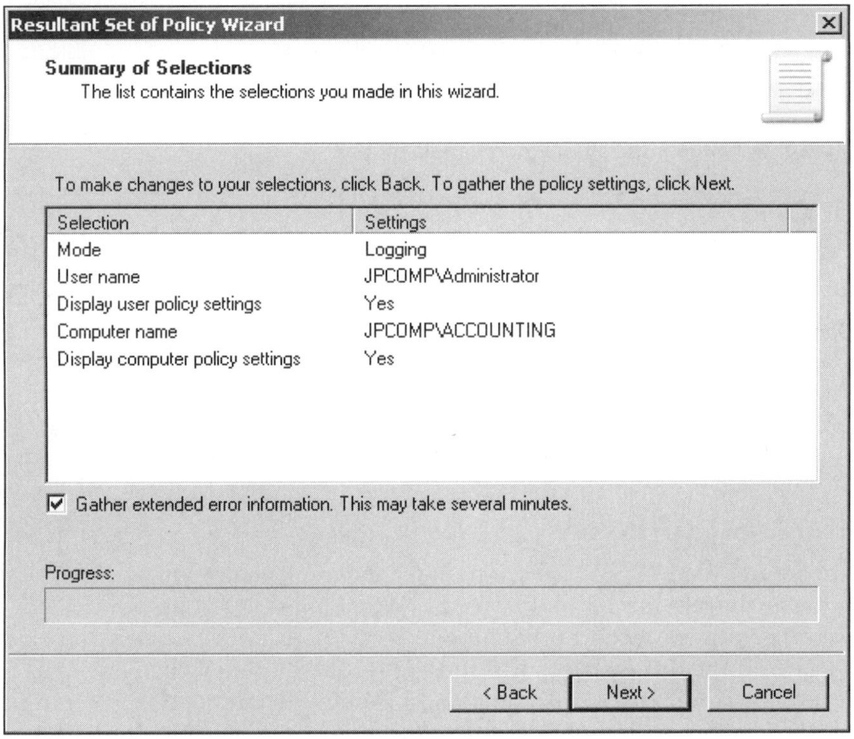

Figure 10-21 Summary of selections

13. Click **Finish.**

    - What are the options now displayed in the right pane?

14. In the middle pane, double-click **Computer Configuration.**

15. Double-click **Windows Settings.**

16. Double-click **Security Settings.** You'll see the security settings options displayed in the middle pane, as shown in Figure 10-22.

Console1 - [Console Root\Administrator on ACCOUNTING - RSoP\Computer Configuration\Wi...]

File   Action   View   Favorites   Window   Help

Name	Description	Actions
Account Policies	Password and account lockout policie	**Security Setti...** ▲
Local Policies	Auditing, user rights and security opt	More Acti... ▶
Event Log	Event Log	
Restricted Groups	Restricted Groups	
System Services	System service settings	
Registry	Registry security settings	
File System	File security settings	
Wired Network (IEEE 802.3) P...	Wired Network Policy Administration.	
Network List Manager Policies	Network name, icon and location grou	
Wireless Network (IEEE 802.1...	Wireless Network Policy Administratio	
Public Key Policies		
Software Restriction Policies		
IP Security Policies on Local C...	Internet Protocol Security (IPsec) Ad	

Console Root
- Administrator on
  - Computer C
    - Softwar
    - Window
      - Sec
    - Adminis
  - User Config
    - Softwar
    - Window

Figure 10-22   RSoP report for security settings

17. Double-click **Account Policies** in the middle pane and then double-click **Password Policy**. You should see a report of the same policies you configured earlier in this chapter for the domain, with no conflicts.

18. Close the console window and click **No** (to not save the settings).

Using the *cipher* Command

As you learned in Chapter 5 when you deploy NTFS you can use the Encrypt attribute to protect folders and files, enabling only the user who encrypts the folder or file to read it. An encrypted folder or file uses Microsoft's Encrypting File System (EFS), configuring a unique private encryption key that is associated with the user account that encrypted the folder or file. This capability might be used at a government facility that has servers housing top secret data. If a hard drive is stolen or discarded because it is malfunctioning, data on the hard drive is protected from unauthorized users.

In Chapter 5 you learned that you can set the Encrypt attribute on a folder or file through working with that folder's or file's properties. Another option that you learn in this section is to use the *cipher* command from the Command Prompt window. You can use the *cipher* command with the parameters listed in Table 10-2. If you do not specify any parameters with the command, it displays the encryption status of the current folder.

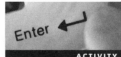

Activity 10-14: Using the *cipher* Command

Time Required: Approximately 10 minutes
Objective: Use the *cipher* command in the Command Prompt window.

Description: This activity enables you to use the *cipher* command to view which folders and files are encrypted on your system.

1. Click **Start** and click **Computer**.

2. Double-click an NTFS formatted volume on which you can create a folder, such as **Local Disk (C:)**.

Table 10-2 Common *cipher* command-line parameters

Parameter	Description
/?	Lists the *cipher* commands
/e	Encrypts the specified folder so any files added to the folder are encrypted
/d	Decrypts the contents of the specified folder and sets the folder so that any files added to the folder are not encrypted
/s	Applies other *cipher* options used with the /s option to the contents of the current folder and the contents of subfolders under it
/h	Enables you to view which folders and files use the hidden or system attributes
/k	Provides the account employing *cipher* with a new encryption key, meaning that previous keys associated with other accounts are no longer valid—use with extreme caution
/n	With the /u option, ensures that encryption keys are not modified, but that you can view the currently encrypted folders and files
/u	Updates the *cipher* user's encryption key
/r	Invokes a recovery agent key so that the server administrator can set up a recovery policy
/w	Purges data from disk space that is flagged as unused (but which still contains data that could be recovered)
/x	Copies encryption key and certificate data to a file that is encrypted for use by the *cipher* user

3. Click the **File** menu, point to **New**, and click **Folder**.

4. Type **Encrypt** plus your initials, such as *EncryptJR*. Press **Enter**.

5. Right-click the folder you created and click **Properties**.

6. On the **General** tab, click **Advanced**.

7. Click **Encrypt contents to secure data**. Click **OK**.

8. Click **OK** in the folder's Properties dialog box and close the drive window, such as Local Disk C:\.

9. Click **Start**, point to **All Programs**, and click **Accessories.**

10. Click **Command Prompt**.

11. At the prompt, type **cd ** and press **Enter** to change to the root directory.

12. Type **cipher** and press **Enter**.

- Do you see any files or folders that are encrypted, as signified by an E? How do you know if a file or folder is not encrypted?

13. Type **exit** and press **Enter** to close the Command Prompt window. (Ask your instructor about whether or not to delete the folder you created.)

Using BitLocker Drive Encryption

BitLocker Drive Encryption is a relatively new security measure for protecting hard drives. It was first introduced in Windows Vista Enterprise and Ultimate for encrypting bootable drives. Windows Server 2008 adds the ability to encrypt nonbootable drives, such as a drive connected to a server and recognized by Plug and Play that contains databases. Windows Server 2008 BitLocker Drive Encryption also supports EFI-based computers as well as computers using BIOS.

BitLocker Drive Encryption uses Trusted Platform Module for one approach to security. **Trusted Platform Module (TPM)** is a security specification for a hardware device that can be used to secure information on a different hardware device, such as a hard drive. The hardware device with the security specification can be a chip or microcontroller on a motherboard that contains the security capabilities. When used to protect a hard drive, TPM verifies that the computer to which the hard drive is connected has authority to access that hard drive. This means if a hard drive is stolen, it cannot be accessed by another computer. Security at the hardware level, such as TPM, is thought to be more foolproof than software security.

TPM security chips can be obtained from companies such as Broadcom, Infineon, and STMicroelectonics. Server manufacturers including Dell and Hewlett-Packard offer server models that have a TPM chip.

If a computer is not equipped with a TPM chip, BitLocker Drive Encryption can be used with a USB flash drive that contains a personal identification number (PIN). When the computer is booted, the user must insert the flash drive, or else hard drives cannot be accessed and the operating system does not start. Additionally, if the computer has gone into hibernation it is necessary to insert the flash drive to resume computer operation.

BitLocker Drive Encryption encrypts the entire drive, including the operating system, programs, and data files. When the system is booted and while the system is running, BitLocker Drive Encryption checks to ensure that files have not been tampered with or accessed by any sources that do not have the proper physical-device key. If it detects unauthorized access, it locks the files on the drive.

You will need to disable BitLocker Drive Encryption when you update the operating system and then enable it after the update.

Activity 10-15: Installing BitLocker Drive Encryption

Time Required: Approximately 10 minutes
Objective: Set up BitLocker Drive Encryption.

Description: This activity enables you to install BitLocker Drive Encryption. You will need to reboot the computer after it is installed, so make sure you have no other open programs or windows before you start. You do not need a TPM chip or flash drive with a PIN for this activity, because you do not enable BitLocker Drive Encryption after it is installed.

1. Click **Start**, point to **Administrative Tools**, and click **Server Manager**.

2. Click **Add Features** in the Features Summary section.

3. Click **BitLocker Drive Encryption** and click **Next**.

4. Click **Install**.

5. Click **Close**.

6. Click **Yes** to restart the computer.

7. Log back on. (You might see the Add Features Wizard again when you reboot and need to click Close and then close Server Manager.)

8. Control Panel now has a new configuration utility for configuring BitLocker Drive Encryption. Because your computer might not be equipped with a TPM chip or you might not have a flash drive with a PIN, you will only view where to configure these. Click **Start** and click **Control Panel**.

9. In the Control Panel Home view, click **Security** and look for *BitLocker Drive Encryption*. In the Classic view, look for the *BitLocker Drive Encryption* applet (see Figure 10-23).

10. Close Control Panel.

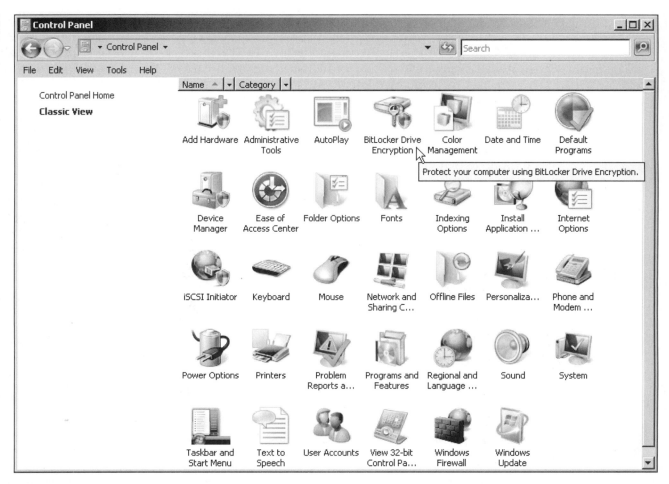

Figure 10-23 BitLocker Drive Encryption applet in Control Panel

In Step 9, if your system has a TPM chip or a flash drive with a PIN, you can click *BitLocker Drive Encryption*, click *Turn On BitLocker*, and follow the steps in the BitLocker Setup Wizard. BitLocker Drive Encryption can also be disabled from the Control Panel BitLocker Drive Encryption option by clicking *Turn Off BitLocker* (if it has previously been enabled).

Configuring NAT

Network Address Translation (NAT) serves two important functions:

- It enables an organization to automatically assign its own IP addresses on an internal network without having to set up many globally unique addresses for use over external networks.

- It protects computers on an internal network so that computers on external networks, including the Internet, cannot identify their true IP addresses on the internal network.

NAT uses a pool of private addresses for its internal network, which is a network separated from the outside world by a router or firewall, for example. Because the internal addresses are not viewed by the outside world, there is no need to have a large pool of IP addresses that can also be used over an external network. Only one or a very small pool of globally unique IP addresses are needed for outside communications. As a by-product, this means that fewer IPv4 global addresses are needed, which has kept the networking world from running out of the limited number of globally available IPv4 addresses.

One reason for developing IPv6 was to enable the use of more globally available IP addresses. The widespread use of NAT has meant that organizations can delay going to IPv6.

NAT is also a good security technique because internal IP addresses are concealed from the outside world. In a typical installation, NAT acts like a firewall so that the outside world (external networks) sees only one address, such as 129.52.0.1. However, the internal network contains many computers with addresses such as 192.168.22.1, 192.168.22.2, 192.168.22.3, 192.168.22.4, and so on. When the computer with IP address 192.168.22.4 sends a communication to the outside world, it's translated into the address 129.52.0.1. (NAT can also use a set of addresses for translation to the outside world.)

When RAS or VPN services are enabled (see Chapter 9 "Configuring Remote Access Services," you can also configure NAT for networks offering remote access through RRAS by using the Routing and Remote Access tool.

Activity 10-16: Configuring NAT

Time Required: Approximately 10 minutes
Objective: Configure NAT for the VPN you set up in Chapter 9.

Description: This activity enables you to set up NAT on an existing VPN.

1. Click **Start**, point to **Administrative Tools**, and click **Routing and Remote Access**.
2. If necessary, click the **plus sign** in front of the server to expand the items under it so you can view IPv4.
3. Click the **plus sign** in front of IPv4, if necessary to view the items under it.
4. Right-click **General** under IPv4 and click **New Routing Protocol** in the menu.
5. Double-click **NAT**, as shown in Figure 10-24.
6. In the tree under IPv4, right-click **NAT** and click **New Interface**.
7. Select the interface, such as **Local Area Connection** and click **OK**.

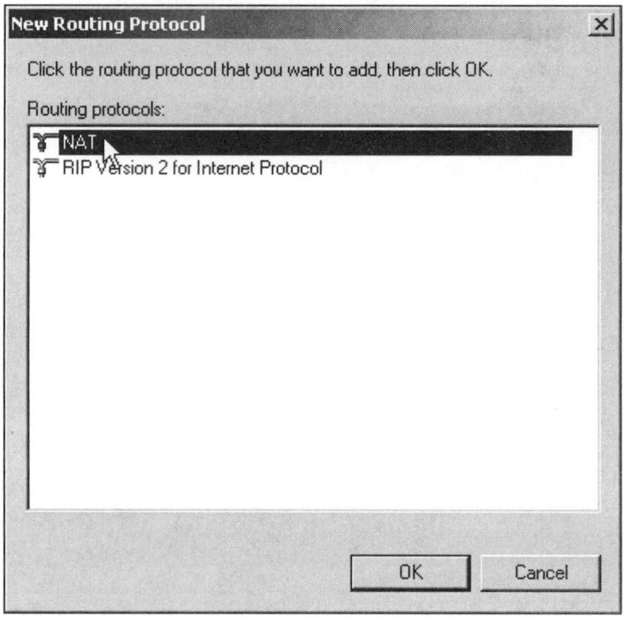

New Routing Protocol   ☒

Click the routing protocol that you want to add, then click OK.

Routing protocols:

NAT
RIP Version 2 for Internet Protocol

[OK]   [Cancel]

Figure 10-24 Selecting NAT

10

8. In the Network Address Translation Properties dialog box, click **Private interface connected to private network,** if it is not already selected. Note that the other selection is *Public interface connected to the Internet,* which enables you to shield internal network addresses from Internet-based attackers. Click **OK.**

9. Close the Routing and Remote Access window.

Windows Firewall

The Windows Firewall used in Windows Server 2008 is the same firewall technology first implemented in Windows XP with Service Pack 2 and Windows Server 2003 with Service Pack 1. It is also used in Windows Vista. The improvements made in this firewall compared with the previous version include the following:

- Protects incoming and outgoing communications
- Merges firewall filters with IPsec settings to avoid settings conflicts
- Includes the *Windows Firewall with Advanced Security* MMC snap-in
- Has firewall exceptions or rules for several kinds of managed objects

In Chapter 2, "Installing Windows Server 2008," you enabled Windows Firewall as one of the first configuration settings for a server. The next step is to configure exceptions and advanced features. Exceptions are programs that you choose to allow through the firewall in both directions (incoming and outgoing communications). When considered as a group, the exceptions are a set of rules. They can be configured for the following:

- TCP and UDP ports
- All or only specified ports
- IPv4 and IPv6
- All or only specified network interfaces
- Services by providing the path to the service

You can configure basic exceptions and advanced features from Control Panel. Specific inbound and outbound communications can be configured from the Windows Firewall with Advanced Settings MMC snap-in.

Activity 10-17: Configuring Windows Firewall via Control Panel

Time Required: Approximately 10 minutes
Objective: Configure Windows Firewall from Control Panel.

Description: In this activity, you configure Windows Firewall exceptions and network connections through Control Panel.

1. Click **Start** and click **Control Panel.**

2. In the Control Panel Home view, click **Security** and click **Allow a program through Windows Firewall.** In Classic View, double-click **Windows Firewall** and click **Allow a program through Windows Firewall.**

3. Scroll through the programs or ports that can be marked as exceptions (see Figure 10-25).
   - How can you enable VPN access through the firewall? What options are available for DHCP related activities?

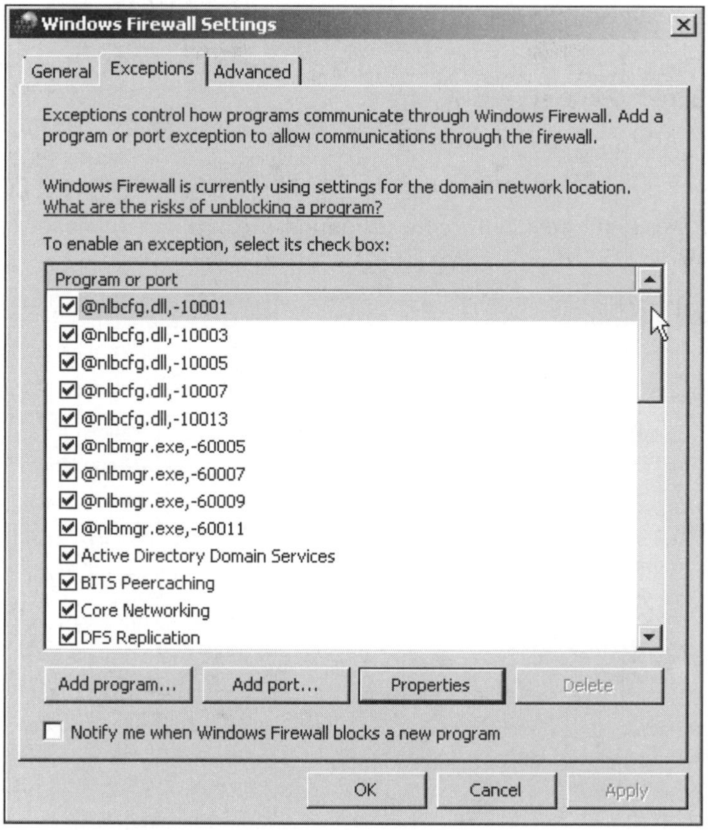

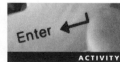

Figure 10-25 Viewing firewall exceptions

4. Click **Add program** to view programs that can be added to the exceptions (the programs listed will depend on what is installed on your computer). Click **Cancel**.

5. Click **Add port**. Notice that you can add TCP or UDP ports. Be cautious about adding ports because attackers use open ports as a way into your system. You can find a listing of TCP and UDP ports at *www.iana.org/assignments/port-numbers*. Click **Cancel**.

6. Click the **Advanced** tab in the Windows Firewall Settings dialog box.

   • For what network connections can you configure the Windows Firewall?

7. Click **Cancel** in the Windows Firewall Settings dialog box.

8. Close the Windows Firewall window if it is open and close Control Panel if it is open.

Activity 10-18: Configuring Windows Firewall Using the Snap-In

Time Required: Approximately 10 minutes
Objective: Use the Windows Firewall with Advanced Security MMC snap-in.

Description: In this activity, you view where to configure incoming and outgoing communications through Windows Firewall.

1. Click **Start** and click **Run**.

2. Type **mmc** in the *Open* text box and click **OK**.

3. Click the **File** menu and click **Add/Remove Snap-in**.

4. Click **Windows Firewall with Advanced Security** and click the **Add** button.

5. In the Select Computer dialog box, leave **Local computer (the computer this console is running on)** selected and click **Finish**.

6. Click **OK** in the Add or Remove Snap-ins window.

7. In the tree, double-click **Windows Firewall with Advanced Settings on Local Computer**.

8. Click **Inbound Rules** in the tree. Notice the inbound rules in the middle pane (see Figure 10-26).

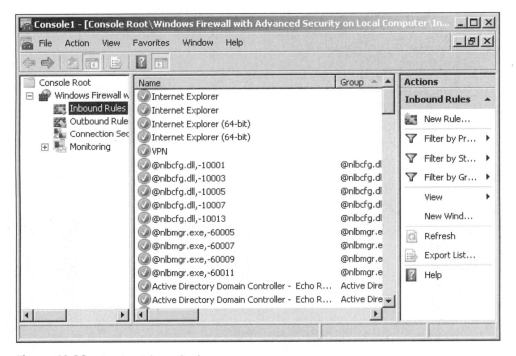

Figure 10-26 Viewing inbound rules

9. Click **Outbound Rules** in the tree and examine the outbound rules in the middle pane.

10. Close the console window.

11. Click **No** so that you don't save the settings at this time.

12. Click **Start**, point to **Administrative Tools**, and click **Server Manager**.

13. In the Security Information section, click **Go to Windows Firewall**. Notice that the middle pane shows profile and other information about the Windows Firewall (see Figure 10-27).

14. Scroll down in the middle pane to the *View and create firewall rules section*. Click **Inbound Rules**. Notice that you can view the same rules as in the Windows Firewall with Advanced Settings MMC snap-in.

15. Click one of the rules in the middle pane, such as **DNS (TCP, Incoming)**. Notice in the right pane the options to *Disable Rule* and *Delete*. As you can see, you can manage Windows Firewall advanced settings from Server Manager as well as from the Windows Firewall with Advanced Settings MMC snap-in.

16. Close Server Manager.

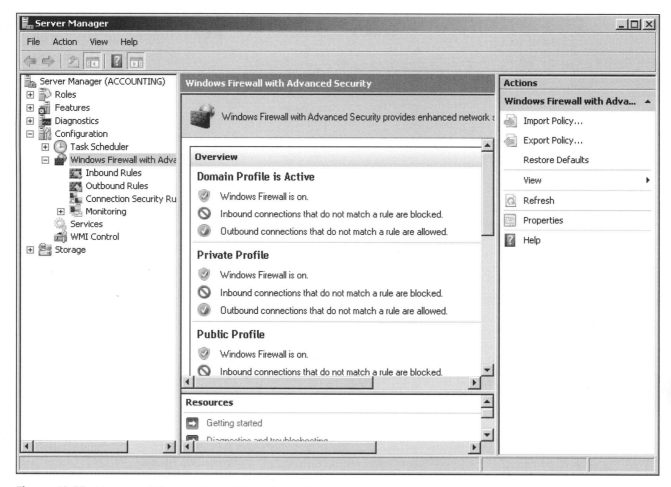

Figure 10-27 Managing Windows Firewall from Server Manager

Network Access Protection

Network Access Protection (NAP) is one of the new features of Windows Server 2008 that security conscious network administrators consider to be a vital addition for maintaining a healthy and secure network. In terms of NAP, "healthy" refers to ensuring that all authenticated computers on the network have the most recent updates and comply with network security policies. To review from Chapter 1, NAP can be used to keep a network healthy in the following ways:

- Identifies clients and other computers on a network that do not comply with the security policies set through Windows Server 2008

- Limits access by noncompliant computers, such as by not allowing access to resources, not permitting logon, or by quarantining a noncompliant computer to specific resources or portions of a network

- Automatically updates or configures a noncompliant computer to match the security policies required for access, such as by changing policy settings on the client or updating the client operating system to have the latest security patches

- Continuously checks throughout the entire network and server connection session to ensure that computers remain in compliance, even after they have been given access to the network, server, and resources

NAP can be used to ensure compliance with network security policies in the following areas:

- IPsec
- VPN
- DHCP
- Terminal Services Gateway
- 802.1X

IPsec

Through IPsec, NAP allows computers that are considered noncompliant to access the local network. However, in conjunction with NAP, IPsec ensures that noncompliant computers are ignored by computers that are compliant. In this way noncompliant computers are basically quarantined so they cannot spread problems, such as a virus, or provide a back door for an attacker. To determine compliance, NAP uses a server that is a **Health Registration Authority (HRA)**. All network clients must contact the HRA server and submit information about their security policy status and recent upgrades—called a **Statement of Health (SoH)**. After the HRA server validates a client's SoH, the client is given a certificate to enable normal operations in the network.

The HRA server is configured through a Network Policy Server (NPS). In Chapter 9, you installed Network Policy Server in Activity 9-1 and then configured a remote access policy for a VPN in Activity 9-6 using the Network Policy Server tool. Through these activities, you've already performed the beginning steps in using the NAP capabilities of a Network Policy Server.

VPN

NAP works through a VPN by enforcing the remote access policy configured for the VPN. In Chapter 9, you already learned how the remote access policy is used to verify a client. In simplified terms, the client attempts to connect, the client is checked against the remote access policy configured in the NPS server, and if the client properly verifies, the client is granted access. This process is part of the NAP initiative to maintain a secure network.

DHCP

DHCP has always been a vulnerable protocol because it is basically simple and comes without much security. DHCP with NAP provides a way to secure the DHCP process. DHCP with NAP is configured through a Network Policy Server. When configured with NAP, DHCP relies on the HRA server to determine the health status of a client. If the client is fully compliant, DHCP issues the following:

- IP address
- Subnet mask
- DNS IP address information
- Gateway IP address information

If the client is noncompliant, DHCP issues only the following:

- IP address
- Subnet mask

Also, if a remediation server is present on the network, DHCP issues to the noncompliant computer the IP address of the remediation server. A **remediation server** is one that can provide updates and security policy changes to the client to bring that client into compliance. Once the client is in compliance, it can submit a new SoH to be granted full network access and DHCP information.

TS Gateway

Terminal Services (TS) Gateway is another new feature of Windows Server 2008 that you learned about in Chapter 9. TS Gateway ensures secure access and communication when Terminal Services are used over the Internet. It does this through using HTTPS, the secure protocol for the Internet. TS Gateway combined with NAP uses the HRA server to ensure that a client is compliant with the health and security policies on a network. However, TS Gateway does not enable communications with a remediation server so that a noncompliant client can be updated. If a computer is noncompliant, it cannot gain full network access through TS Gateway.

802.1X

NAP can also work in conjunction with 802.1X. **802.1X** is a wired and wireless authentication approach offered by the IEEE (Institute of Electrical and Electronics Engineers) and is supported in modern Windows operating systems including Windows XP, Windows Vista, and Windows Server 2003/2008. 802.1X is a physical communication, port-based form of authentication. When 802.1X is enabled, the network port through which communications occur allows unauthenticated communications only until a client has been verified as NAP compliant. After the client is verified, the port becomes a controlled (secure) port permitting only authenticated communications via that client. Nonauthenticated communications are blocked. The communications through a controlled authenticated port require a special key. 802.1X is based on the use of EAP (Extensible Authentication Protocol; see Chapter 9).

The term *port* when used with 802.1X refers to a physical port on a wireless access point (such as a router or switch) or a port on a router/switch on a cabled network.

When implemented through NAP, 802.1X authentication uses the HRA server to determine compliance. If a client is not compliant, then the port on the router/switch is closed by 802.1X or the port is opened only to allow a communications path to a remediation server through which the client can be updated and then reevaluated through the HRA server.

This is a greatly simplified picture of NAP, but it is intended to give you a starting point from which to learn more. To find out more about NAP, download the NAP Platform Architecture white paper from Microsoft at *www.microsoft.com/technet/network/nap/naparch.mspx*.

Activity 10-19: Using Network Policy Server to Configure NAP

Time Required: Approximately 10 minutes
Objective: Learn about using Network Policy Server for NAP configuration.

Description: NAP can be complicated to configure, but it is important to begin by gaining a general understanding of NAP upon which to build as you become comfortable in the network server administrator role. In this activity, you view where to configure NAP using Network Policy Server, and you practice setting a NAP policy for DHCP. Network Policy Server should already be installed from when you completed Activities 9-1 and 9-6 in Chapter 9.

1. Click **Start**, point to **Administrative Tools**, and click **Network Policy Server**.

2. Click **NPS (Local)** in the tree.

3. In the right pane, click **Configure NAP**.

4. Click the **down arrow** in the *Network connection method* box, as shown in Figure 10-28. Notice the options to configure the following:

- Dynamic Host Configuration Protocol (DHCP)

- IPsec with Health Registration Authority (HRA)

- IEEE 802.1X (Wired)

- IEEE 802.1X (Wireless)

- Virtual Private Network (VPN)

- Terminal Services Gateway (TS Gateway)

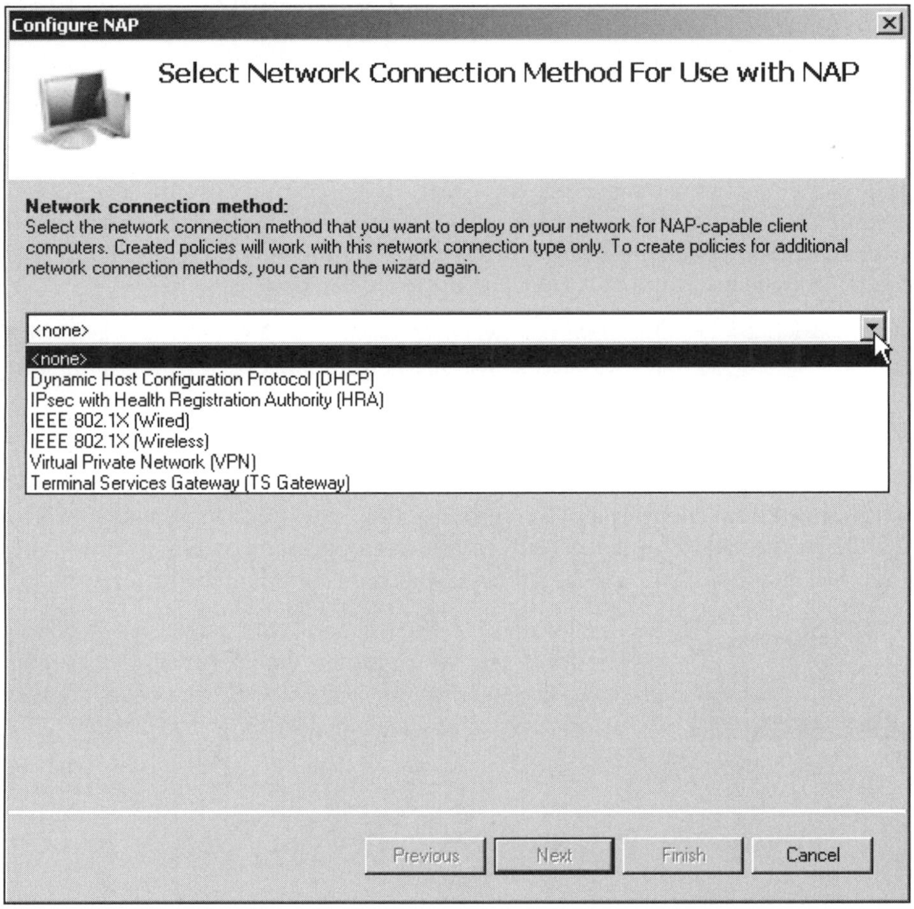

Figure 10-28 Connection method options

5. To configure NAP for a specific type of connection, you can select any of these options. After you select the option, the NAP installation process guides you through a specific configuration. For practice, click **Dynamic Host Configuration Protocol (DHCP)**.

6. Click **Next**.

7. In the next window, you could add this server to be a RADIUS client. Because RADIUS is not presently used on your network, click **Next**.

8. Leave the *DHCP scopes* box empty so that the NAP policy applies to all DHCP scopes. Click **Next**.

9. In the Configure User Groups and Machine Groups window, you can specify groups for the NAP policy. Click **Next**.

10. In the Specify a NAP Remediation Server Group or URL window, you can specify remediation computers that clients can access. Click **Next**.

11. The Define NAP Health Policy window enables you to configure the implementation of the health policy. In this window, you can enable automatic remediation and specify network access for NAP-ineligible clients (see Figure 10-29). Click **Next**.

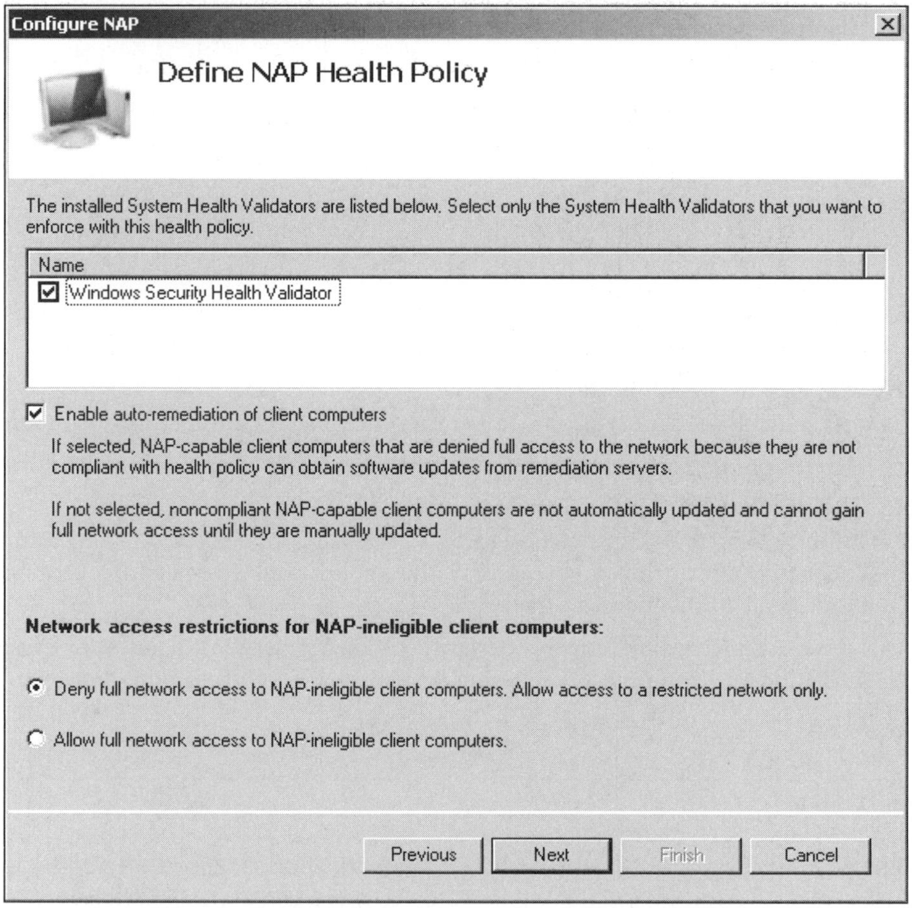

Figure 10-29 Defining the NAP health policy

12. Review the NAP information and click **Finish**.

13. Close the Network Policy Server window.

Chapter Summary

- Windows Server 2008 has many new or enhanced security features. These include Server Core, new group policy options, Windows Firewall enhancements, Network Access Protection, Security Configuration Wizard, User Account Control, and BitLocker Drive Encryption. Some of these features are discussed earlier in the book and others are introduced in this chapter.

- Group policy offers a way to standardize security across a domain, OU, site, or local server.

- Configure account policies to include security features such as password security, account lockout, and Kerberos authentication.

- Use audit policies to track how resources are accessed, such as folders, files, or user accounts.

- User rights policies enable you to create specific security controls over privileges and logon access.

- Security options are specialized policies for accounts, auditing, devices, domain controllers, logon, clients, network security, system shutdown, system settings, and others. Windows Server 2008 offers 78 new specialized policies.

- Configure IPsec security policy for strong client authentication.

- Implement Active Directory Rights Management Services for application-level security.

- Use the Security Templates and Security Configuration Analysis snap-ins to configure consistent security policies for an Active Directory container such as a domain.

- For better control over the activities of clients, configure security policies on the local server or in the domain that applies to clients.

- Use Resultant Set of Policy to plan and troubleshoot group policy settings.

- The *cipher* command is a valuable tool for implementing the Encrypting File System from the Command Prompt window.

- BitLocker Drive Encryption is a security measure for protecting entire hard drives.

- Network Address Translation is used to disguise IP addresses on an internal network from the outside world.

- Windows Firewall can be configured to allow traffic exceptions and to manage incoming and outgoing traffic, so you can use the applications you need but still close doors that don't need to be open to attackers.

- Network Access Protection is designed to keep a network healthy by ensuring that authenticated computers' operating systems are kept up to date and by enforcing security policies.

Key Terms

802.1X   A wireless and wired port-based authentication standard offered by the IEEE.

Active Directory Rights Management Services (AD RMS)   A server role that works with client applications that can take advantage of RMS safeguards. *See* Rights Management Services (RMS).

Advanced Encryption Standard (AES)   A relatively new standard adopted by the U.S. government to replace DES and 3DES, and that employs a private-key block-cipher form of encryption.

assigning applications   (or software)   Means an application is automatically represented on the user's desktop, for example as a Start menu option or as an icon on the desktop, and which initially is really a link to a central application distribution server. The first time the user tries to open the application is the point at which it is fully installed from the distribution server and can be used from that point on.

BitLocker Drive Encryption   A security measure for protecting hard drives in Windows Vista Enterprise and Ultimate as well as Windows Server 2008. It can use a TPM chip on a computer or a flash drive with a PIN to enforce security. *See* Trusted Platform Module (TPM).

demilitarized zone (DMZ)   A portion of a network that is relatively less secure because it is between two networks, such as between a private network and the Internet.

group policy   A set of policies that govern security, configuration, and a wide range of other settings for objects within containers in Active Directory.

group policy object (GPO)   An object in Active Directory that contains group policy settings for a site, domain, OU, or local computer.

Health Registration Authority (HRA)   A server that network clients contact to provide their Statement of Health (SoH). On the basis of the SoH, the HRA server grants a certificate to enable the client to use network services. *See* Statement of Health (SoH).

inherited rights   User rights that are assigned to a group and that automatically apply to all members of that group.

IP security (IPsec)   A set of IP-based secure communications and encryption standards created through the Internet Engineering Task Force (IETF).

Kerberos   A security system developed by the Massachusetts Institute of Technology to enable two parties on an open network to communicate without interception from an intruder, by creating a unique encryption key for each communication session.

publishing applications   (or software)   Involves setting up software through a group policy so that the application is available for users to install from a central distribution server, such as through the Add/Remove Programs capability via the user's desktop.

remediation server   A server that can issue updates and security policy changes to a client computer to bring that client into Network Access Protection (NAP) compliance.

Resultant Set of Policy (RSoP)   A Windows Server 2008 tool that enables you to produce reports about proposed or current group policy settings for the purpose of planning and troubleshooting when multiple group policies are in use (such as for OUs and domains).

Rights Management Services (RMS)   Security rights developed by Microsoft to provide security for documents, spreadsheets, e-mail, and other types of files created by applications.

RSA   Developed by Rivest, Shamir, and Adleman, an encryption technique that uses public and private keys along with a computer algorithm that relies on factoring large prime numbers.

service ticket   In Kerberos security, a permanent ticket good for the duration of a logon session (or for another period of time specified by the server administrator in the account policies) that enables the computer to access network services beginning with the Logon service.

Statement of Health (SoH)   Information that a client provides to a Health Registration Authority (HRA) to enable it to gain access to network services. The information includes security policy and recent update verification. This is part of Microsoft's Network Access Protection (NAP) capabilities. *See* Health Registration Authority (HRA).

Trusted Platform Module (TPM)   A security specification for a hardware device used to secure information on another device, such as on a hard drive. The TPM hardware device is typically a chip.

User Account Control (UAC)   Enables software and device installations in standard user mode while still ensuring authorization from the administrator. UAC is intended to further remove these activities from access to the kernel to protect the operating system and make it difficult to destabilize through malware and intrusions.

Windows NT LAN Manager version 2 (NTLMv2)   An authentication protocol used in legacy Windows NT Server systems and retained in all Windows systems for backward compatibility for clients that cannot support Kerberos.

Review Questions

1. Your IT director has read that Windows Server systems use NTLMv2 for default authentication, but he would rather have Kerberos as the authentication from the Windows Server 2008 domain controllers on the network. Which of the following do you mention to the IT director?

   a. NTLMv2 offers better authentication security than Kerberos.

   b. Windows Server 2008 does not support Kerberos because it is not compatible with Windows Vista.

   c. Kerberos is only available for Windows Server 2008 as an extension obtained from open source software providers.

   d. Kerberos is installed by default on Windows Server 2008 DCs.

2. In Windows 2000 Server, you installed drivers for a new laser printer and the installation altered some of the system files so that you had to reinstall Windows 2000 Server. Which of the following is designed to help prevent this from happening in Windows Server 2008?

   a. User Account Control

   b. Device Stability Wizard

   c. Driver Monitor

   d. Device Manager

3. You have received a Word memo from your supervisor outlining the five-year strategic plan for your company, which operates in a very competitive field. When you try to copy the memo or print it out, you discover you don't have the rights to complete these actions. What Windows Server 2008 and Word capability did your supervisor use to safeguard the memo?

   a. NAP application protection

   b. GUID access

   c. Rights Management Services

   d. XPS View Control

4. A Statement of Health is issued by a client to a _____ server.

5. Your company is considering the use of Network Address Translation for remote access communications. Which of the following are advantages of Network Address Translation? (Choose all that apply.)

   a. It doubles the speed of network protocol transfer.

   b. It enables an organization to automatically assign its own IP addresses on an internal network without having to obtain a globally unique address.

   c. It broadcasts the IP addresses of internal network computers so they can be registered on DNS servers throughout the Internet for faster lookup.

   d. It changes MAC addresses to the loopback address for disguising clients.

6. The _____ authentication method uses a key distribution center and a _____ ticket.

7. You need to lock down a server and ensure that only necessary TCP and UDP port communications are used for inbound and outbound network communications. What tool enables you to lock down communications through these ports?

   a. Port Switch Service

   b. NAT

   c. Windows Firewall

   d. Group Policy Editor

8. A TPM chip is used with _____ Encryption.

9. Attackers have been breaking into accounts on your server by using password-guessing software that goes through thousands of passwords before succeeding in finding combinations that work for particular user accounts. Which of the following security policies can you configure to block this type of intrusion?

   a. enforce password history

   b. reversible password encryption

   c. password detection

   d. account lockout

10. To apply a security template, you can import it into the _____ tool and then apply it from that tool.

11. You are in the Command Prompt window and decide to encrypt a folder. Which of the following commands do you use?

    a. *cipher /e*

    b. *attrib /s*

    c. *cipher /k*

    d. *attrib /c*

    e. There is no Command Prompt command to encrypt a folder.

12. In your company, users are responsible for updating their own Windows client computers. However, in the past week two client computers on the network have been hacked by attackers through the Internet. In both cases, the users had not recently installed updates that would have prevented the attacks. What can you do to address this problem?

    a. Switch to using global network RMS.

    b. Set user rights security to lock out computers that are behind on updates.

    c. Configure to use NAP and establish a remediation server.

    d. After all users have received an IP address from DHCP, disable DHCP so that intruders cannot access the network.

13. You have configured security policies for the domain and for nested OUs. After completing the configuration, users in two OUs do not have the access to resources that they need. What tool can you use to quickly troubleshoot the problem?

    a. Security Templates snap-in

    b. Resultant Set of Policy tool

    c. Network Access Protection Analysis tool

    d. Group Policy Object Editor

14. Which of the following can be set up as security policies to govern how users manage their account passwords? (Choose all that apply.)

    a. Passwords must use MS-CHAPv2

    b. Passwords must meet complexity requirements

    c. Minimum password length

    d. Maximum password age

15. Name two advantages of Advanced Encryption Standard (AES).

16. Your company employs a part-time person whose sole job is to install software for users. That person is now leaving and the company wants to automate the process so that users can reliably install their own software. Which of the following Windows Server 2008 capabilities can you use?

    a. publishing applications

    b. Automated Application Installation Wizard

    c. Pushing applications

    d. GPO application installation

17. Your assistant wants to audit all kinds of activities on a server, from every time someone accesses the server to every time a file or printer is used. What is your response?

    a. Auditing all of these activities is vital for good server security.

    b. It is not possible to audit logon events.

    c. Auditing access to all processes should be added to the list.

    d. Use auditing sparingly; it creates high maintenance for the security logs.

10

18. Which of the following areas have security enhancements in Windows Server 2008? (Choose all that apply.)

   a.   group policy

   b.   reduced attack surface through Server Core

   c.   Network Access Protection

   d.   NIC driver encryption

19. Name two Internet communications protocols that IPsec can help secure.

20. What tool can you use to configure NAT for a virtual private network?

Case Projects

CASE PROJECTS

People's Bank and Trust is a full-service, privately owned community bank. The bank is divided into the following departments: Customer Service, Loans, Business Services, and Investment Services. The bank is presently upgrading its servers from Windows Server 2003 to Windows Server 2008. Also, it is gradually upgrading client computers from a mix of Windows 2000 and XP to Windows Vista. The cash drawers at the tellers' booths are connected to Windows XP computers, which are networked into the servers. The bank uses Active Directory with one small domain and with OUs for each department. All of the servers at the bank are configured as DCs.

In addition to walk-in and drive-up services, People's Bank offers ATM services and Internet banking. The Internet banking is performed through a Windows Server 2003 Web server located at the bank. The bank also offers automated telephone banking services that are tied into its Windows servers.

The bank auditors have recently raised concerns in several areas of computer and network security that the bank wants to address at the same time as it upgrades the client and server computers. The IT director at the bank has retained you via Aspen Consulting to assist with the transition to Windows Server 2008 and to help resolve the security issues raised by the audit.

Case Project 10-1: Password Security

Inadequate password security is one of the areas that the auditors believe needs improvement. The audits raised the following concerns:

- Some bank employees have used the same user account password for several years.

- Many of the existing passwords are only four or five characters in length.

- Several bank employees regularly change their passwords, but rotate between the same three or four passwords with each change.

- An employee who has forgotten a password can keep trying different combinations for as long as they like, until they hit upon the password or give up trying.

What capabilities in Windows Server 2008 enable the bank to address the auditors' concerns? Create a detailed report of your recommendations for the bank's Audit Response Committee. Also, for the IT manager who is a committee member, note what tool can be used to implement your recommendations.

Case Project 10-2: Using Windows Server 2008 Auditing

The Audit Response Committee would like to know in what ways Windows Server 2008 can provide audit information, because no auditing is currently in use. The committee would like you to create a report that provides examples of what can be audited. Also, the IT director wants you to create a set of general instructions for how to set up auditing changes to files.

Case Project 10-3: Managing Client Computers

The auditors would like to see more standardization of each user's desktop and curtail the ability to change some important settings. Specifically they would like to:

- Prevent Windows XP and Windows Vista clients from using Control Panel after computers have been set up.
- Ensure that all Windows XP and Vista clients start the most recent version of Microsoft Excel when they click on a file with an .xls extension.
- Prevent users from changing information about their network connections.
- Remove the My Music icon from the Start menu.

For any of these that are possible, include general instructions for the IT Department about how to implement them.

Case Project 10-4: Solving a Problem with Security Updates

The bank auditors have mentioned in several places in the audit that the network is only as secure as its weakest link. One of their concerns is that many users never take the time to update their computers as a way to apply the latest security patches. They consider regular client computer updates to be as vital as applying regular operating system updates on the bank's servers. What Windows Server 2008 capability can address this concern? Create a report for the Audit Response Committee with your recommendations and include a brief description of any security features that accompany the capability you discuss.

10

chapter 11

Server and Network Monitoring

After reading this chapter and completing the exercises, you will be able to:

- Understand the importance of server monitoring
- Monitor server services and solve problems with services
- Use Task Manager for server monitoring
- Configure and use Performance Monitor
- Set up and use Data Collector Sets for performance and diagnostic information
- Use Reliability Monitor
- Implement the SNMP service for network management

When you hike a favorite trail repeatedly, you grow in your knowledge and appreciation for that trail. You come to understand and see things on your hikes that newcomers or those who aren't paying attention miss completely. The same thing is true about monitoring a server and its network over time. The more you use monitoring tools, the more you come to understand how a server and its network perform in all kinds of situations. This chapter introduces you to tools that enable you to truly know your server and network as an expert. After your server is up and running, this knowledge will make you a proficient server administrator who can quickly spot and solve problems, often before anyone experiences them.

In this chapter, you begin by learning about the importance of monitoring. You learn to monitor server services and how to fix problems with the services. You go on to use Task Manager as a basic tool for monitoring and managing applications, processes, services, system performance, network performance, and users. Next, you learn to use Performance Monitor, which is a versatile tool you'll come to rely on for monitoring your server and network inside and out. Along with Performance Monitor, you use Data Collector Sets to check on server and network performance and to quickly diagnose problems. Next, you use Reliability Monitor for a quick picture of how reliable your system is over time, so you can work on improving reliability. Finally, you implement the SNMP service for network management.

Introduction to Server Monitoring

Server monitoring is performed for several reasons. One reason is to establish a baseline of performance so problems can be more easily identified when they occur. It may be difficult to diagnose a problem or determine if there is a resource shortage unless you first know what performance is typical for your server. Other reasons to monitor servers are to prevent problems before they occur and to diagnose existing problems. Monitoring enables you to pinpoint problems and identify solutions, for example by tracking disk errors and replacing a hard disk before it fails.

The most important way to get to know your server is to use monitoring tools to establish normal server performance characteristics. This is a process that involves establishing benchmarks. **Benchmarks** or **baselines** provide a basis for comparing data collected during problem situations with data showing normal performance conditions. This creates a way to diagnose problems and identify components that need to be upgraded or replaced.

The best way to get a feel for a server's performance is to establish a baseline and then frequently monitor server performance, comparing the data collected with that in the baseline. Performance indicators can be confusing at first, so the more time you spend observing them, the better you'll understand them.

Sample benchmarks that you might establish include the following:

- Test benchmarks of disk, CPU, memory, and network response before releasing a new operating system, server hardware, or a complex application to users
- Slow, typical, and heavy usage of disk, CPU, memory, and other server resources for each server
- Slow, typical, and heavy usage of the combined network and server resources
- Growth of use of network and server resources at specific intervals, such as every six months to a year

In the sections that follow, you'll explore all types of techniques to monitor resources for benchmarks, to help avoid problems and to fix problems as they occur.

Monitoring Server Services

Servers are always running a number of services. The exact number of services depends on the number and types of components you have installed. Table 11-1 describes some of the services typically in use in Windows Server 2008.

Table 11-1 Sample Windows Server 2008 services

Service	Description
Active Directory Domain Services	Enables Active Directory services for a network and must be running to enable users to log on to the network (when Active Directory is installed)
Computer Browser	Keeps a listing of computers and domain resources to be accessed
DHCP Server	Enables clients to obtain leased IP addresses (when the DHCP Server role is installed)
DNS Server	Enables resolution of DNS names and IP addresses (when the DNS Server role is installed)
File Replication	Replicates the Active Directory elements on multiple DCs (when Active Directory is installed)
Intersite Messaging	Transfers messages between different Windows Server 2008 sites
IPsec Policy Agent	Enables IPsec security and enforces IPsec policies
Kerberos Key Distribution Center	Enables Kerberos authentication and the server as a center from which to issue Kerberos security keys and tickets
Microsoft iSCSI Initiator Service	Manages access to iSCSI devices, such as hard drives in a Storage Area Network (SAN)
Netlogon	Maintains logon services such as verifying users who are logging on to the server or a domain
Network Access Protection Agent	Permits clients to use NAP capabilities (when NAP is installed)
Plug and Play	Enables automatic detection and installation of new hardware devices or devices that have changed
Print Spooler	Enables print spooling
Protected Storage	Enables data and services to be stored and protected by using private key authentication
Remote Procedure Call (RPC)	Provides remote procedure call services
Remote Procedure Call (RPC) Locator	Used in communications with clients using remote procedure calls to locate available programs to run
Remote Registry	Enables the Registry to be managed remotely
Resultant Set of Policy Provider	Enables use of Resultant Set of Policy to determine group policy settings
Security Accounts Manager	Keeps information about user accounts and their related security setup
Server	A critical service that supports shared objects, logon services, print services, and remote procedure calls
System Event Notification Service	Enables the detection and reporting of important system events, such as a hardware or network problem
Task Scheduler	Used to start a program at a specified time and works with the software Task Scheduler
TCP/IP NetBIOS Helper	Activated when TCP/IP is installed, and used to enable NetBIOS name resolution and NetBIOS network transport
User Profile Service	Loads and unloads user profiles and is necessary for users to log on or off
Windows Event Log	Enables server events to be logged for later review or diagnosis in case problems occur
Windows Firewall	Enables Windows Firewall to control incoming and outgoing communications
Windows Time	Enables updating the clock
Windows Update	Enables the operating system to obtain updates
Workstation	Enables network communications and access by clients over the network via the Server Message Block (SMB) protocol (SMB is used to access shared resources such as folders and printers)

11

Accessing Server Services

As you have learned previously, you can access server services through Server Manager or the Computer Management tool (see Figure 11-1).

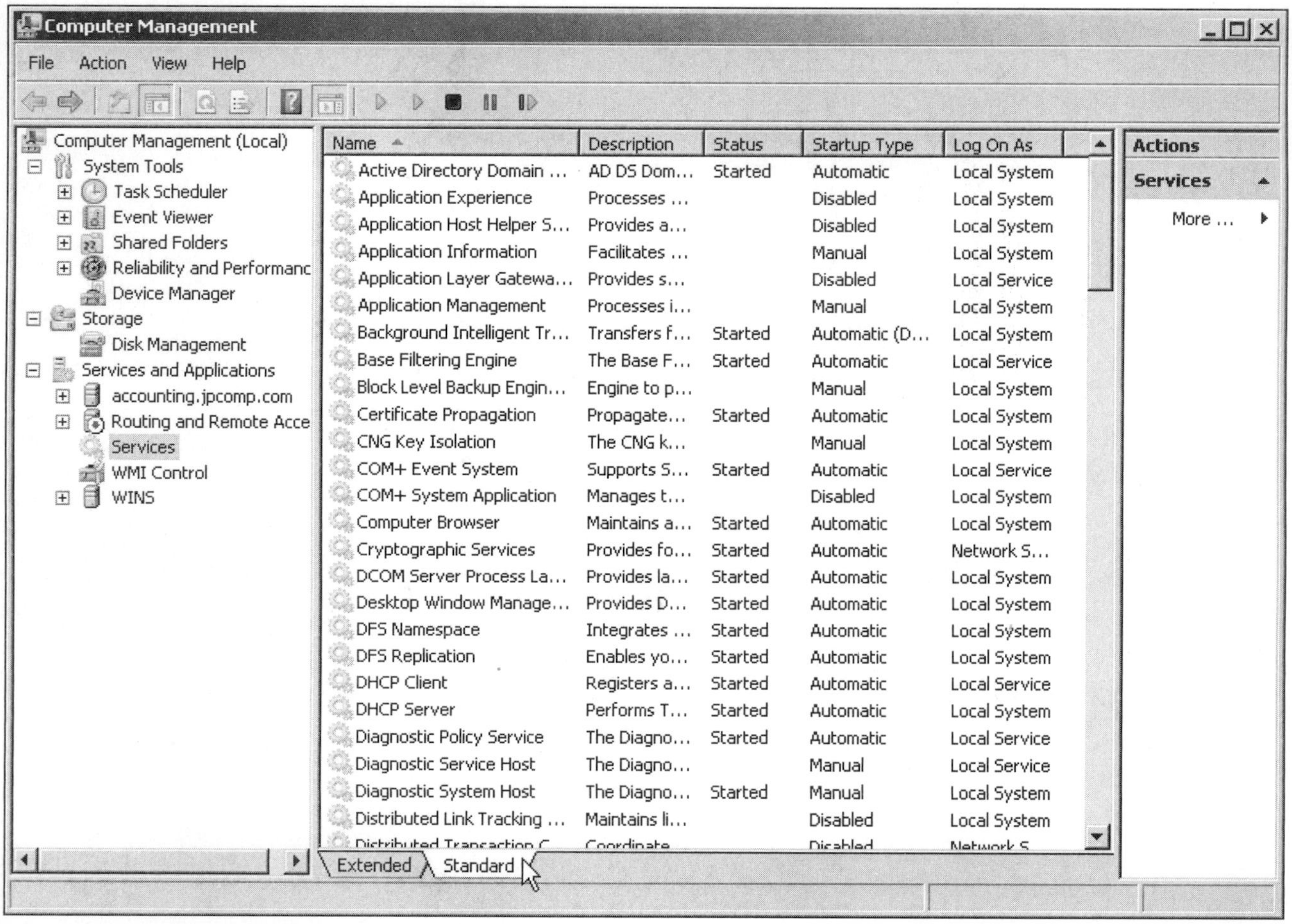

Figure 11-1   Computer Management tool

When you click the Standard tab, as shown in Figure 11-1, the services are displayed in the middle pane in five columns of information. The Name column shows services listed alphabetically. A short description of each service is provided in the Description column. The Status column indicates the current status of the service as follows:

- *Started* shows that the service is running.
- *Paused* means that the service is started, but is not available to users.
- A blank means that the service is halted or has not been started.

The Startup Type column shows how a service is started when the computer boots. Many services are started automatically when the server is booted. Some services are started manually because they might not be needed until a given time. Services that are not set to start automatically or manually are disabled. The Log On As column specifies the account under which the service is running. Most services log on to a Local System account. Some network-related services, such as Network Access Protection Agent, log on to a Network Services account.

Solving a Problem with a Service

When you experience a problem on a server that is associated with a service, check the status of the service to make sure that it is started or set to start automatically. You can start, stop, pause, resume, or restart a service by right-clicking it and clicking any of these options. For example, occasionally a service does not start properly when the server is booted or hangs while the server is running, such as the Print Spooler service. The Server Manager and Computer Management tools provide a way to monitor this situation. Even if the Print Spooler shows that it is started, if you determine that you want to restart it, right-click the service and click Restart (keep in mind, though, that you will lose print jobs in the print queue).

 Use the Stop option carefully, because some services are linked to others. Stopping one service will stop the others that depend on it. For instance, stopping the Workstation service affects these other services: Computer Browser, DFS Namespace, Netlogon, and Terminal Services Configuration. The system gives you a warning when other services are affected by stopping a particular service.

CAUTION

You can check dependencies by double-clicking a service and clicking the Dependencies tab (see Figure 11-2).

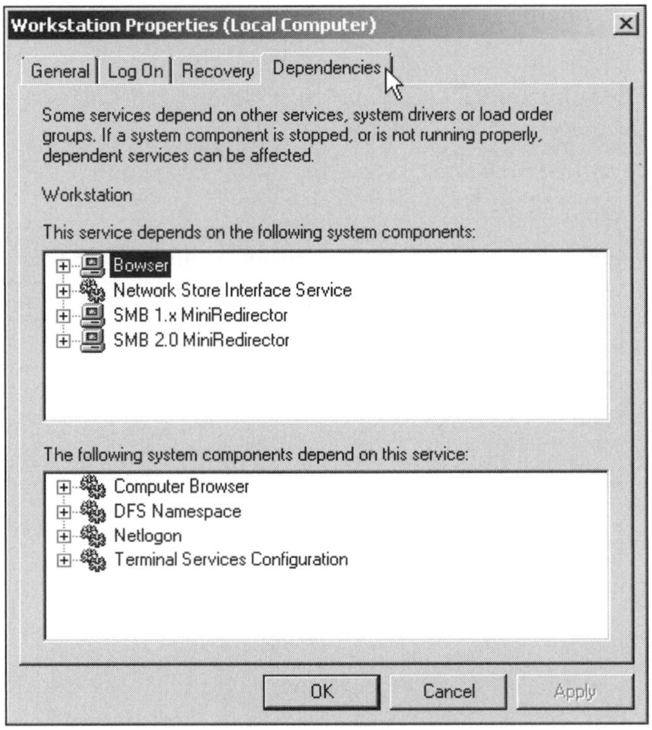

Figure 11-2 Workstation service dependencies

 Several services are linked to the Server and Workstation services, including logged-on users. If it is necessary to stop one of these services—for example, to diagnose a problem—give the users advance warning or stop the service after work hours.

NOTE

Pausing a service takes it offline to be used only by Administrators or Server Operators. A paused service is restarted by right-clicking it and clicking Restart.

Another way to manage a service is to double-click it to view that service's properties (see Figure 11-2). For example, you can set a service to start automatically by double-clicking the service, accessing the General tab, and setting the Startup type box to Automatic.

For all of the activities in this chapter, you'll need an account with Administrator privileges. Also, these activities can be completed on a virtual server or computer, such as in Hyper-V.

Some steps in the activities in this book include bulleted questions with space for you to record your responses/answers.

Activity 11-1: Monitoring and Managing a Service

Time Required: Approximately 10 minutes
Objective: Use the Computer Management tool to monitor and manage a Windows Server 2008 service.

Description: In this activity, you practice monitoring, starting, and stopping a service. You also view a service's dependencies.

1. Click **Start,** point to **Administrative Tools,** and click **Computer Management.** (You can also open the Computer Management tool as an MMC snap-in.)

2. Double-click **Services and Applications** in the tree in the left pane.

3. Click **Services** in the tree.

4. Ensure that the **Extended** tab is selected at the bottom of the middle pane.

5. Scroll to and click the **Server** service. Read the description of this service in the middle pane.

6. Click the **Standard** tab at the bottom of the middle pane.

7. Expand the middle pane to the right into the Actions pane so that you can see the five columns in the middle pane.

8. Scroll through the services and notice the information available in the columns.

9. Double-click the **Server** service.

10. Click the **Dependencies** tab and wait for a few seconds.

    • What services depend on the Server service? On what services does the Server service depend?

11. Click **Cancel.**

12. Click the **Extended** tab at the bottom of the middle pane.

13. Click the **Workstation** service to view its description in the middle pane.

    • Why is this service important?

14. Double-click the **Microsoft iSCSI Initiator Service.** Set this service to start when the server is booted by selecting **Automatic** in the Startup type list box (it is set to Manual by default), as shown in Figure 11-3. Click **Apply.**

15. Click the **Dependencies** tab to determine if any other service(s) must be started prior to starting this service. Notice that this service does not depend on any other services and no other services depend on it.

16. Click the **General** tab and then click **Start.**

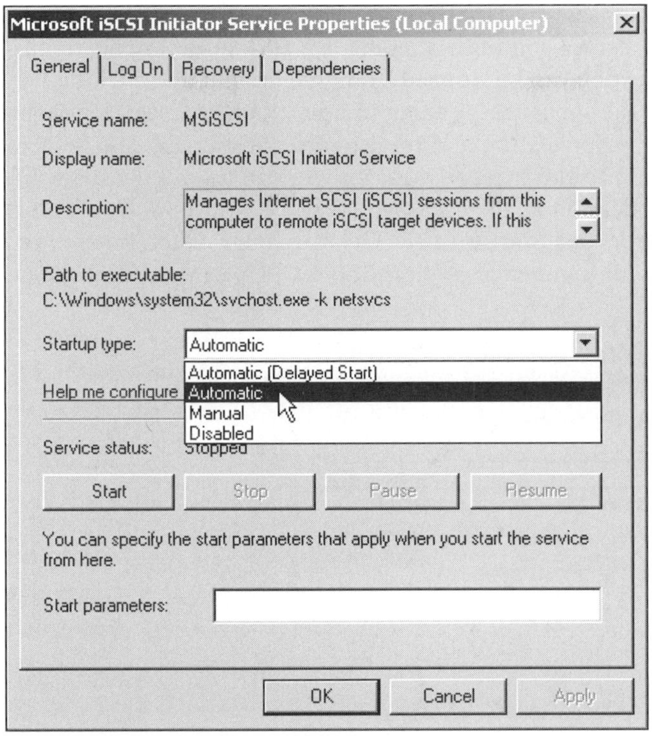

Microsoft iSCSI Initiator Service Properties (Local Computer)   ☒

| General | Log On | Recovery | Dependencies |

Service name: MSiSCSI

Display name: Microsoft iSCSI Initiator Service

Description: Manages Internet SCSI (iSCSI) sessions from this
computer to remote iSCSI target devices. If this

Path to executable:
C:\Windows\system32\svchost.exe -k netsvcs

Startup type: Automatic   ▼

> Automatic (Delayed Start)
> **Automatic**
> Manual
> Disabled

Help me configure

Service status: Stopped

| Start | Stop | Pause | Resume |

You can specify the start parameters that apply when you start the service
from here.

Start parameters: [   ]

| OK | Cancel | Apply |

Figure 11-3 Configuring the Microsoft iSCSI Initiator Service to start automatically

11

17. Click **OK** in the Microsoft iSCSI Initiator Service Properties (Local Computer) dialog box. Click the **Standard** tab in the middle pane. Notice that the Microsoft iSCSI Initiator Service is now started and set to start automatically.

18. Double-click **Microsoft iSCSI Initiator Service**.

19. Click **Stop** to practice stopping the service. Click **OK**.

   • Even though the service is stopped now, what will happen when you reboot the computer?

20. Close the Computer Management window.

 Frequently monitor services to learn which ones you need and which you don't need. Disable services you don't need. This not only helps your server boot faster and run more efficiently, it also provides better security because it closes possible entryways that an attacker or malware can use to access your system.

Using Task Manager

Sometimes a server component, such as an application or process, hangs or consumes server resources, slowing overall server performance. Windows Server 2008 includes the Task Manager tool that can be used to monitor applications and processes running on a server.

Monitoring Applications

You can use Task Manager to view applications running on the server by pressing CTRL+ALT+DEL while logged on as Administrator or as a member of the Administrators group. Click Start Task Manager, which displays a dialog box with six tabs: Applications, Processes, Services, Performance, Networking, and Users (an alternate way to start Task Manager is to right-click an open space on the taskbar and click Task Manager).

When you select the Applications tab, shown in Figure 11-4, you'll see all of the software applications running from the server console, including 32- and 64-bit applications if you are running an x64 server. Any application can be stopped by highlighting it and clicking the End Task button. If an application is hung (no longer responding to user input), you can select that application and press End Task to stop the application and release server resources. The Switch To button brings the highlighted application to the front so you can work in it, and the New Task button enables you to start another application at the console, using the Run option, which is the same option that you would access from the Start button. The status bar at the bottom of the screen shows information about the total number of processes, the CPU usage, and physical memory in use.

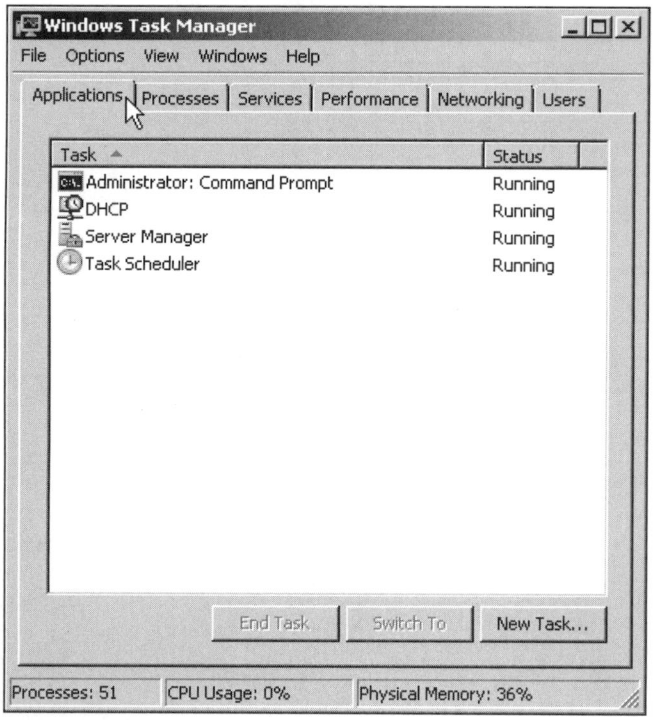

Figure 11-4 Task Manager Applications tab

If you right-click an application, several active options appear in a shortcut menu, as follows:

- *Switch To*—Takes you into the highlighted program.
- *Bring To Front*—Maximizes and brings the highlighted program to the front, but leaves you in Task Manager.
- *Minimize*—Causes the program to be minimized.
- *Maximize*—Causes the program to be maximized, but leaves you in Task Manager.
- *End Task*—Stops the highlighted program.
- *Create Dump File*—Creates a dump file to reflect activity by the application, which is stored by default in \Users\ADMINISTRATOR\AppData\Local\Temp as the file named *programprocessname*.DMP, then goes to the process on the Processes tab that is associated with the program. For example, if you make this selection for the Command Prompt program, the dump file is called cmd.DMP and the process on the Processes tab is cmd.exe. Creating a dump file is useful when you are having a problem with an application, for example if the application crashes or freezes and you want to look for error information in the dump file as a clue to the problem. This is a new feature in Windows Server 2008 and Windows Vista.
- *Go To Process*—Takes you to the Processes tab and highlights the process associated with the program.

When you create a dump file (.dmp), you'll need a debugging tool to open and read the file. Use a 32-bit debugging tool for 32-bit programs and a 64-bit debugging tool for 64-bit programs on an x64 computer. At this writing, you can download the 32-bit *WinDBG* debugging tool from Microsoft at *www.microsoft.com/whdc/devtools/debugging/installx86.mspx*. Go to *www.microsoft.com/whdc/devtools/debugging/install64bit.mspx* for 64-bit debugging tools for x64 computers, including Itanium computers. Creating the dump file can save you a lot of time in troubleshooting a problem with an application.

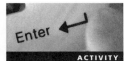

Activity 11-2: Working with Applications in Task Manager

Time Required: Approximately 10 minutes
Objective: Use Task Manager to monitor and manage applications.

Description: In this activity, you start an application and then use it to learn about Task Manager functions for controlling applications, including ending an application.

1. Click **Start,** point to **All Programs,** click **Accessories,** and click **Calculator.**
2. Press the **CTRL+ALT+DEL** keys at the same time.
   - What options are displayed on the screen?

3. Click **Start Task Manager.**
4. Click the **Applications** tab, if it is not displayed already.
5. Right-click **Calculator** and notice the active options on the shortcut menu (see Figure 11-5).

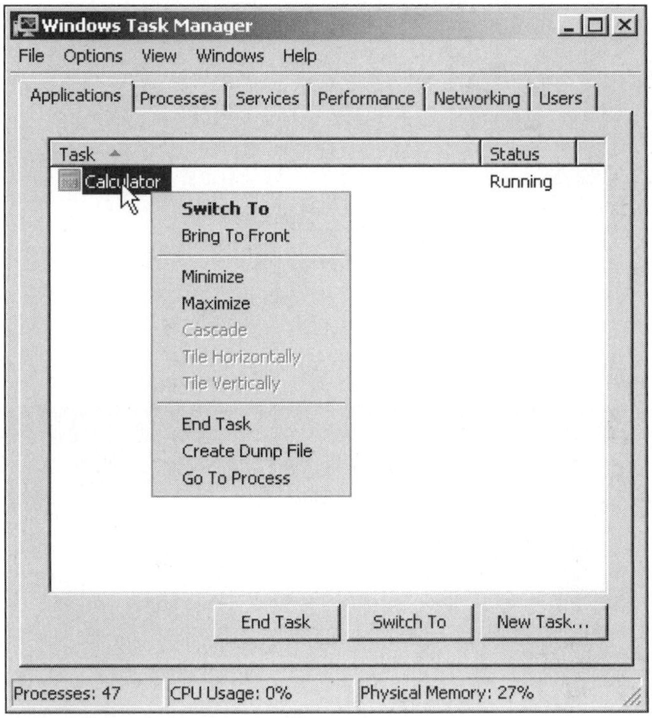

Figure 11-5 Shortcut menu options

6. Click **Switch To.**
   - What happens?

7. Click **Windows Task Manager** in the taskbar.

8. Click **Calculator,** if it is not still selected. Click **End Task** to close the Calculator application.

9. Leave Windows Task Manager open for the next activity.

Monitoring Processes

The Processes tab lists the processes in use by all running applications (see Figure 11-6). If you need to stop a process, simply highlight it and click End Process. The Processes tab also shows information about each started process, as summarized in Table 11-2.

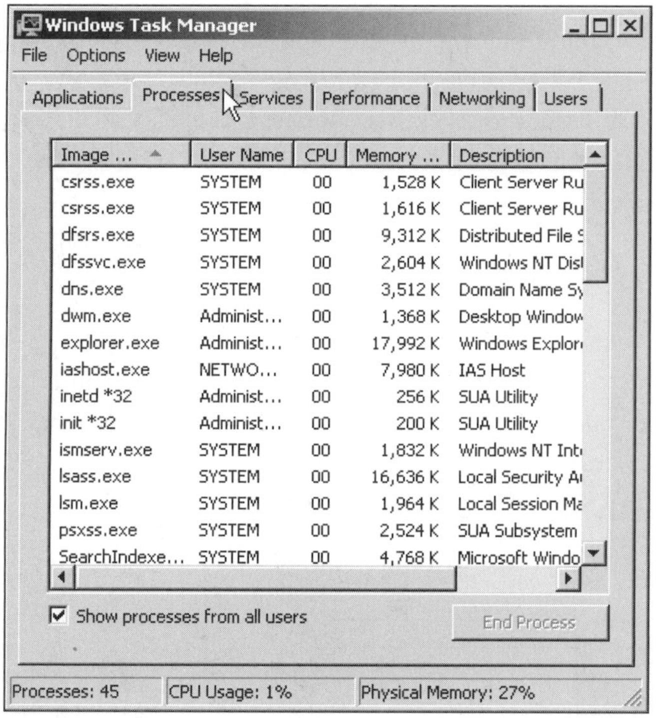

Figure 11-6 Processes tab

Table 11-2 Task Manager process information

Process information	Description
Image Name	The process name, such as WINWORD.EXE for Microsoft Word
User Name	The user account under which the process is running
CPU	The percentage of the CPU resources used by the process
Memory (Private Working Set)	The amount of memory the process is using
Description	Full or formal name of the process, such as Client Server Runtime process

Table 11-2 lists only the default information that is displayed on the Processes tab. You can change the display to view other information, such as page faults, base priority, and threads (all described later in this chapter) by clicking the View menu and then clicking Select Columns.

Many different processes may be running on a system, with some variation related to the Windows operating system, Microsoft, and third-party applications that are running. Table 11-3 presents some common processes that you may see on your system.

Table 11-3 Sample processes

Process	Description
csrss.exe	Critical process used for graphics and graphic commands (do not stop)
dfssvc.exe	Enables the Distributed File System
dwm.exe	Desktop Window Manager for the GUI effects of open windows (do not stop)
explorer.exe	Process that runs Windows Explorer
lsass.exe	Process for implementing logon and security policies that is vital to the server (do not stop)
mcc.exe	Process to run the Microsoft Management Console
SearchIndexer.exe	Noncritical process for Windows searches
services.exe	Important service for starting and stopping processes while the operating system is running, booting, and shutting down (do not stop)
slsvc.exe	Manages software licensing (do not stop)
smss.exe	Session Manager Subsystem and a vital service for a server (do not stop)
spoolsv.exe	Part of the spooler subsystem for printing
svchost.exe	Vital for running.dll files that provide a foundation for Windows operating systems (you are likely to see many instances of this process running and you should not stop them)
System	Windows kernel and system process (do not stop)
System Idle Process	Shows a tally of the amount of the CPU resources available for use (not truly a process and cannot be stopped)
takeng.exe	Process that enables the Task Scheduler to run tasks when scheduled, such as backing up the system at a certain time (do not stop)
taskmgr.exe	Process to run the Windows Task Manager
TrustedInstaller.exe	Used for Windows operating system and software updates (do not stop)
winlogon.exe	Important process that enables users to log on and log off the system (do not stop)

Regularly monitoring processes enables you to learn which ones are normal for your system. If you see a process you cannot identify, check it out because it could be malware. You can find out more about processes by visiting *www.processlibrary.com*.

Setting Priorities

Using the Processes tab within Task Manager, you can also increase the priority of a process (or processes) in the list so that it has more CPU priority than what is set as its default. Suppose, for example, that you want to increase the priority for Windows Explorer, which is process explorer.exe. To start, right-click explorer.exe, displaying a shortcut menu in which you can choose from the following:

- Open File Location
- End Process
- End Process Tree (end that process and all subprocesses associated with it)
- Create Dump File
- Set Priority
- Set Affinity (displayed if your server has two or more processors and allows you to select the CPU on which to run the process)

When you point to Set Priority, you can use the priority options to allocate more or less CPU priority to that process (see Figure 11-7).

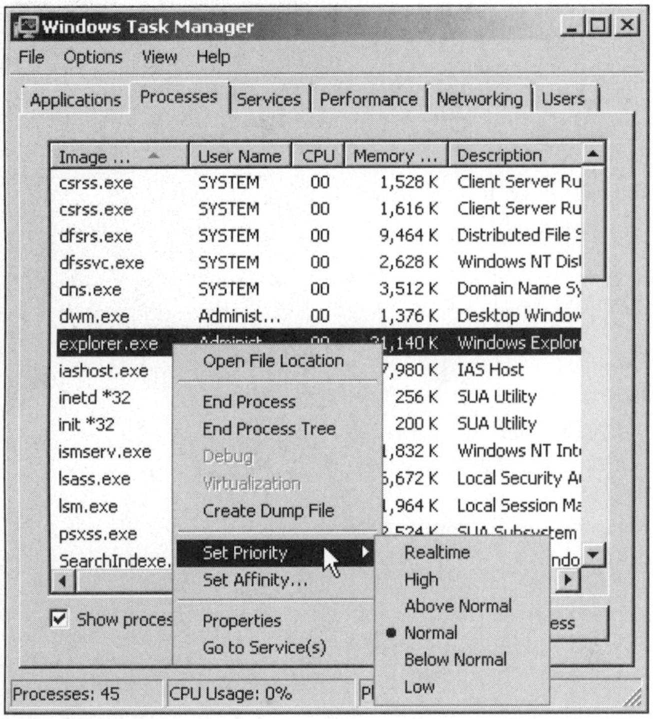

Figure 11-7   Setting the priority of a process

Normally, the priority at which a process runs is set in the program code of the application, which is called the **base priority class.** If the base priority class is not set by the program, a normal (average) priority is set by the system. The server administrator always has the option to set a different base priority. As shown in Figure 11-7, the administrator can change the priority to any of six options: Low, Below Normal, Normal, Above Normal, High, or Realtime. You might think of these processes as being on a continuum, with Normal as the midpoint, which is 0. Low is −2, Below Normal is −1, Above Normal is +1, and High is +2. Realtime is given an extra advantage at +15. For example, a Low priority means that if a process is waiting in a queue—for example, for processor time, disk access, or memory access—all processes with a higher priority will go first. The same is true for Below Normal, except that processes with this priority will run before those set at Low, and so on.

Use the Realtime priority with great caution, because it is like running on steroids. If assigned to a process, that process may completely take over the server, preventing work by any other processes. For instance, you might want to assign a Realtime priority when you detect a disk drive that is about to fail and you want to give all resources over to the backup process so you can back up files before the disk fails.

Activity 11-3: Working with Processes in Task Manager

Time Required: Approximately 10 minutes
Objective: Use Task Manager to monitor processes and to reset the priority of a process.

Description: In this activity, you use Task Manager to learn about how a process is functioning and then to reset the priority of that process.

1. Start the **Calculator** program, as you did in Activity 11-2.
2. Open **Task Manager**, if it is closed, and, if necessary, click the **Applications** tab.
3. Right-click **Calculator** and click **Go To Process**.
4. Right-click **calc.exe** and notice the options.
5. On the shortcut menu, point to **Set Priority**.
6. Click **Above Normal** (see Figure 11-7).
7. Click **Change priority** in the information box.
8. Position the Calculator program and Task Manager so that you can view both. Click several numbers in rapid succession on the Calculator and watch the CPU column for calc.exe. If you watch carefully, you'll notice a temporary change in the CPU use, such as between 01 to over 22 (depending on the speed of your CPU, it is possible it will remain under 01).
9. Click **calc.exe** and click **End Process**. Click **End process** in the information box.
10. Close Task Manager.

Monitoring Services

The Services tab in Task Manager shows the services that are started, stopped, or paused. In addition to Server Manager and the Computer Management tool, this is another place where you can monitor services. However, unlike Server Manager and the Computer Management tool, the management options from Task Manager are limited to starting or stopping a service. To start or stop a service, you do the following:

1. Right-click the service.
2. Click Start Service or Stop Service (see Figure 11-8).

If you want to manage services using more management options, click the *Services* button to open the Services window, which provides management options identical to those you can perform through Server Manager or the Computer Management tool.

Because of display limitations, Task Manager does not use totally consistent names for services when you compare them with Server Manager, the Computer Management window, and the Services window. For example, SamSs in Task Manager is shown as Security Accounts Manager in the other tools. PlugPlay in Task Manager is Plug and Play in the other tools. If you are not sure about a service, maximize Task Manager and expand the Description column to view the description of a service.

The services on the Services tab might not be displayed in alphabetical order. You can put them in alphabetical order by clicking the *Name* column heading.

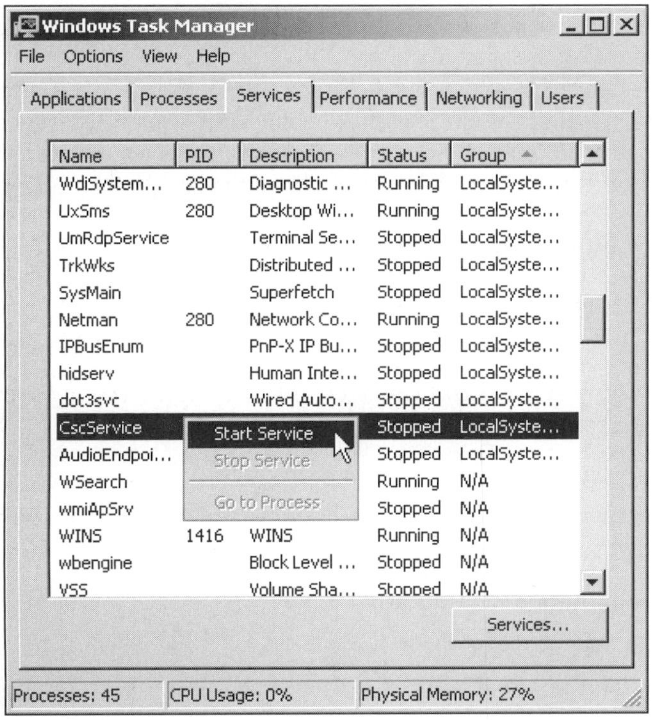

Figure 11-8   Starting a service from Task Manager

Monitoring Real-Time Performance

The Performance tab shows vital CPU and memory performance information through bar charts, line graphs, and performance statistics (see Figure 11-9). The CPU Usage and Memory bars show the current use of CPU and page file use. To the right of each bar is a graph showing the immediate history statistics. The bottom of the Performance tab shows more detailed statistics, such as

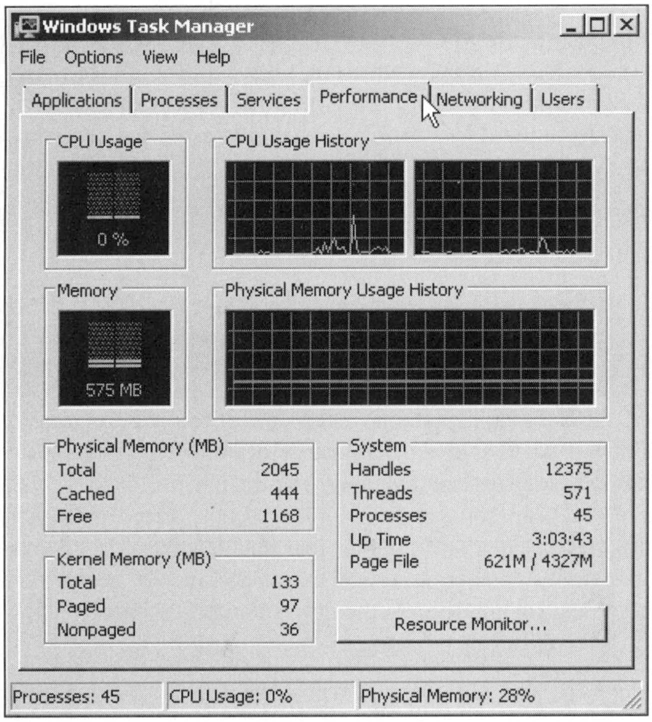

Figure 11-9   Performance tab

those for handles and threads, which are described in Table 11-4. A **handle** is a resource, such as a file, used by a program and having its own identification so the program is able to access it. **Threads** are blocks of code within a program.

Table 11-4 Task Manager performance statistics

Statistic	Description
Physical Memory Total	Amount of RAM installed in the computer
Physical Memory Cached	Amount of RAM used for file caching
Physical Memory Free	Amount of RAM available to be used
Kernel Memory Total	Amount of memory used by the operating system
Kernel Memory Paged	Amount of virtual memory used by the operating system
Kernel Memory Nonpaged	Amount of RAM memory used by the operating system
Handles	Number of objects in use by all processes, such as open files
Threads	Number of code blocks in use, in which one program or process may be running one or more code blocks at a time
Processes	Number of processes that are active or sitting idle
Up Time	Amount of time since the server was last booted
Page File	The size of the page file

When you click the Resource Monitor button, the Resource Monitor window is displayed (see Figure 11-10). The Resource Monitor provides a real-time collection of resources used for the following:

- CPU
- Disk
- Network
- Memory

This tool can be very useful for a first quick analysis of a problem, such as when users report that their connection response to the server is slow. Slow response could be related to CPU use, disk use, network activity, and memory. If you receive a call from a user about slow response, you can quickly look at these statistics to get a general idea of the problem or an initial clue,

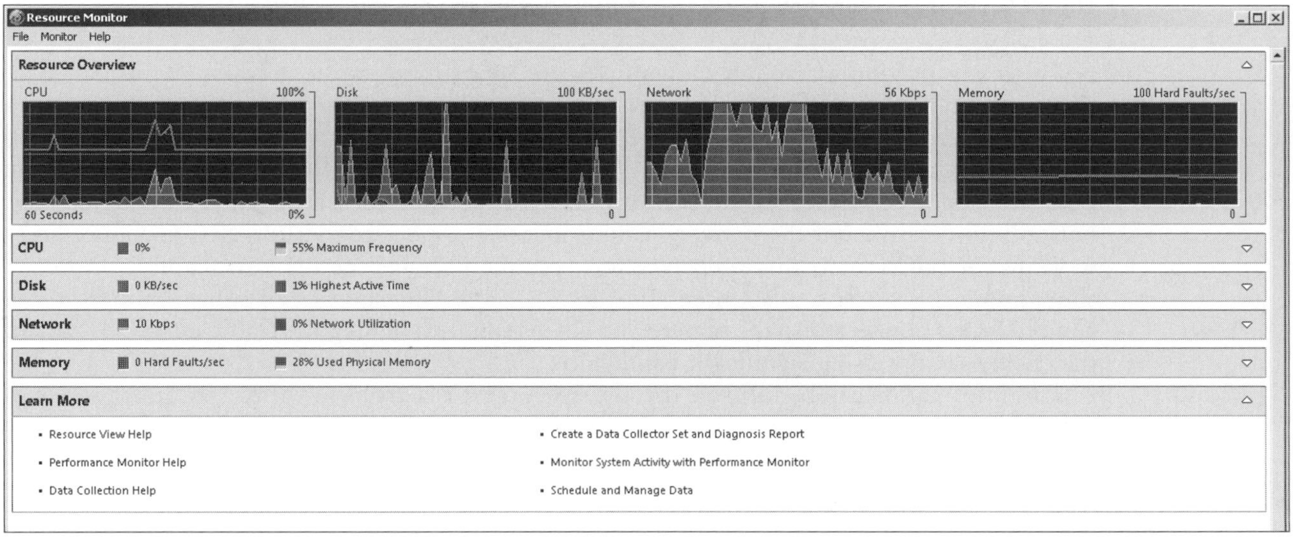

Figure 11-10 Resource Monitor

which might consist of one or a combination of factors. For example, a Terminal Services user might experience slow response because the application she is using maximizes CPU use, creates excessive network activity at the server, or both. Or, the application might be very memory-intensive. If the NIC on the server is malfunctioning by sending out constant network communications, you can get a first clue about this problem by checking the Resource Monitor. In this case, the only high-use area might be the network utilization as measured at the server.

Monitoring Network Performance

The Networking tab in Task Manager enables you to monitor network performance on all NICs installed in the server. A graphical representation shows the total network utilization, which is roughly the percentage of the network bandwidth in use. In Figure 11-11, the Networking tab shows network utilization on a computer with two NICs (Local Area Connection 2 and Local Area Connection).

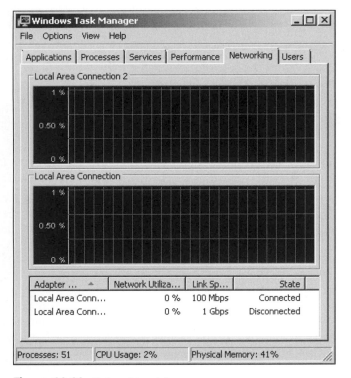

Figure 11-11 Networking tab

The lower portion of the tab shown in Figure 11-11 displays the network performance data across each NIC. It lists the name of the adapter (or connection), the network utilization detected by the adapter (from 0% to 100%), the speed of the network link, such as 100 Mbps, and the operational state of the adapter. Figure 11-11 shows one active NIC that is connected and one NIC that is not connected to the network. The Networking tab can be a quick diagnostic tool not only to determine if the network is busy but also to ensure that the NIC is connected and working. A NIC that is disconnected, for example because the network cable is loose, will show up on this display. Also, note that the connected NIC shows 0% utilization even though computers are connected to the server. The NIC is simply handling the traffic efficiently, because the clients are not using significant bandwidth.

This information can be valuable if you suspect there is a problem with a NIC in the server and you want an immediate determination if it is working. The information on the tab also can be an initial warning that something is causing prolonged high network utilization—80% to 100%, for instance.

If the percent of network utilization is frequently over 40%, that means the network is experiencing collisions and there may be bottlenecks due to the network design, possibly indicating the need to create subnets. Network utilization that is regularly over 60% to 70% indicates a serious need to modify the network to address bottlenecks or increase network speed. Network utilization that is over 90% for a sustained period requires immediate attention in terms of locating the network problem or redesigning the network.

Monitoring Users

The Users tab provides a list of the users currently logged on. You can log off a user by clicking that user and clicking the Logoff button, which ensures that any open files are closed before the user is logged off. Another option is to Disconnect a user, which you might use if the Logoff action does not work because the user's connection is hung.

Plan to regularly monitor the users on a server. Over time, this gives you a good idea about user load at particular times of day. If you see the user load increasing, you can take this into consideration as you plan hardware and software upgrades for your server. Also, regularly monitoring users makes it easier to identify suspicious use of an account, such as when an attacker has taken over an account.

Using Performance Monitor

One of the most versatile tools used to help detect and troubleshoot performance issues on a Windows Server 2008 server is **Performance Monitor**. Performance Monitor can be used to monitor components such as hard disks, memory, the processor, a network interface, a started process, and the paging file. For example, you might monitor memory and the paging file to determine if you have fully tuned the paging file for satisfactory performance and to determine if you have adequate RAM for the server load.

Capturing Data Using Performance Monitor

Performance Monitor is a tool within the Reliability and Performance Monitor. You can open the Reliability and Performance Monitor in the following ways:

- From the Administrative Tools menu
- From Server Manager
- As an MMC snap-in
- From the Command Prompt window or the Start button, Run option by using the *perfmon* command

After the Reliability and Performance Monitor is opened, click Performance Monitor under Monitoring Tools, as shown in Figure 11-12. The default view is in the line mode, showing a grid that you use for graphing activities on the server. In Figure 11-12, Performance Monitor is graphing the % Processor Time that is in use. When you gather data for your analysis, select one or more objects to monitor. A Performance Monitor object may be memory, the processor, or another part of the computer. Other objects are added as you install services and applications.

For each object, one or more counters can be monitored. A **counter** is an indicator of a quantity of the object that can be measured in some unit, such as percentage, rate per second, or peak value, depending on what is appropriate to the object. For example, the % Processor Time counter for the Processor object measures the percentage of processor time that is in use by nonidle processes. (It is not uncommon for % Processor Time to occasionally be very high, but this often just means that an application is using the processor very efficiently.) Figure 11-13 shows % Processor Time selected under Processor while configuring Performance Monitor. Pages/sec is an example of a

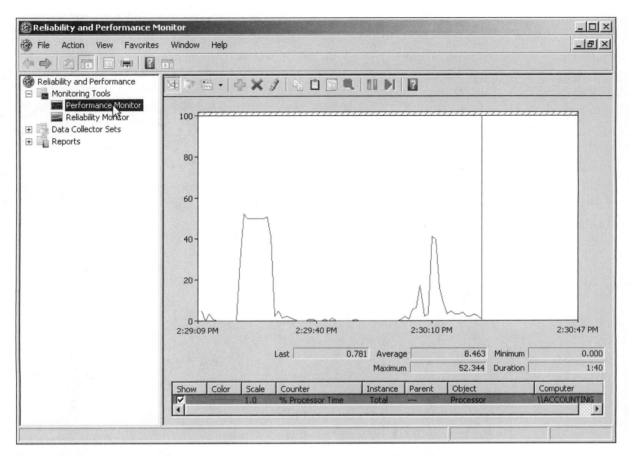

Figure 11-12 Performance Monitor (started from the Administrative Tools menu)

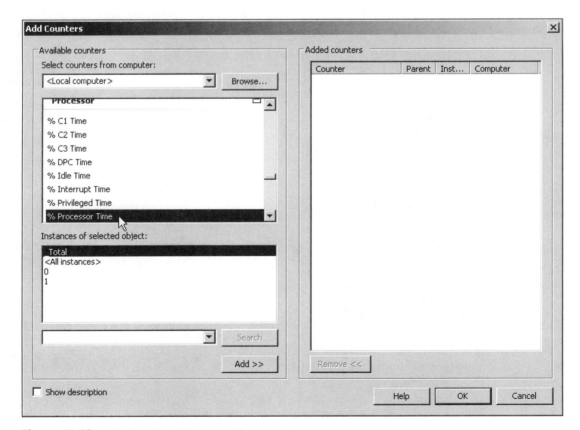

Figure 11-13 Selecting the % Processor Time counter

counter for the Memory object that measures the number of pages written to or read from virtual memory per second. The processor is one of the common objects to monitor when a server is slow. Table 11-5 gives examples of some of the most frequently used counters for the Processor object.

Table 11-5 Sample processor counters in Performance Monitor

Counter	Description
% DPC Time	Processor time used for deferred procedure calls, for example for hardware devices
% Interrupt Time	Time spent on hardware interrupts by the CPU
% Privileged Time	Time spent by the CPU for system activities in privileged mode, which is used for the operating system
% Processor Time	Time the CPU is busy on all nonidle activities
% User Time	Time spent by the CPU in user mode running software applications and system programs
Interrupts/sec	Number of device interrupts per second

TIP When you regularly see % Processor Time at 70% or more, investigate the other counters shown in Table 11-5 as well as the System object using the Processor Queue Length counter. For example, on a single-processor computer when the % Processor Time is regularly at 80% or higher and the System object Processor Queue Length counter is often over 4, it is likely time to upgrade to a multiprocessor server to handle the load.

Sometimes instances are associated with a counter. An **instance** exists when there are different elements to monitor, such as individual processes when you use the Process object, or when a process contains multiple threads or runs subprocesses under it for the Thread object. Other examples are when it is possible to monitor two or more disks or multiple processors. In many cases, each instance is identified by a unique number for ease of monitoring.

Performance Monitor offers several buttons to choose actions and to set display options. After the tool is opened, click the Add button (represented by a green plus sign) on the button bar just above the tracking window (refer to Figure 11-12). This opens the Add Counters dialog box (see Figure 11-13) from which to select objects to monitor, counters, and instances.

You can monitor one or more objects at a time as a way to get a better understanding of how particular objects interact, for example by monitoring both memory and the processor. Also, you can monitor the same object using different combinations of counters. You stop monitoring by clicking the Delete button (represented by an X) on the button bar.

You can use three view modes when monitoring objects: line, histogram bar, and report.

- The line mode is a running line chart of the object that shows distinct peaks and valleys. For example, when you use the line mode and monitor for different objects, a line with a unique color, such as red or green, represents each object.

- The histogram bar mode is a running bar chart that shows each object as a bar in a different color.

- The report mode simply provides numbers on a screen, which you can capture to put in a report.

Each of these options is set from the Change graph type button on the button bar just above the tracking window. You can change the view mode at any time by clicking the appropriate selection. Figure 11-14 illustrates the use of the histogram bar mode to monitor several counters.

Each object combination is displayed using a different color, so they are easily identified. For example, if Figure 11-15 (shown in larger view to see the full line graph) were in color you would see that Page/sec is red, Avg. Disk Queue Length is green, and % Processor Time is blue.

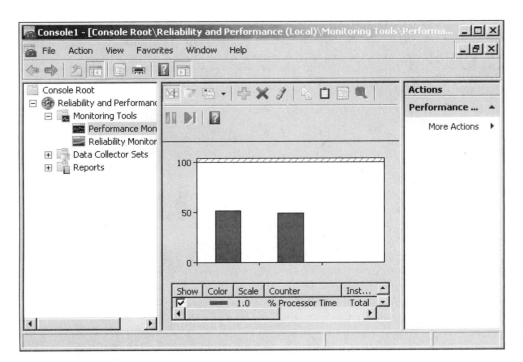

Figure 11-14   Histogram bar mode (from the MMC snap-in)

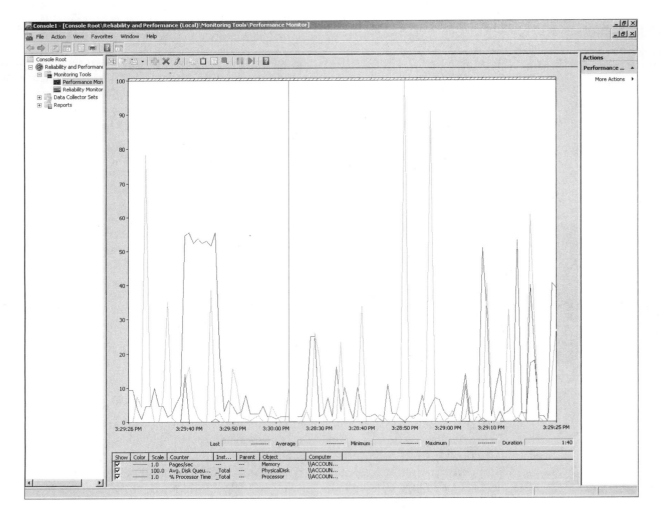

Figure 11-15   Monitoring multiple objects (MMC snap-in enlarged view)

The counters are shown at the bottom of the screen with a key to indicate the graphing color for each one. When you click a counter, the status information just above the counters shows the following for that counter:

- *Last*—The current value of the monitored activity
- *Average*—The average value of the monitored activity for the elapsed time
- *Maximum*—The maximum value of the activity over the elapsed time
- *Minimum*—The minimum value of the activity over the elapsed time
- *Duration*—The amount of time to complete a full graph of the activity

Monitoring System Components

When monitoring the performance of a server, four objects are often used:

- Processor
- Memory
- Physical disk
- Network interface

As you add different components, other objects and counters will be added that can also be important to monitor, but these four are particularly important for monitoring server performance. Table 11-6 provides a sampling of object/counter combinations that you can use initially for monitoring computer system performance.

Table 11-6 Sample objects and counters for performance monitoring

Object	Counters / Descriptions
Processor	% Processor Time — Percentage of time for threads to process
	% Privileged Time — Time spent by the CPU for system activities in privileged mode
	% User Time — Percentage of time spent processing user threads
Memory	Available Bytes — Physical memory currently available for use
	Committed Bytes — Amount of virtual memory currently being used
	Pages/sec — Number of hard page faults per second
Physical Disk	% Disk Time — Amount of time the disk spends working
	Avg. Disk Bytes/Transfer — Average number of bytes transferred between memory and disk during read and write operations
	Disk Bytes/sec — Speed at which bytes are transferred
	Current Disk Queue Length — Number of requests waiting to be processed
Network Interface	Bytes Total/sec — As measured across the NIC, number of bytes sent and received per second

The Memory row in Table 11-6 refers to the concept of a page fault. **Page faults** occur whenever memory pages must be called from disk (from the paging file).

Activities 11-4 and 11-5 enable you to explore how to use Performance Monitor and then how to troubleshoot processor difficulties. In Activity 11-6, you'll learn how to enable Performance Monitor to track disk activity through activating the Disk Performance Statistic Driver.

Activity 11-4: Exploring Performance Monitor

Time Required: Approximately 10 minutes
Objective: Examine available options in Performance Monitor.

Description: This activity gives, you an opportunity to practice viewing objects, counters, and instances in Performance Monitor.

1. Click **Start**, point to **Administrative Tools,** and click **Reliability and Performance Monitor.**

2. When the tool starts, you see the Resource Overview, which is the same as the Resource Monitor you learned about earlier in this chapter.

3. Click **Performance Monitor** in the tree in the left pane under Monitoring Tools.

   • What objects and counters are displayed in the right pane by default?

4. Move your pointer over each of the buttons on the button bar to view its description.

5. Click the **Add** button (a plus sign) in the button bar in the right pane.

   • What computer is selected by default for monitoring? How would you monitor activity on a different computer?

6. Scroll through the objects in the box under the computer that is selected.

7. Click the **plus sign** to the right of **Processor.** Scroll to view the counters associated with the Processor object.

   • What are the first five counters listed? What instances are listed? (There should be enough to represent each processor in the server.)

8. Next, select to view the Server counters under **Server** (click the **plus sign**). Scroll through the counters for Server to view them all.

9. Select to view **Process** as the object and view the counters associated with Process.

10. Choose to view the **TCPv4** object. Click the **Segments/sec** counter and click the **Show description** check box. Notice the description of this counter displayed at the bottom of the window.

11. Observe two more objects and their associated counters and instances.

12. Click **Cancel** in the Add Counters dialog box, but leave the Reliability and Performance Monitor window open for the next activity.

Activity 11-5: Monitoring for Processor Problems

Time Required: Approximately 15 minutes
Objective: Learn how to monitor for processor bottlenecks.

Description: In this activity, you use Performance Monitor to check for processor bottlenecks, such as the processor's ability to handle the server load and possible problems caused by hardware.

1. Make sure that the Reliability and Performance Monitor window is already open, and if not, open it to display Performance Monitor.

2. If any object/counter combinations are currently running—by default % Processor Time should still be running—right-click anywhere in the right pane, click **Remove All Counters** (see Figure 11-16), and click **OK.**

Add Counters...
Save Settings As...
Save Image As...
Save Data As...

Clear
Zoom To
Show Selected Counters
Hide Selected Counters
Scale Selected Counters
Remove All Counters

Properties...

Figure 11-16 Removing counters

3. Click the **Add** button in the button bar to add counters.

4. Scroll to find **Processor** and click its **plus sign**.

5. Click **% Processor Time** (refer to Figure 11-13). Leave **_Total** as the default for instances.

    • What information does this counter provide for the Processor object? How would you find out, if you didn't know?

When you monitor % Processor Time, sustained values of 80-85% or higher indicate a heavily loaded machine; consistent readings of 95% or higher may indicate a machine that needs to have its load reduced or its capabilities increased (with a new machine, a motherboard upgrade, or a faster CPU).

6. Click the **Add** button in the Add Counters dialog box.

7. Click **% Interrupt Time** as the counter for Processor and leave **_Total** as the instance. Click **Add.**

% Interrupt Time is useful to monitor because it measures the amount of the processor's time that is used to service hardware requests from devices such as the NIC, disk, CD/DVD drives, and serial and parallel peripherals. A high rate of interrupts when compared with your baseline statistics indicates a possible hardware problem, such as a malfunctioning NIC.

8. Scroll the counters list for the Processor object and click **Interrupts/sec.** Leave **_Total** as the instance and click **Add.**

The Interrupts/sec counter measures the average number of times per second that the CPU is interrupted by devices requesting immediate processing. Network traffic and system clock activity establish a kind of background count against which this number should be compared. Problem levels occur when a malfunctioning device begins to generate spurious interrupts, or when excessive network traffic overwhelms a network adapter. In both cases, this usually creates a count that's five times or greater than a lightly loaded baseline situation.

9. Scroll to find the **System** object and click its **plus sign**.

10. Click **Processor Queue Length**. Click **Add**.

 The Processor Queue Length counter for the System object measures the number of execution threads waiting for access to a CPU. If this value is frequently over 4 on a single CPU, it indicates a need to distribute this machine's load across other machines, or the need to increase its capabilities, usually by adding an additional CPU or by upgrading the machine or the motherboard. When the value is over 2 per each CPU on multiple-processor systems, you should consider adding processors or increasing the processor speed.

11. The Add Counters dialog box should now look similar to the one in Figure 11-17.

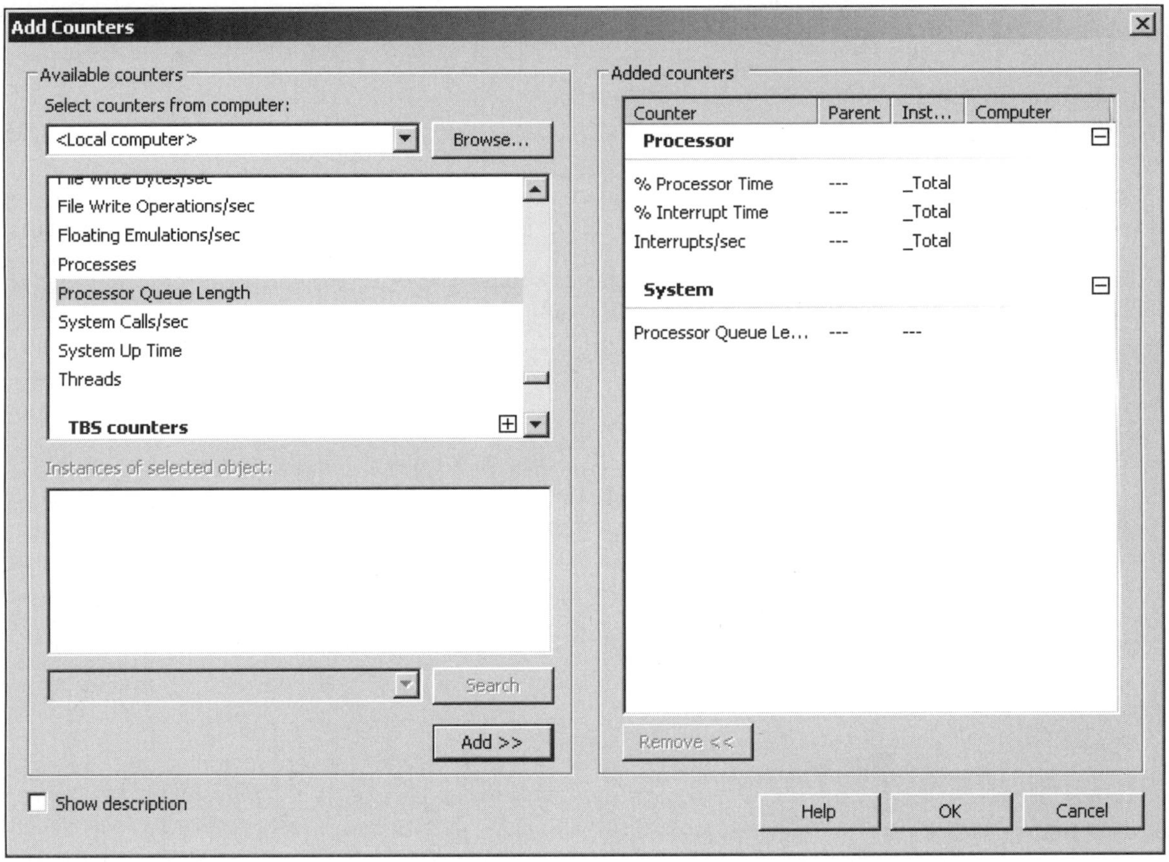

Figure 11-17 Selections in the Add Counters dialog box

12. Click **OK**.

13. Monitor the system for several minutes to determine if there are any processor problems. Record any problems that you diagnose from using Performance Monitor.

14. Click the **Change graph type** button down arrow just above the graph's box and click **Histogram bar** to see this mode. Monitor in this mode for a few minutes.

15. Click the **Change graph type** button down arrow and click **Report** to see this mode. Monitor in this mode for a few minutes.

16. Click the **Change graph type** button down arrow and click **Line**.

17. Right-click anywhere in the right pane, click **Remove All Counters,** and click **OK**.

18. Leave the Reliability and Performance window open.

Activity 11-6: Verifying the Disk Counters

Time Required: Approximately 5 minutes
Objective: Learn to check the status of *diskperf*.

Description: Monitoring disks through Performance Monitor is accomplished by using the Disk Performance Statistic Driver, which is enabled through the command-line program *diskperf*. Normally, hard disk Performance Monitor counters are enabled by default. If they are not enabled, you can start them by typing *diskperf -y* and pressing Enter in the Command Prompt window. Or, to disable the disk counters you would type *diskperf -n*. In this activity, you use *diskperf* to verify the status of the hard disk performance counters to see if they are enabled.

1. Click **Start**, point to **All Programs**, click **Accessories**, and click **Command Prompt**.

2. In the Command Prompt window, type **diskperf** and press **Enter**. If the disk counters are enabled, you'll see the counters are automatically enabled on demand.

3. Close the Command Prompt window.

Using Data Collector Sets

The Data Collector Sets tool is another vehicle that is used to monitor performance and to consolidate performance information. A **data collector set** is a collection of diagnostic and performance information in the form of a report or log. There are three basic types of data collection tools and formats:

- Performance counters and performance counter reports
- Traces and trace reports
- System configuration data

One data collector set can produce only one type of log or it can produce data for all three reporting formats. A **performance counter report** tracks information using objects, counters, and instances. A **trace** monitors particular events, and a **trace report** contains only those instances when the events occur. For example, you could create a trace to record each time disk input/output activity occurs or when an Active Directory Kerberos security event is triggered.

The system configuration data that can be obtained using data collector sets includes information on the following:

- Operating system
- Processor
- System services
- BIOS
- Controllers
- Port classes
- Storage classes
- Printing classes
- Video classes
- User accounts
- Startup programs
- Disk settings
- Processes

11

Data collector sets can be created in several ways. One way is to use a predefined data collector set, such as the following:

- Active Directory Diagnostics (if Active Directory is installed)
- LAN Diagnostics
- System Diagnostics
- System Performance

Using a predefined data collector set helps to take the guesswork out of what to monitor. However, when you select any of the predefined data collector sets, you still can configure specific counters from Performance Monitor to include in your collector set. The Data Collector Sets tool also enables you to start a wizard and select a template to use for creating a data collector set. Templates are XML files that are stored on the local computer. In addition to using templates that come with your operating system, you can import a template created on another computer. Yet another way to create a data collector set is to do so manually.

In addition to using counters, traces, and system information, each data collector set consists of properties that you can configure as follows:

- *General*—Enables you to create a description for the data collector set and add keyword descriptors or use a default description. You can also specify from which user account to run the data collection process, but the account must have Administrator privileges (the default account is System).
- *Directory*—Enables you to specify the directory path and naming convention for the reports after they are generated.
- *Security*—Enables you to set up permissions to control who can run the data collector set for creating a report.
- *Schedule*—Enables you to create a regular schedule on which to run the data collector set, such as at 10:00 a.m. every weekday.
- *Stop Condition*—Enables you to specify conditions under which to stop or limit the duration of the data gathering, such as when the report contents reach a specific size.
- *Task*—Enables you to specify a task that runs as soon as the data collection stops.

After a data collector set has been configured, you can start it and collect data for a specific period of time, such as five minutes, as configured in the properties of the set. The data collector set process also can be manually stopped before the preset stop time. You can run a data collector set session multiple times or on a regular schedule to take snapshots of a server system. Also, you can view the report results from the Reliability and Performance Monitor tool after a data collection session is stopped.

Using a Wizard and a Template to Create a Data Collector Set

One of the easiest ways to get started using the Data Collector Sets tool is to rely on a predefined template. Four templates that are similar to the predefined data collector sets mentioned earlier can be deployed from the Create new Data Collector Set Wizard:

- *Active Directory Diagnostics*—Collects data about Active Directory activities and can combine performance counters and trace events
- *Basic*—Collects data using performance counters
- *System Diagnostics*—Collects information about the status of processes, hardware, system response times, and other measures, and provides ideas for improving system performance
- *System Performance*—Collects information similar to the System Diagnostics template and reports problem areas

The Create new Data Collector Set Wizard steps you through deploying one of these templates, or you can skip the templates and use the wizard to manually configure your own options.

To start the wizard, right-click the User Defined folder under Data Collector Sets in the Reliability and Performance Monitor tool, click New, and click Data Collector Set.

Activity 11-7: Using a Template for a Data Collector Set

Time Required: Approximately 20 minutes
Objective: Create a data collector set from a template.

Description: In this activity, you use the System Performance template to create a data collector set.

1. Ensure that the Reliability and Performance Monitor window is already open, and if not, open it.
2. Click the **plus sign** in front of **Data Collector Sets** in the tree in the left pane.
3. Right-click **User Defined,** point to **New,** and click **Data Collector Set.**
4. In the *Name* box, enter **System Performance** plus your initials, such as *System Performance JR.*
5. Ensure that **Create from a template (Recommended)** is selected, as shown in Figure 11-18.

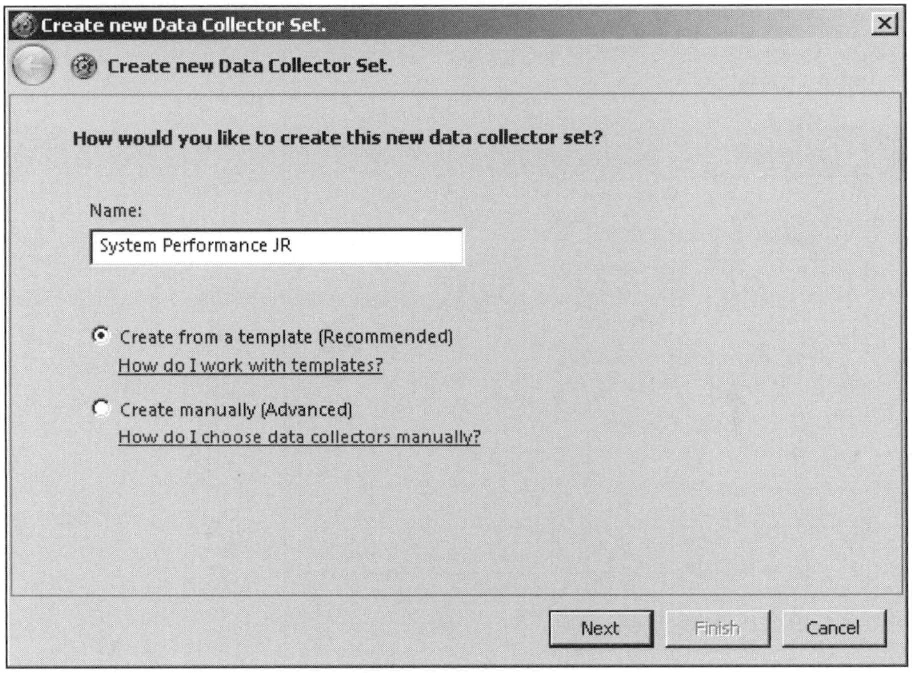

Figure 11-18 Selecting to use a template

6. Click **Next.**
7. Click **System Performance** under Template Data Collector Set and click **Next.**
8. Use the default location in which to save the data and click **Next.**
9. Click **Save and close,** if it is not selected already.
10. Click **Finish.**
11. Click the **plus sign** in front of **User Defined** in the tree, if it is not expanded, and notice the data collector set that you created is listed under User Defined.
12. Click the data collector set you created in the tree. In the right pane, notice that it includes *NT Kernel,* which incorporates a trace session of real-time CPU activity, memory, disk, and network activity. The second tracking element is *Performance Counter,* which is a combination

of counters for processes, physical disk, CPU, memory, system, server, and many network counters.

13. Right-click the data collector set you created, such as *System Performance JR*.

   • What options do you see enabled on the shortcut menu?

14. Click **Properties**.

15. Click the **Stop Condition** tab.

16. Under *Overall duration*, set the value to **5** and leave the *Units* value as **Minutes**. This means five minutes of data is collected each time you start the data collector set (see Figure 11-19).

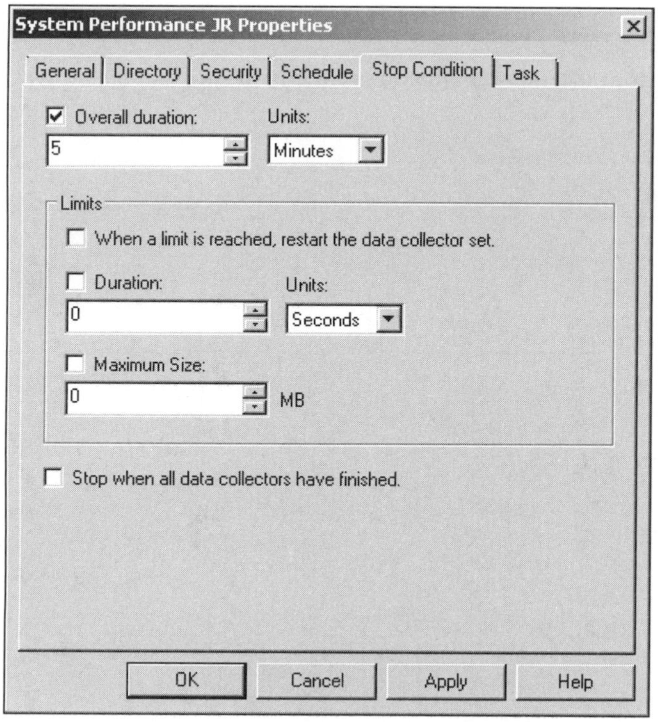

```
System Performance JR Properties                          [X]

General | Directory | Security | Schedule | Stop Condition | Task |

 ☑ Overall duration:        Units:
 [5              ][▲▼]      [Minutes    ▼]

 ┌─ Limits ──────────────────────────────────────────┐
 │  ☐ When a limit is reached, restart the data collector set. │
 │                                                    │
 │  ☐ Duration:            Units:                     │
 │  [0            ][▲▼]    [Seconds   ▼]              │
 │                                                    │
 │  ☐ Maximum Size:                                   │
 │  [0            ][▲▼]    MB                         │
 └────────────────────────────────────────────────────┘

 ☐ Stop when all data collectors have finished.




          [  OK  ]   [ Cancel ]   [ Apply ]   [ Help ]
```

Figure 11-19 Establishing the duration of a data collection session

An alternative is to set limits for the data collection. For example, you might set the duration under Limits as 5 minutes and choose to have the data collector set restart right after it stops. Or, if disk space is a concern, you might have the data collector set stop after the log size reaches 2 MB.

17. Click the **Schedule** tab. This tab enables you to schedule a regular start time for collecting data.

18. Click the **Add** button on the Schedule tab.

19. In the Folder Action dialog box, the default time is 12:00 AM. However, because you are monitoring system performance, it makes more sense to gather data when the system is in full work mode, such as at 10:00 a.m. or 2:00 p.m. or whatever time is more appropriate for your organization. For this activity, change the Start time to **10:00:00 AM**. Also, remove the check marks from Saturday and Sunday.

20. Click **OK** in the Folder Action dialog box.

21. Click **OK** in the Properties dialog box.

22. In the tree, right-click the data collector set you created, such as *System Performance JR*, and click **Start** to commence gathering data.

23. Wait a few minutes (you don't have to wait for five minutes because you can manually stop the data collection sooner). Right-click the data collector set in the tree and click **Stop**.

24. Right-click the data collector set in the tree again and click **Latest Report**.

25. In the right pane, you'll see the report of information you have collected so far (see Figure 11-20).

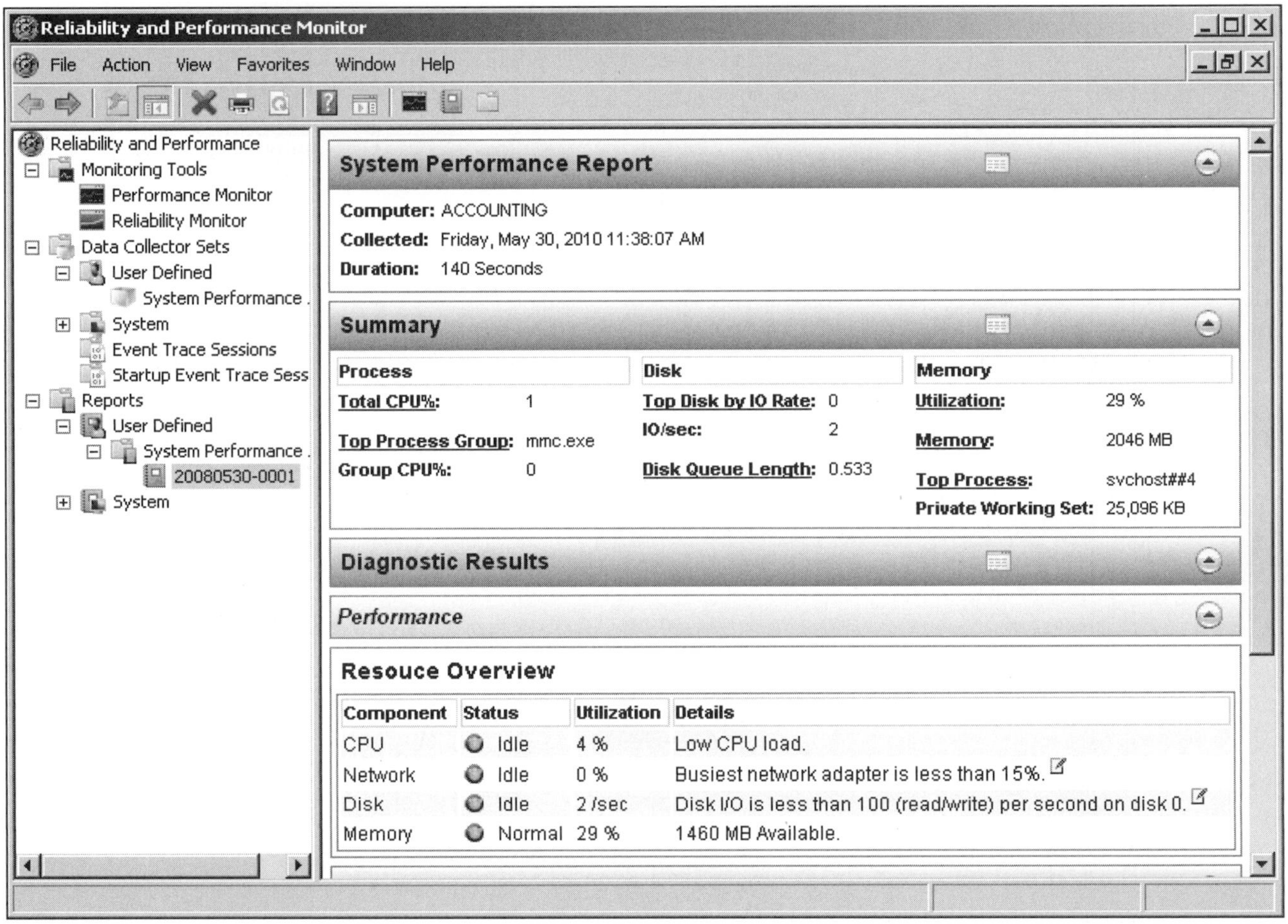

Figure 11-20   Viewing the data collection report

26. Use the scroll bar in the right pane to view the report information. Click the **CPU** heading if it is not expanded. Notice that CPU information is divided into Process, Services, and System. Click the down arrow for **Services** under CPU to expand its view and notice the services listed and CPU% value for each service. Click the **up arrow** to close the view of **Services**.

27. Click the **down arrow** for **Memory**. Click the **down arrow** for **Counters**.

    • How many performance counters are used for the memory object? How many handle count instances are monitored?

28. Click the **down arrow** for **Report Statistics** and review the information about the report, including the Computer Information and Collection Information. Notice you can determine how long the data collector set gathered information by looking under Collection Information.

29. In the tree, click the data collector set you created, such as *System Performance JR*.

30. In the right pane, right-click **Performance Counter** and click **Properties**.

31. In the Performance Counter Properties dialog box, notice that the counters preselected by the template you used are listed under *Performance counters*. If you wanted to remove a particular counter from the data collector set, you could click it and click Remove.

32. Click the **Add** button.

33. In the next dialog box, you can select one or more performance counters to add to the data collector set, as shown in Figure 11-21. Click **Cancel**.

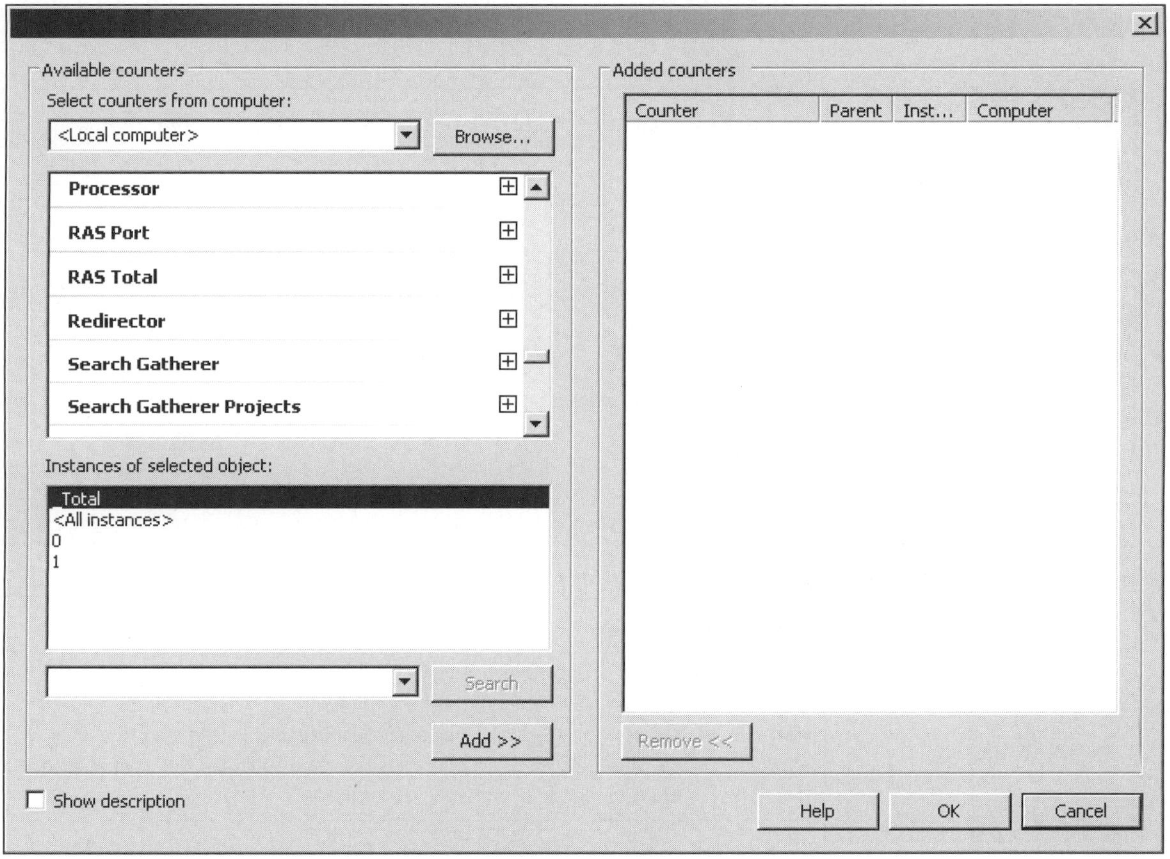

Figure 11-21 Dialog box for adding performance counters

34. Click **Cancel** in the Performance Counter Properties dialog box.

35. Leave the Reliability and Performance Monitor open for the next activity.

Returning to a Report and the Importance of Network Data

After you create a report, you can go back to it by finding that report under Reports in the tree within the Reliability and Performance Monitor tool. For example, the report you created in Activity 11-7 contains valuable information about network performance. Monitoring the network is one of the monitoring tasks you should set out to do early on. This is important because it provides a way to determine baselines and later to compare baseline data with current system performance statistics to locate a problem source. For example, consider a workday afternoon on which several users call to report that the system is slow. Your next step is to determine if the source of the problem is the network or the server. If you regularly monitor the network and the server, you can view your data collector set reporting data to help locate the problem source faster.

For network performance, it helps to establish baselines from which to diagnose problems. Plan to gather data such as the following:

- *Network Interface performance counter*—Shows network traffic at the network interface (NIC), including bytes and packets sent and received, bandwidth data, and network error data

- *IPv4 and IPv6 performance counters*—Shows inbound and outbound IPv4 and IPv6 traffic and packet errors

- *TCPv4 and TCPv6 performance counters*—Shows connection and transmission data, including connection failures

Begin gathering benchmarks so that you have an understanding of what network activity is typical. Also, gather benchmarks on typical network error levels, so that you know at what point an increase in network errors signals a problem.

The report you created in Activity 11-7 contains NIC, IP, and TCP information about network performance that you can use to help create network performance baseline data.

Activity 11-8: Viewing a Report

Time Required: Approximately 5 minutes
Objective: Learn how to go back to view a report you have already created.

Description: In this activity, you reopen the report you created in Activity 11-7 so that you can review the network performance data.

1. Open the Reliability and Performance Monitor if it is not still open.

2. In the tree in the left pane, click the **plus sign** for **Reports**, if necessary.

3. Also in the tree, click the **plus signs** for **User Defined** then for **System Performance**, if necessary. Click **System Performance** in the tree.

4. In the right pane, you will see one report listed with a green icon and a number that represents the date of the report, such as 20090610 for June 10, 2009, and a version number, such as 0001. Double-click the report.

5. Scroll down to the **Network** category and click its **down arrow**. You'll see categories of information for Interface (the NIC), IP, TCP, and UDP.

6. Click the **down arrow** for **IP**. Notice the counters showing performance data for IPv4 and for IPv6 (if it is enabled).

7. Click the **down arrow** for **TCP**. Review the performance data for TCPv4 and TCPv6.

   - What data might you use to determine if there are connection problems?

8. Leave the Reliability and Performance Monitor open for the next activity.

Using a Predefined Data Collector Set

As you learned earlier, the Reliability and Performance Monitor has several predefined data collector sets that you can run at any time without first creating them through the Create new Data Collector Set Wizard. Several of the templates, such as the System Performance template you used in Activity 11-7, are based on these predefined data collector sets.

For diagnosing network problems, particularly hardware problems, and for performing network system checks the predefined LAN Diagnostics data collector set is particularly valuable. Activity 11-9 enables you to use the LAN Diagnostics data collector set (but similar steps can be used to run any of the predefined data collector sets).

Activity 11-9: Using the LAN Diagnostics Data Collector Set

Time Required: Approximately 15 minutes

Objective: Use the predefined LAN Diagnostics data collector set.

Description: The LAN Diagnostics data collector set offers a good starting point for monitoring your network and gathering benchmarks about network use. This is a well-rounded data collector set in that it combines the use of performance counters, traces, and system configuration information into one report. This activity assumes you are using a wired network connection. If you are using a wireless connection, look for appropriate options to view information about that type of connection.

1. Open the Reliability and Performance Monitor if it is not already open.
2. Click the **plus sign** in front of **System** (under Data Collector Sets) in the tree.
3. Notice the predefined data collector sets you can run from under the System folder in the tree.
4. Click **LAN Diagnostics** in the tree.
5. In the right pane, notice the combination of trace, configuration, and performance counter elements included in the LAN Diagnostics data collector set.

   • How many trace elements are shown and what are their names?

6. Right-click **Performance Counter** in the right pane and click **Properties**.
7. On the Performance Counters tab, notice that all of the preselected performance counters are for network monitoring, as shown in Figure 11-22. The asterisk at the end of each object means to use all of the counters for that object. Click **Cancel** in the Properties dialog box.

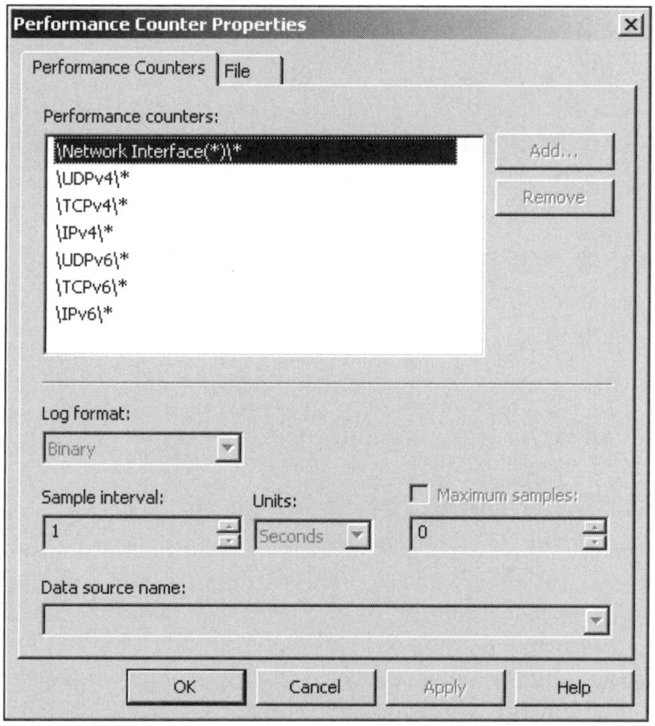

Figure 11-22 Preselected performance counters

8. Right-click **LAN Diagnostics** in the tree in the left pane and click **Start**.

9. Wait for a few minutes.

10. Right-click **LAN Diagnostics** in the tree and click **Stop**.

11. Right-click **LAN Diagnostics** in the tree and click **Latest Report**.

   - Were any problems found under the Diagnostic Results category? Did the system pass as reported under Basic System Checks?

12. Click the **down arrow** for **Wired Networking Troubleshooting Information**.

13. Click the **down arrow** for **Wired Trace**.

14. Click each of the trace files, one at a time, to open a Notepad window to see if any information was recorded about the trace. Close the Notepad file after you view it.

15. Click **Hardware Configuration** to view the information about your computer and its adapters.

16. Leave the Reliability and Performance Monitor window open for the next activity.

Using Reliability Monitor

Reliability Monitor tracks the combined hardware and software reliability of a system from the time the system was installed. Using the Reliability Monitor helps you to judge the overall system reliability while taking into account multiple factors. It presents a running System Stability Chart that enables you to view the overall reliability over the last month to many months at a glance. The System Stability Chart is created from tallying problems or changes as recorded in the following System Stability reports:

- *Software (Un)Installs*—Represents all forms of installs and uninstalls including for applications, application components, drivers, Windows updates, and service packs

- *Application Failures*—Records software that has stopped working or is not responding, that has terminated unexpectedly, or that you have terminated using Task Manager

- *Hardware Failures*—Represents hardware failures such as disk or memory failures

- *Windows Failures*—Records operating system failures and failures that occur when the system is booted

- *Miscellaneous Failures*—Records any other failures, such as when the system goes down because of a power outage

Figure 11-23 shows an example of the Reliability Monitor information. In the top portion of the right pane, you see the System Stability Chart that tracks reliability on a day-by-day basis by plotting points on the chart. The points range from 0 to 10 with 10 representing optimum reliability and 0 representing the lowest reliability level. Figure 11-23 also shows the **System Stability Index**, which is 5.78 (out of 10). The System Stability Index provides a single number summary of recent reliability. The 0 to10 scale is determined by weighting reliability events. For example, a recent hardware or software failure brings the number down. As time passes and no failures or serious warnings occur, the rating gradually goes up, representing improvement.

When a problem has occurred, the lower portion of the chart displays a problem or informational symbol for that date. A red circle with an *x* inside represents a failure condition, such as an application that has stopped working or a NIC that has failed. A yellow yield sign with an exclamation point is a warning event, such as that a new driver installation has failed but the device is still working with the old driver. A white comment symbol with an *i* inside is simply informational, such as that you have successfully installed a new hard drive or software application. In Figure 11-23, notice the two informational symbols representing the successful installation of two software applications (on two different dates). Also note the failure symbol showing that

11

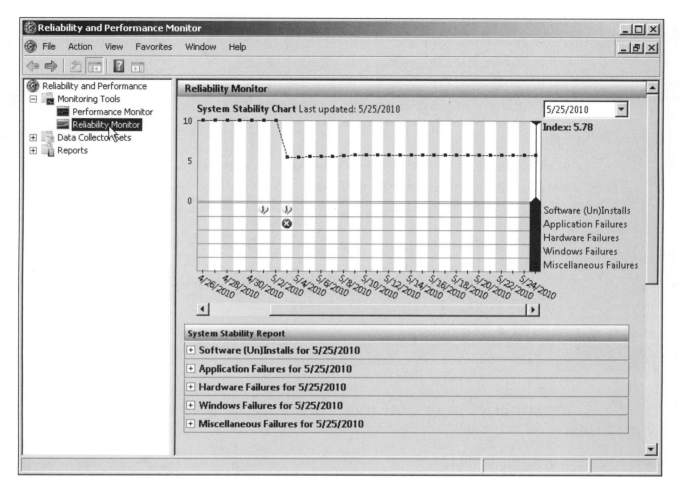

Figure 11-23 Reliability Monitor

an application has failed. When you click a failure, warning, or informational symbol in the chart, information is shown under the chart that provides details about the event.

Notice in Figure 11-23 that the System Stability Chart is plotted using dots. This means that the system has not been running long enough for Reliability Monitor to gather enough data for a representative picture of system reliability. It needs to gather data over many months before a truly representative picture is available. The lines connected by dots are replaced by a solid line when data has been collected over a long enough period to be representative.

As you review the chart and System Stability Index, take into account that the index value goes down when you successfully implement operating system updates, update applications, and add hardware. If you regularly use Windows Update, the reliability index goes down even though the updates make your system more secure. If you remove problematic software or update a driver because the old one had bugs, the index goes down. This is because any form of update or software removal represents a change, and change implies some risk of instability.

The bottom portion of Figure 11-23, which is the System Stability Report section, enables you to view details by date of the specific reports used by Reliability Monitor. For example, in Figure 11-24 when you scroll to and open the Application Failures report for a specific date on which an application failed, you can view the information about which application failed.

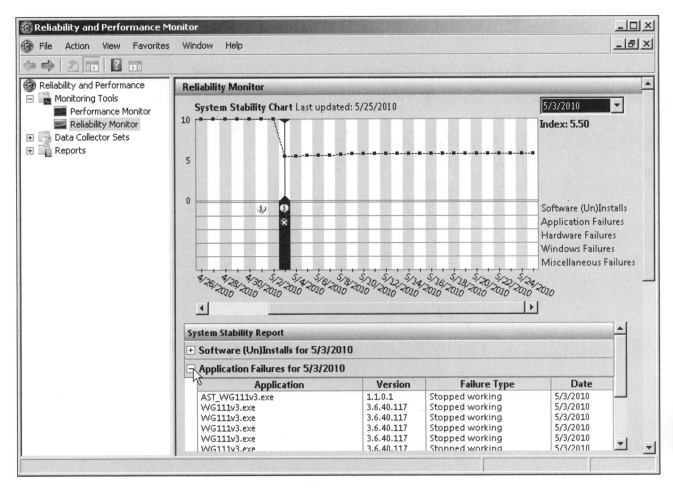

Figure 11-24   Viewing the Application Failures report for a specific date

Reliability Monitor is valuable for tracking the reliability of a server over an extended period of time so that you have a general idea about the overall stability of that server. If you work in an organization and sometimes have problems with a certain server you may get questions from others about its stability. Even though the server has only had a couple of recent problems, such as from a memory failure that you have since fixed, some users or a manager may wonder why the server is "always causing problems." You can use information from Reliability Monitor to show that the server has been reliable until having memory problems and is again reliable now that you've replaced the malfunctioning memory.

The System Stability Reports in Reliability Monitor are also a valuable tool for troubleshooting problems. If an application often becomes unresponsive, you can determine this in the reports and take steps to update or replace that application. If you bought a server computer that has a pattern of hardware problems and proves to be a "lemon," the System Stability Reports will help you determine this quickly.

Activity 11-10: Using Reliability Monitor

Time Required: Approximately 15 minutes
Objective: Learn how to use Reliability Monitor.

Description: In this activity, you use Reliability Monitory to determine the stability of a server.

1. Make sure that the Reliability and Performance Monitor window is already open, and if not, open it.

2. Click **Reliability Monitor** in the left pane in the tree under Monitoring Tools (refer to Figure 11-23).

   • What is the System Stability Index for your computer? What types of events or failures (or lack of these) have contributed to the index value?

3. If you see a date in the System Stability Chart (in the right pane) with a failure, warning, or informational icon, click the column for that date. You should see information about the event or events displayed under the appropriate report for that date in the lower half of the right pane (see Figure 11-24 as an example).

4. Click any other dates that might have a failure, warning, or informational icon and read the reported information about those events.

5. Find the horizontal scroll bar in the middle of the right pane under the System Stability Chart (if your system has been up long enough to have historical data going beyond the last month). If the data is available, scroll to view information in the chart for past months.

6. Close the Reliability and Performance Monitor window.

Implementing the SNMP Service

The **Simple Network Management Protocol (SNMP)** is used for network management on TCP/IP-based networks. It provides administrators with a way of centrally managing workstations, servers, hubs, and routers from a central computer running management software. SNMP can be used for the following:

   • Configuring network devices

   • Monitoring the performance of a network

   • Locating network problems

   • Monitoring network usage

SNMP provides network management services through agents and management systems. The SNMP management system (a computer running management software) sends and requests information from an SNMP agent. The SNMP agent (any computer or network device running SNMP agent software) responds to the management system's request for information. The management systems and agents can be grouped into communities for administrative and security purposes. Only those management systems and agents in the same community can communicate with each other.

 Some examples of network management systems and software applications that use SNMP include AdventNet Web NMS (commercial software), Multi Router Traffic Grapher (open source software), and Network Monitor (network monitoring software available from Microsoft).

When a network management station is set up on a network, the following Microsoft operating systems and components are compatible with SNMP:

   • Windows Server 2008

   • Windows Server 2003

   • Windows 2000 Server

   • Windows 2000, XP, and Vista

   • WINS servers

   • DHCP servers

- Internet Information Services servers
- Microsoft RAS and IAS servers

At this writing, Windows Server 2008 does not come with a full-fledged SNMP network management system application. However, the Windows Management Instrumentation (WMI) Software Development Kit (SDK) enables SNMP applications to access SNMP data.

Activity 11-11: Installing SNMP Services

Time Required: Approximately 5 minutes
Objective: Install SNMP.

Description: In this activity, you use Server Manager to install the SNMP Services feature in Windows Server 2008.

> TCP/IP must be installed in an operating system before you can install SNMP.

1. Click **Start,** point to **Administrative Tools,** and click **Server Manager.**
2. Scroll to the **Features Summary** section and click **Add Features.**
3. Check the box for **SNMP Services.** Click **Next.**
4. Click **Install.**
5. Click **Close.**
6. Leave Server Manager open for the next activity.

After you install the SNMP service, make sure that it is started, is set to start automatically, and is set up to have a **community** of hosts that share use of the service and a **community name,** which is similar to having a rudimentary password used among the hosts.

Activity 11-12: Configuring the SNMP Service

Time Required: Approximately 10 minutes
Objective: Learn how to configure the SNMP service.

Description: In this activity, you learn how to configure the SNMP service and the SNMP Trap service.

1. Open Server Manager, if it is not already open.
2. In the tree, click the **plus sign** for **Configuration** to expand it.
3. Click **Services** in the tree under Configuration.
4. In the right pane, double-click **SNMP Service.**
5. On the General tab, make sure *Startup type* is set to **Automatic** and that the service is started.
6. Click the **Security** tab (see Figure 11-25). From here you can configure the accepted communities for the agent. For example, Public is a community name that is often accepted by SNMP implementations. You would click the Add button in the upper half of the dialog box to configure community names. Also, by default the SNMP agent is configured to accept SNMP packets from localhost. You can configure the SNMP agent to accept SNMP packets from additional hosts by clicking the Add button in the lower half of the dialog box. Additional hosts are specified by host name, IP, or IPX address of the host from which the agent can accept SNMP packets.

11

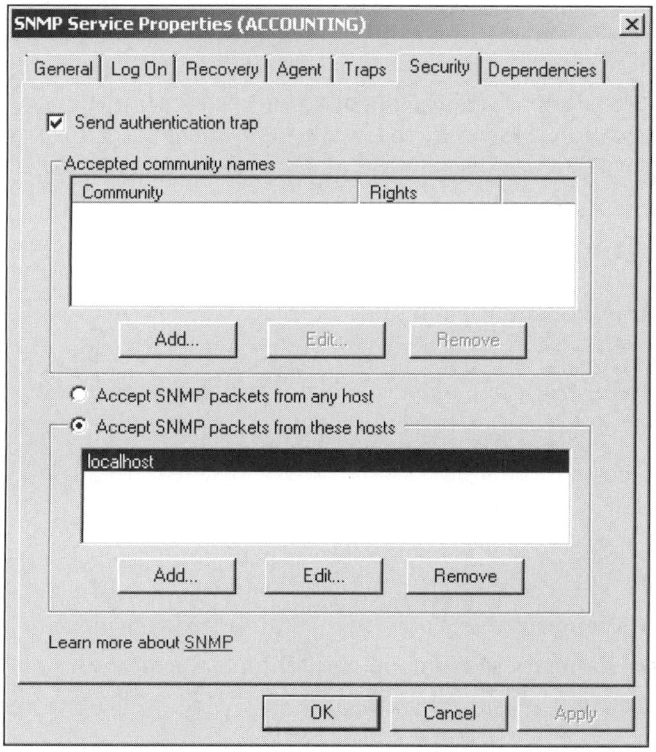

Figure 11-25   SNMP security parameters

7. Click the **Traps** tab. When a certain type of event occurs on an SNMP agent (such as the system being restarted), the agent can send a message known as a **trap** to a management system. The management system that receives the trap is known as the trap destination. To configure a trap, you would type in the name of the community that the SNMP agent will send trap messages to and click **Add to list**. Next, you would click **Add** in the Trap destinations and type in the host name, IP, or IPX address of the management system that will receive the trap messages.

8. Click **Cancel** in the Properties dialog box.

9. Double-click the **SNMP Trap** service in the Server Manager window. If you plan to create traps, you need to configure this service, which is set to Manual by default. Set the *Startup type* to **Automatic**, so that you do not have to remember to start the service after every reboot of the system. Click **Apply**.

10. Click **Start**.

11. Click **OK** in the Properties dialog box.

12. Close the Server Manager window.

Chapter Summary

- Server monitoring enables you to establish benchmarks or baselines to help identify areas that need improvement and to identify problem areas.

- A server has many services running at the same time. Services can be monitored to ensure the necessary ones are started and working correctly and unnecessary services are turned off. Monitoring services also enables you to determine what services depend on others.

- Task Manager enables you to monitor applications, processes, services, system performance, network performance, and logged-on users. If a problem is occurring with a particular application or process, you can use Task Manager to stop the application or process. Task Manager can help identify system performance problems, show if more memory is needed for the computer, or even be used to log off a hung user connection.

- Performance Monitor is one of a suite of tools offered through the Reliability and Performance Monitor. Performance Monitor uses objects such as the processor or memory for monitoring. For each object you can monitor from an array of counters that are specialized measurement options. Performance Monitor offers the ability to monitor your system and network in depth, to set baselines, and to troubleshoot problems.

- A data collector set is another tool in the Reliability and Performance Monitor that enables you to collect data about a server or network and compile the data into a report. The type of data compiled and how it is rendered into a report is established through creating the data collector set. Several predefined and template-based data collector sets are available to help you get a running start with this powerful tool.

- The Reliability Monitor is yet another tool in the Reliability and Performance Monitor. This tool helps you track the hardware and software reliability of a server. Tracking reliability can help you identify problem patterns, such as a particular NIC model that keeps failing, so that you can replace it with a different, more reliable model.

- Windows Server 2008 offers the SNMP service, which you can choose to install. The SNMP service enables network agents to gather network performance data on TCP/IP networks for use by network management software. It also provides a way to manage and configure specific network devices.

Key Terms

base priority class   The initial priority assigned to a program process or thread in the program code.

benchmark (or **baseline**)   A measurement standard for hardware or software used to establish performance measures under varying loads or circumstances.

community   A group of hosts that share the same SNMP services.

community name   In SNMP communications, a rudimentary password (name) used by network agents and the network management station (or software) in the same community so that their communications cannot be easily intercepted by an unauthorized workstation or device.

counter   Used by Performance Monitor, a measurement technique for an object, for example, for measuring the processor performance by percentage in use.

data collector set   A combination of techniques for gathering performance and diagnostic data that is rendered in a report or log format. The basic data gathering techniques can be one or a combination of performance counters, event traces, and system configuration data.

handle   A resource, such as a file, used by a program that has its own identification so the program is able to access it.

instance   An individual occurrence of an element that is being monitored in Performance Monitor; exists when two or more types of elements can be monitored, such as two or more threads or disk drives.

page fault   Event that occurs whenever memory pages must be called from disk (from the paging file).

performance counter report   Output of information gathered via Performance Monitor objects, counters, and instances configured within a data collector set.

Performance Monitor   The Windows Server 2008 utility used to track system or application objects. For each object type, one or more counters can be logged via a data collection set for later analysis, or tracked in real time for immediate Performance Monitoring.

Simple Network Management Protocol (SNMP)   Used for network management and performance monitoring on TCP/IP-based networks.

System Stability Index   A figure between 0 and 10 that represents the current system reliability when taking into account software installation, software removal, application failures, hardware failures, Windows system failures, and other miscellaneous failures.

thread   A block of program code executing within a running process. One process may launch one or more threads.

trace   Capture of a specific event when it occurs, such as a page fault or input to a disk.

trace report   Contains results of monitored trace events generated by a data collector set and contains only those instances when the events occur, such as creating a trace to record each time disk input/output activity occurs or when an Active Directory Kerberos security event is triggered. *See* trace.

trap   A specific situation or event detected by SNMP that a network administrator may want to be warned about or to track via network management software, for example, when a network device is unexpectedly down or offline. *See* Simple Network Management Protocol (SNMP).

Review Questions

1. Your company has purchased a network management system that it plans to use from Windows Server 2008. Which of the following Server Manager features should you install to use with it?

   a.   SNMP service

   b.   NTLM hosts file

   c.   Kerberos version 4.5

   d.   EventSystem service

2. Your company uses an inventory program that seems to be stuck in a programming loop and will not let you shut it down. What tool can you use to immediately shut down this program which is consuming CPU resources?

   a.   Server Monitor

   b.   Performance Monitor

   c.   Task Manager

   d.   Control Panel System and Maintenance option

3. Your advertising firm is expecting a new client to visit in about 15 minutes. In preparation, you have been printing out reports and graphics for the meeting, but the print process has been slow because the server is so busy. What can you do to best help ensure the printouts are finished on time?

   a.   Decrease the priority of all processes, except the print spooler process, to Low.

   b.   Increase the priority of the print spooler process to Above Normal or High.

   c.   Quickly increase the page file size by 1–2 MB to handle the printouts.

   d.   Log all other users off, even if there is not time to give them sufficient notification.

4. Briefly explain the concept of a thread and mention where you can monitor thread activity in Windows Server 2008.

5. One of your company's users has logged out, but your monitoring shows that the user is still logged on. What tool can you use to log off the user's server session?

   a.   User Manager

   b.   Active Directory Users and Computers tool

   c.   Task Manager

   d.   Reliability Monitor

6. The System Stability Index provides a measurement between _____ and _____.

7. Which of the following can be an SNMP agent? (Choose all that apply.)

    a. Windows Server 2008

    b. Windows Vista

    c. DHCP servers

    d. IIS servers

8. Name three tools that can be started from within the Reliability and Performance Monitor.

9. While practicing, your assistant changed the priority of Windows Explorer and now the server response for all users is extraordinarily slow. What priority did he most likely set?

    a. High

    b. Normal

    c. Realtime

    d. Low

10. Briefly explain how to view a running application in Task Manager and then determine its associated process.

11. Your IT department head wants you to gather daily performance data on system performance for a new Windows Server 2008 server. You create a data collector set for this purpose. How can you set the data collector set to run at 2:00 p.m. every workday?

    a. Use the Performance Monitor Schedule option to schedule the start and stop times of the data collector set.

    b. Use the Monitor Scheduler MMC snap-in.

    c. Set the new Task Clock in Windows Server 2008.

    d. Set a schedule and stop condition in the properties of the data collector set.

12. Your server is running slowly and you suspect that a disk drive is the bottleneck. You've decided to use Performance Monitor to monitor the disk drive. Which of the following do you set up in Performance Monitor?

    a. the Harddisk instance

    b. the Physical Disk counter

    c. the MemDisk counter

    d. the % Disk Write counter

13. Which of the following reporting elements can be part of a data collector set? (Choose all that apply.)

    a. Reliability test report

    b. System configuration data

    c. Trace report

    d. Performance counter report

14. Which of the following are System Stability reports available in Reliability Monitor? (Choose all that apply.)

    a. Windows Failures

    b. Management Failures

    c. Update Errors

    d. Application Failures

15. Name three things that can be done with SNMP.

16. While you are checking to ensure you can see all network servers from your Windows Vista workstation, you notice that one of the servers seems to disappear, then reappear, then disappear. You decide to go to the console of that server to run some diagnostics. Which of the following tools can you use to help diagnose a network connectivity or resources access problem at the server? (Choose all that apply.)

    a. Services listing accessed through the Computer Management tool

    b. Event Diagnostics template used as a data collector set

    c. Network Performance tab in Task Manager

    d. Network Interface counter in Performance Monitor

17. An application developer in the IT department at your company has written a purchase order program that often stops responding when the Vendor Listing screen is displayed. Which of the following can you offer to do to help her diagnose the problem with this program? (Choose all that apply.)

    a. Use Task Manager to lower the priority of the *appmanager* service, which is used to run all applications in Windows Server 2008.

    b. Use Performance Monitor to allocate more memory to the program so that it has more reserved memory.

    c. Use Task Manager to print a dump file for the program.

    d. Use Performance Monitor to create a *diskperf* report showing the interaction between disk speed and application access timing.

18. Your assistant recently made some changes to Active Directory and since then there have been several Active Directory problems. Which tool can you use to diagnose Active Directory problems? (Choose all that apply.)

    a. Resource Monitor using the Active Directory tab

    b. Computer Management tool using the tools under the Active Directory folder

    c. Task Manager using the System Performance tab

    d. Data Collector Sets using the Active Directory Diagnostics data collector set

19. Name the three modes you can use to view Performance Monitor activity.

20. Which of the following are areas for which you can obtain system configuration data by using the Data Collector Sets monitoring capability? (Choose all that apply.)

    a. processor

    b. startup programs

    c. port classes

    d. controllers

Case Projects

CASE PROJECTS

Alterrain manufactures high-end mountain bikes with models for general recreational use and specialty models for racing. Alterrain products are sold throughout North America and Europe. The company operates from an office building adjacent to its manufacturing building. A centralized server and network operations room in the office building is fully networked, as is the manufacturing building.

The office building houses management along with the Marketing, Accounting, and Research and Design departments. The Manufacturing, Inventory, and Shipping departments are housed in the manufacturing building. Network communications in the office building are largely wireless, but the servers use cable connections to the network and are protected behind a router. The manufacturing building has a cable network because the machinery used in the building and the building structure are not well suited for dependable wireless communications.

Alterrain has 12 Windows Server 2008 servers that include Standard, Enterprise, Web Server, and Datacenter Editions. The company employees use a combination of Windows Vista, Windows XP, and Linux desktop computers.

Because the company has recently experienced network and server problems, management has decided to launch a Computer Reliability initiative. The goal of this program is to minimize computer interruptions and maximize user productivity. As part of the initiative, they have hired you through Aspen Consulting to help put into place reliability measures.

Case Project 11-1: Obtaining Baselines

The Alterrain IT Department does little server monitoring because most if its resources have been spent upgrading servers and network equipment as well as responding to user needs. You recommend starting the Computer Reliability initiative by developing a plan for gathering baseline performance data on each server. Prepare a report or slide presentation for the IT director that describes the baseline data you would gather.

Case Project 11-2: Using Monitoring Tools

Alterrain is hiring a new computer administrator who will have computer reliability as one of her job duties. In preparation for her arrival, the IT director asks you to prepare an overview for her of Windows Server 2008 monitoring tools, which includes:

- Task Manager
- Performance Monitor
- Reliability Monitor
- Data Collector Sets

Case Project 11-3: Monitoring Database Reliability

A group of users in the Inventory Department has expressed a concern that the server with the inventory database recently has been down too often. Most of the downtime has seemed to be related to database upgrades and patches. No one has kept a log of the downtime, but the Alterrain management group is interested in obtaining further information so they can make a decision about keeping the present database software or changing to a different vendor. What can you do to provide the information requested by management?

Case Project 11-4: Creating a Performance Monitor Strategy

The IT director asks you to prepare a document to help the company standardize Performance Monitor data gathered from each server. Create a recommendation for consistent use of five or six Performance Monitor objects that can be used to help establish baseline data and enable fast troubleshooting of problems that may develop in the future. For each object you propose using, also discuss two or three counters to use with those objects.

11

Managing System Reliability and Availability

After reading this chapter and completing the exercises, you will be able to:

- Understand general problem-solving strategies
- Resolve boot problems
- Use and configure Event Viewer
- Troubleshoot network connectivity
- Remotely administer a server using Remote Desktop
- Remotely administer multiple servers using Remote Server Administration Tools

The most successful server and network administrators are often barely known to the users who rely on them. This means the users' systems work reliably or are fixed nearly as soon as they break down. You can be this kind of administrator once you perfect your problem-solving skills and learn to use the tools in Windows Server 2008 to diagnose and fix problems. In Chapter 11, "Server and Network Monitoring," you learned how to use several tools to address server problems. This chapter teaches problem-solving skills and gives you more tools for your arsenal.

In this chapter, you learn to develop basic problem-solving strategies, including techniques for solving problems step-by-step. Boot problems can represent a serious risk, so you learn how to troubleshoot a server that won't boot. You learn to use Event Viewer, which is the repository of logs used for troubleshooting problems. You also learn many tools for diagnosing network connectivity problems. Finally, you learn to use tools for remotely managing a server to give you greater flexibility compared with working only from the server console.

General Problem-Solving Strategies

The best approach to solving server and network problems is to develop effective troubleshooting strategies. Four general strategies are:

- Understanding how a server and the network interact
- Training your users to help you solve problems
- Solving problems step-by-step
- Tracking problems and solutions

Understanding How Servers and the Network Interact

You can take various steps to better understand the environment in which a server operates. Many server and network administrators create a diagram of the entire network or diagrams of different portions of a network and then update the diagrams each time an aspect of the network changes. Figure 12-1 is a sample diagram of a portion of a network that shows cabled and wireless links.

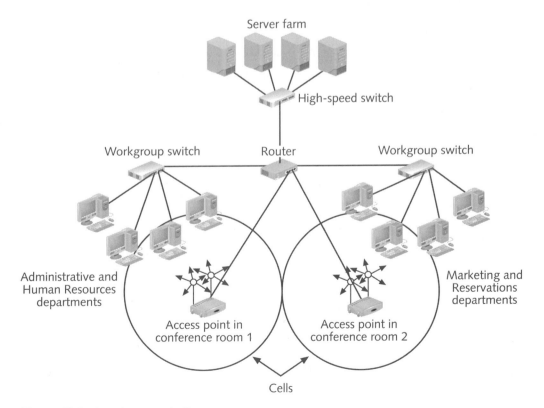

Figure 12-1 Sample network diagram

A network diagram should include the following elements:

- Servers and any mainframes
- Workstations and network printers (unless the network is too large to include these)
- Wireless network devices
- Cabled network devices
- Telecommunications links
- Wireless links
- Remote links
- Building locations

A server does not exist in a vacuum, but is a member of a larger community of networked workstations and users. Gathering benchmarks, as discussed in Chapter 11, helps you understand your server and how it is affected by the network context. For example, slow server performance can look like a network problem, and slow network performance can look like a server problem. The more you know about the server's network context, the faster you'll be able to resolve a problem, such as slow server performance.

Understanding the community that uses a server is vital. For example, because users are dependent on a server, it is important to wait until off-peak hours to perform server maintenance, including software upgrades or the installation of new devices. Some organizations reserve specific off-peak hours for server maintenance, such as very early in the morning, and users know in advance that they cannot access servers during those hours.

Training Users to Help

Another valuable strategy is to train network users to be your partners in reporting problems. If you encourage users to be troubleshooting allies, they are more likely to feel they can take action to deal with a problem, rather than wait impatiently for you to detect and solve it. When you train users to gather information and report it to you, they become troubleshooting partners who can advance you several steps toward the solution. You can train users to take a variety of actions to help you and themselves. For example, they should:

- Save their work at the first sign of a problem
- Record information about a problem as the problem is occurring
- Report any protocol information, such as error messages about a protocol or an address
- Quickly report a problem by telephone, or by voice mail if you cannot be reached immediately
- Avoid sending e-mail about urgent problems

Solving Problems Step-by-Step

Equipped with knowledge of your network context and help from trained users, you can use the following step-by-step techniques to solve server and network problems:

1. Get as much information as possible about the problem. If a network user reports the problem, listen carefully to his or her description. Even if he or she does not use the correct terminology, the information is still valuable. Part of your challenge is to ask the right questions to get as much information as possible.

2. Record the error message at the time it appears or when a user reports it to you. This is an obvious but sometimes overlooked step. If you try to recall the message from memory, you might lose some important information. For example, the error "Network not responding" can lead you to a different set of troubleshooting steps than the message "Network timeout error."

The first message might signal a damaged NIC, whereas the second message could mean that a database server is overloaded and the application is waiting to obtain data.

3. Determine if anyone else is experiencing the problem. For example, several people might report they cannot load a word-processing software package. This might be due to a problem at the server they use to load the software. If only one person is experiencing this problem, it might point to trouble on her or his workstation.

4. Check the Windows Server 2008 event logs for signs of a problem (it's always a good idea to regularly check the logs anyway; you'll learn how to do this later in the chapter).

5. Use Performance Monitor, Reliability Monitor, Data Collector Sets, Task Manager, Server Manager, and the Computer Management tool to help you troubleshoot problems.

6. Check for power interruptions. Power problems are a common source of server and network difficulties. Even though the server is on an uninterruptible power source (UPS), its network connection can still be a source of problems, because the network cable can carry current to the server's NIC during a lightning storm, or because of a major power-related problem.

7. Take the information you have gathered and define the problem, such as that the server is not connecting to the network.

8. Determine possible solutions for the problem.

9. Consider the best or most likely solutions, which may well be the simplest ones. For example, the solution to a problem might be as simple as connecting a cable or power cord.

 In some cases, you might be completely stumped by a problem, for example because it is a rare problem or a bug that only the vendor knows how to fix. In these cases, contact the vendor for solutions. It can be less expensive for you to contact the vendor sooner and pay a modest support fee than to spend hours working on a problem that you might not be able to solve alone.

10. Determine how the solution will affect users. For example, if the solution is to install an operating system update, plan to implement it when the server is not busy or during regularly scheduled server maintenance time when no one expects to use the server.

11. After your solution is implemented, continue monitoring the server to ensure there are no further problems.

 One experienced Windows Server instructor teaches students to do the following when deciding on the best solution: Know what to do, know how to do it, and consider the consequences for users before implementing a solution.

Tracking Problems and Solutions

An effective troubleshooting tool is to keep a log of all network problems and their solutions. Some server administrators log problems in a database created for that purpose. Others build problem logging into help desk systems maintained by their organization. A **help desk system** is application software designed to maintain information on computer systems, user questions, problem solutions, and other information that members of the organization can reference.

The advantage of tracking problems is that you soon accumulate a wealth of information on solutions. For example, to jog your memory about a solution, you can look up how you handled a similar problem six months ago. The log of problems also can be used as a teaching tool and reference for other computer support staff. Problems that show up repeatedly in the log might indicate that special attention is needed, such as replacing a server that experiences frequent hardware problems.

It is also good practice to keep a change log, a record of changes made to a server's hardware and software. Sometimes problems arise when configuration changes are made to a server, such as the installation of new hardware and/or software or a change in settings. Documenting changes provides a reference for troubleshooting if problems should arise later. This is especially important if you are not the only server administrator and someone else is also troubleshooting the problem.

Resolving Boot Problems

Sometimes a server encounters a hardware problem and cannot be booted, displays an error screen during the boot process, or hangs. Several things can lead to boot problems, such as the installation of new software, drivers, or hardware problems. Some of the common causes of boot failures include the following:

- Disk failure on the drive or drives containing the system and boot files
- A corrupted partition table
- A corrupted boot file
- A corrupted Master Boot Record
- A disk read error

In most cases, the first step is to power off the computer and try rebooting it. Often this will work in instances where there is a temporary disk read error or memory error during the first boot attempt, which is corrected on the second try. Also, one or more data storage registers might be out of synchronization in the CPU, causing a transient problem. Rebooting resets the CPU registers. If the computer has multiple drives, a disk controller might need to be reset, which is accomplished by rebooting.

The best way to reboot for clearing a temporary error is to turn the power off, wait several seconds for the hard disk drives to fully come to a stop, and then turn on the power. This causes all components to completely reset. If, instead, you reboot using a reset button, some components might not fully reset.

Troubleshooting by Using Safe Mode

If a simple reboot does not fix the problem, or if you have installed new software or drivers, or changed the server configuration, and the server does not properly boot, try using the advanced options for booting—accessed by pressing F8 as soon as the computer boots—which include starting the computer in Safe Mode. **Safe Mode** boots the server using the most generic default settings (for example for the display, disk drives, and pointing device) and only those services needed to boot a basic configuration. After you boot into Safe Mode, you have the opportunity to further troubleshoot the problem.

For example, if you install software or a driver that causes a problem with the boot process, then you can boot into Safe Mode and remove that software or driver. Or, perhaps you have replaced the mouse with a trackball and installed the new driver for the trackball, but after you reboot, there is no pointer on the screen when you move the new trackball. You can boot into Safe Mode, reinstall the old driver and mouse, and contact the trackball vendor for a solution or new driver. Or, if you changed the server's configuration, for example by setting up an additional page file or installing a Windows component, and the server does not properly boot, you can restore the original page file settings or remove the Windows component while in Safe Mode.

If you contact a Microsoft technician for help with a server problem, often she or he will ask you to boot in Safe Mode in order to execute troubleshooting steps.

Table 12-1 lists the advanced booting options available when you press F8 at the beginning of the boot process. Also, Figure 12-2 illustrates these options.

Table 12-1   Advanced Boot Options menu options

Booting option	Description
Safe Mode	Boots the system using the minimum configuration of devices and drivers, and does not have network connectivity
Safe Mode with Networking	Boots the system using the minimum configuration of devices and drivers, and does have network connectivity
Safe Mode with Command Prompt	Boots the system into the command mode using the minimum prompt configuration of devices and drivers, and does not have network connectivity
Enable Boot Logging	Creates a record of devices and drivers that started, so you can check a log for points of failure—look for the log in the \Windows folder with the name ntbtlog.txt
Enable low-resolution video (640 x 480)	Boots the system using the fewest resources for video
Last Known Good Configuration (advanced)	Boots the system using the last configuration before any changes to the configuration were made and implemented in the Registry
Directory Services Restore Mode	Reboots the server into a local mode so that the server is not available to users as a domain controller; enables the administrator to log on to validate, work on, or restore the Active Directory database
Debugging Mode	Boots the system while transmitting debug data to be viewed at another computer over a serial connection, which can be used by Microsoft technicians to troubleshoot problems
Disable automatic restart on system failure	Does not automatically restart the system if it fails
Disable Driver Signature Enforcement	Enables drivers without the proper digital signature to be installed (which might be needed on older hardware or when you have a driver you know is safe, but does not have a digital signature)
Start Windows Normally	Starts the system without any special options
Reboot	Reboots the system
Return to OS Choices Menu	Returns to the regular operating system menu from which to select to boot into Windows Server 2008 (or another operating system on a dual-boot system)

To access the Advanced Boot Options menu:

1. Reboot the computer. (Be sure all users are logged off before doing this.)
2. Press F8 as soon as the computer boots.
3. Select the option you want to use, such as Safe Mode, and press Enter.

Use the advanced option that is the most appropriate for the kind of problem you are troubleshooting. For example, if the problem is only that you have installed a new monitor driver and cannot use or see the display when you boot, select *Enable low-resolution video (640 x 480)*. If the problem is related to the most recent software or configuration change you have made, such as installing an additional SCSI adapter or an additional network interface, boot using the *Last Known Good Configuration (advanced)*. The *Last Known Good Configuration (advanced)* is the Windows Server 2008 configuration that is stored in the Registry (HKEY_LOCAL_MACHINE\ System\CurrentControlSet). This configuration is the one in effect prior to making a system, driver, or configuration change after the last time the computer was booted. For those times when you are not sure why the system is having problems, or you have installed multiple new drivers or several new software programs, use the Safe Mode or the Safe Mode with Networking option so that you can access the Windows Server 2008 desktop to work on the problem.

```
                     Advanced Boot Options

Choose Advanced Options for: Windows Setup
(Use the arrow keys to highlight your choice.)


    Safe Mode
    Safe Mode with Networking
    Safe Mode with Command Prompt

    Enable Boot Logging
    Enable low-resolution video (640x480)
    Last Known Good Configuration (advanced)
    Directory Services Restore Mode
    Debugging Mode
    Disable automatic restart on system failure
    Disable Driver Signature Enforcement


    Start Windows Normally


Description: Start Windows with only the core drivers and services. Use
             when you cannot boot after installing a new device or driver.




ENTER=Choose                                              ESC=Cancel
```

Figure 12-2 Advanced Boot Options menu

If you use Safe Mode, but are unable to troubleshoot the problem, or a failed driver message is displayed during the boot process, use the Enable Boot Logging option so that you can create a log that you can later check for problems. For example, you might boot so that the log is created, and then boot again into Safe Mode so that you can view the contents of the log.

The Safe Mode with Command Prompt option is particularly useful when you can solve a problem by executing a command, such as by running *chkdsk* to repair damaged files or by running *sfc* to locate critical system files that have been overwritten and then restore them.

If you have Active Directory installed and suspect that it is damaged, or that the **SYSVOL** shared volumes (see the following Note) are corrupted, use the Directory Services Restore Mode to restore damaged files and folders.

When you set up Active Directory, a domain controller is automatically set up with the SYSVOL shared folder, which contains scripts, Group Policy Objects (GPOs), and software distribution files. The GPOs can be important for access to the domain. SYSVOL is technically recognized as part of the operating system. The contents of SYSVOL are replicated between DCs, by the older File Replication service, when Windows 2000 Server and Windows Server 2003 DCs are intermixed on the network with Windows Server 2008 DCs. If only Windows Server 2008 DCs are on the network and the domain functional level is raised to reflect this, then the newer Windows Server 2008 Distributed File System (DFS) Replication capability is used for more reliable and efficient replication.

Some steps in the activities in this book include bulleted questions with space for you to record your responses/answers. Additionally, for all of the activities in this chapter, you'll need an account with Administrator privileges. These activities can be completed on a virtual server or computer, such as in Hyper-V.

Activity 12-1: Booting into Safe Mode

Time Required: Approximately 15 minutes
Objective: Learn how to boot into Safe Mode.

Description: In this activity, you practice accessing the advanced menu options on a server and then you boot into the Safe Mode.

1. Make sure all users are logged off Windows Server 2008.

   • What tool would you use to check that all users are logged off?

2. Shut down and then reboot the computer (click **Start**, point to the **right-pointing arrow** at the bottom of the Start menu, click **Restart**, select the appropriate option in the Shut Down Windows dialog box, and click **OK**—or power off the server and reboot).

3. Press F8 as soon as the computer boots.

   • What option would you use to boot to fix a monitor driver problem? Which one would you use to run *chkdsk*?

4. Select **Safe Mode** and press **Enter**.

   • What information is displayed as the system boots? How might this information prove helpful in troubleshooting a problem?

5. Press **CTRL+ALT+DEL** and log in with your username and password.

   • How is the Windows Server 2008 desktop display different in Safe Mode from when you boot normally? Record your observations about Safe Mode.

6. Shut down the computer and then reboot normally.

Troubleshooting by Using the Installation DVD

In Windows Server 2003, you could install the Recovery Console to access the command line in situations in which the server would not boot. Windows Server 2008 does not use the Recovery Console, but includes a similar capability on the Windows Server 2008 installation DVD along with other recovery options as follows:

• Windows Complete PC Restore

• Windows Memory Diagnostic Tool

• Command Prompt

Windows Complete PC Restore   When you create a VSS full backup using the Windows Server Backup tool (see Chapter 7, "Configuring and Managing Data Storage"), this creates a backup of the data and program files and the system state data. You can create such a backup on a removable disk or on a backup disk permanently connected to the server, for example. The data and program files are files you have put on the server as you have installed programs and stored data on the server. The **system state data** includes the operating system plus extra components and information that reflect the currently configured state of the server, depending on what features are installed. This includes elements such as the following:

- System and boot files
- Protected system files
- Active Directory
- SYSVOL folder (when Active Directory is installed)
- Registry
- COM+ Class Registration information
- DNS zones (when DNS is installed)
- Certificate information (when certificate services are installed)
- Server cluster data (when server clustering is used)
- IIS metadirectory (if the Web Server role is installed)

All of the system state data is backed up as a group because many of these entities are interrelated.

 Keep in mind that you can only back up system state data from the local computer, which means that the backup medium, such as a local or removable drive, must be physically attached to that computer.

When you back up the system state data, you also are backing up the system protected files, which are the files used to start up the operating system when you boot.

In Chapter 7, you learned that you can use the restore capability in the Windows Backup tool to restore from a full backup. Unfortunately, it is often true that the time when you need to do a full restore is when you cannot get the server to boot and so the Windows Backup tool is unavailable, such as when it has been necessary to replace one or more disk drives. This is why Windows Server 2008 offers the capability to perform a Windows Complete PC Restore from the Windows Server 2008 installation DVD. This option restores the data and program files as well as the system state data.

The general steps for performing a Windows Complete PC Restore are as follows:

1. If you are using a removable hard drive, ensure that it is attached to the computer.
2. Insert the Windows Server 2008 installation DVD.
3. Power off the computer.
4. Turn on the computer, and if necessary press the key combination to boot from the CD/DVD drive.
5. The DVD might take a few moments to load.
6. When the Install Windows window appears, specify the language to install, such as English, in the Language to install drop-down box. In the Time and currency format box, make your selection, such as English (United States). In the Keyboard or input method box, make your selection, such as US.
7. Click Next.
8. Click the link for *Repair your computer* (see Figure 12-3).
9. Ensure that *Microsoft Windows Server 2008* is highlighted in the System Recovery Options box. Click Next.
10. Click *Windows Complete PC Restore* (see Figure 12-4).
11. If a valid backup location is not found automatically, you'll see a warning box. Click Cancel.
12. If necessary, click *Use the latest available backup (recommended)*. Provide the location, date and time, and computer information. Click Next and follow any further instructions for performing the restore, such as completing the *Select the location of the backup* window information.

Figure 12-3 Selecting the option to *Repair your computer*

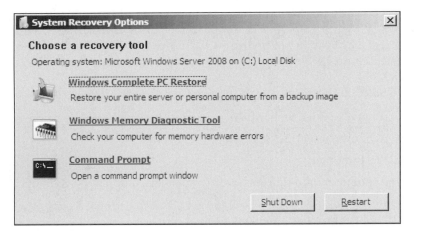

Figure 12-4 System recovery options

Windows Memory Diagnostic Tool The Windows Memory Diagnostic Tool is another tool available from the *Repair your computer* option on the Windows Server 2008 installation DVD. This tool is used to test the RAM in your computer. When you run the tool, you can either have the computer restart immediately and check the memory when it boots, or you can check the memory the next time the server is booted.

Activity 12-2: Performing Memory Diagnostics

Time Required: Approximately 15 minutes
Objective: Learn how to test RAM.

Description: If you suspect there is a memory problem with your server, for example if you see a memory error message, you can use the Windows Server 2008 installation DVD to test the memory, as you do in this activity.

1. Insert the Windows Server 2008 installation DVD.

2. Shut down the computer.

3. Turn on the computer, and if necessary press the key combination to boot from the CD/DVD drive.

4. When the Install Windows window appears, specify the language to install, such as **English**, in the Language to install drop-down box. In the Time and currency format box, make your selection, such as **English (United States)**. In the Keyboard or input method box, make your selection, such as **US**.

5. Click **Next**.

6. Click the link for **Repair your computer** (refer to Figure 12-3).

7. Ensure that **Microsoft Windows Server 2008** is highlighted in the System Recovery Options box. Click **Next**.

8. Click **Windows Memory Diagnostic Tool** (refer to Figure 12-4).

9. Click **Restart now and check for problems (recommended)**, as shown in Figure 12-5.

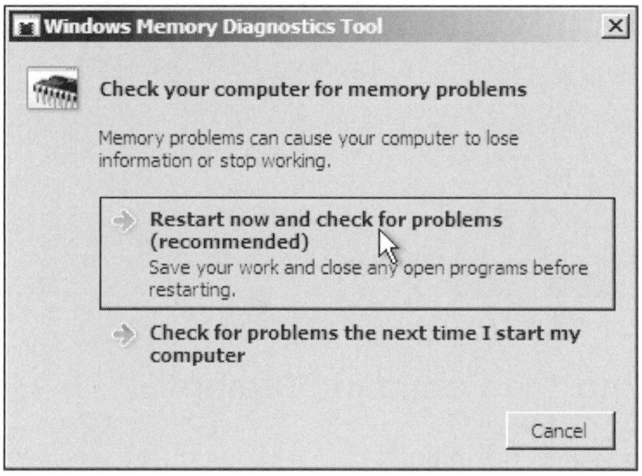

Figure 12-5 Starting the Windows Memory Diagnostic Tool

10. Wait for a few minutes for the computer to reboot.

11. You'll see the Windows Memory Diagnostics Tool that tracks the progress of the diagnostic. The Status information in yellow print will show if any problems are found.

12. When the diagnostics are completed, the computer will reboot. Log back on after it reboots.

Using the Command Prompt

Using the Command Prompt When you insert the installation DVD, you can use it to access the command prompt so that you can repair a disk problem or copy a critical file back to the server. Another reason for using the command prompt is to copy off the server important files you have not yet backed up because the system failed before starting the backup. The command prompt capability can be vital when you cannot boot into your server.

When you open the Command Prompt window, you start in the \Sources folder on the Windows Server 2008 installation DVD. You can execute many commands from the command prompt, such as the *copy* command to copy a file or the *chkdsk* command to check for disk errors and repair them. For any command, you can enter *help /?* to view its online documentation. Table 12-2 provides a sampling of the commands.

Table 12-2 Sample command prompt commands

Command	Description
attrib	Manages folder and file attributes
cd (or chdir)	Changes to a different directory (folder), to the parent directory, or shows the directory you are in
chkdsk	Verifies and fixes files (requires access to the Autochk.exe file)
cls	Reinitializes the display
copy	Copies files
del	Deletes files
dir	Lists the contents of a directory (folder)
diskpart	Partitions a disk and manages multiple partitions on a system
exit	Closes the Command Prompt window and returns to the System Recovery Options box
expand	Uncompresses a file
format	Formats a drive
md (mkdir)	Creates a new directory
more	Shows a file's contents one screen at a time
rd (rmdir)	Deletes a directory
ren (rename)	Modifies a file's name
type	Shows a file's contents

Activity 12-3: Using the Command Prompt

Time Required: Approximately 15 minutes
Objective: Learn how to access the command prompt from the Windows Server 2008 installation DVD.

Description: If you have an area of disk damage or a corrupted system file and cannot boot a server, using the installation DVD to access the command prompt can be critical. In this mode you can attempt to replace a system file, fix the boot problem, or copy important files off of the server. In this activity, you use the Windows Server 2008 installation DVD to access the command line.

1. Insert the Windows Server 2008 installation DVD, if it is not already in the CD/DVD drive.
2. Shut down the computer.
3. Turn on the computer, and if necessary press the key combination to boot from the CD/DVD drive.
4. On the Install Windows window, specify the language to install, such as **English.** In the Time and currency format box, make your selection, such as **English (United States).** In the Keyboard or input method box, make your selection, such as **US.**
5. Click **Next.**
6. Click **Repair your computer** (refer to Figure 12-3).
7. Ensure that **Microsoft Windows Server 2008** is highlighted in the System Recovery Options box and click **Next.**
8. Click **Command Prompt** in the System Recovery Options box (refer to Figure 12-4).
9. You'll see a Command Prompt window similar to Figure 12-6.

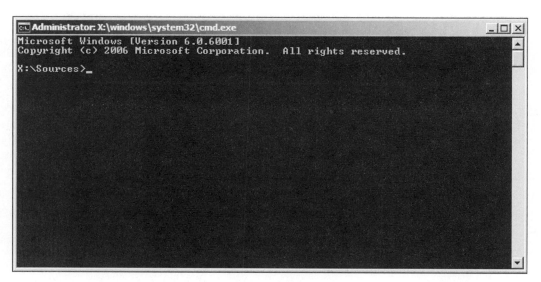

Figure 12-6 Command Prompt window

10. Type **dir C:** (or use another drive designation if your main files are not on drive C:) and press **Enter** to list the contents of the main folder on the server.

11. Type **dir C:\Windows** and press **Enter** to view the files and subdirectories in the \Windows directory (containing system files).

12. Type **copy /?** and press **Enter** to view the documentation for the copy command. Press the **spacebar**, if necessary, to display the remaining documentation.

13. Type **chkdsk C:** (or use another appropriate drive letter for the server) to check the file system and press **Enter**.

 When *chkdsk* is finished, you are likely to see the message "Failed to transfer logged message to the event log with status 50.", because *chkdsk* cannot write to the event log in this mode.

14. Type **exit** and press **Enter** to close the Command Prompt window.

15. On the System Recovery Options dialog box, click **Restart** to restart the server.

16. Log back onto the server.

General Tips for Fixing Boot Problems

Using the Safe Mode, the Windows Server 2008 installation DVD, and other techniques, Table 12-3 and Table 12-4 provide tips for fixing boot problems and responding to Stop messages. A Stop message is an error message displayed when the server experiences a serious problem and then stops functioning.

Table 12-3 Troubleshooting boot problems

Boot problem	Solutions
A message appears when booting, such as one of the following: Inaccessible Boot Device; Invalid Partition Table; Hard Disk Error; Hard Disk Absent or Failed.	The boot sector on the NTFS partition is corrupted or the hard drive is damaged. This can be caused by a virus, a corrupted partition table, a BIOS setting change, or a corrupted disk. Check the BIOS setup to make certain it is correct. Correct any improper settings (also make sure the CMOS battery is working—it is not working if the BIOS settings are zero, null, or incorrect).
	If no BIOS problems are present, use the Windows Server 2008 installation DVD to boot the system into the command prompt, then run a virus scanner on the server or insert a virus scanner in a CD/DVD drive and attempt to scan the hard disk for viruses. If a virus is found, remove it.
	If the disk cannot be accessed, determine if the problem is the hard disk, disk controller, or a SCSI adapter and replace the defective part (make sure to check that a SCSI adapter is properly terminated). If the hard disk must be replaced, reinstall the operating system.
The system hangs when booting.	Power off and on the computer to reboot. Try rebooting a couple of times.
	If rebooting does not work, check the BIOS settings to be sure they have not changed and that the CMOS battery is working. If many of the BIOS settings are incorrect, replace the battery and restore the proper settings.
	For an SMP computer, the hal.dll file might be corrupted. Boot from the Windows Server 2008 installation DVD into the command prompt from the repair mode. Reinstall the hal.dll file from the manufacturer's CD/DVD.
Changes were made to the system configuration when last logged on and now the computer will not boot.	Stop the boot process immediately and reboot using the Last Known Good Configuration (advanced) option (press F8 when you boot) on the Advanced Menu Options screen. Once logged on, check the configuration and fix any problems, such as a bad or removed device driver.
The screen display goes blank or is jumbled as the computer begins booting into Windows Server 2008.	Immediately stop the boot process. Restart the computer, accessing the BIOS setup before starting Windows Server 2008. Check the video BIOS setup to make sure it is correct and restore any settings that are changed. Reboot the computer.
	If no BIOS problems are present, reboot using the Enable low-resolution video (640x480) option on the Advanced Menu Options screen (press F8 when you boot). Once logged on, check and reinstall the display driver. Alternatively, boot into the command prompt repair mode from the Windows Server 2008 installation DVD and reinstall the display driver.
A driver is missing, but you are not sure which one, or the operating system is having trouble recognizing all hardware components on the computer when it boots.	Boot using Safe Mode (press F8 when you boot) and watch for a problem as the drivers are loaded, or boot using the Enable Boot Logging option from the advanced menu options and examine the \Windows\ntbtlog.txt file. (The ntbtlog.txt file is a log of drivers that are successfully loaded or not loaded when Windows Server 2008 boots.)

Table 12-4 Troubleshooting boot problems associated with Stop messages

Stop message*	Solutions
0x00000023 NTFS File System	Boot into Safe Mode or the command prompt via the Windows Server 2008 installation DVD and run *chkdsk* to repair any damaged files.
	If you have recently installed a virus scanner or a disk defragmenter that is not from Microsoft or compatible with Windows Server 2008, boot into Safe Mode or using Last Known Good Configuration (advanced) and remove that software.
0x0000001E and the message Kmode_Exception_Not_Handled	If you have recently installed a new video system and associated drivers, remove the new hardware, and reboot into the Safe Mode to remove the new drivers (or boot using the Enable low-resolution video (640x480) option on the Advanced Menu Options screen). Do the same if you have installed any new drivers.
	Verify the video setup in the computer's BIOS or install any updated BIOS software offered by the computer vendor.
	Reboot using Safe Mode or the command prompt from the Windows Server 2008 installation DVD and make sure that you are not out of disk space. (From the command prompt, type *dir C:* and press Enter to view if free disk space is available.)
0x000000B4 and the message Video Driver Init Failure	If you have recently installed a new video system and associated drivers, remove the new hardware, and reboot into the Safe Mode to remove the new drivers (or boot using the Enable low-resolution video (640x480) option on the Advanced Menu Options screen).
0x0000007B and the message Inaccessible_Boot_Device	Boot into Safe Mode or boot into the command prompt via the Windows Server 2008 installation DVD and check for a virus.
	Boot into Safe Mode or boot into the command prompt via the Windows Server 2008 installation DVD and run *chkdsk* to repair any damaged files.
0x0000002E and the message Data Bus Error or 0x0000007F and the message Unexpected Kernel Mode Trap	Use the Windows Server 2008 installation DVD to run the Windows Memory Diagnostic Tool and replace any defective memory.
0x0000000A and the message IRQL Not Less or Equal	Suspect a hardware resource conflict caused by a new device or card you have added. If you can boot using the Safe Mode, check the system log. If you cannot boot into Safe Mode, remove the new device or devices and boot using Last Known Good Configuration (advanced).
0x00000058 and the message Ftdisk Internal Error	Suspect that the main volume in a mirrored set has failed. Boot using the secondary volume and use the Disk Management tool to attempt to repair the main volume and resynchronize it with the secondary volume.
	If you cannot repair the volume, use the Disk Management tool to break the mirrored set, replace the damaged disk, and then recreate the mirrored set.
0x000000BE and the message Attempted Write to Readonly Memory	Boot using the Enable Boot Logging option and then boot again into Safe Mode (or the command prompt) so you can examine the \Windows\ntbtlog.txt log for a driver that did not start or that is causing problems, then reinstall or replace the driver using the Safe Mode or by copying it into the system using the command prompt via the Windows Server 2008 installation DVD.

*Information in this table is based on Microsoft's help documentation.

12

Using and Configuring Event Viewer

A valuable tool for diagnosing all kinds of server problems is Event Viewer (see Figure 12-7). Event Viewer houses the **event logs** that record information about all types of server events, in the form of errors, warnings, and informational events. Windows Server 2008 event logs are divided into three general categories: Windows logs, applications and services logs, and Microsoft logs.

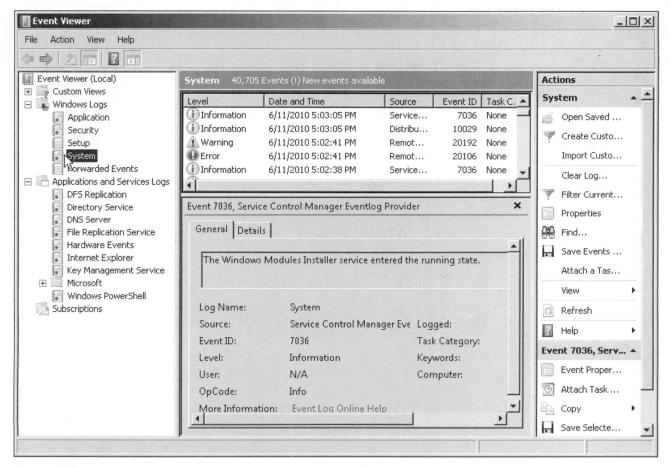

Figure 12-7   Event Viewer

Windows generates four logs for reporting general operating system and software application events:

- **System log**—Records information about system-related events such as hardware errors, driver problems, and hard drive errors.

- **Security log**—Records access and security information about logon accesses and file, folder, and system policy changes. If you have auditing set up, for instance file auditing, use the security log to track each audited event, such as a successful or failed attempt to access a file. If you choose to audit an account or folder, the audit data is recorded in the security log.

- **Application log**—Records information about how software applications are performing, if the programmer has designed the software to write information into the log.

- **Setup log**—Contains a record of installation events, such as installing a role or feature through Server Manager. For example, if a software error occurs, it may be recorded in the log.

The applications and services logs are largely a combination of what Microsoft calls admin and operational logs. **Admin logs** are designed to help give the system administrator information about a specific problem and its causes and may suggest how to solve the problem. For example, it might report that the DFS Replication service (for DFS and DC replication) has failed and that this might be caused by the Windows Firewall configuration. An **operational log** tracks occurrences of specific operations, such as when a disk drive is added.

The specific applications and services logs available in Event Viewer depend in part on which roles and features are installed. Here is a sampling of these logs:

- *DFS Replication log*—Records events for the Distributed File System Replication services, such as when DFS Replication service is started and records any events in which the service fails.

- *Directory Service log*—Records events that are associated with Active Directory, such as updates to Active Directory, events related to the Active Directory database, replication events, and startup and shutdown events.

- *DNS Server log*—Provides information about instances in which (1) DNS information is updated, (2) there are problems with the DNS service, and (3) the DNS Server has started successfully after booting.

- *File Replication Service log*—Contains information about (1) changes to file replication, (2) when the service has started, and (3) completed replication tasks.

- *Hardware Events*—Records events related to hardware including the CPU, disk drives, memory, and other hardware.

- *Internet Explorer*—Records events related to Internet Explorer, including if it terminates unexpectedly or if there are problems accessing the Internet.

- *Key Management Service*—Tracks events related to Kerberos key distribution, when a server functions as a key distribution center. Check this log if users are having trouble logging on, for example, to be sure there are no problems with the key distribution services.

In addition to the logs already described, you also can choose whether to display the analytic and debug logs. These logs are mentioned last because they contain more complex information. The **analytic logs** relate to how programs are operating and are typically used by application or system programmers. The **debug logs** are used by application developers to help trace problems in programs so they can fix program code or program structures.

Several elements are related to working with event logs and are discussed in the next sections:

- Viewing log events
- Creating filters
- Maintaining event logs

Viewing Log Events

Log events are displayed in Event Viewer with an icon that indicates the seriousness of the event. An informational message, such as notification that a service has been started, is prefaced by a blue "i" displayed in a white comment circle; a warning, such as that a DVD is not loaded, is depicted by a black "!" (exclamation point) that appears on a yellow caution symbol; and an error, such as a defective disk adapter, is indicated with a white exclamation point that appears inside a red circle (Figure 12-7 shows examples of the icons).

When you view log events under the Roles Summary section in Server Manager, the error icon is a white "x" (instead of an exclamation point) displayed in a red circle. This is a discrepancy that Microsoft may well fix through an update so the error icon consistently contains either an "x" or an "!" inside.

Each log displays descriptive information about individual events, such as the following information provided in the system log:

- Description of the event
- Name of the log in which the event is recorded
- Source of the event, which is the software application or hardware reporting it
- Event ID, so the event can be tracked if entered into a database (associated events might have the same number)
- Level of the event—information, warning, error
- User associated with the event, if any
- OpCode of the event
- Link for more information
- Date and time the event was logged
- Task category of the event, if one applies, such as a system event or logon event
- Name of the computer on which the event occurred

Event Viewer can be opened from the Administrative Tools menu, as an MMC snap-in, from the Computer Management tool, and from Server Manager. Event Viewer contains options to view all events or to set a filter so only certain events are viewed, such as error events.

To view the contents of a log, click that log in the tree under Event Viewer. To view the detailed information about an event, double-click the event (see Figure 12-8). Read the description of the event for more information.

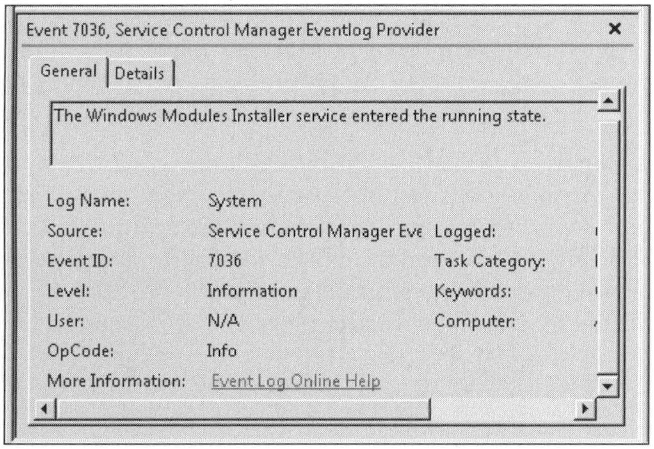

Figure 12-8 Viewing an event

The event logs are a good source of information to help you troubleshoot a software or hardware problem. For example, if Windows Server 2008 crashes unexpectedly, reboot and look at the logs as a first step. A memory allocation or disk problem can be found quickly through the help of the system log. If a software application hangs, check the application log for information.

Using the Event Viewer Filter Option

All of the event logs in Event Viewer have a filter option to help you quickly locate a problem. For example, you can set up a filter to show only events associated with a particular user or only events that occurred on the previous afternoon. The events can be filtered on the basis of the following criteria:

- When the event was logged, such as in the last seven days
- Event level, such as information, warning, error, critical, and verbose

- By log, such as the system or security log
- By source of the event, such as a particular service or software component
- Task category of the event, such as a security change
- Keywords, such as Audit Failure and Audit Success
- User associated with the event
- Computer associated with the event
- Date range
- Time of day range

Maintaining Event Logs

The event logs quickly fill with information, and you should establish from the beginning how you want the logs maintained. Logs can be maintained using several methods, as follows:

- Size each log to prevent it from filling too quickly.
- Overwrite the oldest events when the log is full.
- Archive the log when it is full.
- Clear the log manually (does not overwrite events).

Some network administrators prefer to save the log contents on a regular basis, such as weekly or monthly. Others prefer to allow the logs to overwrite the oldest events. It is recommended that you develop a maintenance schedule to save the log contents for a designated time period, because the logs contain valuable information about historical server activity.

Some organizations print certain logs daily, such as the system and security logs, and then clear them.

To tune the event logs, open Event Viewer and right-click each log you want to tune, one at a time, and click Properties. On the General tab, set the log size in the *Maximum log size (KB)* box. Set the maximum log size to match the way you want to handle the logs. The default size is 20,480 KB. For example, if you want to accumulate two weeks of information, set the size to enable that much information to be recorded, for instance 24,000 KB. You will need to test this setting for a few weeks to make sure that the size you set is adequate. A common way to make sure that an event log is never completely filled is to use one of these options: *Overwrite events as needed (oldest events first)* or *Archive the log when full, do not overwrite events.*

If the server is a busy domain controller on which auditing is enabled, even a large-sized security log might contain only enough space to record a few hours of audited events. In this situation, besides setting a large log size, consider auditing only what is necessary or regularly viewing the log for the information you are seeking.

Options to save and clear the individual logs are also available. To save a log, right-click the log in the tree, click *Save Events As*, enter a name for the log file, and click Save. You can save the log as one of the following kinds of files:

- *.evtx*—which is saved in event log format
- *.xml*—which is saved in XML format
- *.txt*—which is saved as a tab-delimited text file that can be imported into a spreadsheet
- *.csv*—which is saved as a comma-delimited text file that can be imported into a spreadsheet

When you are logged on as Administrator, the event log files are saved by default in the folder \Users\Administrator\Documents. To clear a log, right-click the log in the tree and click *Clear Log*. You'll see options to save the log before you clear it, to clear the log without first saving it, and to cancel.

Activity 12-4: Using Event Viewer

Time Required: Approximately 10 minutes
Objective: Use Event Viewer to view system log events.

Description: In this activity, you use Event Viewer to examine system log events, and you practice using a filter.

1. Click **Start**, point to **Administrative Tools**, and click **Event Viewer**.
2. Click the **plus sign** in front of **Windows Logs** in the tree in the left pane to view the logs listed under Windows Logs.
   - What logs do you see?

3. Click each log to view the information displayed for it in the middle pane.
   - What two boxes of information do you see in the middle pane for each log, and what do the boxes contain?

4. Click **System** in the left pane to view the system log. Briefly scroll through the listed events.
   - Are any errors or warnings reported? If so, find out more about one or two of the errors or warnings by clicking them and viewing the details.

5. Click the **plus sign** in front of **Applications and Services Logs** in the left pane. Click each log to view its contents in the middle pane and click on one or two events for each log.
6. Click the **View** menu at the top of the window and click **Show Analytic and Debug Logs**, if there is no check mark already in front of this selection.
   - What new folders are displayed under Applications and Services Logs?

7. Click the **plus sign** in front of **Encrypting File System** in the tree. Notice the debug log displayed under Encrypting File System.
8. Right-click **System** under Windows Logs in the tree and click **Properties** (see Figure 12-9).
9. The default selection for managing the system log is to *Overwrite events as needed (oldest events first)*. Click **Archive the log when full, do not overwrite events**. This option enables you to keep historic log information, but you will need to periodically delete archived logs you do not need. Notice the location of the system log as shown in the *Log path* box. This is useful information so that you know where to maintain the logs.

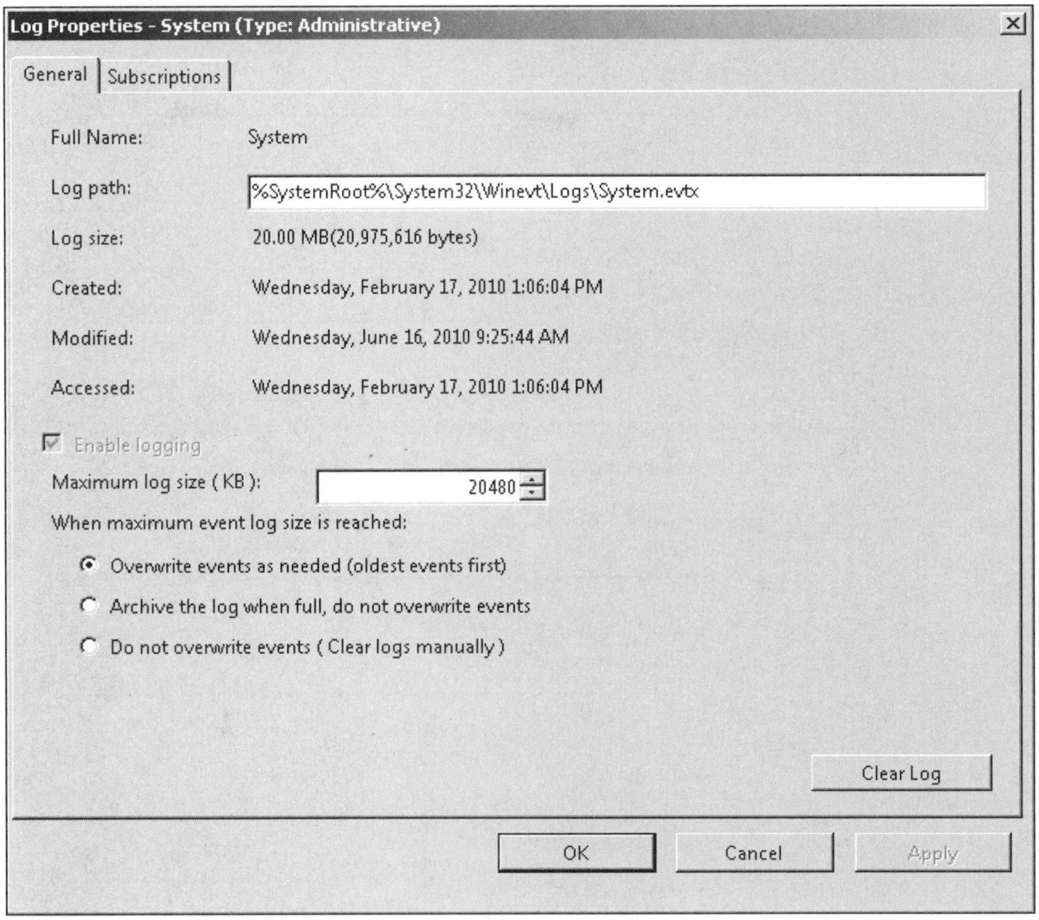

Figure 12-9 System log properties

10. Change the **Maximum log size (KB)** to **22016**.

11. Click **OK** in the Log Properties – System (Type:Administrative) dialog box.

12. Click **System** under Windows Logs in the tree, if it is not already selected.

13. In the right pane, click **Filter Current Log**.

14. Click the **down arrow** for **Event sources** to view the options you can use for filtering. If you were to select one or more of these options, only events for these sources would be displayed in the system log (but the events for other sources would still be tracked and saved so you could change the filter to view them later). Click the pointer in a blank area of the dialog box to close the listing.

15. Click the **down arrow** for **Keywords** and notice the keywords you can use to build a filter (events containing the keywords you select would be displayed). Click the pointer in a blank area of the dialog box to close the listing of keywords.

16. Assume that you only want to view the error messages in the system log. Click the box for **Error,** as shown in Figure 12-10.

17. Click **OK** in the Filter Current Log dialog box.

   • How does using the filter change what you view in the system log? Does this mean that the events you viewed before creating the filter are deleted, or simply not displayed?

18. Close Event Viewer.

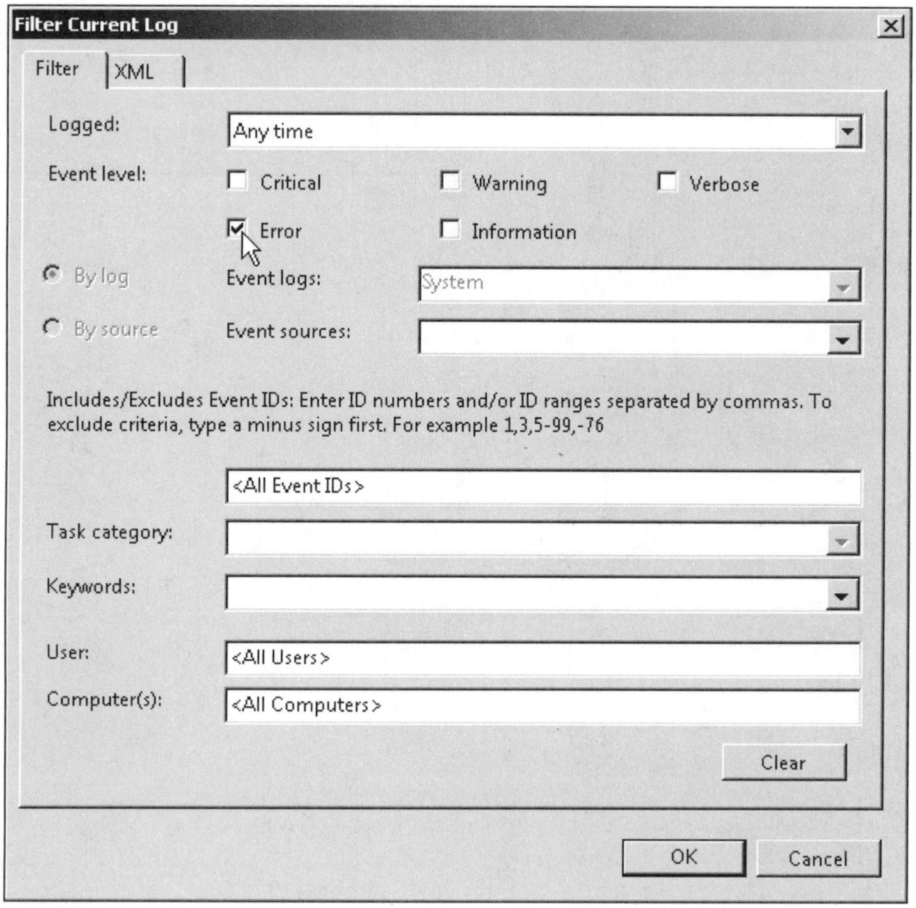

Figure 12-10 Creating a filter

Troubleshooting Connectivity

One area that server and network administrators often troubleshoot is TCP/IP connectivity. For example, a common problem is the use of duplicate IP addresses. This can happen in situations where static IP addressing is used, with the network administrator or user typing in the IP address and subnet mask when the computer is set up. If two computers are using the same IP address, one or both will not be able to connect to the network at the same time; or both are likely to experience unreliable communications such as sudden disconnections.

Both command-line tools and graphical tools are available for troubleshooting Windows Server 2008 connectivity. You learn about these tools in the next sections.

Command-Line Tools

Some TCP/IP utilities, such as Telnet, have IP troubleshooting tools built in. The same is true for workstations and servers running TCP/IP-compatible operating systems, such as Windows Server 2008 and Windows Vista. You can test the IP address of a Windows computer (when you are at that computer), such as Windows Server 2008 or Windows Vista, by opening the Command Prompt window and typing *ipconfig* to view a dialog box showing the adapter address (MAC or Ethernet), IP address, subnet mask, and other information for that computer (see Figure 12-11). If the server is using an IP address that is identical to the address used by another networked computer that is turned on, the subnet mask value is 0.0.0.0 when you run one of these utilities. Also, *ipconfig* shows when there are multiple network adapters in a computer and it can show when the media is disconnected, such as on one adapter as in Figure 12-11.

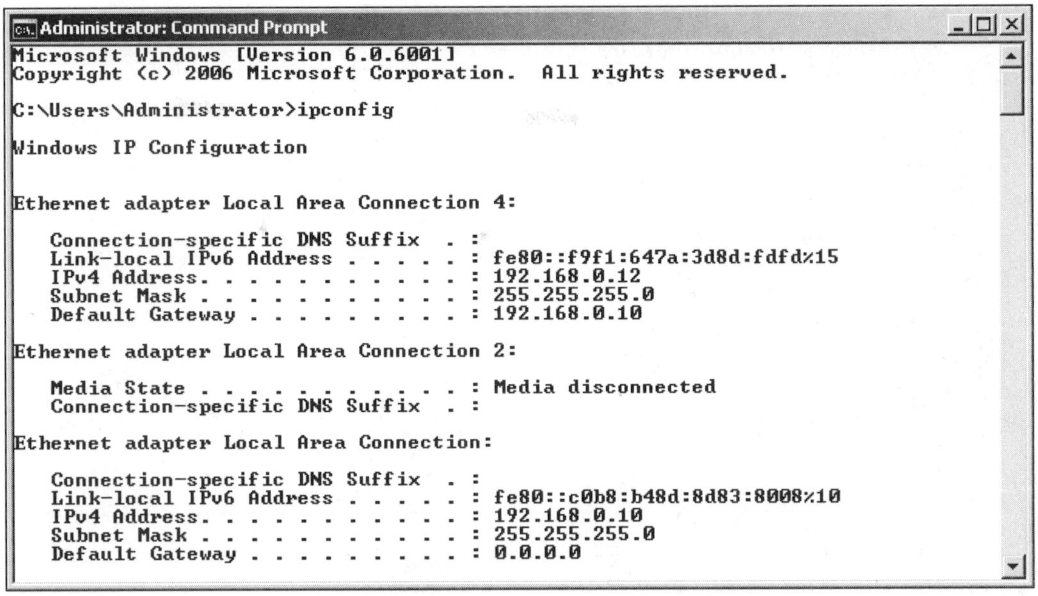

```
Administrator: Command Prompt
Microsoft Windows [Version 6.0.6001]
Copyright (c) 2006 Microsoft Corporation.  All rights reserved.

C:\Users\Administrator>ipconfig

Windows IP Configuration


Ethernet adapter Local Area Connection 4:

   Connection-specific DNS Suffix  . :
   Link-local IPv6 Address . . . . . : fe80::f9f1:647a:3d8d:fdfd%15
   IPv4 Address. . . . . . . . . . . : 192.168.0.12
   Subnet Mask . . . . . . . . . . . : 255.255.255.0
   Default Gateway . . . . . . . . . : 192.168.0.10

Ethernet adapter Local Area Connection 2:

   Media State . . . . . . . . . . . : Media disconnected
   Connection-specific DNS Suffix  . :

Ethernet adapter Local Area Connection:

   Connection-specific DNS Suffix  . :
   Link-local IPv6 Address . . . . . : fe80::c0b8:b48d:8d83:8008%10
   IPv4 Address. . . . . . . . . . . : 192.168.0.10
   Subnet Mask . . . . . . . . . . . : 255.255.255.0
   Default Gateway . . . . . . . . . : 0.0.0.0
```

Figure 12-11 Using *ipconfig* in Windows Server 2008

Another tool for testing TCP/IP connections is the *ping* utility. You can poll the presence of another TCP/IP computer from the Windows Server 2008 or Windows Vista Command Prompt window by typing *ping* and the IP address or computer name of the other computer. Many server administrators use *ping* to quickly test the presence of a server or computer from their office when there are reports of connection problems to that computer. Pinging a server on a network in another state or remote location also enables you to quickly test if your Internet connectivity is accessible from your office workstation. Figure 12-12 illustrates the *ping* utility as used from Windows Server 2008.

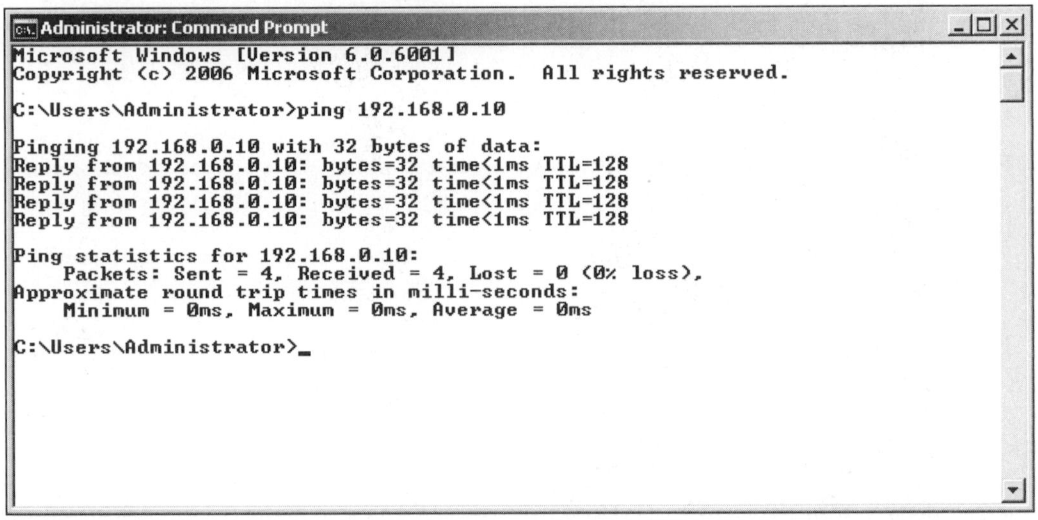

```
Administrator: Command Prompt
Microsoft Windows [Version 6.0.6001]
Copyright (c) 2006 Microsoft Corporation.  All rights reserved.

C:\Users\Administrator>ping 192.168.0.10

Pinging 192.168.0.10 with 32 bytes of data:
Reply from 192.168.0.10: bytes=32 time<1ms TTL=128
Reply from 192.168.0.10: bytes=32 time<1ms TTL=128
Reply from 192.168.0.10: bytes=32 time<1ms TTL=128
Reply from 192.168.0.10: bytes=32 time<1ms TTL=128

Ping statistics for 192.168.0.10:
    Packets: Sent = 4, Received = 4, Lost = 0 (0% loss),
Approximate round trip times in milli-seconds:
    Minimum = 0ms, Maximum = 0ms, Average = 0ms

C:\Users\Administrator>_
```

Figure 12-12 Using *ping* in Windows Server 2008

netstat is a utility available in Windows Server 2008, Windows Vista, Windows XP, and other Windows operating systems and is a quick way to verify that a workstation or server has established a successful TCP/IP connection. This utility provides information about TCP and UDP connectivity. Sometimes a TCP/IP session to a server or mainframe computer hangs. You can determine this by entering *netstat -e* from the Command Prompt window at that computer (see Figure 12-13). Two columns of received and sent data are displayed. If these columns contain

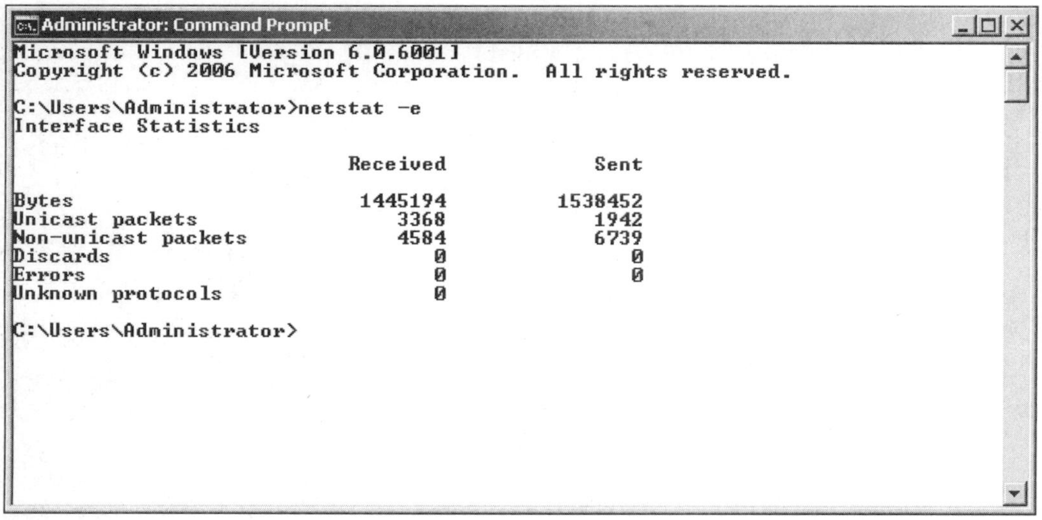

```
Administrator: Command Prompt                                          _ □ ×
Microsoft Windows [Version 6.0.6001]
Copyright (c) 2006 Microsoft Corporation.  All rights reserved.

C:\Users\Administrator>netstat -e
Interface Statistics

                          Received              Sent

Bytes                       1445194           1538452
Unicast packets                3368              1942
Non-unicast packets            4584              6739
Discards                          0                 0
Errors                            0                 0
Unknown protocols                 0

C:\Users\Administrator>
```

Figure 12-13 Using the *netstat -e* command in Windows Server 2008

0 bytes, it is likely the connection is hung. If the connection is hung, use the Network and Sharing Center (in Windows Server 2008 and Windows Vista), as described in the "Graphical Tools" section, to disable the computer connection and then to reconnect.

The *netstat -e* command also provides a quick indication of the number of transmission errors and discarded packets detected at that computer's NIC. For a more comprehensive listing of communication statistics, type *netstat -s*. Table 12-5 lists some useful diagnostics available from the Command Prompt windows in Windows Server 2008, Windows Vista, and Windows XP.

Table 12-5 Windows Server 2008, Vista, and XP diagnostic commands for TCP/IP connectivity

Diagnostic command	Function
arp	Displays Address Resolution Protocol (ARP) information, such as using the *arp -a* command to view the *arp* cache information at a computer (see Chapter 1)
ipconfig	Displays information about the TCP/IP setup at that computer (enter *ipconfig /?* to view all of the options for this command)
nslookup	Shows information about DNS servers
pathping	Polls another TCP/IP node showing the path through routers along the way (including packet loss through routers; see Chapter 1)
ping	Polls another TCP/IP node to verify you can communicate with it (enter only *ping* to view all of the options for this command)
netstat (-a, -e, -s)	Displays information about the TCP/IP session from that computer (enter *netstat /?* to view all of the options for this command)
nbtstat (-n)	Shows the server and domain NetBIOS names registered to the network (enter only *nbtstat* to view all of the options for this command)
tracert (server or host name)	Shows the number of hops and other routing information on the path to the specified server or host (enter only *tracert* to view all of the options for this command)

Activity 12-5: Using TCP/IP Connectivity Troubleshooting Tools

Time Required: Approximately 10 minutes
Objective: Learn how to use *nbtstat* and *netstat*.

Description: In this activity, you have an opportunity to use *nbtstat* to view computers (NetBIOS names) on the network and then *netstat* to view all connections.

1. Click **Start**, point to **All Programs**, and click **Accessories**.

2. Click **Command Prompt**.

3. At the command prompt, enter **nbtstat -n** and press **Enter**.

   • What information is displayed?

4. Next, type **nbtstat -s** and press **Enter**.

   • What information is displayed by this command?

5. Now type **netstat -a** at the command prompt and press **Enter**.

   • What information is produced by this command?

6. Type **ipconfig** and press **Enter** to view the results of this command.

7. Find your IP address from the *ipconfig* results. Type **ping** plus your IP address and press **Enter**.

   • How can you use the *ipconfig* command to verify your own TCP/IP connection? What is the purpose of the *ping* command?

8. Close the Command Prompt window.

Graphical Tools

In addition to using commands from the Command Prompt window, you can use a GUI (graphical user interface) tool for diagnosing and repairing network problems. For example, if you use the *netstat -e* command as described earlier and determine that a network connection is hung, use the following steps through the Network and Sharing Center to disable and then enable the connection:

1. Click Start and click Network.

2. Click Network and Sharing Center.

3. Click Manage network connections.

4. Right-click the connection, such as Local Area Connection, and click Disable (see Figure 12-14).

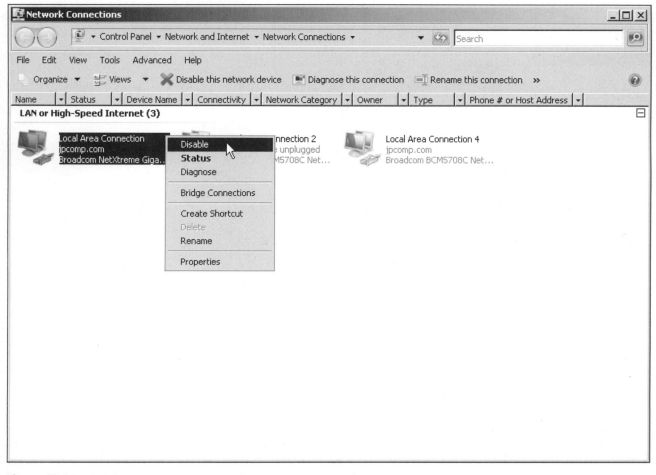

Figure 12-14   Disabling a connection in Windows Server 2008

5. Right-click the connection again and click Enable.

6. Close the Network Connections window and the Network and Sharing Center.

Disabling the connection (or rebooting) will reset the NIC and the TCP/IP connectivity to make sure you have a clean connection.

The Network and Sharing Center also can provide a simple GUI representation of the network to show if network connectivity problems exist between your server and the network or the Internet. The general steps for using this diagnostic are as follows:

1. Click Start and click Network.

2. Click Network and Sharing Center.

3. Click the red x in the diagram of the network (which indicates a problem), wait for a few minutes for the diagnostic to finish, and view the information in the Windows Network Diagnostics dialog box (see Figure 12-15). (An alternative is to click the Diagnose and repair link in the Network and Sharing Center.)

4. Click Cancel to close the Windows Network Diagnostics dialog box.

5. Close the Network and Sharing Center.

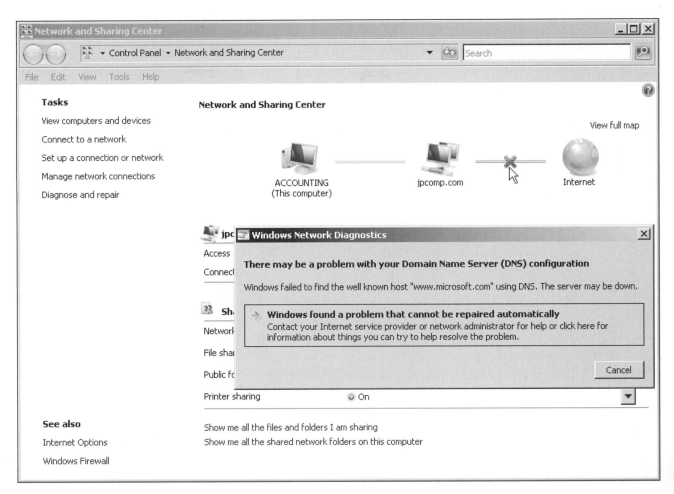

Figure 12-15   Using the Network and Sharing Center to diagnose a connectivity problem

12

Yet another way to use the Network and Sharing Center is to have it diagnose a specific connection, such as the Local Area Connection from the Network Connections window. The general steps for diagnosing a connection are as follows:

1. Click Start and click Network.

2. Click Network and Sharing Center.

3. Click Manage network connections.

4. Right-click the connection you want to check and click Diagnose.

5. Wait a moment for the diagnostic to finish and read the analysis in the Windows Network Diagnostics dialog box (see Figure 12-16).

6. Click Cancel to close the Windows Network Diagnostics dialog box.

7. Close the Network Connections window when you are finished.

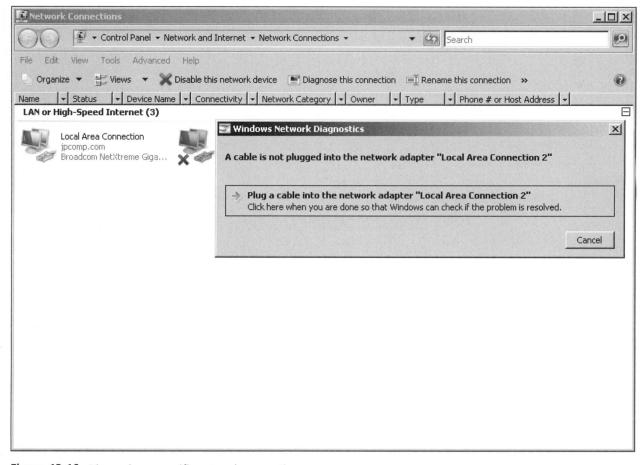

Figure 12-16   Diagnosing a specific network connection

Remotely Administering a Server

In some organizations it is important for server administrators to be able to remotely access a server in order to solve a problem. The remote access may be from another building, from home, or while traveling. The primary way to facilitate remote access is through using the Remote Desktop client capability.

You can use the Remote Desktop client to remotely access and manage the server, such as through a dial-up line and via a RAS or VPN server. Use the Remote Desktop client at your workstation to log on to your regular account that you use for administration (see Chapter 9, "Configuring Remote Access Services"). At this writing, up to two Remote Desktop connections are supported without installing a terminal server.

You can configure Remote Desktop using Server Manager or the System applet in Control Panel to access the System Properties dialog box, as shown in Figure 12-17. In the System Properties dialog box, click either *Allow connections from computers running any version of Remote Desktop (less secure)* or *Allow connections only from computers running Remote Desktop with Network Level Authentication (more secure)*. As you learned in Chapter 9, Network Level Authentication (NLA) is designed to discourage man-in-the-middle attacks and is supported by Windows Server 2008, Windows Vista, and Windows XP.

Also, make sure that you have configured a strong password for the account from which you perform administration. Microsoft defines the following characteristics of a strong password:

- Contains seven or more characters (eight is better)
- Does not reflect qualities about you that others might guess, such as your name, information about your family, or the name of your organization

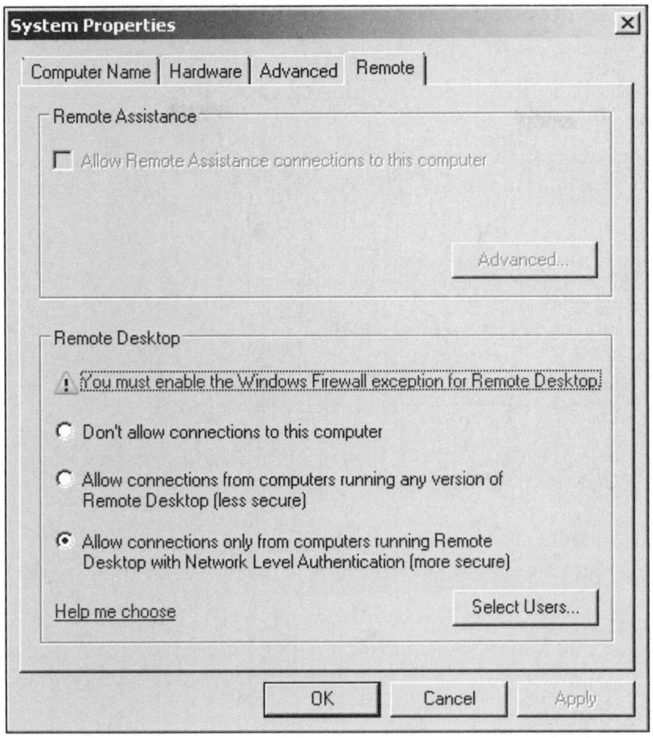

Figure 12-17   System Properties dialog box

- Is not a word that could be found in a dictionary
- Is changed at regular intervals without repeating a previously used password
- Contains a combination of upper- and lowercase characters, numbers, and symbols

Activity 12-6: Configuring to Enable Remote Access Through Remote Desktop

Time Required: Approximately 10 minutes
Objective: Enable access to Windows Server 2008 through Remote Desktop.

Description: In this activity, you configure Windows Server 2008 to be accessed from Windows Vista or Windows XP through Remote Desktop and using NLA.

1. Click **Start**, point to **Administrative Tools**, and click **Server Manager**.

2. In the Server Summary section, click the link for **Configure Remote Desktop**.

3. Click **Allow connections only from computers running Remote Desktop with Network Level Authentication (more secure)**, if it is not already selected (see Figure 12-17).

4. Click **OK**.

5. If you see the Remote Desktop dialog box, click **OK** to confirm that the Remote Desktop Firewall exception will be enabled. Click **OK** again in the System Properties dialog box.

6. Close Server Manager.

7. Click **Start** and click **Control Panel**.

8. In the Control Panel Home view, click **Allow a program through Windows Firewall**; or in the Classic view, double-click **Windows Firewall** and click **Allow a program through Windows Firewall**.

9. Ensure that the Exceptions tab is displayed.

10. Check the boxes for **Remote Administration** and **Remote Desktop,** if they are not checked (see Figure 12-18).

11. Click **OK** in the Windows Firewall Settings dialog box.

Windows Firewall Settings   ×

| General | Exceptions | Advanced |

Exceptions control how programs communicate through Windows Firewall. Add a program or port exception to allow communications through the firewall.

Windows Firewall is currently using settings for the public network location.
What are the risks of unblocking a program?

To enable an exception, select its check box:

Program or port

☑ Netlogon Service
☑ Network Discovery
☑ Performance Logs and Alerts
☑ Remote Access Quaratine
☑ Remote Administration
☑ Remote Desktop
☑ Remote Event Log Management
☑ Remote Scheduled Tasks Management
☑ Remote Service Management
☑ Remote Volume Management
☑ Routing and Remote Access
☑ Routing and Remote Access Remote Management
☑ Secure Socket Tunneling Protocol

| Add program... | Add port... | Properties | Delete |

☐ Notify me when Windows Firewall blocks a new program

| OK | Cancel | Apply |

Figure 12-18   Configuring the Windows Firewall

Remote Server Administration Tools

Remote Server Administration Tools enable you to manage multiple servers from one Windows Server 2008 server. These tools raise important possibilities. For example, you might have one server in a computer operations room that is used round-the-clock by server operators to manage other servers, so that the operators do not have to go to the console of a specific server. Another possibility is to have a Windows Server 2008 server in your office that you use as a personal workstation and from which to manage servers in a remote computer room; or you might use it to manage servers in different locations throughout a company. Remote Server Administration Tools can make you more productive by allowing you to remain in one location to administer remote servers.

The Remote Server Administration Tools are offered through Server Manager. A subset of the Remote Server Administration Tools, called the Remote Administration Tools, is typically automatically installed when you install the Web Service (IIS) role. If the Remote Server Administration Tools are not installed, you can install them through Server Manager. You can also use Server Manager to install additional pieces of the full Remote Server Administration Tools suite, such as Feature Administration Tools.

Before you install the Remote Server Administration Tools, you must first install the Web Server (IIS) role services. Also, it is necessary to configure Remote Administration as a Windows Firewall exception (see Step 10 in Activity 12-6).

Using the Remote Server Administration Tools, you can remotely manage both Windows Server 2008 and Windows Server 2003 servers. Because Windows Server 2008 is role-based, the Remote Server Administration Tools enable you to manage roles and features that are installed on a server. The role-based tools included for remote management are as follows:

- Active Directory Certificate Services Tools
- Active Directory Domain Services Tools
- Active Directory Lightweight Directory Services Tools
- Active Directory Rights Management Services Tools
- DHCP Server Tools
- DNS Server Tools
- FAX Server Tools
- File Services Tools
- Network Policy Access Services Tools
- Print Services Tools
- Terminal Services Tools
- Universal Description, Discovery, and Integration Services Tools
- Web Server (IIS) Tools
- Windows Deployment Services Tools

Most Windows Server 2008 servers also have a combination of features installed as well as roles. To accommodate remote administration of features, the Remote Server Administration Tools also include the following tool sets:

- BitLocker Drive Encryption Tools
- BITS Server Extensions Tools
- Failover Clustering Tools
- Network Load Balancing Tools
- SMTP Server Tools
- WINS Server Tools

To manage these features, make sure you install the Feature Administration Tools when you install the Remote Server Administration Tools in Server Manager.

In addition to all of these tools, you can use other management tools remotely. For example, you can use Event Viewer to view logs on a remote server. Or, you can use the Reliability and Performance Monitor to monitor a remote server.

If you have completed the activities in this book so far, Remote Server Administration Tools should already be installed on your server. If the tool set is not installed, you can install it using the following general steps:

1. Click Start, point to Administrative Tools, and click Server Manager.

2. Check the Roles Summary section to ensure that the Web Server (IIS) role is already installed. If it is not, click Add Roles and install the Web Server (IIS) role (see Chapter 8, "Managing Windows Server 2008 Network Services").

3. In the Features Summary section, click Add Features.

4. Click Remote Server Administration Tools. (If you see the Add Features Wizard dialog box, click Add Required Role Services to add any needed Web Server (IIS) role services. Click Next three times until you reach the Confirm Installation Selections window.)

5. Click Install and follow the instructions for installing this feature.

With the Remote Server Administration Tools installed, managing remote services is relatively transparent. All you have to do is to open the management snap-in you need to use and indicate that you want to connect to a specific remote Windows Server 2008 or Windows Server 2003 server.

Activity 12-7: Using the Remote Server Administration Tools

Time Required: Approximately 10 minutes
Objective: Learn how to use the Remote Server Administration Tools capability.

Description: Many of the MMC snap-ins can be implemented using the Remote Server Administration Tools capability. In this activity, you learn how to use the remote administration capability via two sample snap-ins, the DNS and the Reliability and Performance MMC snap-ins. It is not necessary to have another server to remotely access, because you'll simply learn how to use the remote access capability.

1. Click **Start** and click **Run**.

2. Type **mmc** in the Open text box and click **OK**.

3. Click the **File** menu and click **Add/Remove Snap-in**.

4. In the Add or Remove Snap-ins dialog box, click **DNS** and click the **Add** button.

5. Click **Reliability and Performance Monitor** and click **Add**.

6. Click **OK** in the Add or Remove Snap-ins dialog box.

7. In the Console1 – [Console Root] window, click **DNS** in the tree.

8. Click the **Action** menu and click **Connect to DNS Server**.

9. You see the Connect to DNS Server dialog box (see Figure 12-19). To connect to another server that offers DNS services, you would click the option button for *The following computer* and then enter the name of the server on which to use the DNS management tool. In this case, the Connect to DNS Server dialog box represents the implementation of the Remote Server Administration Tool, DNS Server Tools (which is transparent other than using this dialog box to remotely connect). Click **Cancel**.

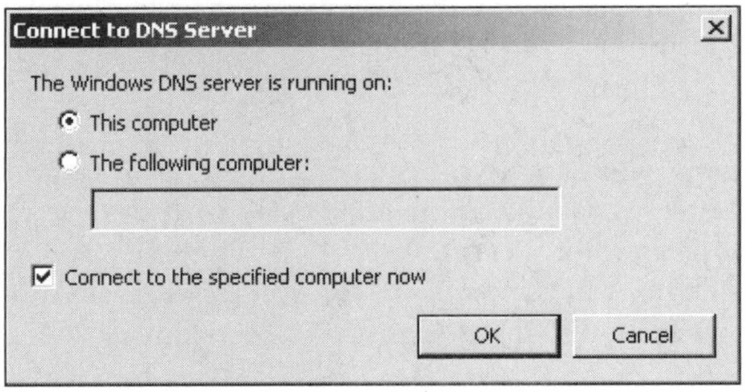

Figure 12-19 Connect to DNS Server dialog box

10. Another way to remotely connect to a server to use the DNS Server Tools is to use the right pane. In the right pane, click **More Actions** under DNS and click **Connect to DNS Server**.

11. When you see the Connect to DNS Server dialog box, click **Cancel**.

12. Click **Reliability and Performance (Local)** in the tree.

13. Click the **Action** menu and click **Connect to another computer**.

14. You see the Select Computer dialog box (see Figure 12-20). In this dialog box you can select to connect to the local computer or to a remote computer. To connect to a remote computer, you can type its name in the box or use the Browse button to find and select the local computer on the network.

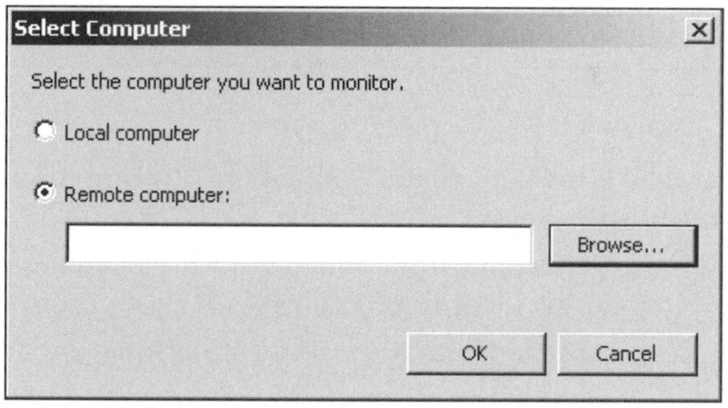

Figure 12-20 Select Computer dialog box

15. Click the **Browse** button. You should see the name of your server and any other servers on the network. Click **Cancel**.

16. Click **Cancel** in the Select Computer dialog box.

17. Click **More Actions** in the right pane and click **Connect to another computer** to view another way to open the Select Computer dialog box.

18. Click **Cancel** in the Select Computer dialog box.

19. Close the Console1 – [Console Root] window.

20. Click **No** so that the console settings are not saved.

Chapter Summary

- Before problems occur, develop a problem-solving strategy that includes understanding your server and network, training users to help, step-by-step problem solving, and tracking problems.

- A server that won't boot can mean big trouble. Window Server 2008 gives you the Advanced Boot Options menu for times when you have boot problems. The Safe Mode is one of the most recognized options available from this menu. Another well-known option is to boot using the Last Known Good Configuration (advanced) option. These are just a few of the options available.

- The Windows Server 2008 installation DVD offers options to recover a system, or work with a system that won't boot.

- Regularly perform a full backup, which includes system state data, so that you can fully recover a system that has failed.

- Event Viewer is a storehouse of logs from which you can monitor a system and diagnose problems. The three main categories of logs are Windows logs, applications and services logs, and Microsoft logs.

- Regularly use Event Viewer to monitor the contents of logs. Also, learn to maintain the logs and to set filters to make the information in logs more useful for specific situations.

- Windows Server 2008 contains command-line and graphical tools for troubleshooting network connectivity problems. Some command-line tools, such as *ping*, enable you to test the connectivity of remote computers as well as the local computer. The GUI tools can analyze a connection and give you a short diagnostic report with suggestions for fixing a problem.

- You can use the Remote Desktop client capability, such as from Windows Vista, to remotely manage a Windows Server 2008 server.

- Windows Server 2008 comes with the Remote Server Administration Tools for managing multiple Windows Server 2008 or Windows Server 2003 servers from one Windows Server 2008 server.

Key Terms

admin log   A type of event log that gives the system administrator information about a specific problem and its causes, and might also suggest how to solve the problem.

analytic log   An event log often used by application and system programmers to help analyze how specific programs are running and to identify problems with those programs.

application log   An event log that records information about how software applications are performing.

debug log   An event log used by application developers to help trace problems in programs so they can fix program code or program structures.

event logs   Logs that you can view through Event Viewer that record information about server events, such as errors, warnings, or informational events.

help desk system   Application software designed to maintain information on computer systems, user questions, problem solutions, and other information that members of an organization can reference.

operational log   A type of event log that tracks occurrences of specific operations, such as when a disk drive is added.

Safe Mode   A boot mode that enables Windows Server 2008 to be booted using the most generic default settings, such as for the display, disk drives, and pointing device—and only those services needed to boot a basic configuration.

security log   An event log that records access and security information about logon accesses, file, folder, and system policy changes.

setup log   An event log that contains a record of installation events, such as installing a role or feature through Server Manager.

system log   An event log that records information about system-related events such as hardware errors, driver problems, and hard drive errors.

system state data   Operating system and boot files, plus extra components and information that reflect the currently configured state of the server, depending on what features are installed. The system state data can be backed up using the Windows Server Backup tool.

SYSVOL   A shared folder set up when Active Directory is installed that contains scripts, Group Policy Objects (GPOs), and software distribution files, several of which are needed for domain access. SYSVOL folders are replicated among DCs.

Review Questions

1. Your server has some damaged disk areas and won't boot or run *chkdsk* automatically when you try to boot. Which of the following options should you try to fix the disk?

   a. Boot from the BIOS boot mode and run the analyze disk option in the BIOS.

   b. Boot from a Windows 98 floppy or CD boot disk and run *diskpart*.

   c. Each Windows Server 2008 drive has a boot sector. Change the BIOS to boot from the boot sector of a different drive.

   d. Boot from the Windows Server 2008 installation DVD and access the command prompt to run *chkdsk*.

2. You are training a new server administrator and are discussing common boot problems. Which of the following do you mention? (Choose all that apply.)

   a. disk read errors

   b. corrupted boot file

   c. corrupted partition table

   d. disk failure on a drive containing boot files

3. You've just added a new monitor and driver to your server, but when you reboot, the display on the monitor is unreadable and distorted. Which of the following can you do to help troubleshoot the problem?

   a. Reboot into the Display Debugging Mode.

   b. Use Enable Boot Logging.

   c. Reboot into the Enable low-resolution video (640x480) mode.

   d. Shut down the computer, reattach the old monitor, and boot normally.

4. Name three problem-solving strategies for addressing a problem with Windows Server 2008.

5. The security log contains hundreds of entries. However, you only want to track the audited logon activities of a single user. Which of the following can you use?

   a. Set up a filter.

   b. Set up a trap.

   c. Turn off recording of all other events related to other user accounts.

   d. View the log using Reliability Monitor.

6. Name five elements that compose system state data.

7. Many users are reporting messages about memory errors on your company's server. Which of the following can you do to find out more about possible memory problems without taking down the server? (Choose all that apply.)

   a. Run the memory diagnostics from the Windows Server 2008 installation DVD.

   b. Check the system log for memory errors.

   c. Check the hardware events log.

   d. Use the Safe Mode RAM Diagnostics option.

8. Name three options that are available when you boot into the repair mode from the Windows Server 2008 installation DVD.

9. Which of the following might be part of your problem-solving strategy? (Choose all that apply.)

   a. Regularly check the logs.

   b. Reboot the server once or twice a day to prevent problems and reset all registers.

   c. Use the Computer Management tool to periodically stop and restart the Workstation, Server, and Logon services throughout the day.

   d. Look for the simple solutions first.

10. What information are you likely to find in the setup log?

11. Your Windows Server 2008 server is having trouble booting, and you suspect that it is related to a driver or service that is not properly starting. How can you track each of the startup actions of the server so that you can later go back and review each one for problems?

    a. Select the Debugging Mode from the Advanced Boot Options menu options when you boot.

    b. Enable Boot Logging as a group policy and examine the file boot.log after the system is rebooted.

    c. Select Enable Boot Logging from the Advanced Boot Options menu options when you boot.

    d. Configure driver signing to be in the verbose mode.

12. Your company's server won't boot. The Management Council just completed the five-year strategic plan and placed the only copy on the server before it crashed. Which of the following can you do to try and retrieve the file containing the plan?

    a. Boot into Safe Mode to obtain a copy of the plan from the application log.

    b. Boot into Disk Mode and perform a disk dump onto a DVD.

    c. Use the Recovery repair option to recover the file onto a flash drive.

    d. Boot into the command line and use the *copy* command to copy the file off of the disk.

13. Which of the following file types can be used for saving an event log to disk? (Choose all that apply.)

    a. .txt

    b. .xml

    c. .doc

    d. .evtx

14. You walk into the computer room one morning and notice a message at the server console stating that the application log is full. Which of the following might be true? (Choose all that apply.)

    a. The application log properties are set at *Do not overwrite events*.

    b. The application log is not enabled.

    c. The application log needs to be set to a larger size.

    d. The security log contents are set to spill into the application log when the security log is full.

15. When you use Remote Desktop client from Windows Vista to remotely access Windows Server 2008, plan to use it with _____ Authentication for stronger security.

16. What key or key combination do you press to boot into the Advanced Boot Options menu?

    a. CTRL+ALT

    b. F8

    c. DEL

    d. CTRL+A

17. Your server is not successfully using Windows Update to update the operating system when you try to do a manual update. It appears that it is connecting to the local network, but not to the Internet. Which of the following tools can you use to help diagnose the problem? (Choose all that apply.)

    a. Network and Sharing Center

    b. *ping* command

    c. *net test* command

    d. *nbtest* command

18. You want to set up a command center for the server operators in your company so they can use one Windows Server 2008 server to monitor the other 28 servers in the operations room and spread throughout the company. Which of the following features should you make sure is installed at the command center server?

    a. Universal Server Manager tool

    b. Active Directory Computers tool

    c. Remote Server Administration Tools

    d. Remote Console Tool

19. Your server won't boot and you suspect it is likely caused by a memory problem. What tool can you use to test the memory?

20. Users report that they cannot log on to a server because they are getting messages about a Kerberos error. Which of the following can best help you track down the problem?

    a. *tracert* command-line command

    b. DFS Replication log

    c. *ping* command-line command

    d. Key Management Service log

Case Projects

Chelos is a chain of popular Mexican food restaurants throughout the southwestern United States. The restaurant headquarters is in Dallas. The Chelos national headquarters is in one multistory building that houses the management offices and the Chelos Kitchens. The management offices consist of the Marketing and Franchising, Accounting, Operations, and IT departments. The Chelos Kitchens unit produces a variety of prepackaged foods used by all Chelos restaurants.

Each department and the Chelos Kitchens unit have Windows Server 2008 servers at their locations. An additional small computer operations center contains the Web, e-mail, DNS, DHCP, and master Active Directory servers. All servers in the company have recently been put under the control of a small team of server operators who work in two shifts. The company has a total of 22 Windows Server 2003 and 2008 servers.

The two system programmers who set up the servers and were responsible for training the server operators have just left to start their own business. Chelos has hired two new system programmers, but they are new to Windows Server 2008, although they have some experience with Windows Server 2003.

The IT director has retained you through Aspen Consulting to assist with the training of the system programmers and to help develop troubleshooting expertise among the system programmers and server operators. Network problems and problems with hardware failures that have delayed operations have been reported, and Chelos wants to improve the server support so that problems are solved more quickly.

Case Project 12-1: Developing a Troubleshooting Strategy

When you arrive at Chelos, your first analysis of their situation is that very few of the IT staff have much troubleshooting expertise. Most of the troubleshooting done in the past was by the two system programmers who have moved on. You decide to develop a written troubleshooting strategy customized for Chelos that can be used by the new system programmers and the server operators. Create a strategy that can be presented either in a document, a slide presentation, or both.

Case Project 12-2: Troubleshooting a Hardware Crash

While you are at the Chelos headquarters, one of the servers suddenly crashes with what appears to be a disk failure. Because you are working on the problem, you also see this as an opportunity to help train the system programmers and server operators currently on duty. Address the following questions as you are working with these staff members:

- Where would you look first for a clue about what happened?
- How would you explain the steps and tools you would use in handling the crash?
- If it is truly a system disk crash, how can you restore the system?

Case Project 12-3: Using Event Viewer

The system programmers and server operators are not very familiar with using Event Viewer to be proactive to prevent problems or even for using it to diagnose a problem. They ask you to develop a report or slide show that addresses the following:

- Different ways to open Event Viewer
- Key Windows logs to check in Event Viewer
- The kinds of information available in Event Viewer
- How to quickly view only specific events
- Developing a regular schedule of checking logs

Case Project 12-4: Working with a Connectivity Problem

As you are discussing event logs with one of the server operators, several calls come in that a server in the Marketing Department cannot be contacted over the network. When the server operator calls someone in the Marketing Department, it is reported that the server seems to be up and running normally but not accessible through the network. What tools can you use to immediately test connectivity from the server operator's location several floors below the Marketing Department? If the server operator decides she has to go to the server to fix it, what command-line and GUI tools can she run to diagnose possible connection problems?

Case Project 12-5: Server Management

It is inconvenient and time consuming for the server operators to go all over the building to manage the servers in each department. What is your recommendation to them for reducing the trips they have to make to the servers spread throughout the building?

Appendix A

Windows Server 2008 Virtualization

Virtualization is generating as much interest today as networking generated when it first caught on. It's hard to pick up a computer publication or go to a computing news Web site without seeing many stories about virtualization. So what is virtualization and what is all of the excitement about? This appendix gives you a short background of virtualization and introduces Microsoft Hyper-V virtualization software that is included with the principal Windows Server 2008 editions.

What Is Virtualization?

Virtualization involves turning a single computing platform, such as an operating system or computer, into two or more virtual computing platforms. The popular application of this is to install software on one computer that has one operating system, so that multiple operating systems can be run from that single computer. Instead of one operating system running at one time from one machine, two, three, or more operating systems can be running from a single machine. For example, if three operating systems are running on one physical machine, this means there are three virtual machines.

Several recognized forms of virtualization include:

- *Server virtualization*—Running multiple server operating systems on a single server computer. For instance, this form of virtualization might include having two Windows Server 2008 operating systems and one Linux operating system on one server. Microsoft Hyper-V is an example of server virtualization.

- *Workstation or PC virtualization*—Running multiple workstation operating systems, such as Windows XP, Windows Vista, and UNIX, on one computer.

- *Application virtualization*—Running single applications in their own virtual machine environments. On a Windows operating system, this means running applications to have their own file system and Registry. For example, if you are converting to a new accounting system, you might have the old accounting software in one virtualized application environment and the new accounting software in another virtualized application environment on the same physical computer. The old accounting software is used until the new software system is fully tested and operational.

- *Storage virtualization*—Setting up multiple networked disk storage units to appear as one unit. You've already learned about storage virtualization as Storage Area Networks (SANs) in Chapter 7, "Configuring and Managing Data Storage."

- *Hardware or CPU virtualization*—Using the CPU to perform virtualization tasks by having virtualization processes work inside a specially designed CPU. AMD implements this through AMD-V technology in some of its CPUs, and Intel does the same through Intel Virtualization Technology (VT) in some CPUs.

To learn more about AMD-V, visit *www.amd.com/us-en/Processors/ ProductInformation/0,,30_118_8796_14287,00.html*, and for Intel VT, see *www.intel.cc/technology/virtualization/index.htm*.

- *Network virtualization*—Dividing a single network into multiple channels or bandwidths so that the network appears as multiple networks.

Of these options, server virtualization has aroused significant interest among those who work with server operating systems and is the focus of Microsoft Hyper-V. In the next section, you learn why server virtualization has sparked so much interest.

Advantages of Virtual Servers

Server virtualization offers several advantages, including the following:

- Enables server consolidation
- Uses hardware effectively
- Provides hardware independence
- Enables using different operating systems on one computer
- Provides effective development environments
- Offers business advantages

Each of these advantages is discussed in the following sections.

Ability to Consolidate Servers

One of the reasons why virtual servers are appealing is that they offer the ability to reduce the number of servers needed to run a business. Over time, businesses and organizations continue to add servers for new functions. For example, this can include adding a Web server (or servers), additional DNS servers, and servers for new databases and software. The sprawl of servers has become known as a server farm, because servers seem to sprout up everywhere.

Server proliferation requires more work in maintaining servers, resulting in the need to hire additional people to manage them. Locating space to store the servers is also a problem. As the number of servers grows, it doesn't take long until space runs out in an operations center or server room; it becomes necessary to invest in more space. Additional expenses are incurred for physical security, air conditioning, and heating to keep the servers in a secure, controlled environment. Further, the cost of electricity is rising, and more server hardware translates into higher electric bills.

The use of virtual servers enables an organization to consolidate servers into fewer physical computers, generally cutting the number of computers by two-thirds or three-fourths. Server consolidation means that significant money can be saved on personnel, space, security, and electricity.

Uses Hardware Effectively

An organization might have a number of computers that are underutilized. For example, many individual file servers, DNS servers, DHCP servers, and other servers barely take advantage of the full power of their hardware. Making these systems virtual servers can save money on hardware and hardware maintenance, because hardware can be used to capacity.

Enables Hardware Independence

The specific hardware used to house virtual servers is less important, because the operating system runs inside the virtual server. The hardware is primarily important to the virtual server host operating system. For example, if the host is Windows Server 2008 in the Hyper-V role, then the computer must be compatible with Windows Server 2008 and Hyper-V. The server operating systems running inside Hyper-V are not as affected by hardware compatibility, other than to make sure that sufficient RAM, disk space, and network connectivity are available. This also means that you can move a virtual server from one host computer to another without worrying about hardware compatibility.

Freedom from hardware compatibility issues has several advantages. One advantage is that it makes disaster recovery easier. If a computer operating as a virtual server host goes down at one site, such as due to a tornado or flood, the virtual servers that it hosts can be exported to other off-site host computers (such as through backups) with fewer hardware concerns. Your organization might even use off-site virtual servers as standby backup computers, so the organization has very little downtime when a disaster strikes.

Another advantage is that hardware upgrades are smoother. When you upgrade the hardware, such as for more processing power or disk space, it is easier to transfer a virtual server from one computer to another. The operating system in the virtual machine needs little or no reconfiguration.

Although virtual networking provides hardware independence, you still need to pay close attention to the hardware needed on a computer that hosts multiple virtual machines. The virtual machines on the host will share the same processor used by the host. Make sure you outfit the host computer with a fast processor. Some host systems, such as Windows Server 2008 with Hyper-V, support SMP computers, which offer more processing power. Another important factor to consider is the RAM installed in the host. Make sure you install enough RAM for the needs of all virtual machines that will be running on the host. For example, consider outfitting the host with at least 2 GB of RAM, but preferably much more for each virtual machine you plan to put on the host.

Ability to Use Multiple Operating Systems

Many organizations use a combination of operating systems, such as Windows Server 2003, Windows Server 2008, Linux, and UNIX. These organizations can reduce the number of servers they maintain by using virtual server systems that support the implementation of different operating systems on the same computer.

This is a major improvement from the days when you had to have certain hardware for each operating system, such as a specialized computer for a UNIX-based Web system and a different type of computer for Windows Server systems. Dedicated hardware often meant an organization had to have specialized staff to manage each type of system and its hardware. Also, each type of hardware required separate support agreements. All of this translated into higher expenses.

Provides Effective Development Environments

Many organizations develop their own software. Other organizations purchase software packages, but need to test those packages before bringing them into live production. In the past, organizations have purchased separate computers for software development and testing. Some organizations with limited budgets have even performed development on production computers, which is a risky approach.

Organizations that use a separate development server can spend considerable time adapting the development software to a new computer system. Using a virtual server as a development environment can ease the hassles of bringing new software live. Developing software on a virtual server presents few or no hardware considerations because you simply transfer the newly developed software to another virtual server. Further, before the software is brought into production, users can test it in a server environment that already looks similar or identical to the one they are accustomed to using. When the new software is brought into live production, users will need to make fewer adjustments.

Organizations that purchase software packages can use a virtual server to test the packages before bringing them into production. Users who help with the testing can do so in a safe environment and take their time to get used to the new software. Bringing the new software into production is simpler and cleaner, just as it is for organizations that develop their own software on a virtual server.

Offers Business Advantages

To stay competitive and attractive to stockholders, businesses must always pay attention to the bottom line. Any business that requires multiple servers can typically save money by deploying virtual servers. You've already learned some of the ways virtual servers can save money, but it's important to reiterate that savings can come from:

- Lower hardware costs
- Paying lower utility bills, including costs for running computers, air conditioning, and heating
- Reduced staff costs
- Reduced costs for space
- Reduced software development costs
- Reduced software implementation costs
- Reduced costs for implementing systems on new hardware
- More disaster recovery options

Disadvantages of Virtualization

When an organization considers the advantages of virtualization, it is also important to be aware of the disadvantages. One disadvantage is that the server hardware can be a single point of failure. Plan to build in hardware fault tolerance and disaster recovery to reduce the impact of hardware failure. For example, consider purchasing server hardware that contains redundant power supplies, CPUs, memory, network interfaces, and RAID level 1 or level 5 disk storage fault tolerance. Another option is to have a backup server computer on hand in case the main one fails. As a disaster recovery step, the backup computer might already be set up with virtual machines to match those on the primary server; you can regularly back up data from the virtual machines on the primary server to those on the backup server. If the primary server goes down, the backup server can take over. For better disaster recovery, place the backup server computer in a different location from the primary server.

Another disadvantage of virtualization is that backing up all of the virtual machines on a single computer can be a much slower process than backing up a single server with a single operating system and no virtual machines. Backing up virtual machines can stress network, CPU, and memory resources on a single computer. You can reduce some of the burden by employing incremental backups, as you learned in Chapter 7. Another option is to purchase software designed to expedite backups on virtual machines.

Several Microsoft software partners offer software for virtual systems, including Acronis, Invirtus, Portlock, Ultrabac, VERITAS software, and others.

Features of Hyper-V

Windows Server 2008 Hyper-V offers features to make this a strong virtual machine platform now and into the future. These features include the following:

- Ability to load 32-bit and 64-bit guest operating systems
- Option to load Windows Server, UNIX, and Linux operating systems on the same computer
- 64-bit performance for faster response, manageability, and security
- Support for SMP computers (with up to four processors)
- Enhanced access of the CPU, video, disk, and networking capabilities of the host computer
- Ability to perform network load balancing through the use of its virtual switch capabilities, so the load can be spread equally among virtual servers
- Option to scale up to larger and faster hardware platforms and capabilities for implementing more virtual machines
- Hyper-V Manager tool for installation and management of virtual machines
- Ability to take advantage of AMD-V and Intel VT CPU technology
- Ability to take virtual machine snapshots of a particular virtual server state, so that you can quickly return to a prior working state if configuration changes create a problem or don't work (also important for creating backups that can return to a prior state)
- Designed so that third-party vendors can develop tools and specialized utilities for Hyper-V

Requirements of Hyper-V

Hyper-V can be installed on a computer that matches the basic requirements for Windows Server 2008 systems (see Table 1-1 in Chapter 1, "Introduction to Windows Server 2008"). Beyond this, the requirements are as follows:

- An x64 computer (Hyper-V does not run on x86 computers because Microsoft anticipates that x64 is the platform of the future)
- Data Execution Prevention (DEP) enabled (see Activity 3-7 in Chapter 3, "Configuring the Windows Server 2008 Environment")
- A processor with AMD-V or Intel VT (hardware virtualization)
- A clean installation of the Windows Server 2008 edition that you use (Standard Edition, Enterprise Edition, or Datacenter Edition)—not really required, but highly recommended by Microsoft

Installing Hyper-V

Hyper-V is a role that you install through either the Initial Configuration Tasks window or Server Manager. The general steps for installing Hyper-V are as follows:

1. Click **Start**, point to **Administrative Tools**, and click **Server Manager**.
2. Scroll to the Roles Summary section and click **Add Roles**.
3. If you see the Before You Begin window, click **Next**.
4. Click **Hyper-V** and click **Next**.
5. Click **Install**.
6. Click **Close**.
7. Close **Server Manager**.

Using Hyper-V Manager

After Hyper-V is installed, you can access the Hyper-V Manager tool from the Administrative Tools menu or as an MMC snap-in. With Hyper-V Manager you can:

- Install virtual machines
- Configure virtual machines
- Install guest operating systems
- Manage virtual machines, including starting and stopping them
- Manage network communications through virtual machines
- Troubleshoot virtual machines

In Chapter 2, "Installing Windows Server 2008," you learned how to install Windows Server 2008 as a virtual machine in Hyper-V by using the New Virtual Machine Wizard. When you use this wizard, you specify:

- The amount of RAM to allocate to the virtual machine
- The network interface to use for the virtual machine
- The virtual disk to use, such as a disk attached to the server or disk storage in a location you specify

After you install an operating system, you can start it by right-clicking the operating system in the Virtual Machines section of the middle pane of Hyper-V Manager and clicking Start, as shown in Figure A-1. Next, double-click the operating system in the Virtual Machine section to open a window from which to access and manage the operating system.

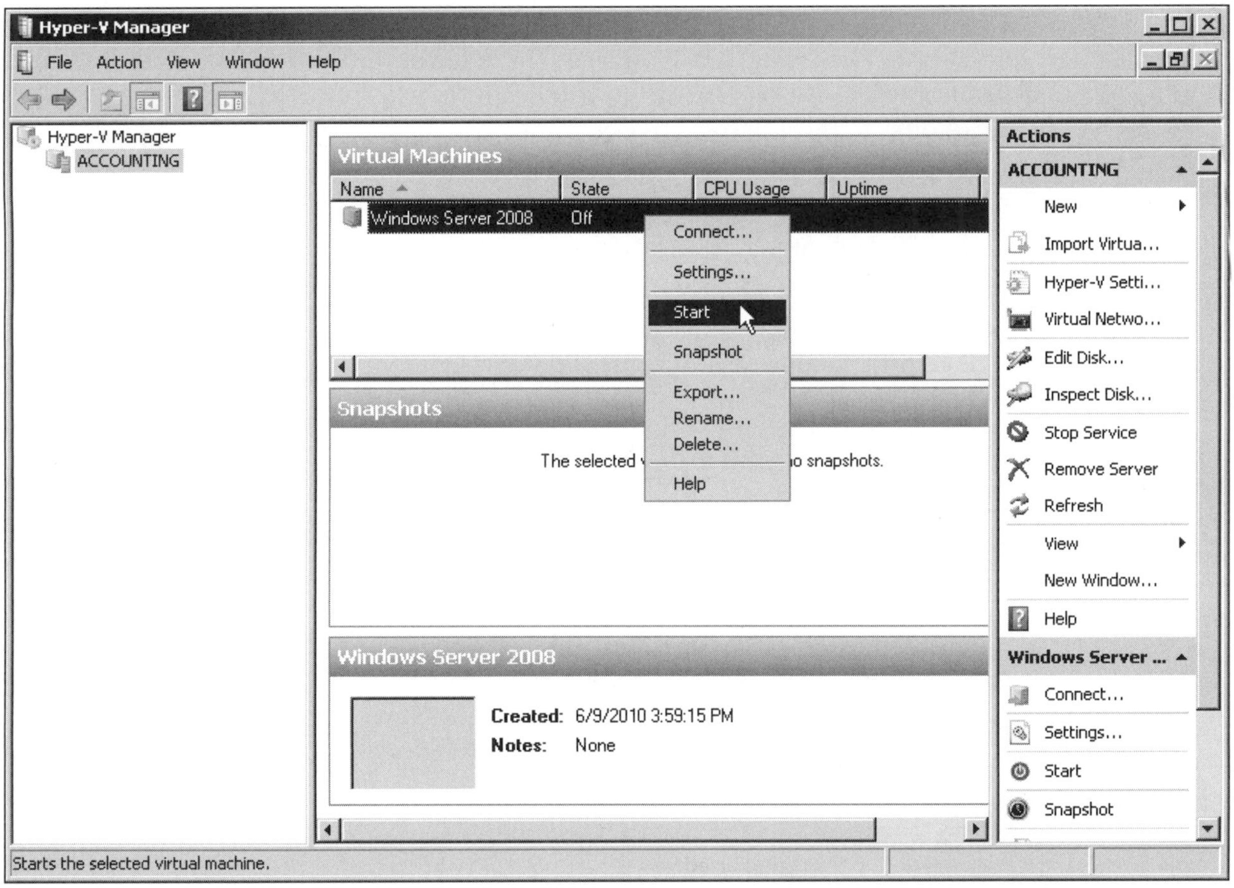

Figure A-1 Starting a virtual machine

The right pane in Hyper-V Manager provides links to tools you can use to:

- Import a virtual machine from another computer
- Configure the settings for Hyper-V (virtual disks, virtual machines, keyboard, and other settings)
- Configure the settings for virtual networks (external, internal, and private networks)
- Edit virtual disk settings via the Edit Virtual Hard Disk Wizard
- Inspect a virtual disk
- Start or stop the Hyper-V service
- Remove a server
- Configure the view
- Manage a specific virtual machine

When you manage a specific virtual machine from the right pane, the options depend on if the virtual machine is started. For example, if it is not started, you can:

- Change the settings
- Start the virtual machine
- Take a snapshot of the current state of the virtual machine
- Export the virtual machine to a different computer with Hyper-V
- Delete the virtual machine

If the virtual machine is started, you can do the following from the links in the right pane of Hyper-V (see Figure A-2, which is for a Windows Server 2008 Standard Edition virtual server):

- Connect to the virtual machine (which opens a window from which to access it)
- Configure settings
- Turn off the virtual machine
- Shut down the virtual machine
- Save the virtual machine
- Pause the virtual machine
- Reset the virtual machine
- Take a snapshot of the current state of the virtual machine
- Rename the virtual machine

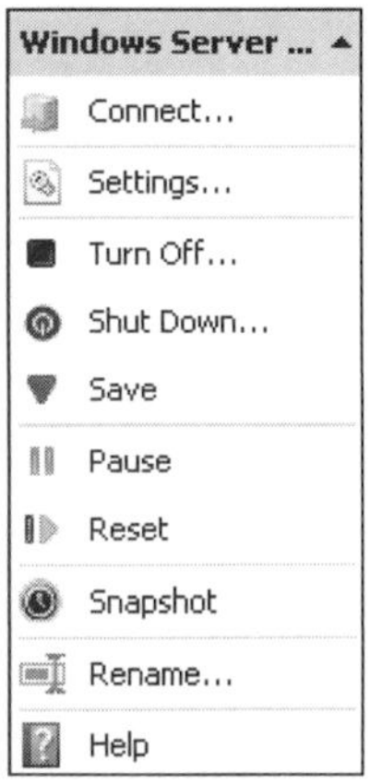

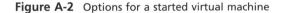

Figure A-2 Options for a started virtual machine

When you open a window to connect locally to the virtual machine, you can maximize the window so that you have a full view of the operating system you are using through the virtual machine. A control bar remains at the top of the screen to minimize the window or close it.

Conclusion

The Hyper-V role is a new addition to Windows Server 2008 that makes this operating system even more versatile for all kinds of server environments. When you purchase the Standard, Enterprise, or Datacenter editions of Windows Server 2008, you can add Hyper-V for a minimal extra cost. In the long run, your investment in Hyper-V can save thousands of dollars and make your server operations more efficient. Even if your organization requires only two or three servers, Hyper-V can make sense in terms of cost savings. For example, you can now purchase one x64 computer for about the same amount of money as an x86 computer. For just a little more, you can purchase an x64 SMP computer. This means you can implement two servers for about half the hardware cost by using Hyper-V. For a medium- or large-sized business, this translates into thousands of dollars saved.

A Step-by-Step Guide to Using Server Virtualization Software

Virtualization enables a school or an individual student to get the most out of computer resources. Schools can use virtualization to turn a single server-grade computer into a virtual server that can host two, three, or more operating systems. For example, one computer can house three virtual servers running Windows Server 2008. This capability saves the school money on servers and enables more students to be able to work on their own operating systems.

Another capability of virtualization is the ability for a school or individual student to turn a single PC into a virtual system on which to run another operating system—without having to alter the current operating system running on the PC. A single computer lab PC or a student's home PC can be turned into a host for Windows Server 2008. This is ideal, for example, when your textbook comes with an evaluation copy of Windows Server 2008. You can install virtualization software and then install Windows Server 2008 for completing hands-on projects and activities. You can use your originally installed operating system, such as Windows XP or Vista, and also use Windows Server 2008 in a virtual "window" or "session," for example. When you are finished learning Windows Server 2008, you simply remove the virtualization software and you're back where you started with your original operating system.

This appendix is a step-by-step guide for turning a single computer into a virtual system housing one or more virtual machines. The main focus is on three popular virtualization systems that are available for free:

- *Microsoft Virtual PC*—Intended for a workstation-grade PC to host another operating system, such as a Windows Server 2008 virtual machine
- *Microsoft Virtual Server*—Intended for a server-grade computer to host multiple virtual machines, including Windows Server 2008 and other operating systems
- *VMware Server*—Intended for server-grade computers to host multiple virtual machines, such as Windows Server 2008

For each of these virtualization systems, you learn how to:

- Obtain a free download version
- Install it
- Create a virtual machine
- Install a guest operating system, such as Windows Server 2008, in the virtual machine, and then how to access that virtual machine's operating system
- Install ISO images
- Configure virtual networking
- Configure hardware components

At the end of the appendix, a brief look at VMware Workstation 6 and Microsoft Hyper-V is also provided.

Microsoft Virtual PC

Microsoft Virtual PC can be installed in Microsoft Windows XP, Vista, and Windows Server 2003 operating systems. At this writing, it is not adapted to be installed in Windows Server 2008. Although Microsoft Virtual PC is intended to host workstation operating systems as virtual machines, you can also use it to create a Windows Server 2008 Standard Edition virtual machine.

Microsoft Virtual PC is available from Microsoft as a free download. From the individual reader's or student's perspective, this is ideal for running the Windows Server 2008 Standard Edition evaluation DVD (available from Microsoft at *www.microsoft.com*) on a Windows XP or Windows Vista computer. It works equally well on Windows XP or Windows Vista computers in a student computer lab.

Requirements for Microsoft Virtual PC

At this writing, Microsoft Virtual PC 2007 with Service Pack 1 (SP1) is the most recently available version. It can be loaded on the following operating system hosts:

- Windows XP Professional with SP2 or SP3
- Windows Server 2003 Editions SP2 (x86 or x64)
- Windows Vista Business Edition (x86 or x64 versions with or without SP1)
- Windows Vista Enterprise Edition (x86 or x64 versions with or without SP1)
- Windows Vista Ultimate Edition (x86 or x64 versions with or without SP1)

The hardware requirements for Microsoft Virtual PC 2007 SP1 are as follows:

- *CPU*—Intel Celeron, Pentium II, Pentium III, Pentium 4, Core Duo, or Core 2 Duo CPU or AMD Athlon or Duron CPU (400 MHz or faster; x86 or x64).
- *RAM*—Enough RAM for at least the minimum requirements of the total number of operating systems you will be running. For example, if you are running Windows XP Professional (128 MB minimum) and want to load Windows Server 2008 (512 MB minimum) as a virtual machine, you'll need a minimum of 640 MB to 1 GB of RAM. If Windows Vista is the host and you want to run a Windows Server 2008 Standard Edition virtual machine, you'll need a minimum of 1 GB of RAM.
- *Disk space*—Enough disk storage for the operating systems you plan to run. For example, Windows XP requires at least 1.5 GB, Windows Vista requires at least 15 GB, and Windows Server 2008 requires at least 10 GB (but 15 GB to 20 GB is better for using different roles and services).

Virtual Machine Operating Systems Supported

After Virtual PC 2007 SP1 is loaded, you can run any of the following operating systems as virtual machines (guests) within Virtual PC 2007 SP1:

- Windows 98 and 98 SE
- Windows Me
- Windows 2000 Professional
- Windows XP Home or Professional with SP1, SP2, SP3 (or no service pack)
- Windows Vista Business Edition (x86 or x64 versions with or without SP1)
- Windows Vista Enterprise Edition (x86 or x64 versions with or without SP1)
- Windows Vista Ultimate Edition (x86 or x64 versions with or without SP1)
- Windows Server 2008 Standard Edition
- OS/2 Warp

How to Download Microsoft Virtual PC

Microsoft Virtual PC can be downloaded from Microsoft's Web site for no cost. The steps to download Microsoft Virtual PC 2007 SP1 are as follows (what you click is presented in bold):

1. Log on to your computer.

2. Create a folder in which to download the setup.exe file for Microsoft Virtual PC (such as a temporary folder or a folder under your Program Files folder).

3. Open a Web browser, such as Microsoft Internet Explorer.

4. Go to the URL **www.microsoft.com/downloads** or **www.microsoft.com/downloads/ Search.aspx?displaylang=en** (for English).

Web links and specific instructions change periodically. You might need to search *www.microsoft.com* for the most current link if these links do not work.

5. Look for Microsoft Virtual PC in the Popular Downloads or Recommended Downloads sections (also check the New Downloads section in case a new version is available). If you find it in one of these sections, click the link for **Microsoft Virtual PC**. If you do not see a link, click **Windows** under the Product Families heading. Click the **down arrow** in the Show downloads for: box, and click **Microsoft Virtual PC**. Click **Go**.

6. Click the link for **VPC 2007 SP1**.

To use Microsoft Virtual PC 2007 with Windows Server 2008 or Windows Vista as the virtual machine (guest) operating system, you must use the download containing SP1.

7. Click the **Download** button for the setup.exe file that is appropriate for your computer, which is 32 BIT\setup.exe for an x86 computer or 64 BIT\setup.exe for an x64 computer.

8. Click the **Save** or **Save File** button.

9. Select the folder you created in which to save the setup.exe file.

10. Click **Save**.

11. Click **Close** in the Download complete box.

12. Close your Web browser.

How to Install Microsoft Virtual PC

Microsoft Virtual PC 2007 SP1 is easy to install. The installation steps are as follows:

1. Browse to the folder in which you saved the setup.exe file for Microsoft Virtual PC.

2. Double-click **setup.exe**.

3. Click **Next** after the Microsoft Virtual PC 2007 SP1 Wizard starts (see Figure B-1).

4. Click the option button for **I accept the terms in the license agreement**. Click **Next**.

5. Enter your username and name of your organization (if an organization name is appropriate). Notice that the product key should already be provided. Also, if you see this option, leave **Anyone who uses this computer (All Users)** selected. Click **Next**.

6. Click **Install**. The installation process will take a few minutes to complete.

7. Click **Finish**.

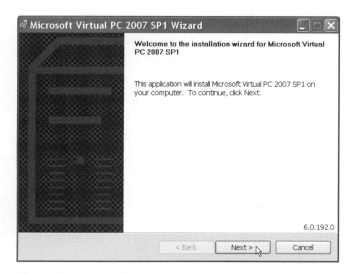

Figure B-1   Microsoft Virtual PC 2007 SP1 Wizard

Creating a Virtual Machine and Installing a Guest OS

After Microsoft Virtual PC 2007 SP1 is installed, the next step is to create a virtual machine in which to install a guest operating system.

 Microsoft Virtual PC 2007 SP1 might not be compatible with hardware virtualization on some CPUs. If you experience a crash dump when configuring the virtual machine or loading the guest OS, first make sure you have enabled hardware virtualization in Step 12. If this does not work, try disabling hardware virtualization in the BIOS and restart these steps from the beginning.

The following are sample steps for setting up the virtual machine with Windows Server 2008 Standard Edition as the guest operating system:

1. From the host operating system, such as Windows XP or Windows Vista, click **Start**.

2. Point to **All Programs** and click **Microsoft Virtual PC**.

3. The New Virtual Machine Wizard opens (see Figure B-2). Click **Next**.

Figure B-2   New Virtual Machine Wizard

4. Ensure that **Create a virtual machine** is selected and click **Next.**

5. Provide a name for the virtual machine, such as **Windows Server 2008.** Click **Next.**

6. Ensure Windows Server 2008 is selected as the operating system to install and click **Next.**

7. Ensure that at least 512 MB to 1 GB of memory is allocated for the virtual machine. If necessary, click **Adjusting the RAM** and use the slider bar to allocate enough memory. Click **Next.**

8. Ensure that **A new virtual hard disk** is selected and click **Next.**

9. Make sure that the virtual hard disk is sized to meet your needs, or leave the default size (you'll need 15 GB for Windows Server 2008 and might use at least 20–40 GB, for example). Click **Next.**

10. Click **Finish.**

11. You should see the Virtual PC Console open on the desktop. If it is not open, click **Start,** point to **All Programs,** and click **Microsoft Virtual PC.**

12. You can configure options at this point by clicking the **File** menu and clicking **Options** on the shortcut menu. Click each option to see what it does and configure any options as necessary. When you are finished, click **OK.** The options are as follows:

   - *Restore at Start*—Pauses a running virtual machine when you exit the console and restores the virtual machine when you reopen the console.

   - *Performance*—Specifies how the CPU time is allocated to virtual machines and specifies what happens when a Virtual PC is a process running in the background.

   - *Hardware virtualization*—Enable hardware virtualization, if your CPU has this capability.

   - *Full-Screen Mode*—Enables the screen resolution to be adjusted so it is the same for the host and guest OSs (note the caution if this is enabled).

   - *Sound*—Configures virtual machine sound. Sound is muted by default. If you enable it, the sounds from the host and guest OS can be difficult to differentiate.

   - *Messages*—Turn off error and informational messages from Virtual PC.

   - *Keyboard*—Specifies the host key for the guest operating system. The default host key is the right ALT key. When you press this key, you can switch the mouse between the guest and host windows and you can execute guest key combinations, such as pressing ALT+DEL to send the CTRL+ALT+DEL key combination to the guest OS for logging on.

   - *Mouse*—Specifies how the pointer is captured for use in the virtual machine window.

   - *Security*—Determines how to control access to Virtual PC functions.

   - *Language*—Specifies the language to use for Virtual PC.

13. Insert the Windows Server 2008 Standard Edition installation DVD.

At this point, you could install any of the supported guest operating systems. If you are installing a different operating system, you would insert the CD/DVD now, complete Step 14, and then Steps 15 through 30 (or whatever steps are required) would be unique to the operating system you are installing.

14. Click the **Start** button in the Virtual PC console window. This opens a second larger window, which is the Microsoft Virtual PC 2007console window. Wait for a few minutes for the DVD to start loading. Click in the console window to enable the mouse to be operative within the console. (If necessary, you can switch the mouse movement back so that it can go all over the screen by pressing the right ALT key, which is the "host" key.)

Occasionally, the mouse might seem stuck, move slowly, or stop functioning in the active portion of the console window. If this happens, close all console windows and go to Step 11 to start again. Also, some installation processes take longer to install in a virtual machine. Don't close the window or stop the installation prematurely, even if you seem to be stuck on a black screen for several minutes.

15. Select the language to install, such as **English,** in the Language to install drop-down box. In the Time and currency format box, make your selection, such as **English (United States).** In the Keyboard or input method box, make your selection, such as **US.** Click **Next.**

16. Click **Install now.**

17. Select **Windows Server 2008 Standard (Full Installation)** and click **Next.**

18. Read the license terms, click the box for **I accept the license terms,** and click **Next.**

19. Click **Custom (advanced).**

20. You'll see the amount of unallocated disk space highlighted, which is the disk space you specified when you configured the virtual machine. Ensure it is highlighted and click **Next.**

21. The installation program begins installing Windows Server 2008. You'll see progress information about Copying files, Expanding files, Installing features, Installing updates, and Completing installation. This part of the installation can take 30 minutes or longer.

22. The installation program restarts the operating system.

23. You see the message: *Please wait while Windows sets up your computer.*

24. Next, you see the Install Windows window in the Completing installation phase.

25. The system reboots again.

26. You'll see the message (a red circle with a white x in it): *The user's password must be changed before logging on the first time.* Click the **OK** button (you might have to click inside the active portion of the console window first to have the mouse function within it).

27. Enter a new password for the Administrator account and then enter the same password again to confirm it. Click the **blue circle** with the white right-pointing arrow inside.

If you enter a password that is not a strong password, you'll see the message: (with a white x in a red circle) *Unable to update the password.* This means that the value provided for the new password does not meet the length, complexity, or history requirements of the domain. Click OK and enter a different password that is over seven characters and uses letters, numbers, and characters such as &.

28. When you see the message, *Your password has been changed,* click **OK.**

29. At this point, the Windows desktop is opened and the Initial Configuration Tasks window is displayed.

30. You can configure Windows Server 2008 as you would in a nonvirtual environment.

31. When you close the Microsoft Virtual PC 2007 console window, you can either turn off the virtual machine or save its current state. Unless you want to save its state, a good practice is to shut down the server prior to closing the window. (Saving the state means to keep the server in its current state, without shutting it down.) When you shut down the server in this way, the Microsoft Virtual PC 2007 console window closes, but leaves the Virtual PC 2007 console window still open. Also, to restart the virtual machine, open the Virtual PC Console window, click **Start,** and wait for the system to boot in the Microsoft Virtual PC 2007 console window.

When you log in to Windows Server 2008 from the console window, the normal CTRL+ALT+DEL key sequence does not work. Instead, click the Action menu and press CTRL+ALT+DEL. Another alternative is to press and hold the right ALT key and press the DEL key.

Installing an OS from an ISO Image

An ISO file is an optical disc (CD/DVD) image file that ends with the .iso file extension. An ISO file can be accessed in several ways, such as from a CD/DVD, a hard drive, or as a shared network file. Typically when you download an operating system, such as an evaluation copy of a Windows operating system, you download an ISO file. One advantage of using an ISO file for installing a guest operating system into a virtual machine is that the installation process can go faster. Microsoft Virtual PC enables you to install from an ISO file by using the following general steps:

1. Follow Steps 1 through 12 in the previous section, "Creating a Virtual Machine and Installing a Guest OS."

2. Click the **Start** button in the Virtual PC console window.

3. After the Microsoft Virtual PC 2007 window opens, press the **right ALT** key if necessary to access the menu at the top of the window.

4. Click the **CD** menu and click **Capture ISO Image**.

5. Navigate to the ISO file, click the file, and click the **Open** button.

6. You return to the Microsoft Virtual PC 2007 window from which you should restart the virtual machine.

Configuring Networking and Hardware Options

You can configure a range of networking and hardware options in Microsoft Virtual PC. For example, if the host computer has two or more NICs, you can specify which NIC to use for a virtual machine. In another example, you might need to create one or more additional virtual hard disks for a virtual machine.

Use these steps to configure networking and hardware options:

1. Open the Virtual PC console, if it is not open. Also, ensure that the virtual machine is turned off before you start.

2. Click the **Settings** button, or click the **Action** menu and click **Settings** (see Figure B-3).

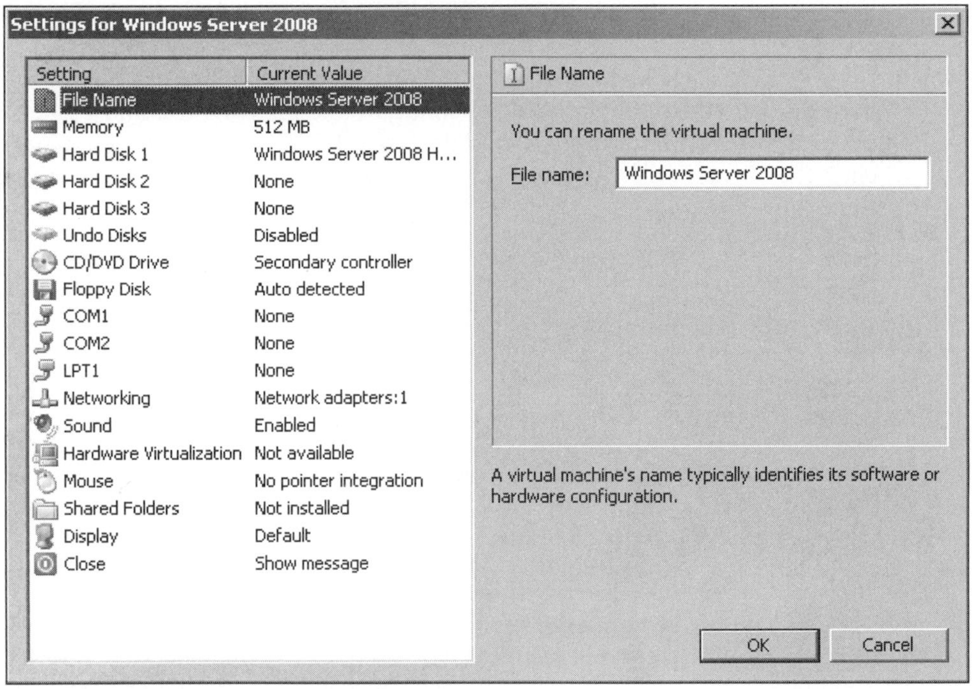

Figure B-3 Settings for a virtual machine

3. Click **Networking** in the left pane. If your computer has multiple adapters, you can select the specific adapter (or multiple adapters) to associate with a virtual machine.

4. In the right pane, click the down arrow for the adapter that is selected by default. The following options are available:

   - *Not connected*—Used if you do not intend to enable the virtual machine to access a network (including the Internet) and so that it cannot be accessed from a network.

   - *Local*—If two or more virtual machines are set up, they can access each other; however, virtual machines cannot access the network.

   - *NetworkInterfaceName*—The actual name of a NIC model, such as an Intel or Broadcom NIC, that the virtual machine is directly connected to for regular network and Internet access. With this selection, network configuration tasks that apply to other network computers also apply to the virtual machine. If a DHCP server is on the network or if the network uses a router with Network Address Translation (NAT), the virtual machine's network connection can be configured to use these. The same applies if a DNS server is set up.

   - *Shared Networking (NAT)*—Used to create a private Virtual PC network which has a virtual DHCP server and a virtual NAT-enabled router or firewall. Typically the first virtual computer created acts as the DHCP server and provides NAT services. In this arrangement, Microsoft Virtual PC performs as a virtual DHCP server, leasing IP addresses for virtual machines in the range of 192.168.131.1 to 192.168.131.253. Further, the virtual machines appear as computers within a private NAT-protected network. A connection to the Internet is shared among the virtual machines and is protected in a way similar to a NAT-enabled router or firewall.

   - *Loopback Adapter*—You will see this option if the operating system is configured to have a Microsoft loopback adapter (configured as a network adapter, such as through the Add Hardware option in Control Panel). This option is used in two contexts. One context is when no physical network connection is present, but you want to simulate network connectivity between the host and all virtual machines. A second context is when you are creating a network with many routers and firewalls as well as many virtual machines.

5. Make the networking selections that are appropriate to your situation.

6. Click **Memory** in the left pane. Notice that you can increase the memory allocation for the virtual machine by using the slider bar in the right pane.

7. In the left pane, click **Hard Disk 1** and notice that the right pane shows the path to the virtual hard disk file. Also, notice you can configure the Hard Disk 2 and Hard Disk 3 options for additional virtual hard disks. To do this, click Hard Disk 2 in the left pane, for example, and click the Virtual Disk Wizard button in the right pane. (A virtual machine can have up to three hard disks.)

8. Click **CD/DVD Drive** in the left pane and notice you can attach a CD or DVD drive via the right pane.

9. Click **Hardware Virtualization** in the left pane and notice in the right pane that you can configure to enable hardware virtualization, if your computer supports it.

10. Notice you can configure additional hardware, such as communication (COM) ports, a floppy disk, printer (LPT) ports, sound, the mouse, the display, and others.

11. When you are finished with the configurations, click **OK**.

Host Key Options

Because a virtual machine represents an operating system running inside an operating system, it is necessary to have a way to use the keyboard so that the keys you press communicate directly with the guest operating system. For example, you'll notice that pressing CTRL+ALT+DEL brings up the Windows Security box or a menu of options, depending on which version of Windows is the host operating system. It does not take you to a logon screen in the guest operating system.

Microsoft Virtual PC enables you to communicate with the guest operating system by using the host key, which is the right ALT key by default. Table B-1 lists important host key combinations you can use while you are accessing a virtual machine.

Table B-1   Host key options for Microsoft Virtual PC

Keyboard combination	Result
HostKey	Enables you to move the mouse outside of the window area used by the guest OS (move the mouse back into the guest OS display and click when you want to work in the guest OS)
HostKey+DEL	The virtual machine OS responds to this as CTRL+ALT+DEL
HostKey+P	Toggles the virtual machine between pause and resume
HostKey+R	Causes the virtual machine to reset
HostKey+A	Selects all items in the active window in the guest OS
HostKey+C	Copies selected text and items in the active window in the guest OS
HostKey+V	Pastes text and items in the active window in the guest OS
HostKey+ENTER	Switches between full screen and window modes
HostKey+DownArrow	Causes the virtual machine to minimize
HostKey+I	Enables you to install virtual machine additions

Microsoft Virtual Server

Microsoft Virtual Server 2005 is intended to host server operating systems as virtual machines. At this writing, Microsoft Virtual Server 2005 R2 SP1 is the most recent version. This version supports hardware (integrated in the CPU) virtualization, such as AMD CPUs equipped with AMD-V and Intel CPUs with Intel VT. Other new features include the following:

- Can be installed in x64 operating systems
- Provides support for Internet Small Computer System Interface (iSCSI), which is a technology used in Storage Area Networks (SANs)
- Has the ability to cluster the virtual servers on a single computer
- Provides enhanced Active Directory support by publishing Virtual Server binding data through service connection points

Other features of Microsoft Virtual Server include the following:

- Virtual disks can expand dynamically
- Supports most popular x86 operating systems
- Can mount a virtual disk on a different operating system
- Enables the use of Volume Shadow Copy Service (VSS) for backups (used in newer versions of Windows operating systems, such as Windows Server 2008 and Vista)
- Offers virtual server management through Virtual Server Web console
- Can use scripting to control virtual machine setups
- Memory access can be resized

Microsoft Virtual Server Guest Operating Systems Supported

Microsoft Virtual Server can house virtual machines for popular Windows and Linux server and workstation operating systems. The following operating systems can be guests:

- Windows Server 2008 Standard, Enterprise, Datacenter, and Web Server (x86 and x64)
- Windows Server 2003 Standard, Enterprise, Datacenter, and Web Server SP1 or SP2 (x86 or x64)
- Windows Server 2003 Standard, Enterprise, Datacenter, and Web Server R2 (x86 or x64)
- Windows Small Business Server 2003 (Standard and Premium Editions)
- Windows 2000 Server
- Windows XP Professional SP2
- Windows Vista Business, Ultimate, and Enterprise
- Red Hat Enterprise Linux versions 2.1 – 4.0
- SUSE Linux Enterprise Server 9.0
- SUSE Linux versions 9.2 – 10.0

 Other operating systems may also run experimentally in Microsoft Virtual Server.

Microsoft Virtual Server Host Operating Systems Supported

Microsoft Virtual Server can be installed into the following Windows host operating systems:

- Windows Server 2008 Standard and Enterprise (x86 or x64)
- Windows Server 2003 Standard, Enterprise, and Web Server with SP1 or SP2 (x86 or x64)
- Windows Server 2003 Standard, Enterprise, and Web Server R2 (x86 or x64)
- Windows Small Business Server 2003 (Standard and Premium Editions, also R2 versions)
- Windows 2000 Server with SP3 or SP4
- Windows XP Professional (x86 and x64)
- Windows Vista Business, Ultimate, and Enterprise Editions

Requirements for Microsoft Virtual Server

The hardware requirements for Microsoft Virtual Server 2005 R2 with SP1 are as follows:

- *CPU*—Intel Celeron, Pentium III, Pentium 4, Xeon, or AMD Opteron, Athlon, Athlon 64, Althon X2, Duron, or Sempron (550 MHz or faster; x86 or x64).
- *RAM*—Enough RAM to match at least the minimum requirements of the total number of operating systems you will be running. For example, if you are running Windows XP Professional (256 MB minimum required for Virtual Server) and want to load Windows Server 2008 (512 MB minimum) as a virtual machine, you'll need a minimum of 768 MB to 1 GB of RAM. If Windows Server 2003 R2 Standard Edition is the host and you want to run a Windows Server 2008 Enterprise Edition virtual machine, then you'll need a minimum of 768 MB to 1 GB of RAM.
- *Disk space*—Enough disk storage for the operating systems you plan to run. For example, Windows Server 2003 R2 Standard Edition requires at least 3 GB, and Windows Server 2008 requires at least 10 GB (but 15 to 20 GB enables you to load more roles and services).

How to Download Microsoft Virtual Server

You can download Microsoft Virtual Server from Microsoft's Web site for free. To download Microsoft Virtual Server:

1. Log on to your computer.

2. Establish a folder in which to store the download (such as a temporary folder or a folder under your Program Files folder).

3. Start your Web browser, such as Internet Explorer.

4. Go to the URL **www.microsoft.com/downloads** or **www.microsoft.com/downloads/ Search.aspx?displaylang=en** (for English).

 Web links and specific instructions change periodically. You might need to search *www.microsoft.com* for the most current link if these links do not work.

5. Look for *Microsoft Virtual Server* in the Popular Downloads or Recommended Downloads sections (also check the New Downloads section in case there is a new version). If you find it in one of these sections, click the link for **Microsoft Virtual Server.** If you do not see a link, ensure that you set the search box near the top of the Web page to **Windows,** if Windows is not already selected. Enter **Virtual Server** in the blank box next to the Go button, and click **Go.**

6. Click the link for **Virtual Server 2005 R2 SP1.**

7. Click the **Continue** button to register for the free download.

8. The information you provide next will depend on whether you have already signed up for Windows Live ID or if you already have an MSN Hotmail, MSN Messenger, or Passport account. If you already have an account, provide your e-mail address and password for the Windows Live ID information, click **Sign in** to verify your information (and answer any required questions), and click **Continue.** If you do not have an account or do not have a Windows Live ID, follow the steps to sign up for a Windows Live ID.

9. Click the **Download** button for the setup.exe file that is appropriate for your computer, which is 32 BIT\setup.exe for an x86 computer or 64 BIT\setup.exe for an x64 computer.

10. Click the **Save** or **Save File** button.

11. Select the folder you created in which to save the setup.exe file.

12. Click **Save.**

13. Click **Close** in the Download complete box.

14. Close your Web browser.

How to Install Microsoft Virtual Server

The general steps used to install Microsoft Virtual Server into the host operating system are as follows:

1. Browse to the folder in which you saved the setup.exe file for Microsoft Virtual Server.

2. Double-click **setup.exe.**

3. Click **Install Microsoft Virtual Server 2008 R2 SP1** (see Figure B-4).

4. Click **I accept the terms in the license agreement.** Click **Next.**

5. Enter your user name and the name of your organization (if you represent an organization). Notice that the Product Key information is provided by default. Click **Next.**

6. Ensure that **Complete** is selected for the Setup Type, as shown in Figure B-5, and click **Next.**

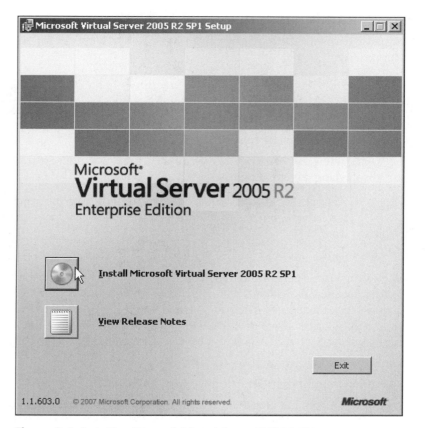

Figure B-4   Installing Microsoft Virtual Server 2005 R2 SP1

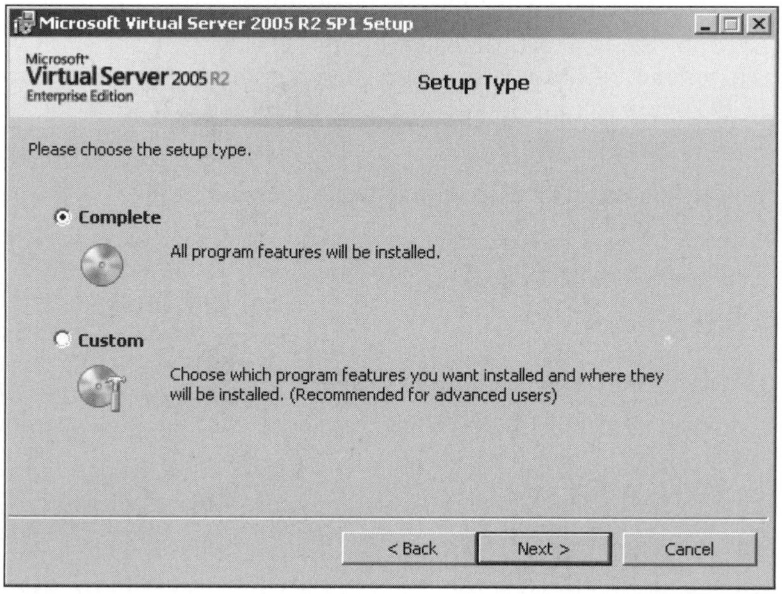

Figure B-5   Selecting the setup type

7. Notice that the Virtual Server Administration Website will be added to Internet Information Services (IIS), and the default Website port is 1024. Further, if you see the option **Configure the Administration Website to always run as the authenticated user (Recommended for most users)**, ensure that it is selected. Click **Next**.

After you click Next, you might see the informational message: *The installed version of Internet Information Services (IIS) does not allow multiple websites.* The Virtual Server Administration Website will be added as a virtual directory under the default site.

8. If the Windows Firewall is enabled on your computer, you can have the setup process create firewall exceptions for Virtual Server. Make sure **Enable Virtual Server exceptions in Windows Firewall** is selected and click **Next.**

9. Click **Install.**

10. If the required IIS components needed for the Virtual Server Administration Website are not already installed, click **Yes** to install them. Click **Install** again, if necessary. You'll see a dialog box showing that the components are being installed.

If instead of the installation box in Step 10 you see a message that the installation program needs to have the IIS World Wide Web service installed and there is no option to install it, this typically means the Virtual Server installation program cannot install IIS. Click OK when you see the message, click Cancel to stop the installation, and follow the steps for your host OS to install IIS (you might need the host OS installation CD/DVD). Start the Virtual Server installation again from Step 1.

11. You'll see a box showing Microsoft Virtual Server 2005 R2 SP1 is being installed.

12. Click **Finish** and close any open windows.

Creating a Virtual Machine and Installing a Guest OS

After Microsoft Virtual Server is installed, you can use the Virtual Server Administration Website tool to configure Microsoft Virtual Server, configure a virtual machine, and install a guest operating system.

Here are the steps for creating a virtual machine and installing a guest operating system (using Windows Server 2008 as the guest operating system):

1. Click **Start,** point to **All Programs,** and click **Microsoft Virtual Server.**

2. Click **Virtual Server Administration Website.**

3. Provide a username and password (for an account that has administrator privileges), when you see the Connect to dialog box and click **OK.**

4. If you are using a recent version of the Windows Firewall, you might see the Internet Explorer box to enable you to add this Web site to the list of trusted sites. (You are likely to see this dialog box the first time you access the Virtual Server Administration Website tool.) Click the **Add** button. In the Trusted sites dialog box, click the **Add** button for the site you are adding and click **Close.** Also, if you see the Microsoft Phishing Filter dialog box, select whether or not to turn on the Phishing Filter (turning the filter on is recommended) and click **OK.**

5. The Virtual Server Administration Website tool is displayed through Internet Explorer, as shown in Figure B-6. Notice that the left pane contains options to navigate, create and add virtual machines, manage virtual disks, manage virtual networks, and manage the virtual server.

6. In the left pane under Virtual Machines, click **Create.**

7. Enter the name for the virtual machine. Also, set the virtual machine memory. For Windows Server 2008, you should set this for at least 512 MB to 1024 MB. Also, select to **Create a new virtual hard disk** with at least 15 GB (more is better) for Windows Server 2008. Finally, specify the virtual network adapter, such as an external network interface. Click **Create.**

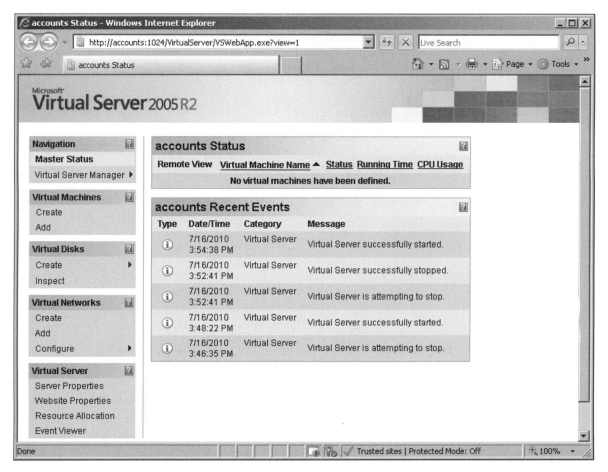

Figure B-6 Virtual Server Administration Website tool

The virtual network adapter options are: Not connected, External Network, and Internal Network. Not connected (the default) does not provide any type of connection so you can only access the virtual machine directly from the server. External Network means users can connect to the virtual machine through the computer's network interface card. Internal Network means that there can be a connection between the virtual machines on the same computer.

8. If you see a box to turn AutoComplete on (to remember your entries used in Web forms), select whether or not to use this feature by clicking **Yes** or **No**.

9. In the right pane, review the configuration information for your test server. Notice that you can use this pane to make changes to the configuration. (See the section that follows, "Configuring Networking and Hardware Options," for more information about configuring these options.)

10. So that you can access a window in which to use the virtual server, click **Server Properties** under Virtual Server in the left pane.

11. In the right pane, click **Virtual Machine Remote Control (VMRC) Server**.

12. Ensure that **VMRC server** is checked for **Enable** and that the TCP/IP address of the host server is entered. (If you have trouble connecting after entering the TCP/IP address of the host server, try leaving the TCP/IP address setting at "All unassigned.") Also, ensure that Authentication is set to **Automatic**. Remove the check mark from the **Enable** box for **Disconnect idle connections** (so you are not disconnected during the OS installation). Check the **Enable**

box for **Multiple VMRC connections** and check **Enable** for **SSL 3.0/TLS 1.0 encryption**. If necessary, set the SSL 3.0/TLS 1.0 certificate to **Keep** or **Request** (if Keep is disabled). Make sure that the host name is the same as the name of the computer you are using. Click **OK** in the lower-right corner of the window. (If you have any problems using VMRC Server, remember that you can come back to this screen to adjust any parameters.)

13. In the left pane, point to **Configure** under Virtual Machines and click the name of the virtual machine you created.

14. Next, you need to turn on the virtual machine. In the right pane, click the screen thumbnail for the virtual machine to turn on the virtual machine.

You might see a message that you need to configure Internet Explorer security to proceed. Make the necessary security configurations. Also, if you see a message from Internet Explorer to install an add-on, click the message and click Install ActiveX Control and follow the directions to continue.

15. Insert the Windows Server 2008 installation DVD.

16. If necessary, click the thumbnail again for the virtual machine. If you see a security message, click **Yes** to proceed.

17. Enter your user name and password (using an account with administrator privileges). Click **OK**.

18. If you see another security message, such as for NTLM Authentication, click **Yes** to proceed.

19. If necessary, scroll down to view the information for working in the Remote Control window. Notice the options to Pause, Save State, Turn Off, and Reset the virtual machine.

20. Scroll back to the top of the Remote Control window.

21. You should see a beginning installation screen for Windows Server 2008. Move the mouse pointer into that screen area (the mouse becomes a small black dot). Click in the area until you see the normal arrow for your mouse. Notice that you can work only within the console for the virtual machine. Press the **right ALT** key (the default host key) to be able to use the mouse throughout the Remote Control window. Remember that you can always use the right ALT key to leave the console area as needed. (Also, to work back inside the console, click the mouse pointer inside the console.) In the upper-right corner of the Remote Control portion of the window, click the down arrow for **Remote Control**. Review the options on the menu, such as Special Keys, Connect To Server, and the other options.

When you point to Special Keys, note that pressing the host key (the right ALT key) with the DEL key can be used to send the CTRL+ALT+DEL key sequence to the virtual machine (this is important to know later for logging in after you have installed Windows Server 2008).

22. Move the mouse pointer back into the console area and click it so that you can work in this area again. You can now proceed with the installation of Windows Server 2008.

23. In the Install Windows window, specify the language to install, such as **English,** in the Language to install drop-down box. In the Time and currency format box, make your selection, such as **English (United States)**. And in the Keyboard or input method box, make your selection, such as **US**. Click **Next**.

24. Click **Install now**.

If your connection stops before the installation is finished, use the left arrow at the top of the window to go back to the main Status window. Click the virtual machine thumbnail to open a new connection via the Remote Control window. Respond to any security messages, log back in, and respond to any additional security messages. The installation should still be running.

25. Select **Windows Server 2008 Enterprise (Full Installation)** (or select a different full installation edition, such as Standard Edition if it is available) and click **Next**.

26. Read the license terms, click the box for **I accept the license terms,** and click **Next**.

27. Click **Custom (advanced)**.

28. You'll see the amount of unallocated disk space highlighted, which is the disk space you specified when you configured the virtual machine. Ensure it is highlighted and click **Next**.

29. The installation program begins installing Windows Server 2008. You'll see progress information about Copying files, Expanding files, Installing features, Installing updates, and Completing installation. This process will take 30 minutes or more.

30. The installation program restarts the operating system.

31. You see the message: *Please wait while Windows sets up your computer*.

32. Next, you see the Install Windows window in the Completing installation phase.

33. The system reboots again.

34. You'll see the message (a red circle with a white x in it): *The user's password must be changed before logging on the first time*. Click the **OK** button (you might have to click inside the active portion of the console window first to have the mouse function within it).

35. Enter a new password for the Administrator account and then enter the same password again to confirm it. Click the **blue circle** with the white right-pointing arrow inside.

 If you enter a password that is not a strong password, you'll see the message: (with a white x in a red circle) *Unable to update the password*. This means that the value provided for the new password does not meet the length, complexity, or history requirements of the domain. Click OK and enter a different password that is over seven characters and uses letters, numbers, and characters such as &.

36. When you see the message, *Your password has been changed*, click **OK**.

37. At this point, the Windows desktop is opened and the Initial Configuration Tasks window is displayed. From here you can start configuring Windows Server 2008.

38. You can close the Remote Control window (the Virtual Machine Remote Control Server) or the Status window (the Virtual Server Administration Website) at any time. The virtual machine continues running in the background. Also, when in the Remote Control window, you can go back to the Administrator window by clicking the left-pointing arrow at the top of the Remote Control window.

 You can shut down a server by first logging on through the Remote Control window. Also, you can use this window and the Status window to turn off a virtual machine (but make sure you shut down the server first).

 To access the documentation for Microsoft Virtual Server, click Start, point to All Programs, click Microsoft Virtual Server, and click Virtual Server Administrator's Guide.

Installing an OS from an ISO Image

If you have an ISO image file for the guest operating system, you have the option to install it instead of performing a traditional installation through the installation DVD. Here are the general steps for installing an ISO image file in a virtual machine within Microsoft Virtual Server:

1. Follow Steps 1 through 13 in the previous section, "Creating a Virtual Machine and Installing a Guest OS."

2. The bottom portion of the right pane should now show the configuration options for the virtual machine.

3. Click the link for **CD/DVD.**

4. Under Virtual CD/DVD Drive 1, click the option button for **Known image files.** Next, click the **down arrow** for **Known image files** and select the image file. If the ISO image file is not listed, then enter the path to the ISO image file in the box for **Fully qualified path to file.**

5. Click **OK** (the display returns to the Master Status listing).

Configuring Networking and Hardware Options

The Microsoft Virtual Server Administration Website offers the ability to configure virtual networks. For example, as you learned earlier, a connected network has two default virtual network options: external network and internal network. You can customize settings for both types of networks, such as settings for a virtual DHCP server. You can also create a new virtual network with properties you define.

 A virtual network is one used by virtual machines within a network and is independent of other virtual networks. In Microsoft Virtual Server, the number of virtual machines connected to a virtual network is unlimited.

The Microsoft Virtual Server Administration Website also provides options to configure hardware settings, such as adding more memory for use by a virtual server. In the next sections, you learn how to configure virtual networking and to configure hardware for a virtual machine.

Configuring Virtual Networking In the following steps, you examine how to configure virtual networking:

1. Open the Microsoft Virtual Server Administration Website tool, if it is not open. (Click **Start,** point to **All Programs,** click **Microsoft Virtual Server,** and click **Virtual Server Administration Website.**)

2. In the left pane under Navigation, click **Master Status,** if necessary. Access each virtual server that is running (if any) and shut it down. To do this, point to the server name (that has a right-pointing arrow) under Virtual Machine Name in the right pane, click **Turn Off,** and click **OK.** (You can configure virtual networking while virtual machines are running, but it is advised to turn them off first.)

3. In the left pane under Virtual Networks, point to **Configure** and click **View All.**

4. In the right pane, point to **External Network (*NICname*)** and click **Edit Configuration.**

5. Review the information in the right pane.

6. In the right pane, click the link for **Network Settings.**

7. Review the properties information, including information about the NIC. Click **OK.**

8. In the right pane, click the link for **DHCP server.**

9. You can use the right pane to configure a virtual DHCP server that leases IP addresses through Microsoft Virtual Server (see Figure B-7). To enable the virtual DHCP server, check the **Enabled** box in the right pane. When you enable the virtual DHCP server, you can configure the following:

   - *Network address*—Enter the network address for the virtual network.

   - *Network mask*—Enter the network mask.

   - *Starting IP address*—Enter the beginning address for the range (scope) of IP addresses that can be leased.

   - *Ending IP address*—Enter the ending address for the range of IP addresses that can be leased.

   - *Virtual DHCP server address*—Enter the IP address of the virtual DHCP server.

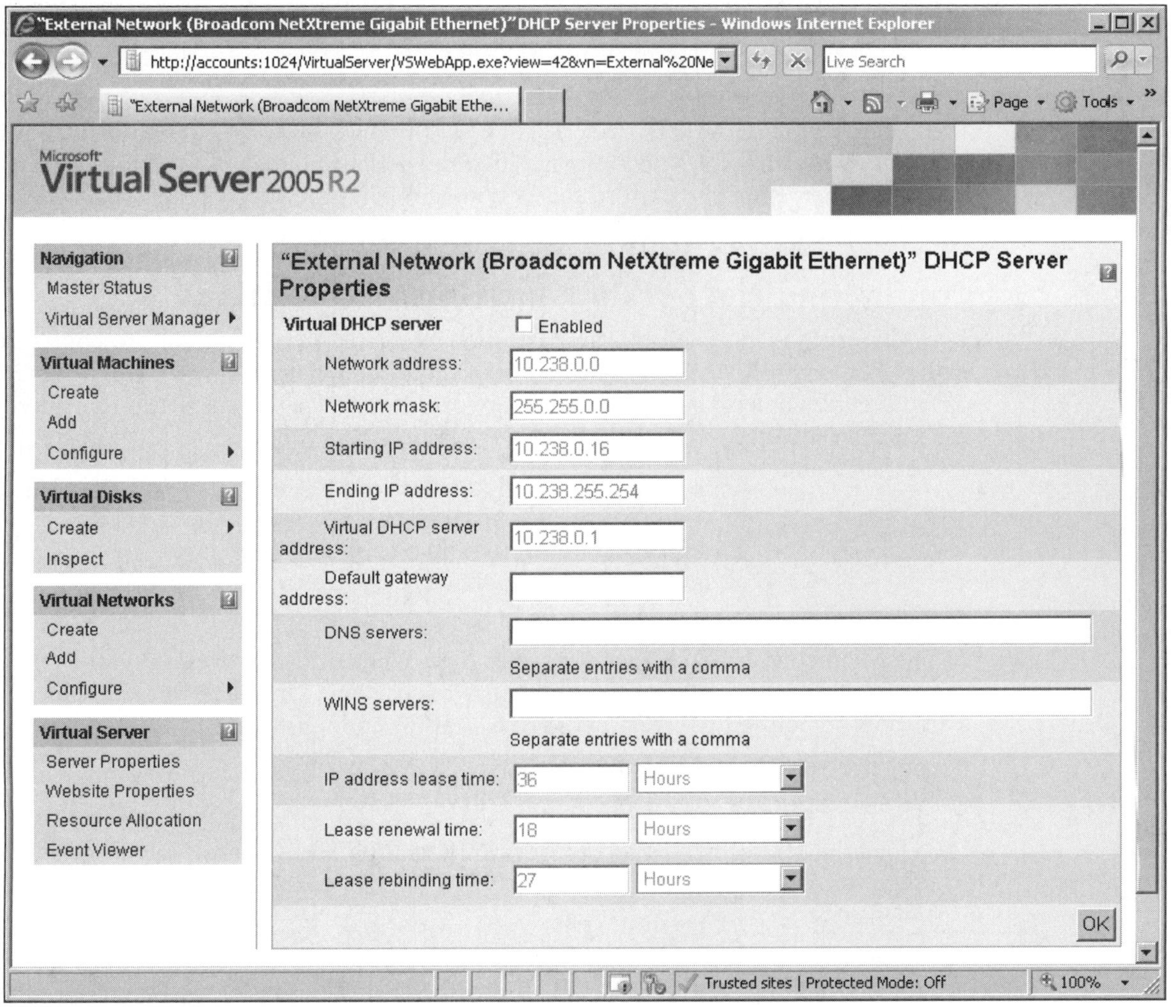

Figure B-7 Virtual DHCP server configuration options

- *Default gateway address*—Enter the IP address of a router that transports packets beyond the virtual network.
- *DNS servers*—Enter the IP address of one or more DNS servers already on the network.
- *WINS servers*—Enter the IP addresses of any Windows Internet Naming Service (WINS) servers (for converting NetBIOS computer names to IP addresses).
- *IP address lease time*—Enter the amount of time that an IP address can be leased, which can be set in days, hours, minutes, or seconds (typically you would set this for one or more days).
- *Lease renewal time*—Enter the amount of time in which the client can contact the virtual DHCP server to renew a lease (in days, hours, minutes, or seconds, but with a minimum of 30 seconds).
- *Lease rebinding time*—Enter the amount of time it takes to enable the client to contact another server to renew its lease, when the main leasing server cannot be reached (in days, hours, minutes, or seconds, but with a minimum of 45 seconds).

10. In the left pane under Virtual Networks, point to **Configure** and click **Internal Network**.

11. Review the information provided in the right pane for the virtual network properties.

12. Click **Network Settings** in the right pane and review the information provided.

13. Click the **back arrow** at the top of the window.

14. Click **DHCP Server** in the right pane and notice that you can enable a virtual DHCP server and configure it.

15. Leave the window open for the next set of steps.

Configuring Hardware for a Virtual Machine In addition to configuring a virtual network, you can configure hardware and other options for a virtual machine. In the following steps, you examine the options that can be configured:

 The virtual machine you select in the steps that follow should be turned off before you start.

1. Ensure that the Microsoft Virtual Server Administration Website tool is open.

2. In the left pane under Virtual Machines, point to **Configure** and click the name of the virtual server you have configured.

3. Scroll to the configuration section in the right pane. Review the options that can be configured, which include the following:
    - General properties
    - Virtual Machine Additions
    - Memory
    - Hard Disks
    - CD/DVD
    - SCSI adapters
    - Network adapters
    - Scripts
    - Floppy drive
    - COM ports
    - LPT ports

4. In the right pane, click **General properties**. If your computer supports hardware-assisted virtualization, notice that you can enable it here. You can also specify a user account under which to run the virtual machine, and you can specify what action to take when the Virtual Server stops. If you make changes, click the **OK** button in the lower-left side of the window.

5. Click the **back arrow** at the top of the window to return to the previous configuration display in the right pane.

6. In the right pane, click **Memory**. Now in the right pane you can change the amount of memory allocated to the virtual machine. If you make changes, ensure that you click the **OK** button.

7. Click the **back arrow** at the top of the window.

8. In the right pane, click the link for **Hard disks**. In the right pane, you see the configuration of the virtual disk used by the virtual machine. Notice the option to *Enable undo disks*. When you select this option, configuration and other changes on the virtual machine are saved so that you can undo those changes, if necessary. Also, notice that you can add a new virtual disk by clicking the Add disk button. If you make changes, remember to click the **OK** button so they take effect.

9. Click the **back arrow**.

10. Click **CD/DVD** in the right pane. In the right pane, you can click the Remove box to remove a CD/DVD drive, and you can click the Add CD/DVD Drive button to add a new drive. If you make changes, click **OK**.

11. Click the **back arrow**.

12. Click each of the remaining Configuration options in the right pane to view what they cover. In particular, notice that you can add NICs by using the Network adapters option.

13. Close the Microsoft Virtual Server Administration Website tool when you are finished (or restart your virtual server so it is in use).

Host Key Options

Microsoft Virtual Server designates the right ALT key as the default host key and offers host key options that are similar to those offered by Microsoft Virtual PC. Table B-2 lists important host key combinations you can use while you are accessing a virtual machine.

Table B-2   Host key options for Microsoft Virtual Server

Keyboard combination	Result
HostKey	Enables you to move the mouse outside of the window area used by the guest OS (move the mouse back into the guest OS display and click when you want to work on the guest OS)
HostKey+DEL	The virtual machine OS responds to this as CTRL+ALT+DEL
HostKey+C	Displays the Connect to server box for connecting to a specific virtual machine (or if you have selected text first, it can be used to copy the text)
HostKey+A	Toggles to the Administrator display window
HostKey+I	Shows the VMRC Connection Properties box with information about the connected virtual machine
HostKey+B	Provides information about the VMRC Client software
HostKey+V	Pastes text and items saved in the Clipboard into the active window in the guest OS
HostKey+H	Enables you to configure a different key as the host key

VMware Server

VMware Server enables you to set up virtual machines to run Windows or Linux operating systems. VMware Server version 2 is a significant update compared with previous 1.x versions. The new features of VMware Server 2 include the following:

- Ability to manage virtual machines from either the Web Access management interface or the non-Web-based VMware Remote Console
- Ability to configure different levels of permissions
- Ability to configure which operating systems will be started when VMware is started
- Editors for hardware devices
- New support for Windows Vista, Windows Server 2008, Red Hat Enterprise 5.0, and Ubuntu Linux up through version 8.x.
- Ability to handle increased memory (to 8 GB) and more NICs (up to 10) in the host machine
- Supports 64-bit guest operating systems on 64-bit (x64) host computers
- Hot-add capability for new SCSI and tape devices (without shutting down a virtual machine)

- Supports VSS for backups on Microsoft guest systems
- Enables use of Firefox 3 or Internet Explorer for the Web Access management interface
- Supports hardware virtualization, such as through AMD CPUs that have AMD-V capability and Intel CPUs with Intel VT
- Supports multiple monitors (to see different virtual machines on different displays)

VMware Server Guest Operating Systems Supported

VMware Server supports the following guest operating systems:

- Windows Server 2008 Standard, Enterprise, Datacenter, and Web Server (x86 or x64)
- Windows Server 2003 Standard, Enterprise, Datacenter, and Web Server with SP1 or SP2 (x86 or x64)
- Windows Server 2003 Standard, Enterprise, Datacenter, and Web Server R2 (x86 or x64)
- Windows Small Business Server 2003 (Standard and Premium Editions)
- Windows 2000 Server and Professional
- Windows XP Professional
- Windows Vista Business and Ultimate (x86 and x64)
- Red Hat Enterprise Linux Server and Desktop versions up through version 5 (x86 and x64)
- Ubuntu 6.x to 8.x
- SUSE Linux Enterprise Server up to 10.x (x86 and x64)
- SUSE Linux versions up to 10.x (x86 and x64)
- Novell NetWare
- Solaris

VMware Server Host Operating Systems Supported

VMware Server 2.x runs inside more different kinds of host operating systems than Microsoft Virtual PC or Server. This is because it can run on several different Linux distributions. It also runs on x86 and x64 computers. The list of VMware host operating systems includes the following:

- Windows Server 2008 Standard, Enterprise, Datacenter, and Web Server (x86 or x64)
- Windows Server 2003 Standard, Enterprise, Datacenter, and Web Server with SP1 or SP2 (x86 or x64)
- Windows Server 2003 Standard, Enterprise, Datacenter, and Web Server R2 (x86 or x64)
- Windows Small Business Server 2003 (Standard and Premium Editions)
- Windows 2000 Server and Professional with SP3 or SP4
- Windows XP Professional and Home through the current service pack
- Windows Vista Business and Ultimate (x86 and x64)
- Red Hat Enterprise Linux Server and Desktop versions up through version 5 (x86 and x64)
- Ubuntu 6.x to 8.x
- SUSE Linux Enterprise Server up to 10.x (x86 and x64)
- SUSE Linux versions up to 10.x (x86 and x64)
- Mandrake Linux up to 10.x

VMware Server also can run on other Windows and Linux distributions, such as other Windows Vista editions or Fedora Linux, but these should be considered as "experimental" because they might not be fully tested.

For Windows host operating systems, you must download the VMware Server version for Windows, which is in .exe format. For Linux host operating systems, you must download the VMware Server version for Linux, which is in .tar format.

Windows Server Core is not a supported host at this writing.

Requirements for VMware Server

VMware Server has the following hardware requirements:

- CPU—Any standard x86 or x64 computer, including the following processors: dual- or quad-core Intel Zeon, Intel Core 2, AMD Opteron or Athlon (733 MHz or faster)
- *RAM*—A minimum of 512 MB, but must include enough RAM for at least the minimum requirements of the total number of operating systems you'll be running (host and guest)
- *Disk space*—Enough disk storage for the operating systems you plan to run (host and guest)
- *Console Web Access*—Internet Explorer 6.0 or above (for Windows hosts) or Mozilla Firefox 2.0 or above (for Linux hosts)

VMware Server 2.x virtual machines can connect to hard, optical, and floppy drives. VMware 2.x also supports USB 2.x connections.

How to Download VMware Server

VMware Server can be downloaded from VMware's Web site at no cost. To download VMware Server:

1. Log on to your computer.
2. Establish a folder in which to store the download (such as a temporary folder or a folder under your Program Files folder).
3. Start your Web browser, such as Internet Explorer.
4. Go to the URL **www.VMware.com/products/server.**

Web links and specific instructions change periodically. You might need to search for the most current link at *www.VMware.com* if this link does not work.

5. Click **Download Now.**
6. Find the latest version of VMware Server (if multiple versions are listed) and click **Download** or **Download Now.**
7. If asked to provide registration information, complete the registration form.
8. Read the licensing information and click **Yes** or **Accept.**
9. Record the serial number for the Windows version (you'll need this later when you install VMware Server).
10. Click the link to download the Binary (.exe) file for VMware Server for Windows Operating Systems.
11. Click the **Save** button.

12. Select the folder you created in which to save the file.

13. Click **Save.**

14. Click **Close** in the Download Complete box.

15. Close your Web browser.

How to Install VMware Server

The general steps to install VMware Server into the host operating system are as follows:

1. If possible, connect to the Internet so that updates can be installed automatically during the installation process.

2. Browse to the folder in which you saved the install file for VMware Server.

3. Double-click **VMware-server-2.x.x-xxxxxx** (where 2.x.x-xxxxxx is the version of VMware Server).

4. You'll see a box noting it is preparing for the installation followed by the Windows Installer box.

5. When the Installation Wizard for VMware Server starts (see Figure B-8), click **Next.**

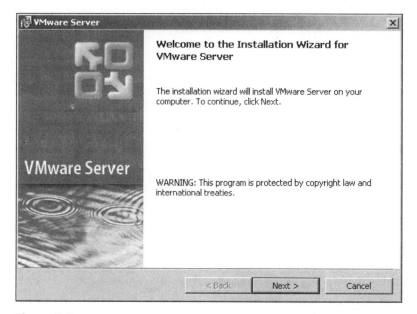

Figure B-8   VMware Server installation wizard

6. Read the license agreement, click **Yes, I accept the terms in the license agreement,** and click **Next.**

7. Verify that the VMware server files will be written to the appropriate destination folder (you can click the Change button to select a different destination). Click **Next.**

8. Verify the fully qualified domain name for the host computer, and verify that the Server HTTP (port 8222) and Server HTTPS (port 8333) Ports are selected by default. Make any changes as needed, such as to the host and domain names (leave the defaults for the ports). Click **Next.**

9. Ensure the desired shortcuts are selected, as shown in Figure B-9. Click **Next.**

10. Click **Install.**

11. You'll see a message that the installation might take several minutes.

12. If you see one or more boxes to install device software, click **Install.**

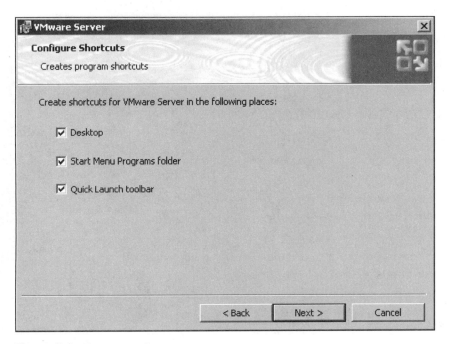

Figure B-9   Shortcut options

13. For the registration information, enter your name and the name of your company (or school), if appropriate. Next, enter the serial number you obtained when you downloaded the software. Click **Enter**.

14. Click **Finish**.

15. Ensure that all programs are closed and click **Yes** to restart the system.

Creating a Virtual Machine and Installing a Guest OS

Now that VMware Server is installed, the next step is to create a virtual machine and install the guest operating system. Here are the general steps using Windows Server 2008 as the guest:

 The VMware Remote Console that you use later in these steps requires that the VMware virtual server (host computer) be resolvable through Domain Name System (DNS). Before you start, make sure that your server can be resolved through DNS on your network (or that DNS is installed on the host). For example, there should be a host address (A) resource record in the DNS server for the host computer.

1. Double-click the **VMware Server Home Page** icon on the desktop or in the taskbar. (Alternatively, you can click **Start,** point to **All Programs,** click **VMware Server,** and click **VMware Server Home Page.**)

 You might need to resolve security requirements for Internet Explorer, such as providing a digital certificate, answering whether or not to set up a phishing filter, and adding this site to make it a trusted site. These are all issues related to Internet Explorer.

2. Log in using your host computer account name (or the administrator account) and provide the password. (Use the same account that you used to install VMware Server.)

3. You see the VMware Infrastructure Web Access window, as shown in Figure B-10.

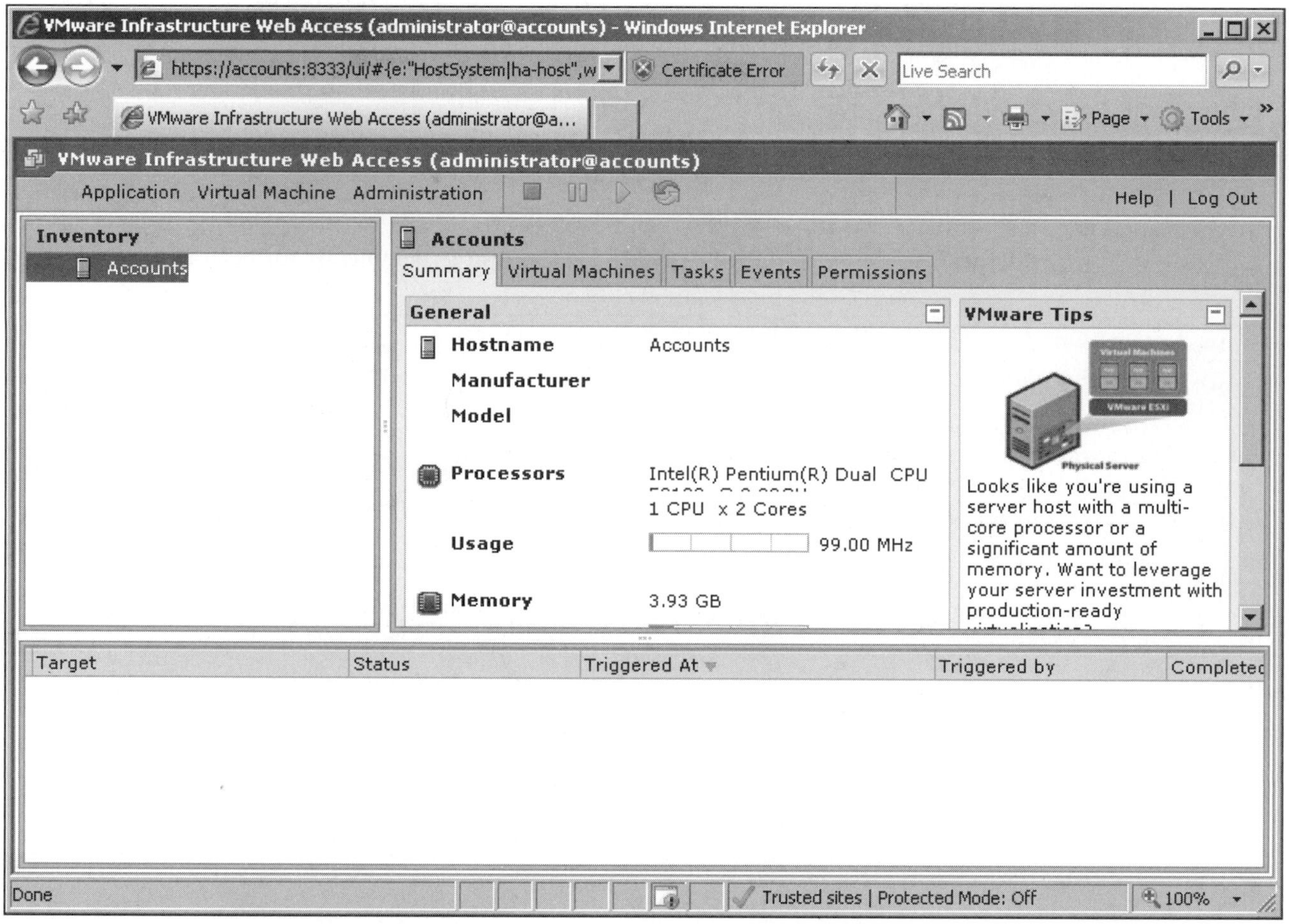

Figure B-10   VMware Infrastructure Web Access window

NOTE   Notice that there is a certificate error reported in Figure B-10, because this new site does not yet have a trusted certificate. If you experience this problem, you might be able to import a certificate by clicking the Certificate Error box at the top of the window, clicking the link for View certificates, and clicking Install Certificate. Another option is to talk to your network administrator about importing a certificate.

4. Ensure that your virtual server computer is highlighted in the left pane.

5. Click the **Virtual Machines** tab.

6. In the right pane under the Commands heading, click **Create Virtual Machine**.

7. Enter the name for the virtual machine and click **Next**.

8. Ensure that **Windows operating system** is selected for the type of guest operating system, select the operating system (in the Version box), and click **Next**.

9. Set the memory size to **512 MB** or higher (1024 MB is the default when installing Windows Server 2008). Also, if your system has a dual- or quad-core CPU or is an SMP system, you can select the number of processors to use. Notice, however, that you should not reconfigure the setting for number of processors after the virtual machine is set up. Click **Next**.

10. Select the virtual disk to use, such as by clicking **Create a New Virtual Disk** (a disk on the current computer). (The other option is to Use an Existing Virtual Disk, which is a disk on a shared drive or hard disk on a different computer.) Enter the capacity for the virtual

disk, such as **20 GB** (see Figure B-11). Adjust any parameters as needed, which include the following:

- *Location for the virtual disk file*—A file location other than the default
- *File Options*—Ability to allocate disk space now and ability to split the disk into two files
- *Disk Mode*—Ability to create independent disks not affected by snapshots
- *Virtual Device Node*—Ability to select the SCSI or IDE adapter and device
- *Policies*—Ability to optimize either for safety (the default) or for performance

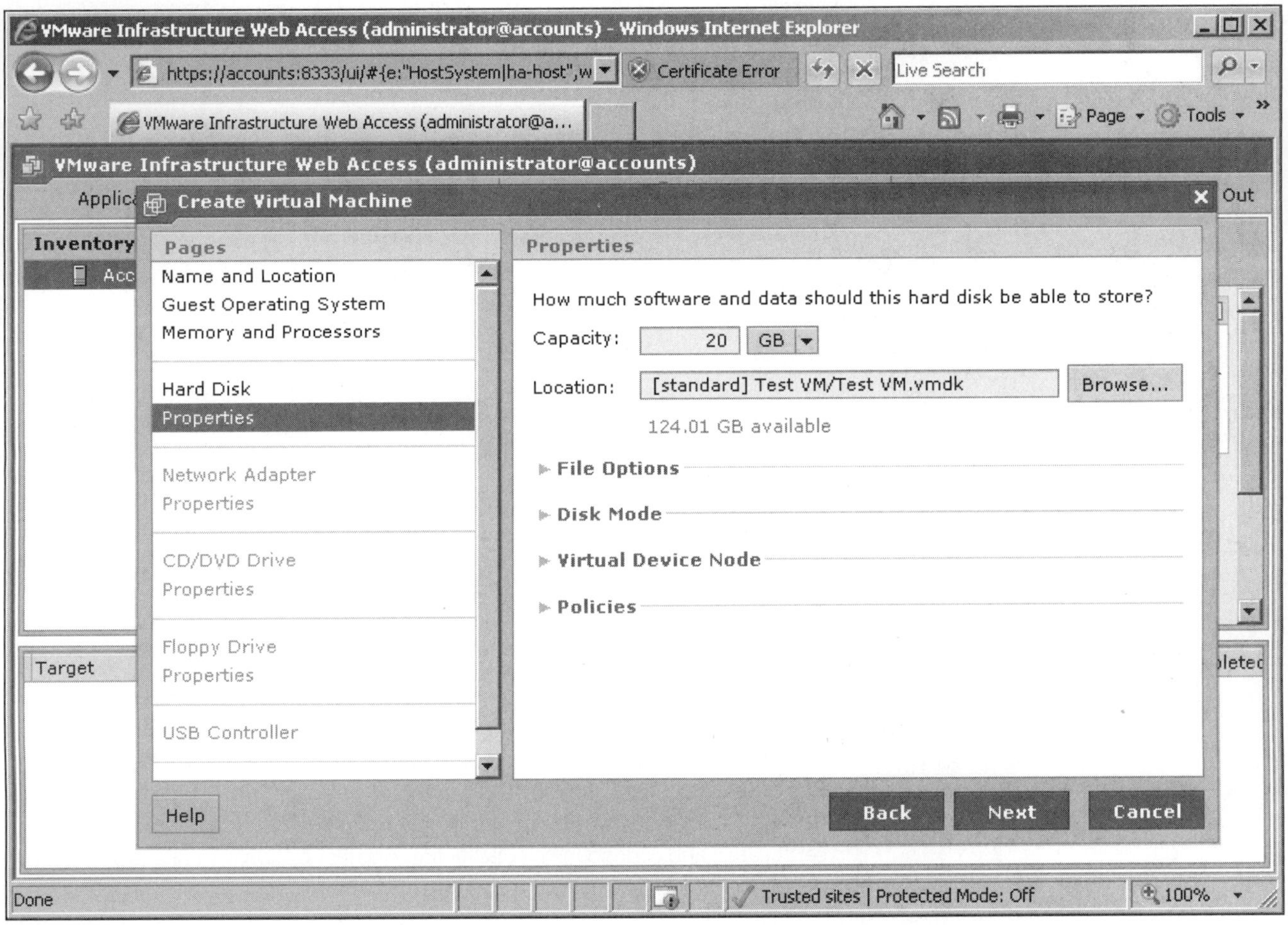

Figure B-11 Configuring virtual disk properties

11. Click **Next**.
12. In the next window, you can add a network adapter for access over a network. Click **Add a Network Adapter**. If you do not want to use the default settings for Network Connection (Bridged) and for Connect at Power On (Yes), configure those settings. The network settings that you can configure for the *Network Connection* parameter are as follows:

- *Bridged*—This setting gives the virtual machine its own network identity (so that it is seen as a different computer than the host), which enables other computers on the network to communicate with it. The bridged setting also means the virtual machine can access the Internet through the local network.
- *HostOnly*—With this setting, only the host computer and other virtual machines on the same host can access the virtual machine, which means the virtual machine is not accessible through the local network.

- *NAT*—The virtual machine and host use the same IP and MAC addresses, which means that the virtual machine does not have its own identity on the local network. This selection might be made if IP addresses are in short supply for the specific network or because an organization's network policy is to allow only one IP address for a specific computer.

13. Click **Next**.

14. You can configure whether to enable access to a CD/DVD drive or to use an ISO image for the installation of the operating system. For this sample set of steps, click **Use a Physical Drive**. Ensure that the correct CD/DVD drive is selected, such as drive E, and ensure that Connect at Power On is set to **Yes**. Click **Next**.

15. If your computer has a floppy drive, you can configure to use it to provide an image for the operating system. Select the appropriate configuration options (to install Windows Server 2008, click **Don't Add a Floppy Drive**). Click **Next,** if necessary. (Depending on your selection, you might need to configure additional properties.)

16. In the next window, you can configure whether to add a USB controller, such as to access a flash drive. Make your selection and click **Next,** if necessary.

17. Review your configuration selections and click **Finish**.

18. In the bottom pane, you should see Success under the Status column to show that you successfully created the virtual machine.

 In some cases, if you have selected different configuration options and then clicked the Back button to go back to the preceding steps, VMware Server might give you an error message or you might not end up with an installed virtual machine. If this happens, start from scratch and avoid undoing selections you have made.

19. Insert the Windows Server 2008 installation DVD.

20. In the left pane, click the new virtual machine name under the host server name (you might first have to expand the entries under the host server name).

21. Ensure that the **Summary** tab is selected in the right pane.

22. In the right pane, scroll to the Hardware section. Click the **down arrow** within the icon in front of CD/DVD Drive 1 (*drivetype*) and click **Edit**.

23. Review the preselected parameters for the host media (CD/DVD drive), make any needed changes, and click **OK**.

24. In the right pane, click the **Console** tab.

25. Click **Install plug-in** to install the Remote Console plug-in.

 If you see a box about noticing the Information Bar, click Close. Also, if the plug-in is not successfully installed in Internet Explorer, you might see a message at the top of the window that you must click to continue. Click the message and click to install the elements required by Internet Explorer, such as to Install the ActiveX Control. Next, click Install plug-in again, and, if necessary, click Install.

26. In the right pane, click **Powered off** (this is like a switch to turn on or off the virtual machine).

27. Click anywhere in the reduced console area in the right pane to start the console.

28. In the Install Windows window, specify the language to install, such as **English,** in the Language to install drop-down box. In the Time and currency format box, make your selection, such as **English (United States)**. In the Keyboard or input method box, make your selection, such as **US**. Click **Next**.

29. Click **Install now**.

30. Select **Windows Server 2008 Enterprise (Full Installation)** (or select a different full installation edition, such as Standard Edition if it is available) and click **Next**.

31. Read the license terms, click the box for **I accept the license terms,** and click **Next**.

32. Click **Custom (advanced)**.

33. You'll see the amount of unallocated disk space highlighted, which is the disk space you specified when you configured the virtual machine. Ensure it is highlighted and click **Next**.

34. The installation program begins installing Windows Server 2008. You'll see progress information about Copying files, Expanding files, Installing features, Installing updates, and Completing installation. This process takes 30 minutes or longer.

35. The installation program restarts the operating system.

36. You see the message: *Please wait while Windows sets up your computer.*

37. Next, you see the Install Windows window in the Completing installation phase.

38. The system reboots again.

39. You'll see the message (a red circle with a white x in it): *The user's password must be changed before logging on the first time.* Click the **OK** button (you might have to click inside the active portion of the console window first to have the mouse function within it).

40. Enter a new password for the Administrator account and then enter the same password again to confirm it. Click the **blue circle** with the white right-pointing arrow inside.

If you enter a password that is not a strong password, you'll see the message: (with a white x in a red circle) *Unable to update the password.* This means that the value provided for the new password does not meet the length, complexity, or history requirements of the domain. Click OK and enter a different password that is over seven characters and uses letters, numbers, and characters such as &.

41. When you see the message, *Your password has been changed,* click **OK**.

42. At this point, the Windows desktop is opened and the Initial Configuration Tasks window is displayed. From here you can start configuring Windows Server 2008 or log out and use the Remote Control window later to access Windows Server 2008.

43. You can close the VMware Remote Console window at any time (the virtual machine keeps running).

44. Close the VMware Infrastructure Web Access window when you are finished using it. (The virtual machine will also continue running, unless you shut it down in the VMware Remote Console window and power it off in the VMware Infrastructure Web Access window.)

You can access online help documentation while you are in the VMware Infrastructure Web Access window. Click the Help option near the upper-right corner of the window.

Installing an OS from an ISO Image

VMware Server supports installing an operating system via an ISO image file. The general steps for this type of installation are as follows:

1. Follow the steps to create a virtual machine.

2. In the left pane under Inventory of the VMware Infrastructure Web Access window, click the virtual server you have created.

3. Click the **Summary** tab in the right pane.

4. Scroll down the right pane to view the Hardware section.

5. Click the **down arrow** for the **CD/DVD Drive 1** section and click **Edit**.

6. Under the Connection section, click the option button for **ISO Image**.

7. Enter the optical disk image path or use the **Browse** option to find and select it.

8. If necessary, select the appropriate device node in the Virtual Device Node section.

9. Click **OK**.

10. Click the **Console** tab.

11. Power on the virtual machine, if necessary.

12. Click inside the console and follow the instructions from the operating system.

Configuring Networking Options

As you learned earlier, the three network connection options are Bridged, HostOnly, and NAT. Each of these types of networks has a default name as follows:

- Bridged is called VMnet0.
- HostOnly is called VMnet1.
- NAT is called VMnet8.

You can configure virtual networking, including VMnet0, VMnet1, and VMnet8, using the Virtual Network Editor tool. For example, you can configure to use the VMware internal DHCP server capability for HostOnly and NAT networks. Bridged networks use an external DHCP server, such as a Windows Server 2008 server configured for this service.

To explore the Virtual Network Editor tool:

1. Click **Start,** point to **All Programs,** click **VMware,** click **VMware Server,** and click **Manage-Virtual Networks.**

2. The Virtual Network Editor is a window with the following tabs (see Figure B-12):

   - *Summary*—Provides a summary of the virtual networks, including VMnet0, VMnet1, and VMnet8

   - *Automatic Bridging*—Controls bridging between the VMnet0 network and the network adapter

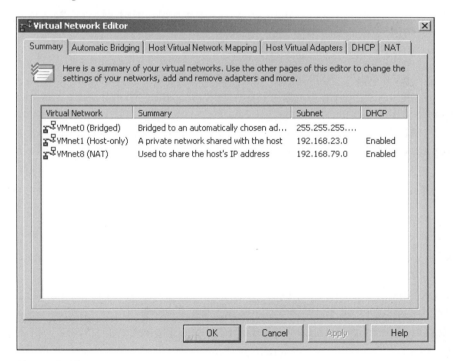

Figure B-12 Virtual Network Editor

- *Host Virtual Network Mapping*—Enables you to link virtual networks to physical network adapters and virtual network adapters, as well as configure subnet and DHCP properties

- *Host Virtual Adapters*—Shows virtual adapter connections, virtual networks, and the status of the connections

- *DHCP*—Enables you to configure DHCP for VMnet1 and VMnet8

- *NAT*—Enables you to control the NAT service and configure NAT settings

3. Click each of the tabs to view what it does.

4. Click the **DHCP** tab again.

5. Click **VMnet1** and click **Properties**.

6. In the DHCP Settings box, notice that you can configure the range of IP addresses to use (Start and Stop IP addresses). You can also configure the lease duration parameters for clients. Click **Cancel**.

7. Notice that you can start, stop, and restart the DHCP service from the DHCP tab.

8. Click the **NAT** tab. You can use this tab to associate the NAT service with a virtual network. Also, you can start, stop, and restart the NAT service from this tab.

9. Close the Virtual Network Editor when you are finished.

Configuring Hardware Options

After you set up a virtual machine, you might want to go back and configure hardware options. For example, you might change the configuration of the network and decide to go from a Bridged network to a HostOnly network.

The following steps enable you to configure hardware:

1. Open the VMware Infrastructure Web Access window, such as by clicking the VMware Server Home Page icon on your desktop.

2. In the left pane under Inventory, expand to view the virtual machines under the host server, if necessary.

3. Under Inventory, click the virtual machine you want to configure.

4. To configure hardware, you first need to ensure that the virtual machine is turned off. Use the Console tab to shut down the OS. Also, click **Virtual Machine** in the button bar and click **Power Off**.

5. In the right pane, click the **Summary** tab.

6. Scroll down in the right pane to view the Hardware section.

7. Click the down arrow for **Processors** and click **Edit**. You'll see a note that advises against changing the number of virtual processors, if you have more than one processor. Click **Cancel**.

8. Click the down arrow for **Memory** and click **Edit**. Notice the recommended size information for memory allocation. Also, you can use the Size (in multiples of 4) box to change the memory allocation. Click **Cancel**.

9. Click the down arrow for **Hard Disk 1** and click **Edit**. You can configure to increase the virtual disk capacity, configure the Virtual Device Node, configure the Disk Mode, and configure Policies. Click **Cancel**.

10. Click **Network Adapter 1** and click **Edit**. You can change the type of Network Connection, such as from Bridged to HostOnly. Information about the connection status, MAC address, and virtual device is also displayed. Click **Cancel**.

11. Click the down arrow for **CD/DVD Drive 1** and click **Edit**. Review the properties you can set and the connection status information. Click **Cancel**.

12. Review information about any other hardware devices.

13. Restart the virtual machine when you are finished.

Installing VMware Tools

VMware tools is an add-on that provides additional ways to manage a virtual machine and that can improve its performance. The elements of VMware tools include the following:

- *VMware Tools control panel* to conveniently change virtual machine settings and connect devices
- *VMware user processes* for Linux and Solaris guest operating systems
- *Device drivers* for enhanced video, audio, mouse, network, and SCSI disk performance
- *Tools service* that provides a variety of tools for messaging, mouse performance, screen resolution, and others

When you install the VMware tools, the virtual machine must be started and you should be logged on to the guest operating system account from which you manage the virtual server software. This is because the tools, including drivers, are installed into the guest operating system and you can access them from Control Panel in Windows Server 2008 (and other Windows operating systems).

To install the VMware tools:

1. Open the VMware Infrastructure Web Access window.
2. Click a virtual machine under Inventory in the left pane.
3. Ensure that the guest operating system is running and if it is not, start it. Log on to the Administrator account or an account that has Administrator privileges.
4. On the VMware Infrastructure Web Access window, click **Install VMware Tools** in the Status column of the right pane for the virtual machine.
5. Click **Install**.
6. Open the virtual machine console by clicking the **Console** tab and clicking inside the console.
7. It might take several minutes for the AutoPlay box to appear in the guest operating system desktop within the console. Click the option to **Run setup.exe**.
8. You'll see the Windows Installer box with the message, *Preparing to install*. This might take several minutes.
9. Click **Next** in the Welcome to the installation wizard for VMware Tools window (see Figure B-13).
10. Select the setup type option from the following options:
    - *Typical*—If you plan to use only VMware Server
    - *Complete*—If you plan to use VMware Server and other VMware products
    - *Custom*—If you want to choose the specific features to install
11. Click **Next**.
12. Click **Install**.
13. If you see the message *Windows can't verify the publisher of the driver software,* click the option **Install this driver software anyway**. (You might see this message several times.)
14. If you see a Windows Security box asking if you want to install this device software, click the box for **Always trust software from "VMware, Inc."**. Click **Install**.
15. Click **Finish**.
16. Save any work you have open on the virtual machine and click **Yes** to restart.
17. Log back on to the guest operating system in the console window.
18. In the guest operating system (Windows Server 2008), click **Start** and click **Control Panel**.
19. Click **Classic View** and click the new applet for **VMware Tools**.
20. You'll see the VMware Tools Properties dialog box, as shown in Figure B-14.

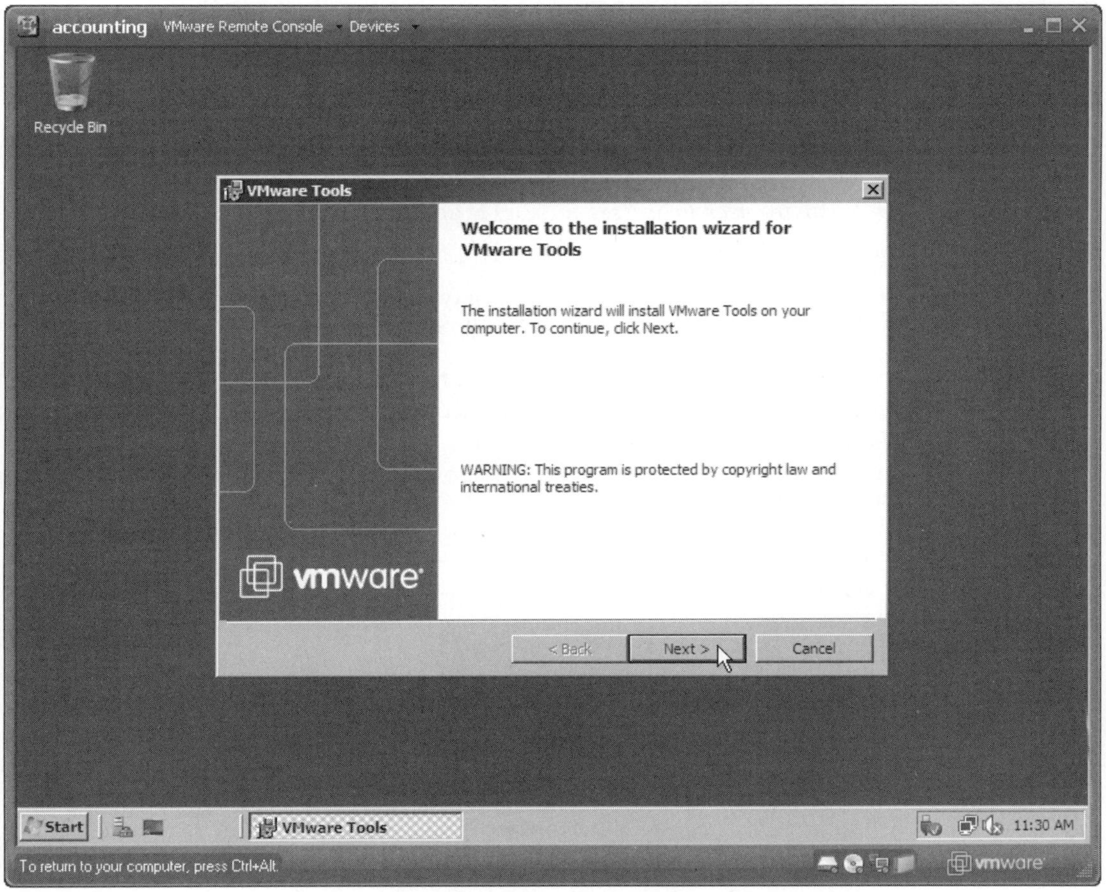

Figure B-13 Installation wizard for VMware Tools

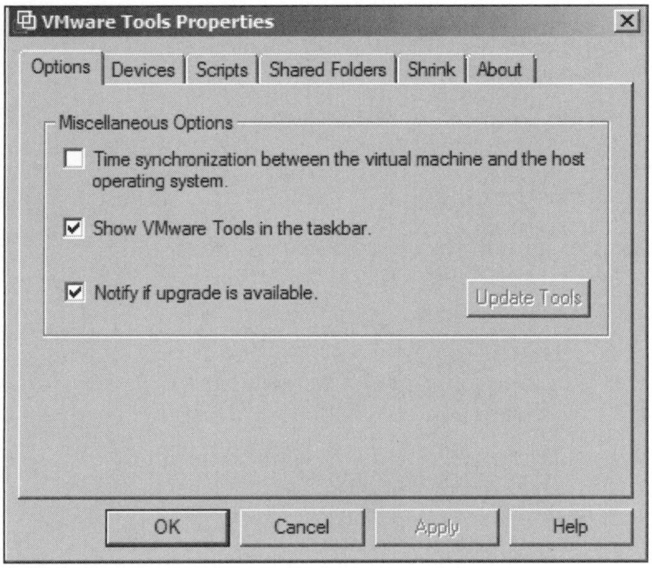

Figure B-14 VMware Tools Properties dialog box

21. Click each tab to see what it does.

22. Click the **Help** button to learn more about VMware Tools capabilities.

23. Close the VMware Tools Help window when you are finished with the Help feature.

24. Click **Cancel** to close the VMware Tools Properties dialog box.

25. Notice that a new icon is displayed in the guest operating system's taskbar in the tray near the clock, which can also be used to open the VMware Tools Properties dialog box.

26. Close Control Panel in the guest operating system.

Other Virtual Systems

This appendix has focused on virtualization systems that are free. Other systems are available at a cost and enjoy popular use. On the desktop side, VMware Workstation has grown in use along with desktop virtualization. Another system is Microsoft Hyper-V, which is new to Windows Server 2008. The following sections give you a brief overview of these systems, but are not intended to provide instructions about how to use them.

VMware Workstation

VMware workstation is popular among software developers and testers because it provides a safe environment in which to write and test development software before it is released to live production. It is also used by individuals who need to run multiple operating systems on one workstation-class computer, including legacy operating systems. This can be useful to enable a user to run old software without having to convert it for a new operating system. It's also useful for learning a new operating system.

VMware Workstation 6.04 (and above) supports Windows, Linux, and other operating systems as host and guest OSs. Newer operating systems supported as both hosts and guests include:

- Windows Server 2008 Standard, Enterprise, and Datacenter (x86 and x64)
- Windows Vista Home Basic, Home Premium, Enterprise, Business, and Ultimate (x86 and x64)
- Red Hat Enterprise Linux up to 4.6 (x86 and x64)
- Ubuntu Linux up to 7.10 (x86 and x64)
- SUSE Linux Enterprise Server 10 (x86 and x64)
- openSUSE Linux up to 10.3

VMware Workstation has several of the same new features as VMware Server, which include:

- Handles increased memory (to 8 GB)
- Supports 64-bit guest operating systems on 64-bit host computers
- Supports hardware virtualization, such as through AMD CPUs that have AMD-V capability and Intel CPUs with Intel VT
- Supports USB 2.0 (including on Linux operating systems)
- Supports multiple monitors (to see different virtual machines on different displays)

As with VMware Server, you can configure hardware for the virtual machine including multiple processors, memory, hard disks, USB access, floppy access, and other hardware elements. You can also configure to use Bridged, HostOnly, and NAT virtual networks. A virtual DHCP server can be configured when you use HostOnly and NAT virtual networking. Setting up a virtual machine is also accomplished through a step-by-step wizard.

Also, like VMware Server you can install VMware tools that include specialized drivers, such as drivers for enhanced video and audio functions for the guest operating system. VMware Workstation offers a console display for accessing the guest operating system that resembles the VMware Server console.

VMware Workstation is specifically designed for workstation host machines and offers a wider range of host and guest operating system compatibility than Microsoft Virtual PC (at this writing). You can download a 30-day free evaluation version at *www.vmware.com/products/ws*.

Microsoft Hyper-V

Microsoft Hyper-V was released just a few months after Windows Server 2008. Unlike the other virtualization systems discussed in this appendix, Microsoft Hyper-V is intended to run only on Windows Server 2008. It is loaded through the Windows Server 2008 Server Manager tool like any other role in Windows Server 2008. In this regard, Windows Server 2008 offers perhaps the smoothest installation process of any of the virtual systems discussed in this appendix. Also, unlike the other systems in this appendix, Hyper-V only runs on x64 computers, which means the host systems include only the following:

- Windows Server 2008 Standard Edition x64
- Windows Server 2008 Enterprise Edition x64
- Windows Server 2008 Datacenter Edition x64

 For a general introduction to server virtualization and the features and requirements of Hyper-V, see Appendix A, "Windows Server 2008 Virtualization."

You can purchase any of Windows Server 2008 Standard, Enterprise, or Datacenter Editions with Hyper-V (for an extra $28 at this writing) or you can purchase Hyper-V separately (also for $28). The low cost and seamless installation and integration with Windows Server 2008 are designed to make this virtualization system particularly appealing to Windows Server 2008 users.

The guest operating systems that can be installed in Hyper-V include:

- Windows Server 2008 Standard, Enterprise, Datacenter, and Web Server (x86 or x64)
- Windows Server 2003 Standard, Enterprise, and Datacenter (x86 or x64)
- Windows Server 2003 Web Edition
- Windows 2000 Server and Advanced Server with SP4
- Windows Vista Business, Enterprise, and Ultimate (x86 and x64)
- Windows XP Professional with SP2 or SP3 (x86)
- Windows XP Professional with SP2 (x64)
- SUSE Linux Enterprise Server 10 with SP1 or SP2 (x86 or x64)

After Hyper-V is installed as a server role, you can open the Hyper-V Manager as a Microsoft Management Console (MMC) snap-in or you can open it from the Administrative Tools menu—all steps familiar to Windows Server 2008 administrators. Use of Hyper-V Manager is relatively intuitive because it is designed in the same format as is used by most Windows Server 2008 administrative tools. For example, to create a new virtual machine, click the New option in the right pane of Hyper-V Manager and follow the steps provided by the New Virtual Machine Wizard.

To configure hardware and management settings for a virtual machine, click Settings under the name of the virtual machine in the right pane of Hyper-V Manager. The Settings window (see Figure B-15) enables you to add hardware, configure hardware, and configure management capabilities.

You can access the Virtual Network Manager from Hyper-V Manager to configure a virtual network. There are three types of virtual networks:

- *Private*—Offers communication only between virtual machines on the same virtual server
- *Internal*—Enables communication between virtual machines and the host virtual server
- *External*—Offers communication between virtual machines and the physical network (using a network adapter)

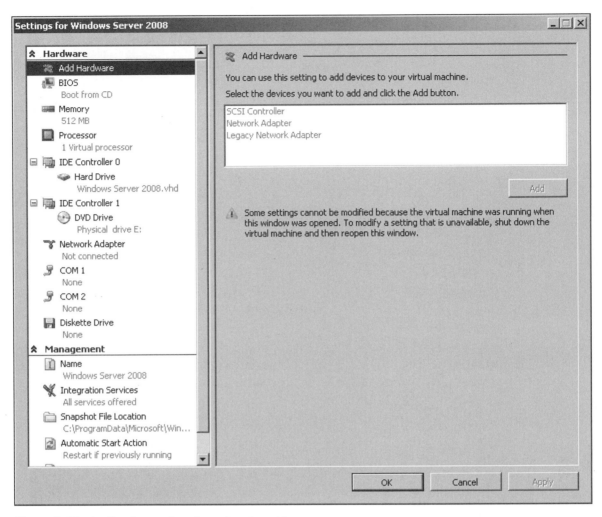

Figure B-15   Configuring settings for a virtual machine

For an external virtual network, you can specify a virtual LAN identification number. This is a unique number used for communications through the network adapter that distinguishes the virtual network from other networks.

The guest operating system appears in a console window that has an Action menu from which to send CTRL+ALT+DEL for logging on, and which can start, turn off, shut down, or pause a virtual machine (as well as other options). You also can expand the console to completely fill the desktop display. The console window can be started by clicking its thumbnail. When the console window opens, it provides a message about how to start the guest operating system.

At this writing, Hyper-V does not include as extensive a range of guest and host operating systems as other virtualization systems. However, it is a good fit with Windows Server 2008 environments and more guest operating systems likely will be added in the future. Windows Server 2008 administrators will find that installation and administration is very consistent with how other server roles are installed and administered.

Glossary

802.1X A wireless and wired port-based authentication standard offered by the IEEE.

access control list (ACL) A list of all security descriptors that have been set up for a particular object, such as for a shared folder or a shared printer.

access server A device that connects several different types of communications devices and telecommunication lines to a network, providing network routing for these types of communications.

Active Directory A central database of computers, users, shared printers, shared folders, other network resources, and resource groupings that is used to manage a network and enable users to quickly find a particular resource.

Active Directory Rights Management Services (AD RMS) A server role that works with client applications that can take advantage of RMS safeguards. *See* Rights Management Services (RMS).

active partition The partition from which a computer boots.

Address Resolution Protocol (ARP) A protocol in the TCP/IP suite that enables a sending station to determine the MAC or physical address of another station on a network.

admin log A type of event log that gives the system administrator information about a specific problem and its causes, and might also suggest how to solve the problem.

Advanced Encryption Standard (AES) A relatively new standard adopted by the U.S. government to replace DES and 3DES, and that employs a private-key block-cipher form of encryption.

aggregated links Linking two or more communications channels, such as ISDN channels, so that they appear as one channel, but with the combined speed of all channels in the aggregate.

analytic log An event log often used by application and system programmers to help analyze how specific programs are running and to identify problems with those programs.

application log An event log that records information about how software applications are performing.

assigning applications (or software) Means an application is automatically represented on the user's desktop, for example as a Start menu option or as an icon on the desktop, and which initially is really a link to a central application distribution server. The first time the user tries to open the application is the point at which it is fully installed from the distribution server and can be used from that point on.

asynchronous modem A modem from which communications occur in discrete units, and in which the start of a unit is signaled by a start bit at the front, and a stop bit at the back signals the end of the unit.

attribute A characteristic associated with a folder or file used to help manage access.

auditing In Windows Server 2008, a security capability that tracks activity on an object, such as reading, writing, creating, or deleting a file in a folder.

Automatic Private IP Addressing (APIPA) Windows Server 2008 supports Automatic Private IP Addressing (APIPA) to automatically configure the TCP/IP settings for a computer. The computer assigns itself an IP address in the range of 169.254.0.1–169.254.255.254, if a DHCP server is not available.

Bandwidth Allocation Control Protocol (BACP) Similar to BAP, but is able to select a preferred client when two or more clients vie for the same bandwidth. *See* Bandwidth Allocation Protocol (BAP).

Bandwidth Allocation Protocol (BAP) A protocol that works with Multilink in Windows Server 2008 to enable the bandwidth or speed of a remote connection to be allocated on the basis of the needs of an application, with the maximum allocation equal to the maximum speed of all channels aggregated via Multilink.

base priority class The initial priority assigned to a program process or thread in the program code.

basic disk In Windows Server 2008, a partitioned disk that can have up to four partitions and that uses logical drive designations. This type of disk is compatible with MS-DOS, Windows 3.x, Windows 95, Windows 98, Windows NT, Windows 2000, Windows XP, Windows Vista, and Windows Server 2003 and 2008.

basic input/output system (BIOS) A program on a read-only or flash memory chip that establishes basic communication with components such as the monitor and disk drives. The advantage of a flash chip is that you can update the BIOS.

benchmark (or baseline) A measurement standard for hardware or software used to establish performance measures under varying loads or circumstances.

bidirectional printing The ability of a parallel printer to conduct two-way communication between the printer and the computer, such as to provide out-of-paper information; also, bidirectional printing supports Plug and Play and enables an operating system to query a printer about its capabilities.

BitLocker Drive Encryption A security measure for protecting hard drives in Windows Vista Enterprise and Ultimate as well as Windows Server 2008. It can use a TPM chip on a computer or a flash drive with a

PIN to enforce security. *See* Trusted Platform Module (TPM).

boot partition Holds the Windows Server 2008 \Windows folder containing the system files.

bridgehead server A domain controller at each Active Directory site with access to a site network link, which is designated as the DC to exchange replication information. There is only one bridgehead server per site. *See* site.

broadcast A message sent to all computers on a network (but usually blocked to other networks by a router).

cable modem A digital modem device designed for use with the cable TV system, providing high-speed data transfer.

Challenge Handshake Authentication Protocol (CHAP) An encrypted handshake protocol designed for standard IP- or PPP-based exchange of passwords. It provides a reasonably secure, standard, cross-platform method for sender and receiver to negotiate a connection.

CHAP with Microsoft extensions (MS-CHAP) A Microsoft-enhanced version of CHAP that can negotiate encryption levels and that uses the highly secure RSA RC4 encryption algorithm to encrypt communications between client and host.

CHAP with Microsoft extensions version 2 (MS-CHAP v2) An enhancement of MS-CHAP that provides better authentication and data encryption and that is especially well suited for VPNs.

client A computer that accesses resources on another computer via a network or direct cable connection.

client access license (CAL) A license to enable a workstation to access a Windows Server.

clustering The ability to increase the access to server resources and provide fail-safe services by linking two or more discrete computer systems so they appear to function as though they are one.

cmdlet A command-line tool available in Windows PowerShell. *See* Windows PowerShell.

COM+ An enhancement to COM that enables publishing and subscriber services for applications, load balancing, and other services.

community A group of hosts that share the same SNMP services.

community name In SNMP communications, a rudimentary password (name) used by network agents and the network management station (or software) in the same community so that their communications cannot be easily intercepted by an unauthorized workstation or device.

compiler A program that reads lines of program code in a source file and converts the code into machine-language instructions the computer can execute.

Component Object Model (COM) A set of standards for building software from individual objects or components; COM provides the basis for Object Linking and Embedding (OLE) and ActiveX, for example.

Compressed Serial Line Internet Protocol (CSLIP) A newer version of SLIP that compresses header information in each packet sent across a remote link. *See* Serial Line Internet Protocol (SLIP).

connection-oriented communication Also called a connection-oriented service, this service provides several ways to ensure that data is successfully received at the destination, such as requiring an acknowledgement of receipt and using a checksum to make sure the packet or frame contents are accurate.

connectionless communication Also called a connectionless service, a communication service that provides no checks (or minimal checks) to make sure that data accurately reaches the destination node.

container An Active Directory object that houses other objects, such as a tree that houses domains or a domain that houses organizational units.

contiguous namespace A namespace in which every child object has a portion of its name from its parent object.

counter Used by Performance Monitor, a measurement technique for an object, for example, for measuring the processor performance by percentage in use.

custom backup Enables you to configure backups differently for each volume, using either a full backup or an incremental backup.

data collector set A combination of techniques for gathering performance and diagnostic data that is rendered in a report or log format. The basic data gathering techniques can be one or a combination of performance counters, event traces, and system configuration data.

Data Encryption Standard (DES) A data encryption method developed by IBM and the National Security Agency in cooperation with the National Bureau of Standards (now called the National Institute of Standards and Technology) as an encryption technique using a secret key between the communicating stations. Triple DES (3DES) employs three secret keys combined into one long key.

Data Execution Prevention (DEP) A security feature that monitors how programs use memory and stops programs that attempt to use memory allocated for system programs and processes. This is intended to foil viruses, Trojan horses, and worms that attempt to invade system memory.

data type The way in which information is formatted in a print file.

debug log An event log used by application developers to help trace problems in programs so they can fix program code or program structures.

default gateway The IP address of the router that has a connection to other networks. The default gateway address is used when the host computer you are trying to contact exists on another network.

defragmenting A software process that rearranges data to fill in the empty spaces that develop on disks and makes data easier to obtain.

demilitarized zone (DMZ) A portion of a network that is relatively less secure because it is between two networks, such as between a private network and the Internet.

Device Specific Module (DSM) A software interface between the Multipath I/O capability in Windows Server 2008 and the hard disk hardware.

DFS topology Applies to a domain-based DFS model and encompasses the DFS namespace root, shared folders, and replication folders.

dial-up networking Using a telecommunications line and a modem to dial in to a network or specific computers on a network via a modem at the other end.

digital certificate A set of unique identification information that is typically put at the end of a file, or that is associated with a computer communication. Its purpose is to show that the source of the file or communication is legitimate.

digital subscriber line (DSL) A technology that uses advanced modulation technniques on regular telephone lines for high-speed networking at speeds of up to about 52 Mbps between subscribers and a telecommunications company.

directory service A large container (database) of network data and resources, such as computers, printers, user accounts, and user groups, that enables management and fast access to those resources.

Directory Service Client (DSClient) Microsoft software for pre-Windows 2000 clients that connect to Windows 2000 Server, Windows Server 2003, and Windows Server 2008 and enables those clients to view information published in Active Directory.

discretionary access control list (DACL) An access control list that manages access to an object, such as a folder, and that is configured by a server administrator or owner of the object.

disjointed namespace A namespace in which the child object name does not resemble the parent object name.

disk duplexing A fault-tolerance method similar to disk mirroring in that it prevents data loss by duplicating data from a main disk to a backup disk; but disk duplexing places the backup disk on a different controller or adapter than is used by the main disk.

disk mirroring A fault-tolerance method that prevents data loss by duplicating data from a main disk to a backup disk. Some operating systems also refer to this as disk shadowing.

disk quota Allocating a specific amount of disk space to a user or application with the ability to ensure that the user or application cannot use more disk space than is specified in the allocation.

Distributed File System (DFS) A system that enables folders shared from multiple computers to appear as though they exist in one centralized hierarchy of folders instead of on many different computers.

distribution group A list of users that enables one e-mail message to be sent to all users on the list. A distribution group is not used for security and thus cannot appear in an access control list (ACL).

DNS dynamic update protocol A protocol that enables information in a DNS server to be automatically updated in coordination with DHCP.

domain A grouping of resource objects—for example, servers, computers, and user accounts—to enable easier centralized management of these objects. On Windows Server 2008 networks, a domain is contained within Active Directory as a higher-level representation of how a business, school, or government agency is organized.

domain controller (DC) A Windows Server 2003 or 2008 server that contains a full copy of the Active Directory information, is used to add a new object to Active Directory, and replicates all changes made to it so the changes are updated on every DC in the same domain.

domain functional level Refers to the Windows Server operating systems on domain controllers and the domain-specific functions they support. Depending on the functional level, one, two, or all of the following operating systems are supported: Windows 2000 Server, Windows Server 2003, and Windows Server 2008.

domain local security group A group that is used to manage resources—shared folders and printers, for example—in its home domain, and that is primarily used to give global groups access to those resources.

Domain Name System (DNS) Also called Domain Name Service, a TCP/IP application protocol that enables a DNS server to resolve (translate) domain and computer names to IP addresses, or IP addresses to domain and computer names.

domain-based DFS model A DFS model that uses Active Directory and is available only to servers and workstations that are members of a particular domain. The domain-based model enables a deep, root-based, hierarchical arrangement of shared folders that is published in Active Directory. DFS shared folders in the domain-based model can be replicated for fault tolerance and load balancing.

dotted decimal notation An addressing technique that uses four octets, such as 10000110.11011110. 01100101.00000101, converted to decimal (e.g., 134.222.101.5) to differentiate individual servers, workstations, and other network devices.

driver signing A digital signature incorporated into driver and system files as a way to verify the files and to ensure that they are not inappropriately overwritten.

DSL adapter A digital communications device that links a computer (or sometimes a router) to a DSL tele-communications line.

dynamic addressing An IP address that is automatically assigned to a client from a general pool of available addresses and that might be assigned each time the client is started, or it might be assigned for a period of days, weeks, months, or longer.

dynamic disk In Windows Server 2008, a disk that does not use traditional partitioning, which means that there is no restriction to the number of volumes that can be set up on one disk or to the ability to extend volumes onto additional physical disks. Dynamic disks are only compatible with Windows Server 2008, Windows Server 2003, and Windows 2000 Server platforms.

Dynamic Domain Name System (DDNS) A form of DNS that enables client computers to update DNS registration information so that this does not have to be done manually. DDNS is often used with DHCP servers to automatically register IP addresses on a DNS server.

Dynamic Host Configuration Protocol (DHCP) A network protocol that provides a way for a server to automatically assign an IP address to a workstation on its network.

Dynamic Host Configuration Protocol for IPv6 (DHCPv6) A version of DHCP that can be used with IPv6 implementation on a network.

dynamic-link library (DLL) files A library of files containing program code that can be called and run by Windows applications (and with SUA, also used by UNIX/Linux applications). *See* Subsystem for UNIX-based Applications (SUA).

Encrypting File System (EFS) Set by an attribute of NTFS, this file system enables a user to encrypt the contents of a folder or a file so that it can only be accessed via private key code by the user who encrypted it. EFS adheres to the Data Encryption Standard's expanded version for data protection.

enhanced metafile (EMF) A data type for printing used by Windows 95, 98, Me, NT, 2000, XP, Vista, Server 2003, and Server 2008 operating systems. EMF print files offer a distinct advantage in Windows operating system environments because they are very portable from computer to computer.

event logs Logs that you can view through Event Viewer that record information about server events, such as errors, warnings, or informational events.

extended partition A partition that is created from unpartitioned free disk space and is linked to a primary partition in order to increase the available disk space.

Extensible Authentication Protocol (EAP) An authentication protocol employed by network clients that uses special security devices such as smart cards, token cards, and others that use certificate authentication.

Extensible Firmware Interface (EFI) A firmware alternative to BIOS that includes the use of GPT disks. *See* Globally Unique Identifier (GUID) Partition Table or GPT.

fault tolerance Techniques that employ hardware and software to provide assurance against equipment failures, computer service interruptions, and data loss.

fault tolerant memory sync Enables memory to resynchronize after transient memory problems so there is no interruption to current computing activities.

Fibre Channel A subnetwork technology used primarily for SANs that enables gigabit high-speed data transfers. *See* Storage Area Network (SAN).

File Transfer Protocol (FTP) A TCP/IP application protocol that transfers files in bulk data streams and that is commonly used on the Internet.

folder target A path in the Universal Naming Convention (UNC) format, such as to a DFS shared folder or to a different DFS path.

forest A grouping of Active Directory trees that each have contiguous namespaces within their own domain structure, but that have disjointed namespaces between trees. The trees and their domains use the same schema and global catalog.

forest functional level A forest-wide setting that refers to the types of domain controllers in a forest, which can be any combination of Windows 2000 Server,

Windows Server 2003, or Windows Server 2008. The level also reflects the types of Active Directory services and functions supported.

formatting A process that prepares a hard disk partition for a specific file system.

forward lookup zone A DNS zone or table that maps computer names to IP addresses.

fragmented Having files spread throughout a disk with empty pockets of space between files; a normal and gradual process in the functioning of an operating system, addressed by using a defragmentation utility.

frame A unit of data that is transmitted on a network that contains control and address information, but not routing information.

frame relay A WAN communications technology that relies on packet switching and virtual connection techniques to transmit at rates from 56 Kbps to 45 Mbps.

full backup A backup of an entire system, including all system files, programs, and data files.

global catalog A repository for all objects and the most frequently used attributes for each object in all domains. Each forest has a single global catalog that can be replicated onto multiple servers.

global security group A group that typically contains user accounts from its home domain, and that is a member of domain local groups in the same or other domains, so as to give that global group's member accounts access to the resources defined to the domain local groups.

globally unique identifier (GUID) A unique number, up to 16 characters long, that is associated with an Active Directory object.

Globally Unique Identifier (GUID) Partition Table or GPT A method for partitioning disks that allows for theoretically unlimited partitions and use of larger disks. In Windows Server 2008, the maximum number of partitions on a GPT disk is 128, and the maximum partition size is up to 18 exabtyes.

graphics device interface (GDI) An interface on a Windows network print client that works with a local software application, such as Microsoft Word, and a local printer driver to format a file to be sent to a local printer or a network print server.

group policy A set of policies that govern security, configuration, and a wide range of other settings for objects within containers in Active Directory.

Group Policy Object (GPO) An object in Active Directory that contains group policy settings for a site, domain, OU, or local computer.

handle A resource, such as a file, used by a program that has its own identification so the program is able to access it.

hard link Enables you to create one file and then establish links to that file in other folders, as though the file is in all of the folders.

Health Registration Authority (HRA) A server that network clients contact to provide their Statement of Health (SoH). On the basis of the SoH, the HRA server grants a certificate to enable the client to use network services. *See* Statement of Health (SoH).

help desk system Application software designed to maintain information on computer systems, user questions, problem solutions, and other information that members of an organization can reference.

hive A set of related Registry keys and subkeys stored as a file.

home directory or home folder A server folder that is associated with a user's account and that is a designated workspace for the user to store files.

host address (A) resource record A record in a DNS forward lookup zone that consists of a computer or domain name correlated to an IP version 4 (or 32-bit) address.

hot-add memory Memory that can be added without shutting down the computer or operating system.

hot-add processor The ability to add a processor to an empty processor slot on a multiprocessor system while the system is running.

hot-replace processor The ability to replace a processor in an SMP system without taking the system down.

Hyper-V Virtualization software developed by Microsoft that can be included with most versions of Windows Server 2008. *See* virtualization.

Hypertext Transfer Protocol (HTTP) A protocol in the TCP/IP suite of protocols that is used to transport Hypertext Markup Language (HTML) documents and other data transmissions over networks and the Internet for access by Web-compliant browsers.

Hypertext Transfer Protocol Secure (HTTPS) A secure form of HTTP that uses Secure Sockets Layer to implement security.

I/O address The address in memory through which data is transferred between a computer component and the processor.

incremental backup Backs up only files that are new or that have been updated.

inherited permissions Permissions of a parent object that also apply to child objects of the parent, such as to subfolders within a folder.

inherited rights User rights that are assigned to a group and that automatically apply to all members of that group.

instance An individual occurrence of an element that is being monitored in Performance Monitor; exists when two or more types of elements can be monitored, such as two or more threads or disk drives.

Integrated Services Digital Network (ISDN) A telecommunications standard for delivering data services over digital telephone lines with a current practical limit of 1.536 Mbps and a theoretical limit of 622 Mbps.

Internet Authentication Service (IAS) Used to establish and maintain security for RAS, Internet, and VPN dial-in access, and can be employed with RADIUS. IAS can use certificates to authenticate client access.

Internet Information Services (IIS) A Microsoft Windows Server component that provides Internet, Web, FTP, mail, and other services to make the server into a full-featured Web server.

Internet Printing Protocol (IPP) A protocol that is encapsulated in HTTP and that is used to print files over the Internet.

Internet Protocol (IP) The Internet layer protocol responsible for addressing packets so that they are delivered on the local network or across routers to other networks or subnets.

Internet Protocol Version 4 (IPv4) The most commonly used version of IP, which has been in use for many years. IPv4 has a limitation in that it was not designed to anticipate the vast numbers of networks and network users currently in existence.

Internet Protocol Version 6 (IPv6) The newest version of IP that is designed for enhanced security and that can handle the addressing needs of growing networks.

Internet Server Application Programming Interface (ISAPI) A group of dynamic link library (DLL) files that consist of applications and filters to enable user-customized programs to interface with IIS and to trigger particular programs, such as a specialized security check or a database lookup.

Internet Small Computer System Interface (iSCSI) A high-speed technology used in SANs that employs TCP/IP communications and SCSI disk drives. *See* Storage Area Network (SAN).

interrupt request (IRQ) line A hardware line that a computer component, such as a disk drive or serial port, uses to communicate to the processor that it is ready to send or receive information. Intel-based computers have 16 IRQ lines, with 15 available for computer components to use.

IP address A logical address assigned to each host on an IP network. It is used to identify a specific host on a specific network.

IP Security (IPsec) A set of IP-based secure communications and encryption standards created through the Internet Engineering Task Force (IETF).

IPv6 host address (AAAA) resource record A record in a DNS forward lookup zone that consists of a computer or domain name mapped to an IP version 6 (or 128-bit) address.

journaling The process of keeping chronological records of data or transactions so that if a system crashes without warning, the data or transactions can be reconstructed or backed out to avoid data loss or information that is not properly synchronized.

Kerberos A security system developed by the Massachusetts Institute of Technology to enable two parties on an open network to communicate without interception from an intruder, by creating a unique encryption key for each communication session.

Kerberos transitive trust relationship A set of two-way trusts between two or more domains (or forests in a forest trust) in which Kerberos security is used.

kernel An essential set of programs and computer code that allows a computer operating system to control processor, disk, memory, and other functions central to its basic operation.

Layer Two Tunneling Protocol (L2TP) A protocol that transports PPP over a VPN, an intranet, or the Internet. L2TP works similarly to PPTP, but uses an additional network communications standard, called Layer Two Forwarding, that enables forwarding on the basis of MAC addressing. *See* Point-to-Point Tunneling Protocol (PPTP).

leased lines Telecommunications lines or bandwidth on telecommunications lines that can be leased from a telecommunications company.

load balancing On a single server, distributing resources across multiple server disk drives and paths for better server response; and on multiple network servers, distributing resources across two or more servers for better server and network performance.

local area network (LAN) A network of computers in relatively close proximity, such as on the same floor or in the same building.

local print device A printer, such as a laser printer, physically attached to a port on the local computer.

local security group A group of user accounts that is used to manage resources on a stand-alone computer.

local user profile A desktop setup that is associated with one or more accounts to determine what startup programs are used, additional desktop icons, and other customizations. A user profile is local to the computer in which it is stored.

logical unit number (LUN) A number that identifies a physical SCSI drive or logical SCSI targets (which can be volumes, IP addresses, adapter ports, and other connections depending on the SAN technology). *See* Small Computer System Interface (SCSI).

mandatory user profile A user profile set up by the server administrator that is loaded from the server to the client each time the user logs on; changes that the user makes to the profile are not saved.

Master Boot Record (MBR) Data created in the first sector of a disk, containing startup information and information about disk partitions.

media access control (MAC) address Also called a physical or device address, the hexadecimal number permanently assigned to a network interface, and used by the MAC sublayer (a communications sublayer for controlling how computers share communications on the same network).

member server A server on an Active Directory managed network that is not installed to have Active Directory.

Microsoft Point-to-Point Encryption (MPPE) A starting-to-ending-point encryption technique that uses special encryption keys varying in length from 40 to 128 bits.

Microsoft Virtual Network Switch Protocol Used with the Hyper-V role at the server's network interface card(s) (NICs) to bind or associate the virtual network services to the NICs and enable the use of a virtual switch between the parent partition containing the main operating system, Windows Server 2008, and child partitions containing other operating systems.

mirrored volume Two dynamic disks that are set up for RAID level 1 so that data on one disk is stored on a redundant disk.

modem A modulator/demodulator that converts a transmitted digital signal to an analog signal for a telephone line. It also converts a received analog signal to a digital signal for use by a computer.

mounted drive A physical disk, CD/DVD, removable drive, or other drive that appears as a folder and that is accessed through a path like any other folder.

multicast A single message is sent from one location and received at several different locations that are subscribed to receive that message.

Multilink or Multilink PPP (MPPP) A capability of a remote access server to aggregate multiple data streams into one logical network connection for the purpose of using more than one modem, ISDN channel, or other communications line in a single logical connection.

multimaster replication Windows Server 2003 and 2008 networks can have multiple servers called DCs that store Active Directory information and replicate it to each other. Because each DC acts as a master, replication does not stop when one DC is down, and updates to Active Directory continue, for example creating a new account.

Multipath I/O A set of drivers in Windows Server 2008 that can be used with device and network architecture to set up multiple paths between a server and its disk storage to achieve fault tolerance.

multitasking The capability of a computer to run two or more programs at the same time.

multithreading Running several program processes or parts (threads) at the same time.

name resolution A process used to translate a computer's logical or host name into a network address, such as to a dotted decimal address associated with a computer—and vice versa.

namespace A logical area on a network that contains directory services and named objects, and that has the ability to perform name resolution.

namespace root The main container that holds DFS links to shared folders in a domain.

NetBIOS name A name or identifier used in older Windows systems to uniquely identify a computer.

network A communications system that enables computer users to share computer equipment, software, and data, voice, and video transmissions.

Network Access Protection (NAP) A collection of security protection features that monitor and manage a server and its clients so that access to network and server resources is carefully controlled to match security policies.

Network Address Translation (NAT) Used by Microsoft Routing and Remote Access Services and by firewalls, NAT translates IP addresses on an internal or local network so that the actual IP addresses cannot be determined on the Internet, because the address seen on the Internet is a decoy address.

network interface card (NIC) An adapter board or device to connect a workstation, server, or other network device to a network medium. The connection can be wired or wireless.

Network Level Authentication (NLA) A security method that enables authentication to take place before a Terminal Services connection is established and that involves verifying the user account, client computer, and network server.

network print device A printing device, such as a laser printer, connected to a print server through a network.

New Technology File System (NTFS) The file system that is native to Windows Server systems and that supports features such as security, compression, disk quotas, encryption, self-healing from disk damage, and others.

object A network resource, such as a server or a user account, that has distinct attributes or properties, is defined in a domain, and exists in Active Directory.

Open Database Connectivity (ODBC) A set of database access rules used by Microsoft in its ODBC application programming interface for accessing databases and providing a standard doorway to database data.

operational log A type of event log that tracks occurrences of specific operations, such as when a disk drive is added.

organizational unit (OU) A grouping of objects within a domain that provides a means to establish specific policies for governing those objects, and that enables object management to be delegated.

ownership Having the privilege to change permissions and to fully manipulate an object. The account that creates an object, such as a folder or printer, initially has ownership.

packet A unit of data transmitted on a network that contains control and address information as well as routing information.

page fault Event that occurs whenever memory pages must be called from disk (from the paging file).

paging Moving blocks of information, called pages, from RAM to virtual memory (the paging file) on disk.

paging file Disk space, in the form of a file, for use when memory requirements exceed the available RAM.

partition table Table containing information about each partition on a disk, such as the type of partition, size, and location. Also, the partition table provides information to the computer about how to access the disk.

partitioning Blocking a group of tracks and sectors to be used by a particular file system, such as NTFS.

Password Authentication Protocol (PAP) A nonencrypted plaintext password authentication protocol. This represents the lowest level of security for exchanging passwords via PPP or TCP/IP.

peer-to-peer networking A network on which any computer can communicate with other networked computers on an equal or peer basis without going through an intermediary, such as a server or host.

performance counter report Output of information gathered via Performance Monitor objects, counters, and instances configured within a data collector set.

Performance Monitor The Windows Server 2008 utility used to track system or application objects. For each object type, one or more counters can be logged via a data collection set for later analysis, or tracked in real time for immediate performance monitoring.

permissions In Windows Server 2008, privileges to access and manipulate resource objects, such as folders and printers; for example, the privilege to read a file or to create a new file.

Plug and Play (PnP) The ability of added computer hardware, such as an adapter or modem, to identify itself to the computer operating system for installation. PnP also refers to the Intel and Microsoft specifications for automatic device detection and installation. Many operating systems, such as Windows-based, Macintosh, and UNIX/Linux support PnP.

Point-to-Point Protocol (PPP) A widely used remote communications protocol that transports PPP as well as legacy protocols such as IPX and NetBEUI. PPP is used for dial-up connections between a client and Windows Server 2008.

Point-to-Point Tunneling Protocol (PPTP) A remote communications protocol that enables connectivity to a network through the Internet and connectivity through intranets and VPNs.

pointer (PTR) resource record A record in a DNS reverse lookup zone that consists of an IP (version 4 or 6) address correlated to a computer or domain name.

portable operating system interface (POSIX) Standards set by the Institute of Electrical and Electronics Engineers (IEEE) for portability of applications.

PostScript printer A printer that has special firmware or cartridges to print using a page-description language (PDL).

Preboot Execution Environment (PXE) An environment in which a client computer has software or hardware to enable its network interface card to connect to the network and communicate with a server (or boot from the server) without having to first boot from an operating system on the client's hard disk.

preemptive multitasking Running two or more programs simultaneously so that each program runs in an area of memory separate from areas used by other programs.

primary DNS server A DNS server that is used as the main server from which to administer a zone, such as updating records in a forward lookup zone for a domain. A primary DNS server is also called the authoritative server for that zone.

primary partition The partition or portion of a hard disk that is bootable.

print client The client computer or application that generates a print job.

print job A document or items to be printed.

print queue A stack or lineup of print jobs, with the first job submitted at the top of the stack and the last job submitted at the bottom, and all of the jobs waiting to be sent from the spooler to the printer.

print server A network computer or server device that connects printers to the network for sharing and that receives and processes print requests from print clients.

Printer Control Language (PCL) A printer language used by non-PostScript Hewlett-Packard and compatible laser printers.

printer driver Contains the device-specific information that Windows Server 2008 requires to control a particular print device, implementing customized printer control codes, font, and style information so that documents are converted into a printer-specific language.

printer pooling Linking two or more identical printers with one printer setup or printer share.

privileged mode A protected memory space allocated for the Windows Server 2008 kernel that cannot be directly accessed by software applications.

process A computer program or portion of a program that is currently running. One large program might start several smaller programs or processes.

protocol A strictly defined set of rules for communication across a network that specifies how networked data is formatted for transmission, how it is transmitted, and how it is interpreted at the receiving end.

publish Making an object, such as a printer or shared folder, available for users to access when they view Active Directory contents and so that the data associated with the object can be replicated.

publishing applications (or software) Involves setting up software through a group policy so that the application is available for users to install from a central distribution server, such as through the Add/Remove Programs capability via the user's desktop.

RAID-5 volume Three or more dynamic disks that use RAID level 5 fault tolerance through disk striping and creating parity blocks for data recovery.

RAW A data type often used for printing MS-DOS, Windows 3.x, and UNIX and Linux print files.

Read-Only Domain Controller (RODC) A domain controller that houses Active Directory information, but cannot be updated, such as to create a new account. This specialized domain controller receives updates from regular DCs, but does not replicate to any DCs because it is read-only by design. *See* domain controller (DC).

redundant array of inexpensive (or independent) disks (RAID) A set of standards designed to extend the life

of hard disk drives and to prevent data loss from a hard disk failure.

Registry A database used to store information about the configuration, program setup, devices, drivers, and other data important to the setup of Windows operating systems, such as Windows Server 2008.

Registry entry A data parameter in the Registry stored as a value in hexadecimal, binary, or text format.

Registry key A category of information contained in the Windows Registry, such as hardware or software.

Registry subkey A key within a Registry key, similar to a subfolder under a folder.

Reliable Multicast Protocol Used on Windows-based networks to facilitate multicast transmissions for multimedia communications.

remediation server A server that can issue updates and security policy changes to a client computer to bring that client into Network Access Protection (NAP) compliance.

Remote Authentication Dial-In User Service (RADIUS) A protocol and service set up on one VPN or dial-up RAS server, for example in a domain, when there are multiple VPN or dial-up RAS servers to coordinate authentication and to track remote dial-in statistics for all VPN or dial-up RAS servers.

Remote Desktop Connection (RDC) Software on a client computer that enables it to connect to a terminal server. This was originally called Terminal Services Client.

replication group A grouping of shared folders in a DFS namespace root that are replicated or copied to all servers that participate in DFS replication. When changes are made to DFS shared folders, all of the participating servers are automatically or manually synchronized so that they have the same copy.

resource On a network, this refers to an object, such as a shared printer or shared directory, which can be accessed by users. On workstations as well as servers, a resource is an IRQ line, I/O address, or memory that is allocated to a computer component, such as a disk drive or communications port.

Resultant Set of Policy (RSoP) A Windows Server 2008 tool that enables you to produce reports about proposed or current group policy settings for the purpose of planning and troubleshooting when multiple group policies are in use (such as for OUs and domains).

reverse lookup zone A DNS server zone or table that maps IP addresses to computer or domain names.

Rights Management Services (RMS) Security rights developed by Microsoft to provide security for documents, spreadsheets, e-mail, and other types of files created by applications.

roaming profile Desktop settings that are associated with an account so that the same settings are employed no matter which computer is used to access the account (the profile is downloaded to the client from a server).

root key Also called a subtree, the highest category of data contained in the Registry. There are five root keys.

router A device that connects networks, is able to read IP addresses, and can route or forward packets of data to designated networks.

Routing and Remote Access Services (RRAS) Microsoft software services that enable a Windows Server 2008 server to provide routing capabilities and remote access so that off-site workstations have access to a Windows Server 2008 network through telecommunications lines, the Internet, or intranets.

RSA Developed by Rivest, Shamir, and Adleman, an encryption technique that uses public and private keys along with a computer algorithm that relies on factoring large prime numbers.

Safe Mode A boot mode that enables Windows Server 2008 to be booted using the most generic default settings, such as for the display, disk drives, and pointing device—and only those services needed to boot a basic configuration.

schema Elements used in the definition of each object contained in Active Directory, including the object class and its attributes.

scope A range of IP addresses that a DHCP server can lease to clients.

scope of influence (scope) The reach of a type of group, such as access to resources in a single domain or access to all resources in all domains in a forest (*see* domain local, global, and universal security groups). (Another meaning for the term scope is the beginning through ending IP addresses defined in a DHCP server for use by DHCP clients; see Chapter 8.)

script A file of shell commands that are run as a unit within the shell. The shell interprets the commands to the operating system one line at a time. Usually to run the contents of a script, the name of that script must be entered at the command line. Scripts save time because commands don't have to be typed individually by the user. Another advantage is that the users do not have to memorize the exact sequence of a set of commands each time they want to accomplish a certain task.

secondary DNS server A DNS server that is a backup to a primary DNS server and, therefore, is not authoritative.

Secure Sockets Tunneling Protocol (SSTP) A remote access communications protocol used in VPN communications and that employs PPP authentication techniques along with Web-based communications transport and encryption through Hypertext Transfer Protocol and Secure Sockets Layer. *See* Secure Sockets Layer (SSL).

Secure Sockets Layer (SSL) A data encryption technique employed between a server and a client, such as between a client's browser and an Internet server. SSL is a commonly used form of security for communications and transactions over the Web and can be used by all Web browsers.

Security Configuration Wizard (SCW) A configuration tool that creates or modifies security policies for Windows Server 2008 servers.

security group Used to assign a group of users permission to access network resources.

security log An event log that records access and security information about logon accesses, file, folder, and system policy changes.

Serial Line Internet Protocol (SLIP) An older remote communications protocol that is used by some UNIX and Linux computers. The modern compressed SLIP (CSLIP) version uses header compression to reduce communications overhead. *See* Compressed Serial Line Internet Protocol (CSLIP).

server A single computer that provides extensive multiuser access to network resources.

Server for Network Information Services A service that Subsystem for UNIX-based Applications (SUA) can add to Active Directory to make a Windows Server 2008 server a Network Information Services server for coordinating management of user acccounts and groups between UNIX/Linux computers and Windows Server 2008 servers on the same network. *See* Subsystem for UNIX-based Applications (SUA).

Server Manager A comprehensive server management tool offered through Windows Server 2008.

server-based networking A model in which access to the network and resources, and the management of resources, is accomplished through one or more servers.

service pack (SP) A major update for an operating system that includes fixes for known problems and provides product enhancements.

service ticket In Kerberos security, a permanent ticket good for the duration of a logon session (or for another period of time specified by the server administrator in the account policies) that enables the computer to access network services beginning with the Logon service.

setup log An event log that contains a record of installation events, such as installing a role or feature through Server Manager.

share permissions Permissions that apply to a particular object that is shared over a network, such as a shared folder or printer.

shared directory A directory on a networked computer that other computers on the network can access.

shell A command-line environment, also called a command interpreter, that enables communication with an operating system. Commands that are run within a shell are typically specific to that shell (although different shells sometimes use the same or similar commands, particularly in UNIX and Linux).

Shiva Password Authentication Protocol (SPAP) A proprietary version of Password Authentication Protocol used on Shiva systems. *See* Password Authentication Protocol (PAP).

Sigverif A tool used to verify system and other critical files to determine if they have a signature.

Simple Mail Transfer Protocol (SMTP) An e-mail protocol used by systems having TCP/IP network communications.

Simple Network Management Protocol (SNMP) Used for network management and performance monitoring on TCP/IP-based networks.

simple volume A portion of a disk or an entire disk that is set up as a dynamic disk.

site An option in Active Directory to interconnect IP subnets so that the server can determine the fastest route to connect clients for authentication and to connect DCs for replication of Active Directory. Site information also enables Active Directory to create redundant routes for DC replication.

Small Computer System Interface (SCSI) A 32- or 64-bit computer adapter that transports data between one or more attached devices, such as hard disks, and the computer.

spanned volume Two or more Windows Server dynamic disks that are combined to appear as one disk.

spool file A print file written to disk until it can be transmitted to a printer.

spooler In the Windows environment, a group of DLLs, information files, and programs that process print jobs for printing.

spooling A process working in the background to enable several print files to go to a single printer. Each file is placed in temporary storage until its turn comes to be printed.

stand-alone DFS model A DFS model in which no Active Directory implementation is available to help manage the shared folders. This model provides only a single or flat level share.

Statement of Health (SoH) Information that a client provides to a Health Registration Authority (HRA) to enable it to gain access to network services. The information includes security policy and recent update verification. This is part of Microsoft's Network Access Protection (NAP) capabilities. *See* Health Registration Authority (HRA).

static addressing An IP address that is assigned to a client and remains in use until it is manually changed.

Storage Area Network (SAN) A grouping of storage devices that forms a subnet. The storage devices are available to any server on the main network and appear to the user as though they are attached to the server they are accessing.

stripe set Two or more basic disks set up so that files are spread in blocks across the disks.

striped volume Two or more dynamic disks that use striping so that files are spread in blocks across the disks.

striping A data storage method that breaks up data files across all volumes of a disk set to minimize wear on a single volume.

stub zone A DNS zone that contains only the SOA record zone, name server (NS) records for authoritative servers, and A records for authoritative servers.

subnet mask Used to distinguish between the network part and the host part of the IP address and to enable networks to be divided into subnets.

Subsystem for UNIX-based Applications (SUA) A set of services that can be installed in Windows Sever 2008 to create a UNIX-like environment for UNIX and Linux clients.

subtree Same as root key.

symmetric multiprocessor (SMP) computer A computer that uses more than one processor.

synchronous modem A modem that communicates using continuous bursts of data controlled by a clock signal that starts each burst.

system control ACL (SACL) An access control list that contains settings to audit the access to an object, such as a folder.

system environment variables Variables defined by the operating system and that apply to any user logged on to the computer.

system log An event log that records information about system-related events such as hardware errors, driver problems, and hard drive errors.

system partition Partition that contains boot files.

System Stability Index A figure between 0 and 10 that represents the current system reliability when taking into account software installation, software removal, application failures, hardware failures, Windows system failures, and other miscellaneous failures.

System State data Operating system and boot files, plus extra components and information that reflect the currently configured state of the server, depending on what features are installed. The System State data can be backed up using the Windows Server Backup tool.

SYSVOL A shared folder set up when Active Directory is installed that contains scripts, Group Policy Objects (GPOs), and software distribution files, several of which are needed for domain access. SYSVOL folders are replicated among DCs.

T-carrier A dedicated leased telephone line that can be used for data communications over multiple channels for speeds of up to 400.352 Mbps.

terminal A device that consists of a monitor and keyboard to communicate with host computers that run the programs. The terminal does not have a processor to use for running programs locally.

terminal adapter (TA) Popularly called a digital modem, links a computer or a fax to an ISDN line.

terminal server A server configured to offer Terminal Services so that clients can run applications on the server, similar to having clients respond as terminals.

TEXT A data type used for printing text files formatted using the ANSI standard that employs values between 0 and 255 to represent characters, numbers, and symbols.

thin client A specialized personal computer or terminal device that has a minimal Windows-based operating system. A thin client is designed to connect to a host computer that does most or all of the processing. The thin client is mainly responsible for providing a graphical user interface and network connectivity.

thread A block of program code executing within a running process. One process may launch one or more threads.

total cost of ownership (TCO) The cost of installing and maintaining computers and equipment on a network, which includes hardware, software, maintenance, and support costs.

trace Capture of a specific event when it occurs, such as a page fault or input to a disk.

trace report Contains results of monitored trace events generated by a data collector set and contains only those instances when the events occur, such as creating a trace to record each time disk input/output activity occurs or when an Active Directory Kerberos security event is triggered. *See* trace.

transitive trust A trust relationship between two or more domains in a tree, in which each domain has access to objects in the others.

Transmission Control Protocol (TCP) This transport protocol, which is part of the TCP/IP suite, establishes communication sessions between networked software application processes and provides for reliable end-to-end delivery of data by controlling data flow.

Transmission Control Protocol/Internet Protocol (TCP/IP) The default protocol suite installed with Windows Server 2008 that enables network communication.

trap A specific situation or event detected by SNMP that a network administrator may want to be warned about or to track via network management software, for example, when a network device is unexpectedly down or offline. *See* Simple Network Management Protocol (SNMP).

tree Related domains that use a contiguous namespace, share the same schema, and have two-way transitive trust relationships.

Trusted Platform Module (TPM) A security specification for a hardware device used to secure information on another device, such as on a hard drive. The TPM hardware device is typically a chip.

two-way trust A domain relationship in which both domains are trusted and trusting, enabling one to have access to objects in the other.

unicast A message that goes from one single computer to another single computer.

Uniform Resource Locator (URL) An addressing format used to find an Internet Web site or page.

Universal Naming Convention (UNC) A naming convention that designates network servers, computers and shared resources. The format for a UNC name is, for example, \\servername\namespace\folder\file.

Universal PnP (UPnP) A supplementation to PnP that enables automated configuration for devices connected through a network.

universal security group A group that is used to provide access to resources in any domain within a forest. A common implementation is to make global groups that contain accounts members of a universal group that has access to resources.

User Account Control (UAC) Enables software and device installations in standard user mode while still ensuring authorization from the administrator. UAC is intended to further remove these activities from access to the kernel to protect the operating system and make it difficult to destabilize through malware and intrusions.

User Datagram Protocol (UDP) A connectionless protocol that can be used with IP, instead of TCP.

user environment variables Environment variables that are defined on a per-user basis.

virtual directory A URL-formatted address that provides an Internet location (virtual location) for an actual physical folder on a Web server that is used to publish Web documents.

Virtual Disk Service (VDS) Used to enable management of disk volumes in SANs through one interface at a server.

virtual memory Disk storage allocated to link with physical RAM to temporarily hold data when there is not enough free RAM.

virtual private network (VPN) A private network that is like a tunnel through a larger network—such as the Internet, an enterprise network, or both—that is restricted to designated member clients only.

virtualization Software that enables one computer to run two or more operating systems that are live at the same time and in which one application running in one operating system does not interfere with an application running in a different operating system.

volume A logical designation of one or more physical disks partitioned and formatted with one file system. One volume can be composed of one or more partitions. In Windows Server 2008, a volume can be a basic disk partition that has been formatted for a particular file system, a primary partition, a volume set, an extended volume, a stripe set, a stripe set with parity, or a mirror set. A volume can also be a dynamic disk that is set up as a simple volume, spanned volume, striped volume, RAID-5 volume, or mirrored volume.

volume set Two or more formatted basic disk partitions (volumes) that are combined to look like one volume with a single drive letter.

Volume Shadow Copy Service (VSS) Backup service used in Windows Server 2003 and Windows Server 2008 to create stable images of files and folders on servers based on the point in time when the image is made.

Windows Deployment Services (WDS) Services in Windows Server 2008 that enable Windows Server 2008 and Windows Vista (and certain other Windows operating systems) to be installed on multiple computers using automated techniques.

Windows Internet Naming Service (WINS) A Windows Server service that enables the server to convert Net-BIOS computer names to IP addresses for network and Internet communications. (NetBIOS is an applications programming interface to provide programs with a consistent command set for using network services.)

Windows NT LAN Manager version 2 (NTLMv2) An authentication protocol used in legacy Windows NT Server systems and retained in all Windows systems for backward compatibility for clients that cannot support Kerberos.

Windows PowerShell A Windows command-line interface that offers scripting capabilities as well.

Windows Server Catalog of Tested Products A list of computer hardware and software tested by Microsoft and determined to be compatible with a specific Windows Server operating system, such as Windows Server 2008.

workgroup As used in Microsoft networks, a number of users who share drive and printer resources in an independent peer-to-peer relationship.

workstation A computer that has its own central processing unit (CPU) and may be used as a stand-alone or network computer for word processing, spreadsheet creation, or other software applications.

X.25 An older packet-switching protocol for connecting remote networks at speeds up to 2.048 Mbps.

XML Paper Specification (XPS) An advanced way of printing documents for multiple purposes, including viewing electronic pages and printing pages in a polished format.

zone A partition or subtree in a DNS server that contains specific kinds of records in a lookup table, such as a forward lookup zone that contains records in a table for looking up computer and domain names in order to find their associated IP addresses.

Index

Note: Page numbers referencing figures are italicized and followed by an "f".